T0327410

Fixed Income Trading and Risk Management

Fixed Income Trading and Risk Management

ALEXANDER DÜRING

WILEY

Library of Congress Cataloging-in-Publication Data is Available:

ISBN 9781119756330 (hardback)
ISBN 9781119756354 (ePub)
ISBN 9781119756347 (ePDF)

Cover Design: Wiley
Cover Image: © Husjak/Shutterstock

Set in 10/12pt, STIXTwoText by SPi Global, Chennai, India

10 9 8 7 6 5 4 3 2 1

Contents

Foreword   xv

PART ONE
Preliminaries

CHAPTER 1
Introduction   3

CHAPTER 2
Money, Credit and Banking   9

    2.1   Abstract properties of money   9
    2.2   Early forms of money   11
         2.2.1   *Paper money and bank notes*   14
    2.3   Fiat money   15
         2.3.1   *Fiat money and trade*   15

CHAPTER 3
Banks   17

    3.1   Banks and bank money creation   17
    3.2   Categories of banks   18

CHAPTER 4
Bank Money Creation   20

    4.1   Single-bank introduction   20
    4.2   Extension to multiple banks   22
    4.3   Transfer settlement in central bank money   25
    4.4   Trade and non-bank credit   28
         4.4.1   *Non-cash trading instruments*   29
         4.4.2   *Discounting*   30
         4.4.3   *Delineating payment instruments from money* 30

4.5   Digital token monies and cryptocurrencies   31
4.6   The money multiplier   32

CHAPTER 5
The Role of Central Banks   **34**

5.1   Introduction   34
5.2   Monetary financing   39

CHAPTER 6
Monetary Policy   **40**

6.1   Objectives of monetary policy   40
6.2   Monetary policy under inflation targeting   43
6.3   Central bank operational frameworks   46
     6.3.1   *Symmetric interest rate corridors*   47
     6.3.2   *Asymmetric lending corridors*   49

CHAPTER 7
Operational Frameworks   **50**

7.1   Control of the money supply   50
7.2   Liquidity provision: Rediscounting, outright purchases and
     Lombard lending   51
7.3   Liquidity absorption: Asset sales and reverse repos   52
7.4   The impact of FX operations   52

CHAPTER 8
Interaction between Frameworks and Policy   **54**

8.1   Volatility   54
8.2   Collateral   55

CHAPTER 9
Non-Standard Monetary Policy   **57**

9.1   Quantitative easing   57
     9.1.1   *The Monetary Effect of Large-Scale Asset Purchases*   61
     9.1.2   *Market liquidity and central bank asset purchases*   62
     9.1.3   *Helicopter money*   63
     9.1.4   *Choice of methods and assets*   65
9.2   Practical experience   67
     9.2.1   *QE, money multipliers and FX*   67
     9.2.2   *Bank of Japan 2013 QE experience*   71
     9.2.3   *Lessons from the initial BoJ quantitative easing*   72
9.3   Negative interest rates   73
9.4   The specific situation of the ECB   74

PART TWO
Cash Instruments

CHAPTER 10
Contract and Instrument Types   **79**
10.1   Securities and bilateral contracts   79
10.2   Security identifiers   81
    10.2.1   ISIN codes   81
    10.2.2   CUSIP codes   83

CHAPTER 11
Trading and Settlement   **85**
11.1   Trading   85
    11.1.1   Trading and price formation   85
    11.1.2   Trading venues   86
    11.1.3   The OTC trade lifecycle   87
       The trade inquiry   89
       Negotiation   89
       Agreement   90
       Recording   91
       Enrichment   92
       Reporting   92
       Pre-confirmation   93
       Allocation   93
       Confirmation   94
       Settlement instructions   94
       Fails   95
       Reconciliation   96
    11.1.4   The exchange trade cycle   96
    11.1.5   Trading in competition versus single dealer inquiries and orders   97
       Mistrades   98
11.2   Settlement   98
    11.2.1   Settlement mechanisms   99
    11.2.2   Settlement conventions   99

CHAPTER 12
Central Clearing   **101**
12.1   Direct clearing   101
12.2   Indirect clearing   106
    12.2.1   Agency clearing   106

12.2.2   *Principal clearing*   107
12.2.3   *Hybrid clearing models*   107
12.3   Contract value adjustments (xVA)   108
12.3.1   *Credit Value Adjustment*   108
12.3.2   *Funding Value Adjustment*   109
12.3.3   *Debit Value Adjustment*   110

CHAPTER 13
The Money Market   **111**

13.1   Money market instruments   111
13.2   Discount factors   112
13.3   Daycount conventions   114
13.4   Money market interest rates   115
13.5   Compounding   116
13.6   LIBOR, Euribor, and friends   117
13.7   Overnight benchmarks   119
13.8   Benchmark reform   120
13.9   Money market futures and futures trading   121
13.9.1   *Money market futures*   121
13.9.2   *Identification of futures contracts*   122
13.9.3   *Futures trading basics*   124
13.9.4   *Convexity adjustment*   124

CHAPTER 14
The Repo Market   **126**

14.1   The repurchase market   126
14.2   Haircut   128
14.3   Variations of repurchase transactions   128
14.4   Rehypothecation   130

CHAPTER 15
Spot and Forward Rates   **131**

15.1   Forward rates   131
15.2   No-arbitrage calculations   131
15.3   Official rates versus term rates   133
15.3.1   *The turn premium*   133
15.3.2   *Matching policy expectations to market rates*   134

CHAPTER 16
The Bond Market   **137**

16.1   Introduction   137
16.2   Cashflow types   138
16.2.1   *Bullet bonds*   138
16.2.2   *Zero coupon bonds, perpetuals and annuities*   139

16.3   Issuer types   142
        16.3.1   *Joint issuance*   144
        16.3.2   *Supranationals*   146
16.4   Governing law and contractual clauses   147
16.5   Bond markets   151
        16.5.1   *The primary market*   153
        16.5.2   *The secondary market I: (interdealer market)*   157
        16.5.3   *The secondary market II: (customer-facing market)*   158
16.6   Accrued interest   158
16.7   Yield   159
        16.7.1   *Running yield*   160
        16.7.2   *Simple yield*   160
        16.7.3   *Compound yield*   160
        16.7.4   *Bond-equivalent yield*   161
16.8   Interest rate risk   163
16.9   Convexity   164
16.10 Bond value decomposition   165
16.11 Carry   167

CHAPTER 17
Floating-Rate Notes   **169**

17.1   Coupon reset mechanics   170
17.2   Libor and OIS-linked notes   171
17.3   Discount margin   173
17.4   CMS and CMT floaters   174

CHAPTER 18
Asset Markets and Liquidity   **176**

18.1   Concepts   176
18.2   Liquidity measurement   180
        18.2.1   *Taxonomy of liquidity measures*   181
18.3   Examples   183
18.4   Liquidity premium   185
18.5   Liquidity and volatility   187

CHAPTER 19
Curves and Curve Models   **189**

19.1   Models   190
19.2   Yield curve representation and interpretations   191
        19.2.1   *Discount factors versus par curves*   191
19.3   Market-based curve representations   193
        19.3.1   *Bootstrapping*   193
        19.3.2   *Reverse bootstrapping*   195
19.4   Parametric curve models   196
        19.4.1   *The Nelson-Siegel and Nelson-Siegel-Svensson splines* 197

	19.4.2	Polynomial splines	198
	19.4.3	The exponential spline	199
	19.4.4	The Vasicek spline	200
	19.4.5	Composite models	202
19.5	Fitting curve models		203

CHAPTER 20
Curve Analysis   **205**

20.1	Expectations		205
20.2	Convexity bias		209
20.3	Term risk premium		211
20.4	Preferred habitat		212
	20.4.1	Asset–liability matching	212
	20.4.2	Regulatory constraints	213
	20.4.3	Passive investing	214
	20.4.4	Central bank reserve portfolios	215
	20.4.5	Market technicals	215

CHAPTER 21
Carry and Roll-Down   **217**

CHAPTER 22
Curve Spreads   **220**

22.1	Z-spread		220
22.2	Par spread		221
22.3	Swap spreads		222
	22.3.1	Asset swap spreads	222
	22.3.2	I-spreads	223
	22.3.3	The TED spread	224

PART THREE
Inflation-Linked Debt

CHAPTER 23
Inflation-Indexed Bonds   **227**

23.1	Introduction		227
	23.1.1	Cashflows of inflation-linked bonds	230
	23.1.2	Quotation of index-linked bonds	232
23.2	Rebalancing, rebasing and revision of CPI indices		232
23.3	Inflation seasonality		234
23.4	Price formation in inflation-linked markets		238
23.5	Return measures of inflation-linked bonds		240
23.6	Breakeven inflation		241

23.7   Carry on inflation-indexed bonds   244
23.8   Comprehensive inflation modelling   245
23.9   Inflation models and expectations   249

PART FOUR
Defaultable Claims

CHAPTER 24
Credit Risk   255

24.1   Default, insolvency, and bankruptcy   255
24.2   Seniority and subordination   256
       24.2.1   *Time subordination and acceleration*   256
       24.2.2   *Contractual subordination*   256
       24.2.3   *Statutory subordination*   257
       24.2.4   *Joint liabilities and credit support*   258
       24.2.5   *Sovereign debt*   259
24.3   The default process   259
       24.3.1   *Collective action clauses*   261
       24.3.2   *Debt exchanges and consent solicitations*   262
       24.3.3   *Managed defaults*   263
       24.3.4   *Wind-downs*   263
24.4   Credit ratings   264
       24.4.1   *Rating migration*   266
       24.4.2   *Alternative rating approaches*   270

CHAPTER 25
Covered Bonds   272

25.1   Statutory covered bonds   277
25.2   Danish covered bonds   279
25.3   Structured covered bonds   281
25.4   Covered bond credit risk analysis   282

CHAPTER 26
Asset-Backed Securities   284

26.1   The ABS issuance process   285
26.2   Default risk of ABS   286
26.3   Maturity of ABS   287

CHAPTER 27
Residential Mortgage-Backed Securities   289

27.1   Residential mortgage prepayments   290
27.2   Prepayment modelling   292

PART FIVE

Derivatives

CHAPTER 28
Bond Futures   301

28.1 Introduction   301
28.2 Futures trading patterns   303
    28.2.1 *Open interest and trading volume*   303
    28.2.2 *CFTC data for US futures contracts*   307
28.3 Valuation of physically delivered bond futures   310
    28.3.1 *Basis and implied repo rate*   310
    28.3.2 *Conversion factors and the notional coupon*   312
    28.3.3 *The cash-and-carry arbitrage*   314
    28.3.4 *The quality option*   315
    28.3.5 *Hedging with futures*   316
28.4 Futures rolls   321
    28.4.1 *Roll ratios*   324
    28.4.2 *Advanced futures delivery models*   325
28.5 Delivery windows   326
28.6 Interaction between futures and bonds   327
28.7 Futures squeezes   329
28.8 Cash-settled futures   331
    28.8.1 *Exchange-for-physical transactions*   332
28.9 New bond issues   332

CHAPTER 29
Swaps   334

29.1 Introduction   334
29.2 Plain vanilla swaps   336
29.3 Trade compression and re-couponing   338

PART SIX

Standard Trading Strategies

CHAPTER 30
Trading Principles   343

30.1 Definitions   343
30.2 Trade identification   345
30.3 Trade portfolios   346

CHAPTER 31
Curve Trading   347

31.1 Simple curve trades   350
    31.1.1 *Outright Trades*   350

31.1.2 Steepeners and Flatteners   350
31.1.3 Butterflies   353
31.1.4 Condors   354
31.2 Intrinsic curve movements   354
31.2.1 Alternative specifications   360

CHAPTER 32
Bond Trading   **362**

32.1 Bond relative value   362
32.2 Relative value strategies   363
32.2.1 Spread widener/tightener   363
32.2.2 Basis trade   364
32.2.3 Bond spread   365
32.2.4 Bond spread with curve hedge   365
32.2.5 Alternative strategies   366

PART SEVEN
Risk Management

CHAPTER 33
Principal Component Analysis   **371**

33.1 PCA as generalised regression   373
33.2 Measuring data complexity with PCA   375

CHAPTER 34
Bond Index Mechanics   **378**

34.1 Bond index principles   378
34.2 Index rebalancing   380

CHAPTER 35
Portfolio Risk Management   **381**

35.1 Risk-neutral portfolios   381
35.2 Index tracking   383
35.2.1 Factor analysis and spanning sets   385
35.2.2 Friction effects   387

CHAPTER 36
Hedging   **389**

36.1 Introduction   389
36.2 Duration-neutral hedges   390
36.3 Regression hedges   391
36.4 Yield curve model hedges   392

CHAPTER 37
Mean-Variance Optimisation   **395**

CHAPTER 38
Portfolio Rebalancing   **403**
   38.1 Passive and semi-passive strategies   404
         38.1.1 *No reallocation*   404
         38.1.2 *Passive management*   404
         38.1.3 *Index replication*   405
         38.1.4 *Constant asset allocation*   405
         38.1.5 *Trend-Following*   406
         38.1.6 *Mean reversion*   406
   38.2 Numerical examples   407

PART EIGHT
References

CHAPTER 39
Selected Global Bond Markets   **413**
   39.1 Euro area   413
         39.1.1 *Austria*   414
         39.1.2 *Belgium*   415
         39.1.3 *Finland*   416
         39.1.4 *France*   416
         39.1.5 *Germany*   418
         39.1.6 *Greece*   421
         39.1.7 *Ireland*   422
         39.1.8 *Italy*   423
         39.1.9 *The Netherlands*   424
         39.1.10 *Portugal*   425
         39.1.11 *Spain*   426
   39.2 Iceland   427
   39.3 Japan   428
   39.4 Sweden   430
   39.5 United Kingdom   431
   39.6 United States of America   433

Bibliography   **435**

Index   **439**

Foreword

Source: ALEXANDER DÜRING

This book about fixed income has been inspired by over two decades of work in the market from offices in London, Frankfurt and Tokyo. During this time, the author had the good fortune to be close to, and sometimes involved in, an eclectic mix of events. Although working for a large investment bank and the European Central Bank has made it possible to collect this experience, the book does not represent the views of either. Any opinions about central banking should in particular not be taken as those of the Eurosystem.

This book is also inspired by a building, namely the British Museum in London, a detail of which is pictured above. This inspiration has three aspects. The first is that the architecture of the building cannot be understood by looking only at its historic base, or only at Sir Norman Foster's modern additions. Fixed income markets can similarly not be properly understood by considering only their conventions, or only the modern mathematical apparatus that has been created to analyse them. Although this book will present complex mathematics determining the risk characteristics of various instruments, some design features of these instruments are archaic. These features remain today for no better reason than that there was never a need to change them.

Second, the museum is open to all and free in principle, although a small donation is encouraged. Children can walk in and experience artefacts that once were created for the exclusive use of priests and kings. In the world of fixed income, the efforts of statistics offices, central banks, trade associations and others have made a wealth of data available to the general public. Freely available numerical libraries and advances in computers make it possible for everyone to analyse, and learn from that data. Understanding of markets has thus been democratised in ways that were unimaginable even a decade ago. This book, written at home using only freely available and self-developed software, is built on these foundations and encourages such exploration.

Third, the British Museum is not uncontroversial, as are some of the exhibits shown there. The ideas of debt, of trading debt, and of banking are similarly the subject of debate and argument. This book gives some space to this debate although the author would not claim to be neutral in it. The financial industry is part of the service sector, however else it may be portrayed in popular culture. People working in it cannot be oblivious to their role in society, and take it as granted that their actions will not be questioned by others.

Books not only require inspiration, but also enablement. In this case, this has been provided by my family who kindly tolerated the amount of time I spent on writing it and whom I thank for their forbearance. Erwin, Reiko and George at Deutsche, and Julian at the ECB helped me to develop a somewhat non-conformist approach to financial markets. Tamio and Henry at Deutsche Securities Inc. encouraged me to teach, as did Toto, Christophe and Ralph at the ECB. Those who attended these classes and asked questions will hopefully find them answered here. To them, and many not named, go my thanks for making work in financial markets the joy it is.

As this is a textbook, literature references are given here extensively with the aim of encouraging further reading rather than striving for completeness in representing the state of the art.

Preliminaries

CHAPTER 1

Introduction

This book deals with the fixed income markets and the best point to start is to define what this means. The book will follow market usage by defining fixed income instruments as contracts that specify payment obligations that are not linked to the economic situation of the obligor. It also excludes from the scope contracts that establish payments depending on the performance of physical assets, such as commodities or weather. The book will further discuss a range of fixed income derivatives, namely contracts that specify obligations that depend on the performance of fixed income instruments.

Fixed income instruments can be broadly divided in to bilateral contracts and securities. Securities differ from bilateral contracts in that they are transferrable without the consent of all parties. Note that some features of securities may be linked to bilateral contracts. Table 1.1 lists various fixed income instruments in these two categories.

In German, fixed income instruments are referred to as 'Renten' and the same word is also used to refer to pensions. In the English vernacular, the scope of the word 'rent' to signify income streams has been narrowed down significantly to refer to payments linked to the use of physical assets. The Latin translation of the word 'rent', 'pension', is now used in English to designate the income stream that accrues to people after a lifetime of work. On the other hand, 'Pension' in financial German refers to the renting out of financial assets[1]. This etymological divergence between otherwise related languages highlights an important point, namely that the notion of fixed income instruments is not new but underwent several changes of connotation over time.

TABLE 1.1 Non-exclusive list of instrument types

Bilateral contracts	Securities
Deposits	Bonds
Loans	Commercial paper
Swaps	Certificates of deposit
Futures	Asset-backed securities

---

[1] It has to be admitted that few people today use the word Wertpapierpensionsgeschäft.

Apart from commodity contracts, the definition above rules out common and preferred equity instruments where the issuer has some discretion about the timing and amount of payments. This is a strong restriction because the party to the contract that is obliged to make a payment has no rights versus the payee. The very word 'equity' implies an equitable relationship between payer and payee, whereas in the fixed income setting, the obligor usually has limited discretion.

The ancient Greeks despised money lending, as evidenced in Aristotle's Politics:

> There are two sorts of wealth-getting, as I have said; one is part of household management, the other is retail trade: the former necessary and honourable, while that which consists in exchange is justly censured; for it is unnatural, and a mode by which men gain from one another. The most hated sort, and with the greatest reason, is usury, which makes a gain out of money itself, and not from the natural object of it. For money was intended to be used in exchange, but not to increase at interest.

The three book religions, Judaism, Christianity, and Islam, severely restrict the lending of money against interest and hence the majority of fixed income instruments. In scriptural terms, only Judaism permits charging interest at all, and only in the case of Jews charging interest to gentiles according to the usual intepretation of Deuteronomy 23:19–20:

> Thou shalt not lend upon usury to thy brother; usury of money, usury of victuals, usury of anything that is lent upon usury. Upon a stranger thou mayest lend upon usury; but unto thy brother thou shalt not lend upon usury; that the LORD thy God may bless thee in all thou settest thine hand to in the land whither thou goest to possess it.

For Christians, the encyclical Vix pervenit [88] issued by Benedict XIV. on 1 November 1745 opened a legal distinction between usury and lending money at interest, although it reaffirmed the general prohibition of usury. Even earlier, the Pax Westphalica [67] in 1648 casually refers to fixed interest obligations. Today, the issue presents no particular problem for Christians. However, many countries retain prohibitions on excessive interest charges that relate back to usury concepts.

In contrast, Islamic law (*Shar'iah*) has retained its prohibition to lending at interest (*riba*), or indeed unconditional repayment obligations. Together with *gharar* (uncertainty) and *maysir* (gambling), such practices are strictly forbidden by the Qur'an. This rules out investing money for interest (but not the earning of profits from equity investments) and also the concept of pure options. These restrictions present an obstacle for Muslim investors to interact with the western financial system. Accordingly, a system of Islamic finance has developed that allows profitable investments at low risk.

In order to understand why fixed income is apparently such a new concept, it is instructive to study the prohibitions above, setting aside the issue of divine inspiration. For instance, in Exodus 22:25, Jews are instructed:

> If thou lend money to any of my people that is poor by thee, thou shalt not be to him as an usurer, neither shalt thou lay upon him usury.

The implication is that a lender of money is somebody with surplus cash while a borrower is in an emergency situation and needs cash to make ends meet. Exploiting such an emergency situation is morally reprehensible and therefore forbidden. Aristotle's aversion to lending is similarly explained in that he abhors the idea of a necessary social process being abused for pecunary gain. Human beings have to trade in order to exist, but the act of trading does, in his eyes, not contribute to the production of goods. Profiting from something that is not actually increasing the store of wealth of humankind is therefore despicable.

These arguments do not sound too unfamiliar today and debts are still viewed negatively in some parts of the political spectrum [43]. The innovation of some newer critical authors is to draw a distinction between social convention of debts that have to be served unconditionally on one hand, and more flexible moral notions of obligations on the other. The latter are alleged by these authors to be more in line with human development. Setting aside the question whether there is indeed an anthropological basis for distinguishing between morals and social convention, there remains a question as to whether lenders are willingly absorbing an ambiguity in their relationship with borrowers, or instead view their claims as legally absolute. An argument made in Henry V [74] (4.1) may be instructive:

> KING HARRY So, if a son is by his father sent about merchandise do sinfully miscarry upon the sea, the imputation of his wickedness, by your rule, should be imposed on his father, that sent him. Or if a servant, under his master's command transporting a sum of money, be assailed by robbers, and die in many irreconciled iniquities, you may call the master the author of the servant's damnation. But this is not so. The King is not bound to answer the particular endings of his soldiers, the father of his son, nor the master of his servant, for they purpose not their deaths when they propose their services.

Similarly, most lenders do not 'purpose' inability to repay when they lend money and indeed tend to prefer to lend to borrowers who repay on schedule. A pensioner who has invested in a mortgage does not seek the destitution that may befall the borrower who is dispossessed upon default and would usually prefer not to face the risk of his or her own destitution should the process of liquidating the property faily to reproduce the originally expected income stream.

What has changed in recent times is that lenders are no longer necessarily rich and borrowers are not necessarily poor. People now generally accept that individuals need to put money aside to prepare for their old age and that if they were unable to do so without being paid interest, inflation and credit risk would erode the value of their savings. They also have no reason to enter a relationship based on equity with whoever has use of their money at the time. The association of fixed income with pension in the German word 'Rente' is therefore now quite natural. On the borrower side, it is now also common to borrow money for convenience, such as in a mortgage, or to invest in a new business. Many business owners do not want to form equitable partnership with capital providers. They prefer to pay interest on that capital and retain the profits they expect from their venture. In addition, interest payments are tax-deductible in many jurisdictions. In the times when the great religious books were written, large multigenerational families would have handled equivalent transfers internally, whereas businesses nowadays have to conclude external contracts.

The sometimes shady area of consumer finance shows, however, that inequity is still an issue in money lending. This means that the debate about the moral implications of fixed income liabilities is not likely to end. So-called predatory lenders, who do seek out borrowers that can be expected not to repay and can therefore be pursued for their assets following default, do exist. Most modern legal codes provide some safeguards against such abuses of the legal system, such as upper limits on interest rates, or know-your-client rules.

At the same time, some supposedly new arguments about wealth distribution can be traced to insufficient awareness of what are essentially fixed income assets. Popular studies of wealth disparity tend to focus on traceable forms of assets, such as accumulated income, real estate, etc [68]. However, Mr Darcy is described in 'Pride and Prejudice' as having £10,000 a year. Earlier, Sir Toby in 'Twelfth Night' justifies the description of Sir Andrew Aguecheek as 'as tall a man as any in Illyria' with 'he has three thousand ducats a year'. This description of a person's assets in terms of the annuity they generate, instead of their current value, was quite common at the time these books were written. Using this approach today can be eye-opening.

Mayer Amschel Rothschild, founder of the Rothschild banking dynasty and arguably one of the richest men in the world at his time, died on 16 September 1812 of an infection [35]. An affliction of this kind would be trivial to cure today, and that cure would be free of charge to even the poorest British citizen. The National Health Service (NHS) of the United Kingdom had an annual budget of £116.4bn in 2015/16, equivalent to around £1,800 per head of the UK population. The NHS is free of charge at the point of use, so every person registered with the NHS has the right to consume services, if they require, that are worth around £1,800 per year. Assuming for illustration an average remaining life span of 30 years and a discount rate of 1.8% (the long-term yield at that time), a person wishing to obtain an equivalent income stream would have to invest an amount of about £41,400 using the annuity formula Equation (16.1). Simply by registering with the NHS, an average UK resident therefore in effect acquires an asset that is equivalent to £41,400. This asset is of course only valuable to the extent that illness creates a need to draw on it. The point is, though, that a person *outside* the NHS would have to accumulate that amount of wealth to be able to purchase the services and goods available to the average NHS user.

Although the NHS-implied assets are invisible on citizens' balance sheets, their counterpart on the national balance sheet of the United Kingdom is not. The NHS has to be funded either through taxes or government debt. Of the latter, the United Kingdom carried £29,400 per head of the population in 2016.

Germany provides a monthly stipend that in 2017 was €409 and occasional additional payments to single people with no dependants unconditionally on previous earned income. Using current 30 year interest rates, a 30 year annuity of this magnitude had a present value of €127,000. A person with savings of this amount would be considered reasonably well off even though few would consider the equivalent income stream as attractive. Absent this welfare system, one would have to accumulate this very substantial sum to obtain an equivalent income stream. Universal free or subsidised education is another example of a valuable claim on society that is in principle open to all but not valued as an asset.

Classically, wealthy citizens were called upon to fund common expenses and in return earned rights to future distributions of national wealth [57], for instance through the interest on government bonds. Although wealthy persons have been encouraged to provide for the poor by way of charity in many ethical frameworks, this has always been an exhortation rather than an obligation. From the viewpoint of the recipients, such charitable giving was a blessing, not a right. Traditionally, therefore, societies put a lot of value on either income-earning assets or opportunities for work that would create meaningful income streams. The onus to pay for goods and services, in other words, has traditionally been on the consumer.

Modern societies legislate unconditional claims on society that are not the result of prior contributions, such as welfare or universal health care. Because such liabilities of the national budget ultimatively have to be backed by corresponding tax assets, tax payers, who are the ultimate contingent debtors in this relationship, may at some point feel aggrieved. Claimants on social redistribution in effect have claims on taxpayers and government bond investors that resemble those that creditors have on debtors, namely claims on a fixed income stream.

No extreme point in this virtual creditor–debtor relationship presents an obvious optimum for overall welfare. Denying any form of redistribution would not only create social unrest, but would in most ethical frameworks be considered immoral. It would also be economically ruinous because it would consign potential consumers to destitution, reducing the scope for producers to earn an income. Taken too far, redistribution on the other hand would instead discourage producers from earning (or at least declaring) taxable income. The optimal extent of redistribution is open to debate (known in supply-side economics as the Laffer curve), but does most certainly depend not only on general measures such as welfare expenditure relative to gross domestic product, but also on the specific form in which redistribution takes place [27].

Islamic finance, which is developing borrowing and lending instruments based on *shar'iah* notions of equity, could provide interesting lessons in this regard. The pricing of Islamic banking products can generally be translated into terms that would be familiar to Western bankers, but the legal relationships between lenders and borrowers follow different rules. As Muslim nations grow in economic importance and the Islamic finance sector expands, at some point it will perhaps start to influence Western notions of banking. Already at this time, the Ecological and Social Responsibility (ESR) investment trend shares some similar ideas.

This book has been designed as course material and, with the exception of the last chapter, can be read from front to back. Industry practitioners might hopefully find it useful as a general vade mecum afterwards. The chapter arrangement follows a fairly conventional structure. Beginning with money, banking and monetary policy (Chapters 2–9) it then moves to how transactions take place (Chapters 10–12). Having thus covered the infrastructure of financial markets, the next part deals with the money and bond markets (Chapters 13–18). Several ideas linked to valuation follow in Chapters 19–22. The next parts, presented in Chapters 23–27 are detours into more complex parts of the bond market, dealing with inflation, credit risk, and mortgage prepayments. The essential derivatives markets, bond futures and swaps are presented in Chapters 28 and 29. With the complete set of instruments in hand, Chapters 30–32 introduce trading strategies, while Chapters 33–38 address standard portfolio and risk management strategies. Chapter 39 is a reference to various bond markets provided mostly to illustrate the variety of products that exist.

As a general approach, this book does not only present and explain concepts but also critically discusses their shortcomings. Like any human endeavour, fixed income analysis uses imperfect tools. Imperfections do not invalidate tools, but make it incumbent on their user to know when not to trust them.

A quick word on charts

This book uses a particular form of scatter plot, for instance the one shown here.

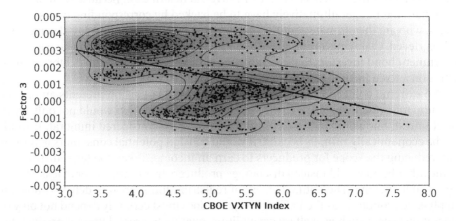

In this plot, the actual observations are augmented by information about their probability density. When many points fall closely together in the same area, the human eye tends to see them as just one point. This optically overvalues outliers. In the scatter plots here, a two-dimensional Gaussian is calculated for each individual data points using the observed variance in the x and y direction of the chart for all data points. These individual Gaussians are then evaluated on a regular grid and added up for all data points. The resulting probability density function is represented in a greyscale behind the usual dots of the scatter plot. In line with topographic maps, isolines are added to give additional flavour to the resulting shape.

CHAPTER 2

Money, Credit and Banking

Money is ubiquitous in society but the definition of money is still perenially being debated by economists and anthropologists. As this is a finance textbook, a somewhat unconventional approach will be taken here. Starting from abstract properties of money, the concrete items that can be used as money will be explained in a roughly historical order. Starting from the abstract definition has the advantage of being able to focus on essential features before getting side-tracked by ancillary properties.

2.1   ABSTRACT PROPERTIES OF MONEY

Money is a tool that enables people to trade goods and services against a standard *means of exchange*. This function makes money an abstract commodity in the sense that is received and given as payment for all other goods or services without necessarily having a material value in itself[1]. Just what constitues money in this sense in a given society is decided by common agreement because everybody involved in trading needs to accept a particular form of money for it to be effective. There does not have to be a unique money in a given society. Multiple commodities can serve as money in parallel and most modern monetary systems use at least two forms of money.

When transactions involve money on one side, it makes sense to express the value of assets in terms of the amount of money they can be exchanged against. This leads to the use of money as a *unit of account*.

A concomitant requirement of a means of exchange is that it holds its value, at least over short periods. This requirement means that the rate at which money can be exchanged into goods and services does not fluctuate too much from one day to the next. Sellers of goods or services against money need to have confidence that the money received will purchase a known quantity of other services in the near future. Money can therefore serve as a *store of wealth*.

The use of money is therefore intrinsically linked to the notion of credit: By accepting money (instead of goods or services) for payment, a seller of goods defers consumption in a way that would not be automatic in barter trade. Money can in this sense be

---

[1]This definition does not rule out that money can also be a concrete commodity with an intrinsic value.

thought of as an obligation of society as a whole to provide goods and services to holders of currency[2].

The credit aspect of money implies that money is not in itself wealth but merely a claim on actual goods and services. A society can choose to increase the amount of money in circulation but will not usually find itself richer as a result. Most successful instances of money creation for the purpose of economic stimulus can be traced to increases of credit, i.e., an increase in economic activity not tied to current expenditure. However, the creation of excessive amounts of currency (fiat or specie) can lead to lower economic activity. For instance, inflow of specie from the Americas was argued to have depressed economic activity in the countries that directly benefited from these inflows (Portugal and Spain) (cf. Cantillon in [60]).

Money is therefore a social construct creating an asset that can be used in exchange, as a unit of account, and as a store of value. Among the assets that serve as money, there is generally a subset known as cash that has has crucial specific properties that are sometimes overlooked by classical economists:

Immediate finality of payment Cash transfers are non-reversible and therefore final as soon as they occur unless there is an obvious evidence of theft. In contrast, even simple non-cash transactions such as credit card payments are subject to potential unwind risks related to uncovered obligations.

Anonymity Two parties can transact in cash without knowing the identity of the other party.

Decentralisation Cash transactions do not rely on third parties, in particularly not on a bank providing account services.

Indentifiability Users should be able to readily identify the asset and distinguish it from counterfeits.

Cash transactions incur significant costs related to the safe storage, distribution, collection and counting of cash. Because cash can be transferred quickly and anonymously, there is much more of an incentive to steal cash than any other asset. Stocking cash machines in a remote location of a large country, and returning cash taken in the shops of that location to the central bank requires a lot of transportation in special trucks. Users of the cash usually do not consider such costs which are, however, intimately related to these four properties.

---

[2]Some economists assume instead that money is an obligation of the central government under a theory called chartalism or, more optimistically, Modern Monetary Theory (MMT). Such thinking might be encouraged by evidence like Section 16 of the Federal Reserve Act [34] which states that bank notes 'shall be obligations of the United States'. The motivation for this statement is likely to have been that in 1913 when the Federal Reserve System was set up bank notes were issued by private banks which could be subject to defaults. By explicitly putting the credibility of the federal government behind the 'greenback', the stability of the new paper currency was enhanced. This does not negate the self-referential nature of fiat money. The link between government debt and currency is contradicted not only by cases where currency is used even though the central government has no credibility (the Somali Shilling at the time of writing), but also cases where societies use money issued in other jurisdictions, i.e., cases of dollarisation.

2.2   EARLY FORMS OF MONEY

The oldest form of money is physical and many still think of money in physical terms. As long as there is sufficient stability in the supply of any commodity and its value in terms of other commodities can therefore be reliably assessed, it can be used as money. Money that is based on the value of the commodity of which it is made is known as commodity money. In the larger Asian and Western societies, money used to be associated with precious metals, namely gold and, to a smaller degree, silver. It is therefore common to think of money as something that has value in and of itself, leading to the idea that the 'gold standard', gold-based money, is something inherently desirable. Other cultures used standard commodities, such as rice or grain, to express and settle obligations. However, the exclusive use of commodities as money is neither the historical origin of money, nor is it its apparent direction. Before discussing the basics of modern monies for the purposes of trading in the money market, it is instructive to spend some time on the history of money.

Seen as a tool, cash should be reasonably portable, easily recognisable and difficult to counterfeit. In central Europe, where mining was introduced fairly late, commodities such as salt played the role of money for a long time. Salt was sufficiently scarce to give small amounts of it appreciable value; it can be kept for a long time; and it is difficult to forge. Salt is also an essential food ingredient, so salt obtained in trade could be consumed if it wasn't needed for as a store of wealth. This is only one example for using consumables as money. Islamic law recognises six commodities that must be traded 'equal for equal, and hand to hand' (gold, silver, wheat, barley, dates and salt). Islamic law referring to these six commodities is deemed to apply to money in general and therefore governs, for instance FX transactions.

When an item used as money has an idiosyncratic value, for instance under the gold standard, the credit element of money can be obscured. Receivers of money then receive a valuable asset as well as an abstract commodity. However, the production value of gold, or any other form of commodity money, can fluctuate relative to that of other commodities, for instance as a result of advances in mining technology. The historical stability of a commodity as a means of payment is therefore probably at least in part due to its function of money. Users of commodity monies accept the commodity with a view to its future value for purchases, i.e., its monetary value, rather than for its intrinsic value alone. The validity of this argument is difficult to prove conclusively with historical data. It amounts to the statement that stability of prices under a gold standard is not just the result of the value of gold anchoring the value of other goods, but that conversely the value of gold is also anchored by the value of other goods. In the current, post-metallic currency system, the predominant role of the US dollar as an international trade invoice currency is likely to stabilise its exchange value[3].

The volatility of gold prices since the demonetisation of gold in the second half of the 20th century is an illustration, albeit an imperfect one, of this point. Figure 2.1 shows the ratio of the gold price in dollars to the urban consumer price index, which

---

[3]This is the essence of the 'exorbitant privilege' enjoyed by the US, although the deep liquidity of the dollar-denominated capital markets also support the external value of the dollar.

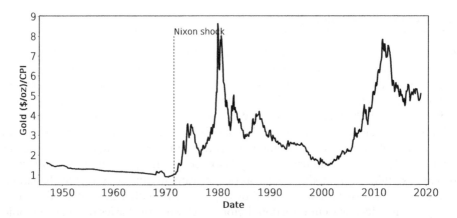

FIGURE 2.1   Gold price (London fixing) in US dollars divided by the US Urban Consumer Price index. Data retrieved from FRED.

is a measure of the price of a standard basket of goods and services in the US. A stable exchange ratio between gold and goods and services would imply a low volatility of this series. The data appears to bear out the idea that monetary use of gold may have stabilised this ratio before the suspension of dollar convertibility into gold by President Nixon on 15 August 1971 made it more volatile.

However, the technical background is more complex. Under the Bretton Woods system, the dollar was pegged to gold which required the active control of gold supply and demand by central banks. The dollar prices of other goods and services meanwhile followed other economic trends, including the policies of the Federal Reserve System. Stability of gold relative to goods and services in the US was therefore due to a common anchor, namely the US dollar. The higher volatility of gold relative to other prices following the suspension of gold convertibility is therefore not only due to changes in market mechanisms but the result of changed government policies. At the same time, gold sometimes outperforms other assets in times of crisis because some investors expect it to become more valuable as a monetary commodity.

Metals, especially precious metals, make the best commodity monies because they are easy to store, count, and transfer. However, at most times in history, commodity monies in practice have traded at a premium or discount to the actual commodity. If money can be made from the metal and turned back into the non-monetary metal itself (viz. the minting and melting of coins), the cost of minting or melting provides a corridor around the inherent metal value within which the commodity money can trade. Normally, minted money is slightly more expensive than its commodity value because it is more convenient to use as a means of payment. In some cases, minting is restricted to certain workshops operated or licensed by a sovereign and money creation is subject to a special form of tax, known as seigniorage [71]. The value V of a coin is then given by the following inequality involving the inherent metal value V_i, minting cost V_M, melting cost V_m and seigniorage S:

$$V_i - V_m \leq V \leq V_i + V_M + S \tag{2.1}$$

If a coin is trading below the lower of these boundaries, scrap metal merchants would find it attractive to melt it down, while if coins are trading above the boundary, it would be attractive to mint new coins. The use of coins introduces a number of interesting economic problems, but these are of no interest for the financial markets. The interested reader is referred to the literature, in particular [71].

A legal concept called *lex monetae* stipulates that each sovereign can legislate what constitutes money in its own jurisdiction. This concept is at the same time trivial and misleading. A sovereign can certainly legislate what types of assets can be used to discharge debts stated in monetary terms, at least as far as court-enforced payments are concerned. Such assets are referred to as legal tender or forced money. Given that sovereigns are usually able to levy taxes, and therefore command large payment flows, prescribing legal tender can lend significance to assets by legal fiat. While *lex monetae* in this sense is not written legislation, its operation can be found already in old international treaties. The Pax Westphalica, the peace treaty that in 1648 ended the hostilities of the 30 Years War and set important precedents for international law in Europe, specified restitution payments in the local currency of the respective sovereigns [67]. That being said, those sovereigns were all using gold as the base of their currencies at the time. On this evidence, *lex monetae* amounts to the acknowledging that sovereigns have the right to stamp their own coinage.

Beyond this trivial scope of *lex monetae*, societies can find themselves in situations where the legislated money is unsuitable for daily transactions and choose to use other means of exchange, such as money issued in other jurisdictions. The misleading aspect of *lex monetae* therefore is that it can suggest that full control of a sovereign over the money used in its jurisdiction is at all times assured. Taken to the extreme, it would seem to extend to giving sovereigns the right to change the value of monetary claims by changing the national currency[4]. While possible in some national laws, the absence of *lex monetae* in international treaties means that this option is unavailable in cross-border funding.

Depending on the money used, the actual inherent metal value was sometimes difficult to estimate because coins with different degrees of purity were in circulation, or the weight of a coin could not easily be assessed. When a government deliberately brings coins of lower purity into circulation this is called debasement of a currency[5]. Various techniques to achieve the same effect were invented by private forgers. For instance, until Sir Isaac Newton invented the rolling of coins, the practice of cutting off the edges of coins (clipping) was used to reduce the weight of coins relative to their nominal value.

In other parts of the world, island tribes in the Carribean used sea shells or curiously shaped stones as money, known as wampun. The conceptual importance of wampun

---

[4]During the euro crisis in 2010, some commentators suggested that *lex monetae* would give euro area member states the right to repay euro-denominated debts in devaluated domestic currencies without being in default.

[5]It is the history of debasements conducted in order to reduce government debt that excited the aficionados of lex monetae at the height of the euro crisis. Reverting to a national currency which would then be devalued against the euro was seen as a way to reduce excessive debt burdens in some euro members states. The fundamental flaw with this argument, as far as EU Law is concerned, is that article 118 of the Treaty on the Functioning of the European Union states that the euro is the currency of the European Union. Whatever rights *lex monetae* may be conferring, euro area member states have signed them away. In addition, changing the denomination of an existing security to the detriment of bond holders is likely to be an illegal unilateral contract modification in most legal systems.

relative to the use of precious metal is that wampun has no inherent commodity value at all. It is therefore money that derives its value purely by social agreement. Money that is defined purely through social agreement in this way is known in economics as fiat money[6]. All modern currencies are fiat monies in this sense. However, the discussion about commodity money above shows that even commodity monies usually have a value component that is no different from fiat money. In particular, seigniorage introduces such a component into a commodity money. The act of minting is only important if there is a social convention to use particular coins, or a particular advantage in doing so.

2.2.1 Paper money and bank notes

Transacting large amounts of trading using physical coins is difficult and between the 9th and 11th centuries, the Chinese monetary system introduced paper money to make trading easier. In addition, frequent episodes of debasement eroded the faith in the coins of some jurisdictions. This created an incentive for merchants to establish payment instruments linked to metal of a known purity and weight. When paper money is discussed in the context of commodity money, the underlying commodity is usually referred to as specie.

Two very different forms of paper money exist, namely certificates and bank notes. A certificate is documentary evidence of a particular amount of metal (or other commodity money) that is stored somewhere in physical form. Certificates are therefore simply a more convenient way of transacting trades in commodity money and this is the original form of paper money used in China. Certificates are always fully backed by the physical commodity and holders of the certificate can easily exchange the paper for the physical commodity.

A bank note in the current sense, however, is merely a document stating the promise of a particular issuing bank to pay a certain amount of money. In other words, bank notes are debt certificates that are payable on demand. Among the major currencies, the English pound is one of the few to still retain this notion and pound notes state this payment promise explicitly, as shown in Figure 2.2.

Bank notes in Europe developed naturally from certificate monies. The point at which a depositary receipt becomes a bank note is when the issuer of the note can lend the physical money to a third party, i.e., when the trustee becomes a banker. The transition from the sole use of specie or certficates for payment towards bank notes represents an important transition in the definition of money: When paper money is accepted as payment in transactions, the banks issuing this paper create money. As a result, two parallel monies exist in the economy, namely the original specie (outside money) and the paper money and deposit money issued by banks (inside money). These two monies are in principle interchangeable, at least as long as the public has no doubts as to the ability of banks to pay out specie on demand.

---

[6]Fiat is latin for 'let there be'.

FIGURE 2.2 Detail of an old five pounds sterling bank note. Because this note was legal tender in England, the Bank of England could keep the promise by returning the note to the bearer. Source: Bank of England.

2.3 FIAT MONEY

The last step in the creation of modern money is to realise that the deposit of specie does not actually need to exist as long as some form of bank note is generally accepted as a means of payment. Indeed, as Kynaston pointed out [53], the suspension of cash (gold) payment on Bank of England notes in 1797 marked the transition to paper money, and this transition was made possible by concomitant declarations by merchants that they would accept the paper notes as payments despite their suspended convertibility into specie[7].

To stay with the English pound as an example; the promise shown in Figure 2.2 is economically meaningless because anybody delivering this note to the Bank of England with the demand to repayment could in practice be given the same note back. The note is a legal instrument for discharging debts in England (legal tender) and therefore the obligation of the Bank would be fulfilled by the return of the note. For this reason, the US dollar notes simply state that they are legal tender, and the notes of most other currencies, including euros and yen, simply state a nominal amount. Through the circuituous route of metal-based money, modern economies now have established a cash system that is based purely on social contract. The use of token monies in this system is similar to wampun.

2.3.1 Fiat money and trade

For a metal-based currency to work, there must be enough physical metal available to withstand a bank run. Banks in a metallic system generally hold a so-called reserve of

---

[7]Technically speaking, 1797 was not the first time the Bank of England suspended payments in specie because such an episode occurred already more than a hundred years earlier. What made 1797 special is that the suspension was mandated by law. Proponents of the gold standard would do well to remember that such currency arrangements tend to be suspended just when they are supposed to be most attractive, namely in times of crisis. In 1797, the immediate cause of the crisis was the onset of the Napoleonic Wars.

specie that is designed to cover redemption requests, as well as specie required for inter-bank transactions. This reserve can be held individually or through a central reserve bank, but must be sufficient to satisfy the expected maximum amount of notes that could be presented for payment. The ratio of reserves held to the amount of banknotes outstanding is called the reserve ratio.

This requirement creates a straightjacket for money creation because the reserve ratio, and hence the monetary multiplier in Equation (4.3) cannot easily be altered. In effect, the amount of money that can be created in such an economy is limited by what that economy can source in terms of reserve metal. For this reason, some economists advocate the return to a metal-based monetary system because they see pure fiat cur-rencies as an easy temptation for inflationary policies (see e.g. Friedman [37] for an entertaining discussion). Indeed, when sovereigns have replaced metal-based curren-cies with fiat money, the intention was often to raise funds at the expense of the general population through deliberate debasement, leading to bouts of high inflation. In par-ticular, episodes of paper money in economies that were otherwise using metal-based currencies are usually associated with wars.

However that may be, the mathematical realities of modern economies make the idea of meaningful commodity links unrealistic in any case. The 'straightjacket' men-tioned above has become too tight for the world economy. At the time of writing, the quarterly trade deficit of the United States of America alone is in the same order of magnitude as the annual world gold production[8]. In international commerce, where national laws regarding bank reserves are largely irrelevant, this trade deficit would have to be covered with large outflows of physical gold[9]. Even if the monetary gold holdings of the USA were able to cover this outflow for a sustained period, the loss of reserve metal would lead to an eventual contraction of the monetary base in the USA[10].

By instead settling international trade in fiat money, trade volumes are not con-strained by the availability of a specific physical commodity. The physical constraint is replaced by one based on expectations. A persistent large large trade deficit creates doubts about the value of holding the currency of that country. This will over time lead to a cheapening of that currency, hopefully making the country more competitive in international trade, and correcting the trade imbalance. Whether either of these two adjustments works in practice is a matter of conjecture because every exchange rate involves two currencies, and cross-border fund flows can also be affected by investment in financial instruments and real assets.

---

[8]The US trade deficit in 2019 averaged USD 51.4bn per month while the 2018 world gold produc-tion of 3,332 tons had a market value of around USD 135.5bn using the average London fixing (Source: World Gold Council, FRED).

[9]Persistently large gold outflows were the driver for the suspension of dollar gold convertibility by President Nixon on 15 August 1971.

[10]The opium wars between the UK and China are often linked to the drain of sterling silver from the UK to India which had to be offset by silver income from selling drugs to China.

CHAPTER 3

Banks

3.1 BANKS AND BANK MONEY CREATION

Although the word bank has been used several times already, no definition has been provided. A good reason to defer this definition is that it is not easy to provide one given on one hand the many functions banks perform, and on the other hand the many banking functions performed by non-banks. In a very narrow sense, a bank is an institution that holds itself out as offering the service of paying cash on demand to its customers. This cash can be money held at the bank after having first been placed there by the customer, or money that is created through the provision of credit, as outlined below.

The core function of banks as depositary institutions is that they offer the service of accepting deposit money from the public and paying back these deposits, usually on demand. Deposits that are repaid only after a set period are known as time deposits, those that can be reclaimed at any time as demand deposits or sight deposits. In the United States, so-called checking deposits are demand deposits that can be drawn on by writing cheques. Banks in some cases offered to certify deposited amounts through pieces of paper, called bank notes.

Many bank functions are related to this core definition. Banks for instance offer securities dealing and custody services which require cash payments to purchase securities, and crediting of interest and dividend payments to the customer accounts. Some non-banks can perform very similar functions. Insurance companies and asset managers also hold client assets but may have different rules for accessing these assets and turning them into cash.

The functions performed by banks pre-dated the existence of banks as an institutional species. For instance, the Knights Templar operated a financial service network that can be compared to modern-day travellers cheques. Another impetus for the development of banking was that merchants employed their capital in the form of loans to other merchants as an alternative to risking it in their own ventures. Merchants had the choice to charter a ship, send it to a faraway destination with goods and money for exchange, and try selling the goods returned, if any, for a profit using their own capital. Providing partial financing to a similar venture by another merchant offered different risks and returns and gave rise to the business of merchant banking [84].

3.2   CATEGORIES OF BANKS

Banks are usually set up for particular purposes that are narrower than the general definition above. Some banks are set up to collect funds for particular types of investments. The Banque de France of John Law and the Bank of England were set up to fund government expenditure [41,53]. Schlesische Landschaften, Deutsche Pfandbriefbank and Kreditkassen for Husejerne i Kjøbenhavn started as institutions to collect funds for real estate projects of various types. Many commercial banks, meanwhile, focus on trade financing. At the same time, banks are also founded with a focus on their liability side, namely as vehicles to invest funds from particular communities. Mutual and savings banks in Europe, the regional banks in Japan, and US community banks are as much concerned with managing the liquid assets of their communities as they are with particular asset side business. Last but not least, some banks serve as infrastructure providers to other financial institutions and are less well known outside this industry. Such institutions would comprise the Continuous Linked Settlement Bank (CLS Bank) offering settlement services in the FX market, or State Street and Bank of New York acting as custodians for the asset management industry.

It should be noted that setting up a bank to fund a particular type of economic activity does not mean that this activity has free access to funds. Like any enterprise, banks need to be able to earn their cost of capital to remain in business indefinitely. At the same time, banks compete in the market for customer assets, both among each other and against other types of asset manager, or indeed non-financial investments. When specialist banks are set up to conduct promotional lending, such as development banks, the advantage they provide to their clientele versus other lenders stems from lower cost of capital. This is usually provided through a non-profit nature (which means that the paid-up capital does not carry an equity risk premium), and guarantees for their funding (which reduces the credit risk premium of their debt). Brecht's famous pseudo-koan 'What is the robbing of a bank compared to the setting up of a bank?' is therefore flawed.

Some jurisdictions create different classes of banking businesses and prevent single legal entities from engaging in more than one of them. The original separation principle was the US Glass-Stegall Act of 1933 which prevented securities underwriters from conducting regular banking business. One motivation of this law was to police the conflicts of interest that arise when a bank can decide to lend to a firm on its own risk, or invite customers to assume this risk. The Glass-Stegall Act was repealed under President Clinton in 1999 but at the time had only limited practical effect. Japan retains a clear separation between banks, trust banks, and securities firms, and requires this separation to be explicit in the names of the legal entities. Firms of different types are permitted, however, to be held within the same holding companies. Germany and France retain specialist bank designations (Sparkassen, Banques Populaires, Sociétés de crédit foncier) but Germany abolished its specialist Pfandbriefbank designation in 2005. As a result of the 2008 financial crisis, the United Kingdom introduced a concept of ring-fencing which requires that the assets and liabilities of retail banks need to be isolated from those of a wholesale bank in the same group. This is an advanced form of segregation designed to protect retail customers from the supposedly riskier parts of a bank. Other jurisdictions achieve similar effects by requiring 'living wills', i.e., continuously updated plans for an orderly wind-down of a complex and significant financial entity.

Banking separation is a principle that must not be confused with the idea of 'narrow banking', also known as 'positive money'. This concept in political economics seeks to address financial risks by prohibiting the creation of private credit money as discussed below. In essence, narrow banking amounts to total government control over the money supply, which, given the fluctuations in money demand, means government control over the allocation of credit.

CHAPTER 4

Bank Money Creation

This section outlines the process of money creation via the extension of private bank credit. The money so created is known as credit money, or inside money. The vast bulk of money used in modern societies is created in this way, rather than through the actions of central banks. However, as will be outlined below, this money is convertible into central bank money, including bank notes, making it virually economically equivalent. To reflect current practice, electronic book-entry money is used here instead of the historical private bank notes.

The presentation here is based on double-entry book-keeping to make it easier to understand. The double entry principle means that every increase in an asset is accompanied by an increase in a liability or decrease of another asset by an equal amount. In the same way, an increase in a liability required an increase in an asset, or decrease of another liability. As usual, assets are shown on the left and liabilities on the right.

4.1 SINGLE-BANK INTRODUCTION

The essential process in creating money is for a bank extend a loan to a customer by crediting the customer's current account with the loan amount. The loan is a new asset for the bank and this increase of assets is accompanied by an increase in deposit liabilities. The process is shown in Figure 4.1.

It should be noted that, for now, this process has no impact on any economic actor aside from the bank and its customer. The loan exists only as a bilateral contractual relationship between these two entities, as does the balancing deposit.

The nominal amount of the deposit need not be the same as that of the loan. For instance, a Danish mortgage is created by the sale of a new mortgage bond so that the deposit amount is linked to the *market* price of that security at the time. The borrower is responsible for the repayment of his or her share of the bond at its *nominal* value[1].

The key to understanding why money has been created lies in the business model of a bank. Because deposits can readily be converted into cash or transferred, they are effectively means of payment. Bank deposits have a certain degree of credit risk but for most bank customers, this risk is outweighed by the convenience of not having to look

---

[1]The impact of the loan on the balance sheet of the bank is also simplified here because the bank may recognise certain fees immediately as profit and loss so that they go into the equity portion of the right-hand side of the bank's balance sheet.

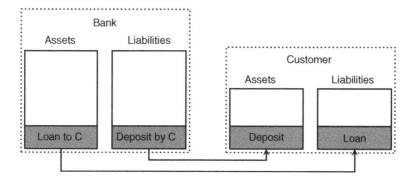

FIGURE 4.1 The money creation process. A bank lends money to a customer and credits this money to the customer's current account. The arrows link corresponding assets and liabilities on the balance sheets of bank and customer.

after and handle physical cash. Still, while bank deposits are denominated in currencies that are legal tender (such as euros, dollars or yen), they are not identical to cash.

In practice, most modern economies restrict this process through reserve requirements. Such requirements oblige the bank to hold central bank money in an amount that covers a certain minimum fraction of a subset of their deposits. Historically, the reserve of a bank was the amount of physical specie it held against redemption requests of bank notes it had issued. Because physical specie is difficult to increase in times of high redemptions (which usually coincide with crises of confidence), reserve holdings had to have a prudent size. In modern economies, central bank money is predominantly electronic and can be created instantly. Reserve requirements are therefore now mainly a means for the creation of a structural demand for central bank money, and therefore a monetary policy tool.

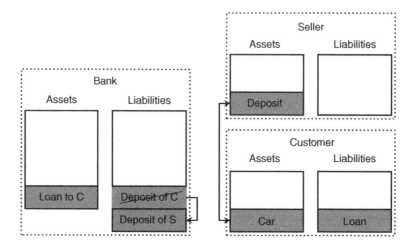

FIGURE 4.2 Transfer of a deposit between two customers of the same bank as part of a sale transaction.

In the simplest case, the customer can use the deposit to purchase an asset, like a car, via a transfer to a seller who has a current account at the same bank. The purchase reduces the bank liability linked to the customer desposit but increases the deposit liability to the seller by the same amount (cf. Figure 4.2).

While this transaction is simple and, as far as money is concerned, only involves the manipulation of book entries in the bank, it has an important precondition: Both customers of the bank need to be willing to transact in the money of this bank, and in this case have current accounts with it. This is a very strong condition and unrealistic in practice. The logical next step is therefore to consider transactions involving multiple banks.

4.2 EXTENSION TO MULTIPLE BANKS

Deposits at different banks, even in the same currency, are at first sight non-equivalent. Since deposits are private current liabilities where the debtor is a bank, they carry the name-specific credit risk of the bank they are held at. Seen as assets, anyone asking somebody else to accept money deposited in a bank for payment in effect asks the payee to accept that bank's credit risk. This includes transfers between deposits at different banks: a customer asking to credit an account with money held at a different bank asks the receiving bank to accept the credit of the bank the holds the original deposit. In the days of private-issue bank notes and cheques, a customer paying a banknote issued by one bank, or a check drawn on it, into an account held at a different bank would in effect ask the receiving bank to accept the credit of the issuing bank.

As discussed in the context of deposits at a single bank, the reason why deposits at different banks in the same currency are largely fungible is that each bank stands ready to pay out deposits in legal tender. A natural limit to the payments a bank can expect to make is that many customers keep money at the bank for a considerable amount of time as part of their savings. A second factor is that banks receive payments as well as make them. This factor leads to the idea of netting.

The amount of interbank credit that customer transfers force banks to extend can be reduced through netting. In simple bilateral netting, two banks A and B work out the net flow between them, i.e., the positive difference of money sent to B from A on one hand, and from A to B on the other. The bilateral flow would then be reduced to the difference of these amounts. More netting efficiency can be obtained through multilateral netting because then flows through intermediaries can be included in the netting calculation. Assuming four banks A, B, C, and D take part and f_{AB} denotes the money sent from A to B, and so on, one can set up a matrix of flows and net across all payment flows as shown in Figure 4.3.

This type of netting was indeed performed for paper cheques by placing cheques on a large table subdivided in the same way as the matrix in Figure 4.3. Because the reduction of payment obligations is a joint benefit of the participating banks, they have an interest to set up and optimise this form of cooperation despite competing for the underlying business that creates the payment obligations in the first place. Netting is more effective when done over a larger volume of payments. This argues for holding

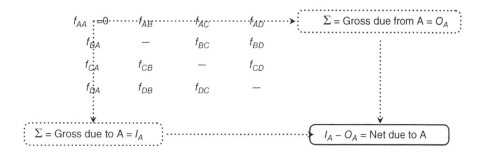

FIGURE 4.3 Netting across multiple interbank transfers. The final receivable or payment obligation of bank A is calculated by first summing up inflows and outflows separately and then netting the result. The net payments of all banks add to zero.

payments for some time, netting them and then processing the net amounts. A longer netting period, however, allows for more imbalances to build up which increases risk in the system. However, even after netting is performed and interbank payment obligations are reduced in this way, the net amounts will not be zero at the end of each day. Over time, payments between banks should more or less balance out, but that does not reduce the need to process payments.

It is therefore still necessary to have mechanisms that allow a change of obligor through interbank transfers. There are two ways to arrange this, both of which are in common use. One is based on bilateral relationships where banks hold deposits for each other, the other involves central clearing banks. The latter can be central banks, and this is indeed the form of interbank transfer that is the most prevalent in developed economies. As will become clear, the second type of transfer is simply a special form of the first.

The first transfer mechanism uses so-called nostro accounts which are current accounts held by one bank at another bank[2]. When bank A is asked to make a payment to a customer S banking at bank B where bank A holds a sufficient amount of money in a nostro account, it will ask B to transfer money from that nostro account into the account of S. Viewing this in terms of the four balance sheets affected, the following picture emerges:

Customer C The deposit (asset) at bank A is reduced by the transfer amount, this is offset by the inflow of whatever asset has been purchased from S.

Customer S The deposit (asset) at bank B is increased by the transfer amount, this is offset by the outflow of whatever asset has been sold to C.

Bank A The deposit of A (liability) is reduced by the transfer amount, this is offset by the reduction in the nostro account balance (asset) by the transfer amount. The size of bank A's balance sheet contracts by the transfer amount which is intuitive because the transfer is an outflow of assets.

Bank B The nostro account balance of A (liability) is reduced by the transfer amount, this is offset by an equal increase of the deposit of S (liability).

---

[2]'Nostro', meaning 'ours', refers to the account holding bank viewing it as their asset held somewhere else.

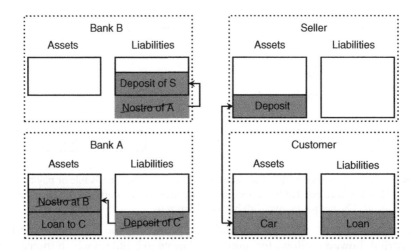

FIGURE 4.4   Transfer of a deposit between two customers of two different banks using a nostro account. For bank B, this transfer is an internal transaction between the deposits of two customers (S and bank A).

The transfer is depicted graphically in Figure 4.4.

An important question is how nostro account balances are created in the first place. These balances are inside money, which is in this case created by bank B. A simple way to create such money is for bank A to simply ask for a loan from bank B. Such a loan would usually be collateralised in some form so that when bank B discounts (cf. Section 4.4.2) a bill drawn on bank A, B does not accept unprotected the credit risk of bank A. Alternatively, bank A could sell an asset, or a debt obligation to the public and deposit the funds so raised in its nostro account at bank B. last but not least, bank A can receive payments into its nostro account at B if the reverse transaction to the one presented here is executed between customers like C and S.

Nostro accounts used in this way pay an important role in cross-border finance because not every bank will have an equal presence in every market. If bank A is active in one part of the world but would like to offer regular payment services to its clients in a different jurisdiction, it can do so by engaging the services of a bank B active in that jurisdiction as explained here. For instance, even a small manufacturer would typically need to pay suppliers and receive payments from costumers in other countries. As it would be impractical for the manufacturer to maintain accounts at banks in every jurisdiction involved, or to bank with a bank that is active in all of them, it will instead use a bank that has correspondent banking relationships to process these payments[3].

Nostro accounts have the disadvantage of consuming balance sheet for the banks involved. They need to hold sufficient funds to deal with usual cumulative flows

---

[3]It should be mentioned that correspondent banking is not without problems. Because the correspondent bank makes payments on behalf of another bank without having full knowledge of the underlying transaction and (in the example here) one of the customers involved (C), it may unwittingly aid the flow of illegally obtained funds.

between two banks and these funds lie idle unless, and until, there is a customer payment requiring their use. Banks can reduce idle balances in nostro accounts by regularly sweeping them into other assets but the balance sheet benefit of doing so is still limited.

Instead of settling interbank payments bilaterally between the two banks involved, a more efficient mechanism has arisen where third-party payment processors centralise the payment flows between sets of banks. In the UK, these central payment processors are large private banks known as money-centre banks. The German savings banks use regional central banks (Girozentralbanken and Landeszentralbanken) that are jointly owned by the participating savings banks and their regional governments. The smaller Japanese banks use their jointly owned respective central treasuries (Norinchukin, Shinkin Chukin, Shoko Chukin, etc.)[4].

The central payment processor can be seen as a bank in which every participating bank has a nostro account. The net payments arising after a netting process as shown in Figure 4.3 are executed by crediting and debiting these nostro accounts. In this arrangement, instead of every bank having to maintain a nostro account at every other participating bank, it only maintains one account at the central payments processor.

It follows from this setup that the central payments processor must have a superior credit relative to that of the participating bank because its central role requires that every participating bank treats a deposit at the central processor as free of default risk. The standard way of ensuring this superior credit is to restrict the activities of this institution or equip it with strong guarantees of a highly trusted entity. Today's financial systems rely on central banks to perform this role so that the mechanism can be explained in that context.

4.3 TRANSFER SETTLEMENT IN CENTRAL BANK MONEY

The final step in the evolution of modern payments processing is the merger of the central payments processing function with that of a central bank (central banks are discussed in detail in Chapter 5). A deposit at a central bank is money and there is therefore no credit risk associated with such a deposit[5]. The larger central banks offer interbank payments systems that enable banks to transfer deposits held at the central bank between each other. Banks may choose to conduct netting as discussed in

---

[4]In the German system in its prime, the savings bank in one region used their regional Landesbank to process payments between them, while payments between regions were handled by a central bank for the Landesbanken. The successor of this bank is now known as DekaBank Deutsche Girozentrale. Its central role of payments processing has become less important, however, through the advent of the ECB's TARGET2 system. DekaBank now handles mostly central securities-related tasks and the German payments system has evolved from a three-tiered to a two-tiered structure.

[5]It should be remembered, however, that credit risk in this sense refers to the risk of money not being available when called for. Even a central bank deposit carries the risk that the money it refers to loses acceptance in the private market, i.e., the risk of a currency devaluation or capital controls.

TABLE 4.1 The main real time gross payments systems.

Central bank	Name	Access
Federal Reserve	FedWire	Federal Reserve member banks, depositary intitutions, foreign bank branches
ECB	TARGET2	Eurosystem counterparties (MFIs)
Bank of Japan	BOJ-NET	Banks (banks, trust banks, shinkin banks, etc.), branches of foreign banks, securities firms, securities finance firms, money market brokers
Bank of England	RTGS/CHAPS	Banks, building societies, investment firms and central counterparties
People's Bank of China	High-value payment system	Banks, PBoC branches

Figure 4.3 but such netting, if it occurs, is of no concern to the central bank. Transfers between current accounts at a central bank are executed as instructed, which implies that they are viewed as gross transfers by the central bank. To enable efficient use of the deposits, transfers are executed in real time or near real time.

The essential difference between using central payments processors and central banks for interbank payments is that accounts held at a central bank are economically identical to legal tender. Payment in central bank money, or transfers between central bank current accounts, therefore achieve immediate finality, i.e., transfers of assets that are not subject to the credit risks of the parties involved.

On the other hand, when the central payment processor is a bank then the liquidity generated in this bank (in other words, the credit balances held by the participating banks) is potentially cheaper than central bank liquidity. Jointly owned clearing banks would distribute interest earned on debit balances (after costs) to their owners, which are at the same time the users of the system. If the same users had to source central bank cash at the prevailing policy rate, the same interest earned at the central bank would be paid out to someone else (usually the government). As mentioned above, the downside is that the participants assume convertibility risk, i.e., the risk that the clearing bank fails and balances held there cease to be convertible into central bank money. Usually, therefore, the joint owners of such clearing banks also guarantee them jointly.

Some payments systems provide intraday credit, which in essence means that while in principle only transfers between positive account balances can be made through these systems, the central bank providing such accounts allows them to be overdrawn during the day.

The practical reason to allow such overdrafts is to make the system robust against the reordering of transactions. Table 4.2 shows an example of how the ordering of transactions can determine whether an overdraft is required or not.

Incentivising payment participants to re-order transactions in order to avoid the recourse to intraday overdrafts can be counterproductive. Every participant would seek to delay outgoing payments and accelerate incoming flows although the incoming flow for one participant is an outgoing flow for another.

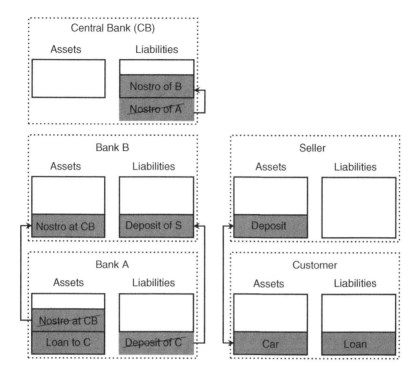

FIGURE 4.5 Transfer of a deposit between two customers of two different banks using a central clearer or central bank. In essence, part of the balance sheet of bank A is transferred with finality to the balance sheet of bank B. The central bank balance sheet size is unaffected because only the designation of an existing liability changes.

TABLE 4.2 Example for the effect of transaction ordering on intra-day cash balances. Changing the timing of the transaction marked in bold makes the difference between requiring an intraday overdraft or not.

Case A			Case B		
Time	Payment	Balance	Time	Payment	Balance
6:00		100	6:00		100
8:15	50	150	8:15	50	150
9:23	**−200**	**−50**	10:01	100	250
10:01	100	50	**11:04**	**−200**	50
12:03	50	100	12:03	**50**	100
19:00		100	19:00		100

At the same time, allowing overdrafts exposes the payment system to the risk that a participant turns out to be unable close a negative balance at the end of a payment day. This is the reason why direct participation in central bank operated payments system is generally restricted to monetary policy counterparties. Such institutions have in any case recourse to funds-providing facilities of the central bank that grants the overdraft.

Any negative balances left at the end of a trading day can be covered with new central bank money. However, the recourse to such a facility may be seen as negative by the central bank and be sanctioned. System participants would normally be expected to arrange for end-of-day balances to be covered by normal means, including regular funding operations by the central bank.

As a result, payment systems without overdraft can encourage higher cash holdings at participating banks. In essence, these banks substitute overdrafts at the payment system with higher cash reserve holdings. From a systematic point of view, the intraday liquidity provision is done in the private sector, rather than at the central bank. Whether this is preferrable is in essence a matter of belief. From a monetary policy viewpoint, the transactional money demand is a distraction from the central banks stance. Having to accommodate such demand visibly through overnight cash, rather than implicitly through intraday credit in the payment system, can therefore sometimes conflict with the intended signalling effect. In the US, where the Fed normally targets the overnight rate through daily open market operations, this downside is less pronounced than in the euro area, where the main pre-crisis operation was a weekly repo tender. This may be one reason why TARGET2 with intraday overdrafts and FedWire without this facility form stable equilibria with the respective operational frameworks.

4.4 TRADE AND NON-BANK CREDIT

Trading as a source of lending in the economy is often neglected in macroeconomic analyses. Most of the trade between companies, and sometimes between companies and customers, is conducted on credit. Sellers of goods and services tend to invoice customers in arrears. This is related to the idea that a trader buying a good needs some time to resell it before the maker could be paid from the proceeds. From an economic viewpoint, delivering a good or service for later payment amounts to a loan granted by the producer to the trader. The terms of this loan, in particular the currency and duration, can be negotiated freely between the trading partners.

The extent of trade credit can be measured on a single company level by the accounts payable and accounts receivable items on corporate balance sheets, at least on reporting days. By comparing the sales of a company (i.e., the flow of receivables through the company's accounts) to its accounts payable balance sheet item, one can calculate the the average time between finalising a sale and eventual payment. This is known in corporate finance as the collection period [13, 46]:

$$\text{Collection period} = \frac{\text{Accounts receivable}}{\text{Total sales}} \tag{4.1}$$

Note that accounts are usually published on a quarterly basis and corporations may have incentives to manage balance sheet items up or down around reporting dates. For instance, a company might prefer to be paid before December 31st on a particular invoice in order to reduce accounts receivable at year end. Doing so would shorten its collection period as defined in Equation (4.1). In other circumstances, leaving an outstanding balance with a customer may offer a better return than depositing cash with a bank and a later payment would be preferable.

Although most markets have established conventions on invoice currencies and payment terms, there is a considerable degree of freedom for corporate treasuries to manage the currency and maturity composition of their accounts payable and receivable. Deviations from market standards may incur extra costs but may be outweighed by the benefits, whether it be through appreciation by users of published accounts or through economic returns. As a result, terms of payment are not simply a matter of convention but can be part of active balance sheet management.

It is even possible to vary invoice periods by currency. A company that pays invoices quickly in currency A but allows for invoices in currency B to be paid to itself over longer periods replicates a short A, long B position. Such a position can be difficult to spot in corporate accounts, and therefore in international balances of payments.

4.4.1 Non-cash trading instruments

Trading on credit can take the form of trading on account or the form of negotiable non-cash instruments such as bills of exchange and cheques. When trading on account, the seller maintains an account for each customer. Deliveries to the customer lead to debits against the account while payments from the customer are credited to the same account. Accounts can be in surplus (as a result of overpayment by the customer) but are usually in debit or flat. Trading on account is common when traders interact with non-traders because the relationship is strongly asymmetric.

Bills of exchange are payment instruments that represent an unconditional obligation of the party that it is drawn on, the drawer. Bills are payable on demand after their stated first payment date on presentation to the drawer. Usually, the seller of a good would issue a bill and present it to the buyer for acceptance in exchange for handing over the goods. Once accepted, the bill becomes unconditional. Due to this property bills themselves are being used as means of payment between traders. The payee of a bill can transfer it as payment to another trader by means of endorsing it to the recipient. For bills in paper form, this involves a simple signature on the back of the bill. Endorsement does not change the payment amount or payment date of the bill. However, it creates a conditional liability on the trader that endorsed it. If the original drawer of the bill refuses to, or is unable to, pay the bill as specified, the holder of the bill can seek redress from the trader who endorsed the bill. As such, by using a bill drawn on a third party as payment does not release a trader from a final obligation to pay in full for goods or services received.

If a bill is accepted by a banker on behalf of the ultimate payee, it is called a Banker's acceptance, or BA. By accepting the bill, the banker acts as both agent to the acceptor and, usually, guarantor to the issuer of the bill. A cheque is a payment instrument drawn on a bank subject to sufficient funds in the account of the payer. Cheques can be post-dated to prevent conversion into cash before a set date. As such, a banker's acceptance and a cheque are similar in that a bank provides additional security to payees accepting them for payment. They differ in who is the legal obligor and in the conditionality of payment.

4.4.2 Discounting

A trader can sell a bill to a banker for an immediate cash payment. This is known as discounting and represents one of the oldest forms of bank credit as well as the origin of the word discount in finance. When the banker buys the bill, the cash amount paid will normally be lower than the face value of the bill. The ratio between the two is known as the discount factor:

$$\text{Discount factor} = \frac{\text{Cash payment}}{\text{Face value}} \tag{4.2}$$

The discount factor is usually expressed in the form of an interest rate, known as a discount rate.

A bank that has discounted a bill may re-sell it to another bank. This is known as rediscounting. Typically, central banks used to inject liquidity through rediscounting (see Section 7.2).

4.4.3 Delineating payment instruments from money

Traders can use bills and cheques drawn on third parties to pay each other which raises the question whether there is a difference between money and these non-cash payment instruments.

As usual in economics, the answer is complex. In corporate finance, bills held are separated from the balance sheet category of 'Cash and Cash Equivalents' on the asset side but both of them are counted towards the wider category of 'Current Assets'. Monetary aggregates do not count bills of exchange or cheques as money but this may simply be due to the difficulty in measuring the relevant outstanding amounts. Note that no bank is able to quantify the nominal amount of cheques drawn on it until they are presented for payment.

However, when a bill or cheque becomes payable, they do represent claims payable in money. This property is what enables them to be used in transactions. A number of differences between non-cash payment instruments are noteworthy although they do not explain their omission from monetary aggregates:

No legal tender Payees can refuse to accept bills or cheques as payment for debts payable. This is one of the motivations for discounting a bill, namely the operation of transforming a bill into legal tender, subject to an appropriate discount.

Immediacy A bill is payable by the drawer upon presentation. Unlike cash, this delays payment. The payee has to present the bill at a given location at a given time to receive cash. This cash may in any case be refused and would have to be recovered through redress from intermediate endorsers of the bill.

Limitations Bills normally cannot be claimed beyond a certain period after their due date (usually one year). Cash, in contrast, has no such limitation.

4.5 DIGITAL TOKEN MONIES AND CRYPTOCURRENCIES

In recent decades, virtual currencies known as cryptocurrencies such as Bitcoin or Ethereum have been created. Such currencies not only do not have a nominal anchor, but are not even tied to any given jurisdiction. The are used as means of exchange through distributed databases that allow anonymous and nearly instantaneous[6] transfers between participants. The way in which cyber-currencies seek to achieve the store of value property required of money is by tying the creation of currency units to complex mathematical calculations which have a meaningful execution cost (so-called proof-of-work problems). Overall, cryptocurrencies are more than new currencies. They depend for their functioning on a complex ecosystem of users willing to provide storage and computing power, mathematical laws that guarantee a limited supply, and protocols that solve attendant problems, such as how to prevent the same crypto-asset being spent twice in two separate transactions [62]. The reason why Bitcoin succeeded as well as it did is that the economic incentives for all participants were carefully balanced, or rather, the Bitcoin incentives were balanced in a way that led to its success.

Cyber-currencies replicate the salient features of cash transactions through cryptographic means. In general, this is achieved through the use of a cryptographically safe public transaction log that is replicated across the entire network of participants in which every single transaction is recorded (the so-called blockchain). Transactions are considered final once they are recorded in the blockchain for a sufficient amount of time; participants are anonymous because they are only identifiable by the public part of their asymmetric keys, and the replication of the blockchain removes the need for central recording of monetary assets, such as bank accounts.

The main criticism of cryptocurrencies is that they expend a very large amount of physical assets (electricity and specialised hardware) on achieving aims that in the majority of cases could be achieved in much less elaborate ways. Immediate finality of payment combined with a reasonable degree of anonymity and decentralisation has been achieved in commercial settings through pre-paid electronic monies such as Suica in Japan (2001) long before cryptocurrencies became popular. Some technical concepts used in cryptocurrencies, such as the blockchain, are interesting in other settings and may speed up certain transaction types in other contexts. However, a blockchain does not create a currency and digital payments can be handled, and have been handled for many years, without the use of a blockchain.

Digital token currencies are substantially different from cryptocurrencies because they do not seek to replace the entire institutional infrastructure of modern monies and may even be issued by central banks. As a concept, these monies replace classical physical tokens, such as numbered bank notes, with digital equivalents. The transfer of such tokens can be organised through centralised or distributed databases depending on which system provides better usability and cost efficiency.

---

[6]In practice, money transfers in cryptocurrencies appear to be instantaneous but are in fact not final until some considerable time (up to several hours) later. This compares to near immediacy of bank-based transfers in most developed and some developing nations.

4.6   THE MONEY MULTIPLIER

Because bank notes are debt, there is in theory no limit as to how much of them (in terms of nominal amounts) can be issued by a given bank. This is unlike certificates where the total amount in circulation is, by definition, equal to the physical amount of physical commodity money in storage[7]. Because bank notes are sometimes cashed, issuers needed to hold a certain amount of physical metal against such repayment demands. This amount of physical cash is called the reserve. For reasons discussed below, bankers have an economic interest to hold as small a reserve as possible, but prudence suggests as large a reserve as possible. No matter how large an actual reserve is, there is always a risk of more bank notes being presented for payment than the size of the reserve. Such a large repayment demand is known as a bank run[8].

The economic importance of banking is less the creation of bank notes than the lending of the deposits. By doing so, the bank in effect creates new money because not only are the bank notes in circulation, but also the cash deposit that the bank has lent to a third party. Furthermore, the cash that has been lent on can later end up as another deposit, i.e., new bank notes. To give a simple example, imagine 10 gold coins being deposited with a bank. The bank issues a 10 coin note against it. Assuming that the bank generally holds a 10% reserve against deposits, up to nine coins can be lent by the banker to a borrower. The borrower may purchase some goods with this money and the seller of those goods could deposit the nine coins against a bank note for nine coins. The total amount of money now in circulation is equivalent to 19 coins, namely the two bank notes of 10 and 9 coins. Again the banker can lend part of the deposit (8.1 coins given the 10% reserve), which may again be deposited and so on, ad infinitum. In total, the maximum amount of paper money that can be based on the 10 physical coins is equivalent to 100 coins. Mathematically, the maximum amount of money M that can be based on an initial deposit of one coin with a reserve ratio of r is given by:

$$M = \lim_{n \to \infty} \sum_{k=1}^{n} \frac{1}{(1+r)^k} = \frac{1}{r} \qquad (4.3)$$

The number M is known as the monetary multiplier and the coins in the example are known as high-powered money because an increase in the number of coins leads to an M-fold increase in the amount of money in circulation. The limit $n \to \infty$ suggests that the number M is theoretical, but although the actual amount of money in circulation may be lower than suggested by the theoretical M, the relationship between this amount, the amount of high-powered money, and the reserve ratio r, is intact. Not least, this is because there is no reason for loans to be paid in coins. The bank could

---

[7]Perhaps the most well-known remaining certificate money is the paper money used in Scotland, Northern Ireland, and the Channel Islands. Aside from small 'authorised issues', these bank notes issued by private banks are backed by identical stores of English pound notes specially issued by the Bank of England. These special issues have a denomination of one million pounds.

[8]One way to reduce the risk of bank runs is to create a lender of last resort, cf. Chapter 5.

easily create 100 coins worth of notes upon the deposit of 10 coins, and use 90 of these for lending.

However, interbank payments normally have to be settled in specie (or, in modern times, central bank money) instead of the bank notes issued by the banks themselves. This requirement for settlement money creates an additional limit on the money multiplier M. In practical terms, therefore, the money multiplier has little relevance.

The problem of bank runs has led to the establishment of banks that act as a lender of last resort to banks subject to a run. The banks in London deposited part of their reserves with the Bank of England (against interest) with the understanding that the Bank would lend the accumulated reserves to banks that were subject to a bank run [5]. Although the total bank reserves were much lower than the total amount of bank notes in circulation, any one bank could survive a bank run by borrowing from that central repository. A similar system was established as a reaction to bank failures in the 1920s in the United States in the form of the Federal Reserve Bank System.

The pooling of physical specie (which after all, incurs a cost and pays no interest) reduces the cost of maintaining a sufficient reserve compared to each bank holding a sizeable amount of specie. This pooling is one avenue along which the notion of central banks, discussed further below, has evolved.

CHAPTER 5

The Role of Central Banks

For readers of a technical book like this, the relevant aspect of central bank activity is not so much why central banks act, but how and when they do it. Central banks are such large actors in the market that their operations affect various aspects of market microstructure. With the advent of unconventional monetary policy tools, central bank operations have extended along the yield curve and across asset classes. This chapter will spend only a minimum amount of space on the monetary policy aspect of central banks (what Bindseil [10] would call the 'white collar' part of central banking) and focus more on monetary policy tools and frameworks (the 'blue collar' aspect of their work). Readers looking for deeper insights into the policy aspects have access to a variety of good textbooks, including from practitioners like Bernanke [9], Issing [51] and Shirakawa [75].

5.1 INTRODUCTION

Central banks are banks that act as lenders and deposit takers to other banks. Most central banks also offer similar services to their own government (usually with tight restrictions or outright prohibitions on lending) and other customers, for instance foreign central banks or governments. While the history of central banks goes back several centuries, some countries came to central banking only late, notably the United States [3].

The designation central bank implies that these institutions play a fundamental role in their respective economy. Aside from this implication, however, there is not only no uniform definition of what exact function makes a bank a central bank, but also no consensus in economics about the necessity of central banks. The general public is also sometimes confused as to which institution are central banks. While the Bank of England and the Bank of Japan are central banks, Bank of Ireland and Deutsche Bank are private institutions[1]. The National Bank of Slovakia is a central bank while the National Bank of Greece is not.

Ownership is also not a reliable guide. Most central banks are owned by sovereigns but not all. The US Federal Reserve Banks are privately owned, as is the Banca d'Italia,

---

[1]The central banks of Ireland and Germany are the Central Bank of Ireland and the Deutsche Bundesbank, respectively. Bank of Ireland is government-owned at the time of writing.

and the Central Bank of Greece is listed on the Athens Stock Exchange. The nationalisation of the Bank of England in 1946 did not fundamentally change its position in the UK financial system.

A usual starting point for the definition of a central bank is that of a bank of issue, i.e., a bank that issues money. Bindseil [11] adopts this definition, with extra provisions so that a central bank is indentified by three characteristics: it issues financial money of ultimate quality, it is based on a public charter, and it has been set up with the aim of public policy objectives. These three elements need further clarification, however. The money issued by the central bank need not be physical currency but can also be book entry (giro) money.

As Figure 5.1 shows, some currency systems exist today where bank notes are issued by private, non-central banks. Meanwhile, US Dollar notes, shown in Figure 5.2, are issued by the US Treasury, not the central bank.

FIGURE 5.1   A Hong Kong Dollar note issued by the Hongkong and Shanghai Banking Corporation (HSBC). The central bank of Hong Kong is the Hong Kong Monetary Authority (HKMA) which does not issue currency itself but governs the note issuance of private banks. Source: HSBC/HKMA.

FIGURE 5.2   A US Dollar note bears the seal of the Federal Reserve System but is issued by the US Treasury and signed by the Treasury Secretary. Source: US Treasury.

The Bindseil definition does include these two institutions when one considers the clearing accounts offered by both to the banks in their respective jurisdictions[2]. Physical paper money is merely the form of money used by the general public but the bulk of transactions is conducted in electronic form.

Other authors, such as Goodhart [42] link the central bank definition less to the mechanical issuance of currency but to the aims of such issuance, which is generally linked to the provision of liquidity in times of stress, known as the lender of last resort (LOLR) function. The difference with the other definition is that this function is historically newer and so creates a somewhat arbitrary starting date for the emergence of central banks. As authors such as Bindseil [11] or Roberds and Velde [70] highlight, some central bank functions can be shown to have existed as early as the 15th century. Considering these institutions as central banks means that the emergence of the modern LOLR central banks (usually associated with the creation of the Swedish Riksbank, then known as Riksens Ständers Bank) was an evolutionary step rather than a revolution. It is more plausible, particularly in the light of the tightly integrated trading relationships in Europe even in the late middle ages, that central banking developed gradually, one innovation at a time, across multiple countries over a longer period. In this approach, the Riksbank retains its claim to be the *oldest* central bank, but it is not the *first*.

One could therefore argue that the LOLR function is not always part of the charter of a central bank. The Banque de France and the Federal Reserve are examples of central banks that were chartered as LOLR banks (although for very different purposes), while the LOLR role of the Bank of England was only legislated after it had evolved *de facto*.

Whether one sees the LOLR function as the defining feature of a central bank, or takes the wider view of Bindseil, a central bank is defined via its liability side while the asset side is less specified. A central bank is therefore not necessarily a bank that funds the state, as is sometimes claimed. Indeed, the credibility of a central bank is often linked to its independence from the state, which underpins the separation between money and state debt.

Not all economists agree with this focus on the liability side. Funding of government expenditure, stability anchor for the financial system, and other roles compete for the ultimate reason for the existence of central banks in the literature.

This disagreement reflects the varied history of the institutions that make up the current line-up of central banks. Some of them were indeed created to ensure stable government funding, i.e., with an asset-side focus, like the Banque de France. Others were set up for the LOLR function in response to particular financial crisis, such as the Federal Reserve System in the United States. The Bank of England was set up with legal privileges, but its central function in the London financial market evolved in ways

---

[2]An additional quibble one might have with this definition is the precise nature of the phrase 'public charter'. At the times when some of the early central banks were set up, there was no universal suffrage which means that a charter would be issued by a monarch or, in the city states, a body representing a small group of eminent citizens. The latter setting is not very different from a joint stock company. Many private banks were also set up with royal charters, for instance the first Pfandbrief issuer, Schlesische Landschaften, or Deutsche Bank.

that were not always predetermined by these legal arrangements. That being said, it is difficult to argue against the need for a publicly chartered LOLR bank given that any other currency arrangements (so-called free banking) has tended to end up in trouble.

As mentioned earlier, banking in Europe started from the business of taking deposits in the form of specie (precious metal) against the issuance of negotiable paper certificates, or the provision of transferrable giro credit. Because these paper certficates or giro credit could be exchanged back into specie on demand, they took on the role of money itself. However, the use of paper money in daily transactions meant that paper currency could remain in circulation instead of being frequently exchanged back into specie. This had the important side effect of leaving specie in circulation rather than tying it up in bank reserves. What made central bank-issued money different from any other monies in the economy is that the central bank money is of higher quality, either because it has legislative support, is more widely accepted, is convertible into specie of more reliable quality, or because the credit quality of the central bank is higher. In any case, holders of non-central bank money would prefer to convert it into central bank money.

The development of bank money requires two separate preconditions. First, the specie into which the bank money could be exchanged has to be widely accepted. This is a condition on the social contract valid at the time. The use of bank money does not in itself represent a change in currency. When bank money is used under a gold standard, gold remains the basic means of exchange. In the current fiat money regimes, private issue bank notes, where they exist, and private bank giro money merely represent, but do not replace, the basic means of exchange which is the liabilities of the central bank.

Second, because the obligation to exchange paper into specie rests with the issuing bank, users of the paper currency must have trust in the credit of that particular bank, i.e., its ongoing ability to convert its paper into specie on demand. This is all the more important in a system of fractional reserve banking where banks by construction are unable to redeem all outstanding notes for specie at the same time.

While this setup has evolved in the context of historical currency arrangements, it remains valid in today's world of fiat currencies and electronic transactions. Individuals are willing to be paid in the liabilities of individual private banks by accepting payments into their bank accounts. These bank accounts are not substantially different from paper bank notes issued by banks in the past. Individuals can also use these same bank liabilities to make payments when they transfer money electronically.

The second condition is more complex when one considers a banking system comprised of many banks rather than a few big names. Users of paper currency issued by multiple banks need to trust every single issuing bank. In practice, this has meant that only certain types of private paper money were accepted widely, leading to the natural emergence of oligopolies.

The need for the existence of a central bank and a privileged legal tender is sometimes disputed, as is the creation of money by private banks [42]. On one extreme, proponents of free banking suggest that private banks should be allowed to issue bank notes freely and that the role of central banks should be limited [44]. In this model, the users of currency would be deciding which banks to trust, which would then put pressure on bank managers to behave in a demonstrably prudent way[3].

On the opposite side of free banking is the idea of positive money, called Vollgeld in Germany, where this theory has some following. In this type of banking model, private banks do not have the right to create money. Instead, they need to borrow any money they wish to advance as loans from the central bank. While central bank money retains the features of a fiat currency (the central bank would have the right to issue as much of its money as it sees fit), the amount of money in circulation would be decided by the state, not private actors. Banks would be mostly providers of payment and other services and any risky lending activity would in essence mirror the operation of asset managers. If one allows for the assumption that it does not matter which private bank advances a particular loan, positive money is merely the extreme where the amount of total credit in the economy is exactly controlled by the government. As will be discussed later on, central banks can influence the amount of private money creation in various ways even not as precisely as positive money advocates would view as desirable. The Bundesbank operated under a regime that targeted a given rate of money supply growth[4] and the US Federal Reserve had tight money supply targets during its Friedmanite episode between 1979 and 1982. Some economies experienced government targets for credit growth, for instance the window guidance employed in Japan in the 1980s and China in the early 2000s [38].

Giving authority to decide on money creation to the largest borrower in the economy (the government) is seen as sensible on the grounds that governments are appointed by the collective wisdom of the population through democratic elections[5]. Control over the money supply, which can be implemented through positive money, could allow the government to reduce the cost of its debt by conducting monetary policy in such as way as to reduce the function of money as a store of value. While this use of monetary policy for the augmentation of government finances is also possible in fractional reserve banking systems [28], positive money eliminates the alternative of private monies.

It should not be surprising that the relative popularity of these schools of thought is somewhat cyclical. When the economy is doing well, private actors feel less inclined to submit to government oversight. Free banking then tends to be advocated as a natural expression of private enterprise. Conversely, in a recession many people wish

---

[3]The idea that publishing a bank's situation encourages good management can be seen in pillar III of the Basel framework.

[4]Some authors argue that while money supply may have been the stated target, actual policy measures were more in line with inflation targeting [28], or at least on the road to it [9].

[5]It should be noted in this context that the fundamental ideas of positive money actually predate modern democracies, cf. for instance the creation of the Banque de France under Napoleon [42].

for more state intervention and positive money concepts become more popular[6]. The co-existence of private monies with a controlling role of central bank monies in most modern economies is a compromise between these two extremes.

5.2 MONETARY FINANCING

The term monetary financing describes the creation of money with the aim of funding fiscal expenditure and is older than central banking. A government typically raises money from the populace through taxes, levies, and tariffs. On the back of these revenue streams, the government can also borrow money, and, as pointed out elsewhere, historically these revenue sources were not as clearly separated as they are today [57].

In a metal standard currency, monetary financing does not require that the government issues money that is legislated as a means of exchange (forced money), or forces the central bank to issue money on its behalf. The same economic effect has historically been achieved by diluting the specie content of a standard coin (debasement), or by seizing the specie reserves of a money-issuing bank. In all of these cases, the precious metal amount that a given monetary unit can be converted into will be less than expected, and may even be zero. The problem is that a government, and in particular a non-democratic one, can override the public interest in stable money.

This loss of conversion value is why monetary financing is problematic for money because it impedes the store-of-value function. In medieval times, monetary financing was in some cases avoided by sheltering the money-issuing central bank in a religious institution [11]. Today's approach is to make central banks independent and rule out monetary financing by law. Central banks are either completely forbidden from lending to their sovereigns (Europe) or can only do so to a very limited degree (US and Japan). Where monetary financing is not expressly forbidden in law, it tends to be ruled out as a matter of policy because it clashes with the aim of maintaining stable money.

Practically all central banks are authorised to buy and sell bonds issued by their sovereigns and many do so as part of their operational framework. As will be discussed below, non-standard monetary policy tools require large-scale purchases of sovereign debt. Because a holder of a debt instrument acts as a lender to the issuer of that instrument, the question arises how such holding can be reconciled with a prohibition on monetary financing.

---

[6]It tends to be forgotten in these arguments that government-controlled banks can collapse as well as private ones. To a larger extent than the more general criticisms of central planning (e.g. [44]), any default of a public bank should create severe doubts about the ability of governments to police the financial system. Planning a whole economy centrally is a computationally complex task and failure to do so successfully in the former Eastern bloc can be explained away by this complexity. Running a German or Austrian Landesbank, in contrast, is not evidently more complex than running a private bank. The observed cases of failures to do so better than private management cannot as easily be separated from general control abilities in the public sector.

CHAPTER 6

Monetary Policy

6.1 OBJECTIVES OF MONETARY POLICY

Monetary policy is the active control of financial conditions by the central bank. It now generally has the objective of ensuring that the domestic currency has the qualities associated with money, i.e., that it can serve as a unit of account, store of value and medium of exchange. This objective generally requires that the future purchasing power of the currency can be anticipated by the general public and that the technical means of exchanging the currency (banknotes, electronic payment systems) work reliably. Modern monetary policy therefore tends to be geared towards some form of price stability which can be defined in various ways. In the policy mode known as inflation targeting, price stability is defined as a given positive inflation rate (zero inflation is undesirable due to measurement issues and asymmetric risk concerns [9]). In the related price level targeting approach, the central bank defines a target path for the price level and therefore explicitly commits to compensate any past deviations in the future. This commitment is at best implicit in inflation targeting. Over time, both the understanding of price stability, and the best way to express it, have evolved across different central banks.

Some central banks, for instance the US Federal Reserve and Reserve Bank of Australia, operate on a mixed mandate that targets the correlated but distinct aims of price stability and maximum employment.

The existence of a monetary policy target suggests that monetary policy is essentially a control problem, and some central bankers have indeed sought to describe their approach in such terms. The idea of reducing economic problems to the solution of mathematical equations could be linked to the suggestion by Karl Marx that 'a science can only be considered to be fully developed when it reached the stage where it can utilise mathematics'. In practice, the large number of parameters such a model would have to incorporate, while the number of observations is limited by the low frequency of collection of the relevant data, precludes the proper calibration of such an ambitious model. In addition, it may be incorrect to assume that central banks have sufficient tools to act in an optimal way even if they had sufficient information.

One can indeed argue that the existence of a complete model of optimal monetary policy under a rational expectations framework would in fact contradict the idea of active monetary policy. By way of *reductio ad absurdum*, if a complete model existed, it would eventually be known to all economic actors. The central bank would under these

FIGURE 6.1   Example of a Japanese castle wall (Osaka Castle). Source: ALEXANDER DÜRING.

circumstances not have any way in which to influence the decisions of others, having to follow a policy path that is known to everybody else[1]. In essence, this would be a world of real business cycle models where the only uncertainty stems from random jumps in productivity.

This raises the question whether the absence of a perfect monetary policy approach is a drawback for the economy. The answer is not immediately obvious and instead depends on one's economic model. Followers of the Minsky theory of the business cycle [58] would argue, for instance, that the shocks generated by occasions when monetary policy decisions later turn out to have been mistaken can flush out elevated leverage before it becomes excessive.

An illustration of this idea can be found in the construction of Japanese castle walls (Figure 6.1). Unlike European castles, the slope of Japanese walls becomes progressively steeper towards the top. The common justification for this design is that it creates an adverse selection process for attacking soldiers attempting to climb these walls. Less capable soldiers are likely to fail close to the bottom and may sustain minor injuries when they fall. The most capable soldiers will not fall off the wall until they reach a height at which their fall will result in major, or even fatal, injuries. The wall design therefore selectively apportions the maximum damage to the most dangerous enemies[2]. In the realm of monetary policy, a central bank may be able to offset incoming shocks

---

[1]In economics, these arguments are known as the Lucas Critique (historical correlations are not a good guide to future reactions to monetary policy) and Goodhart's Law (an indicator becomes non-informative when it is chosen as a policy target).

[2]An unkind observer with a mind focused on physics might argue instead that the inward slope offsets the pressures generated by a quasi-liquid soil in case of an earthquake, and that the absence of this consideration in Europe explains the special design of Japanese castles. However, a perfectly reasonable alternative explanation is no excuse to dismiss a good story.

to the economy by a well-executed monetary policy path. However, this could leave the economy even more exposed to shocks that are either beyond the capacity of the central bank to react, or could not have been foreseen by the central bank.

The lesson of the Japanese castle wall is that there is a trade-off between the steady state performance of an economy and its resilience to shocks. A central bank that can hold its economy close to a state of maximum output (however defined) may find that it is least able to prevent sharp deteriorations in economic conditions simply because there is more room to fall. In other words, the longer an economy grows beyond potential, the more time there is to build up excessive risk positions.

Put more bluntly, active monetary policy may have a purpose not because it is always right but precisely because it may on occasion be wrong. Authors like Cooper [26] who perceive a conflict between the notion of efficient financial markets on one hand, and the need for a central bank on the other, may therefore be missing two important points. First, the provision of money by central banks needs to be carefully managed to endow this money with the qualities expected of it, namely its role as a store of value. If this non-trivial management is not provided in a reliable fashion, markets cannot work. Second, even if the central bank occasionally makes mistakes in this management, these may not always have negative long-term consequences.

That being said, central banks tend to interpret their mandates as leaning against the business cycle instead of aggravating it[3], in other words, as dampening volatility instead of ensuring a certain level of uncertainty. As will be discussed later, the relationship between the proclaimed stance of the central bank, and the amount of uncertainty it allows to occur around it, are an important consideration for monetary policy frameworks.

It should be realised that this 'leaning against the cycle' is a good textbook concept but translates into diffcult decisions in real life. A central bank looking to dampen aggregate demand in a higher inflation situation may appear to be trying to manage a macroscopic variable. The economic variable of lower aggregate demand, however, translates into a loss of employment for a macroscopically significant number of workers. Explaining to the affected families that their personal income levels need to be reduced to protect the greater good of price stability is a difficult task, especially because this apparent link suffers from a fallacy of decomposition. The central bank does not terminate individual employment contracts, but merely changes probabilities.

In today's world, this has led to a structural change in how central banks communicate with the public. In the not too recent past, central banks shrouded themselves in an aura of mystique and revealed only a limited amount of information about the motives behind their actions. Famously, the Fed did not even disclose its target rate until February 1994 [33]. When the ECB started regular press conferences after Governing Council meetings, and later tied the meeting schedule to the press conference schedule, this level of transparency was unique[4]. Today, even the Fed has regular press conferences. To date, this increased level of transparency has not hurt the credibility of central banks.

---

[3]Former Federal Reserve Chairman William McChesney Martin memorably described this task as 'to take away the punch bowl just as the party gets going'.

[4]Visitors to Frankfurt am Main may notice that the Bundesbank building is located on a hill at some distance from the city centre while the original ECB building is very central. In this case, the visible location choices are symbolic for communication approaches.

6.2 MONETARY POLICY UNDER INFLATION TARGETING

In order to discuss the impact of active monetary policy on inflation, it is instructive to start from the basic quantity equation of the price level:

$$MV = PY \tag{6.1}$$

Here, M is the money stock, V the velocity of money, P the price level, and Y the total volume of traded goods and services. For all practical purposes, Y can be thought of as a proxy of GDP; the only difference between the two is changes to inventories. The equation expresses simply that the total volume of things paid for during a given period (PY) is equal to the money handed over in exchange (MV).

Solving for P and taking the total differential gives:

$$dP = \frac{M}{Y}dV + \frac{V}{Y}dM - \frac{MV}{Y^2}dY \tag{6.2}$$

The price level therefore depends on three control variables in this model: Higher prices can be obtained by higher velocity of money, a larger money stock, or lower output. Note that the total differential makes no assumption about correlation, or indeed causal relationships, between the three control variables.

Economists generally agree only that the term dV is unsuitable for monetary policy because it is impossible to control the way in which money is used in the economy. V can react substantially to changes in investment climate as liquidity preferences change. Beyond this point, economists split into monetarists and Keynesians[5] according to the logical precedence assigned to the dM and dY terms.

A Keynesian economist views the dY term as central to official guidance of the economy and there are many factors in which this term can be controlled, including monetary policy. An important endogenous determinant of the near-term evolution of dY is the current output gap, i.e., the difference between actual and potential (however defined) output [22]. Because there is an assumption that the output gap is mean-reverting to some degree[6], monetary policy can use measures of the output gap (unemployment rate, capacity utilisation, investment spending) as clues for monetary policy. On this basis, the policy interest rate set by the central bank is determined by the natural rate of interest for the economy r^* on the one hand, and the distance of inflation from its target on the other. Keynesians regard the dM term as reacting passively to dY. This view is supported by the observation that most of M in the usual definitions (M2 and M3) is not central bank money, but monies created by commercial banks. In the euro area, only about 10% of M3 are currency in circulation and bank reserves (M0); the rest are largely deposits. However, changes in M can have effects on the economy even in this framework, if largely through relative asset prices and signalling. The difficulty of this approach is that it relies on unobservable variables, such as the output gap, to judge the appropriate direction for monetary policy.

---

[5]Apologies to any economists who object to being subsumed into these two groups despite having subtle but important differences with either. Neo-classical economics are subsumed here under the Keynesian school.
[6]Mean-reversion is sometimes implicit in the use of Hodrick-Prescott filters in the estimation of the output gap.

For monetarists, the dM term is paramount for central bankers because the dY term is not subject to central bank control. The output gap is rejected as a monetary policy indicator because it cannot reliably be measured in real time[7]. Monetarists agree that dY has an influence on the price level; the contention is simply that a central bank should not look to intervene in real variables[8]. In this world view, money growth dM is simply given by a desired inflation level dP plus an a term that accounts for the growth in money demand arising from economic growth dY and shifts in money usage (velocity), given by dV. This is the theoretical background behind the money growth target approach that was taken by the Bundesbank. As long as the coefficients of Equation (6.2) are reasonably stable, a central bank that targets money growth is indistinguishable from one that targets inflation [28]. The problem with money growth targeting is that the target quantity must be reasonably wide so as to be less sensitive to short-term fluctuation related to transaction money demand (which tends to be inside M0). Even so, there are multiple reasons to hold money other than in order to spend it on goods and services.

All that being said, the left side of Equation (6.1) is somewhat of a fiction. There are multiple definitions of M (M0–M3, M2+CD, base money) vying for the attention of central bankers, and V is unobservable. The equation is therefore not much more than a definition of V, rather than a useful guideline to monetary policy.

Brushing aside this technical difficulty, one finds central banks with inflation targets in agreement on a hierarchy of price level control, shown in the chart below:

$$\begin{array}{c} \text{Quantity (open market operations or lending)} \\ \Downarrow \text{(III)} \\ \text{Price (interest rates on central bank money)} \\ \Downarrow \text{(II)} \\ \text{Quantity (money supply)} \\ \Downarrow \text{(I)} \\ \text{Price (goods and services)} \end{array} \qquad (6.3)$$

Central banks control the price level of consumer goods by adjusting the money supply M, ie., the quantity of money (I). This quantity cannot be controlled directly by the central bank because most of M is not central bank money. Instead, central banks control the demand for M (II) via interest rates (monetarist explanation) or signal their stance on the real economy via interest rates (Keynesian explanation). The ECB refers to (II) as the monetary transmission mechanism. Interest rates are simply a price of money and by changing the price, central banks can look to influence demand for money.

Note that relationships (I) and (II) operate with a long and variable lag. The creation of the money components outside M0 require decisions of private actors to borrow, and changes in the availability of money may feed into price setting mechanisms only slowly, given imperfect information and market rigidities. A useful benchmark is a lag of 12–18 months.

---

[7]This measurement problem explains why the Taylor rule works well as an ex-post explanation of central bank action but much less well as a forecasting tool.

[8]The tradition of monetarism in Germany is part of the explanation of why the court cases filed in that country against ECB monetary policy usually allege that the ECB oversteps the mandate of a central bank by acting in ways that affect real variables, instead of only nominal ones. To a Keynesian, it is absurd to assume that the two can be cleanly separated.

Given that there are two mutually exclusive intepretations of central banking, the European Central Bank had to choose one to guide its own policy decisions when it was set up in 1999. In line with the behaviour of other European institutions in similar situations it adopted both. The two pillars of the ECB policy framework are a monetarist M3 analysis and a potentially Keynesian inflation analysis. While the early chief economists at the ECB used to interpret the second pillar narrowly and use output gap measures mainly as a quality control tool of macro-economic forecasts, more recent communications put more emphasis on the 'slack in the economy' which can be interpreted as Keynesianite references to the output gap[9].

Under normal circumstances (standard monetary policy), some, but not all, central banks control the relevant interest rates via quantities (III), namely the amount of daily open market operations. The Fed and the Bank of Japan fall into this group; the ECB uses a mix of instruments but under normal circumstances influences interest rates directly via the minimum rate at which it allocates cash at the main refinancing operations.

Demand for money can change due to purely technical factors such as tax and wage payments, holiday gift shopping seasons, etc. At high frequencies money demand is not perfectly responsive to policy interest rates[10].

The alteration between quantity and prices in the control hierarchy Figure 6.3 can cause breakdowns when for some reason one of the relationships no longer works as anticipated. For instance, price levels may become insensitive to money supply when households simply hoard cash. In the framework of Equation (6.2) one could find that:

$$\frac{M}{Y}dV = -\frac{V}{Y}dM \qquad (6.4)$$

so that the effect of changing M would simply be offset by an opposing change of V. Another way in which this relationship can break down is when $V \to 0$ which implies $\partial P / \partial M \to 0$. This situation arises when the general economy loses faith in the domestic curreny and resorts to barter or the use of a substitute currency (dollarisation). Price levels then become independent of the domestic money supply simply because domestic money is no longer in use.

Two specific forms of Goodhart's Law may apply to inflation targeting. The first is that long-term inflation expectations of the public should, if the central bank is credible, converge to the central bank's target. Public expectations of inflation would then no longer be informative for policy makers as to the actual outlook for inflation which would remain subject to various shocks and require monetary policy action. The second is that some policy tools can affect market measures of future inflation such as derivatives linked to future price level changes. In such cases, these market measures can also become non-informative.

---

[9]Keen readers of the ECB's Introductory Statements will note that the economic analysis comes before the monetary analysis, both of which are then cross-checked.
[10]This is essentially why the Friedmanite episode of the Fed ended in failure (inelastic money supply led to volatile market interest rates) and why the Bundesbank operated more as an inflation-targeting central bank despite its professed money supply framework [28].

6.3   CENTRAL BANK OPERATIONAL FRAMEWORKS

Central banks can use various tools to control the supply of liquidity to private banks. Each central bank will typically choose a subset of the available tools according to the specific situation of its domestic banking market. The chosen set of tools and the way the are implemented is called the operational framework of the central bank. Factors such as the structure of the banking system, the size and structure of the relevant securities markets, and the relevance of net foreign trade can all influence the design of the operational framework. Note that the framework itself need not be tied to a particular monetary policy objective. The same objectives might be achieved with various frameworks, and the same framework can be used for different, or changing, monetary policy objectives.

In general, however, there are certain common desiderata for operational frameworks (cf. e.g. [10]), as outlined below.

Parsimony Frameworks should not make use of an excessive number of distinct instruments and instead have a small number of clearly understood mechanisms to achieve standard aims (liquidity provision, liquidity absorption, emergency lending, etc.). A surfeit of instruments is likely to confuse market participants as to the exact monetary policy objective inherent in the choice between two similar instruments. Similarly, a central bank should avoid the simultaneous use of discretionary instruments with opposing monetary effects.

Stability Operational frameworks can and should change over time to adapt to changes in the operating environment. Changes to standard tools should, however, not occur without a well-understood and well-communicated justification. One can therefore observe a certain amount of hysteresis in how central banks interact with the market as the side effects of a useful small adjustment may outweigh the potential benefits. It may be noted that the specific institutional setup of a central bank itself is usually also the result of specific historic circumstances rather than the result of an extended period of careful design [53].

Moderation Central banks must apply instruments in order to achieve the desired effects but should do so with the minimum of disruption to private market interactions. This is not only a question of of limited mandates, but has financial stability effects. For instance, it is useful to force private banks to 'test their name' in the private market on a regular basis, instead of providing liquidity to them from the central bank, so as to gain insights as to the public opinion about their strength.

A potential drawback of moderation is that it creates a stigma for the use of non-standard liquidity facilities, such as the Fed discount window or the ECB dollar-providing operations. Banks may be reluctant to make use of such facilities when there is a tacit or explicit understanding that doing so is a sign of crisis. Given that risk premia charged by private funds providers are normally higher than what a central bank can provide, avoiding the stigma of a central bank facility will normally mean higher funding costs for the bank in question. Whether this is in the long-term interest of financial stability is not an easy question to answer and central banks take different stances on this issue.

Separation Instruments in the framework should be used for clearly defined purposes, and these purposes should be clearly delineated. For instance, emergency lending should be conducted in ways other than through regular lending operations such as not to confuse the monetary policy signal of the latter.

The separation principle has been blamed for the slowness of the European Central Bank in adopting non-standard monetary policy measures [47]. Such criticism is probably misplaced because hesitation was a global feature of the use of non-standard measures and may be linked to the dictum of then-chairman Ben Bernanke 'The problem with quantitative easing is that it works in practice, but not in theory.' Central bank models of the economy before the economic crisis that started in 2008 generally suffered from a Keynesian disdain for financial matters and did therefore not incorporate transmission channels of monetary policy that are the hallmark of non-standard measures, namely bank equity and investment portfolio allocations.

6.3.1 Symmetric interest rate corridors

Central banks outside crisis situations tend to operate in a setting that can be described as a symmetric corridor system. In this setup, interbank interest rates fluctuate inside a range, and central bank liquidity[11] provision is minimal, designed to cover exactly the aggregate needs created by bank notes, reserve requirements and transactional account holdings of central bank cash. Such a system requires a minimum of three tools, namely one to provide the bulk of liquidity, one to absorb any excess and a third to cover any shortfalls. The interest rates on these three tools then describe the centre of the corridor, and its lower and upper bounds.

Liquidity provision can take the form of regular auctions or open market operations. Where auctions are used, the volume supplied must match the banking system demand at the desired interest rate. To judge this demand, all factors of liquidity demand must be forecast, and particularly the demand for transactional liquidity can be subject to large fluctuations.

When multiple liquidity-providing operations exist, their combined quantitative effect needs to be taken into account. In principle, all of the banking system's *aggregate* liquidity needs should be exactly covered by these operations. Banks should then distribute among themselves on a daily basis this liquidity to cover *individual* requirements which fluctuate more than the aggregate demand.

Participation in the liquidity provision operations is ensured by keeping the banking system structurally short liquidity. Traditionally, this has been achieved through reserve requirements that force banks to borrow central bank funds which

---

[11]To recall, the term 'liquidity' is here used in the sense of central bank funds provided, generally into current accounts held by commercial banks at the central bank. In the US, this is known as 'reserves'.

then need to be kept at the central bank[12]. In today's market, this requirement is no longer necessary to generate bank demand for central bank liquidities as transactional funds demand has risen.

Standing facilities can then be used to cover situations where liquidity does not match expectations, either in aggregate or for individual banks. Excess liquidity can be absorbed either in a specific facility (like the ECB's Deposit Facility) or remunerated at a lower rate (the Fed's Interest on Excess Reserves). When aggregate or individual needs exceed the amount of liquidity available, this can be covered through a specific lending facility. In the case of the ECB, this is the Marginal Lending Facility and for the Federal Reserve the Discount Window.

The use of standing facilities should be the exception, not the norm. There are two reasons for such usage. The first is unexpected liquidity demand, i.e., a forecast error by the central bank. The risk of such errors occurring rises with the time horizons of liquidity provision, so it is least for daily operations and higher for longer ones. More concerning is a situation where both facilities are used at the same time because that means that at least one bank has a liquidity surplus that it is unwilling to lend to at least one other bank with a liquidity shortfall. The distance between the interest rates on the two facilities should be large enough to discourage such behaviour.

Stigmatisation of lending facilities outside the main operations is a constant topic in money markets. On one hand, banks should trade among each other, and a regular use of standing facilities by any one bank can be sign of weakness. In the US, recourse to the Discount Window has traditionally been seen as negative, although at the time of writing the Federal Reserve is encouraging banks not to view it as such. In a similar way, some of the long-term fund supplying operations of the ECB were initially seen as stigmatised.

It should be noted that because the Fed's Open Markets desk in principle conducts daily operations, there should be less risk of an aggregate liquidity shortfall. Therefore, access to the Discount Window may more readily be seen as a sign of individual, rather than aggregate, circumstances. In addition, the Eurosystem has a designated instrument known as Emergency Liquidity Assistance that is reserved for solvent banks with specific liquidity problems. The clear separation between this instrument and the Marginal Lending facility may serve to de-stigmatise the use of the latter.

During the financial crisis, it became obvious that the euro area interbank market had become less efficient than before. As part of the response, the ECB narrowed the interest rate corridor between the Marginal Lending and Deposit Facilities. In principle, this lowers the cost to the banking system of using the Eurosystem balance sheet as a

---

[12]Traditionally, these reserves would be in specie, or be payable in specie by the central banks, and serve to ensure that a bank can pay out specie on its liabilities on demand. This is the historic reason why the US market refers to current account holdings at the Fed as reserves while the European market simply refers to them as liquidity. In Japan, they are known as current account holdings.

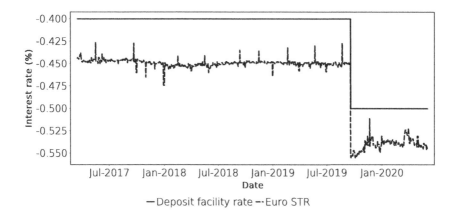

FIGURE 6.2 ECB deposit facility rate and pre-€STR and €STR. Source: From ECB SDW, ECB deposit facility rate and pre-eSTR and eSTR. The information may be obtained free of charge through: https://sdw.ecb.europa.eu/. © 2020, European Central Bank.

central counterparty in the money market. At the current juncture, however, there is such a high level of excess liquidity in the system that the corridor is now of lesser relevance, as will be discussed below.

6.3.2   Asymmetric lending corridors

With the financial crisis, and the wider adoption of non-standard monetary policy measures, most central banks' operating frameworks have in principle become asymmetric. In this setting, the market rate of interest does not fall in the middle of a corridor between standing facility rates, but is instead permanently pinned to one side of the corridor. Currently, this is the liquidity-absorbing side, i.e., its lower boundary.

In this setup, the level of liquidity in the banking system is no longer dependent on main refinancing, or standard open market operations. Instead, the banking system operates with a liqudity surplus generated by non-conventional liquidity injections.

One of the side effects of purchase programmes in particular is that central bank reserves were injected in exchange for assets held by non-banks. The non-bank sector therefore had an increasing need to desposit cash with commercial banks which lowered the rates at which such funds traded outside the banking system. This is visible, for instance, in the euro short-term rate (€STR) which includes non-bank transactions with banks and has been consistently below the ECB's deposit facility rate since it has been produced (cf. Figure 6.2). In the US, the Federal Reserve has introduced a new facility, the overnight reverse repo (ON RRP) to absorb liquidity from a wider range of counterparties in order to prevent market rates from falling below the target rate.

CHAPTER 7

Operational Frameworks

7.1 CONTROL OF THE MONEY SUPPLY

The short-term liabilities of central banks, whether it is bank notes issued by them, or the accounts held by commercial banks at the central bank, form the basis of money, also known as base money in most developed economies. Central banks have some, but not unlimited, control over these liabilities. One can classify actions of central banks into three groups according to the effect they have on their total liabilities. Some actions have no effect, for instance the exchange of current account holdings at the central bank into bank notes. Some actions increase central bank short-term liabilities, such as the purchase of assets by the central bank. These are known as liquidity providing operations. The third group are actions that reduce short-term liabilities, such as asset sales, known as liquidity absorbing operations.

Each central bank has a set of pre-defined operations that fall into each of these categories and together form the operational framework of that central bank. Because they are predefined, market participants, notably commercial banks, can form reasonable expectations about the conduct of these operations and the risk of unintended side effects is minimised. While the operational frameworks of central banks tend to exhibit strong hysteresis, some desirable common features can be identified. A good framework should at the same time be wide enough to cover potential emergencies without the need to introduce ad hoc tools, and parsimonious enough to do so with the minimum of complexity [10]. As a result, operational frameworks can be broadly divided into three parts. The first are standard operations which are intended to be used on a regular basis and the parameters of which signal the general monetary policy stance in normal times. A second set of operations is used in emergency situations as part of the LOLR function of the central bank. The third set are non-standard operations that are used broadly, but only at times of particular economic exigency. Each central bank can assemble these three sets of operations in different ways. For instance, a standing lending facility may be part of the standard operations for one central bank, while it forms part of the LOLR framework of another.

The following two sections describe some standard monetary operations tools with no claim to completeness.

7.2 LIQUIDITY PROVISION: REDISCOUNTING, OUTRIGHT PURCHASES AND LOMBARD LENDING

Central banks can in principle provide liquidity to commercial banks by lending to, or buying assets from, them. When central banks lend to commercial banks, they generally do so against collateral[1].

Central banks provide liquidity by discounting the commercial bills presented by banks, i.e., by purchasing these bills for cash. This is known as rediscounting. This term is based on the idea that the commercial bank in question first obtained the bill by discounting it. It should be borne in mind that the legal mechanics of bill trading imply that the bank presenting the bill for rediscounting can be subject to claims for redress from the central bank if the draftee of the bill refuses payment. The central bank therefore has recourse to both the bank it advances cash to, through rediscounting, and to the ultimate borrower. The practice of rediscounting bills has become less prevalent in modern-day central banking but explains terms such as the discount window at the United States Federal Reserve.

The rediscounting of a bill provides liquidity to the general economy for as long as the bill is outstanding because the payment of the bill to the central bank will amount to a reduction of the asset and liability sides of the central bank. Given the short-term nature of bills, the central bank tends to be passive in the repayment profile of its assets and would have to offset this passivity through an active purchase strategy to target a given liquidity supply.

Central banks can choose instead to purchase long-term assets from the market and resell them before maturity to gain better control over the total amount of liquidity in the banking system. The buying and selling of securities in the open market is known as open market operations or outright operations. This is the standard operating mode of the Fed.

In another type of liquidity provision, the central bank advances cash against securities posted for the duration of the lending operation. This was known as Lombard lending but today the term is somewhat archaic. In modern financial markets, the equivalent transaction is a sale combined with a simultaneous repurchase of the same security for future settlement. This type of trade is known as repurchase or simply repo trading. Where central banks lend against collateral, rather than purchasing it outright, they nowadays do so in line with repo market practice. The ECB and Bank of Japan operate in this manner in normal circumstances.

Rediscounting and open market operations are similar in the sense that the central bank becomes outright owner of an asset in exchange for liquidity injected into the banking system. They differ in that the instrument purchased is usually held to maturity in rediscounting operations while it may be sold in open market operations. Open market operations are similar to repo operations in that the maturity of the operation is shorter than that of the instrument used, but they differ because the maturity of a

---

[1]Lending without any form of security would create unacceptable moral hazard. Banks could advance loans to related parties and then cover any losses through borrowing from the central bank and ultimately socialise any losses.

repo operation is usually fixed while the re-sale of an asset purchased in an open market operation is at the discretion of the central bank. Open market operations, unlike repos, expose the central bank to price risk.

Although the recent large-scale asset purchase programmes have blurred the lines somewhat, it can be said that the US Federal Reserve relies mostly on open market operations while other central banks use repos for their liquidity providing operations.

7.3 LIQUIDITY ABSORPTION: ASSET SALES AND REVERSE REPOS

Just as asset purchases by central banks supply liquidity to the economy, asset sales by the central bank pull liquidity back from the economy. Central banks can sell securities issued by other entities provided that they have previously been purchased by the central bank, or they can issue securities themselves and sell those. As with asset purchases as a liquidity absoprtion tool, the maturity of the securities involved creates a predefined maturity patterns to the liquidity effect that can be counteracted by active portfolio management by the central bank.

Repo operations, in contrast, decouple the maturity of the securities involved from the maturity of the liquidity impact. This decoupling can only be taken so far given that the repo markets are liquid only up to horizons of a few months.

7.4 THE IMPACT OF FX OPERATIONS

Central banks, or other national authorities tasked with managing the external value of the currency, routinely transact in the foreign exchange market. When they buy foreign currency from domestic entities in order to manage their own currency downwards, they create central bank liabilities. Sales of foreign currency conversely reduce central bank liabilities. Interventions in the FX markets therefore interact with the purely domestic factors affecting liquidity in the domestic money market. Such operations can clash with the primary mandate of the central bank in question, such as inflation targeting.

This problem can be solved to some extent by sterilisation of FX interventions. This type of operation reduces liquidity by exchanging a liquid asset for a less liquid asset. For example, the Ministry of Finance of Japan, which is responsible for intervening in the FX market, has accumulated large amounts of foreign currency. In order to buy this foreign currency, it has to pay Japanese Yen. Because the Ministry of Finance is not the central bank, it obtains the required Yen amounts by issuing so-called Foreign Exchange Fund Financing Bills. Selling these bills on the open market turns cash into less liquid bills. The selling of Yen against foreign currency therefore does not increase the amount of Yen cash in the market because it is offset by the issuance of financing bills.

For a central bank that issues domestic currency for FX intervention purposes, the more direct way to sterilise the impact on the domestic money supply is to buy domestic long-term assets. Again, while in the first instance liquidity is created for the purpose of buying foreign currency, it is in a second step transformed into less liquid assets on the balance sheet of the private sector. This type of transaction is a large contributor to the so-called NMP (non-monetary policy) portfolios of some euro area central banks.

FX interventions are symmetric in the sense that they involve both currencies in a currency pair. A central bank that sells, for instance, euros to buy dollars on the open market increases the supply of euro liquidity in the private sector while reducing the supply of dollars. If the central bank in question were the ECB, the sterilisation on the increased euro liquidity would be in the interest of the ECB, and presumably managed by it, because that liquidity impact might affect its inflation mandate. The impact on the dollar market, meanwhile, would have to be managed by the US Federal Reserve. As a result, FX interventions among the major currency areas are usually coordinated in order to contain the spillover effects on the money markets concerned.

A case in point is Japan, which has a persistently positive current account. This means that Japanese entities tend to earn more money abroad than they have to spend domestically. This leads to an interconnection between the overseas and domestic money markets. Generally, interest rates in Japan are depressed by a generous availability of yen funding versus a variable supply of dollar funding. It can be argued [80] that this restricts the ability of the Bank of Japan to control effective short-term interest rates in its own currency. The interest rates on short-dated Japanese government debt turned negative even before the Bank of Japan cut its own policy rates below zero.

CHAPTER 8

Interaction between Frameworks and Policy

O perational frameworks have a bearing on the monetary policy stance. For instance, central banks used to move policy rates in 1/4 percent steps in most developed economies before the financial crisis. Since then, some central banks have started moving policy rates in 0.1% steps. For the operational frameworks this means that they need to ensure a much tighter range on actual market rates in order to make sure that the changed policy has any actual effect.

8.1   VOLATILITY

The volatility of the market rate corresponding to the policy rate is an obvious point of concern for the monetary policy stance. Volatile interest rates generate risk premia which, *ceteris paribus*, lead to a steeper yield curve. More significantly, the efficacy of a policy rate change would be diminished if actual market rates were to fluctuate wildly around that rate.

On a wider view, interest rates, the natural domain of central banks, are not the only factors affecting the decisions that monetary policy might want to encourage. For instance, in countries where workers have a large part of their assets in pension funds invested in equities (like the US), falls in equity prices can lead to reduced consumer expenditure (the so-called wealth effect) which could be dis-inflationary. That would suggest that central banks should be mindful of equity valuations, and in fact take measures to stabilise them. This is the intellectual underpinning of the 'Fed Put' concept. At the same time, excessive equity (or for that matter, any other asset) valuations may store up trouble for the future. This suggests, as is sometimes done, that central banks should lean against higher asset prices as well as higher inflation.

That being said, volatility is important for markets. Without volatility, there would be no need for trading or risk management[1] which would diminish the ability of a market to manage volatility when it returns. Volatility also acts as a brake on excessive risk-taking among financial and non-financial actors. Overall, therefore, the market

---

[1] Or, coincidentally, this book.

volatility needs to be a concern for the monetary policy stance, and not just for the operational framework.

Central banks can manage market volatility through a variety of means, such as operations to control short rates, or longer-dated yields through outright purchases. Communications is an important channel because the better the public understands the likely actions of the central banks, the less it will react to surprises with outsized market moves.

One part of non-standard measures has been forward guidance. This policy tool is designed to dampen volatility by extending the forecast horizon of central bank action beyond the next policy announcement. In a now-famous paper [19], Campbell et al. distinguished between two types of forward guidance, which they termed Delphic and Odyssean. In the Delphic model, the central bank communicates its economic forecasts and the likely policy reaction if these outcomes materialise. The Odyssean model, on the other hand, binds the central bank unconditionally to a particular path of action. A full implementation of the Odyssean model with long horizons is unlikely to be credible given that it may cause the central bank to act against its mandate, for instance by hiking in the face of deflation based on an earlier commitment. The credibility of the Delphic model, on the other hand, depends on public trust in the superior forecasting ability of the central bank. Despite these caveats, forward guidance appears to have worked well [65] and is likely to remain a policy tool.

8.2 COLLATERAL

For central banks that use repo operations for liquidity provision, the choice of acceptable collateral is not purely an operational concern. From the operational standpoint, the range of collateral needs only to be large enough to ensure that enough of it is held by the banking system to absorb the liquidity that the central bank wishes to supply. One would in practice make the collateral range somewhat wider so that inevitable fluctuations in bank holdings, and of liquidity needs, do not require changes in the collateral criteria but still accept only the highest quality collateral available in that volume. Wider collateral ranges should be acceptable for the lender-of-last-resort function because banks requiring such support are less likely to hold large amounts of the highest quality collateral.

The Eurosystem has chosen a different approach. It accepts a very wide range of collateral for standard operations. While some authors view this as exposing the central bank to too much risk (e.g., [64]), the Eurosystem in fact manages collateral risk not only via collateral selection, but also through an aggressive use of haircuts[2] and daily margining. This wider collateral framework has a monetary policy stance aspect because it ensures access to central bank liquidity across a wide range of financial institutions. If the framework were narrower, there would be a need for the private banking system to establish channels of liquidity transmission to banks not holding the highest

---

[2]See Section 14.2 on page 128 for a discussion on haircuts and relative credit strength.

quality collateral. Any tightening in the lending conditions of this private transmission channel would affect the transmission of monetary policy.

Some observed cases of changes to collateral frameworks therefore have had policy stance aspects. The Fed's Term Securities Lending Facility (TSLF, see page 129) amounted to a collateral widening action by the central bank even though the Fed itself conducts only a limited amount of repo for liquidity provision. The ECB widened collateral eligibility criteria on several occasions as part of managing the financial crisis, and also unwound some of this widening when calm returned to the markets.

CHAPTER 9

Non-Standard Monetary Policy

9.1 QUANTITATIVE EASING

Quantitative easing (QE) is the best known but far from the only non-standard form of monetary policy. In conventional monetary policy frameworks, the operational policy target is an interest or foreign exchange rate and the balance sheet of the central bank reacts, through monetary policy operations, passively to changes in market supply and demand to bring the market clearing rate in line with the target.

Quantitative easing can be understood as a shift to operational targets for specific quantities related to the balance sheet of the central bank, such as bond holdings or base money. Employing non-standard tools is appropriate when policy action is necessary but the standard tools do not work, for instance when interest rates have reached a lower bound or no longer stimulate aggregate demand as expected [65].

Seen in this way, QE is simply the continuation of standard monetary policy by other means. The extreme nature of QE is then simply a product of the extreme circumstances in which the central bank finds itself. Standard monetary policy tools are supposed to work in a wide range of usual circumstances. A central bank resorting to non-standard tools then must be operating in a very non-standard set of economic conditions. That being said, Figure 9.1, using Japanese data, shows that central bank balance sheet expansion is not necessarily a substitute for lower rates. The chart has been formatted suggestively so that the start of the 2001–2006 quantitative easing episode appears as a continuation of the rate cuts that started in March 2001. The reduction of excess reserves in 2006 also appears like a precursor to the rate hike that occurred in July of that year. However, the response to the financial crisis that started in 2007[1] did not follow this simple narrative. Excess reserve holding increased around the time of the first rate cuts as a result of liquidity hoarding. The central bank adjusted operational targets for liquidity-supplying operations to accommodate such behaviour. In 2016, when the Bank of Japan cut the short-term interest rate target to negative (with an introduction of a tiered deposit system), the tool of excess reserve expansion had been used extensively for two years.

---

[1] In due fairness, the tightening in 2006 was seen at the time as premature by some observers. The decline of nominal GDP shown in the chart, which began well before the onset of the global crisis, would then not be entirely due to external shocks but may have had an endogenous component.

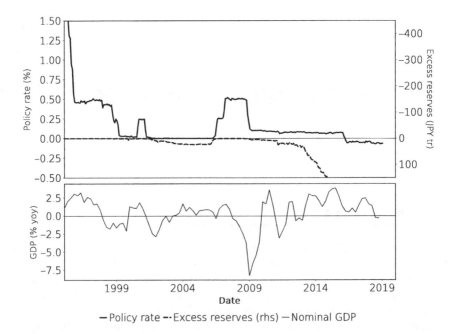

FIGURE 9.1 Monthly averages of the Japanese yen unsecured overnight (mutan) rate and excess reserve holdings at the Bank of Japan. The annual rate of change in the nominal GDP is shown for reference. Sources: Bank of Japan, Cabinet Office.

An interesting example of the distinction between quantitative easing and mere accomodation of market fluctuations was the introduction of T-bill purchases by the Fed in autumn 2019. These purchases amount to an injection of central bank liquidity into the banking system similar to the outright purchases of Treasuries that were undertaken as part of various QE earlier programmes. However, the purchases were a passive reaction to an increased demand in the US repo market, not a change in monetary policy stance. The purchases run in parallel with repo operations. Because T-bills have short maturities, the time frame over which the purchases inject liquidity into the market is longer than that of a normal repo operation but shorter than a Treasury purchase.

Just as, in Tolstoy's words, all happy families are alike, but each unhappy family is unhappy in its own way, central banks operating with a standard tool set operate in similar and well understood ways; central banks employing non-standard tools find themselves in more unique circumstances. Although experience with QE has been gathered in many currency areas, they all differ in what are probably important parameters, such as importance of the banking system, current account balance, and external debt position. Copying from other countries is therefore unlikely to succeed. Constructing a theory of QE from first principles is an alternative and more promising approach.

Quantitative easing in the monetarist sense becomes useful when the breakdown is in the link between interest rates and the money supply (II). The central bank can in such situations simply attempt to bypass the bank money creation process and control M

more directly by creating more base money. This idea was the intellectual basis for the first QE programme conducted in Japan 2001–2006. At the time, the BoJ targeted base money in the form of the excess reserves held by Japanese banks in their BoJ accounts, eventually reaching a volume of around JPY 29tr.

It should be noted that it is difficult for a central bank to assess breakdowns in the monetary transmission mechanism in real time because the quantitative nature of that link is not static. Every monetary policy action causes a reaction in the money supply (which may be zero). The best a central bank can do is to predict that reaction with some model. When the actual outcome deviates from the prediction, the reasons could be that:

- the model is incorrect or a structural change means that the model parameters no longer correspond to the new market regime;
- while the model is correct, time lags and inevitable forecast and measurement errors lead to a temporary deviation that will eventually mean-revert;
- the money market has changed in such a way as to make it unreactive to monetary policy.

Only the last situation could be characterised as a breakdown in the monetary transmission mechanism. Whether this warrants other measures by the central bank is not immediately obvious. In modern democracies the central bank is an agent of economic policy. When this particular agent can no longer work with the set of tools allocated to it, the implications are wider than a simple change of strategy at the agent[2]. At the same time, democratic processes do not lend themselves to timely adjustments of the tool set of the agent.

While quantitative easing, in the sense of increasing M by central bank fiat, is immediately meaningful in a monetarist interpretation, it would be completely meaningless to a Keynesian[3]. To understand why a central bank might want to conduct quantitative easing even when it is not monetarist, other possible channels of operation must be considered. Below is a listing of channels through which asset purchases could affect the price level.

> **Quantity effect (A)** As outlined in Equation (6.2), more money should, *ceteris paribus*, increase the price level.
>
> **FX market (B)** More supply of the domestic currency should devalue it in the FX market and thereby push up import prices. Assuming the economy contains a price-competing export sector, higher external demand for these products should also support higher inflation. See Figure 9.3 for some historical data.

---

[2]Some central bankers have gone as far as advocating higher inflation targets to reduce the probability of reaching the lower bound on interest rates in low growth environments. This is an alternative expression of the same dilemma. An agent is given tools to achieve an aim. When the tools do not suit the target, or vice versa, the decision to change either lies with the principal, not the agent.

[3]A major obstacle to the understanding of the monetary transmission mechanism in a Keynesian/neo-classical setting is that the related economic models tend to ignore the role of the financial sector in the economy.

Signalling (C) By using its potentially unlimited balance sheet for asset purchases, the central bank signals strong commitment to its price or inflation target.

Relative pricing (D) By intervening in asset markets, the central bank affects the relative pricing of different capital sources in the economy. This can stimulate some sectors relative to others, or subsidise some forms of lending relative to others.

Portfolio effect (E) Because the central bank removes assets from the portfolios of private investors, these investors must reallocate cash to other assets. Even though the central bank itself does not target these alternative assets (as in the relative pricing effect above), they benefit from the spillover of the extra liquidity.

Bank capital formation (F) By increasing asset prices, the central bank can create permanent new equity capital in banks because it allows them to sell assets above amortised cost.

Risk-weighted assets (G) If the central bank buys assets with non-zero risk weights from banks, it frees up existing bank equity.

Lower Volatility (H) Central bank buying can dampen the price volatility in the affected asset markets. This can free up bank equity (via lower VaR measures), flatten the yield curve (due to lower term risk premia), and stimulate investment (due to more certain present values of future cashflows). Because all these effects are indirect and already listed above, these are not separate operational channels of QE. It should also be noted that prolonged low volatility can be detrimental to financial stability. While some investors will increase leverage to achieve the same risk-adjusted returns, banks have to disinvest from their market making operations. Should volatility then return due to some external shock, large deleveraging would occur in an environment of depleted market-maker balance sheets.

Pure monetarists would agree only with the first two channels (A) and (B), and also disagree with the second sentence in (B). A more Keynesian interpretation of QE would deny (A). Point (C) was made by the Bank of Japan in its explanation of the current QE programme. The 'relative pricing' (D) aspect is most prominently reflected in the Fed's 'Operation Twist', which was targeted directly at lowering long-term interest rates, and the Fed's purchases of mortgages, as well as the Bank of Japan's yield curve control (YCC). Any such thinking would meanwhile be anathema to an ordoliberalist economist[4].

The two channels (F) and (G) are particularly important for markets where the breakdown in the control relationship (II) is caused by a lack of bank capital and where banks provide the bulk of funding to the real economy. That said, central bank policy that is explicitly geared to supporting bank capital levels would run counter to the general principle that the role of a central bank is the provision of liquidity, not of capital[5].

---

[4]This school of economics is not structurally tied to either monetarism or the neo-classical school but its representatives tend to be monetarists.

[5]The standard prescriptions of central bank crisis tools remain Walter Bagehot's exhortations to the Bank of England [5]: 'that in time of panic it must advance freely and vigorously to the public out of the reserve [...] and the advances should, if possible, stay the panic. And for this purpose

While some politicians and economists view the FX channel as important, the evidence for the stimulative effects of a weaker currency on exports depends on the nature of industry and non-price competitiveness. It is quite possible that FX depreciation simply creates windfall benefits for highly competitive companies while companies without a viable growth model are unable to enjoy improved cost competitiveness.

The variety of possible channels of QE into the real economy means that it is difficult to specify a required size for such a programme before specifying what mechanisms and assets it should target. A purely monetary interpretation of QE would imply sizes that are meaningfully large relative to the existing money stock, and by implication, GDP. A more Keynesian programme targeted at specific asset classes could operate on sizes that are large relative to the pool of eligible assets yet small compared to the total money stock (and indeed would not be seen as quantitative easing by a monetarist observer for that reason). It is therefore useful, at least for a non-monetarist observer, to distinguish between quantitative easing (aimed at addressing a breakdown in the relationship (II) above) and asset purchases (which may have more specific targets). Note that the Bank of Japan conducted quantitative easing with an emphasis on repos, not asset purchases, between 2001 and 2006. In practice, the ability of central banks to adjust purchase programmes during their implementation means that the inevitable forecasting errors regarding their impact does not diminish their justification. The forecasts need to be accurate enough to weigh the advantages and disadvantages of conducting such operations, versus the available alternatives, with a reasonable degree of certainty.

9.1.1 The Monetary Effect of Large-Scale Asset Purchases

When central banks purchase macroscopically large amounts of assets, the impact is not limited to the banking system, i.e., the direct counterparties of the central bank, as would be the case with standard operations. Banks looking to sell assets to the central bank have to source them from other asset owners, such as funds, insurance companies or households. This creates a conceptual problem because these actors are unable to hold directly the asset created by the central bank in exchange, namely new central bank liquidity. Instead, the asset sellers merely substitute these assets with claims against banks. This means that the banking system in aggregate acts not only as an intermediary in the asset transfer, but is forced to lengthen its aggregate balance sheet to accommodate these new claims.

Figure 9.2 demonstrates this graphically. In economic terms, the increase in outside money (the quantitative easing effect) is matched by an increase in inside money.

This mechanism means that asset purchases potentially have an additional side effect. If the security purchased by the central bank is of very high credit quality, a simple bank deposit (which exposes the depositor to the credit risk of the bank) may not be an acceptable substitute. The asset manager may instead ask for the deposit to be collateralised, i.e., a repo transaction. While in principle this repo only amounts to swapping

---

there are two rules: First. That these loans should only be made at a very high rate of interest. [...] Secondly. That at this rate these advances should be made on all good banking securities, and as largely as the public ask for them. [...] No advances indeed need be made by which the Bank will ultimately lose.'

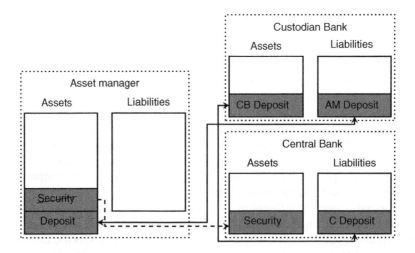

FIGURE 9.2   Balance sheet effect of large-scale asset purchases. Corresponding assets and liabilities are paired by arrows; the dashed arrow denotes the transfer of the security purchased by the central bank.

central bank deposits against securities elsewhere in the system, the repo market may not at all times be efficient enough to accommodate these transactions without friction costs. These friction costs may explain in part why general collateral repo rates can decline as a result of large-scale asset purchases.

9.1.2   Market liquidity and central bank asset purchases

The modern asset management industry is driven by market indices which are used either as performance benchmarks, or strict asset allocation guidelines, depending on the amount of tracking error targeted by a given asset manager. Exchange-traded funds (ETFs) in particular are closely tied in their asset allocation to a given bond index. The index weight of a given bond is given simply by the market value of the asset, divided by the sum of all market values. An index-neutral asset allocation would therefore be one where each asset is held in direct proportion to its outstanding volume.

In practice, such an index-neutral asset allocation is impossible to realise because there is a structural demand preference for certain assets by investors who do not follow a broad market index. Foreign reserve managers at central banks, for instance, tend to prefer the most liquid assets regardless of expected returns. This is because the main concern for such portfolios is not their return, but the ease with which they can be turned into cash in times of crisis. Other investors, such as insurance companies, follow investment strategies that are based on particular return targets linked to liabilities. At times of lower market yields, such portfolios purchase riskier assets.

Central bank asset purchases can exacerbate this problem even when they follow market weights. As an example, assume a segmented market consisting of two types of asset, each of which comprises 50% of the total market volume. One asset is of very high quality and 40% of the asset is held by investors who are constrained to hold such high quality assets. The other asset is perceived as more risky and consequently no forced holders are present in this asset. As a result 60% of the first, and 100% of the second asset are held by value-oriented investors that can buy or sell depending on market prices. If the central bank now steps in and buys 30% of the total market volume in proportion to the outstanding amount, it will reduce the free float of the first asset by half but the free float of the second by less than a third. The price impact of the purchases is therefore likely to be larger for the first asset.

Central banks can, and do, mitigate the distorting effects of such local imbalances in various ways [25]. For instance, large purchase programmes have securities lending facilities so that the availability of special repo collateral is not negatively affected by central bank holdings. Purchases are also conducted in ways that avoid excessive security-specific price effects. Depending on the central bank, the way in which this is done varies. For central banks using auctions, some form of relative value analysis takes place when offers are evaluated. Others may incorporate such analysis in bilateral operations. The way in which implementation frameworks across central banks differ does not only apply to the mode of purchase, but also to information disclosure about purchases. The experience from large-scale asset purchases around the world is that there are multiple optimal combinations of purchase mode, flexibility of purchase, and information disclosure. Which of these optima is chosen depends on local market usances. In every case, however, central banks have made adjustments to their programme implementation in order to protect market functioning. Doing so requires a large amount of market monitoring and analysis.

9.1.3 Helicopter money

Quantitative easing as described here remains a monetary policy tool in the sense that it provides an aggressive, but temporary, injection of liquidity into the economy. The next escalation step could therefore be to make the liquidity injection permanent. At that stage, however, monetary policy crosses into the fiscal policy realm because the idea of controlling the money supply in order to preserve the store of value property of money would be subordinated to other aims, such as dealing with a debt overhang. By permanently expanding the money supply, the central bank would engineer a jump in the price level, according to Equation (6.2).

The most graphic description of this approach is the idea of dropping banknotes from a helicopter, put forward by Milton Friedman in 1969. As Ben Bernanke pointed out in 2002, the same concept could be implemented by fiscal measures that are funded by monetary expansion[6].

What appears to be misunderstood is that this approach is actually very straightforward and to some degree already implemented. Some authors (e.g. Nyborg [64])

---

[6]The unsung hero of economic education, Douglas Adams, popularised this concept in 'The Restaurant at the End of the Universe' [1] as follows:

'How can you have money,' demanded Ford, 'if none of you actually produces anything? It doesn't grow on trees you know.' [...] 'Since we decided a few weeks ago to adopt the leaf as legal tender, we have, of course, all become immensely rich.' [...]

make the assumption that helicopter money requires the explicit cancellation of government debt by the central bank, or the conversion of debt held by the central bank into infinite maturity zero coupon bonds. The actual mechanism can be much simpler. Most developed nation central banks are required by law to remit any profits over a certain threshold to their respective governments. Coupon payments by the government to the central bank are therefore ecomically neutral because they will be remitted after the end of the fiscal year. The level of coupons held by the central bank is therefore more or less irrelevant, aside from pull-to-par effects. In addition, the maturity of a government bond is not equivalent to a fiscal contraction simply because the redemption amount will normally be covered by the issuance of a new government bond. Instead of accepting perpetual bonds, a central bank can simply commit, implicitly or explicitly, to reinvesting any maturing principal in new government bonds. In other words, the transition between quantitative easing and helicopter money need not be tied to the shape in which the initial liquidity injection takes place, or the types of bond acquired by the central bank. Instead, it is dependent on the evolution of central bank involvement in the sovereign debt market.

The Bank of Japan is a useful example. It has purchased Japanese government bonds outright since at least 1967 [81]. To the extent that the volume of government bonds held by the BoJ never fell to zero, these purchases are economically indistiguishable from helicopter money. A debt that has been rolled over for in excess of 50 years is simply not very different from a perpetual asset. That being said, the Bank of Japan until 2013 applied a 'banknote rule' that limited the amount of JGB it could hold to the total volume of banknotes in circulation. In doing so, it limited the amount of 'helicopter money' roughly to the amount of seigniorage remitted to the country. According to the US Federal Reserve, outright holdings of US Treasury assets have over the last 15 years also never fallen below USD 500bn. These 500bn, equivalent to about 2.75% of current nominal GDP, are also hard to separate from helicopter money. To put this into some context, foreigners hold physical US dollars outside the US without the intent to present them for payment in the US itself. The seigniorage associated with this money accrues to the United States. A report by the St. Louis Fed [4] gives an estimate of USD 500bn for such notes, which is the same amount as that contributed by the Treasury holdings of the Federal Reserve. While both factors create a fiscal boost, the monetary of these two factors is subtly different because helicopter money adds to domestic liquidity while notes held abroad diminish it[7].

'But we have also,' continued the management consultant, 'run into a small inflation problem on account of the high level of leaf availability, which means that, I gather, the current going rate has something like three decidious forests buying one ship's peanut.' Murmurs of alarm came from the crowd. The management consultant waved them down. 'So in order to obviate this problem,' he continued, 'and effectively revalue the leaf, we are about to embark on a massive defoliation campaign, and ... er, burn down all the forests. I think you'll all agree that's a sensible move under the circumstances.'

---

[7]Indeed the purpose of estimating the volume of physical currency held abroad is to be able to counteract this contraction of domestic liquidity.

In any case, the liquidity effect of the long-term holdings of central banks has so far been minuscule, and certainly too small to have an impact on inflation. In this sense, the practical test of helicopter money has still not occurred.

9.1.4 Choice of methods and assets

The choice of how to conduct quantitative easing and what assets to involve in the implementation depends on the central bank's assessment of how QE works. A purely monetarist central bank looking at effects (A) and (B), or even (C) above can choose freely between repo or outright transactions, and can use any type of financial asset, or indeed non-financial asset, in these operations. The hurdle for the purchase of non-financial assets in the monetarist view is that it influences real economic activity (dY) too much whereas a Keynesian would see the role of the central bank as easing financing conditions for the government to conduct such purchases.

When the central bank takes a more Keynesian view of quantitative easing, the choice of operation becomes very skewed towards outright purchases. While repo operations provide funding and signal central bank intent, the effects linked to portfolio shifts and bank equity rely on outright purchases. Last but not least, if the central bank is targeting bank equity levels (implicitly or explicitly), it must remove assets from bank balance sheets in such a way that they can be de-recognised in accounting terms.

Assuming outright asset purchases are chosen as the implementation method, the choice of assets becomes more important for a number of reasons. First, a central bank choosing to act via relative pricing (D) needs to purchase the relevant assets directly and assume a considerable risk of default; if it is confident that portfolio shifts (E) will be sufficient, it can target other asset classes where, for instance, asset purchases are less distorting or technically easier. Also, the credit risk of outright purchases is much higher than on repo operations with daily margining. The central bank must therefore weigh the cost of credit risk against the benefit of targeting specific asset markets.

With this in mind, one can discuss possible asset classes for outright purchases in terms of the potential effects listed above. Below is a list of assets and a summary of their potential effects in a simple matrix.

Government bonds Due to their superior liquidity, government bonds are the natural choice for executing large-scale asset purchase programmes. Lower government bond rates can also affect funding costs for other actors in the economy such as banks and high-grade corporates. That said, even deep government bond markets can experience low liquidity as a result of central bank asset purchases if these are to be large relative to GDP. Because repo operations would achieve the same monetary expansion goals, such purchases may call into question central bank independence beause future central bank policy may become constrained by the default risk of a large government bond portfolio (this situation is known as fiscal dominance).

Supras, Subsovereigns, Agencies Depending on the market, there may be near-substitutes for government bonds available. Aside from the US agency MBS market, in no market are such securities comparable size and liquidity with government bonds. Purchases of SSA securities are therefore most useful via portfolio allocation shifts.

Covered Bonds Covered bond purchases, in those markets where these bonds are high in volume are a natural extension of repo along the curve because covered bonds also are standardised collateralised bank obligations. However, liquidity in covered bonds is substantially lower than for government bonds in all markets aside from Denmark.

Senior unsecured bank debt Bank debt is an abundant asset class but would pose a risk management dilemma for central banks that use repo as a liquidity provision tool. Holders of bank debt carry credit risk of the issuing bank. Doing so on an unsecured basis for a longer term whilst asking for repo collateral on short term operations is logically inconsistent. Furthermore, any such purchase would require taking a view on spreads which would invariably call into question the impartiality of the central bank vis-à-vis its counterparties, especially where the central bank has superior insight into the situation of each bank issuer.

Corporate debt Corporate bonds are a large asset class but are illiquid in most markets. More concerning for an asset purchase programme is that debt financing is more easily available for companies with a large stock of fixed assets and stable cashflows. High-growth start-up companies operate on very low leverage ratios because they are less able to source debt financing. A breakdown of major bond indices shows a large share of utilities (telecommunications, energy, gas), mining, transportation and car manufacturing companies among the issuers of investment grade bonds. Lowering funding costs for such companies is unlikely to be growth positive which would be a pre-condition for a Keynesian QE approach. Corporate bond purchases also implicitly discriminate by size against smaller and unrated companies. That being said, funding larger corporations through the central bank can free up bank balance sheets for the loan funding of smaller ones.

Bank loans Banks lend under slightly less onerous conditions (albeit potentially at higher rates) than the public markets because they operate under less information asymmetry than bond investors and may have access to collateral. Purchasing bank loans would therefore be more stimulative for high-growth companies than the corporate bond market. Additionally, it would have a beneficial effect on bank equity via RWA reduction and potentially capital gains if banks have loans to sell at book value or above (banks are unlikely to sell loans below book value). However, a purchasing central bank faces a selling bank counterparty with superior information about the loan asset and probably has insufficient analysis capabilities to value large numbers of loans across different jurisdictions.

The only realistic way of purchasing bank loans is therefore likely to be via securitisation where loan pooling and tranching provides a sufficient risk buffer for the purchasing central bank.

Foreign assets A way of focusing QE in the FX channel would be the direct purchase foreign assets without sterilising the resulting liquidity. The structural problem with unsterilised foreign asset purchases is that the targeted amount of FX intervention and increase in the money supply are rigidly coupled. In addition, the central bank could be criticised for taking credit risk in foreign markets, and for spending resources in a way that might benefit foreign economies via the QE channels (D) through (G) above while these effects would be absent for the domestic economy.

In practice, a more serious concern would be that pursuing the FX channel in such an overt fashion would be seen by other countries as unfair.

Equities The Bank of Japan has been purchasing equities through exchange-traded funds (ETFs). Japan is somewhat unique in that it has a large number of listed small companies (the Topix index has nearly 2,200 constituents and the index weights have a Herfindahl index of 0.0064, meaning it is well diversified). For Europe, the points made on corporate bond purchases would also apply to listed equity.

9.2 PRACTICAL EXPERIENCE

9.2.1 QE, money multipliers and FX

The experience of early quantitative easing programmes has been that it is hard to prove efficacy along the lines in which they were designed to act. While the expansion of central bank balance sheets is directly observable, the evidence on broader money aggregates is less convincing. As Figure 9.3 shows, money multipliers dropped during the Japanese and US quantitative easing programmes (essentially suggesting that Equation (6.4) may have held) which raises doubts over the ability to bypass the standard private money creation mechanism[8]. The evidence in the euro area is more mixed in that the money multiplier declined before large-scale balance sheet expansions were undertaken[9].

Of course, the problem with such analyses is that they are by definition relying on counterfactual thinking. It is quite possible that broad money aggregates would have declined if central bank balance sheet expansion had not taken place. Monetary policy loosening is a response to a decline in economic activity and such a decline is likely to coincide with a drop in private money creation. As always in macro-economic problems, the option of conducting experiments with a different policy path but otherwise identical conditions is not available. Furthermore, the idea that a QE programme can have a signalling purpose very much negates the idea of an ex-post quantitative analysis of efficacy. Signalling effects are by definition circular: they work because they work.

As mentioned above, money velocity cannot be measured directly because many monetary transactions are unobservable (or at least unobserved by statisticians). As a proxy, one can use the payments volume in central bank reserves transfer systems. Since physical cash payments are only a small part of total payments in most economies, the interbank transfers of central bank reserves may capture a broader subset of total payments because they are often reflective of customer payment orders.

---

[8]M2 is chosen here because it can be found for all jurisdictions, not because it is the most appropriate money aggregate. The Federal Reserve stopped the publication of M3 as of 23 March 2006.
[9]That being said, the transition to fixed-rate full allotment of ECB main refinancing operations, and the narrowing of the corridor between marginal lending facility and deposit facility can be viewed as a passive balance sheet expansion.

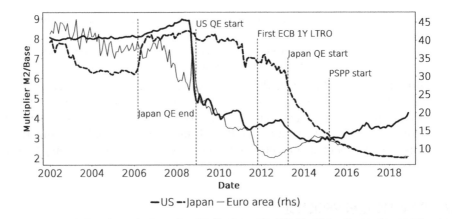

FIGURE 9.3   Money multipliers (M2/Base money) in the US, Japan and the Euro area.
Sources: FRED, Bank of Japan, ECB.

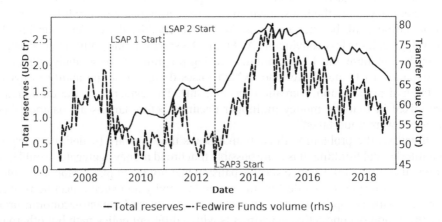

FIGURE 9.4   US total reserves and monthy Fedwire Funds transfer values. The relationship
appears to be strenghening after 2013. Sources: FRB Services, Federal Reserve.

Such reserve transfers systems are operated by central banks (Fedwire Funds by the US
Federal Reserve System, Target2 by the ECB) or private bank associations (the Zengin
System[10] by the Japanese Bankers Association's Zengin-Net, Faster Payments by Faster
Payments Scheme Limited in the UK).

A study by the ECB on the liquidity velocity of central bank money in the Target
2 system (Box 3 in [7]) found a significant decline in money velocity as base money
increased although the relationship does not appear to be a straightforward case
of Equation (6.4). The ECB does not disclose the underlying payments volumes but
such disclosure is available for Fedwire Funds.

---

[10]Zengin is the Japanese short name for the Japanese Bankers Association. The Zengin System is
formally called the Zengin Data Telecommunication System.

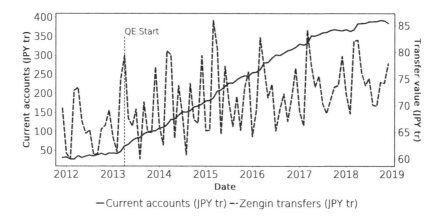

FIGURE 9.5 Monthly average current account holdings of Japanese banks at the BoJ and total small (under JPY 100m) transfer values in Zengin. Sources: BoJ, Zengin-Net.

Figure 9.4[11] suggests that since 2013, there has been a closer relationship between total payments volume and money supply which would contradict Equation (6.4) and support the idea that quantitative easing can have an effect on economic activity. A single dollar in bank reserves turned around in Fedwire Funds 28.9 times on average between 2012 and 2018 with a standard deviation of 9.4%. Between January 2007 (the start of Fedwire Funds data availability) and the onset of monetary easing in 2008, a single reserve dollar moved 6,500 times, with a comparable 9.7% standard deviation. A more stable velocity of reserves (i.e., a small standard deviation) would suggest a higher sensitivity of prices to money supply through Equation (6.1). That being said, Fedwire Funds transfers may also be the result of trading in financial assets which are outside the scope of this equation. One could posit that quantitative easing may be stimulating the trading in financial assets and that this explains the relationship between the size of the Fed balance sheet and payments volumes.

At the same time, one could interpret higher transaction volumes in conjunction with larger central bank balance sheets globally as a sign of lower trust in private banks. To the extent that bank customers wish to reduce their exposure to banks, there will be a shift from transacting in bank money (deposits) towards transacting in securities. This then creates more demand for transactional central bank money.

The Japanese Zengin System data, shown in Figure 9.5, is more in line with Equation (6.4). Because Zengin breaks out the volume of small value transfers[12],

---

[11]The figure uses the official acronym LSAP for large-scale asset purchases. Note that the Fed also conducted lending operations that injected additional liquidity before the start of these outright purchase operations.

[12]Small value transfers are collected and settled in central bank money at designated times through the Bank of Japan's RTGS system. Zengin transfers over JPY 100m are settled in real time through RTGS.

one can make the assumption that such transfers are related to purchases and wage payments which are within the scope of Equation (6.1) while financial instruments transactions are less relevant. To further match the velocity measure to the underlying stock, Figure 9.5 uses only current account holdings at the Bank of Japan because these can be transferred through Zengin. Banknotes and coins in circulation, which are also part of the monetary base, are excluded. Transaction volumes since 2012 have been extremely stable with an average annual growth rate of around 1.7% and apparently unconnected to the evolution of the current account volumes.

The UK data is unfortunately not stable enough to conduct this type of analysis because interbank payments underwent a significant transformation in the last decade. The large-volume CHAPS system was replaced by the faster, and considerably cheaper, Faster Payments system and this transition affected end-user take-up of such transfer systems.

The evidence on on the FX impact of quantitative easing is mixed. Figure 9.6 shows the ratio of the money multipliers in Japan and the US, each defined as M2 divided by base money. This ratio decreases when the money multiplier in Japan falls, for instance as a result of quantitative easing, *relative* to that of the US. Because more easing in Japan could be expected to cheapen the Yen (leading to an increase in the JPY/USD exchange rate), the exchange rate is plotted on a separate, inverted axis.

Some common trends between the two series appear to exist although the correlation cannot be called strong. The relative easing of monetary policy by the Bank of Japan following the bursting of the Japanese bubble occasionally coincides with Yen cheapening but the overall level in 2006 (at the peak of the first QE) is not much weaker than in 2001. The quantitative easing in the US is clearly visible as an increase in the ratio of money multipliers, but the timing and evolution of the post-Lehman appreciation of the Yen does not seem to be fully synchronised. The more recent history again shows a better correlation. Note that FX interventions were a more frequent occurrence during the earlier part of the history shown here.

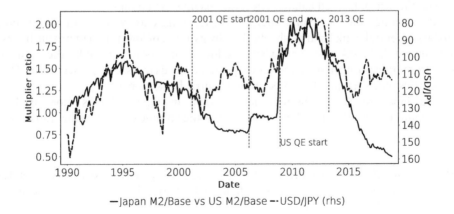

FIGURE 9.6   Long-run series of the ratio of the Japanese and US money multipliers and the JPY/USD FX rate. Sources: Federal Reserve, Bank of Japan.

The sporadic nature of the correlation between QE and FX rates is perhaps a good indication for the limits of central bank policy. Japan has been running a persistent current account surplus (trade and income) over the period shown here. Such a surplus should be positive for the currency to the extent that some of these flows are repatriated rather than reinvested abroad. A central bank can temporarily offset these long-term trends with activist monetary policy but apparently not competely decouple the FX rates from trade fundamentals. The weakening of the Yen to some degree also stems from the deterioration of Japan's trade balance following the Fukushima disaster and not only from Abenomics and BoJ policy. The observation that the Yen depreciated 23% against the USD before QE was started by the BoJ, and since then moved only 7%, is evidence of the relative importance of other factors for the FX rate.

That said, even a temporary suspension of normal price formation mechanisms could in theory be supportive for the real economy in the longer run. A central bank could look to allow capital formation in the manufacturing sector via a policy that depreciates the currency, creates extra external demand, and thus allows more profits to be invested in machinery and bank loan repayments. At the end of this process, the manufacturing sector would be less dependent on labour input and the banking system less leveraged. A re-strenghtening of the currency would then not cause any substantial problems for growth. However, the materialisation of such hysteresis effects is by no means certain.

9.2.2 Bank of Japan 2013 QE experience

The experience of the Bank of Japan's quantitative easing programme in 2013 highlights the importance of technical factors. The Bank of Japan announced on 4 April 2013 a quantitative easing programme across multiple asset classes (JGB, CP, corporate bonds, ETF, REIT) which amounted to the purchase of around 70% of the gross issuance of JGB and thereby more than the net supply of government debt.

Interestingly, interest rates increased after QE was announced which would run counter to the expectation that announcing a programme to buy a particular type of asset would make it more expensive. Over a year after the start of QE, Japanese 10Y yields (0.6%) were still higher than they were before QE was announced. Two factors can be identified to explain this phenomenon besides higher realised inflation.

The first was a communication problem. Bank of Japan Governor Kuroda was ambiguous about the exact channels in which he expected QE to affect the economy and it took some time to clarify that signalling effects were the main channel in which the Bank of Japan expected its policy to work. Because the Governor expressed indifference over the direction of yields (saying that a rise in JGB yields as an expression of higher inflation expectations was understandable), bond market participants had difficulties in interpreting the price signals the BoJ wanted to send. As a matter of fact, the BoJ did not intend to send any such signals.

The second problem was implementation. In its original communication on 4 April 2013, the operational schedule was for 11 operations to be held on 6 days of the month (meaning that the BoJ would conduct two operations on the same day). The size of each operation was to be around JPY 1tr (EUR 7bn) and JPY 300bn (EUR 2bn) in the long end. These sizes were apparently chosen in reference to JGB auctions which are JPY 2.3tr in size for 10Y JGB and JPY 700bn for 30Y JGB. While the immediate reaction of the market was positive, dealers judged these sizes as too large to be able to offer sufficient amounts of securities at each operation. This disappointment is reflected in the sell-off in JGB that followed immediately after the initial rally. The BoJ reacted to this criticism by changing the operations schedule two weeks later. On 18 April, a new schedule was announced that increased the number of operations to 17 on 8 days of the month, with a corresponding reduction in the size of each operation to JPY 700bn. This was further refined on 30 May 2013 to 19 operations to be conducted on 10 days.

Meanwhile, the spike in yields caused problems for Japanese commercial banks who are large holders of JGB for carry purposes. Because the average maturity of the carry portfolio is slightly longer than the maturity of deposits, volatility along the curve has an impact on capital levels. The higher volatility of the 2Y–5Y spread in particular caused problems for these banks.

This encouraged large banks to sell their holdings in intermediate JGB in order to reduce risk. From a monetary policy point of view, while the purchase of more than the net supply of government bonds would of course at some point require the reduction of JGB holdings in the private sector, the rapid nature of this selling, and the attendant increase in volatility, are unlikely to have been part of the planned outcomes.

By now, the Japanese market has adapted to the situation and volatility has fallen to very low levels. The realised volatility of the JGB market is now roughly 0.6% annualised which implies an average daily move of around 4.5 cents across all JGB. Trading volumes have fallen as well and about 7.5% of all trading in JGB is now directly related to either auctions or buy-backs. No single trade in the 10Y benchmark JGB was recorded on 14 April 2014[13].

9.2.3 Lessons from the initial BoJ quantitative easing

These developments raise the question what would happen in the Japanese market if volatility were to reappear suddenly. The experience of the 'VaR shock' of the summer of 2003 is instructive in this respect. At the time, yields and volatility had been falling for some time under the influence of gradual monetary easing by the Bank of Japan. After several years of rallying bonds, traders who would take active short positions had gradually been weeded out of the market. In this situation, US bond yields backed up substantially on the back of an apparent change in Fed policy. The rapid rise in JGB yields that started in June 2003 could not be stopped by filling short positions; instead the existing long positions at dealers came under pressure and were in addition subject to higher VaR charges. Stop-loss selling became inevitable and created a positive feedback loop that accelerated the move upwards in yields; eventually driving a second wave of selling in August 2003. Note that these events occurred during the first quantitative easing episode of the BoJ, not as a result of liquidity withdrawal.

---

[13]While the 10Y JGB is the bellwether of the Japanese bond market, it actually has no natural investor base, being too long for banks and too short for life insurers.

The actual withdrawal of liquidity by the Bank of Japan in 2006 did not immediately disrupt general interest rate levels. The BoJ withdrew liquidity faster than it had injected it. JGB yields increased gradually from around 1.5% to 2%. It should be noted that at the time the Japanese market was, as happens sporadically, used as an easy way to express a global reflationary views via short rates positions. The impact of liquidity withdrawal was more subtle and better observable in the sub-sovereign space.

There were two shocks in the Japanese municipal bond market that provide a clue as to what the end of QE meant for fixed income markets. The first is the Yubari shock of 20 June 2006 when the small town of Yubari in Hokkaido[14] applied for fiscal reconstruction status. The timing of this news coincided with the winding down of excess reserves at the BoJ and various types of sub-sovereign debt experienced spread widening. A second and unrelated episode of municipal stress around year-end 2007, after the liquidity levels stabilised, was much more limited and did not extend to other issuer classes.

The conclusion is that the end of QE removed the certainty of abundant funding that would normally encourage value investors to pick up assets that had declined too much in price. The widening of spreads in summer of 2006 was therefore not the result of liquidity withdrawal itself, but the result of a decline in risk appetite driven by that liquidity reduction. The market was more settled in 2007/2008 so a similar credit event had a very different and more localised impact.

Viewed in a wider context, this evidence from the unwind of the first QE programme in Japan appears to contradict a narrow monetarist interpretation of the impact of QE. Although the operational implementation of the programme used short term operations, the impact of the unwind suggests that private sector investors bridged the liquidity into asset purchases. Exit strategies from large-scale asset purchases communicated by central banks now generally take longer in order to avoid side effects of sudden liquidity withdrawals.

9.3   NEGATIVE INTEREST RATES

Until the financial crisis of 2008, negative interest rates were generally seen as aberrations that only occurred in special market segments, like the repo market for specials. Negative offer rates for deposits were seen in markets where policy rates were near zero and some banks had no desire to increase the size of their balance sheets. None of these observations contradicted the economic intuition that physical cash offers a risk-free investment at an interest rate of zero and so acts as a floor for risk-free interest rates.

As a result of the financial crisis, negative interest rates have become more prevalent for two reasons. First, policy rates declined globally and moved close to zero. In some instances, particularly the Japanese market, cross-currency funding strategies then made it economical to invest in assets at negative interest rates to generate funds in other currencies via the FX swap market [80]. The second reason is that central banks found that cash holdings even at negative policy interest rates do not increase

---

[14]Population at the time was around 12,000 but has since fallen to below 10,000.

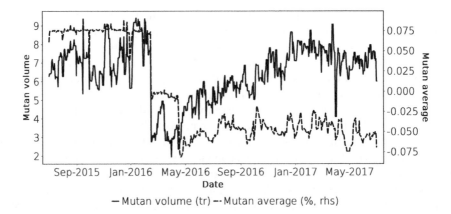

FIGURE 9.7   Japanese daily mutan volumes and average rates July 2015–July 2017. Source: Data from The Tokyo Tanshi Corporation Ltd, Japanese daily mutan volumes and average rates, © THE TOKYO TANSHI CO, LTD.

significantly. As it turns out, cash has storage costs and is more difficult to transact than central bank current account holdings. Central banks can therefore lower policy rates even below zero.

The relevance of negative interest rates is profound. In a multi-currency setting, a floor on interest rates can limit the ability of a central bank to maintain a constant level of accomodation relative to another central bank when that other central bank cuts interest rates. From a signalling point of view, an interest rate floor can lead to a market view that a central bank has limited room for accommodation even in extreme low inflation situations. Yield curve models based on short rate drifts must assign non-zero probability mass to negative interest rates and as a result should predict flatter curves[15] [65].

The transition to negative rates had different effects in different currency areas. While is has been smooth in most countries, the experience in Japan, where negative rates were introduced relatively late and without much prior warning on 29 January 2016, interbank money market volumes declined by 75% from one day to the next and took around one year to recover (Figure 9.7).

9.4   THE SPECIFIC SITUATION OF THE ECB

The decline in inflation following the financial crisis has been uneven across member states that make up the euro area. In the setting of Equation (6.2) on page 43, structural reforms (including a more efficient allocation of labour) imply positive dY and hence a negative contribution to dP. To the extent that such effects explain diverging inflation

---

[15]The significance of the latter effect is debatable because the impact of negative rates on expectations can be offset by other drift terms.

trajectories, they do not create a reason for monetary policy to act. Indeed, positive dY may in a Keynesian setting suggest reasons to tighten before the output gap shrinks too drastically. However, declines in inflation in some euro area countries were also due to weak domestic final demand, partly caused by fiscal consolidation.

Asymmetric inflation declines can be counteracted with targeted quantitative easing programmes and other unconventional policy measures while they are less susceptible to conventional monetary policy tools. Given the institutional constraints of the EU, symmetric fiscal policies are limited in scope, shifting the pressure on the ECB to act in such a way.

One of the features of the EU Treaties, and by implication the design of the monetary union, are the strong restrictions that are placed on the EU institutions. The sovereign nation states that make up the EU have jealously protected their prerogatives and have transferred only limited competencies to the EU. Seen as an institution, the ECB (as opposd to the Eurosystem) conducts only a small amount of market operations, has no independent decision-making authority, and has no single finance ministry with which to coordinate policy. The national central banks, which together with the ECB make up the ESCB[16], have considerable powers and are involved in financial markets to a much larger degree than the ECB itself. The situation of the Fed is not comparable although the Fed also operates in a decentralised fashion. While the Federal Reserve Board in Washington also does not conduct market operations, it has outsourced all of this work to a single Reserve Bank, that of New York. In some of the more recent policy programmes, the Fed was able to obtain fiscal backstops for the credit risk it took in asset purchase programmes.

The financial crisis has highlighted the shortcomings of this institutional arrangement. National interests diverge between countries with large external lending positions, those with large external deficits, and those who had a large financial intermediation sector. It is often said that the monetary union of the euro area is incomplete because it is not flanked by a fiscal union. While true, this statement is not in fact particularly meaningful. Incompleteness must be measured against a benchmark, and a fiscal union is an obvious but not necessary one. So far at least, the monetary union has not turned out to be dysfunctional which arguably is a more important concern than incompleteness.

In this setting, the ECB is faced with the task of acting in a comprehensive manner while having been carefully designed not to be able to act other than in very narrow ways. This classical dilemma has led to an uncomfortable outcome which shows in the terms 'input legitimacy' and 'output legitimacy' used in public communications [72][17]. The concept of 'output legitimacy' is periously close to 'the end justifies the means'. Karl Marx already remarked that if the end justifies the means, then the end is unjustified[18]. In the specific context of examining the actions of a central bank, 'output legitimacy' is

---

[16] European System of Central Banks.

[17] The terms are taken from speeches by former board member Jörg Asmussen but the concepts appear in a number of ECB communications including the submissions to the German Constitutional Court.

[18] 'Wenn der Zweck die Mittel heiligt, dann ist der Zweck unheilig.'

also logically meaningless because only one possible output, namely the present state, can be observed. Any alternative outcomes are necessarily pure conjecture because only one currency area with the specific features of the Eurozone exists. Legitimacy, however, cannot result from conjecture. For this reason, 'output legitimacy' is not a valid framework for judging the admissibility of specific policy actions.

The issue came to the fore in 2020 when the German constitutional court ruled the ECB's Public Sector Purchase Programme to be unlawful (ultra vires) on the grounds that it had not been properly justified ex-ante: 'it would have been incumbent upon the ECB to weigh these effects and balance them, based on proportionality considerations, against the expected positive contributions to achieving the monetary policy objective the ECB itself has set... For this lack of balancing and lack of stating the reasons informing such balancing, the ECB decisions at issue violate Art. 5(1) second sentence and Art. 5(4) TEU and, in consequence, exceed the monetary policy mandate of the ECB deriving from Art. 127(1) first sentence TFEU.' (nos. 176f in [17]). The ECB is not subject to the jurisdiction of the German constitutional court and EU law is assumed to be the exclusive jurisdiction of the European Court of Justice. That court did not share this opinion when it ruled, at the request of the German court, on PSPP in 2018 (ECJ case C-493/17). While questioning the lack of an ex-ante justification of PSPP, the German court did not see a violation of EU Treaties in the execution of PSPP ex-post.

At the time of writing, this particular conflict appears to have been resolved by forwarding additional information about the decision-making process regarding PSPP to the German government and parliament. As discussed above, the issue of communicating not only monetary policy decisions, but also their rationale, is evolving in the global central banking community.

Cash Instruments

Two

Cash Instruments

CHAPTER 10

Contract and Instrument Types

Fixed income markets are governed by a plethora of contracts. These cover the relationships between lenders and borrowers, securities issuers and securities holders, dealers and their customers and so on. In addition to formal contracts, informal customs provide further frameworks to the mutual behaviour of market participants. This chapter introduces some of these concepts.

10.1 SECURITIES AND BILATERAL CONTRACTS

Fixed income instruments can generally be divided into transferrable securities and bilateral contracts[1]. In either case the obligations of the parties to the contract are documented in one or more legal instruments, i.e., physical documents. In most cases, the same parties will conduct a series of very similar transactions, so in the interest of economy, a general legal instrument will outline the common features of all related transactions and each specific transaction will then only require a short document outlining the specific details of this one transaction. Claims against a borrower can be evidenced in a number of ways and such evidence need not necessarily be in the form of a legal instrument. Indeed, in a bond transaction with physical bond certificates (now rare), the actual bond contract would specify the number and denomination of bond certificates to be printed and those certificates would then represent the claims under the bond contract. However, these certificates would only represent evidence of the claim under contract, not the contract itself.

Transferrable securities come in two general forms, namely bearer securities and registered securities. Note that there is an apparent third form, namely book-entry securities, discussed below. In the case of a bearer security, ownership of the beneficial interest is evidenced by possession of the security. This makes bearer securities very easy to trade because all that is needed to transfer the beneficial claim is to transfer pieces of paper. However, bearer securities carry significant risk of destruction, theft, and counterfeiting[2]. Indeed, counterfeiting of bearer securities such as shares and bonds was at

---

[1]The definitions used here are not related to legal definitions of securities or contracts that may differ between different jurisdictions.
[2]The Hollywood movie 'Die Hard' can serve as an example.

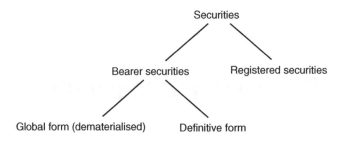

FIGURE 10.1 Security types.

some time more lucrative for criminals than counterfeiting currency. Bearer securities also present a problem in terms of denomination. If they are issued in very small denominations, the cost of printing the certificates in a way that is sufficiently hard to forge is very costly, while issuing large denominations restricts the amounts that can be traded. Last but not least, bearer securities are very useful for criminal activity such as money laundering and tax evasion because proof of ownership does not require any audit trail.

In contrast, registered securities are securities where beneficial interest is recorded by the issuer or an agent of the issuer, the registrar. There may be physical certificates of ownership as well, but unlike bearer securities, holding such certificates does not prove beneficial interest. Trading in registered securities is more cumbersome than for bearer securities because each transaction has to be reported to the registrar for the new owner to be registered. At the same time, trading is technically possible in any denomination.

German law recognises a mixed form of security called a Schuldschein. Translated literally, the term means 'promissory note', but a more accurate description would be 'transferrable loan'. A Schuldschein does by itself not constitute a debt by the issuer, but is evidence of a separate loan contract. Schuldscheine are usually documented to allow a limited number of transfers (usually three) and transfers are registered on the certificate itself. The reason to see a Schuldschein as a mix between registered and bearer securities is that a physical and transferrable certificate evidencing ownership exists, but ownership is still registered and change of registration is limited.

The ease of trading in a security has important implications for the accounting treatment of investments in the security. If trading in a security is difficult, it cannot be assumed that a meaningful market for that security exists and there is therefore no market price. One of the motivations to still issue debt certificates with transfer restrictions, such as German Schuldscheine, is to permit holders to avoid mark-to-market accounting of such securities while permitting liquidation of investments when needed.

Modern securities markets are generally too fast to permit physical transfer of paper certificates although this still happens. Instead, securities are now generally traded in book-entry form. Legally, the securities are issued as bearer securities with only one physical certificate denoting the beneficial interest in the entire issue. This certificate, called a global note is deposited with a trusted intermediary, the custodian which in this case is more appropriately known as a central securities depository (CSD). Such institutions are further divided into local and global CSDs, known as LCSD and GCSD.

Trading in the security is then done through transfers of book entries with a clearer or clearing house. Security clearers are specialist banks that focus on keeping records of beneficial ownership in securities and transfer such ownership, usually though maintaining accounts with an GCSD or being a GCSD themselves. Put differently, the custodian of a global note holds the certificate in trust for one of the large clearers and the chain of ownership from the securities holders to the global note is closed through a trust agreement between the clearer and the custodian. Of course, the clearing houses also act as custodians for a number of securities transactions, but that is not a necessary condition.

There are currently two global firms that handle the bulk of securities transfers, namely Euroclear and Clearstream. While Euroclear is owned by a consortium of banks, Clearstream is a subsidiary of Deutsche Börse AG, the German stock exchange. Other securities clearers exist in local markets and most clearers have links with one another so that transfers of ownership can be handled effectively across different clearers. For instance, Italian securities are usually held in a LCSD called Monte dei Titoli, German government bonds at the Bundesschuldenverwaltung, but all of them can be traded through most clearing systems. This gives investors unfettered access to local markets.

10.2 SECURITY IDENTIFIERS

Securities need to be identified in order to trade them. There are various ways to do that. Between human beings, it is common to use descriptions related to important characteristics of the security such as 'Federal government bond 1% coupon of 2015' for a bond issued in 2015. More commonly, securities have a ticker (short for ticker tape symbol) that identifies the issuer to some degree. The security above could have the tickers T, DBR, or RAGB, depending on which federal government (United States, Germany or Austria) issued the security. Using the ticker, the same bond may therefore be identified as 'DBR 1% 2025' or 'DBR 1% 08/25' where the last part refers to the maturity of the bond which in this case is 15 August 2025. German financial reports somewhat confusingly refer to securities by coupon and issuance date rather than maturity date.

For the automation of settlement procedures, it is vital that securities are identified in a way that does not require human ingenuity to resolve potential misunderstandings. The market has therefore developed security identifier systems that rely on fixed-length codes. ISINs, discussed below, are most widely used in international transfers. The most common domestic systems are the US CUSIP[3], the German WKN (Wertpapierkennnummer), the Japanese meigara code[4].

10.2.1 ISIN codes

ISINs (international securities identification numbers) are security identifiers governed by an ISO standard (ISO 6166:2013) but assigned by a private company. They are the

---

[3]The abbreviation CUSIP stands not for the codes themselves but for the committee that proposed the system, the Committee on Uniform Security Identification Procedures.
[4]The term 'meigara code' can refer in common usage to a 4-digit listed equity identifier, or a 9-digit bond (kōshasaikoyūmei) code. The second usage is intended here.

most prevalent security identifiers in global markets. ISINs are therefore sometimes mistakenly equated with securities themselves. In practice, not every security has an ISIN and not every ISIN corresponds to a security. Not every securities issuer wants to incur the expense and effort to obtain an ISIN for every security issued, while ISINs have also be assigned, for instance, to futures contracts and iBoxx indices.

Adding to the confusion is the practice by some issuers to issue new tranches of existing securities (taps) with a new ISIN. Although the cash flows of the new tranche usually match those of the existing security, the new ISIN ensures that concerns like non-standard settlement dates of the new security (for instance, first settlement 5 days after issuance rather than T+2 for the existing security) can be handled properly. After a certain period of time, the new ISIN is merged (funged[5] in market parlance) into the existing security. The new ISIN therefore ceases to exist and a position in the tap security changes ISIN. In other words, the same security can have different ISINs at different times.

ISINs consist of 12 characters (uppercase letters or numbers) divided into three blocks. The first 2 characters are letters that identify the country of issuance[6] in line with ISO standard 3166-1 (US for United States of America, JP for Japan, DE for Germany, and so on). Note that the country of issuance is not the same as the country of incorporation of the issuer. The special code 'XS' is used for eurobonds. The next nine characters are referred to as national securities identification numbers. These are in most cases domestic security identifiers, padded by leading zeros in case they are shorter than 9 characters. For instance, a German domestic Wertpapierkennnummer (WKN) is six characters long and therefore German ISINs start with DE000 (country code plus three padding characters ahead of the WKN). In the US, CUSIP numbers, which are 9 characters long, are used for the national securities identification numbers. Importantly, this convention is not followed everywhere. Japanese ISINs start with JP but the following 9 characters for bonds are constructed in a way that is completely different from the domestic identifiers (meigara code). As a result, ISINs of Japanese bonds cannot be constructed from the meigara code[7].

The 12th and last character of an ISIN is a check digit calculated from the first 11 characters. The presence of that check number reduces the scope for human error, such as transposed characters. Exchanging any adjacent characters leads to a different check character, as do most changes of a single character. Comparing the check digit calculated from the first 11 characters of an ISIN with the 12th character is therefore a useful check for transmission errors.

The calculation of the check digit is somewhat complicated in modern programming languages. The first step is to write down a numerical representation of the first 11 characters of the ISIN, using 0 for the digit 0 and so on, and the digits 1 and 0 for the letter A, the digits 1 and 1 for the letter B and so on. For instance, the 11 characters starting the ISIN of JB321:

J P 1 1 0 3 2 1 1 C 3

---

[5]The verb 'funge' does not exist in most English dictionaries but the derived adjective 'fungible' does.
[6]More precisely the country of residence of the central securities depository holding the security.
[7]The 9 domestic characters of a Japanese ISIN are known in Japan as the 'New security code' (shinshōken kōdo).

become:

1 9 2 5 1 1 0 3 2 1 1 1 2 3

By construction, the result of the first step is a series of numbers. In the next step, every other number, starting with the second, is doubled. In the example above, this doubling and again replacing every 2-digit result by 2 single-digit numbers (shown in bold) delivers:

2 1 **8 2 1 0** 1 2 0 6 2 2 1 2 2 6

Next, these digits are added up in a simple sum, resulting here in the number 44. The 10s modulus of this sum, here 7, is subtracted from 10 and the 10s modulus taken again on the result (3), so that the check digit and therefore the 12th character of this ISIN is 3[8].

10.2.2 CUSIP codes

A CUSIP is a 9-character code. Like ISIN codes, CUSIPs have an internal structure, including a check digit at the end. The first 6 characters of a CUSIP identify the issuer, the next 2 an individual issue, and the last is a check digit. Of the 6 issuer code characters, the last 3 may be alphanumeric while the first 3 are always numeric. Some issuer id combinations are reserved, and multiple issuer ids may be given to large-scale issuers like the US Federal Government. That being said, the large number of possible issue codes means that at the time of writing, the issuer codes 912796 for bills and 912810 or 912828 for bonds and TIPS suffice to cover the extant US government securities.

The issue code is fully numeric for equity securities and contains at least 1 letter for debt securities, with the letters O and I as well as the numbers 0 and 1 omitted for fixed income securities to avoid confusion[9], making it straightforward to distinguish between debt and equity instruments.

The CUSIP check digit serves the same purpose as the ISIN check digit but is calculated in a subtly different way[10]. Using a US Treasury example (T 8.75% 08/20), the CUSIP starting with 912810EG is first translated into a series of numbers, where digits retain their value and letters become numbers starting with 10 for A. This CUSIP therefore becomes:

9 1 2 8 1 0 14 16

Similar to the ISIN calculation, every other of these 8 numbers is then doubled:

9 2 2 16 1 0 14 32

---

[8]The final modulus operation ensures that if the 10s modulus of the last sum is 0, the check digit is 0 instead of 10, or A.

[9]This allows for 100 equity and 1008 debt securities per issuer id.

[10]The difference is indeed so subtle that one wonders whether it is the result of deliberation or confusion.

The resulting digits are then added up:

    9+2+2+1+6+1+0+1+4+3+2

which here results in the number 31. The 10s complement of this number, calculated in the same way as for an ISIN, is the check digit 9. The full CUSIP is therefore 912810EG9.

CHAPTER 11

Trading and Settlement

The process of trading is the process of negotiating and agreeing the details of a transaction in securities and derivatives between two counterparties. After trading, the next step is settlement where the transaction is finalised. The steps undertaken to manage settlement and any ongoing obligations between the parties are known as clearing.

11.1 TRADING

Financial markets have evolved over time and are still evolving in response to changing social conditions and technological process. Trading in financial instruments first resembled trading in physical markets where traders met physically in a market place to negotiate transaction details. Various market places were specialised in particular types of financial instruments and became formalised over time from sections of particular streets or coffee houses to more formal bourses [35, 59]. Traders with no direct access could make use of intermediaries who would trade on their behalf in remote markets.

11.1.1 Trading and price formation

Trading involves agreement on the price at which an exchange of asset happens. The negotiation of this price is to some degree subject to the incentives of the counterparties involved. Many investors are in some cases strongly incentivised to conclude a transaction quickly. For instance, a fund manager tracking an index will at times find it necessary to invest coupons received to re-establish a carry position in line with the index. On the other hand, an investor may judge available market prices to be advantageous for establishing a new position and thus be more concerned with price than with timing. In practice, the bargaining over the transaction price involves a trade-off between immediacy of transacting and the optimisation of price.

This notion has an important consequence for how new information is incorporated in market prices. It is unrealistic to assume that new information can immediately affect negotiated prices across all securities in a market. Instead, all markets have a hierarchy of instruments where news affects the most liquid instruments first and prices of other instruments react through the repricing of these most liquid instruments. In the US market, the most liquid instruments are the on-the-run (most recently issued) Treasury securities, followed by on-the-run agency mortgage bonds. In Europe and Japan, the most liquid instruments are bond futures contracts.

Market makers will typically build pricing models that reflect the liquidity hierarchy in order to provide real-time pricing of less liquid instruments. Actual prices of such instruments will then be a combination of the output of such hierarchical models and adjustments for recent supply and demand information. This latter component reflects the time and price preferences of investors in the market as much as can be observed by a particular dealer.

The pricing hierarchy is self-reinforcing because investors who express macroeconomic views through fixed income positions will react to data releases by trading the most liquid instruments first. In contrast, pricing for less liquid instruments can become opaque immediately after data releases before the more liquid instruments settle on a new price. This can have the side effect of a permanent liquidity premium carried by benchmark bonds. Such a premium is observed in the US but is more or less absent for the on-the-run securities in Europe or Japan given the more dominant role of futures contracts in those markets.

11.1.2 Trading venues

Most modern trading venues can be seen as structures that lie between two extremes. The first is a public exchange operating on the basis of a public order book. Exchange members can place orders in this public book and such orders are matched according to rules set by the exchange. Trades occur when opposing orders are matched against each other (fully or partially, depending on the exchange) and the exchange acts as intermediary. Because the most basic order type is a limit order ('execute a trade in xxx securities at *a price of yyy or better*'), such exchange structures are also known as a central limit order book or CLOB.

Some exchange-type trading venues allow for the posting and matching of orders without making these orders public. Such dark pools enable trading but do not serve the purpose of price discovery by the wider public or even the exchange members.

The opposite trading model to an exchange is the over-the-counter or OTC market. In this market structure, a special type of trader known as a market maker advertises a willingness to provide prices for certain financial instruments and to trade on these prices on a bilateral basis. Market makers typically provide prices only to known clients to protect against various risks. In an OTC market, every dealer has a bilateral relationship with every customer. Most exchanges instead provide intermediation services that mean that each participant only faces the exchange as a counterparty.

The concept of market making is not tied to that of a liquidity provider in a public market. A liquidity provider is a market participant who is generally willing to trade in response to price movements. In contrast to a market maker, the role of liquidity provider can be less formal and not advertised. Significantly, some market participants act as liquidity providers only in normal market environments but may consume liquidity in crisis situations.

In market parlance, a firm price is a price quote at which a trader (usually a market maker) is willing to execute while an indicative price does not necessarily imply a willingness to trade at that price. Generally, market makers provide indicative prices on a continuous basis but firm prices only on request. A price request must include the the trade size but not necessarily the side (buy or sell) that the requestor wishes to execute. A price is said to be two-way if it includes a bid and an ask (prices at which the trader market maker would buy or sell the instrument, respectively), a bid or ask price by itself correspondingly is a one-way price. A (very rare) quote in which bid and ask price are the same is known as a choice price[1].

In practice, the extremes of exchange trading on the one hand and OTC trading on the other do rarely exist in these pure forms. Most public exchanges are in fact operating a mixed model where for at least some products, or trade sizes over a certain limit (so-called block trades), trades are negotiated outside the public order book and only published later. Exchanges also occasionally employ schemes where exchange members are financially incentivised to make markets in listed products by maintaining presence in the public order book. On the other hand, frequent and large issuers of bonds tend to ask investment banks to act as market makers in their bonds and monitor their activity. This establishes market structures that allow for easier price discovery and thereby move OTC markets closer to the setting of public exchanges.

11.1.3 The OTC trade lifecycle

The trade lifecycle is the sequence of steps between the initial trade negotiation and the final settlement of the resulting obligations between the trade counterparties. There is some variation in the trade lifecycles of trades in different instruments and contracts but the aim of them is always identical: any asset transfers must faithfully reflect the intentions of the contracting parties at the time the trade was negotiated. At the same time, firms must protect themselves from unintentional errors and fraud. This requires a sufficient number of independent checks. Figure 11.1 shows a schematic overview of the parties involved and their main interactions in the lifecycle.

Generally speaking, a trade in the OTC market consists of the following steps which will be described in more detail later:

Inquiry A price taker (customer) inquires for a firm quote (one-way or two-way) from one or more market makers.

Negotiation Some form of communication between the parties takes place until the price taker accepts or rejects a price.

Agreement The market maker confirms that a trade at the negotiated price has taken place. *Only after this step are both parties bound by the trade agreement.*

Recording Customer and market maker record the trade in their systems.

Enrichment The original trade records are augmented with additional information, such as settlement instructions.

Reporting Some jurisdictions require the reporting of trades to regulators and potentially to data dissemination platforms (trade repositories).

---

[1]It is not always irrational for a trader to provide a firm choice price even though this implies that the trader does not intend to benefit from buying at a lower price and selling at a higher price. A choice price maximises the chance of executing a trade. This can provide valuable information about market direction. It should be remembered that there is limited public disclosure of trading conditions in OTC markets.

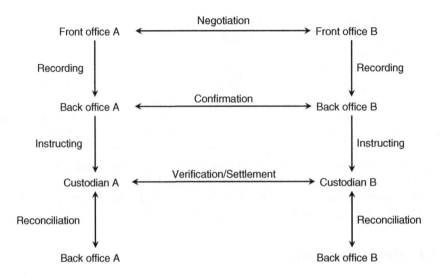

FIGURE 11.1 The actors and interaction processes in the OTC trade lifecycle between 2 counterparties, A and B. Note that A and B may be using the same custodian in which case the Verfication/Settlement step would be internal to that custodian.

Pre-confirmation The front offices of customer and market maker exchange settlement instructions. Both sides compare the instructions received with instructions sent to spot discrepancies.

Allocation Institutional fund managers regularly execute trades for a number of funds in parallel and then ask the dealer to split the trade into pieces which are then allocated to various funds.

Confirmation After the trades have been agreed by the front offices, the middle offices of both counterparties exchange transaction details and report discrepancies.

Settlement instructions Both counterparties instruct their respective custodians to make the required payments and securities transfers.

Reconciliation Both counterparties compare the cash and securities positions reported by their custodians with the positions implied by the transactions that have taken place as recorded in their internal systems.

Before counterparties can transact, they generally conclude a so-called master agreement. Such agreements are highly standardised and templates are provided by industry organisations. An important aspect of the securities market is that communication between the parties can take place in a variety of forms (trading platforms, chats, email, telephone, fax). Whatever channel is used, instructions are considered binding if the other side reasonably understands them. Clarity in the language used is therefore essential to avoid miscommunication.

The trade inquiry

An OTC trade starts when a customer asks one or more market makers to price a particular trade. At this stage of the process it is important that all parties are fully aware of all price-relevant information. At a minimum, this would be the security or contract details, the trade size, and the side of the transaction (buy or sell for securities, pay or receive for swaps, etc.). The latter is sometimes known as the verb. Some other details, such as settlement date or venue, can be left unspecified as long as they follow the market conventions that exist precisely for the purpose to simplify the trade process.

A trade inquiry normally is not binding the customer in the sense that the customer has the option to reject all prices shown in response to the inquiry. However, because pricing an inquiry is not completely cost-free for market makers, it is considered detrimental to the relationship when customers frivolously ask for firm prices without any real intent to trade. A customer can ask explicitly for an indicative price to signal that a trade may not be intended. Conversely, a firm price inquiry signals an intent to trade and therefore reveals information about the direction in which the customer intends to adjust positions. As a result, the trade inquiry is an exchange of information. The customer reveals information about what security and size he or she is interested to trade in, and in case of a one-way quote inquiry, the direction of the trade interest. The market maker, by responding, reveals his or her estimate of a market-clearing price.

Trade inquiries usually are done 'in competition' ('in comp' in market vernacular) which means that a customer asks multiple dealers at the same time to quote on a particular trade. In some cases, this is mandated by regulation or internal trading rules. Whether such inquiries ultimately benefit the customer is not always obvious. On one hand, multiple dealers will compete to provide the best prices to the customer. On the other hand, the winning dealer will be subject to winner's curse which means not only that he or she sold at the lowest, or bought at the highest, price but also that the other dealers in the competition will be aware of the likely position of one of their competitors. A dealer might therefore adjust the quote depending on whether or not the inquiry is in competition or not. In addition, by alerting a larger number of dealers to the trade interest, the client might move the market in an adverse direction.

Negotiation

A customer is free to ask a dealer to improve a quote and it is in any case assumed that a dealer will update a quote according to changing market conditions while the customer is considering the responses. Electronic trading platforms tend to impose minimum lifetimes for market maker quotes in the order of seconds, when trades are negotiated over the phone or electronic chats, less formal rules apply.

A quote is called subject when the dealer states explicitly the he no longer feels bound by it, be it because too much time has passed since providing the quote or because the market has moved too much. In bilateral communication a dealer may indicate a quote going subject by stating 'subject' or 'your risk'.

In bilateral communication, a customer may attempt to guide a dealer by revealing information about other dealers' quotes ('seeing better away', etc.). Given that such statements are generally unverifiable, a dealer may discard such communication depending on the customer–dealer relationship. It is in any case up to the dealer to decide whether to move a quote in favour of the customer.

Agreement

By convention, it is the customer who accepts a quote. On electronic platforms this is done by pressing a button, in bilateral communication by stating the relevant equivalent of 'mine' or 'yours' in whatever language is used to communicate. Important in this step in the communication is to reaffirm the intended side of the original inquiry. A customer who asked by phone or chat for a bid (indicating a willingness to sell) and then states 'mine' (indicating a buy confirmation) violates standard trade protocol and would signal a failure in the negotiation process.

By stating 'mine' or 'yours', the customer is bound to trade in the specified security in the specified size at the price quoted by the dealer unless the dealer rejects the trade.

Again by convention, a dealer must confirm the conclusion of the trade by some equivalent of 'done' or signal that the trade has not been concluded by some form of 'off that' etc. This convention gives the dealer an option to reject a trade that has already been accepted by the customer. In the FX market, this option is known as a last look but that term has a different meaning in the fixed income markets[2]. It is considered bad form to reject a trade unless there is an obvious reason such as a significant market move, late acceptance of a quote by the customer, and so on. A dealer can signal during the negotiation phase that a quote is no longer binding as mentioned above. Generally, unless a dealer confirms a trade with 'done' or the local language equivalent, no trade has been concluded. Whether a failure to honour a quote is a relationship issue between customer and dealer is not trivial.

It is not essential to follow the conventions outlined above. Trades executed away from electronic platforms involve human beings which implies a certain degree of freedom in how communication is structured. What is essential, however, is that both parties at all times are clear about what has taken place. The purpose of conventions is to reduce the incidence of misunderstandings and the main information-theoretical tool to achieve this is redundancy. For instance, the side the client wishes to deal on is evident both in the initial price request (asking for an offer signals the client will buy, asking for a bid means the client wishes to sell) as well as in the acceptance (a buying client accepts with 'mine', a selling client with 'yours'). In other words, the conversation conventions in the market involve deliberate duplication of information in different forms so that inconsistencies can be spotted easily. Electronic platforms can reduce such redundancies in the communication but need to replicate it in the user interfaces they present to human operators. For this reason, a sell transaction screen will usually not only have

---

[2]In the fixed income market, a 'last look' means that a customer who has asked multiple dealers for a price is giving one dealer an option to take a last look and improve the price to conclude a trade. In other words, a last look is an option granted to one specific dealer selected by the client while in the FX world it is granted to the market maker by default.

the word 'Sell' in a prominent location, but would normally also use a different colour scheme from a buy transaction screen.

Recording

After a trade has been concluded (both customer and dealer agree that a trade has been done and on the trade details), the next step is for both customer and dealer to record it in their respective book-keeping systems. Electronic trading platforms automatically record trades on behalf of both sides of the trade and offer mechanisms to forward that information into the electronic booking systems used by client and dealer, known as straight-through processing, or STP. For trades concluded on the phone or via electronic chats, this step has to be performed manually. Phone lines are now generally taped and electronic chats also recorded so that the recording step at least in principle does not introduce room for misunderstandings. The following example of a perfectly normal conversation illustrates the relevance of trade recording:

> **Customer:** How are you left for 10 mio?
>
> **Dealer:** 110.14
>
> **Dealer:** Off that
>
> **Customer:** Refresh pls
>
> **Dealer:** 110.16
>
> **Customer:** Mine 10 mio for 110.16
>
> **Dealer:** OK, done.

In this case, customer and dealer would have executed a trade already (possibly on a different platform) and are therefore aware of the security involved and the side the customer wishes to trade on (here, customer buys). None of this information is evident from this chat protocol alone. The customer asks for a price and the dealer responds, only to revoke the quote shortly after. The customer asks for a refreshed price and accepts the response.

The recording step in the trade lifecycle is where the trader at the customer side and the relevant contact person at the dealer enter the trade into their relevant systems. In the example above that would require that both enter the security that was left out of the conversation above, and that both record the respective counterparties.

Clarity of communication is essential in avoiding situations where counterparties record conflicting versions of what has taken place. Because records of all communications exist, it is possible to reconstruct what exactly passed between counterparties when there are conflicting versions of what happened. A customer might respond 'Lovely!' to a quote in order to sarcastically indicate that a price is unacceptable while the counterparty would interpret it as 'Mine' and respond with 'Done'. A subsequent examination of phone tapes or chat protocols would do little to disentangle that sort of misunderstanding. The better route to correct trade recording is to stick to standard language. For instance, the customer above confirms size and price explicitly, and uses the words 'mine' and 'for' which both indicate a buy transaction. A sale would normally be confirmed with 'yours' and 'at'. Note that different markets use very different conventions, such as quoting yields or yield changes instead of prices[3].

Enrichment

Once a trade has been recorded, the bare trade information has to be augmented with the information required to successfully settle the trade. Normally, this is possible using information that both counterparties hold about each other in their respective counter-party databases. Such informaton would include standard security settlement instructions (SSIs) such as custodian and account details. For internal purposes, companies may add information about credits to be given to particular sales contacts or other statistical data. Generally, this process is automatic but front office staff have the option to override parts of the result, for instance specifying different custodian details from those filled in by default.

Reporting

Many jurisdictions require trades to be reported and reporting obligations have increased since the financial crisis. Trade reporting can serve multiple purposes:

Price discovery The general public may have an interest to learn about the prices at which trades in certain securities have been concluded. Regulators therefore sometimes require market makers to report trades that have been concluded to central price dissemination platforms (known as a consolidated tape). Dealers in the OTC market generally oppose such price discovery on the grounds that they hold a balance sheet position as a result of the trade just concluded and would like to be able to unwind the position at a profit. It is therefore usually the case that large trades are disseminated to the wider market with a delay. The length of this delay, as well as the size cut-off for such delayed dissemination, are chosen to allow the dealer, at least in principle, to unwind or hedge the position without being taken advantage of by the wider market.

Public interest Aside from the narrow price discovery aim, the general public may have an interest in knowing about more general trends in financial markets. This would include aggregate trade volumes in classes of securities, types of counterparties involved etc., but may not involve price discovery on specific securities.

---

[3]While trader communication is usually portrayed as terse, deliberate redundancies in fact abound in market vernacular. As Umberto Eco remarked (on page 249 in [32]) 'in a characteristic language, for every unit of one expression one is obliged to find a corresponding content-unit.' Trader language therefore stops short of becoming so terse as to make every possible statement meaningful. The general public may not be aware of these subtleties because the use of words in trader language has evolved away from their everyday meanings. This, however, is not specific to financial markets. The expression 'from time to time' means something very different to a lawyer than to a layman.

Systemic risk Regulators have an interest in knowing about interlinkages between financial firms. Knowing about trades that have been concluded can help in this endeavour, albeit only to the extent that regulators are able to analyse the resulting data sets. Such data on financial interlinkages is generally considered to be too sensitive for public disclosure.

Fraud and money laundering Given the limited public discovery of OTC trading, there is a risk that traders collude to defraud their firms, or that trading is used to launder the proceeds of illegal activity. Financial firms generally have procedures in place that are designed to catch such activity but regulators may feel that they are better placed to conduct the required analysis. Regulators are in the advantageous position of having access to the data from multiple institutions. This advantage is, however, alloyed with the difficulty of having to analyse large sets of data coming from multiple institutions.

Note that for globally operating financial institutions a specific form of the trade reporting function is essential to manage their global risk management functions. While the various subsidiaries may be able to function more or less autonomously, they must report all the trades they conclude to their headquarters for aggregation and analysis.

Pre-confirmation

Counterparties normally exchange trade pre-confirmations at the front office level as soon as trade details have been recorded internally, usually a few seconds or minutes after a trade has been concluded. The purpose of this process is to ensure that the trade and settlement details recorded in the systems of both parties match. Such matching is a precondition of successfully settling the transaction and costs will arise if problems are not caught at this early stage. Commercial providers offer standard tools for this process that integrate the pre-confirmation process into standard communication tools.

A small but significant portion of trades fails at this stage because manually recorded trade details do not match. This is usually the result of misunderstandings about trades conducted outside electronic platforms and can easily be rectified. Electronic trading platforms automate the pre-confirmation process because there is no uncertainty about trade details.

Allocation

Allocation is an optional step in the trade lifecycle that is related to how institutional fund managers operate. Typically a manager is responsible for multiple funds that follow similar or even identical strategies but are legally separate. A trade executed by such a manager may therefore be meant for several such funds at the same time. In order to achieve maximum separation of the funds concerned, the fund manager may ask the dealer to split an agreed ticket into multiple parts and allocate them to several individual funds. The total amount of securities traded, and the total consideration paid, are unaffected by this process.

For the trade recording systems of both dealer and fund manager, the allocation process represents a meaningful complication. A single recorded trade has to be replaced with a multitude of trades for settlement purposes, and the relationship between these new trades and the original trade (which will never settle) needs to be preserved in case disputes arise at a later stage.

Confirmation

Once the front offices of both counterparties have agreed the enriched trade details, they forward them to their respective middle offices for processing. The first stage of this process is for the middle offices to send confirmation messages on a pre-agreed platform, such as S.W.I.F.T. or fax. Any discrepancies discovered in this stage of the trade lifecycle are more costly to resolve because open questions have to be sent to the respective front offices for clarification which takes up valuable time. On the other hand, successful confirmation at the confirmation stage elevates a trade from an agreement between the front office staff to an agreement between the contracting firms.

When trade details cannot be matched at this stage, a counterparty's middle office may notify the other counterparty that it does not know the trade. The phrase 'don't know', or simply DK, is generally used in the English-speaking world to reject a trade confirmation that cannot be matched against any internally recorded transaction[4]. It should be borne in mind that to DK a transaction at this stage is not a free option to walk away from an unfavourably priced transaction for either party. Because so much data is recorded in the trade negotiation process by either party, a legitimately concluded trade can easily be reconstructed. Failure to agree on trade details at the confirmation stage are most likely to arise from human error, multiple recording of the same trade by one counterparty, or the failure to retract confirmation of amended trade details when errors were spotted in the pre-confirmation stage.

Settlement instructions

Following succesful confirmation, both counterparties will instruct their custodians to settle the transaction. The custodians typically require shorter instruction periods than the standard trade cycles (e.g. T+2 in Europe) so that settlement instructions need not be given as soon as confirmation has been successful. However, by instructing early, counterparties can use the pending transactions on their custodian accounts to check again that the transaction will settle as expected.

Custodians will not process transactions unless instructions received from the two counterparties match to a reasonable degree. After the pre-confirmation and confirmation cycle, this provides a third check on mismatched transactions. Because this check happens last, it is the most costly to unwind transactions at this stage. Counterparties therefore have a strong economic incentive to resolve any problems at the pre-confirmation stage.

---

[4]As a result, the pseudo-verb 'to DK' has taken on a wider meaning in the financial sector as indicating the repudiation of a presumed contractual relationship.

Fails

It sometimes happens that the seller of a security (either outright or in either leg of a repo transaction) fails to deliver that security to the other counterparty. This is known as a fail and is in principle an event of default. A partial fail is a situation where the seller can deliver some, but not all of the amount transacted. Some buyers accept partial settlement, some do not. Because fails can have multiple legitimate causes, it is extremely rare to declare a default on a failing counterparty. A typical cause for a fail is a clerical error in a repo financing transaction where a market maker has lent out inventory for funding and recalls that inventory from repo when it has been sold to a customer. If the internal interaction with the repo desk, or the external with the repo counterparty results in a delay, the outright sale will fail as a result of the repo fail. Less commonly, a market maker may believe that a particular bond is available in repo and sells it in the course of quoting to a customer, only to find out that it is not available after all. Various forms of settlement discipline exist to discourage fails.

The basic approach to discourage fails has been to let the economics of an agreed trade stand as they are even when a fail occurs. This means that if the buyer transfers the same amount of cash, and receives the same amount of the security, at a later date, then the fail is said to be cured. Because the seller of the security receives the same cash later, he or she loses the interest that could otherwise be earned on it while the fail continues. In essence, the seller lends cash to the buyer at a rate of 0% with the security as collateral. In other words, the seller borrows the security at a repo rate of 0% while the fail continues. When interest rates were higher, this was a sufficient incentive to encourage speedy fails mitigation. At the time of writing, interest rates are low, or even negative, so that this disincentive no longer exists to the same degree.

In the European market, this incentive was insufficient even when rates were higher because, as is discussed for instance in Chapter 28, specials rates can be very low relative to GC. It is not uncommon for bonds to trade 5% or more special. This implies negative repo rates for such special collateral even when rates are reasonably positive. Being able to borrow a special security at 0% by the simple expedient of not delivering would not be a sufficient disincentive. For quite some time, therefore, the European market has seen fails charges that reflect the actual cost of a fail. The US market only introduced such charges in May 2009 [39] in the form of a flat 3% fee. Fails charges are the most common way to disincentivise fails but do not cure fails. An additional disincentive is bilateral: A fund manager may simply choose not to interact in future transactions with a counterparty that has a consistently high fails rate. The loss of business should also incentivise that counterparty to improve its inventory management practices.

Multiple ways to cure fails exist, listed below:

Fails mitigation lending is a facility offered by some CSDs where a failing transaction is cured automatically by borrowing the security for delivery from a pool of collateral providers. Such lending is generally very expensive because the CSD sees this as a source of profit, while the collateral providers would not make their securities available in such a way if they did not earn at least the going market rate for lending them.

Dollar rolls and coupon swaps are the standard ways of dealing with fails in the US mortage market when TBA transactions cannot be settled as expected due to insufficient production.

Bilateral O/N and T/N repos are securities lending transactions with settlement terms that are shorter than the standard spot settlement. A trader finding that securities will not be available as expected can borrow them in time for spot (T+2) settlement even at T+1 or even T+2 through non-standard repo terms. This can cure a fail, but obviously only if these transactions settle on time.

Buy-ins are transactions where the clearer or the counterparty that is being failed to buys the security in the open market to settle the transaction, with the purchase consideration being charged to the failing counterparty. Usually a buy-in is an option available to the securities buyer under some conditions set in the master agreement between the two counterparties. Buy-ins are extremely costly, easily subject to dispute over the execution terms, and may even fail if the security in question is indeed not readily available. In these cases, both the original seller (who is still trying to settle) and the buy-in agent are looking for the same security in the same market. The European Union has made buy-in transactions mandatory for transactions that fail beyond a certain period in the Central Securities Depositories Regulation (CSDR) as of 1 February 2021[5].

With the exception of buy-ins, the failing counterparty can make some economic choice between continuing to fail, or use one of the available avenues to cure the fail. That being said, fails contradict the fundamental principle of bond markets, *dictum meum pactum* and market participants agree that fails should be rare exceptions.

Reconciliation

Once a transaction has been settled, each counterparty will conduct a process of reconciliation between its internal books and the account statements received from its custodian or custodians. For instance, a counterparty that has sold EUR 10 million notional of security A would expect that its holding of this security at the relevant custodian has declined by exactly EUR 10 million while its cash holdings should have increased by the relevant consideration, taking into account all other transactions conducted for the relevant settlement date.

Problems identified at the reconciliation stage are difficult to resolve because they can in principle only arise as a result of errors made by the custodian, given that the relevant settlement instructions were approved by the counterparty itself.

11.1.4   The exchange trade cycle

Trading on a public exchange differs from OTC trading in that both counterparties generally do not know the identity of the other because both face the exchange or, more precisely, its designated clearing house as a central counterparty (cf. Chapter 12).

---

[5]This aspect of the CSDR has been widely criticised by the financial industry.

This generally simplifies trade processing because neither counterparty requires settlement instructions other than those of the exchange. Trade reporting is also generally handled by the exchange. Given that most exchanges nowadays operate on purely electronic platforms, the scope for manual error in the confirmation and reconciliation process is also minimal.

Exchanges generally permit the use of their clearing facilities for trades in listed products that have been agreed outside the exchange trades (so-called off-exchange trades). This such cases two counterparties agree bilaterally the details of the trade and then cross them, bypassing the central limit order book of the exchange. The trade is then entered into the exchange's trade system as a block trade. Exchanges generally impose minimum sizes on such trades because such trades do not contribute to price discovery in the central limit order book. The reason why block trades exist is that they permit the transfer of exceptionally large amounts of risk without the information leakage that would occur if the trade interests were published in the order book before execution.

11.1.5   Trading in competition versus single dealer inquiries and orders

Multilateral trading platforms allow, and many fund management rules mandate, that each trade interest is shown to a group of dealers in competition and that the dealer with the best price is selected for execution.

In case of a tie between two dealers in a competitive quote (multiple dealers show the same price), it is up to the client to select who to award the trade to. It is a common courtesy, but not more than that, to select the dealer who printed the last trade with that customer.

The price shown by a dealer is usually valid only for a limited time period which is in the order of seconds for liquid markets. After this period, the quote is assumed to be subject, i.e., subject to the dealer still being willing to transact at this price.

Following a trade in competition, it is market usance to provide non-monetary rewards to some dealers. The winning dealer, who accepts the risk of the trade, will usually be told what his or her cover was, namely the price quoted by the next best dealer. This information may allow that dealer to adjust the next client quote, bearing in mind that the losing dealers may adjust their quotes as well, and potentially in the opposite direction. The dealer providing the cover price will usually only be told that he or she 'was cover' but with no or only a vague indication of how far they were from winning in order to protect the winning trader. All other dealers are usually told that the trade ended as even the information that the trade concluded ('traded away') may be valuable.

The competitive quote approach follows the logic that it is the fiduciary duty of a trader (who rarely trades his own money) to ensure the best execution of the trade. The countervailing argument to this thinking is that the winning dealer will have acquired a position as a result of the executed trade and will have to hedge or unwind this position. Since multiple dealers were alerted to the trade by the original inquiry, they will be aware of this trade interest and use this information to the detriment of the winning dealer. Any dealer asked to quote a price in competition will therefore factor higher hedge cost into the initial quote, defeating the purpose of best execution.

In practice, this argument has some merit for very large trades where it may indeed be advantageous for a client to ask a single dealer to execute the trade. That dealer can then hedge or unwind the position without the wider market being aware of what is happening. Pricing will generally be done relative to a market benchmark and clients that trade frequently will be able to judge whether they are better off asking for a single quote or trading in competition. For smaller trades, it is unlikely that information leakage is meaningful.

What should be noted, however, is that requiring multiple dealers in competition is not a sufficient precondition for best execution. Unless the dealers selected for the competition are indeed able and willing to provide competitive prices, the overall result may still be poor. As a tool to ensure best execution, a multiple quote requirement is therefore a very blunt instrument unless it is augmented by monitoring which counterparties were selected to compete. That being said, given that it is easy to check mechanically how many dealers were asked for a price on a given trade, it is a tool that lends itself to regulators.

Dealers will sometimes offer clients to work an order instead of quoting a firm price on the spot. Working an order means that the dealer will, on a best effort basis, try to execute the client's trade interest in the market over a period of time. In an illiquid market this may be preferrable to being told that the dealer cannot quote a firm price at all. However, an order provides a number of options to the dealer related to the timing of execution and hedging. A client may choose to grant these options to a trader in order to get the desired transaction done but should remain aware of the value of that option.

Mistrades

A mistrade is a trade that was conducted at a clearly erroneous price. The difference between a mistrade and an erroneous trade confirmation is that with a mistrade, the trader agreed to trade at an off-market price. A mistaken trade confirmation is simply an error later in the trade recording process.

What constitutes a mistrade or fat finger error, and how it is dealt with, depends on the trading venue. Most exchanges and electronic trading platforms have mechanical rules to identify and automatically cancel mistrades. When counterparties interact bilaterally, the situation is less clear and no general rules exist. In principle, a trader who said 'Done' on a given trade is bound by his or her word[6]. In practice, however, it would be unreasonable for counterparties who interact on an ongoing basis not to allow for human error and be willing to set aside trades from time to time. On the other hand, declaring a mistrade should not be a free option to a dealer to cancel trades that in retrospect could have been executed at a more advantageous price.

11.2   SETTLEMENT

Settlement follows the trading of securities and gives finality to the transfer instructions that arise from each trade.

---

[6]Viz. the motto of the London Stock Exchange, which still governs fixed income markets: Dictum meum pactum.

11.2.1 Settlement mechanisms

Settlement involves instructing banks that hold cash and securities to transfer these valuable assets between counterparties. In a bygone era, such instructions would be given independently after a trade had been concluded. For instance, the seller of a security would instruct the custodian to transfer ownership to the buyer, and the buyer would instruct a bank to transfer cash to the seller. The problem with this approach is that if one of the counterparties fails to fulfill its obligations, the other one would face an immediate outflow of an asset (because this side of the instructions would remain valid) but would enjoin other creditors in any attempt to settle the receipt of the other side of the transaction. This type of risk is usually known as Herstatt risk[7] or settlement risk.

Settlement risk remains in place for certain types of transaction where payments occur in different currencies and different locations. In the case of outright foreign exchange transactions, where this risk is most prevalent, a special bank (the CLS, or Continuous Linked Settlement, Bank) was set up to eliminate this risk. The mitigation technique used by this bank and others operating in simpler environments is known as 'delivery versus payment' or DvP. In a DvP process, a trusted bank will accept incoming asset transfers but only execute them if both parties have the necessary assets in account with that trusted bank. This process is similar to the use of escrow accounts in non-financial private sector transactions[8].

The use of DvP involves the holding of assets at the trusted intermediary (which is usually a GCSD) and this warehousing is costly for all involved parties. To reduce this cost, DvP in bond markets is generally conducted not on a continuous basis but in so-called settlement cycles. At predefined times in a trading day, the intermediary will try to match and execute all transactions pending at that time. This process creates a netting benefit similar to that outlined in Figure 4.3 on page 23 while at the same time preserving the benefit of only finalising transactions that can actually settle in full.

11.2.2 Settlement conventions

When talking about time and trading, it is important to distinguish between two dates. The first is the valuation date which is the date on which prices are being observed. If a

---

[7]The insolvency of the Herstatt Bank in 1974 took more than 30 years to resolve and was one of the less salubrious episodes of German banking regulation. The bank was ordered to suspend banking operations on 26 June 1974 but the wider market was not immediately informed. As a result, counterparties continued to pay Herstatt even though the bank would not make any outgoing payments. Some 35 years later, a government-owned German bank earned the newspaper moniker 'Germany's most stupid bank' by making payments to Lehman Brothers the day after the US company declared its insolvency.

[8]For instance, transactions in German real estate usually involve the notary public entrusted with the transaction notifying the land registry of an impending sale. Upon confirmation of this notification, the buyer transfers the purchase price to an escrow account of the notary who then instructs the land registry to transfer title. When the title transfer is confirmed, the notary transfers the cash from the escrow account to the seller. While this process takes more time, it allows the unwinding of any transfers in case of unexpected problems.

trade actually occurs, the same day is also the trade date. However, it takes some time to process a trade once it has been agreed between two parties, so the actual exchange of cash and securities happens usually at a later point in time, the so-called settlement date. Unfortunately, it is also common in the market to trade 'for value of …', meaning 'for settlement on …', so valuation date (trade date) is easy to mix up with value date (settlement date). Note that a security can be sold again regardless of whether the buy transaction has already settled or not. A trader can therefore trade in and out of an issue several times a day. All the required settlement instructions are handled by today's sophisticated back office systems. The only important requirement is that when settlement is set to occur, the necessary cash and securities are in the right accounts. Otherwise, the trade fails and penalties may be incurred.

When settlement is supposed to happen relative to a given trade date is generally decided by market convention although it is possible and common to agree earlier or later settlement between two parties on a case by case basis. By and large, most bond markets settle in T+2, meaning settlement occurs two business days after the trade has been agreed. Because there is a risk that a counterparty defaults during these two days (note that with public holidays, T+2 can easily become almost a week), market participants and regulators usually try to push the settlement times down. For instance, US and UK government bonds (Gilts) can settle T+0, i.e., on the same day, under some circumstances. Money and FX markets usually settle T+2. Note that until settlement, the buyer of a bond earns interest on the cash paid for the bond, while the bond holder accrues interest. Therefore, when settlement is done on a non-standard day, the price at which the bond is bought or sold is adjusted. Economically, the settlement date is the essential date of a transaction.

While shorter settlement periods reduce credit risk, they increase the cost of human error. In modern trading, counterparties' back offices usually confirm trade details to each other within minutes of a trade. This confirmation process ensures that when instructions are sent to the clearer by both counterparties, there is a minimal risk of a mismatch between these instructions (or indeed, that one of them is missing). If the initial confirmation fails, counterparties will seek to find and redress the reasons. The shorter the time between trade and settlement, the more likely it is that trivial misunderstandings can lead to delayed settlement because there is insufficient time for reconciliation.

On a historical note, conventions like T+2 are referred to as rolling settlement because the settlement date is always rolling two days after the trade is done. In the (ancient) past, markets used fixed settlement where all transactions done in a certain period were all settled on a single day [59]. This was more practical when a lot of paper had to change hands, but of course nobody could be certain that the counterparty to any trade would still be able to settle on that day (fixed settlement days could then be spaced 60 days apart).

Incidentally, when two parties in a fixed settlement market agreed to settle on the following settlement day instead of the upcoming one, the trade was said to be back-warded. This term still survives in the word backwardation in the futures market. There, it describes the normal situation where the further away contract is cheaper than the front contract. The opposite of backwardation in this sense is contango.

CHAPTER 12

Central Clearing

12.1 DIRECT CLEARING

Central clearing replaces the $n(n-1)/2$ possible bilateral clearing relationships that are possible between n market participants with only n bilateral relationships, each between a market participant and a central counterparty (CCP[1]). This simplification of relationships goes beyond the mere operational efficiency which comes with the netting possibilities shown in Figure 4.3 on page 43. Each bilateral relationship requires the setting up and maintenance of payment instructions, as well as credit risk management.

Central clearing is a risk-mitigation tool that is most effective for trades that have a long lifespan. This is because a longer lifespan means that a trade can move further from its inception value and therefore create counterparty performance risk. However, at large volumes even short-dated trades, such as the regular T+2 settlement of a repo transaction, can create substantial balance sheet exposures for financial firms. Consequently, central clearing is now pervasive across the financial industry.

Mechanically, trade negotiation between two counterparties is done as normal, but immediately after the trade has been concluded it is 'given up' to the CCP as shown in Figure 12.2. For trades conducted on an exchange, the give-up to the clearing house of the exchange is generally automatic. In the European Union, new regulations demand that clients can specify that a trade is cleared at a CCP of their choosing (so-called 'client-directed clearing'). In practice, derivatives exchanges remain the exclusive clearers of their contracts and have obtained temporary regulatory exceptions to remain in this position.

The advantages of central clearing among frequent trades are sufficiently obvious to have led to a long history of this technique. The Osaka Rice Exchange established in 1697 used central clearing and margining in a similar fashion to modern CCPs.

At the same time, the presence of a central counterparty creates a cost and introduces new types of risk. The cost is related to the setting up and operation of the CCP. Given that the CCP is counterparty to every trade cleared there, a failure of the CCP to perform under a contract would have catastrophic consequences for financial stability. Because the CCP itself does not conduct trades, and therefore does not endogenously

---

[1]Central counterparties are treated by regulators as a form of market infrastructure and this is the keyword to look for when searching for regulatory details.

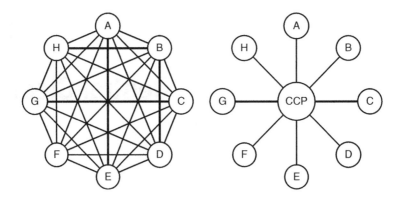

FIGURE 12.1   Clearing relationships with bilateral and central clearing. The 28 possible bilateral relationships between 8 counterparties collapse into just 8 when a CCP is used.

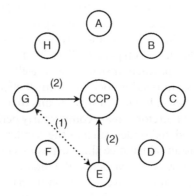

FIGURE 12.2   Trade execution with central clearing. After the trade is concluded (1), it is immediately given up to the CCP (2).

generate any risk of defaulting on a trade-related obligation, the risk for the CCP is that one of its counterparties fails to perform and so the CCP does not have the resources to pay out on the other side of the affected trades. Capitalising a CCP to such a degree that any conceivable risk could be covered with the CCP's own capital would require an economically prohibitive setup cost. This means that measures to reduce the risk exposure of CCPs are critical design features of such arrangements. As will be explained below, some of these mitigation measures create new types of risk for the direct counterparties of the CCP. Such a counterparty is known as a clearing member.

The first step in reducing CCP risk is the frequent exchange of cash margin, known as margining. This means that every trade is revalued on a daily basis using a universally[2] agreed pricing methodology. Such margin payments related to revaluation of existing positions are known as variation margin (VM). Margining in practice

---

[2]The word 'universally' here refers to all direct and indirect users of the CCP.

constrains the type of products that can be cleared centrally to those that on one hand can be priced reliably every day, and on the other hand have sufficiently low volatility to make margin payments practical. Potentially highly volatile derivatives, such as credit default swaps, are therefore difficult to clear, as are exotic derivatives. In essence, variation margining transforms counterparty risk into liquidity risk.

Variation margin is only a partial protection against the implications of market price movements under default risk. It takes some time for a clearing house to deal with a default of a clearing member. During that time, market prices are likely to move further against the position of the defaulting member but that clearing member will no longer be in a position to contribute additional variation margin. Clearing houses therefore charge an additional margin, called initial margin[3] (IM) for new positions. Initial margin is therefore calibrated relative to the expected market movement during an assumed time period corresponding to the time it takes to unwind a defaulting member's positions. In the simplest case, one would set the margin to $\rho\sqrt{t}$ where ρ is the one-day expected variance of a given position and t is the number of days assumed necessary to close out a defaulting member's positions. In practice, CCPs set initial margins in a more complex way to reflect partially offsetting risks. For instance, a clearing house would not simply add initial margins for a paid 11 year swap, received 12 year swap position in the same currency given that the 11 and 12 year swap rates are highly correlated and the positions therefore partially offsetting. CCPs to some extent compete on the efficiency of their margining systems. A CCP that can more realistically reflect the risks of a given portfolio will be more attractive to users than one that charges apparently unnecessary margin against less risky positions. At the same time, stable correlations are the precondition for such risk offsets. Regulators therefore restrict cross-position netting at CCPs to prevent artificially low margin requirements.

While variation margin must generally be posted, and is paid out, in cash, clearing houses accept non-cash collateral for initial margin. As the return on margin is due to the clearing member posting it, this arrangement ensures that the more permanent initial margin is not an undue drag on the income of the posting member. However, the interaction between variation and initial margin is more complex. Large market movements create by themselves a need for rapid variation margin payments and receipts as the CCP revalues existing positions. At the same time, such events change the estimates of market volatility and can therefore lead to increased initial margin.

Margining means that any accrued profit or loss on a transaction (which for the CCP, like any other counterparty, means a claim or obligation to pay, respectively) is frequently settled through cash payments. This resets the exposure value of the trades, and therefore the exposure of the CCP to zero. The reason that CCP margins are paid in cash is that this makes the payments immediately final[4]. Frequent margining also means that the ability to pay of any clearing member is tested frequently. A gradual deterioration of the credit quality of a clearing member will therefore eventually lead to a default on a margin call at a time when there may still be assets to mitigate losses.

---

[3]In bilateral clearing with margining, this margin is known as the independent amount (IA).
[4]Margining is also used in bilateral (non-cleared) trades, and there margin can also take the form of other collateral. In essence, such arrangements reflect the risk management preferences and asset ownership preferences of the two parties involved.

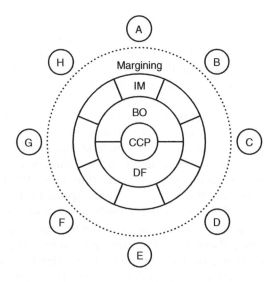

FIGURE 12.3 Standard protection mechanisms for a central counterparty. After margining, the CCP is protected by the initial margin (IM) posted by clearing members, and furthermore by the default fund (DF) and the bidding obligations (BO). Only after all these buffers are exhausted would the CCP itself be threatened by default.

Clearing members can default. Essentially there are two fundamentally different types of such defaults. The first is an external default where the member is declared insolvent by a court or declares insolvency. In this event, there is no uncertainty about whether or not that member can fulfill margin obligations to the CCP because it will simply be legally unable to to so. The second is a failure to make variation margin payments to the CCP as and when required. In such internal defaults, it is essentially up to the CCP to enforce its claims on the member (potentially resulting in an external default) or to postpone such claims. CCPs generally have decision-making structures in place to balance the risks of enforcing an external default or allowing obligations to build up while margin claims remain unmet.

Once a clearing member does default, the CCP is faced with potential losses from unfulfilled payment obligations. The layer of protection after variation margin is the initial margin posted by the clearing member to the CCP. Once a clearing member defaults, the initial margin assets can be realised to pay out variation margin to other clearing members until the positions of the defaulting members are closed out[5]. While a clearing member is in default but the CCP has not yet entered default proceedings, the CCP can pay out variation margin by borrowing against IM assets posted by the member that is failing to pay VM.

The sizing of initial margin is dependent on the prospect of closing out a defaulted clearing member's positions in a set amount of time, and at a maximum loss. This requires that there is a market for such positions at the time the default occurs. To ensure

---

[5]Once these positions are closed, they cease to generate variation margin calls.

the existence of such a market, CCPs impose a bidding obligation on clearing members at closing auctions of batches of positions held by a defaulting member. After a default, the CCP will typically batch positions by maturity and currency and then require the remaining clearing members to bid for these positions. Because the market will have a general idea of the net positions of the defaulted member and therefore move against these positions, the amounts bid will usually be negative, implying that the bidding member asks to be paid to take on the position of the defaulted member. The initial margin posted by the defaulted members should go some way towards covering this cost. Should that be insufficient, the CCP can dip into the default fund, a segregated pool of assets contributed by all clearing members, to cover the amount not already covered by the initial margin posted by the defaulted member. Some CCPs also mandate clearing members to assist with personnel for the closing of positions, meaning that experienced trading staff is posted to the CCP for a short time to execute position transfers.

The mutual nature of the default fund creates a natural incentive for clearing members to post low bids in the closing auctions. A low bid ensures a low likelihood of incurring losses on the future evolution of the positions acquired in the auction while the lower valuation is absorbed by the mutual default fund. This incentive is counteracted by CCPs through an obligation to replenish the default fund after a closing auction. The less a clearing member bids for positions, the more that member has to contribute to the replenishment of the default fund.

Central counterparties need to optimise the sizing of the various protection components with a view to achieving an acceptable level of residual risk with a minimum level of deployed capital. The outcome of this optimisation is dependent on market volatility as well as the type, volume and distribution of business going through the CCP at any one time. CCPs typically run daily stress tests simulating the default of their largest clearing member and adjust margin requirements in response to changes in market volatility.

Bidding obligation and default fund contributions create contigent liabilities for clearing members that are crystallised by the default of another member. In addition, the requirement to post variation margin in cash, and at short notice, can create liquidity stresses. These risks are fundamentally different from usual bilateral trading relationships because it is not clear which clearing member default would trigger which type of close-up auction, and the exposure of the CCP to any given clearing member is only known to that member. The potentially required top-up amount for the default fund is therefore nearly impossible to establish for a clearing member.

As a result of these complex risks, clearing membership creates complex capital requirements for banks. At the same time, many financial and non-financial institutions are unable to become clearing members because they are unable to manage such risks, or do not have, as would for example be the case for pension funds, any capital that could be committed to clearing member obligations. For this reason, central clearing is often accessed through intermediaries. The complexity of risk management do however appear to lead to a rationing of such services rather than to supply that reacts elastically to pricing.

12.2   INDIRECT CLEARING

When a market participant is unable to become a clearing member of a CCP, central clearing can be done indirectly through the services of a clearing member. The clearing member is then said to act as clearing agent for the non-member. This choice of words creates some unfortunate room for confusion because there are at this time two models for the provision of clearing services known as agency clearing and principal clearing. These two models differ in the relationship between the CCP and the non-clearing member and the choice between them is driven more by history than economics. At the time of writing, the US market is dominated by agency clearing while the European and Japanese market is dominated by principal clearing.

An essential new problem introduced by indirect clearing is the separation of obligations of the clearing member and the client. In principal clearing, all obligations towards the CCP are with the clearing member while they are split between clearing member and non-clearing member in the agency model. These differences concern the risks faced by the CCP.

At the same time, non-clearing members face the risk that their clearing agent defaults while holding their assets. In such a situation, assets may be encumbered with the clearing agent while the market risk is in effect still borne by the non-clearing members. An essential element of CCP default management is therefore the transfer of positions from a defaulting clearing agent to non-defaulting agents. The problem here is that clearing agency is a bilateral relationship that is in principle outside the purview of the CCP because it involves the full gamut of bilateral credit risk and lending arrangements possible between a liquidity provider and a client. An essential safeguard in such situation is the segregation of margin assets between the clearing agent and the non-clearing clients.

12.2.1   Agency clearing

In the agency clearing model, the CCP has contractual relationships with non-clearing users but the essential obligations of clearing are delegated to clearing members. This means that the clearing member contracted by a non-clearing user is responsible for posting margin and bidding in close-out auctions. However, the CCP has full visibility on the total positions of every end-user. The services provided by the clearing member acting as agent consist of ensuring that variation margin calls are met and it is between that clearing member and its client to arrange for either delivery of sufficient cash, or the transformation of non-cash collateral into cash through repurchase transactions.

The fundamental benefit of agency clearing is that the CCP has full information about the individual positions held by all beneficial owners of all trades cleared on the CCP. This makes it possible to conduct stress testing on the basis of ultimate ownership of positions rather than on indirect information which may be skewed when non-clearing members use multiple clearing agents.

The downside of agency clearing is that substantial obligations remain with non-clearing users but the CCP has limited information about these entities. In particular, the CCP will usually not be able to judge the ability of a non-clearing member to post sufficient collateral to its clearing agents in case of large market movements.

While this type of risk is in principle the responsibility of the clearing members to manage, the survival of the CCP potentially depends on this type of assessment.

12.2.2 Principal clearing

In the principal clearing model, the CCP has only clearing members and no contractual relationships with non-clearing users. Clearing members act as agents that stand completely between the CCP and the end client. In essence, a clearing member acts as if its own positions and those of its non-member clients form a single block with all attendant obligations. As far as the CCP is concerned, non-clearing members simply do not exist.

In the principal clearing model, CCPs typically offer convenience accounts to clearing members that allow detailed separation between the positions maintained by the clearing member on behalf of individual clients, but there is no pretence that such positions can be aggregated across multiple clearing agents used by the same end-user. In other words, the CCP cannot identify, much less quantify, positions maintained by one non-clearing user who splits clearing business across multiple clearing members. As in the agency clearing model, this exposes the CCP to risks related to defaults of large non-clearing users, or, equivalently, the correlated default of multiple non-clearing users with similar positions.

12.2.3 Hybrid clearing models

Both agency and principal clearing are characterised by a clear separation between clearing members and non-clearing members of a CCP. They differ in whether or not non-clearing members have an explicit contractual relationship with the CCP.

With mandatory central clearing, essentially shortcomings of central clearing have become more apparent. To be a clearing member, a market participant has to have ready access to central bank cash and be able to transfer such cash in a timely manner to and from the CCP. The member must also have sufficient equity to commit to the default fund and have the risk-management expertise to assist in the close-out process of defaulted members. This can entail the management of residual positions which may have contractual maturities extending into decades. While these features are generally in place for financial trading firms, they are less prevalent among many entities that have been mandated in recent years to clear positions, e.g., pension funds or government entities. It is difficult to envision a tax-funded entity managing the 30 year swap book of a defaulted investment bank.

The standard solution, which is to have non-clearing members contract out their obligations to clearing members under the principal or agent clearing model, is limited by the availability of balance sheet at these clearing members. Total market risk is not reduced by redistributing contigent risks from one type of market participant to another. Indeed, given the specific requirements of clearing members, concentrating the liquidity risks of the entire market on a limited set of clearing members is likely to increase, not decrease, financial stability risks. Clearing members tend to prudently ration their provision of clearing services which creates a bottleneck for the clearing of positions. In particular, entities that do not normally hold cash and do not have access to money market or central bank borrowing have to rely on their ability to access the repo market in order to mobilise cash for variation margin payments. The general market risk of non-performance of such entities is therefore not eliminated but only transformed into the risk of their inability to access the repo market in stressed scenarios.

CCPs have responded to this bottleneck by establishing clearing models that separate different obligations of clearing members, for instance Eurex Clearing's ISA Direct model [21]. Under such hybrid models, entities manage the initial and variation margin process themselves but contract the default management obligation to financial services firms. Under current capital requirement and liquidity coverage rules, relieving clearing members from the collateral transformation obligations of the principal clearing model makes a substantial economic difference. However, given the jump risk nature of the default management process, it is not immediately clear that this release of regulatory capital corresponds to an actual decrease in risk.

12.3 CONTRACT VALUE ADJUSTMENTS (XVA)

Central clearing is now the default clearing mechanism for most liquid derivatives contracts, and for many spot transactions including repos. Therefore the prices in the central clearing market are probably the best reference for market prices.

This then raises the question of how to value derivatives that are not cleared centrally. Theoretically, clearing has no impact on valuation because accounting standards specify (here in the phrasing of AG71 of IFRS 39 [48]): 'Fair value is defined in terms of a price agreed by a willing buyer and a willing seller in an arm's length transaction.' In practice, however, different clearing models do imply different costs in terms of capital or margin. More significantly, the value of any one specific transaction can depend on all other transactions that are pending with the same counterparty. This is because each new transaction will change the future expected exposure versus the counterparty and so, if applicable, the expected amount of margin or collateral that needs to be posted in the future.

Financial institutions therefore need to apply valuation adjustments, collectively known as xVA, where the letter x stands for other letters in abbreviations like CVA, FVA, DVA, etc., that will be explained in more detail below.

12.3.1 Credit Value Adjustment

When a transaction is not cleared or margined, any mark-to-market revaluation exposes the party with a positive mark-to-market to default risk of the other counterparty.

Simply speaking, the transaction may have a positive market value, but the risk is that the other counterparty fails to perform as promised.

Traditionally, banks trading derivatives projected future mark-to-market exposures against their counterparties and charged expected exposures against the credit lines approved for these counterparties. With risk-based capital requirements, these credit exposures incur capital charges, and the cost of this capital needs to be assigned to the transaction. This cost is called the credit value adjustment, or CVA.

Structurally, the CVA depends not only on the transaction (as accounting standards would seem to imply), but also on the credit risk of the counterparty, the capital cost of the bank as the other counterparty, and all other transactions between these two counterparties. The latter link arises because a new transaction that reduces future expected exposure between the two counterparties reduces the capital charge and so should carry a negative CVA. While economically correct, this notion contradicts the fundamental idea of accounting fair value because the new transaction has a capital impact that is unique to the two contracting parties. The notion of an 'arm's length transaction' is therefore not applicable in this context. In addition, the notion of a generic 'willing buyer and willing seller' neglects the specific credit risk and capital cost essential to the CVA calculation.

Swap dealers tend to hedge large-scale counterparty risks through the use of credit default swaps. This means that CVA for large counterparties is proxied fairly well through CDS spreads.

12.3.2 Funding Value Adjustment

When a transaction is margined, CVA is no longer appropriate because the credit risk aspect of the transaction is addressed through margining. Instead, counterparties must concern themselves with the cost of providing margin to each other. While CVA incurs a cost to the counterparty that has a positive mark-to-market (due to the credit risk it faces), margining creates a cost to the counterparty that has a negative mark-to-market because it needs to post margin. Margin posted is remunerated by the receiving party.

Margin is usually treated as a cash equivalent, and is remunerated at a cash rate, while the party posting it needs to raise the margin at its own funding cost, the funding value adjustment (FVA) can be sizeable. For instance, a bank funding itself unsecured at an average rate of 50 bps over the overnight average (SOFR, €STR, SONIA, etc.) would have a running cost of 50 bps for cash posted as margin if that cash is remunerated at the overnight rate.

MVA in practice is more complex because margin can in some instances be posted in multiple currencies. The party posting the margin will choose the currency that offers the most attractive remuneration, taking into account cross-currency basis swap rates. The future remuneration rate of posted margin can therefore be a complex option involving funding spreads in different currencies.

FVA can lead to situations where a single derivatives dealer has multiple positions that offset each other in terms of risk, but differ in the margining provisions. This means that the dealer has no market risk, but funding risk resulting from mismatches in how margin is received and posted. Such funding costs can be sizeable relative to the potential profit margins in liquid derivatives markets.

12.3.3 Debit Value Adjustment

In some clearing arrangements, collateral requirements depend on the rating of the counterparties. When downgraded below certain trigger levels, collateralisation, or an increase in collateralisation levels, becomes mandatory in such contracts. This means that a counterparty in effect faces higher costs when its own credit quality deteriorates. Counter-intuitively, this means that financial firms may face an economic need to hedge their own credit risk. Debit value adjustments (DVAs) reflect the economic cost of this obligation to the best estimate of the firm applying it, bearing in mind that an actual hedge is virtually impossible.

CHAPTER 13

The Money Market

Informally, the money market is defined as the market for funds with maturities of up to two years, and the associated derivatives.

The money market is the second largest capital market (the largest is the foreign exchange market). Money markets are extremely efficient and it takes only minutes to raise or place funds when standard documentation is in place.

13.1   MONEY MARKET INSTRUMENTS

Money market instruments come in different shapes. Various instruments are issued by different entities and typically have different conventions. In the same market, almost identical paper may be traded in different ways depending on whether it is classified as CP or CD, so it is very important to make sure to understand what one is dealing with. Here are some examples for cash instruments traded in the money market:

Deposit Non-transferrable deposit with a given bank. Deposits may be callable or putable if this agreed in advance. Callable deposits carry slightly higher interest rates, for instance.

Loan The opposite of a deposit, i.e., cash obtained from a bank. Loans are usually not negotiated on a very short-term basis, but short term loans are used as part of a revolver facility or to bridge finance M&A transactions, bond issues, etc.

Certificate of deposit (CD) Transferrable deposit, usually non-callable and non-putable. The idea of a CD is that the investor can realise cash ahead of the deposit maturity by selling the CD. The extra liqudity usually means that CD interest rates are slightly lower than those on equivalent deposits.

Treasury bill (T-bill) Short term paper issued by a government.

Commercial paper (CP) Short-term bonds issued by corporations and some governments. These instruments are very similar to CDs, but are quoted differently. Typically, a corporate has a programme to issue CP on a regular basis and the programme is backed by a revolver loan (see below) in case the banks arranging the CP sales have temporary difficulties selling the paper. A variation of commercial paper (promissory notes) is known as tegata in the Japanese market.

Asset-backed commercial paper (ABCP) Short-term bonds issued by a special-purpose corporation that holds other assets which provide the cash to service the ABCP.

Banker's acceptance (BA) Effectively a trade receivable, a BA is a certificate from a bank that is backed by the right of a corporate to receive payment for goods sold. The corporate will present papers that evidence the right to receive payments (usually a contract and a bill of lading) to the bank and will receive the BA. The BA can then be sold by the corporate to receive cash immediately instead of when the goods are being paid for. The buyer of the BA faces the credit risk of the bank instead of the corporate or the buyer of the goods, as would be the case if CP was used instead.

Revolver loan, Standby facility Not a loan itself, but the commitment of a bank to make short-term funds available on demand as long as certain conditions are met. A borrower usually pays a commitment fee to the bank as long as the facility exists and the bank is required to set aside capital in case the facility is drawn.

The T-bill and CP markets are functionally fairly similar but some differences exist. Bills are usually sold in auctions like bonds while CP is issued on investor demand (reverse inquiry) at terms set by the issuer. While CP can be traded in the secondary market, the volume of secondary trading activity is substantially lower than for bills and price discovery in the CP market is much more difficult as a result. Issuers sometimes buy back their own CP to help investors liquidate such paper, but are usually under no obligation to do so. CP can also be issued in structured form, for instance with redemption amounts that vary in accordance with some index, or with option features. The two instruments have in common with other short-term instruments that they compete with bank deposits and CDs for short-term funds from a variety of investors such as money market funds, corporate treasuries and banks. As a result, they should be considered near money, and changes in the demand and supply of such paper can have impact on more visible interest rates such as interbank lending and FX swap rates.

13.2 DISCOUNT FACTORS

Monies paid in the future are usually less valuable than money paid in the present. There are a number of reasons for that; for instance:

- Inflation (money will buy less goods in the future than today)
- Credit risk (the risk that the person expected to pay the money in the future will not pay)
- Interest rate risk (the risk that if instead of lending money for a month today, one might be able to lend it at a better rate tomorrow)
- Liquidity preference (the fact that instead of lending money for a month today, one might decide tomorrow that one would rather buy a bicycle).

Mathematically, the time value of money is usually expressed through discount factors, written here as $Df(t)$. A discount factor can be thought of as the value of a payment of one currency unit at a given point in time t. For instance, if one is willing to pay 98 sen for the promise to receive 1 yen from the Japanese government in one year's time, one could write $Df(1) = 0.98$. The 98 sen are also called the present value of the payment of 1 yen. This is related to the idea of 'net present value' in corporate finance.

The discount factor will generally depend on who makes the promise to pay the money. For instance, one would expect a lower discount factor for a corporate's promise to pay than for a government's promise to pay. This is because, for a corporate, there is a smaller or greater chance of the corporate being unable to pay when the sum becomes due. The discount factor therefore reflects not only the time value of the payment itself, but also the probability of loss and the expected size of the loss.

In theory, discount factors are unique. What this means is that for any given time t, there is exactly one $Df(t)$ for each issuer and instrument type. Suppose there were instead two different discount factors $Df'(t) > Df''(t)$. One could then sell, say, $100 * Df'(t)$ yen worth of the instrument trading with discount factor $Df'(t)$, so one would have to pay 100 yen at time t in the future. If one at the same time buys $100 * Df''(t)$ yen (which is less than $100 * Df'(t)$; see above) worth of the instrument trading with discount factor $Df''(t)$, one will get exactly the 100 yen needed to make that payment. The difference $100 * (Df'(t) - Df''(t))$ would be a riskless profit, which, in theory, does not exist. The market would sell so much of the instrument with the higher discount factor and buy so much of the instrument with the lower discount factor that the prices move to reflect the same discount factor.

In practice, different discount factors for comparable cash flows may exist. The first, trivial reason, is the explanation given above: Unless somebody actually does the buying or selling necessary to bring the discount factors in line, there is no reason why they should be. This means that opportunities to make riskless profits (arbitrage) can exist, albeit only for a short time. The time may even be so short as to be useless. The more complex reason is that it may be impossible to actually do the trade. In order to sell an instrument, one has to be able to borrow it from somebody and perhaps nobody is willing to lend it. Even if somebody were willing to lend it, perhaps the premium they are asking may be too expensive to make the trade worthwhile (discussed in Chapter 14 on repo trading). Even if the trade could technically be executed, the time t may be so long that there is little point in exploiting the difference $Df'(t) - Df''(t)$ if it is very small. In the case of cash flows related to bonds, it may be impossible to separate individual payments from the same bond, and trade them against payments from comparable other bonds by the same issuer. Therefore, especially in the money market, instruments can trade at prices that would suggest that discount factors are not unique.

Despite these shortcomings of discount factors, they are the core of fixed income analysis. Everything else, interest rates, option pricing, etc., is built on top of discount factors. Economically, this is rational. At the end of the day, what matters is cash in hand. How much cash in hand is worth compared to cash in the future is given by discount factors.

Discount factors are difficult to work with in daily practice, so the market generally quotes interest rates instead. It is impossible to talk about interest rates as such because the meaning of a given interest rate depends on the instrument and the market. Discount factors, on the other hand, do not have that problem. An essential task of fixed income analysis is therefore the correct translation between different expressions of discount factors.

13.3   DAYCOUNT CONVENTIONS

When calculating interest, one needs to take into account the number of days for which the money is lent. Interest is generally quoted on an annualised basis for easy comparison, but even though a rate is annualised, it is only valid for the stated period. For example, there is no contradiction between being quoted 2.1% for 6 months' money in annualised terms and 2.5% for 1 year of money.

In order to get from the annualised (quoted) interest to the actual interest for the period, the annualised interest rate is multiplied by the daycount fraction *DCF*. As the name suggests, the daycount fraction is a fraction, namely:

$$DCF = \frac{\text{Days in interest period}}{\text{Days in year}} \tag{13.1}$$

Markets use different ways of counting days for both the numerator and denominator of this fraction. The daycount convention describes how this is done and a number of common daycount conventions are outlined below. Different conventions can be used for different instruments in the same market.

To understand some of the strange daycount conventions, one has to be aware that interest rates are older than pocket calculators and computers. In the 1970s, slide rules and logarithm tables were state of the art calculation tools. Therefore, some conventions are driven more by the desire to simplify calculations than logic.

ISDA 30/360 Each month is assumed to have 30 days and each year has 360 days. If the start date falls on a 31st, it is corrected to fall on the 30th. If the end date falls on the 31st and the start date is on the 30th or 31st, the end date is corrected to fall on the 30th.

30E/360 Each month is assumed to have 30 days and each year has 360 days. Both start and end date are always corrected to fall on the 30th when they fall on the 31st. Note that the end date in ISDA 30/360 is only adjusted if the start date falls on a month end.

act/360 (actual/360) The days in the interest period are counted correctly and the result is divided by 360. This means that the amount of interest paid after one year is slightly larger than the one year interest rate (namely 365/360 or 366/360 of that amount).

act/365 Similar to act/360, but the number of days in the year is assumed to be 365.

act/act Actual number of days in the accrual period divided by the actual number of days in the relevant year. A leap year is assumed when the 29th of February is part of the accrual period. This is the most natural way of calculating interest, but also the most complicated for anything but a computer.

Money markets, including Japan's, usually use act/360 as the daycount convention. The main exceptions are the old Commonwealth countries (UK, South Africa, Australia, etc.) where act/365 is used.

Looking a little ahead, bond markets generally use act/act or 30/360, whereas swap markets tend to use act/act, act/365 or 30/360.

13.4 MONEY MARKET INTEREST RATES

There are effectively two ways to quote the price of a money market instrument. The first, and most common, is to de-annualise the interest rate and work out the discounted value of the redemption cashflow. The other method is to treat the interest rate as a discount amount and de-annualise that. The standard method is the simple interest method:

$$P = \frac{100}{1 + r * DCF} \tag{13.2}$$

(Note that prices are always quoted in percent of the notional amount, hence the 100.) The interest rate earned on an asset that is trading at P and pays back 100 is:

$$r = \left(\frac{100}{P} - 1\right)/DCF \tag{13.3}$$

The discount margin method is:

$$P = 100 - r * DCF \tag{13.4}$$

Here, the interest rate for a given price is simply:

$$r = (100 - P)/DCF \tag{13.5}$$

As mentioned, the discount margin method is used only in a few markets. However, a very important one of these markets is the market for US Treasury bills. This is a good example of how conventions can be driven by convenience. Although the discount margin quotation is not very precise, it is very easy to do with a slide rule (especially because the US money market uses act/360 daycount). In fact, it is quite easy to build a slide rule that is marked to make this calculation very easy. The division operation in the simple interest method is quite tricky to do precisely, so tables or a calculator are necessary.

Instruments with a maturity beyond 1 year are special when the daycount convention uses actual days as the nominator and the instrument spans a leap year. The problem is that if the instrument effectively straddles 2 years and 1 of them is a leap year, it is unclear whether 'actual' in the nominator means 365 or 366 days. The solution is to make it mean both. Generally, the instrument is split into 2 parts, namely 1 part that is exactly 1 year long and ends at the final maturity of the instrument, and a second one that starts immediately and ends at the start of the 1 year instrument. Each of the two parts then uses the appropriate nominator, i.e., 365 or 366, depending on which of the 2 contains the 29th of February. This is a first example of the general convention to work backwards from the maturity of an instrument, rather than forwards from its inception. The rationale for this convention is that it improves fungibility between instruments originated on different days.

13.5 COMPOUNDING

So far, interest rates have been discussed in the context of single-period investments. In general, contracts can cover multiple periods and can require interest to be paid at the end of each of them. For instance, a credit card loan typically requires monthly interest payments. While the interest used to calculate the payment amounts are annualised rates, the monthly payment frequency affects the total cost of a loan. Assuming 30/360 daycount for simplicity, a loan of EUR 100 for 1 year at 6% would require repayment of EUR 106 at the end of the year. If interest is charged monthly, it is no longer immediately clear what the total interest cost is. If the borrower pays the interest at the end of each month, the total interest payment is 12 times 0.5%, equal to the stated annual interest of 6%.

If the borrow instead does not pay the interest, it is added to the outstanding loan balance. After the first month, the loan balance would then be EUR 100.50 and so the 6% interest rate would be charged for the following month. The payment obligation at the second month would therefore be EUR 100.50 $*$ 1.005 = 101.0025. After the full year has elapsed, the loan balance would be 100 $*$ $(1 * 6\%/12)^{12}$ $\approx$ 106.17. This addition of interest payable to the outstanding loan balance, and the corresponding increase in the interest obligation, is known as compounding. Compounding can lead to surprisingly high interest charges. At 12% annual interest, monthly compounding generates a total compound interest of 12.68%. In retail lending, many countries therefore require the disclosure of the total interest cost chargeable over 1 year, including the effects of compounding and applicable fees. Such interest rates have names like annual effective rate (A. E. R.). Absent fees and as long as non-business days and daycount conventions do not affect the calculation, the annual effective rate r_{eff} for an annualised rate r is given as:

$$r_{eff} = \left(1 + \frac{r}{n}\right)^n - 1 \qquad (13.6)$$

Interbank lending takes place predominantly on an overnight basis. This makes it useful to consider the limit $n \to \infty$ which is known as continuous compounding. Using the well-known limit relationship:

$$e^x = \lim_{n\to\infty} \left(1 + \frac{x}{n}\right)^n \qquad (13.7)$$

one finds:

$$r_{eff} = e^r - 1 \qquad (13.8)$$

In actual interbank lending, compounding of overnight interest is made more complex by the fact that interest cannot be paid on non-business days. Compounding therefore has no effect on weekends. For a two-week horizon with no holidays, for instance, the total interest using actual/360 is not given by:

$$i_c = N\left(1 + \frac{r}{360}\right)^{14} \tag{13.9}$$

but by the (for positive rates r somewhat smaller):

$$i_c = N\left(1 + \frac{r}{360}\right)^{8}\left(1 + \frac{3r}{360}\right)^{2} \tag{13.10}$$

because the two weekends spanned by the lending period simply require 3 days of linear accrual without compounding.

13.6 LIBOR, EURIBOR, AND FRIENDS

Because trading in money markets is done between institutions and not on an exchange, the market is not very transparent. To provide reference rates for the market as a whole, the British Bankers' Association (BBA) introduced the concept of LIBOR (London Interbank Offered Rate). To find LIBOR, the BBA asked panels of banks to submit the interest rate at which they expect a highly rated bank to be able to borrow unsecured to other high-quality banks at 10am on each London business day over certain horizons. From the quotes obtained, the highest and lowest were thrown out and the average of the remaining quotes (a so-called trimmed mean) was published as LIBOR. There are different LIBOR rates for different time horizons (1M, 3M, etc), and for different currencies (USD LIBOR, GBP LIBOR, etc.). LIBOR is such a useful idea that similar fixings are now done in many places and the term Libor is used to summarise these rates. One would for instance talk about a Libor account in Czech krona even though there is no actual fixing in London. The rates produced in other centres are named very similarly. There are CIBOR (Copenhagen, DKK), TIBOR[1] (Tokyo, JPY), STIBOR (Stockholm, SEK), KLIBOR (Kuala Lumpur, MYR), PRIBOR (Prague, CZK), and so on. Note that both JPY LIBOR and TIBOR exist, but because the panel banks are different, they do not represent the same credit risk.

The bid side of LIBOR is called LIBID, but this rate is rarely used. Typically, LIBID is assumed to be 12.5 bp below LIBOR (1/8th of one percent).

With the introduction of the Euro, the European Bankers' Federation introduced a fixing called Euribor that is very similar to EUR LIBOR, but has a much larger bank panel. For a few months in 1999, there was competition between the two fixings, but by now Euribor has completely superseded EUR LIBOR as the market benchmark.

---

[1]There are two separate TIBOR fixings, one for the on-shore and one for the off-shore yen market.

The LIBOR concept has been extremely successful and many interest rate derivatives, like money market futures and swaps, are linked to this type of benchmark which is generically known as an Ibor. Many loans and FRN coupons are set with a link to Libor or a related rate. The essential weakness of the concept is that traders are invited to provide opinions, rather than actual traded rates. Indeed, unsecured term lending is now comparatively rare; many interbank lending transactions are now overnight and secured. Hence, the quotes submitted to the Libor fixings tend to be simply spread off overnight swaps which are discussed below.

The standard Libor derivative is a forward-rate agreement (FRA). A FRA is a bilateral contract where one party makes a fixed payment while the other one pays a variable amount linked to a Libor fixing at the expiry of the contract. In line with other derivatives, only the net amount is actually paid. The fixed payment is expressed as an interest rate r_{FRA}. With a notional N and a fixing rate r_{fix}, the difference d in interest payable at the end of an accrual period of t days between the fixed and floating rate is:

$$d = N(r_{fix} - r_{FRA})\frac{t}{360} \tag{13.11}$$

where for some currencies, like Sterling, 365 would be used in the denominator. Because the market rate is known at the beginning of the accrual period, the FRA is closed out at that point, and the interest difference d is discounted to the start of the period with a payment that is:

$$p = N\frac{(r_{fix} - r_{FRA})\frac{t}{360}}{1 + \frac{r_{fix}t}{360}} \tag{13.12}$$

The party making the fixed payment is known as the buyer while the other side is the seller, which reflects the money and swap market convention to assume that the buyer takes cash and agrees to pay a certain amount of interest. Higher interest rates r_{fix} therefore are beneficial to the buyer of the FRA, although this would be offset by interest payable on an actual borrowing transaction that the FRA is used to hedge. Money market futures contracts (discussed below) follow the bond market convention where the buyer is a lender, and hence has the opposite exposure.

A FRA is usually labelled by its start and end date. A 6M9M FRA would be a FRA on a deposit covering a period starting in 6 months and ending in 9 months, i.e., a 3 month deposit.

In the course of the financial crisis, it was discovered that some traders colluded with others, in some cases across multiple firms, to manipulate various Libor fixings on certain days[2]. Generally, these manipulations appear to have been undertaken to achieve favourable outcomes on derivatives fixings and there appears to have been no

---

[2]A single trader is perceived as less able to shift the Libor fixing because extreme submissions will be eliminated in the trimmed mean calculation. That being said, the trimmed mean can still move upwards when an extremely high rate is submitted because another submission that would otherwise have been discarded will be included in the mean calculation instead. The reverse is true for a very low submission.

bias to manipulate these rates consistently upwards or consistently downwards. This may explain why money market futures and swap volumes failed to decline substantially as the manipulation was discovered. Most users appear to have taken the extent of manipulation as less significant than the benfits of the benchmarks. That being said, willfully misleading markets on prevailing conditions is morally and legally wrong. Regulators, as a result, have worked globally to reduce the use of Libors for financial products and at the time of writing, various reform processes are underway to replace these benchmark. This process is discussed in a later section.

Before moving to this topic, it should be borne in mind that one can change the benchmark fixing process but the incentives of manipulating the reference rate for cash-settled derivatives are likely to remain. If a trader who pushes up a reference rate would have to carry an overpriced amount of cash for a longer period, the associated cost and balance sheet commitment would be a strong, and perhaps sufficient disincentive[3]. As money market derivatives will for practical reasons remain cash-settled, vigilance on bechmark setting will remain required.

13.7 OVERNIGHT BENCHMARKS

Given the shift of interbank cash trading to overnight markets, several secured and unsecured overnight rate benchmarks have sprung up. The euro area has always had the Eonia (Euro Overnight Index Average) and before that the Japanese market focused on the mutan (literally 'unsecured') overnight rate. More recently, rates like Sonia (Sterling Overnight Index Average), Tonar (Tokyo Overnight Average Rate) and so on have been developed. In the case of Japan, Tonar replaced the mutan rate in December 2016 as overnight benchmark [8]. The main innovation in the US market has been the introduction of SOFR (Secured Overnight Funding Rate) which is based on a broader range of transactions than the traditional Effective Fed Funds[4] rate. The euro area switched to a similarly broader benchmark with the introduction of €STR. Futures markets exist for some of these benchmark rates.

One reason why at the current juncture there is a need for interest rate benchmarks that look beyond the interbank market is that current monetary policy configurations work with an excess liquidity in the banking system. This excess liquidity reduces the need for banks to trade funds between themselves and therefore the volume of interbank transactions. The wider benchmarks extend to transactions where at least one participant is not a bank.

The bridge between overnight rates and term rates is the overnight index swap (OIS) swap market, particular the short end of this market. There is active quasi-arbitrage trading between 3M term rates and 3M OIS swaps, for instance. Such a swap is an

---

[3]Cf. the introduction to Chapter 28 on page 301.
[4]Note the word 'effective'. This rate is the volume-weighted average rate at which federal funds actually trade and are reported. The policy rate of the Federal Reserve is known as the Federal Funds rate. It is the task of the Open Markets desk at the Fed New York to make the Effective Funds Rate trade within the band prescribed for the Federal Funds rate by the Fed's Open Market Committee.

exchange between a fixed payment (corresponding to the term rate) and a floating payment corresponding to the compound interest on an overnight deposit carrying the benchmark rate:

Forward-starting OIS are the natural equivalent of FRAs. At the same time, many large-scale issuers of floating-rate notes are switching to overnight rate benchmarks, and there is an active market in long-term swaps against these very short rates. To some extent, this could obliviate the need for term benchmarks, at least between financial firms. As will be discussed next, however, the same may not be true for non-financial users of short-rate benchmarks.

13.8   BENCHMARK REFORM

The discovery of Libor manipulation, combined with the realisation that there are fewer transactions between financial firms in the unsecured term market, have spurred market regulators into action to encourage the creation of benchmarks that are both more robust against fraud, and more representative of actual transactions. Both these desiderata work in the same direction because a benchmark representing a larger volume of actual trading is presumably harder to manipulate. The initial step taken has been a tightening of supervision for benchmark providers in order to make the benchmark production process more robust. Submitters of benchmark quotes have also made subject to more stringent penalties for wrong-doing[5]. In the longer run, more sustainable solutions need to be found.

Broadly speaking, there are two directions this effort is taking. One is to base term benchmarks to a larger extent on actual trades and less on trader assessments. This is known as the 'hybrid methodology'. The second is to fundamentally shift benchmarks towards overnight trading activity where there is the most volume.

For financial firms and very large corporates, overnight rates are a natural interest rate reference because their treasury operations operate on a high frequency. For private households and smaller firms, there is a need for intermediate rate references that are linked to terms of a week to a few months. As an example, a mortgage borrower with a floating-rate mortgage (common in the UK, Italy and Spain) needs certainty about the interest due some time before the payment date. With a Libor link, this amount is

---

[5]Given that providing quotes to a benchmark fixing is mostly a badge of pride (because only the most active firms in a market are asked to contribute) which has actual costs associated with it, some financial firms reacted to this extra risk by stopping to submit quotes.

known at the start of the interest period. When benchmark rates shift to overnight rates, then there needs to be a replacement for the term rates provided by the Libors.

One obvious solution would be to use OIS swap fixing but one might argue that this would hand the setting of term rates to money market derivatives traders. An alternative is to use lagged compounded overnight rates. In this approach, the floating rate interest payable is determined by observing the compounded overnight interest rate over a period p but lagged by a period l.

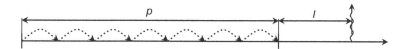

For $l = 2$ (where 2 stands for the T+2 money market settlement convention), the interest payment corresponds to the OIS swap rate and hence the professional money market. As discussed on page 172, the European FRN market is using $l = 5$. In the case where l is equal to the coupon period, the payment at the end of an accrual period of length l would be known at its beginning (as is the case for standard Libor contracts) and if also $p = l$, it would be based on observing the overnight rates over an equal period in the past. One could therefore construct floating rate contracts where, for example, the interest payable on a quarterly leg is determined by the compounded interest on the overnight benchmark during the preceding quarter.

While this approach may sound reasonable, it is a misinterpretation of the observation period p. If l does not match the money market settlement convention, then the interest rate on the term it applies to is not directly linked to overnight market rates over that period, independent of the value of p. More importantly, the length of p does not induce a term risk premium because the averaging is always one of overnight rates which have no term premium. Averaging over more or less periods does not change that. There is therefore no conceptual link between the length of the averaging period p and the term for the term rate one wishes to link to it. Market participants using a lagged averaged overnight rate to set term rates will then probably apply an explicit mark-up that depends on the term (note that there will be in any case a quoted margin on any lending contract).

For a central bank, contracts with lagged rates have the marginal drawback that changes in the policy rate will affect borrowing costs under such contracts only with a delay of around $p/2 + l$. That would be longer than under the current term rate environment where new resets immediately reflect the new policy rate. This may not be a technical problem because economic actors are forward-looking and will factor future borrowing expenses into investment decisions.

13.9 MONEY MARKET FUTURES AND FUTURES TRADING

13.9.1 Money market futures

Moves in short-term interest rates can be hedged using exchange traded contracts. Depending on the underlying currency, these contracts are known as Euroyen,

Eurodollar, Short sterling, or Euribor contracts[6]. The contracts are generally linked to the equivalent of 3 months Libor for the respective currency (Euribor in the case of euros) and the main contract expiries fall on the third Wednesday of every third month in the year (the so-called IMM days). On this day, the final price of the future is determined by the exchange as:

$$\text{Final price} = 100 - \text{Libor fixing} \tag{13.13}$$

Futures contracts can only move in discrete steps specified by the exchange, for instance 0.005 (equal to 0.5 bp) in the case of a Euribor contract. This minimum price move is called a tick. The notional amount of a money market future tends to be USD 1 million or the closest local equivalent (EUR 1 mio for euro-linked contracts and so on). The cash value of a one-tick move on a 3M contract is then about one quarter of half a basis point on one million, which amounts to 12.5 dollars or the local equivalent. Note that Equation (13.13) provides a rates exposure that is opposite in sign to Equation (13.12) so that the *buyer of a FRA* has a position matching that of a *seller of a future*, and vice versa.

13.9.2 Identification of futures contracts

Individual futures contracts are identified by a combination of the underlying and the delivery date. While delivery date identifiers follow a common convention, the identification by underlying can sometimes differ for the same contract across data providers. For instance, the Eurex 10Y Bund contract is known as FGBL[7] on Eurex and Reuters (now Refinitiv) is using the same designation. The data provider Bloomberg instead uses the code RX for the same contract[8]. Money market contracts also follow this pattern on Bloomberg, with Euribor contracts ER, eurodollars ED, and short sterling L_ (note the space, also present in the Gilt contract G_).

The delivery date is specified by a single code letter for the month and a one- or two-digit year. The month code letters, given in the table below, are unfortunately somewhat cryptic[9].

The contracts expiring in the next year are also known as white, the next years as red, green and blue[10], followed by gold, purple, orange, pink, silver and copper, although most traders would struggle to name the contracts past gold. In 2020, the March 2021 expiry would be called 'white March' (or simply 'March'), the March 2022 expiry 'red March' and so on.

---

[6]The reason for the use of the word 'euro' in some of these contracts is explained in Section 16.4.
[7]Future German Government Bond Long, which is in line with the 2Y Schatz contract FGBS and the 5Y Bobl FGBM.
[8]The Eurex Schatz is DU and the Bobl OE on Bloomberg.
[9]One way to remember them is to write down the alphabet starting with F and striking out all those letters that appear in the word WORSTIPLY. Why this should be the case is not immediately obvious.
[10]A useful mnemonic is that a standard RGB colour monitor makes up white light from red, green and blue colours.

TABLE 13.1 Standard future expiry month codes.

January	F	February	G	**March**	**H**
April	J	May	K	**June**	**M**
July	N	August	Q	**September**	**U**
October	V	November	X	**December**	**Z**

Colour codes are not used for bond contracts because bond futures contracts generally expire within 1 year. Instead, one uses the designations front and back for the next and the following expiry.

Bond futures contracts generally expire in March, June, September and December and so it is sufficient to remember the codes H, M, U and Z, marked in bold in the table. A Eurex Bund future for delivery in June 2019 would therefore be identified as FGBMM9 on Reuters and RXM9 on Bloomberg. These designations are called specifics because they identify one individual contract. The downside of working with specifics for analysis purposes is that they exist only for a relatively short time interval, which is usually 9 months for bond contracts, and that they roll down the curve (shorten in remaining maturity) for money market contracts.

In addition to the specifics, therefore, data providers construct data series that span longer periods. The simplest form are serials where active contracts are simply numbered according to their expiry date. The contract expiring soonest is the first, the next the second contract, and so on. Data providers would therefore offer a FGBM1, FGBM2, etc. series[11]. At any given point in time, each serial contract refers to one specific contract but that association changes at each expiry. For instance, in February 2019, the second Bund contract FGBM2 would be the June 2019 delivery FGBMM9 but from the March delivery onwards, the same FGBM2 would refer to FGBMU9. In this sense, the expressions 'front contract' and 'back contract' are serials.

A more subjective series construction is by activity where providers such as Bloomberg designate a 'most active' specific for each underlying. Such series end in A for the most active and B for the next most active. Traders therefore routinely refer to RXA in chats when they do not simply talk about 'the Bund'. The complication of these actives series is that it is not always obvious when the designation changes. Most of the time the first serial contract will also be the most active, but as explained later, trading activity switches from the front to the back contract some time before delivery.

From the traded prices of money market market futures, it is possible to build interest rate curves out to the maturity underlying the Libor rate that is linked to the furthest traded money market contract. In Yen and euros, this is roughly 1–2.5 years, and up to 10 years in the US. To look ahead a little, this is done by solving Equation (15.4) for the term rate rather than the forward rate.

---

[11] On Bloomberg accordingly these would be RX1, RX2, etc.

13.9.3 Futures trading basics

Money market futures are only one example of exchange traded futures. The daily closing price of a contract on an exchange depends on the exchange trading in the contract. For instance, it might be the last traded price or some average of the prices seen over the last few minutes of trading. Given the margining mechanism, this price has limited relevance as it may be corrected on the next trading day. On the last trading day of a futures contract, however, the final price (also called the exchange-determined settlement price EDSP) is given by the Libor fixing, as explained above. This ties the trading of the contract to the underlying money market rate. After the fixing, the exchange will calculate a final margin payment and returns the sum of the last day's variation margin and the initial margin to the investors. Contracts where a fixing determines the final settlement price and closing out is done through the normal daily margin mechanism are called cash-settled contracts as opposed to physically settled contracts, such as most bond futures contracts.

13.9.4 Convexity adjustment

The price calculation of a money market futures contract Equation (13.13) implies:

$$\frac{\partial^2}{\partial r^2} F = 0 \tag{13.14}$$

This is different from a simple money market deposit. By Equation (13.2) the price of the deposit is given by:

$$P = \frac{1}{1 + r * DCF} \tag{13.15}$$

so the second derivative is:

$$\frac{\partial^2}{\partial r^2} P = \frac{2DCF^2(1 + r * DCF)}{(1 + r * DCF)^4} > 0 \tag{13.16}$$

The second derivative of price with respect to interest rate is the convexity of a fixed income instrument. In the derivatives world, the same quantity is called gamma.

Here, the convexity of a deposit is always positive while that of a money market contract would appear to be strictly zero. In practice, the requirement to post variation margin against a futures position means that money market futures do in fact have convexity. A trader holding a long position in the future will have to post additional margin when rates rise because the mark-to-market value of the future declines. If the trader has to fund this margin, it will be at the new, higher, rate. If yields then decline again, the trader will receive variation margin from the clearing house but can only invest this cash at the new, lower, rate. Volatility in rates therefore leads to the trader borrowing at higher rates and investing at lower ones.

The result of this dynamic is that futures-implied rates are not unbiased estimates of future short-term rates. Instead, a trader would only buy a futures contract if the implied rate were higher than his or her expectations of future market rates, and the difference between the futures implied rate and the actual expectation is the compensation for the cost introduced by the marging requirement. This rate difference is known as the convexity adjustment and given by:

$$\Delta r = -\frac{1}{2}\sigma^2 t^2$$

(13.17)

where σ is the interest rate volatility (usually proxied by the implied volatility of options on the contract itself) and t the time to expiry of the contract. Notably, the convexity adjustment increases quadratically with time to expiry and volatility. This makes the adjustment more relevant for long-dated contracts, and more volatile short-rate markets. For the euro and yen strips, convexity adjustment play a small role because the contracts do not extend far enough into the future.

In days gone by, the convexity adjustment of a money market future was the difference between the implied rate on a futures contract and the equivalent forward-rate agreement (FRA). This was because futures contracts had margining while FRAs did not. In today's world of central or bilateral clearing, FRAs also require margining. The convexity adjustment is therefore still relevant for the building of discount curves but FRAs have become more complex to value due to xVA adjustments (discussed in Section 12.3 on page 108).

CHAPTER **14**

The Repo Market

14.1 THE REPURCHASE MARKET

The word repo is a contraction of repurchase agreement which is a sale and simultaneous buy-back, for settlement at a later date, of the same security. In essence, a repo transaction is a temporary exchange of cash against a security which is referred to as collateral in this context. This can be compared to a mortgage in retail finance. The difference between the sale and the buy-back price of the security reflects an interest rate applied to the cash leg of the transaction, known as the repo rate. Because a security changes hands in the opposite direction of the cash, a repo transaction is structurally similar to a secured deposit. The repo market can be divided into three segments, the GC market, the specials market, and the interdealer market. The duration of a repo contract (i.e., the period between sale and buyback) can range from a single day to several months, but short duration trades dominate the overall market volume in both turnover and outstanding volume. Unlike the cash bond market, the settlement of the initial trade leg can be faster than the usual T+2 timing (of course, this does not apply in those bond markets that trade T+1 or even T+0 anyway, such as US Treasuries or UK Gilts). So-called open repo trades remain in place until cancelled, usually by the collateral lender. Such trades do not have an initial maturity and usually have variable interest rates.

The general collateral (or GC) market is where investors place or borrow cash against securities from broadly defined sets, such as 'German, French or Dutch government bonds with a maturity between 1 and 10 years'. In such GC transactions, the party accepting the cash has discretion over what specific collateral is used in the transaction. Specification of collateral happens after the trade, including the repo rate, has been agreed between the parties. The focus of a GC transaction is the cash leg and GC repo is used both by cash lenders and borrowers to transact in a secure way. The GC repo rate is generally lower than the unsecured rate that would apply between the two counterparties which reflects the lower credit risk. As a matter of fact, the volume of unsecured lending between banks has declined drastically in recent years, with a corresponding increase in secured (repo) interbank lending. This shift in transaction terms results partly from increased risk awareness at banks, but also from the regulatory treatment of interbank risk on bank balance sheets.

In the specials market the security used as collateral is specified at the time the transaction is agreed. This market segment is also known as the specific market. A security is called special in the repo market when cash lenders are willing to accept a repo rate below, sometimes substantially below, the GC rate in exchange for that security. Typically this will be the case when there is a large demand to borrow that security, for instance for delivery to a futures exchange, or for market-making purposes.

Lastly, there is an interdealer market that forms the bridge between the GC and specials markets. A given security may have been lent out as GC for a longer term but since then become more sought after. The purpose of the interdealer market is to find such positions and use them to relieve shortages in the security. One reward for this service is the spread between the GC and specials rates.

There are two reasons why the repo market is so important. The first is that it is now much larger than the unsecured bank lending market. Repo reduces the credit risk in lending because collateral is available in case the borrower of the cash defaults. Second, repo makes it possible to sell securities one does not own. In the fixed income world, dealers generally are the counterparty to their customers, so a buy request from a customer is filled by selling the security to the customer with the dealer as the seller. This is very different from the equity world where the buy request is usually just forwarded to the next exchange. The dealer can only deliver the security the buyer asks for if the dealer either owns is or has a way to borrow it. Given the hundreds of bond issues traded actively in most bond markets, holding each of them in inventory would be prohibitively expensive. With an active repo market, the dealer can simply borrow a bond requested by a customer and buy the bond back later in the market or from another customer when it becomes available. In this case, the driving force of the trade is not a cash-rich institution wishing to place cash as in a deposit. Instead, it is a dealer wishing to borrow a security. Hence, traders speak of 'buying a security in repo' instead of calling the same transaction 'lending cash in repo'.

There are different GC rates for different collateral standards. For instance, Italian GC (where any Italian government bond is elegible collateral) trades at a marginally higher rate than German GC because Italian government bonds are seen as having slightly higher credit risk.

However, when there is high demand for borrowing a particular security, the security is said to be special and a lower rate is being paid on the cash that is being lent than in GC transactions. This is because the trader lending the cash is willing to accept a lower income on the cash in return for having that particular security. A given security is said to be '20 bp special' when the cash rate at which it can be bought (borrowed) is 20 basis points lower than the GC rate. A security is usually special only for certain time horizons, e.g., until the next futures contract delivery or until a new bond is being auctioned. Hence, an issue can be '100 bp special in overnight' and '10 bp special in 1 month', meaning that the repo rate for borrowing the issue for one day is 100 basis points below the overnight GC rate but when the issue is borrowed for a whole month, the rate is only 10 bp below the one month GC rate. Because repo is generally quoted in terms of collateral borrowing, the bid rate in repo is higher than the offer rate.

Repo rates depend on the type of clearing used. Centrally cleared repos imply lower balance sheet cost, and therefore structurally lower repo rates, than bilateral repos. A specific form of repo where the securities do not change hands but are instead held at a trusted third party (tri-party repo) has a similar effect as central clearing and is becoming more dominant.

14.2　HAIRCUT

Although the repo rate is the main economic variable in repo transactions, another important factor is the so-called haircut. The haircut is a percentage amount of collateral notional that is disregarded for the purpose of calculating the amount of cash that can be borrowed against this collateral. For instance, at a haircut of 1% and with collateral worth JPY 10bn (market value), only 9.9bn in cash can be borrowed. The haircut protects the cash lender against variations in the collateral value in the period it takes to either unwind the repo transaction, or replenish collateral. The amount of haircut, therefore, depends on collateral quality and the price volatility of the collateral. Government bond collateral usually has haircuts of 0% to 1% depending on maturity while equity haircuts can be around the 50% level.

Haircuts can also depend on the relative credit risk of the contracting parties. Because a higher haircut means that the securities lender transfers more value to the cash lender than the cash amount received, the securities lender is exposed to the risk that the cash lender defaults and the securities lender faces losses on the extra securities lent. This setup is the reason why central banks (who, in theory, cannot default on commitments in their own currency) can impose high haircuts on their counterparties. This ability to enforce asymmetric terms on repo counterparties is important because central banks tend to face wrong-way risk in the securities they receive. This concept refers to the high correlation between the value of the collateral, and the stability of the borrowing bank. Because banks are exposed, in various ways, to the borrowers that issue the collateral they use for funding, the value of the collateral is likely to decline at the same time as the borrowing bank becomes less sound, i.e., when the collateral is most important.

Usually, repo counterparties agree to revalue the collateral on a daily basis and to post or return collateral depending on the observed price changes. This is one example of mark-to-market.

14.3　VARIATIONS OF REPURCHASE TRANSACTIONS

Aside from straight repo, there are a number of other ways of achieving the same effect. The problem with repo is that in many markets the legal system does not recognise that lending the securities and returning them is the same transaction. This means that one counterparty in the trade is not completely covered in case the other side defaults. This problem is particularly important in cross-border lending. There are other transactions that are economically equivalent to repo, but have different legal structures. These are:

Securities lending Almost like repo without the cash leg, the lender lends the security in return for a fee. The fee is calculated from an interest rate that is effectively the spread between GC and the special rate of the security. Securities lending can be collateralised so that the securities lender receives another security for the duration of the lending operation. Such a transaction is also known as a collateral swap, which can have the purpose of collateral transformation. For instance, the holder A of a security X may wish to borrow cash from a lender B with particular lending standards that do not permit X as collateral. This might not be because X is of low quality but perhaps because X is not denominated in a particular currency, or located in a particular CSD.

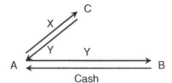

The borrower A can use a collateral swap with a third party C to transform the collateral X into collateral Y which is acceptable to B. In this case, the funding cost for A is equal to the sum of the repo rate charged by B and the lending fee charged by C. For C, normally a large asset manager, the lending fee in effect increases the return on asset Y.

An important case of collateral upgrades was the Term Securities Lending Facility (TSLF) announced by the Fed in June 2009. Under the TSLF, primary dealers could borrow US Treasury securities from the Fed's SOMA portfolio against posting investment grade corporate and mortgage bonds, for a fee that was set at auction. In the middle of the financial crisis, this programme served to increase the quality of the collateral available for private sector repos, and so helped to improve the redistribution of cash between private sector entities.

Sell-and-buyback The repo transaction is documented as an outright sale and a subsequent buyback at a later time. The price at which the buyback is executed is fixed at the time of the initial sale and reflects the repo rate at which the bond is trading. The cash flows and securities flows are the same as in a normal repo, but some problems are introduced. For instance, the seller must realise any capital gains or losses on the securities and faces the possibility that in the case of default, the securities sold will not be returned. Instead, other securities or cash may be returned.

Tri-party repo In this transaction, the collateral securities are not transferred to the cash lender and are instead held in trust by a third party. Usually, that third party is a depository institution or a clearing house. This tri-party repo can eliminate the need to actually transfer securities if both the cash lender and cash borrower are able to use this third party as their clearer. Although tri-party is not really useful for the purpose of borrowing securities, it is much cheaper than standard repo and so more efficient for secured cash lending.

Straight repo is used by many central banks to create money. The ECB main refinancing and longer term lending operations are generally repos although the ECB can also use outright buying and selling of securities to control liquidity. The Bank of

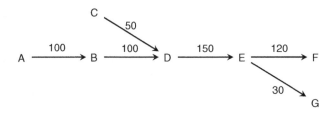

FIGURE 14.1   Example of rehypothecation of a single security. Letters designate counterparties and numbers the amount of collateral posted.

Japan uses repos (gensaki) together with outright buying and selling (formerly known as rinban). The Fed, on the other hand, mainly uses outright purchases and sales. When a central bank uses repo as the main liquidity tool, banks looking to fund in that currency usually have to have a branch in the respective country in order to be able to participate.

14.4   REHYPOTHECATION

It is possible that the counterparty receiving collateral uses the same collateral for another repo transaction until it is due to be returned. In some cases, this can lead to long chains of transactions where the same collateral is reused several times, as shown in Figure 14.1. This is known as rehypothecation and sometimes viewed as problematic. Note that collateral received can be fully or partly rehypothecated, and rehypothecated collateral can come from multiple sources. As long as all transactions settle and mature as planned, rehypothecation presents no issue. A problem arises when one of the counterparties in the chain of rehypothecation trades fails.

Although a counterparty failure presents negligible credit risk due to the collateralisation of a repo trade, it can cause delays in the return of collateral. In the example of Figure 14.1, failure of F could delay the return of collateral to E which would then propagate a failure all the way back to A and C, the original suppliers of the collateral. Note that A and C need not be aware of the existence of F, much less its economic situation. In case of a failure of G, an additional question becomes obvious: the collateral held could have come completely from A, or completely from C, or be a mixture of both. The extent to which A and C should be affected is not clear. A failure of F would clearly have to affect both.

Regulators are now looking into ways to address these issues, and in particular limit the number of links in such chains. The example shows why this is not a trivial issue. E receives collateral from A and C, and in doing so is the third link in the chain starting at A but only the second in the chain starting at C. While modern securities clearing systems can easily track beneficial ownership of individual pieces of securities, tracking such rehypothecation chains would require much more data processing.

CHAPTER 15

Spot and Forward Rates

15.1 FORWARD RATES

Forward rates are the bridge between interest rates of different horizons. One can ask the following question: Assume one can lend money from now (t_0) until t_1 at the rate $r_1(t_0, t_1)$ and until $t_2 > t_1$ at the rate $r_2(t_0, t_2)$. At which future rate $r_f(t_1, t_2)$ does one need to be able to lend money between t_1 and t_2 so one has the same return from lending from t_0 to t_1 and then from t_1 to t_2 as from lending straight from t_0 to t_2? The meaning of these rates is shown in Figure 15.1.

15.2 NO-ARBITRAGE CALCULATIONS

Using discount factors, the answer is quite simple. Discounting a given amount of cash from t_2 back to t_0 gives a present value of $Df(t_0, t_2)$. Discounting the same amount of cash back to t_1 gives the forward present value $Df(t_1, t_2)$. To bring this forward present value back to t_0, one has to multiply by the discount factor $Df(t_0, t_1)$, so the present value is $Df(t_0, t_1)Df(t_1, t_2)$. Because this present value reflects the same future cashflow, the following equation must hold in the absence of arbitrage:

$$Df(t_0, t_2) = Df(t_0, t_1)Df(t_1, t_2) \qquad (15.1)$$

and so trivially the forward discount factor is:

$$Df(t_1, t_2) = \frac{Df(t_0, t_2)}{Df(t_0, t_1)} \qquad (15.2)$$

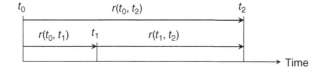

FIGURE 15.1 Relationship of spot and forward rates.

Discount factors are the fundamental building blocks of fixed income mathematics, but the market uses interest rates. Therefore, while forward discount factors are easy to calculate, they need to be translated back into interest rates.

In the money market, the relationship between interest rates and discount factor is given by the prices of pure discount instruments. For instance, the price of a deposit paying 1 yen in six months is equal to the six months discount factor. Depending on the market, these prices are given by Equation (13.2) or Equation (13.4). If simple yields are used, Equation (15.2) becomes:

$$\frac{1}{1 + r(t_1, t_2)DCF(t_1, t_2)} = \frac{1 + r(t_0, t_1)DCF(t_0, t_1)}{1 + r(t_0, t_2)DCF(t_0, t_2)} \tag{15.3}$$

and therefore:

$$r(t_1, t_2) = \frac{1}{DCF(t_1, t_2)} \left(\frac{1 + r(t_0, t_2)DCF(t_0, t_2)}{1 + r(t_0, t_1)DCF(t_0, t_1)} - 1 \right) \tag{15.4}$$

If one instead uses discount rates, Equation (15.2) has the simpler form:

$$1 - r(t_1, t_2)DCF(t_1, t_2) = \frac{1 - r(t_0, t_2)DCF(t_0, t_2)}{1 - r(t_0, t_1)DCF(t_0, t_1)} \tag{15.5}$$

and the forward rate is:

$$r(t_1, t_2) = \frac{1}{DCF(t_1, t_2)} \left(1 - \frac{1 - r(t_0, t_2)DCF(t_0, t_2)}{1 - r(t_0, t_1)DCF(t_0, t_1)} \right) \tag{15.6}$$

Note that, although the equations look very similar, they are in fact subtly different.

As mentioned in the section on money market futures, it is possible, and indeed the normal course of action, to construct spot rates from the current traded values of the Libor futures strip. In this case, the only spot rate taken from the deposit market is the so-called cash stub or stub rate that corresponds to the cash rate until the start of the reference period of the first Libor contract. From that date on, the futures implied interest rate is taken as a forward deposit rate and the spot rate to the end of the first contract's reference period is calculated according to Equation (15.2).

In principle, therefore, the term structure of money market rates is built from the stub rate which is successively extended using money market futures-implied rates using the recursive relationship:

$$1 + r(t_0, t_{i+1})DCF(t_0, t_{i+1}) = (1 + r(t_0, t_i)DCF(t_0, t_i)) *$$
$$(1 + r(t_i, t_{i+1})DCF(t_i, t_{i+1})) \tag{15.7}$$

Note that the futures-implied forward rates require a convexity adjustment following Equation (13.17) before being used to produce the forward rates in Figure 15.2.

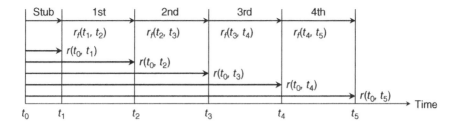

FIGURE 15.2 Relationship of Libor strip with the spot rate term structure.

15.3 OFFICIAL RATES VERSUS TERM RATES

Money creation can be influenced using different means but generally there is a concept of a policy rate or official rate that reflects the opinion of the central bank as to the appropriate level of borrowing rates in the economy. The official rate is most naturally a short rate because the central bank needs to ensure that changes in the policy rate feed quickly through into the economy. The longer existing deposits at the old rate are running off, the slower the impact of a policy change would be.

Because official rates in developed economies tend to be adjusted more frequently than other factors influencing money creation (such as reserve requirements), market attention is focused on the official rates and the front end of the interest rate curve is driven by expectations of changes in the official rates.

In general, official rates refer to the specific interest rates that a central bank can target through its open market operations. These operations do not necessarily start immediately after a change in the official rate has been decided by the central bank. Furthermore, market interest rates are not usually quoted on horizons that are adjusted to central bank policy decisions but in round maturities such as 'three months'. The relationship between official rates and the liquid market rates is therefore not trivial and it is important to understand the exact working of the central bank to understand the relationship.

15.3.1 The turn premium

Before discussing the extraction of policy rates from observed interest rates, it is important to explain a technical effect in the money market known as the turn premium. Banks have daily control over their balance sheet but balance sheet data has to be submitted to regulators on a periodical basis. The most important balance sheet date is year end, which usually coincides with the calendar year, but may be on some other date, such as 1st April in Japan.

Banks have a strong incentive to shrink their balance sheets towards year end, also called the turn[1], in order to report the least risky assets on that occasion. Banks will therefore be more reluctant to conduct business, such as lending, when the transaction

---

[1] This term relates to the expression 'the turn of the year'.

spans a year end than they are when the transaction opens and closes within the same year. As a result, interbank lending rates tend to jump when the horizon of the lending transaction spans year end. For instance, 3M deposit rates in most markets will jump in late September when the maturity changes from December to January. This is the turn effect. Although interest rates move daily, the turn effect is always positive, so it can be distinguished from normal fluctuations. Naturally, the turn premium is also reflected in forward rates and money market futures prices.

The size of the turn premium is not constant and is subject to supply and demand. Given sufficient data points (observable rates), one can establish a forward rate from the last day of the year to the first day of the following year. The difference between this interest rate and the neighbouring overnight rates is the turn premium proper and it usually ranges around a few percent. Exceptionally large turn premia could be observed in some markets on occasions where the new year coincided with market changes, such as the introduction of the euro in 1998/1999, the Y2K worries in 1999/2000, and the introduction of euro cash in 2000/2001. In more recent times, the introduction of the leverage ratio has led to spikes in repo market rates around turn dates. While this regulatory tool remains in place, turn premia have declined as market participants adjusted their behaviour, particularly by funding earlier.

The extent of the turn premium depends to some degree on the instrument used. An unsecured interbank loan has a different balance sheet treatment from a repo transaction, or an overnight index swap. Central banks generally limit the impact of the turn on their policy rate, so different rate instruments will reflect the turn to differing degrees. It is important to keep in mind that the turn premium is unrelated to any changes in the economy, and therefore the 'natural' level of interest rates or the policy rate. Therefore, the turn premium needs to be compensated for when extracting policy rate expectations from market rates.

15.3.2   Matching policy expectations to market rates

The basic way of reconciling policy expectations with observed rates is to use an overnight account and roll this account using the expected path of the policy rate. In doing so, any differences between the policy rate and market rates need to be adjusted for.

In Figure 15.3, there is one assumed path of the policy rate, shown as a thick line near the bottom of the chart. From that policy path, one derives an assumed path of overnight rates, taking into account any expected differences in level and timing of changes. For instance, ECB policy MRO rate changes are decided upon and announced on Thursdays, but only apply to the next MRO which settles on the following Wednesday. At the same time, there may be differences between the policy rate and the market rate. For instance Figure 6.2 on page 49 shows that the overnight benchmark rate in the euro area differed from what was at the time the main policy rate. In addition, actual market rates may have turn effects which also need to be taken into account. With a projected path of overnight rates, one can track the value of a deposit made at time t_0 until time t which is in essence the inverse of the discount factor $Df(t_o, t)$.

From the compounded value of the overnight account, one can extract the complete term structure of interest rates and forwards. The expected policy path, i.e., the sequence

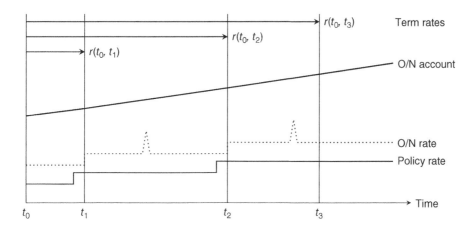

FIGURE 15.3 The hierarchy of matching policy rate expectations to observed market rates. The ordering along the vertical axis does not imply the level of rates.

of imputed policy rate changes, is then adjusted so as to achieve the best possible overall fit with market rates.

Typically, one abstracts away from the discrete nature of policy changes (usually 25 bp) and allows any amount of rate changes. Changes are then interpreted as probabilities of discrete changes, i.e., a 10 bp implied change is interpreted as a 40% probability of a 25 bp change. Note that the resulting probability picture hides the effect of cumulative probabilities. For instance, one may obtain 50% probabilities of a 25 bp change in the policy rate in two successive meetings. This should usually not be interpreted as a 25% probability of two consecutive hikes (as would be possible if the probabilities were strict unconditional probabilities), but rather that the market expects exactly one 25 bp hike, but is split as to the exact timing. Therefore, while talking about probabilities is standard usage, it is important to realise that this is just a loose manner of speaking.

In any case, policy changes on the overnight account are applied only on those days when they could actually occur. This means that the meeting calendar of the respective central bank is part of the inputs to the fitting process. Otherwise, the solution space becomes too large.

As can be surmised from the picture, a number of concerns need to be addressed when using market rates to infer policy changes. These are discussed below.

Basis of cash versus policy rates In some cases, the most liquid cash rate is actually a different instrument from the policy rate. For instance, the policy rate of the ECB is a repo rate while Euribor is an unsecured rate. The credit spread incorporated in unsecured lending will therefore introduce a maturity-dependent basis. The basis can be corrected for using observable spreads that reflect a similar basis, such as the Libor–GC spreads for different terms.

Term structure and other effects As has been discussed when introducing the turn effect, market interest rates are driven by factors other than central bank policy changes. The turn effect is an obvious example, but more significant in economic terms is the impact of the term risk premium. This premium, which is not observable in the market, is a spread over the interest rates that would be consistent with an overnight account rolling at the policy rate. The premium reflects the fact that lenders committing to a term deposit give up the option to reinvest the money elsewhere, which is an option that an overnight investor has. The term risk premium grows with longer investment horizons and is not constant through time. While models for the term risk premium exist, they usually work on timescales that are not relevant for forecasting central bank actions.

Normally, the term risk premium is simply ignored because it is assumed to be growing sufficiently slowly with the maturity of the underlying instrument. This is acceptable for short horizons. However, it is important to keep in mind that a flat term structure reflects rate cut expectations compensating the increasing term risk premium.

Futures vs cash basis There is a basis between the interest rate futures markets and the underlying cash rates that is created by the convexity bias of futures contracts. This is addressed in Equation (13.17).

It should be noted that all of these factors can change, and so can the monetary policy framework. At the time of writing, developed countries' financial markets operate in an environment of excess liquidity which makes the lower end of interest rate corridors binding. In more normal environments, this may not be the case. Such changes would affect the modelling of the translation from policy rates into market rates in Figure 15.3.

CHAPTER 16

The Bond Market

16.1 INTRODUCTION

Bonds are tradeable loans issued by governments, corporations, and financial institutions to raise long-term funds. Strictly speaking, there is no important legal difference between money market paper and bonds but the periodic interest paid on bonds makes the valuation slightly more complicated. While issuers are in principle free to design bonds in any way they wish, it is in practice much easier to raise debt when it has a form that is already kown to potential investors. This is why bonds tend to have certain common cashflow characteristics and why standard terms reappear in the legal documentation of bonds.

Bonds establish payment and other obligations for the issuer, as well as certain actions the issuer can take when interacting with bond holders. The total set of rights and obligations of issuer and bond holder derives from multiple sources. The most important is the governing law of the jurisdiction where the bond is issued because every jurisdiction has a set of laws dealing with debts. For sovereign issuers in their own jurisdiction, a combination of civil code and specific debt issuance laws usually complete the legal conditions of each bond. It should be noted that sovereigns can change the governing law which means that in principle they can change the terms of existing debt. Although this option can be used, and has been used, to reduce debt obligations, sovereigns using this option typically lose access to capital markets for some time.

Private issuers, or sovereign issuers issuing outside their own jurisdiction, generally need to provide more specific legal terms for bonds which is generally done in a document called the prospectus. A prospectus combines information about the issuer with specific legal terms and conditions of one or more bond issues. Typical clauses that can appear in a prospectus are discussed further below. A prospectus is a legal document and the contents of this document are subject to strict regulation in many jurisdictions. Such regulation generally aims at establishing a common minimal set of information disclosure about the issuer rather than specific legal provisions for the bonds themselves. The production of a prospectus is expensive because it requires a lot of legal and accounting work. Issuers can save costs by producing only one prospectus for a series of bonds that they plan to issue. Such a series of bonds is called a programme and correspondingly the prospectus would be called a programme or base prospectus. Depending on the type of debt issued under a programme, the programme itself might be referred to as for instance an EMTN (euro medium-term note) or CP (commercial paper) programme.

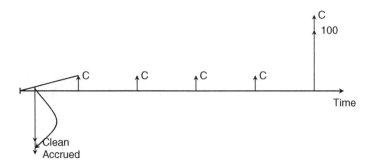

FIGURE 16.1 Simple annual fixed rate bullet bond structure. The bond repays its par amount at the maturity date. The bond has regular accrual periods so every coupon payment is equal to the nominal coupon C. A purchase transaction is indicated with negative cash flows (the consideration paid to the seller of the bond) and the consideration is split into clean price and accrued interest.

When issuing under a programme, issuers issue new bonds with simplified terms and conditions documents that simply reference the relevant programme prospectus.

Bonds can be classified along a number of criteria, such as their cashflow structure, issuer type, or legal features. From an economic point of view, the cashflow structure is the most important feature of a bond because it determines the valuation approach used to price and hedge the security. For visualisation purposes, it is convenient to think of the cashflows as arrows on a timeline as shown in Figure 16.1.

It should always be borne in mind that while cashflows are fungible for the purpose of valuing bonds in the absence of default risk, there is an important legal difference between coupon and redemption payments in defaults. In most jurisdictions insolvency triggers an immediate claim on payment of the remaining principal due to investors, plus any accrued interest. These claims exclude the right to payment of future coupons that have not yet started accruing. The present value of future coupons therefore usually declines when the credit quality of a bond deteriorates because it becomes less likely that they will ever get paid. The present value of the principal might instead even increase because it will get paid earlier (albeit probably only in part).

16.2 CASHFLOW TYPES

16.2.1 Bullet bonds

Bonds usually pay interest in the form of coupons at regular intervals called coupon periods. Depending on the length of coupon period, bonds are classified as annual, semi-annual, quarterly, etc. Coupons are always stated in annualised terms, so a semi-annual bond will pay half the stated coupon twice a year, a quarterly bond will pay a quarter of the coupon four times a year and so on. The distribution of coupons to investors creates an administrative burden which makes more frequent coupons more expensive to manage. On the other hand, both issuers and investors tend to find it inconvenient to deal with few large cashflows per year. This would favour higher coupon frequencies. The compromise eventually chosen by issuers reflects the relative importance of these concerns. Note that institutional bond portfolios (and the liabilities of larger issuers) can avoid bunching of cashflows by diversifying across many bonds.

Coupon rates, expressed in percentages, are in most markets binary, rather than decimal, fractions for historical reasons. Usually, these fractions are multiples of eighths because bonds are often issued in certificates referring to 1,000 in the local currency (euros, dollars, etc), and the smallest fraction that can be paid in whole cents (i.e., the local version of the small denomination) is one eighth[1]. Binary coupons have the added advantage of some redundancy when expressed in decimal form. For instance, a coupon of 3.152 on a bond from an issuer that usually has binary fractions can usually be identified as a typo. Decimal coupons are used for government bonds in Japan, Spain, and other countries, and private issuers sometimes choose decimal fractions down to 1/1,000th of a percent to place new bonds exactly at par value.

Even with fixed rate bullet bonds, cashflow structures can have minor complications. It is quite common that the time period between the first accrual day (the day when a bond begins to accrue an interest payment obligation for the issuer) is longer or shorter than a regular coupon period. In such cases of so-called long first coupon or short first coupon bonds, the first coupon payment is adjusted upwards or downwards, respectively, to reflect the different accrual period. Less commonly, the last coupon period can be shorter than a regular coupon period, with a correspondingy smaller last coupon period. Such structures occur for instance in Japanese municipal bonds.

A related class of bonds, floating-rate notes, have regular coupon payments that are variable. These FRNs are discussed in Chapter 17 because their valuations are very different from fixed coupon bonds. Inflation-linked bonds, where in most cases a fixed coupon is adjusted for changes in some price level, also merit a separate chapter, Chapter 23.

16.2.2 Zero coupon bonds, perpetuals and annuities

A special class of fixed rate bond pays no interest at all and is known as a zero-coupon bond, or zero. The equivalent of interest income for these bonds arises because they are issued below par, generating a capital gain towards redemption.

Aside from money market instruments, zeros tend to be created as the result of stripping coupon bonds, i.e., splitting coupon bonds into separate payments of coupons

---

[1] A sixteenth of a percent of 1,000 euros is 62.5 cents.

and principal[2]. It should be borne in mind that a zero coupon bond is different from a coupon bond with a fixed coupon of 0% even though both only have a single payment flow at maturity. While a zero has no natural coupon frequency, a 0% fixed rate bond has the same coupon frequency as a related bond with a coupon above 0%. For instance, a 0% BTPS (Italian government bond) would naturally have a semi-annual coupon frequency while a 0% OBL (German government bond) would have an annual coupon frequency even though neither actually pays a coupon. The coupon frequency can affect the calculation of yields and is therefore important. For zero coupon bonds, the coupon frequency tends to be derived from related securities but is not as straightforwardly defined.

Another important aspect of zero coupon bonds is their tax and accounting treatment. Many jurisdictions treat interest income differently from capital gains. Some investors also prefer to have income deferred, for instance because they work in a progressive income tax system and would like to be able to pay tax on their investment income when they are retired and in a lower tax bracket. Zero coupon bonds appear ideal from this point of view because investors realise their return when the bond repays. Tax authorities are of course aware of this issue and accordingly tend to treat zeros differently from coupon bonds.

In accounting terms, a zero coupon bond that is a coupon stripped from a coupon-bearing bond is not treated as a long-term liability of the issuer in the same way that the principal obligation is. Interest payable at market rates is recorded differently from the principal obligation, and creating what looks like a principal zero-coupon payment from a coupon does not change the indebtedness of the issuer.

In some way, the opposite of zero coupon bonds are perpetual bonds, also called perpetuals.

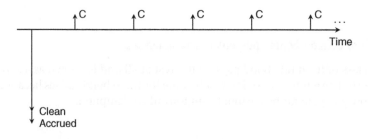

While a zero only makes a principal repayment but pays no coupons, a perpetual bond pays only coupons but never repays the principal. The only way to redeem a perpetual bond is a buy-back by the issuer (here, the holder has to be willing to sell), or, if this is part of the bond prospectus, a call (an early repayment at the sole discretion of the issuer). Sometimes, the word consol is used interchangeably with the word perpetual but this is somewhat inaccurate. A consol, or more explicitly a consolidated loan, is a form of United Kingdom government debt that was created by consolidating various

---

[2]The (most certainly apocryphal) acronym STRIPS stands for Separate TRading of Interest and Principal Securities. The first strips were created by physically stripping coupons from paper bond certificates.

earlier outstanding annuities into a single issue in 1754 [57][3]. Several consols were issued over the years but the oldest remaining consol, the $2\frac{1}{2}$% Annuities, created in 1853, was finally redeemed on 5 July 2015. Other perpetual bonds from private issuers remain, but typically have call features that all but ensure a finite expected lifetime. Perpetuals that could be redeemed at the discretion of the borrower were used in 18th century France as a way of circumventing usury laws because the absence of a fixed repayment date made these instruments look less like a loan [60].

Perpetuals are an example of an annuity, a bond that pays fixed cashflows at regular intervals[4]. While perpetuals have an infinite maturity, other annuities make regular payments that mix principal repayments with interest payments. Because the repayment of principal happens over time, such bonds are also called amortising bonds.

The most common form of a finite maturity annuity is an amortising mortgage where the annuity payments P are calculated according to the formula:

$$P = N_0 \frac{r}{1 - (1 + r)^{-n}} \tag{16.1}$$

for n payments (i.e. for semi-annual payments over N years, $n = 2N$) and an annualised interest rate of $c = fr$ (i.e., $f = 2$ for semiannual payments of $f = 12$ for a usual consumer mortgage). The initial notional of the bond is N_0. Note that banks tend to use this formula when quoting mortgage repayment amounts to customers even when interest rates are reset periodically so that c is not constant over time as assumed in Equation (16.1).

Based on Equation (16.1), one can calculate the remaining principal amount of the annuity in period k ($0 \leq k \leq n$):

$$N_k = N_0 \left[(1 + r)^k - \frac{(1 + r)^k - 1}{1 - (1 + r)^{-n}} \right] \tag{16.2}$$

with the special values $N_k = N_0$ for $k = 0$ and $N_n = 0$. It should be remembered that the standard convention is to quote bond prices in percentages of the remaining principal outstanding. Here, this is would be N_k, not N_0.

The interest amount I_k that is paid on payment date k is simply the product of r and the principal outstanding at $k - 1$, N_{k-1}. Specifically,

$$I_k = N_0 \frac{r[(1 + r)^n - (1 + r)^{k-1}]}{(1 + r)^n - 1} \tag{16.3}$$

The amortisation payment A_k made at payment date k, $P - I_k$ is:

$$A_k = N_0 \frac{r(1 + r)^{k-1}}{(1 + r)^n - 1} = P - I_k \tag{16.4}$$

---

[3]According to the UK Debt Management Office, this 3% annuity was first issued in 1752.
[4]The word annuity does not imply an annual coupon frequency. UK perpetuals were called annuities although they had semi-annual or quarterly coupons.

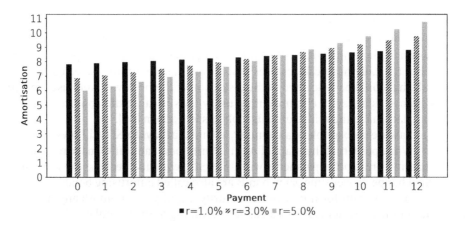

FIGURE 16.2 The amortisation payments A_k of an annuity for different interest rates ($n = 12$). The higher interest rates are the more back-loaded the repayment of principal becomes.

Examples of bonds following this convention are Icelandic Housing Finance Fund (HFF) bonds. These are semi-annual bonds with a quoted interest rate of 3.75%. In this case, $r = 1.875\%$. The payments P depend on the initial maturity of the bonds. For the 2024 bond, which had an initial maturity of 20 years, $n = 40$ so that $P = 3.5759128$ while for the 2034 bond with an initial maturity of 30 years, $n = 60$ and $P = 2.7903945$. This highlights that for finite maturity annuities, the stated interest rate does not provide an immediate clue on the bond cashflows. A 3.75% US Treasury bond would simply pay 1.875% coupons twice a year and par at maturity.

Note that while Equation (16.1) does not allow $r = 0$ directly, one can use the observation that for small r, $1/(1 + r) \approx 1 - r$ to work out that $\lim_{r \to 0} P = N_0/n$. Intuitively, for zero interest rates a finite maturity annuity is simply a repayment of the original principal in equal installments. For higher interest rates, the repayment of principal is pushed backwards (cf. Figure 16.2).

In contrast to annuity bonds following the standard amortisation convention, straight-line amortising bonds have cashflows that comprise interest and a fixed share of the original principal being amortised. Cashflows therefore vary (decline) even when the bonds have a fixed interest rate.

16.3   ISSUER TYPES

Bonds can be issued by a variety of legal entities. Typically, governments issue debt under their own domestic law and these bonds form the reference for debt in that domestic market. However, governments can also issue bonds in different jurisdictions where they compete with other issuers, including the government of that jurisdiction.

In many countries, local entities below the central government, such as regions or cities, also access the bond market under their own name. Typically, funding for such entities is a mix of own-name bond issuance in the so-called municipal or sub-sovereign bond market, loans from special funding vehicles that pool municipal debt and issue in the bond market under their own name, and bank loans of various types. Many countries have government-supported specialist banks that act as funding vehicles for municipalities, such as Dexia Municipal Agency in Belgium, or Agence France Locale in France. For instance, Japanese municipalities (prefectures and large cities) fund through:

- bond issues under their own names,
- joint municipal bond issues in varying compositions,
- loans from the Japanese Funding for Municipalities agency (JFM) which is jointly owned by the municipalities,
- bank loans.

German regional entities (Länder) can raise funds from:

- bond issues under their own names,
- joint Länder issues in varying compositions,
- bank loans.

A single joint issue of the German federal government and the Länder exists but has been judged not to be cost effective. Unlike Japanese municipalities, which are liable jointly for all of the outstanding joint municipal bonds they participate in, German Länder are only liable for their share in each issue which means that each bond issue has a different credit risk structure. In practice, few investors view this as a problem.

In the United States in particular, there is a set of municipal bonds that is tied to specific investment projects, the so-called project bonds. Unlike a standard municipal bond, where investors have the general revenues of the issuing entity as sources of repayment to rely on, project bonds are linked to the revenue of a specific project, such as a toll bridge or sewage system. There may in some instances be some credit support from the issuing municipality, but in all cases investors need to be aware of the specifics of that project and the financing sources. Project bonds have had mixed success in other countries.

Banks form the next larger issuer group and use their bonds to refinance their loan and investment activity. International banks tend to be corporate entities with a large number of subsidiaries, some of which are pure funding vehicles. Investors need to pay attention to the specific legal entity that issues a particular bond, and how that entity is being supported by the overall corporate structure. Various types of support exist, from outright guarantees to so-called letters of comfort which are a weaker form of support. Bank bonds are often held by other banks as a form of investment because bank debt has preferential treatment under some bank capital regulations. A specific form of bank bond, covered bonds, is discussed separately in Chapter 25.

In the US, specialist companies have been set up to source cheap funding for mortgage loans. While these are known in the US as agencies, only some of the issuers are actually government agencies. The two largest issuers, Fannie Mae and Freddie Mac (after their acronyms FHLMC and FRMC) are private-law corporations and therefore more correctly named government-sponsored entities (GSEs). The term agency is in other jurisdictions reserved for issuers that are indeed public sector entities, such as CADES in France or Landesrentenbank in Germany.

Non-financial corporations issue bonds as an alternative to loan funding. As such, only corporations that can successfully appeal to investors have access to the bond market. Such corporations tend to have long-established names, large and stable cash flow, and stable earnings. The largest corporate issuers are therefore utilities, car manufacturers, airlines, etc., while newer technology companies rarely access the bond market. Companies with higher growth rates tend to rely more on bank loans and various classes of equity for funding. As with banks, investors need to be aware that a given corporation may issue bonds from a funding vehicle, a special-purpose company in a tax-friendly jurisdiction[5]. Exactly how the funding vehicle is able to repay bonds from the funds of the parent company is important for investors.

Smaller companies can issue bonds but the market for such debt tends to be less stable. Germany, for instance, has had a relatively vibrant market for bonds issued by medium-sized companies but a spate of high-profile defaults has diminished the standing of this asset class.

In some cases, legal entities are created solely for the purpose of issuing debt that refinances particular assets. Such entities are called special-purpose vehicles, or SPV and the resulting debt instruments are usually called asset-backed securities or ABS. The creation of an SPV can have multiple purposes. The buyer or a particular bond may have a preference for a different cashflow structure and ask an investment bank to repackage that bond with a set of derivatives to change the cashflow structure. In other cases, the SPV is set up to be the legal owner of a set of cashflows and exists to sell these cashflows, after suitable transformation, to investors. In either case, the assets in the SPV, and obligations that the SPV may have besides the debt it issues, are important considerations for investors.

16.3.1   Joint issuance

There are some instances where multiple legal entities issue joint bonds. This means that a single bond provides funding to multiple entities. It also means that multiple entities are responsible for the repayment and coupons of these bonds. Examples of such issues are Länder bonds issued by varying consortia of German states, and joint municipal bonds issued by Japanese prefectures. Beyond such examples of joint issuance by entities of similar properties, there is a single example of a bond issued jointly by some German states and the German federal government.

The proceeds of the bond issuance are shared among the issuing consortia according to some pre-determined key and under normal circumstances that key also determines the relative share of the debt service obligation. When one of the participants of the consortium is no longer able to service the debt, the question arises what happens with the corresponding share of the obligation. There are two fundamental models known as several liability, and joint and several liability. Under several (but not joint) liability, the entities of the consortium are liable for their share of the liability but not those of other members. Under joint and several liability, each member of the consortium is liable for the entire issue. Joint and several liability is a substantial source of

---

[5]The Netherlands are a common jurisdiction for many corporate issuers.

risk for consortium members because they may have to repay the obligations of others. Joint and several liability is therefore more common when there are few and closely connected borrowers, such as married couples entering a mortgage contract. Japanese joint municipal bonds are also issued under joint and several liability, in this case because there is a very strong fiscal redistribution system in Japan that in effect ties the fiscal strengths of the prefectures closely together. The German joint Länder issues, meanwhile, have several but not joint liability.

In a ruling of September 2006 ([15]) the German constitutional court set extremely high hurdles for mutual fiscal support among German states. That ruling drew substantially on the idea of moral hazard to come to the conclusion that federal fiscal redistribution measures are not suited to the remedy of debt sustainability problems. In essence, the German court ruled that local fiscal autonomy is difficult to reconcile with joint fiscal liability. The Japanese local finance system, which was reformed after the Yubari shock of 2007, foresees an increasing level of oversight and control of local authorities when their fiscal situation deteriorates. As a result, local fiscal flexibility is diminished in situations where joint fiscal responsibility may become more necessary. The German argument would therefore not contradict the approach taken by Japan, but just reflects different choices about the limits of local authority.

At the EU level, the issue of joint debt issuance as been discussed multiple times. The European Community (the predecessor of the European Union) reacted to the economic aftermath of the 1970s oil crisis by issuing bonds to refinance loans to energy, industry and infrastructure sectors (Decision 78/870/EEC). Known as the Ortoli facility[6], the loans were made to companies across the European community. The bonds were liabilities of the EC, not of the member states, and their repayment was backed in the first instance by the the repayment of the loans that were made with the funds raised. The European Community budget provided additional credit support to these bonds with the result that they carried AAA credit ratings. Two aspects differentiate these bonds from the German joint Länder and Japanese joint municipal bonds, however. First, the issuing entity is not a consortium but a single entity. Unlike the members of the issuance consortia, the EC members have no explicit obligation to provide the funds to repay the bonds. Instead, the EC member states have an unspecific obligation to provide the EC with funds for the budget, something known as a sufficiency guarantee. Second, the EC bonds were not fiscal instruments used to directly finance expenditure. As a result, there was no need for a fiscal capacity to repay them, such as a tax or tariff arrangement. The bond liability was designed to self-liquidate through the receipt of loan repayments. This model of raising funds for loan provision was so successful that the European Union is still issuing bonds under this model. Now as then, these bonds are obligation of the EU as a single legal entity, not of the member states.

In the aftermath of the 2008 financial crisis, efforts were made to design a new form of common borrowing instrument in the EU, this time for fiscal expenditure purposes, and with some form of joint liability of member states. No model was found to be both workable from a market perspective and compliant with the legal constraints

---

[6]Strictly speaking, the programme was called the 'New Community Instrument' in the ever romantic Brussels vernacular.

of the European Union Treaty framework. The seminal document on this process is the Green Paper on 'stability bonds' [24] which was produced with large-scale involvement of private sector experts. It concluded that joint and several liability structures conflict with the no-bailout clause (Article 125) of the Treaty on the Functioning of the European Union (TFEU), so a Treaty change would be required to implement them. Other models under discussion at the time, such as tranching of government bonds, are unworkable in practice[7].

One way in which to reconcile the prohibition of joint and several liabilities in Article 125 TFEU[8] with the principle of fiscal assistance of Article 122[9] is that triggering mutual guarantees arising from joint and several liabilities amounts to an ex-post fiscal transfer. A member state that wishes to obtain fiscal support from others can receive such support ex-ante through the provisions of Article 122. If joint and several liabilities were available, the same member state could obtain the same money through the issuance of such a debt instrument, and subsequently refuse to repay it. This would trigger corresponding payments from the other borrowers, amounting to ex-post fiscal support. The approach taken by the EU framework is simply that because ex-ante support is available, ex-post support adds nothing as far as mutual support is concerned. At the same time, it creates uncertain future obligations on national budgets that should be avoided.

The extent to which debt in the EU can be mutualised is also a constitutional law question related to the notion of sovereignty for each of the member states. The right to raise taxes, and to decide how they are spent, is a fundamental aspect of sovereignty. The putative motto of the Boston Tea Party, 'No taxation without representation', is an example of that. The EU framework does not provide for a full-scale transfer of national sovereignty to the EU, and fiscal authority is not included in the competencies transferred to the EU. The expenditure of the EU is therefore always pre-approved by the member states. In a 2011 ruling related to the EFSF [16], the German constitutional court opined that not only a transfer of fiscal sovereignty to the EU had not taken place, but that the German parliament was barred from enacting such a transfer by the German Basic Law. This is just one example where, even if EU law were not an obstacle to joint and several liability bonds, national consitutions may stand in the way.

16.3.2　Supranationals

While direct joint debt issuance by multiple sovereigns appears difficult, there are several examples of multi-national entities that can issue debt. In many cases, such debt

---

[7]The problems with tranching of government bonds are discussed in more details in Section 24.2.5 on page 259.

[8]'A Member State shall not be liable for or assume the commitments of central governments, regional, local or other public authorities, other bodies governed by public law, or public undertakings of another Member State, without prejudice to mutual financial guarantees for the joint execution of a specific project.'

[9]'Where a Member State is in difficulties or is seriously threatened with severe difficulties caused by natural disasters or exceptional occurrences beyond its control, the Council, on a proposal from the Commission, may grant, under certain conditions, Union financial assistance to the Member State concerned.'

issuance is backed by commitments of the nations that constituted the entity (labelled here as members). Examples are the World Bank Group (issuing debt out of one of its subsidiaries, the International Bank for Reconstruction and Development, IBRD), the European Investment Bank (EIB), the European Stability Mechanism (ESM) and the European Bank for Reconstruction and Development (EBRD). This segment of issuers is known as the supranationals, or supras. Together with regional and agency borrowers, the bonds issued by supranationals form a bond market segment known as SSA (supras, sub-sovereigns and agencies). The SSA segment is characterised by medium-sized issuance programmes (smaller than most government markets), a reasonable level of secondary market liquidity, and high credit quality compared to private sector issuance. In this sense, the SSA segment forms a bridge between the largest and most liquid government markets and high-grade private sector debt.

Not all supranational institutions issue debt, or at least not debt that is publicly tradeable. Two well-known examples are the International Monetary Fund (IMF) and the Bank for International Settlements (BIS). In both cases, the independence of operations from the vagaries of private debt markets is at least part of the raison d'être of these institutions.

A common feature of a supranational is that it does not have a fiscal function and instead raises funds for on-lending. While this on-lending may have concessionary features compared to direct market borrowing for the recipients of such loans, the loan terms still generally cover the cost of the supranational's funding and other operations. In principle, therefore, a supranational should not be dependent on ongoing support of its members. As a result, commitments of members to the supranationals are not quantifiable contingent liabilities of those members and so do not affect their debt levels directly.

Member support for supranationals usually takes the form of paid-up and callable capital. Paid-up capital is, as it would be for a private bank, invested at least partially in highly liquid assets. This liquidity reserve is designed to ensure timely payment of outstanding bonds without an immediate need to refinance in the bond market. Lending operations are funded by debt issuance. Should the available capital levels fall below requirements, members may be asked to provide additional capital. As a result, the members do not need to guarantee the debt issued by the supranational to ensure high ratings, instead they commit to replenish the capital base of the issuer when needed. Such capital calls should be the exception, not the norm, but depending on the supranational in question, they can have other political motives. If members decide to forgive part of the loans made by the supranational, they have to offset the value lost through new capital injections. In this way, nations can fund debt relief efforts through the injection of new capital into multilateral lending institutions.

16.4 GOVERNING LAW AND CONTRACTUAL CLAUSES

Bonds can be issued in the country where the borrower is resident, using the laws of that particular country to settle potential disputes between the borrower and the bond investors. Such bonds are called domestic bonds. Sometimes, however, it may be more advantageous for the borrower to issue bonds in a different market, or investors prefer to lend money on the terms of a well-known legal system. This has been done for centuries[10], but the market for such off-shore issues got an important boost from capital controls imposed by the US government and in particular the introduction of the Interest Equalization Tax (IET) in 1963. This led many US issuers to issue bonds in the London market and the resulting large market in foreign bond issuance is now called the eurobond market or the euromarket. This is now somewhat confusing because there is also the euro currency and euro bond can mean a euro-denominated issue issued in whatever market or a eurobond issue denominated in whatever currency. When precision is required, one talks about bonds as being euro-dollar, euro-yen, euro-sterling, and so on. This convention is also the reason why interest rate futures on short rates have 'euro' in their names, such as euro-dollar and euro-yen contracts. This means that the short rates refer to off-shore deposits, i.e., desposits in the euromarket. This does not necessarily mean that there are interest rates differences between the on-shore and off-shore markets.

The are informal names for off-shore bond issues issued in a particular country in this country's currency. Such names are yankee (US), samurai (Japan), kangaroo (Australia), bulldog (UK), etc. Conversely, a bond issued by a US entity in the euro market is called a reverse yankee. A particular type of samurai aimed at the Japanese retail market is called uridashi.

Bond investors usually buy bonds with a view to holding them for a long time. This means that they are exposed to changes in the business outlook of the issuer as well as to the conditions of the legal system in which the bond is issued. In order to reduce the risk of a dramatic negative change in the likelihood that the bond will pay as promised, bonds usually carry covenants that restrict the freedom of the issuer to carry out certain actions such as asset disposals, dissolution, and so on. Violating a covenant usually means that the bonds become immediately due and payable and other penalties may apply. The conditions applying to a particular bond are documented in the prospectus of a bond which is circulated to investors at the time a bond is sold. The prospectus usually also contains background and financial information about the issuer that can help making an informed investment choice. The exact requirements for a prospectus depend on the market in which a bond is sold or listed.

Typically, a so-called preliminary prospectus is distributed during the marketing period for a new bond, i.e., before the actual prospectus is distributed. The preliminary prospectus usually has a warning printed in red on its front page, stating that the prospectus is not final. For this reason, preliminary prospectuses are also called reds in the market. Frequent issuers do not produce independent prospectuses for each bond issue. Instead, they establish an issuance programme with a common prospectus that has placeholders for issues of varying conditions. Individual issues under such a programme then simply refer to the programme prospectus and add individual terms and conditions (T&Cs in short) to each issue. Where prospectuses have to be registered with

---

[10]For instance, the first Japanese long-term government bond was a sterling denominated bond issued on 23 April 1870 in order to raise finances for the first railways in Japan. The bond had a volume of 1 million pounds and a coupon of 9 percent. It was collateralised with customs revenues and three railway lines.

supervisor authorities, the use of such omnibus prospectuses is also known as shelf registration.

Sovereign issuers generally do not publish prospectuses for domestic law bonds althought they may publish short terms and conditions for individual issues. This is consistent because the general conditions applicable to domestic debts are generally regulated by the relevant civil law and financing law for the government. Investors need to be aware, however, that sovereigns can change the laws governing domestic debts. One important driver of the importance of the eurobond market is that investors can pursue defaulting issuers in a jurisdiction that is perceived as independent.

Some clauses keep reappearing in bond prospectuses, so one should be aware of them. Here is a selection of the most important.

Governing Law The law by which legal disputes between the bond holders and the issuer are governed (note that this may be different from the laws both the country where the bond is issued and the country where the issuer is domiciled). English Law or New York State Law is most commonly used for international bonds for historical and practical reasons[11].

Jurisdiction The courts that will have jurisdiction over any disputes. This is somewhat different from Governing Law and usually mainly related to the cost of legal representation. Potential plaintiffs generally prefer courts close to their home location because retaining legal representations in other locations may incur additional cost and uncertainties.

Events of default A list of events that will be considered breaches of the contract between the issuer and the investors. Such events will provide reason to pursue the issuer in court. The most important is of course failure to pay, but other possibilities can include breaches of covenants.

Cross-default Statement that defaults on one debt issue are deemed to be events of default on all or all similar debt instruments. This protects bond investors because it means that they are immediately able to enjoin in bankruptcy proceedings even if the next payment under the specific instrument they hold that could be missed is still a long time away.

Collective action clause In the event that the issuer needs to restructure a bond, there are essentially two ways in which to implement such a restructuring. The traditional way is for the issuer to make an offer to bondholders (usually after some discussion with them and their advisers) and force them to seek redress in court if they deem the offer unacceptable. The downside of this approach is that, depending on jurisdiction, individual bond holders can cause substantial problems for the issuer through series of court cases that can delay a successful restructuring. Recently, therefore, bond prospectuses contain clauses that set

---

[11]One has to be aware that different countries can have very different laws and that some legal concepts may not exist in all countries. English law is well known, generally not subject to abrupt changes, and English law courts operate in other countries. English law also recognises a floating charge, i.e. a charge on an unspecified asset. Most jurisdictions only recognise a fixed charge on a specified set of assets.

out rules for collective decisions by bond holders which are then binding on all of them.

Rating triggers Some corporate bonds contain clauses that lead to higher coupon payments in case of credit rating downgrades. Such clauses are designed to protect investors from valuation losses caused by the spread widening that usually accompanies rating downgrades, especially if such downgrades lead to ejection from certain bond market indices. It should be noted that these clauses effectively subordinate the holders of bonds by the same issuer that do not carry these clauses because a larger share of the issuer's cash flow will be diverted away from them after a downgrade.

Negative pledge Promise of the issuer not to pledge any assets as security for future debt issues. This is very important because the assets of the issuer are all that bond investors can look to in case the issuer stops paying on the bond. Negative pledge clauses usually carve out mortgages so that issuers can in the future purchase real estate assets with loans secured by these assets. Such exceptions highlight the substantial impact a negative pledge clause can have on the business activities of an issuer.

Soft bullet When issuers are essentially solvent but cannot manage the redemption payment on an outstanding bond at the time of maturity, they can document the bond in such a way as to permit the redemption at a later date. This is essentially a conditional extension of the bond maturity and may require higher coupon payments during the extension period. Soft bullet structures are essentially a form of credit rating arbitrage. By obtaining an option to pay principal later, the issuer is more likely to make full payment which can support a given credit rating. The downside for investors is that they hold a paper that will give them longer exposure to the issuer precisely at the time when the economic situation of that issuer has deteriorated. In the covered bond market, soft bullets are increasingly being replaced with conditional pass-throughs, discussed in the section on covered bonds (page 272).

Gross-up and tax call This clause used to be standard in Eurobonds. All bond coupons are paid without deducting taxes, but if the issuer is suddenly forced to withhold taxes, the issuer has the choice to either increase the coupon so the net amount paid stays the same (gross-up) or call the bond immediately. Because the European Union has decided to introduce withholding tax, it is no longer practical to have this sort of clause and nowadays bond prospectuses generally specify no gross-up as outlined below.

No gross-up The issuer generally rules out extra payments to compensate for withholding tax.

Indemnity Statement that the law firm drawing up the prospectus and the investment bank distributing it are not liable for actions of the issuer. This does not mean that the investment bank has no responsibility for the prospectus, but it means that an investor trying to sue the bank usually will have to prove that the bank made a deliberate mistake or did not exercise due care and diligence.

A prospectus usually has to be filed with, or even approved, by some regulator before bonds can be sold to the general public. The reds typically are distributed before such approval has been granted, but the content normally is the same as the final version.

16.5 BOND MARKETS

Bonds are traded in public or private markets. In order to trade bonds, it must be possible to agree on the price for a given amount of debt. The most common form of expressing a price is as a percentage of the remaining principal of the bond that is being traded (bonds can amortise and the remaining principal may be different from the borrowed amount). The remaining principal is also referred to as the par amount and prices are therefore usually expressed as percentage of par. A price of 100, i.e., 100% of par, is also referred to as par (e.g. 'this bond trades at par').

Many bonds specify that traded par amounts have to be an integer multiple of a fixed amount. In the past, this was due to bonds being traded in paper certificates of a certain denomination. With the advent of electronic certificates, this technical restriction is no longer valid and most liquid market can trade in any size down to the lowest relevant currency unit (one cent or penny, etc.). Where minimum denominations still play a role is in bonds that are marketed at institutional investors only. By choosing a large minimum denomination (for example, EUR 100,000), the issuer can make it clear that the instrument should be out of reach for retail investors.

Price quotations usually (but not always) exclude accrued interest. Figure 16.1 on page 138 shows that accrued interest is essentially a straight-line interpolation of interest payable between two coupon dates, something that will be discussed in more detail later. The quoted price excluding accrued interest is called the clean price, clean price plus accrued interest is called the dirty price. Dirty price times par amount gives the invoice amount that must be paid in exchange for the given par amount of bonds. Note that every market has rules for the rounding of accrued interest.

While for analytical purposes the dirty price is more useful than the clean price, the clean price has a nicer dynamic relative to yield levels (yields are discussed in more detail later). Figure 16.3 shows that a bond that trades at the same yield as its coupon rate has a clean price close to par while the dirty price shows a saw-tooth pattern. At yields above the coupon rate, the clean price will be below par while the dirty price may be above par. Conversely, at yields below the coupon rate, the bond will trade above par. The yield that makes the clean price equal to par is therefore called the par yield.

Although the correspondence between coupon rate and par yield is close, it is not an identity. Jumping ahead a little bit, Figure 16.4 shows the clean prices of two bonds as a function of time where each bond trades always at a compound yield equal to its coupon. Because accrued interest is calculated in a linear way while yields are used in a power, there is a marginal divergence of the clean price from par in between coupon dates. The difference is larger at higher coupons, and the chart also shows that it is larger in leap years when there is a longer time between coupons.

Market participants tend to agree that it is undesirable to quote bond prices at an arbitrary precision. As a consequence, there is a minimum price increment. In most

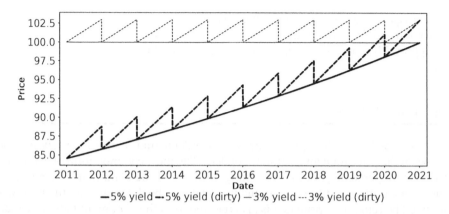

FIGURE 16.3   Clean and dirty prices of the same bond (3% annual coupon) at two different yield levels through time.

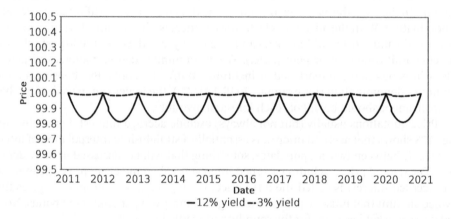

FIGURE 16.4   Clean prices of two bonds (3% and 12% annual coupons) trading at a yield equal to their coupon rate as a function of time.

bond markets this is one tenth of a cent (0.001% of par). The notable exception to this convention is the US bond market which has so far resisted decimalisation and trades in a convention known as thirty-seconds[12]. In the US market, a price might be given as 99-24 (note the dash instead of the decimal point) which in decimal terms is $99 + 24/32 = 99.75$. The modern US system of thirty-seconds has evolved, however, because price increments of 1/32 of one percent of par (around 3 cents in decimalised markets) are too large given the liquidity of the US Treasury market. The first innovation is the plus which is an extra 1/64th (around 1.5 cents in decimal

---

[12]Trading in binary rather than decimal fractions dates back to the days when coins were made out of precious metal and could be split when required. It is simply easier to cut a coin into four parts than into ten. This is also the reason why bond coupons traditionally were binary fractions.

terms) on top of the price in thirty-seconds. In the example above, 99-24+ would be $99 + 24/32 + 1/64 = 99.765625$[13]. For even finer price quotations, thirty-seconds can be augmented by eighths of a thirty-second. These are simply appended to the thirty-seconds quote, so 99-245 would be $99 + 24/32 + 5/256 = 99.76953125$. Note that 99-244 is the same as 99-24+ and neither 99-248 or 99-249 exist (99-248 would be 99-25).

Some CBOT Treasury bond futures options use a different convention where the third digit is the rounded decimal fraction in quarters. Here, the 5 in 99-245 would stand for 0.5 of a thirty-second, i.e. 99.245 in the option would be 99.244 or 99-24+ in bond price terms and 99.247 (99+24.75/32) would be written 99.246 if it was a bond price. Somewhat luckily, 99-242 is the same in either convention.

The Japanese government bond market is an example of a market that trades in yield terms. The minimum price increment is one tenth of a sen (0.001% of par), but in practice yields are quoted in half basis point steps which provides a slightly more coarse price grid.

16.5.1 The primary market

The primary market is the market where bonds are issued and sold to the investor public for the first time. When bonds are sold or bought by investors after they have been placed for the first time, this is referred to as secondary market trading, discussed below.

Bonds are for the most part fairly exchangeable and investors therefore can usually choose whether to buy a new issue in the primary market or a similar bond in the secondary market. This means that issuers need some way to attract investor attention at those times when they wish to place new supply. The foremost incentive is price. New issues are usually sold at a yield that is slightly above the fair value implied by surrounding issues from the same issuer. This yield pick-up, the new issue premium, is an important measure of investor demand. When issuers offer high new issue premia, it can be a sign that investors have concerns about the issuer. New issue premia also affect secondary market levels. When they are sufficiently high, it may be attractive for investors to participate in the primary supply only to immediately sell the new bond in the secondary market[14]. This will then put pressure on the new and old bonds alike.

Investors usually have an interest in large issues because they are traded more actively, leading to more efficient price formation. To achieve this, issuers in many cases sell new bonds in multiple tranches. A new bond is first sold as an initial tranche and then subsequent tap issues are sold that are fungible with the initial tranche. Fungible means that the various tranches are fully exchangeable with each other and fungibility must be specified by the issuer. There are no requirements for each tranche of a bond to be sold in the same way. For instance, it is quite common for governments to syndicate the first tranche of a new bond and then auction subsequent ones. Some issuers offer additional bond tranches on a continuous basis to a group of dealers. The issuer will

---

[13]There is no 'minus' because, for instance, '99-24–' can be expressed as 99-23+.
[14]This practice of flipping also exists in other markets.

then typically give the dealers a pricing grid for a selection of bonds that are available through reverse inquiry.

For corporate bond issuers and smaller sovereigns, the way to sell bonds is to hire investment banks who will market and sell the new bond through a process called syndication. In a syndicated deal, one or more banks are appointed as lead manager and these banks generally work with other banks as sub-distributors. The issuer pays the banks a fee that is a small percentage of the cash raised. Fees depend on the maturity of the deal and the credit risk involved. Depending on issue size, issuers will usually attempt to put together a syndicate group that has global distribution capabilities. This would normally mean picking a domestic bank in the issuer country with a strong domestic distribution network and one or two global investment banks one of which might, for instance, be stronger in Europe and the US and the other stronger in Asia. The hierarchy of investment banks in a given deal is generally is split in lead manager, co-lead and syndicate member. The level of responsibility does not only coincide with the fee distribution, but is also an important marketing factor. Some research firms prepare league tables that show the total number of deals a bank has been involved in, as well as the total deal volume. Such league tables generally place more weight on lead mandates than, for instance, co-leads. Another important reason to prefer lead manager status is that new bonds are sometimes oversubscribed, i.e., there is more investor demand than actual bond supply. After all the investor demand indications have been collected, an allocation process starts where each investor is assigned part of the new issue. The issuer and lead managers can choose to prefer certain clients in the allocation process and although this generally does not have the same economic implication as IPO allocations in the equity world, it is important for banks' client relationships that they are seen as being able to satisfy their client's wishes.

Price formation in the syndicated market can be done in two ways. In a bought deal (also known as a firm underwriting commitment), the lead banks guarantee a price or spread level to the issuer. If the banks are unable to distribute the issue to investors at this price level, the banks purchase the bonds for their own account. This places a high degree of risk on the banks and this is generally reflected in higher underwriting fees. In the alternative best efforts approach, investment banks solicit client interest but do not guarantee placement.

Initially, the banks will decide together with the issuer on the issue size and a so-called spread guidance, i.e., an indicative spread range relative to a well-known benchmark. For instance, spread guidance may be that x bn of bonds will be sold at a spread of 23–25 bp over benchmark B. The investment banks will then solicit bids from investors who may indicate that they would purchase y_1 million at 24 and y_2 at 25 bp spread. This is known as the book-building process. The investor bids are aggregated and if, for this example, there are at least x bn bids at a level of 24 bp over the benchmark, the issue will be priced at this level for all investors. Spread guidance and even the size of the issue can be adjusted during the book-building period which can last from less than a day to a few weeks. Increasing issue sizes during the book-building process is disliked by some investors, and issuers and syndicate banks sometimes rule out this option by marketing a deal as 'no-grow'.

Once sufficient client interest has been collected, the new issue books are closed and the issue is priced by observing the benchmark price and adding the relevant spread. The pricing of a new deal is usually seen as the decisive moment in a new bond deal. The issue price so found is known as the fixed-price reoffer price because the syndicate banks usually commit to buy back the new bonds at this price for a limited time period known as stabilisation. The price effectively remitted to the issuer is the all-in price which is the fixed-price reoffer minus the fees paid to the banks and other costs, such as fees to law firms working on the prospectus or listing fees.

A particular syndication structure called a pot deal has become widespread in Europe after first appearing in the US. In a pot deal, there is one book of investor interest and fees are split according to a fixed formula between the participating banks. This is in contrast to the classic syndication structure where banks do not reveal the names of their clients to the issuer during the book-building. Pot deals put more pressure on the investment banks because the issuer has more information about the progress of the process. At the same time, pot deals avoid situations where one syndicate member tries to 'look good' to the issuer by exaggerating client interest and then ending up buying a large part of the allocation for its own book. When such behaviour occurs, the bank in question will usually attempt to free up its balance sheet by selling the issue in the secondary market after the end of the stabilisation period, which will cause the new issue to underperform and thereby upset investors. Syndicate banks can still participate in pot deal transactions as investors, and the volume absorbed by them is disclosed separately as joint lead interest. Such participation can have various motivations, including the need to have trading inventory available for subsequent market-making in the new issue.

The alternative to syndicated deals is to sell new bonds by public auction. This avenue is only open to large government and sub-sovereign issuers who can rely on enough attention being present when they wish to come to the market. In an auction process, bidders[15] are invited to submit prices (competitive bids) to the issuer or the agent of the issuer who will then allocate the auctioned bonds to the highest bidders. Bidders are usually allowed to submit multiple bids at different prices so their bids can be partially satisfied. In an American auction, each successful bidder pays the price that they bid in the auction while in a Dutch auction[16] each successful bidder pays the same price. This uniform price is determined by the issuer according to predefined rules, e.g. it could be the lowest price at which all bids can be satisfied. Generally, bids at the lowest accepted price are allocated pro-rata among all bids at this price level. Some issuers offer non-competitive bids (bids with no price attached) in conjuction with competitive bids. These non-competitive bids are usually allocated at the average auction price. Confusingly, there is also the concept of non-competitive allocation, discussed below.

The difference between the average price of an auction and the lowest allocated price is called the tail of the auction and in some markets serves as an indication of the strength in demand for the new bond. The longer the tail, the lower the demand because

---

[15] A minimum standard of financial soundness is required for bidders in any auction. The issuer must have certainty that all bidders can actually pay for their share in the auction, and that bids can be submitted in a reliable and secure fashion.

[16] A Dutch auction must not be confused with a Dutch Direct Auction which is the mechanism used by the Dutch State Treasury Agency to place bonds in the market.

it indicates that a large number of defensive bids had to be filled to place the whole issue. Of course, this sort of logic needs to be adjusted for duration risk (longer maturities should automatically have larger tails) and the tail might be completely meaningless in the presence of large non-competitive bids. Another important indicator for the success of a new issue, in addition to new issue premium and auction tail, is the bid–cover ratio, which is the amount of bids received divided by the amount offered. An auction where less bids were received than the amount on offer, i.e., where the bid–cover ratio is less than one, is said to be uncovered. Syndicated deals are often judged on the mathematically equivalent total book size.

No single indicator is sufficient to judge the success of a syndication or auction. An issuer looking to achieve a high bid–cover ratio, or equivalently, a large book, can simply offer a higher new issue premium to entice participation. This risks poor performance of other bonds after the supply, and thereby the alienation of long-term investors. Conversely, the issuer may want to keep the new issue premium low and so potentially face a low bid–cover ratio or even uncovered issuance. Syndicate members individually or collectively may wish to make a deal more successful than it would otherwise be and place larger bids for themselves. This pushes up the bid–cover ratio at a given new issue premium.

Most auctions are conducted in a way that makes them more similar to syndication. The issuers appoint bidding groups of banks and only members of the bidding groups are allowed to submit bids. In some cases, such as Germany, membership in the bidding group is effectively open to all banks, so there is only a marginal relationship between the issuer and the banks. In other cases, the bidding group consists of so-called primary dealers which are banks that have been conferred a special status by the issuer. When there is a primary dealer group, the issuer will usually expect a certain minimum of bonds being taken down by each primary dealer; otherwise the primary dealer status will be withdrawn. The primary dealers are thereby incentivised to place the new supply just as a syndicate member would be. However, primary dealers are only rarely paid fees for auction participation and instead in some cases buy bonds at auctions over the market level at the time. Compensation by the issuer instead happens through syndicated deals, other trading mandates, etc.

Some issuers use non-competitive allocations to compensate successful bidders. In this case, there is a certain point in time after the auction where successful bidders can request additional bonds at the price paid at the auction in proportion to the volume they successfully received at the auction itself, e.g., 10% of that amount. So, successful bidders are given a call option. Generally, the various incentives given to bidding group participants mean that although there is no publicly disclosed payment of syndication fees, the economic relationship can be very similar.

The German government bond supply system stands out from other large issuers such as the US, Japan, or France for the absence of a formal primary dealer group. The requirements to become a member of the 'bidding group' at the German Debt Management Agency are minimal. One reason is that the Agency is itself active in the secondary market for its bonds. It can retain bonds at auction and has therefore an additional parameter to control new issue pricing in addition to the cut-off price and the share of non-competitive bids it allocates. Faced with weak bidding for new bonds, it can set the cut-off price near the top of the bidding range and allocate a high share of non-competitive bids or retain a large share of the new supply. Conversely, it can allocate more competitive bids through a lower cut-off prices and lower non-competitive allocation. In effect, the Agency can use its own balance sheet in a way that is very similar to a dealer syndicate in a bought deal.

When a regular issuer, in particular a government, has a number of bonds outstanding, the most recent issue is called the on-the-run issue and the preceding one the off-the-run. It is also common to talk about the first off-the-run, second off-the-run, and so on, and to attach maturities, e.g. on-the-run 10 year, etc. In some markets, notably the US, Italy, Spain and, to a lesser extent, France, the higher liquidity of on-the-run securities is associated with a liquidity premium (cf. Chapter 18).

16.5.2 The secondary market I: (interdealer market)

Trading in bonds is generally not done on public exchanges although most public bonds are officially listed to satisfy investor constraints or central bank collateral eligibility rules (for instance in the case of the ECB). Some exchanges further require that off-exchange trades are reported to the exchange which will then publish information about those trades. However, trading is generally done by bilateral agreement between two parties, or through broking.

When securities houses deal among themselves, they are sometimes reluctant to do so directly in order to avoid giving away information about their current positioning. This is the reason for the existence of brokers (also called inter-dealer brokers) who try to match buying and selling interest between dealers anonymously. Trades though a broker can involve name giveup where both sides are informed after the trade is agreed as to who the counterparty is, or be completely anonymous with each dealer facing the broker as their counterparty. Brokers are usually paid a small fraction of the traded volume in fees.

Bond brokerages have over the last few years built electronic trading systems that increase the efficiency of the brokerage process. On electronic trading platforms, dealers can display prices anonymously and deal on the prices displayed. In some cases, government issuers have encouraged banks to set up electronic market making platforms such as MTS. Such platforms combine an electronic trading system with commitments to display firm prices on the platform for a certain amount of time per day so as to provide liquidity in the interdealer market. Although the commitments are usually less strict than what would normally be market convention, the presence of such trading systems means that smaller securities firms who would have difficulties risk managing a full trading operation can use a certain minimum level of interdealer liquidity as a backstop when offering liquidity to their customers. This is the reason why government issuers are so interested in supporting the existence of such platforms, while large securities houses face the dilemma that by supporting the interdealer market, they are effectively supporting their competition in dealing with customers. In practice, the volumes traded on such platforms are a fraction of total market volume.

By and large, interdealer platforms bring more advantages to all of their participants than disadvantages. A large gobal investment bank has stress-tested this assumption in 2004 by executing a series of trades in a market making platform called EuroMTS for euro area government bonds that added up to over EUR 15bn bought within a few seconds and then selling part of this amount back to the market a few minutes later. Because the market makers were required to show certain minimum size quotes across a large number of bonds, this bank was able to execute this large volume without giving the other banks the opportunity to adjust the prices to reflect this large demand. In particular, the trade was aimed at executing more volume than was available at that price in the usual hedge instrument for euro area government bonds in this maturity sector, the Eurex Bund futures contract. The initiating bank therefore was probably able to make a sizeable profit from the liquidity mismatch of EuroMTS versus the futures exchange. Consequently the trade was probably the main impetus for tighter market regulation.

However, the important lesson from the episode is that trading on EuroMTS is still continuing. Although some rules have been introduced to limit the scope for such trades reoccuring, dealers seem to value the presence of the platform enough not to withdraw.

16.5.3   The secondary market II: (customer-facing market)

Customers deal with securities houses in a variety of ways. Voice trading is still common, but generally used only when large transaction sizes are executed. Normally clients do not talk to traders directly, but through the intermediation of a salesperson. This is has a few practical as well as compliance-related reasons.

The bulk of customer trading these days is done through electronic platforms because this is vastly more cost-efficient and less error-prone than voice trading. An electronic trading system can automatically feed trade information through to the backoffice systems managing the settlement instructions and the risk management systems of the bank. Among electronic platforms, one distinuishes between quote request and streaming systems, as well as between single-dealer and multiple-dealer platforms. In a quote request system, a client can solicit price quotes from a number of dealers, but then has to arrange execution of the winning quote in other ways. In contrast, a streaming trading system is a system where firm price quotes are displayed on an ongoing basis and a customer can trade on these quotes through the same system.

16.6   ACCRUED INTEREST

Bond coupons are generally paid to the current holder of the bond in one sum. When bonds are traded between coupon dates, this means that although the seller has effectively been lending money to the issuer, the interest since the last coupon payments will be paid in full to the buyer. In trading, the seller therefore generally is compensated for the amount of interest that has accrued since the last coupon payment date.

Bonds generally pay interest only on good business days, but unlike swaps, bonds usually do not adjust the coupon for the actual accrual period.

Accrued interest is calculated exactly like interest on a CD, using the coupon rate C as the interest rate. Hence, accrued interest is simply:

$$I = C * DCF(t_{i-1}, t_s) \tag{16.5}$$

where t_{i-1} is the last coupon payment date and t_s is the settlement date of the bond transaction. The *DCF* here is calculated according to the rules for the respective bond market, which may be (and usually is) different from the convention for the money market. The actual/actual convention is quite common in the bond market, so if there are coupon periods of over one year, the fictitious accrual period outlined in the money market section applies. A good example are German 10Y government bonds which usually have a first coupon period of more than one year.

When a bond is traded only in multiples of a fixed notional amount, the bond has a long or short first or last coupon period and the issuer, in the prospectus, commits to pay a rounded amount on the first or last coupon corresponding to the fixed notional, Equation (16.5) is incorrect for the respective coupon period. Accrued interest is instead calculated on the actual (rounded) coupon payment using the appropriate daycount fraction.

Some bond markets (notably the UK and in some sense Japan) still use ex-dividend periods. These stem from a time when coupons were physical pieces of paper that had to be cut off and mailed to the issuer to receive payment. The ex-dividend period is the time just before the coupon payment date when the coupons are assumed to have been cut off and travel in the mail. If a bond changes hands during the ex-dividend period, on the payment date, the original holder will get the coupon, not the buyer of the bond. For settlement during the ex-dividend period, the accrued interest is negative because the buyer will hold the bond for a few days without getting paid any interest. The formula Equation (16.5) effectively becomes:

$$I = C * DCF(t_i, t_s) \tag{16.6}$$

(Note the change in the index of the coupon date). In Japan, negative accrued interest does not exist because although an ex-dividend period exists, no bond settlement takes place during that period.

Bonds in most markets are quoted on a clean price basis. This means that for the purposes of settling a trade, one has to calculate accrued interest and add it to the price quoted in the market before multiplying with the notional amount. The sum of clean price and accrued interest is called dirty price. Schematically,

$$\text{Dirty price} = \text{Clean price} + \text{Accrued Interest} \tag{16.7}$$

16.7 YIELD

The general idea of a yield is that is should measure the rate of return on a bond investment. Multiple ways of expressing such returns exist and they differ in the underlying simplifications they make. One can follow the evolution of yield measures by adding complexity to the mathematics. The dirty price of a bond in percent of notional will be denoted by P and the coupon C. t_n is the maturity date as used before. Yields are denoted by y.

16.7.1   Running yield

The simplest yield calculation is:

$$y = \frac{C}{P} \tag{16.8}$$

The idea here is that if one pays 101% to receive a coupon of 4% running, one has a rate of return of around $4\%/1.01 \approx 3.96\%$. The running yield is the straightforward equivalent of the dividend yield used by equity analysts.

16.7.2   Simple yield

The difference (or at least one of the differences) between equity and bonds is that bonds usually have a final maturity date. If one pays 101 for a bond today that matures in two years time and therefore pays back 100, the extra 1% of investment is lost unless the coupon makes up for it. The next best yield measure takes this into account by amortising the capital loss over the remaining time to maturity:

$$y = \frac{C - \frac{P-100}{t}}{P} \tag{16.9}$$

This simple yield is the standard yield convention in the Japanese market.

The problem with the simple yield is that it implicitly assigns a capital loss occuring in 10 years time the same value as a capital loss occuring in one year. Ideally, therefore, the capital losses would be weighted by the appropriate discount factor. From this thought, it is just a little step to the idea to weight each cashflow with the appropriate discount factor.

16.7.3   Compound yield

Compound yield is the equivalent of the internal rate of return in corporate finance. Specifically, yield is the solution to the equation:

$$P = \sum_i \frac{Cf_i}{(1+y)^{DCF(t_s,t_i)}} \tag{16.10}$$

A variation used sometimes in Germany is the Moosmüller yield which treats the time period until the first coupon payment as a money market instrument. The price-yield equation in this case becomes:

$$P = \frac{1}{1 + yDCF(t_s, t_1)} \sum_{i=1}^{n} \frac{Cf_i}{(1+y)^{DCF(t_1,t_i)}} \tag{16.11}$$

The Moosmüller yield is not widely used, but has one advantage over the compound yield outlined above. It is market convention (street convention) to treat a bond as a money market instrument during its last coupon period, i.e., when it becomes a pure discount bond. The Moosmüller yield does this automatically because in this case the sum runs over only one term and that term has a discount factor of 1, leaving the discounting to the initial money market term.

Both yields cannot be calculated in a closed form for arbitrary inputs. In other words, there is no formula that gives the compound or Moosmüller yield for a given price in the general case of an arbitrary number of coupons and settlement date. The only way to calculate yields is therefore to try different values for y in Equation (16.10) or Equation (16.11) to see which works. Of course there are clever ways to do this very quickly, but it is still a lot more expensive computationally than simple yields.

While compound yield appears to be comparatively 'scientific', it does in fact have some remaining drawbacks. Equation (16.10) is invariant against changing the timing of cashflows as long as the cashflow is adjusted with the interest rate y. For instance, moving any coupon C of an annual bond forward by one year would not change its present value (dirty price) as long as the coupon is reduced to be $C/(1+y)$. Moving it back one year would also not change the price as long as the coupon is changed to be $C(1+y)$. This implies that y is the implied forward interest rate between the two coupon dates[17]. In this way one can show that y is not only the internal rate of return of all the cashflows, but also the implied forward rate between any two cashflow days. Actual investment returns will differ because investors are unlikely to be able to reinvest coupons they received at this implied interest rate. Indeed, because long-term yields tend to be higher than short-term yields, an investor who holds a bond to maturity and reinvests all intermediate coupons payed by the bond should not expect to achieve a total return equal to the yield.

The implicit time invariance in the rate of return contained in Equation (16.10) also negates the idea of a yield curve, i.e., the concept of different yields for bonds of different maturities issued by the same issuer. Coupons from different bonds by the same issuer should economically be discounted by the same interest rates, no matter which bond they stem. This concept then leads to the idea of discount factor curves which will be discussed later.

16.7.4 Bond-equivalent yield

US government bonds pay interest semi-annually and annualisation is used to arrive at what is known as the bond-equivalent yield y_B with the equation:

$$y_B = 2(\sqrt{1+y} - 1) \tag{16.12}$$

Bond-equivalent yields are always lower than compound yields by an amount of $y^2/4$. When comparing the yields of bonds with different coupon periods, it is important to

---

[17]To be precise, the forward rate would be a money market rate which could then technically be quoted in a different daycount convention, depending on the market, and so have a different numerical value.

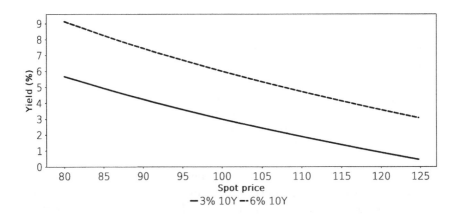

FIGURE 16.5   Price–yield relationship for two 10Y bonds with different coupons.

first translate all yields to the same standard, such as compound or bond-equivalent yield.

In the introduction to this section, it was mentioned that the various yield measures differ in the simplifications they contain, but nothing negative has been said about the compound yield. The problem with any yield-type return measure is the assumption that there is a single interest rate that describes the time value of money. A close inspection of Equation (16.10) shows that any cashflow can be moved forwards or backwards in time as long as the size of that cashflow is adjusted by a discount factor that is always given by the yield y. Inspecting the bond market, however, one finds that bonds of different maturities have very different yields, so the discount factor that needs applied at each point in time is different.

The solution to this problem is to pick one term structure of discount factors that is reasonably realistic, and express differences in returns as spreads to this curve. This is the motivation behind the use of various curve spreads which will be discussed elsewhere.

Yields of fixed coupon bonds generally fall when bond prices increase (cf. Figure 16.5). The shape of this relationship differs between bonds with different coupon rates. Bonds with higher coupons pay more of their total cashflow early in the lifetime of the bond and these cashflows are less sensitive to the discount rate. The bonds with the highest sensitivity to discount rates are therefore zero-coupon bonds. The inverse relationship, i.e., the change in yield corresponding to a given change in price, shown in Figure 16.6, accordingly shows less yield impact of the same price change for lower coupon bonds.

The extreme case of a zero coupon bond best illustrates the trade-off between interest rate sensitivity in absolute and relative terms. As Figure 16.7 shows, the duration (relative price risk) of the zero increases linearly with maturity. However, because the present value of the bond falls, the absolute price risk first increases, but then also falls and eventually converges to zero. Intuitively, an infinite maturity zero coupon bond has no value, no matter what the discount rate is (as long as it is positive).

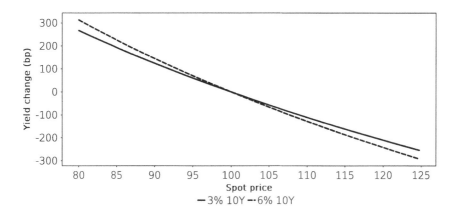

FIGURE 16.6 Yield changes for price changes of two 10Y bonds with different coupons.

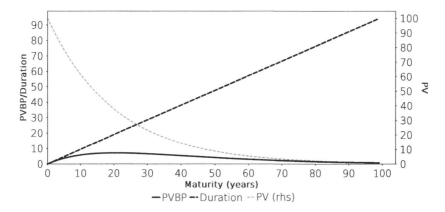

FIGURE 16.7 Price and risk measures for a zero-coupon bond at 5% yield as a function of maturity.

16.8 INTEREST RATE RISK

Equations (16.8) through (16.11) establish mathematical relationships between price and yield. Therefore, changes in yields will drive changes in prices and vice versa. Two sensitivity measures are most common, namely the modified duration D^* defined as:

$$D^* = \frac{1}{P}\frac{\partial P}{\partial y} \tag{16.13}$$

and the PVBP (present value of a basis point), written here as:

$$PVBP = \frac{\partial P}{\partial y} \tag{16.14}$$

Clearly, the only difference between these two measures is the dirty price P. Both measures are used, albeit in slightly different contexts. PVBP is the cash amount by which the market value of a given *notional amount* of bonds changes for a 1 bp change in yields. D^* is the relative price change, but because the notional amount of bonds can be seen as the ratio of market value and dirty price, modified duration is also the cash amount by which the market value of bonds with a given *market value* moves. For a fund manager, it is more important to view portfolio size in terms of the amount of assets under management and modified duration is therefore perhaps a more natural measure. A bond trader monitoring positions, meanwhile, will usually see nominal amounts in the trading book and use PVBP.

16.9 CONVEXITY

Convexity is a common but not very well defined concept in fixed income. It is common because it refers to the idea that the sensitivity of prices to changes in measures such as yields are typically nonlinear. Convexity is the term that describes this nonlinearity. However, there are multiple mathematical definitions of convexity depending on the context. Here, convexity is defined simply as the second derivative of price with respect to yield, i.e.:

$$Conv = \frac{\partial^2 P}{\partial y^2} \tag{16.15}$$

In this way, duration is the slope of the tangent in the price-yield relationship at the current yield, while the convexity is a measure of the curvature of that line at that point.

Convexity is generally seen as beneficial for bond portfolios because for a given amount of interest rate taken, a more convex portfolio provides incremental returns relative to a less convex portfolio when markets are volatile and interest rate is adjusted after yield moves. Market participants know this and factor convexity into their investment decisions (cf. Section 20.2 on page 209).

Although this will be discussed in more detail later, the problem with convexity in this definition is that the concept of yields by construction assumes a flat yield curve.

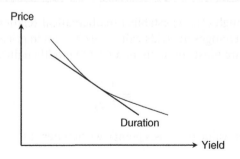

FIGURE 16.8 *Graphical representation of convexity.*

This means that changes in front end interest rates are in principle weighted equally in the DV01 and convexity risk measures as long-term interest rates. These risk measure simply state risk in terms of so many dollars or euros per basis point in yield change with no regard to relative yield volatilities in different curve sectors. Given the normally higher volatility of shorter interest rates, this means that both DV01 and convexity overstate the interest sensitivity of long-dated bonds.

Generally speaking, convexity is used in the market for all kinds of nonlinear relaptionships. For instance, the convexity in the convexity adjustment for money market contracts Equation (13.17) has a very different meaning from the one encountered here.

16.10 BOND VALUE DECOMPOSITION

Present value, PVBP and convexity can be better understood by looking at the breakdown of these measures for bonds of different maturities. We assume 5% coupon bonds of 10, 20, 30, and 40 years maturity trading at par and show the breakdown of the present value (the current market price), PVBP and convexity into the contributions provided by principal and coupons. Given the small coupons, the charts sum the coupon contributions per decade (1st–10th coupon, 11th–20th coupon, and so on).

Figure 16.9 shows the breakdown of the bond present value. What may be surprising is that the present value of the first ten coupons is unchanged across all 4 bonds even though they represent all coupons of the 10Y bond but only one quarter of the coupons of the 40Y bond. Mathematically, this should not be a surprise given that the present value of these cashflows is simply ten flows of 5% of notional discounted at a 5% yield for 1 to 10 years. The present value of these cashflows must therefore be a constant.

Somewhat more meaningful is the interpretation of this observation. A 20Y bond can be thought of as a 10Y bond that will be refinanced by the issue of a new 10Y bond in

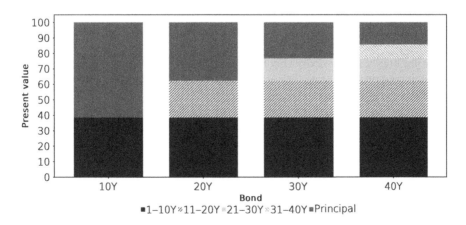

FIGURE 16.9 Breakdown of bond present values by coupons and principals for different bond maturities. All bonds have 5% coupons and trade at par (5% yield).

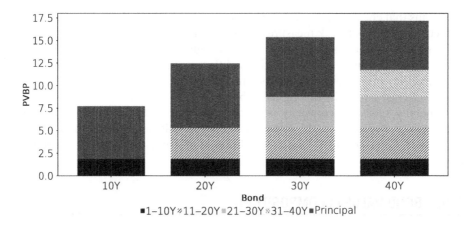

FIGURE 16.10 Breakdown of bond PVBP by coupons and principals for different bond maturities. All bonds have 5% coupons and trade at par (5% yield).

ten years time. The concept of yield as a uniform discount rate therefore implies that an investor in a 20Y bond would be indifferent to investing in a 10Y bond now, and in ten years again in a 10Y provided the expectation that at maturity a bond of equal coupon will again be issued at par.

The breakdown of first-order bond risk (PBVP) in Figure 16.10 is more complex. Longer-dated bonds have more risk and therefore total risk increases with maturity at equal yield. However, the breakdown is not linear. The PVBP of the principal declines with maturity. This is the simple result of the principal itself becoming less valuable when it is being repaid further into the future, something that Figure 16.9 already demonstrated. The PVBP of each coupon block remains constant, again as the simple result of discounting the same cashflows at the same interest rate and then taking a first derivative. In line with the observation on the principal, the PVBP of the coupon blocks declines in the sense that the first ten years of coupons have more PVBP as the next ten years and so on. This again results from the lower present value.

Turning finally to convexity (Figure 16.11), again one observes that the contribution of each coupon block, i.e., the same cashflows at the same time discounted by the same yield is constant. The convexity of longer-dated cashflows is higher, unlike the PVBP. However, the relationship is not monotonous. The convexity of the 40Y principal is lower than that of the 30Y principal. This is a result of the yield calibration used here. Essentially, at very long maturities the decline in present value outweighs the increase in convexity. Taken to an extreme, absent any default risk, an infinite maturity zero coupon bond has zero present value[18] and that present value does not change with the discount rate.

---

[18]The present value of a defaultable principal depends not only on the discount rate but also on expected time to default. This is because principal obligations usually accelerate in defaults.

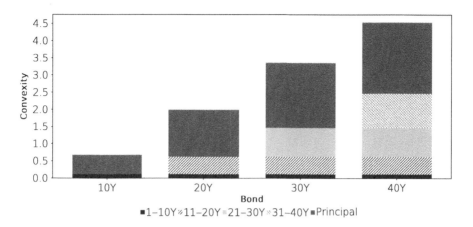

FIGURE 16.11   Breakdown of bond convexity by coupons and principals for different bond maturities. All bonds have 5% coupons and trade at par (5% yield).

16.11   CARRY

Carry is the income earned on a long bond position, taking into account the cost of financing the bond, in other words, coupon income minus financing cost. The usual definition of carry is:

$$\text{Carry} = \text{Spot price} - \text{Forward price} \tag{16.16}$$

Because zero coupon bonds do not accrue any interest but roll up to par, they generally show up as having negative carry in this measure. In some markets, especially the US, one therefore uses yields and:

$$\text{Carry} = \text{Forward yield} - \text{Spot yield} \tag{16.17}$$

Using no arbitrage, the equation to calculate the forward price (under the assumption that no interim coupon is paid) is simply:

$$P_f = \frac{P_0}{Df(t_0, t_f)} \tag{16.18}$$

where $Df(t_0, t_f)$ is given by the repo rate $r(t_0, t_f)$:

$$Df(t_0, t_f) = \frac{1}{1 + r(t_0, t_f)DCF(t_0, t_f)} \tag{16.19}$$

so:

$$P_f = P_0(1 + r(t_0, t_f)DCF(t_0, t_f)) \tag{16.20}$$

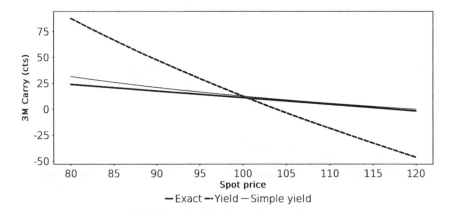

FIGURE 16.12   Carry calculated using the exact method of Equation (16.21) and approximations. Note that using the simple yield gives better approximate results than using the compound yield.

If an intermediate coupon C is paid between t_0 and t_f, there is no immediately obvious forward price because it is not quite clear at which rate the coupon can be reinvested. Standard practice is to use the repo rate $r(t_0, t_f)$ itself, so one has:

$$P_f = \frac{P_0}{Df(t_0, t_f)} - C * DCF(t_{i-1}, t_i)\frac{Df(t_i, t_f)}{Df(t_0, t_f)} \qquad (16.21)$$

with:

$$Df(t_i, t_f) = \frac{1}{1 + r(t_0, t_f)DCF(t_i, t_f)} \qquad (16.22)$$

Note that Equation (16.21) holds no matter which repo rate is being used. The assumption of reinvestment at the repo rate only enters when the same r is used in all discount factor calculations in Equation (16.21).

The carry calculation using Equation (16.21) is cumbersome and one can instead approximate by multiplying the difference between bond yield and repo rate by the holding period, i.e. de-annualising the relevant interest rates, to arrive at the carry. The quality of this approximation is shown in Figure 16.12.

CHAPTER 17

Floating-Rate Notes

Floating-rate notes (FRNs) may appear to sit oddly in a book of fixed income instruments. They are bonds where the coupon is not fixed but is reset, usually at the start of each interest period. However, as will be discussed below, under some circumstances this feature stabilises the value of the bonds compared to other securities. The term variable-rate note is used almost interchangeably with the term FRN but has slight connotation of a coupon structure that is linked to something else than benchmark interest rates.

The cashflow structure of an FRN is shown in Figure 17.1. The specific features of an FRN are the choices for the reference index used to calculate the coupon rate, the coupon frequency, and the timing of the resets. In the majority of FRNs, coupons reset to a 'natural' index at the begining of each coupon period. However, more complex FRNs exist and the full spectrum of FRNs ends at highly structured products. In essence, if one thinks of a bond coupon as a function of some inputs:

$$C = f(\text{something}) \tag{17.1}$$

then the standard bullet bonds discussed so far are the most simple manifestation of this equation, namely:

$$f(\text{something}) = \text{const} \tag{17.2}$$

Floating-rate notes are bonds where f takes a more interesting form. Although the vast bulk of FRNs has a very natural structure for f, some can be very complex.

The typical investor in a floating rate bond is the treasury of a deposit-taking institution, for instance a retail bank. Banks compete against other banks and other products for deposit money. The deposit rate each bank offers is therefore a compromise between wishing to pay a low rate (to save costs) and a high rate (to attract money). At the same time, deposit funding competes with other funding sources that may be available to the bank. As a result, deposit interest rates tend to follow interbank market funding interest rates, albeit usually with a spread that reflects the higher cost of deposits. This extra cost is linked to the need to advertise, retain customer service staff, and maintain buildings that impress the saving public. Although deposit interest rates fluctuate, the deposits themselves tend to remain at a bank for longer periods. Customers do not frequently move deposit money between different banks, and for this reasons deposits are said to be 'sticky'.

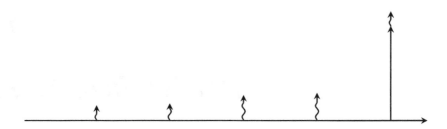

FIGURE 17.1   Simple floating rate note. The bond repays its par amount at the maturity date. The bond has regular accrual periods but coupons are reset at the beginning of each coupon period in accordance with some pre-defined index.

As a result of this economic setting, the liability side of a bank tends to be linked to short-term rates in the interbank market. Banks therefore are natural investors in assets that also pay the variable interbank rates, or use derivatives to transform the cashflow structure of other instruments into a variable-rate structure.

By the same logic, some retail investors purchase FRNs as an alternative to holding term deposits at a bank that roll over periodically. The advantage of doing so can be a higher coupon, but also that a FRN can be sold at any time while a term deposit can usually only be terminated at maturity without incurring extra penalties. Also, only banks can offer term deposits while FRN can be issued by other entities.

17.1   COUPON RESET MECHANICS

FRNs usually reset the coupon at the beginning of the coupon period. There can be a lag between the observation of the benchmark and the reset date. For instance, because money market deposits settle $T + 2$ in most markets, the coupon used for a coupon period starting at T will usually be the reference rate taken at $T - 2$. Some FRNs, particularly more structured ones, have longer lags which sometimes reach 20 business days, i.e., almost a month.

It is possible to fix the coupon later than at the start of the accrual period. Such in-arrears structures can delay the coupon fixing to as late as the payment date. It is meaningless to calculate an accrued interest when the accrual rate is not fixed and in-arrears structures therefore trade on dirty, rather than clean price.

Coupons only rarely set to the benchmark itself, and instead a spread is set at issuance, and then applied at every reset date. This spread is called the quoted margin, called here μ. The coupon on a standard FRN payable over the period starting at t_i would therefore be:

$$C_i = R(t_i - 2) + \mu \qquad (17.3)$$

where as usual all rates are quoted in annualised terms even though FRN coupon periods are frequently shorter than one year. Note that other formulas are possible.

A so-called inverse floater for instance uses a formula like:

$$C_i = \max(0, \mu - R(t_i - 2)) \tag{17.4}$$

so the coupon moves in the opposite direction of the benchmark.

Most jurisdictions do not allow negative coupons which would be payment obligations from the investor to the issuer. In addition, many CSDs are unable to process such payments. Implicitly, therefore, Equation (17.3) is to be read as:

$$C_i = \max(0, R(t_i - 2) + \mu) \tag{17.5}$$

This implicit coupon floor is now standard in bond documentation because there have been frequent instances where the simple formula Equation (17.3) would have led to negative resets. Again, nothing prevents issuers from setting the floor to any other non-negative value and some FRNs have floors above zero. In the same vein, issuers can furnish coupons with a cap.

17.2 LIBOR AND OIS-LINKED NOTES

The 'natural' coupon of a floating rate note is the interbank benchmark rate applying to the period between two coupon resets, as pertaining at the start of the accrual period, and the coupon formula Equation (17.3). A quarterly FRN would therefore have coupon resets linked to the 3M Libor rate applicable in that currency.

If that is the case, then the present value of the FRN at the time of its last coupon reset (i.e., one coupon period before maturity) would be:

$$P = \frac{100 + C * DCF}{1 + rDCF} \tag{17.6}$$

where r is the appropriate discount rate applicable to liabilities of the FRN issuer. This discount rate should be the market rate plus an appropriate spread. A quick comparison with Equation (17.3) shows that if that spread happens to be μ, then $P = 100$ in this equation. At the beginning of the last coupon period, the FRN is therefore worth exactly par if the quoted margin is equal to the credit spread of the issuer. One can now consider the beginning of second-to-last coupon period. At the end of that period, the bond will be worth par (as has just been shown), and an additional coupon will be paid on the end of that period. Equation (17.6) wherefore applies again, only that in this instance the 100 in the numerator refers to the value of the bond, not its redemption amount. It follows that also at the start of the second-to-last coupon period the bond has a value of par. This induction can be continued all the way to the first coupon period. The result is that the value of an FRN is equal to par at the time of each coupon reset if the quoted margin is the correct risk premium for the issuer.

Between coupon resets the FRN value can fluctuate because the market discount rate applicable between the settlement date of any trade, and the market rate when the coupon was fixed can differ. For instance, if the central bank makes a surprise rate cut after a coupon has been fixed, the next coupon payment will reference the older, higher central bank rate, and so the FRN price will increase to reflect the lower discount rate. However, the effect of this mismatch between the coupon fixing and the market rate will end with the next coupon payment. In total therefore, FRNs have a very stable market price as long as the risk premium of the issuer remains constant.

As mentioned in the section on Libor, Section 13.6, unsecured term benchmark rates are being phased out globally because regulators have taken the view that benchmarks based on an economically irrelevant subset of transactions are open to abuse. FRN issuers have therefore switched to coupons that follow overnight benchmark rates. In principle, the coupon payment (not the annualised coupon rate) should amount to the compounded interest on a money market account:

$$c(t-1) = \prod_{t=t_0}^{t_1} [1 + (r(t-2) + \mu)DCF(t, t+1)] - 1 \qquad (17.7)$$

where $r(t-2)$ is the overnight rate observed for each day t applicable to the relevant overnight rate (note that money markets settle T+2) within the coupon period, and $DCF(t, t+1)$ is the applicable daycount fraction[1]. This formula, however, has a structural disadvantage and therefore is not how interest is calculated on actual bonds. The total interest amount is only known at the end of the coupon period and so it would be difficult to define accrued interest during the accrual period. Inconveniently for the issuer, the spread μ would also be compounded, and so be not directly comparable to the quoted margin of a standard Libor FRN.

Instead, Equation (17.7) is used to construct an intermediate term rate which is the annualised compound interest between the last coupon payment and any settlement date within the coupon period, including the next payment date:

$$\rho(t-1) = \frac{\prod_{t=t_0}^{d} [1 + (r(t-l))DCF(t, t+1)] - 1}{DCF(t_0, d)} \qquad (17.8)$$

$\rho(t)$ is then used in the same way as $R(t)$ in Equation (17.3) to calculate the coupon fixing. In this way, the quoted margin μ is not compounded, and the formula can be used to calculate interim accrued interest. This accrued interest is in effect based on the best possible estimate of the eventual coupon payment. Somewhat unintuitively, the standard observation lag l between the overnight rate and its application appears to have been selected in the European market to be five business days rather than two[2].

---

[1]The daycount fraction is not simply 1/360 for most currencies and 1/365 for the Commonwealth markets because there may be a weekend or public holiday between t and $t+1$.
[2]This convention enables a longer-than-standard T+2 settlement while retaining defined accrued interest.

17.3   DISCOUNT MARGIN

Floating-rate notes do not have predictable cashflows and therefore they do not have yields. One approach to compare expected returns of FRNs is the so-called fixed-equivalent yield where future cash flows are projected, either by simply assuming constant coupons, or that future reference index levels can be predicted from some form of forward curve. In the latter case, the actual coupon formula, e.g. Equation (17.3), can be used directly. Once cashflow projections are obtained, a yield can be calculated from this series of irregular cashflows in the same way as for any other bond.

The more common market convention, however, is to calculate a spread known as the discount margin. Conceptually, the discount margin μ' is the quoted margin that would make the price of a given FRN equal to par. That suggests that one should calculate it based on a discount factor term structure as:

$$\mu' = \mu - \frac{P - 100}{\sum_i DCF(t_{i-1} - t_i)Df(t_i)} \tag{17.9}$$

where the denominator of this fraction acts to distribute the difference between the market price and par across each coupon period, bearing in mind that like the quoted margin, the discount margin is quoted in annualised terms and so needs to be de-annualised for the daycount fraction of each coupon period. As presented here, the discount margin is more closely related to the notion of an asset swap spread (cf. Section 22.3.1 on page 222).

Equation (17.9) is straightforward if one has a discount factor curve $Df(t)$ to hand but amounts to relying on external instruments to build that curve. The market convention is to calculate the discount margin from the bond alone. The approach resembles that of the yield calculation, with the added assumption that the benchmark resets in the future will be identical to the current rate. Specifically, the dirty price of the bond P is expressed as:

$$P = \frac{(R(t_l) + \mu)DCF(t_t, t_1)}{1 + DCF(t, t1)(R^*(t) + \mu')} + \sum_{i=2}^{n} Df(j)DCF(t, t_i)(R(t) + \mu) + 100Df(n) \tag{17.10}$$

where the discount factors $Df(k)$ are given by the recursive relationships:

$$Df(k) = \frac{Df(k - 1)}{1 + DCF(t_{k-1}, t_k)(R(t) + \mu')} \tag{17.11}$$

and:

$$Df(1) = \frac{1}{1 + DCF(t, t_1)(R^*(t) + \mu')} \tag{17.12}$$

Here $R(t_l)$ stands for the last fixing of the reference index while $R^*(t)$ is the money market rate between the settlement date and the next coupon date (the so-called stub rate). The discount factors $Df(k)$ amount to the compounded discounted value of a deposit rolling at the frequency of the FRN with an interest rate equal to the current fixing of the benchmark rate plus the fixed spread μ' which is what this nonlinear equation needs to be solved for. The three terms in Equation (17.10) correspond to the discounted values of the next coupon, all subsequent coupons, and the principal, in that order. This equation needs to be solved for μ' using a non-linear solver, similar to calculating a compound yield.

In essence, the difference between Equations (17.9) and (17.10) is that the former would lead to a different result if the forward curve of the reference rate moved, while the latter would not. When the yield curve steepens, the discount factors $Df(t_i)$ in Equation (17.9) decline, so the asset swap spread for a given price increases. The definition Equation (17.10) does not depend on the current yield curve at all (only on the two rates $R^*(t)$ and $R(t)$), so the discount margin is unaffected by curve changes. That means, just as for yields, that it is methodologically incorrect to compare discount margins across bonds of different maturities.

When the FRN is linked to overnight rates like €STR, Equation (17.10) is no longer appropriate because the term rates $R^*(t)$ and $R(t)$ do not exist, and the next coupon $R(t_l) + \mu$ is unknown. The sensible solution is to use the same $\rho(t)$ from Equation (17.8) instead of these term rates.

17.4   CMS AND CMT FLOATERS

Several entities, including the French, Italian and Japanese governments, have issued variable-rate bonds where the coupons are set with reference to a long-term rate. In the French and Japanese cases, that rate was a 10Y government yield, while Italy issued eurobonds with coupons linked to various swap rates, usually the 10Y swap rate. Bonds linked to benchmark yields in the government bond and swap markets are known as constant-maturity treasury (CMT) and constant-maturity swap (CMS) floaters. Private issuers also issue securities with more complex CMS structures, such as coupons linked to the spread between 2Y and 10Y CMS rates[3].

The first question about such bonds is how the relevant rates can be observed, given that bond and swap markets are over-the-counter markets where prices are negotiated in private. For CMT rates, the French market has a well-known benchmark known as the TEC10 which is calculated from price quotations provided by the primary dealers in French bonds. In Japan, the yields seen in the most recent government bond auction, given the large volume transacted in such auctions, give a reliable pricing. For CMS rates, standard fixings exist in the same way as Libor fixings[4]. Such fixing rates are now subject to the same governance rules as other benchmark rates.

Because the fixing rate for the coupon does not coincide with the discount rate applicable to the coupon period, Equation (17.6) does not have the effect of keeping bond prices close to par. Instead, CMT and CMS structures have complex exposures

---

[3]This particular structure would be a 2–10 CMS steepener.
[4]At the time of writing, the Intercontinental Exchange (ICE) provides swap rate fixings for various currencies. These fixings were in the past administrated by the International Swap Dealers Association and are therefore still sometimes colloquially called ISDAfix.

to long-term interest rates given that increasing long-term rates have both the effect of higher forward rates (and thereby expected coupon resets) and lower discount factors. The two effects partly counteract each other in their impact on bond prices so that the convexity adjustment in their pricing is substantial.

CMS structures are generally easier to hedge than CMT structures because paying or receiving swaps has a lower balance sheet cost than holding long or short positions in bonds with the attendant repo operations. As a result, CMT portfolios are usually hedged with CMS structures, exposing the hedge to basis risk. In this case, the risk is a change in the CMS–CMT spread, which is in essence the swap spread of the government bond curve.

CHAPTER 18

Asset Markets and Liquidity

18.1   CONCEPTS

The liquidity of an asset is the ease with which it can be converted into cash when required, or conversely, the ease with which it can be bought for cash. In both cases the focus is on such a conversion taking place without affecting market prices too much. This definition explains why the word liquidity is used in this context in the first place: more generally, liquidity refers to the cash or cash-like instruments held by an entity. Market liquidity then refers to the general liquidity conditions of the assets in that market, e.g., the market for US Treasuries or Japanese municipal bonds.

Liquidity is not constant. While a typical government bond in Europe will see roughly unchanged trading activity throughout its life, turnover in a usual corporate bond will drop by around 90% within the first six months of its life. US Treasury bonds also show declining activity in older securities while in the JGB market liquidity differs across the various types of JGB. Liquidity during a usual trading day tends to be higher in the morning hours than in the afternoon and important economic data releases or other news events can drain liquidity while the market digests the new information.

One aspect of liquidity is tied to a search problem: A seller of an asset needs to find a willing buyer for that specific asset at the current time at a price that is at or near the indications available in the market. Simple combinatorics imply that this search problem is easier when the number of assets is smaller, or the number of potential buyers is larger. Issuers can therefore aid liquidity by restricting the number of securities they issue and produce larger volume securities instead. This is one reason for the relative scarcity of very long-dated bonds: An issuer who issues a new 100 year bond every year will eventually have 100 bonds outstanding and so split market liquidity across so many securities while the sum of the outstanding amounts of these bonds equals the total debt of the issuer. If the same issuer issues 10-year bonds instead, each one can be 10 times larger and is likely to be more liquid as a result[1]. Issuers can also make it easier for a broad range of investors to participate in the market by avoiding artificial constraints related to settlement and custody arrangements.

---

[1]The downside for the issuer is that shorter bonds require more frequent refinancing and so expose the issuer more to interest rate volatility.

The conversion between assets and cash can happen in a variety of ways, two extremes of which are public exchanges and market makers. Public exchanges are sometimes called central limit order books, or CLOBs in reference to the most common technical structure of these venues: Exchange participants send orders to the exchange that specify the asset, the side (buy or sell), a quantity, and a limit price which is the highest purchase price, or the lowest sale price, that the participant will accept. These orders are collected in a central book, and matched up against each other whenever possible. Participants have the option to modify or rescind orders in response to market news.

Market makers, in contrast, hold themselves out to provide prices to their clients in what is known as the over-the-counter (OTC) market, regardless of whether there is an intermediate offsetting trading interest from another client. Two protocols are used for such transactions. The most common by far is the request for quote (RFQ) protocol where a client requests a firm price for a given size and transaction side in a specific security, and the market maker responds with a price, or, less commonly, with a refusal to trade. Trading can take place on electronic platforms or via phone or chat (both the latter are referred to as 'voice' trading). The alternative streaming pricing protocol is one where dealers continuously post executable prices on some electronic platforms and clients can choose to execute at these prices up to a certain maximum size. Regulators prefer the streaming protocol for transparency but in practice dealers have little economic incentive to offer good pricing on such services. It is an essential component of market making that firms offering such a service are willing to warehouse securities for some time until they are able to lay off the positions to some other market participant.

The search problem mentioned above is approached in different ways by exchanges and market making. Exchanges aim for the concentration of a large number of investors in the same venue. Market making essentially eliminates the search problem by producing willing counterparties, albeit at a cost (the bid–offer spread charged by the market maker and any information advantage gained from being in this business). To make this possible, market makers keep their positions secret (at least from the wider market) to prevent infomation leakage.

While public exchanges have been ubiquitous for a long time, their existence in a capitalist economy is worth a second thought. Exchanges are shared utilities of their participants but these participants are by nature competitors. Exchange trading is an obvious zero-sum game where every change in price of a transaction creates a different redistribution of wealth between the two parties that transact. There are two possible explanations why exchanges form despite this natural antagonism of their users. The first is that exchanges divide the total set of investors into one of insiders (exchange members) and outsiders (everyone else). For insiders, any disadvantage created by the succour given to the other insiders is outweighed by the advantages enjoyed collectively by the insiders vis-à-vis the outsiders who do not have access to the trading venue. In economic terms, exchange members form a cartel and enjoy economic rents. An example of such an advantage was the existence of fixed (i.e. non-competitive) minimum commissions charged by members of the London Stock Exchange to the investing public before the 'Big Bang' reforms implemented on 27 October 1986 [59]. A second potential explanation is that the reduction of search costs and collective regulation is a sufficiently valuable public good for the exchange members to offset the disadvantage of supporting one's competitors. Rather than being concerned with the benefits their activity bestows on their competitors, exchange members value the reduction in potential risks to themselves created by the ability to control or lay off risks to other firms. This type of outcome is an example of a network effect[2]. This network effect could be achieved by other means, however. The EuroMTS trading platform is an inter-dealer trading venue where dealers post firm prices to each other. The existence of the platform allows dealers to exit unfavourable positions, but the bid–offer spreads seen on this platform are wider than the general market. The MTS platform is therefore not the optimal pricing venue for dealer trading, and is not designed for that purpose. In any case, dealer has a strong incentive to sell a bond to a client at the market offer rather than at the MTS bid to another dealer. As a result, while MTS provides good price discovery, the actual execution activity on the platform is dwarfed by the overall market volumes.

Public exchanges and OTC markets compete for client trading activity. Investors sending orders to an exchange can look for execution at a transparent venue for comparatively low fees but by sending in their order they make public what trade they are looking to execute. The information disclosure alone can lead to an adverse move in market prices; this effect is called information leakage. In addition, while information leakage is virtually certain to occur, there may be no opposing order in the CLOB that would be match the trading interest so exposed, at least not in a short period of time and near market levels prevailing when the initial order was posted. In this case, the investor has disclosed information but not managed to execute the trade. Sending the order to a market maker in the OTC market discloses the trade interest only to that counterparty but market makers will seek to generate profits by seeking to quote low bid and high offer prices. Investors can try to restrict such behaviour by sending the same pricing request to multiple market makers at the same time ('in competition'[3]). However, market making is overall a business that not only covers the cost of the resources involved but is also profitable. This observation implies that users of the OTC market are paying for the provision of liquidity. The economic trade-off between exchange and OTC execution is therefore essentially tied to search costs. When many investors trade a relatively small number of distinct assets, public exchanges are likely to be an efficient execution venue. When there are too many similar but not fully fungible assets, trading interest is dispersed across them and OTC execution is more likely to be more efficient. This explains why blue-chip equities and bond futures contracts trade comfortably on exchanges, while bonds and small-cap equities trade mostly in the OTC market.

The competition between public exchanges and OTC markets suggests that it is unlikely that market makers are able to extract rents in the same way as exchange members could. Even if one were to argue that market making is not sufficiently competitive,

---

[2]Cities exhibit similar network effects in that traders of related crafts congregate in the same areas because the benefit of finding customers easily outweighs the downside of always being in close competition. Street names like Bread Street in London and areas like Takaracho in Tokyo are reminders of these times.

[3]It is considered polite to disclose the presence of competition to the market maker. Many investors have regulatory obligations to trade in competition ('in comp') involving at least three market makers.

the market could always move to exchanges if trading there was cheaper. Given that the majority of bonds are listed to satisfy formal criteria, trading them on exchange is to all extents already possible but apparently not economical[4].

Exchange trading and market making are not mutually exclusive. Some exchanges occasionally operate compensation models for some products where exchange participants who commit to providing continuous bid and offer prices share in the exchange fees paid by other users who trade on these prices. This is typically done in order to generate an initial trading interest in new products and continues until a natural market is established[5]. In other instances, specialist trading firms (known in the US as principal trading firms, or PTFs) act like market makers in normal times without being formally recognised as such. This does, however, also imply that such firms will not make prices when trading conditions become less favourable for them.

Recently, alternative forms of bridging the gap between public exchanges and market making have emerged. One is algorithmic trading, which is a catch-all term for strategies that execute trades on public exchanges without disclosing the true trade interest to the wider market. When such strategies are used to manage larger trades without disturbing market prices too much, this is generally not viewed as negative. However, the same types of algorithm can also be used to mislead the market about trade interest in order to move prices. Such strategies, known as spoofing, are considered to be market abuse. The other alternative is dark pools, which operate like public exchanges but without a public disclosure of orders[6]. Unlike public exchanges ('lit' markets in this context), dark pools disclose trade interests only when orders can actually be matched. Financial firms that have traditionally been market makers have set up dark pools to augment their market making business, which requires committing balance sheet to the warehousing of positions, with what is essentially a match-making service for clients. For regulators, dark pools detract from the goal of achieving more transparency in financial markets.

From an investor's point of view, the picture is not perfectly clear. Each investor would like to know about each of the other investors' trading conditions while having an interest to conceal her or his own trades from the wider market to prevent information leakage. Both goals cannot be achieved at the same time.

---

[4]The German Bundesbank provides a service which consists of posting prices on German public exchanges based on the liquidity of the OTC market. If exchanges were a superior execution venue, this service would not need to exist.

[5]Such arrangements are not without complications. The exchange is in effect spending funds of exchange users on the creation of trading activity that would not otherwise exist. This may be seen as misleading these users as to the actual liquidity in the products involved. As long as such arrangements are properly disclosed and limited in duration regulators do not normally intervene. However, there has been at least one instance, involving the 10Y OAT contract on Matif in 2000, where regulators did step in to stop what was perceived as an artificial inflation of trading activity [55]. In this case French banks had set up a 'Matif intervention bancaire', inevitably known as the 'Men in black' by its acronym, to generate extra trading activity.

[6]A dark pool is therefore comparable to a broker market, but available to a wider public.

18.2 LIQUIDITY MEASUREMENT

The definition of liquidity has some obvious conceptual problems. There are multiple venues in which assets can be traded and each of them may lead to different assessments of liquidity. Not every investor has access to every public exchange, every dark pool, or is being serviced by every market maker. Liquidity therefore is dependent on the investor, not just on the asset. Practically, most liquidity indicators are therefore measured for a given execution venue and therefore apply to a certain class of investors. This means, however, that contagion across trading venues is by construction not reflected and liquidity may be understated as a result.

Moreover, measuring liquidity relies on one of two counterfactual assumptions, namely 'At what price could a trade take place (while it does not)?' or 'What would the market price be if a trade had not taken place?' These two counterfactuals open two problems: How reliable are price quotations when they are not provided with a firm intention to trade; and, How can price movements caused by actual trades be separated from price movements caused by other factors?

The first concern about the reliability of quotes is related to advertising. Market makers have an incentive to show very competitive quotes on an indicative basis in order to attract requests for firm quotes. Meanwhile, algorithmic trading algorithms operating on public exchanges also are designed to suggest that trading opportunities are available at or near current market prices. In either case, the intent is to incentivise investors to reveal true trade interest. At the time such interest is revealed, the market picture might change. A market maker may refuse to quote on a firm basis, or an algorithm may choose to cancel an order. In either case, the indicated market prices can be unavailable for actual execution.

The second concern above is reminiscent of the Heisenberg Uncertainty Principle in physics. Prices are fundamentally a stock measure in the sense that they are point-in-time assessments of the value of an asset. Trading volumes are, on the other hand, flow measures that reflect the amount of an asset that has changed hands over a certain period of time. To measure flow precisely, it needs to be observed over a certain period of time, while over that period of time other factors, such as economic data releases, can affect prices. This means that price measurement becomes more uncertain if flow is observed over longer time intervals.

Another important concern is about the very notion of trading in the context of defining liquidity (see Figure 18.1). One can treat each transaction as an event by itself

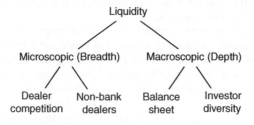

FIGURE 18.1 Multiple aspects of liquidity.

and define liquidity related only to this single trade instance. This microscopic aspect, also called market breadth, is largely related to the competitive environment between market makers and the willingness of non-bank dealers to respond to trade orders or quote requests. In a wider context, however, the totality of transactions performed in a given period will have some common elements, such as dis-investment from a certain subset of securities. This creates a correlation between individual transactions that will be reflected in market pricing. This is the macroscopic aspect of liquidity, called market depth. The ability of the market to absorb correlated flow is related to the aggregate risk absorption capacity of liquidity providers, including non-dealers with active trading operations. The number or competitive situation of liquidity providers is less important in this context than the capacity to hold positions in the face of market volatility.

In this sense, macroscopic liquidity is harder to observe because it is only meaning-ful when trading patterns are less diversifiable. From a market stability point of view, this is somewhat disconcerting because it means that a lack of market depth will only be observed when market depth is needed. Simply relying on microscopic liquidity mea-sures to gauge market depth is however not an option given the arguments made above.

18.2.1 Taxonomy of liquidity measures

There is a multitude of quantitative liquidity indicators used in the market and this requires some form of taxonomy. One approach is to classify indicators by the type of information used, as done in Table 18.1.

What may be surprising is the inclusion of measures that do not rely on trade infor-mation at all. The thinking behind such measures is that a liquid market has secondary properties, such as the absence of obvious arbitrage opportunities. Illiquidity can there-fore manifest itself through the appearance of apparent mis-pricing.

Each type of measure suffers from particular problems. However, in many instances the trends shown by different indicators tend to move in the same direction [36]. When they do not, their divergence may reveal deeper information about changes in mar-ket conditions, such as investor perception of trading conditions as opposed to current liquidity.

Pre-trade measures rely on price quotations that may not be firm, or could be withdrawn before they can be executed on. Liquidity apparent in such prices may also disappear at any time. Most aggregated indicative screen price bid–offer spreads are substantially wider than what could be achieved in actual trading although individual dealers may window-dress their own indications to be tighter than what they are

TABLE 18.1 Liquidity measures by type of information used

Pre-trade information	Post-trade information	No-trade information
Bid–offer spreads	Trade impact	Spline spread dispersion
Order book depth	Trade volumes	Futures dislocation
Repo rates	Quote dispersion	
	Time to quote	
	Trade sizes	

actually willing to quote in firm inquiries. At the same time, algorithmic traders may be hiding the full extent of their trade interest from public order books, so liquidity might actually be better than the visible order book suggests. Last but not least, many markets have minimum price gradations. This introduces quantisation noise into any price measures. Other pre-trade measures are the frequency of price updates (less liquid markets will see fewer updates) but the increasing prevalance of machine pricing means that prices may be updated by an algorithm with no reference to actual trading activity. Commercial providers produce related indicators based on actually transacted prices relative to indicative mid prices. That being said, sample bias can be a significant problem for such measures because in stressed liquidity situation there will be no bid and offer prices for less liquid securities, and trading will be concentrated in the most liquid securities.

Post-trade indicators are based on actual trades, rather than potentially misleading indications. Typically, they relate the price changes observed in a given time period to the observed trade volumes. However, they too may be misleading for three reasons. First, not every trade is observable by every market participant so any measurement will be based on a potentially biased subset of trades that could be observed. Second, the subset of trades that have taken place is itself a biased sample of trades that *could* take place, namely that subset that was deemed both necessary and executable at the time. To the extent that portfolio managers make trading decisions based on their judgement of relative ease of execution (which is incumbent on good portfolio managers), post-trade measures of liquidity may be biased away from illiquid securities. Third, measures related to the price impact of trade volumes additionally may be skewed by the amount of market-moving information, including trades in related markets, that emerged during the observation period. Market prices may move by large amounts even in the absence of any trading when new information arrives. Other post-trade indicators are trade size, number and volume of trades, and so on. Such indicators are also not without problems. A dormant market may burst into activity not just due to improved liquidity, but also because investors feel the need to enter or exit that market.

An interesting post-trade indicator for active trading clients is the dispersion of prices observed in competitive requests for quotes from multiple counterparties. In a liquid market, dealers can be expected to be well aware of the market-clearing price and willing to quote close to it. In a less liquid market, dealers will be both uncertain about the prevailing price level, and more inclined to adjust prices to their current inventory. Given that dealers sometimes use off-market prices to signal an unwillingness to trade, care needs to be taken to disregard such unrealistic responses. As other post-trade indicators, this type of measure suffers from sample bias as portfolio managers select the trades that appear executable, while the execution traders select the counterparties that are likely to offer reasonable prices.

The practical definition of indirect indicators relies on a reasonably reliable implementation of the arbitrage concept. An arbitrage opportunity is always a theoretical concept and may not be present in practice, or the identification of opportunities may be flawed. For instance, spline spreads calibrated on spot market prices may suggest over- and under-valued securities. However, the conditions for borrowing the securities indentified as overpriced for short-selling, or the cost of funding long positions in the apparently underpriced securities, may make it impossible to trade on this perceived

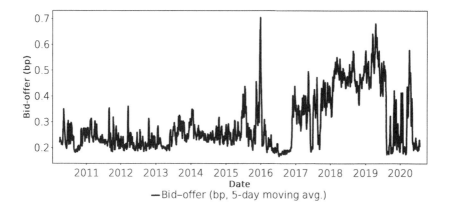

FIGURE 18.2 Bid–offer spreads (in yield basis points) of nominal US Treasuries with remaining maturities of 7–15 years, calculated from data obtained from treasurydirect.gov. Note that the convention to quote Treasuries in 1/256th steps creates an effective lower bound on the bid–offer spread equivalent to around 0.04 bps in this maturity range. European bond markets are less liquid but are quoted in price steps of 1/1,000th (0.1 cents). Source: Data obtained from treasurydirect. Gov.

opportunity. Moreover, the removal of arbitrage opportunities through trades that take advantage of them can only occur to the extent that market participants judge liquidity conditions to be sufficient. Since such judgements can take time to adjust, and can be disturbed by news flow, the link to actual liquidity conditions can be tenuous at times. On the other hand, indirect indicators are not biased by advertisement effect of indicative prices, and less biased by trade selection than the post-trade indicators[7]. In this respect, indirect indicators may be a better measure of macroscopic liquidity, with the caveat mentioned above that, in the absence of undiversified flow, such indicators will not signal a deterioration of liquidity conditions.

To sum up, each type of liquidity indicator has advantages and disadvantages. Indirect indicators may be better at reflecting problems in the macroscopic liquidity, while the pre- and post-trade indicators reflect microscopic liquidity developments. This means that rather than relying on a single indicator, it is useful to monitor a set of diverse indicators and pay as much attention to the divergences observed as to the commonalities.

18.3 EXAMPLES

The production of pre- and post-trade bid–offer indicators is structurally fairly simple as long as the relevant data is available. Figure 18.2 shows an example of average bid–offer spread data for US Treasuries.

As an example of indirect liquidity indicators, Figure 18.3 shows average absolute spline spreads against a Nelson-Siegel spline. The production of such indicators is more

---

[7]Indeed one could argue that indirect indicators reflect the cost of trades that are not done, instead of the trades that actually take place.

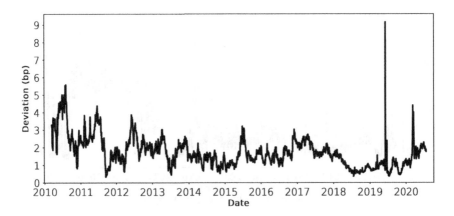

FIGURE 18.3 Average absolute deviations from a Nelson-Siegel spline for US Treasuries with remaining maturities of 7–15 years, calculated from data obtained from treasurydirect.gov. The spline is fitted to maturities from 1 to 30 years and spreads are re-based to average 0 for all bonds in the daily sample. Source: Data obtained from treasurydirect. Gov.

complex than for Figure 18.2. First, a fair value model has to be fitted to the observed market prices. Here, this model has been fitted to the entire curve. The average absolute yield deviation from fair value is then calculated for a subset of bonds so liquidity conditions in different parts of the curve can be assessed independently. To remove the impact of sectoral richness or cheapness, the spreads are first re-centred to a zero average.

Both measures show low liquidity (high indicator values) around the latter stage of the financial crisis and around the time of the 'taper tantrum' of 2013. What is more interesting is the divergence of both indicators in 2015/16. While the microscopic bid–offer spread indicator shows no meaningful deterioration, spline spreads show a greater dispersion. Given that this period coincided with the activation of restrictions on trading introduced by the Dodd–Frank Act, perhaps there could be a connection to lowered provision of dealer balance sheets, particularly in the repo market.

Changing liquidity conditions are often correlated across markets because operating constraints affect dealers in similar ways.

Figure 18.4 shows identically calculated liquidity indicators across the US, Germany and Japan during the worst phase of the market disruption caused by the Covid-19 outbreak in 2020. All three markets show substantial strains going into March. Factors contributing to this development were funding difficulties for some market participants and pressure to reduce risk positions in the face of heightened volatility. On 15 March, the Federal Reserve announced significant measures which were in part aimed at supporting Treasury market functioning, including a market-neutral approach to purchases and extended repo lending of the SOMA portfolio. These measures supported a notable improvement in the US market. The ECB's public-sector purchase programme (PSPP) had already been implemented in a market-neutral fashion since its inception in 2015 which partially explains why the liquidity situation in the Bund market did not deteriorate to the same extent as in the US. Still, the ECB added an additional purchase

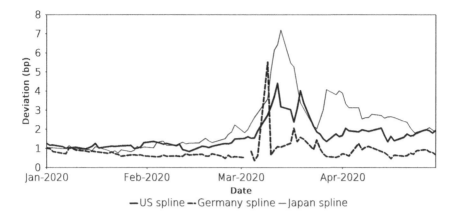

FIGURE 18.4 Spline liquidity indicators for US Treasuries, German Bunds and JGB calculated in the same way as in Figure 18.3 during the worst phase of the Corona virus in 2020. Sources: Data from TreasuryDirect, Bundesbank and JSDA.

envelope to PSPP and on 18 March launched the Pandemic Emergency Purchase Programme and market liquidity also improved.

18.4   LIQUIDITY PREMIUM

The total return of an investment depends on the transaction costs related to entering and leaving the position. Simplistically, the return of a bond is given by:

$$\text{Return} = [\text{Coupon income}] + [\text{Capital gain}] - [\text{Bid} - \text{offer spread}] \qquad (18.1)$$

The items in this equation have different time dependencies. If a bond is bought and sold again immediately, then the first two terms will be zero while the third term, which will usually not be zero, creates a loss. Over very long periods, the first two terms should dominate this equation.

From the perspective of a portfolio manager, the return of the entire portfolio is the sum of such terms for each individual asset held. Because usual portfolios require trading, either to respond to inflow and outflows, or to changes in outlook, trading costs, i.e., the third term in this equation, are of great importance.

Some assets are known to be tradeable with lower transaction costs because they have a deeper market, or because market trading is concentrated in these securities. If that is the case, then a portfolio manager considering the equation above for two securities with different transaction costs (third term) will have to consider an expected holding period to weigh the first two terms agains the third when comparing the securities. For a short holding period, transaction costs are relatively more important, and a more liquid but lower yielding bond may be more attractive than a higher yielding, but less liquid one. Lower transaction costs can therefore generate a yield discount, or price premium, known as the liquidity premium. In some markets, and notably the

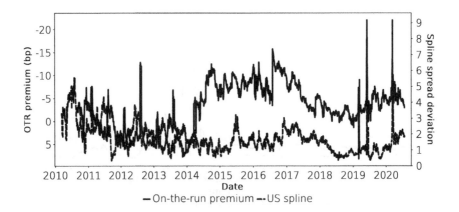

FIGURE 18.5 On-the-run premium and spline spread deviation measures of US Treasury market liquidity. Note that the spline spread deviation is plotted on the inverted right axis so that downwards movements in both series mean a deterioration in conditions. The impact of the repo squeeze in the summer of 2019, and the onset of the Corona pandemic in 2020 are clearly identifiable. Ten-day averages. Source: Data from TreasuryDirect.

US Treasury market, the most liquid securities trade at lower yields compared to more liquid ones.

This relationship between liquidity and premium is not static but changes with perceived holding periods. If investors do not see an immediate need to adjust their portfolio structures, then it would be irrational to accept the lower income associated with the liquidity premium. Conversely, in times of higher market uncertainty, there can always be a need for rapid portfolio adjustment, and liquidity premia increase. The liquidity preium is therefore in itself a measure of market liquidity, and can be used to monitor market developments.

Figure 18.5 shows a comparison of the spline-based liquidity measure discussed above and a liquidity premium measure defined simply as the spline spread of the most liquid US Treasury, the on-the-run 10Y. The two show a strong co-movement[8] but are not identical. The different evolution is related to the conceptual difference between the measures. The spline spread dispersion is largely a measure of potential arbitrage opportunities, and a higher value means that for a larger set of securities investors do not have the means or the confidence to use such opportunities. The spline spread of the on-the-run need not represent an arbitrage opportunity because a higher liquidity premium may be warranted by market volatility. As such, the liquidity premium measures liquidity conditions via the price investors are willing to obtain liquid assets.

Many market participants use simpler measures of the on-the-run premium, such as the spread between the on-the-run and a particular off-the-run, such as the second or third youngest security of the same initial maturity. Such measures are easier

---

[8]Arguably, the spline spread of the on-the-run is part of the average used to calculate the total spline spread deviation. However, its weight is not large enough to dominate the volatility of the average.

to construct than the spline-based measure here but require a trade-off. The closer the on-the-run and off-the-run are in maturity, the more similar they are in liquidity and the smaller and more volatile the spread observed between them. To get a more meaningful measure, one should use older comparables to the on-the-run, but that means a larger difference in maturity dates. This pollutes the liquidity premium measure with curve movements, such as simple steepening/flattening moves. In addition, larger differences in issuance date can mean larger differences in coupon, so that yield spread comparisons are compromised by coupon effects. Both effects can be mitigated by comparing not yields but spline spreads between on-the-run and off-the-run. If one is prepared to go so far, then just using the on-the-run spline spread is simpler. It has the added advantage that idiosyncratic movements of any one off-the-run do not affect the liquidity measure.

The German and Japanese markets do not show the same extent of on-the-run premia because price discovery and duration hedging in these markets takes place in futures contracts. This difference in market structure means that the liquidity advantage of an on-the-run security is not as significant, and there is therefore no associated premium. Technically, the most liquid instruments are the futures' cheapest-to-deliver bonds but that does not always lead to a premium. Instead, when markets exhibit selling pressure, this may first lead to a cheapening of futures contracts, and thereby the CTDs, relative to their respective bond curves.

18.5   LIQUIDITY AND VOLATILITY

Because realistic market prices are usually only observable through trading, liquidity can affect price volatility through an effect known as bid–ask bounce. The mechanics of this effect are shown in Figure 18.6.

The assumption is that mid prices, which reflect the economic value of the instrument given all public known information, follow a stochastic process. As investors buy

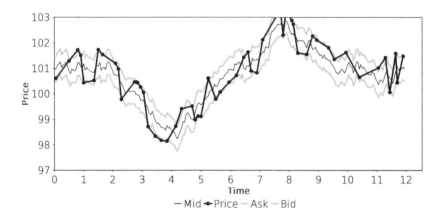

FIGURE 18.6   Observed price evolution for an illiquid instrument. As trading (dots) occasionally switches from the bid to the ask side of the market, prices appear to jump while actual mid price has much lower volatility.

and sell the instrument, however, they trade on ask or bid prices, respectively, that also reflect the liquidity of the instrument. The evolution of traded prices therefore incorporates not only the volatility of the mid price, but also the bid–offer spread. If the bid–ask spread is wide, this second volatility component can dominate the underlying volatility of the mid price.

In practice, there is no mid price that would be known to market makers but unknown to investors. Instead, one can envisage a price at which the market would clear if there was an equal amount of buying and selling interest in the market and consider that to be the mid price. At any given time, however, buying or selling interest will dominate due to the emergence of economic news, or structural factors such as index rebalancing events. Prices then need to move so much as to entice erstwhile buyers to stop buying, or erstwhile neutral investors to consider selling, for instance. This would be equivalent to the transition towards the ask price in Figure 18.6. In this case, the change in flow direction would, via this effective mid-ask or mid-bid transition, generate an apparent price volatility that would not be present in a more liquid market.

CHAPTER 19

Curves and Curve Models

n Section 16.7, on yields, it was pointed out that Equation (16.10):

$$P = \sum_i \frac{Cf_i}{(1+y)^{DCF(t_s,t_i)}}$$

suffers from a fundamental defect, namely that the same discount rate y is applied to every cash flow of a given bond. In a typical market with more than one bond, it will generally be the case that these bonds trade at different yields. Cash flows occuring at the same or similar times from different bonds would therefore be discounted with different rates depending on which bond they belong to. This is somewhat unsatisfactory when one associates yields with the expected rate of return available in the market for investments of a given horizon. One would therefore somehow prefer to change Equation (16.10) in such a way that y becomes a function of time, i.e., $y(t)$.

This of course runs into a mathematical problem, namely that a single equation can only define the value of a single variable. However, these two problems solve each other: By using information about multiple bonds *simultaneously*, one can derive time-dependent discount rates that are consistent with the prices of these bonds. Such a time-dependent set of discount rates is known as a term structure and the model representation of a term structure is a curve.

Therefore, a yield curve is the representation of market information contained in the prevailing prices of a set of fixed-income instruments. It can be seen as a holding bag for instrument definitions and prices. The complexity of this holding bag can differ widely between different representations.

The purpose of using curves is that they allow the pricing of instruments using discount factors. These instruments need not be the same ones as those used to define the curve itself, and they need not even exist at all. Overall, therefore, one has a structure as shown below where instrument definitions and prices are used to form a curve and the curve, and instrument definitions and a curve provide prices:

Instruments+Prices ⟶ Curve ⟶ Prices
↗
Instruments

The concrete representation of a curve is known as a model. Different types of curve models are explained in the next section. In this book, the focus is less on the many varieties of curve models that have been proposed because good literature exists on those ([40, 52, 69] etc.). Instead, the focus is on the use of models for trading.

19.1 MODELS

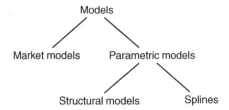

The concept of a curve is fundamental for the comparison of fixed income products over different time horizons. Generally speaking, a curve is the abstract concept of associating interest rates with investment horizons. The concept of interest rate curve of various kinds has already been used implictly when interest rates were treated as time dependent in the sections on money market calculations. It is important to be aware that there are many different ways of representing time-dependent interest rates and that there may be more than one interest rate applying to a given time horizon, namely when credit risk, liquidity factors, and legal issues (such as onshore versus offshore markets) are taken into account.

The simplest theoretical starting point for understanding curves is to consider the discount factor curve, i.e., a mapping from time t to a discount factor $Df(t)$. More generally speaking, a discount factor curve is a function $Df(t_1, t_2)$ of two time arguments t_1 and $t_2 > t_1$ giving the value of a unit payment at t_2 at the investment time t_1. However, if the discount factors are unique, one can always use the reinvestment identity:

$$Df(0, t_1)Df(t_1, t_2) = Df(0, t_2) \tag{19.1}$$

to write the 'forward' discount factors in the form of a single argument function.

In general, one can think of 3 mathematically equivalent representations of the yield curve, namely via discount factors, zero rates, or instantaneous forward rates. The par curve, i.e. the mapping from a maturity time t to the coupon rate of a bond that will be priced at 100% of notional value differs from these 3 equivalent curves in that the par curve depends on bond market conventions, such as coupon frequency, holiday calendar, and daycount convention. The relationship between the 4 curve representations is therefore best represented by Figure 19.1.

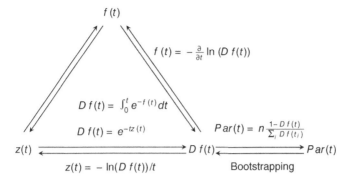

FIGURE 19.1 Curve representations.

19.2 YIELD CURVE REPRESENTATION AND INTERPRETATIONS

19.2.1 Discount factors versus par curves

The discount factor form is the theoretically most natural way of expressing a term structure of discount factors, but it is by no means the only one. A common form of representing the same information is to write discount factors in the form of a par interest rate curve, i.e., as a mapping from a time to maturity to the interest rate (coupon) of a par bond. The price of any fixed coupon bond is given as the total present value of all its cash flows, so for a par bond with a coupon frequency of f:

$$1 = \frac{C}{f} \sum_{i=1}^{N} Df(t_i) + Df(t_N) \tag{19.2}$$

so that the par interest rate $C(t_N)$ of a bond maturing at t_N is:

$$C(t_N) = f \frac{1 - Df(t_N)}{\sum\limits_{i=1}^{N} Df(t_i)} \tag{19.3}$$

This representation is common because fixed rate coupon bonds represent the most common investment universe for bond investors. However, it has a number of obvious drawbacks. First, the par rate is in general dependent on the coupon frequency and it will have a more complicated form when the time to maturity is not an integer multiple of the coupon period. Par curves are therefore usually restricted to node points that are evenly spaced at coupon periods. Furthermore, actual bond coupons are fixed at the time of issuance so that par bonds may not actually be available for investment. The par curve is therefore not directly observable in general. Note also that if the coupon frequency is not annual and the yield convention is not bond-equivalent, the yield of a par bond is not equal to the coupon. One could then alternatively define the par curve as the yield curve of par bonds. The translation between the two definitions is straightforward, however.

Equation (19.3) is a translation from discount factors to par rates. The opposite translation is referred to as bootstrapping, explained in Section 19.3.1.

There are two fundamentally different modes of curve representation. On the one hand, one can treat a curve as a collection of observable and tradeable instruments in the market, together with a prescription of how to calculate interest rates that are not given by these instruments, such as interpolation rules. The second type of representation uses a general functional form for the mapping between maturities and interest rates and this mathematical form is used with a set of parameters which will give discount factors or interest rates that best reproduce the rates observed in the market. The two representations can coincide in the extreme sense that the bootstrapping method above, together with the coupon bond price P_i, the coupon C_i and the maturity point t_i, form a parameter set. The intention of market-based curves is generally to obtain a set of discount factors that reprices all market instruments exactly to avoid apparent arbitrages between the model curve and the actual market. This exact repricing usually requires a large number of inputs and may lead to non-intuitive forwards. Parametric curves, in contrast, are usually chosen to arrive at a reduced number of curve parameters and smooth forward rates. Due to the restricted parameter space, not all market instruments, if any, are repriced exactly by such models. On the other hand, divergences between the prices implied by a parametric model and actual market prices can in some cases represent actual dislocations and parametric models are therefore an important tool to discover such opportunities.

Economists tend to focus on zero rates, which are (unfortunately) also known as spot rates. A zero rate $z(t)$ is the market rate for investing money from today to t when there is no intervening cash flow (as opposed to a par curve, where there is a periodic coupon payment). Zero rates avoid the reinvestment risk associated with coupon payments. The interest rate at which a coupon can be reinvested can differ from the initial yield of a coupon bond. The disadvantage is that zero rates are practically unobservable in the market[1] and need to be extracted from coupon bond prices through bootstrapping or spline fits. The price of a zero coupon bond trading at a rate of $z(t)$ is nothing but the discount factor $Df(t)$, namely:

$$Df(t) = \frac{1}{(1 + z(t))^t} \tag{19.4}$$

Zero rates also allow the easy calculation of forward rates, that is, the arbitrage-free interest rates $f(t_1, t_2)$ that are consistent with zero rates from today to t_1 and t_2. The no-arbitrage condition is:

$$Df(t_2) = Df(t_1)Df(t_1, t_2)$$

$$\frac{1}{(1 + z(t_2))^{t_2}} = \frac{1}{(1 + z(t_1))^{t_1}} \frac{1}{(1 + f(t_1, t_2))^{t_2 - t_1}}$$

---

[1]There are zero coupon government bonds created through the stripping of coupon bonds, i.e., the separation of coupon and principal payments. The low liquidity of such intruments means that their prices are not completely aligned with the liquid market prices of the original coupon bonds.

Therefore:

$$f(t_1, t_2) = \sqrt[t_2 - t_1]{\frac{(1 + z(t_2))^{t_2}}{(1 + z(t_1))^{t_1}}} - 1 \tag{19.5}$$

This formula can be, and frequently is, simplified when all t are integer and one is looking for the one-period forward rate $f(t, t + 1)$. Using the binomial expansion:

$$(1 + z(t))^t = \sum_{k=0}^{t} \binom{k}{t} z(t)^k \tag{19.6}$$

and noting that when $z(t) \ll 1$ the binomial expansion is dominated by its first terms:

$$(1 + z(t))^t = 1 + tz(t) + \dots$$

Noting also that, for small x:

$$\frac{1}{1 + x} \approx 1 - x$$

so that Equation (19.5) becomes:

$$f(t, t + 1) \approx \frac{1 + (t + 1)z(t + 1)}{1 + tz(t)} - 1 \approx (t + 1)z(t + 1) - tz(t) \tag{19.7}$$

19.3 MARKET-BASED CURVE REPRESENTATIONS

As mentioned in the outline, market-based curve models are essentially holding bags for market instruments and their prices, together with rules for extracting discount factors and pricing other instruments.

19.3.1 Bootstrapping

The standard way to extract discount factors from equally spaced market rates, such as government bonds or swap rates, is bootstrapping. This procedure consists of progressively stripping coupon instruments into zero coupon instruments, at each step using the zero rates obtained during the previous steps to take the next one. An example is shown in Table 19.1.

The calculation here assumes annual rates, and a daycount convention of annual/annual for simplicity[2]. Under this assumption, the 1Y swap is a zero coupon instrument paying par plus the coupon of 0.307%, so the 1Y discount factor Df_1 is determined by the 1Y par rate p_1 as:

$$Df_1 = \frac{1}{1 + p_1} \tag{19.8}$$

---

[2]For USD swaps, the fixed rate is actually semi-annual.

TABLE 19.1   Bootstrapping of the USD swap curve on 5 June 2020. For simplicity, swap rates have been assumed to be annual. Source: Data from ICE.

Years	Par rate	Df	$\sum Df$	Spot	Fwd
1	0.307%	0.996939	0.996939	0.307%	0.307%
2	0.299%	0.994047	1.990986	0.299%	0.291%
3	0.346%	0.989687	2.980673	0.346%	0.441%
4	0.424%	0.983193	3.963866	0.425%	0.660%
5	0.517%	0.974469	4.938335	0.519%	0.895%
6	0.614%	0.963761	5.902096	0.617%	1.111%
7	0.704%	0.951749	6.853845	0.709%	1.262%
8	0.783%	0.938982	7.792827	0.790%	1.360%
9	0.854%	0.925545	8.718373	0.863%	1.452%
10	0.915%	0.911883	9.630256	0.927%	1.498%

The 2Y swap then is a coupon payment (here of 0.299%) after 1 year, and a payment of par plus the same coupon after 2 years. The discount factor to the 2Y point is at this stage unknown but the discounted values of the coupon of 0.299% paid after 1Y and the payment of 100.299% after 2 years must add up to par. Therefore,

$$Df_2 = \frac{1 - p_2 Df_1}{1 + p_2} \tag{19.9}$$

Moving on to the 3Y swap, it pays 2 coupons of 0.346% (after 1 and 2 years) which have now known discount factors, plus a final payment of 100.346% after 3 years. Hence,

$$Df_3 = \frac{1 - p_3(Df_1 + Df_2)}{1 + p_3} \tag{19.10}$$

This series continues as:

$$Df_i = \frac{1 - p_i \sum_{j=1}^{i-1} Df_j}{1 + p_i} \tag{19.11}$$

Table 19.1 contains the auxiliary column $\sum Df$ containing the sum of discount factors up to the current line, used in the numerator of Equation (19.11). The zero and forward rates are merely derived quantities in this algorithm. The zero rates are given by:

$$z_i = \sqrt[i]{\frac{1}{Df_i}} - 1 \tag{19.12}$$

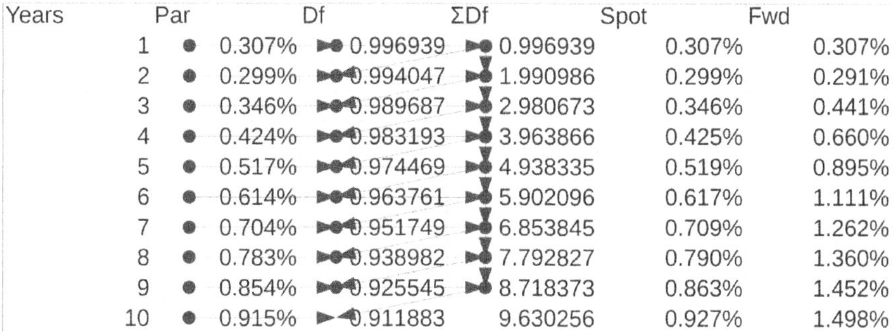

Years	Par	Df	ΣDf	Spot	Fwd
1	● 0.307%	►● 0.996939	►● 0.996939	0.307%	0.307%
2	● 0.299%	►●0.994047	►● 1.990986	0.299%	0.291%
3	● 0.346%	►●0.989687	►● 2.980673	0.346%	0.441%
4	● 0.424%	►●0.983193	►● 3.963866	0.425%	0.660%
5	● 0.517%	►●0.974469	►● 4.938335	0.519%	0.895%
6	● 0.614%	►●0.963761	►● 5.902096	0.617%	1.111%
7	● 0.704%	►●0.951749	►● 6.853845	0.709%	1.262%
8	● 0.783%	►●0.938982	►● 7.792827	0.790%	1.360%
9	● 0.854%	►●0.925545	►● 8.718373	0.863%	1.452%
10	● 0.915%	►●0.911883	9.630256	0.927%	1.498%

FIGURE 19.2 'Bootlacing' representation of the bootstrapping process. Sources: Data from ICE and graphics produced in LibreOffice Calc.

and the forwards starting at period i by:

$$f_i = \frac{Df_{i-1}}{Df_i} - 1 \tag{19.13}$$

When done in a spreadsheet application, the iterative nature of the bootstrapping process can be visualised as a 'bootlacing' by switching on tracing of precedents, shown in Figure 19.2.

In an actual application on coupon bonds, a stub discount factor will apply to the first cashflow which in general occurs earlier than a full coupon period. This stub discount factor carries through to all subsequent cashflows. Similarly, the price of each coupon instrument has been assumed to be par in Equations (19.8, 19.9, 19.10) but this will not generally be the case for actual coupon bonds. These changes can easily be incorporated into the equations and do not fundamentally alter the process.

19.3.2 Reverse bootstrapping

The bootstrapping process outlined above decomposes a regular sequence of coupon instruments into discount factors and zero rates. Occasionally, there is a need to decompose a series of cashflows into par instruments, for instance to translate a given payment obligation into a portfolio of par swaps, or to construct a par bond portfolio with a given payment profile.

Because this decomposition is in some ways the reverse of bootstrapping, it starts at the longest maturity point and progresses towards the shortest. Table 19.2 demonstrates the decomposition of a simple annuity into par swaps using the same curve as in Table 19.1.

Starting at the end, the payment obligation V_6 at the 6Y point is translated into a notional payment plus the par coupon on this notional. The notional is:

$$N_6 = \frac{V_6}{1 + r_6} \tag{19.14}$$

TABLE 19.2 Reverse bootstrapping of a 6-year annuity using the USD swap curve on 5 June 2020. For simplicity, swap rates have been assumed to be annual. Source: Data from ICE.

Years	Par rate	Obligation	Notional	$\sum I$
1	0.307%	1	0.9752964	0.0247036
2	0.299%	1	0.9782906	0.0217094
3	0.346%	1	0.9812157	0.0187843
4	0.424%	1	0.9846107	0.0153893
5	0.517%	1	0.9887854	0.0112146
6	0.614%	1	0.9938975	0.0061025

At the next shorter, the 5Y point, the payment obligation is equal to the 6Y coupon payable on the 6Y swap, plus the 5Y coupon and 5Y notional repayment. Therefore, the notional is:

$$N_5 = \frac{V_5 - N_6 r_6}{1 + r_5} \tag{19.15}$$

Moving on to the 4Y point, this becomes:

$$N_4 = \frac{V_4 - N_6 r_6 - N_5 r_5}{1 + r_4} \tag{19.16}$$

In this form it continues to every shorter point as:

$$N_i = \frac{V_i - \sum\limits_{i=i+1}^{k} N_j r_j}{1 + r_i} \tag{19.17}$$

Again, it is helpful algorithmically to carry the summation term of Equation (19.17) as a separate variable, as done in the last column of Table 19.2.

In this example, a flat annuity has been decomposed into par notionals and as one would expect for positive interest rates, these notionals increase gradually towards longer maturities as the interest payable declines with each maturing par instrument. This calculation differs from the mortgage formula Equation (16.1) on page 141 in that it uses an actual market par curve to discount each cashflow with the appropriate discount factor while the mortgage formula uses a flat interest rate r.

19.4 PARAMETRIC CURVE MODELS

As mentioned earlier, parametric curve models, sometimes also labelled reduced-form models, do not attempt to reprice all market instruments exactly. Instead, their aim is to arrive at a reasonably accurate representation of market rates, and the identification of relative valuation opportunities.

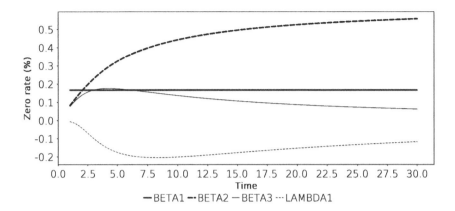

FIGURE 19.3 Sensitivities of zero rates given by a Nelson-Siegel spline to 25% bumps in each curve parameter.

19.4.1 The Nelson-Siegel and Nelson-Siegel-Svensson splines

The Nelson-Siegel spline is a curve model that expresses spot (zero) rates as:

$$z(t) = \beta_1 + \beta_2 \frac{1 - e^{-t/\lambda}}{t/\lambda} + \beta_3 \left[\frac{1 - e^{-t/\lambda}}{t/\lambda} - e^{-t/\lambda} \right] \tag{19.18}$$

The contributions of the 3 terms prefixed by $\beta_{1,2,3}$ represent a constant, an exponentially declining short-term contribution and a hump-shaped medium-term component. The time scale of the second and third components is calibrated by the λ parameter. This easy interpretation means that this type of model is often used by economists, including central banks, to represent bond yield curves in a parsimonious manner.

A useful way to demonstrate the role of each parameter is to fit the curve to a given market so as to obtain a realistic set of parameter values. One can then measure the changes on interest rates induced by changing the value of one parameter at a time. For the Nelson-Siegel spline Equation (19.18), this is done in Figure 19.3 for the example of zero rates.

The Nelson-Siegel-Svensson model is simply the Nelson-Siegel model Equation (19.18) with a second hump term added:

$$z(t) = \beta_1 + \beta_2 \frac{1 - e^{-t/\lambda_1}}{t/\lambda_1} + \beta_3 \left[\frac{1 - e^{-t/\lambda_1}}{t/\lambda_1} - e^{-t/\lambda_1} \right] + \beta_4 \left[\frac{1 - e^{-t/\lambda_2}}{t/\lambda_2} - e^{-t/\lambda_2} \right] \tag{19.19}$$

The additional two parameters (β_4 and λ_2) make the Nelson-Siegel-Svensson model somewhat more flexible. At the same time, the separation between the two λ parameters can be weak, which leads to identification problems between the terms led by β_3 and β_4.

A Nelson-Siegel spline is used in the calculation of the REX index of Germany government bond yields. The REX index is administered by Deutsche Börse AG and the associated REXP performance is used by some German domestic fund managers. Because German government bonds used to exhibit a strong tax-driven coupon effect, the Nelson-Siegel form of a polynomial yield curve is augmented by a second-order polynomial of the coupon for each bond.

The REXP is based on the performance of 30 theoretical bonds with integer maturities of 1, 2, ... 10 years and coupons of 6%, 7.5%, and 9% to calculate the daily performances. The REXP is not representative of the German debt market because it uses fixed weightings for the 30 theoretical bonds instead of actual market weights for the maturity sectors. More fatally for investors looking to replicate the REXP performance, current German government coupons are lower than the theoretical benchmark coupons and the tax effect is such that the yield of higher coupon bonds is higher than that of lower coupon bonds. The running carry of the REXP benchmark basket is therefore higher than what can be achieved with the actual underlying bonds. Managers benchmarked to the REXP index therefore generally carry spread risk to earn back the basis between the benchmark and the actual underlying market.

19.4.2 Polynomial splines

Although the word 'spline' has already been used in the context of the Nelson-Siegel spline, mathematically a spline refers to a narrower class of functions, namely piece-wise polynomials. It is therefore natural to try and use such piecewise polynomials to represent yield curves. To define a spline, one uses a set of N node points t_i where time ordering is assumed for simplicity ($t_i > t_j \ \forall \ i > j$). One can, but does not have to, assume $t_0 = 0$.

A piecewise polynomial of degree n is a set of polynomials defined by:

$$y_i(t) = \sum_{k=0}^{n} \beta_{i,k} t^k \text{ for } t_i < t < t_{i+1} \tag{19.20}$$

This definition provides a set of $N - 1$ basis funtions over the closed intervals $[t_i, t_{i+1}]$ and these basis functions have n coefficients each. To reduce the number of free parameters, one adds the constraint that the first $n - 1$ derivatives of these polynomials should agree at the node points, i.e.,

$$y_i(t_{i+1}) = y_{i+1}(t_{i+1}) \tag{19.21}$$

$$y_i'(t_{i+1}) = y_{i+1}'(t_{i+1}) \tag{19.22}$$

$$y_i''(t_{i+1}) = y_{i+1}''(t_{i+1}) \tag{19.23}$$

...

These constraints can of course be expressed in terms of the polynomial coefficients $\beta_{i,k}$ which then give a system of $(N - 1)(n - 1)$ linear equations. This set of equations is incomplete as long as no additional constraints are posed to resolve the remaining $N - 1$ free coefficients. There are two possible ways to define these equations. The approach taken in computer graphics, where splines are most commonly applied, is to define the values of the polynomials at the node points t_i. Because there are N node points, the most useful choice for a curve model is to leave the value free at $t_N = \infty$. However, the choice of restricting the values at the node points means that one needs to obtain market yields at the node points which generally means that node points are set to correspond to the maturities of benchmark instruments. Replicating the swap curve with such a spline model is unproblematic because swap rates to fixed maturities are observable in daily market data. If cash bonds are used instead, one has to live with the fact that the time to maturity for each node point will be changing every day. Normally, the time to maturity will drop by one business day each business day, but there will be jumps in the node location whenever a new benchmark appears. This may be a problem in some applications, especially because the smoothness condition does not extend far enough to generate continuous forward overnight rates (unless of course overnight rates are used to build the spline). However, a polynomial spline fitted to market par yields in general delivers a yield curve that can be hedged with market instruments (albeit with a number of instruments that is equal to the number of node points). This means that the polynomial spline curve is tradeable; which is, of course, a precondition for using it in curve arbitrage trades.

A polynomial spline was the basis for the now discontinued JEX/JEXP index family produced by Deutsche Börse AG for the German Jumbo Pfandbrief market.

19.4.3 The exponential spline

The exponential spline model is a model that is formulated explicitly in discount factor space. In particular, discount factors are written as:

$$Df(t) = \sum_{i=1}^{n} \beta_i e^{-i\alpha t} \tag{19.24}$$

The boundary condition $Df(0) = 1$ translates directly into:

$$\sum_{i=1}^{n} \beta_i = 1 \tag{19.25}$$

The basis functions of this spline are ever faster declining exponentials, and in the special case of $n = 1$ the model is simply one where the yield 'curve' is given by a constant exponentially compounded interest rate α. For $n > 1$, this interpretation is preserved in the limit of very large t because for $t \gg 1$:

$$\lim_{t \to \infty} Df(t) = \beta_1 e^{-\alpha t} \tag{19.26}$$

α therefore has the natural interpretation as the infinite maturity exponentially compounded zero rate. In practice, however, it is much better to think of α as a time scale parameter similar to the λ parameter in the Nelson-Siegel spline. Larger values of α make the spline more flexible.

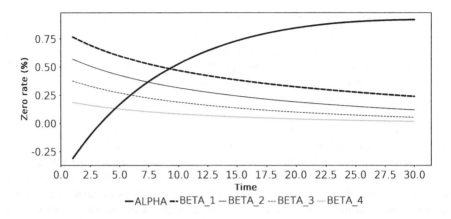

FIGURE 19.4   Sensitivities of zero rates to 25% bumps in α and absolute bumps of 0.1 to the β parameters of the exponential spline model. The role of the β terms as successively faster declining exponential funtions is clearly visible.

The prices of coupon bonds are linear functions of the β_i so that the square errors of bond prices become a quadratic function in the β_i. The equations for the minimum square error, i.e., the first derivatives with respect to the β_i are therefore linear in the β_i which makes the exponential spline very efficient to fit to bond prices.

19.4.4   The Vasicek spline

The Vasicek spline is a simple structural curve model where the evolution of the short rate follows the process:

$$dr_t = k(\theta - r_t)dt + \sigma dW_t \tag{19.27}$$

where W_t is a Wiener process. It has the useful property of allowing a closed-form calculation of the discount factors which means that calculating asset prices does not require a computationally costly numerical integration. This makes the model a useful entry point to structural curve analysis.

Following [12] using two shortcuts $A(t)$ and $B(t)$ as follows:

$$A(t) = \frac{1 - \exp(-kt)}{k}$$

$$B(t) = \exp\left(\theta - \frac{\sigma^2}{2k^2}(A(t) - t) - \frac{\sigma^2}{4k}A(t)^2\right)$$

one has:

$$Df(t) = B(t)\exp(-r_0 A(t)) \tag{19.28}$$

The theoretical beauty of a structural curve model is that the curve shape is determined by the volatility of the short rate, here characterised by σ and the mean-reversion strength k. In principle, therefore, one should find a calibration of the model where

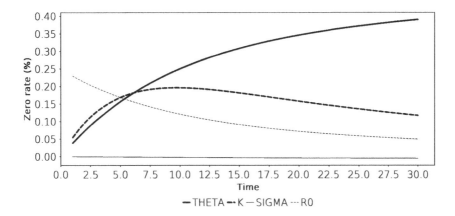

FIGURE 19.5 Sensitivities of zero rates to 25% bumps the parameters of the Vasicek spline model.

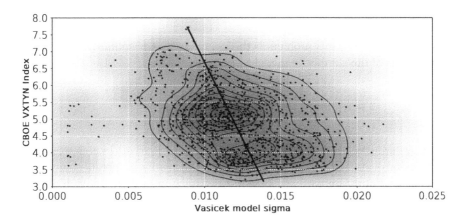

FIGURE 19.6 Scatter plot of the σ parameter of a daily Vasicek spline fitted to the US Treasury curve against the CBEO VXTYN Treasury implied volatility index. History 2014–2019. Sources: Treasury prices from treasurydirect.gov and VXTYN data retrieved from FRED.

the model-implied volatility is somehow related to the observable implied volatilities traded in the market.

However, this is not a trivial task. Figure 19.6 shows the correlation between the σ extracted from fitting a Vasicek spline to daily observations of the US Treasury curve against an index of market-traded volatility (the CBOE VXTYN index)[3]. The R^2 between these two series is less than 0.1. In defense of the Vasicek model it should be noted that the VXTYN is an index of short-dated options on a 10Y Treasury future while the σ

---

[3]The figure deliberately excludes data after July 2019 when the US curve had several bouts of volatility.

parameter of the model is a long-dated volatility of the overnight rate. This mismatch in volatility type is, however, only a partial explanation of the low correlation. In general, it is very difficult to achieve a self-consistent calibration of market interest rates and volatility in a structural model without inserting the interest rate path explicitly, or working with an unwieldy number of parameters.

19.4.5   Composite models

The yield curve models presented so far work well for individual markets but may face some problems when comparing related sub-markets. For instance, the debt of national agencies would normally be expected to trade at slightly higher yields than that of the sovereign due to a small liquidity premium for sovereign bonds. Fitting two independent splines to the sovereign and agency bonds sometimes results in situations where the agency spline is partly below the sovereign spline, usually because there are fewer bonds in the agency market, resulting in over-fitting behaviour. In some cases, there are so few bonds on the agency curve that a reliable calibration of splines with a larger number of parameters is impossible.

A useful solution to this problem is the use of composite splines. One defines the discount factors of the composite model as:

$$Df(t) = Df_B(t)Df_S(t) \tag{19.29}$$

where $Df_B(t)$ are discount factors derived from a base market (in this example the sovereign bonds) and $Df_S(t)$ is constructed to reflect only a spread component so that the agency bonds are correctly priced. An attraction of this approach is that the functional form of $Df_S(t)$ can be much simpler than that of $Df_B(t)$. Instead of a fully fledged Nelson-Siegel-Svensson with 6 parameters for $Df_B(t)$ one could define $Df_S(t)$ simply as:

$$Df_S(t) = \exp\left(-t\sum_{i=0}^{k} c_i t^i\right) \tag{19.30}$$

so that the spread between the 2 curves, expressed as continuously compounded zero rates, is a simple polynomial defined by only $k + 1$ parameters. The calibration of such a spline is a sequential process where the $Df_B(t)$ are first constructed using a model like those discussed earlier and a base market, and in a second step the $Df_S(t)$ are fitted using the spread market bonds. Each step follows standard fitting procedures as discussed in the next section.

Figure 19.7 shows examples of such splines for two Japanese sub-sovereign issuers. Despite the low number of parameters 3 per issuer), the spread splines reflect the issuer yield curves with reasonable accuracy because the main interest rate dynamics are captured in the base JGB spline.

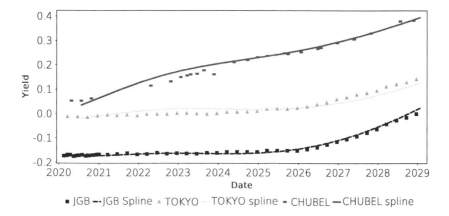

FIGURE 19.7 Spread splines ($k = 2$) calibrated to the 1–10Y bonds issued by the Tokyo Metropolis and Chubu Electric based on the 1–10Y JGB Nelson-Siegel-Svensson spline for 24 January 2019. Source: Data from JSDA.

19.5 FITTING CURVE MODELS

Fitting a curve means finding the set of parameters for a given parametric curve that minimises an appropriately defined error term relative to market data.

When the market data consists of bond prices, the most common approach is to fit bond yields, by defining the error term E as:

$$E = \sum_i (y_i - y_i^{\text{model}})^2 \qquad (19.31)$$

where y_i are the market and y_i^{model} the model-implied yields. Model-implied yields should not be simply taken as the par yields given by the model but be calculated from model prices coming using the actual cashflows of each bond and the model-implied discount factors:

$$P_i^{\text{model}} = \sum_j Cf_{i,j} Df^{\text{model}}(t_j) \qquad (19.32)$$

where the summation index j runs over all future cashflows of bond i. Note that the resulting price in this equation is a dirty price.

Given that, for small price changes, yield changes are well approximated by the DV01 of the bond ($\Delta y = \Delta P / DV01$), the error term above can be approximated as:

$$E = \sum_i \frac{1}{DV01_i^2} (P_i - P_i^{\text{model}})^2 \qquad (19.33)$$

While this may seem like a trivial mathematical trick, it has in practice a significant computational impact. Calculating a yield from a given bond price is a costly operation because it involves a non-linear root search. Most parametric curve models, especially the exponential spline model, can calculate model-implied prices very fast from the bond cashflow structures. Using DV01-weighted prices to derive the error term is therefore usually several magnitudes faster than using yields.

Some applications, including the ECB spline curves, use outlier removal techniques. After minimising the error term Equation (19.31), individual spline spreads are evaluated and bonds that more than a certain number of standard deviations, or more than a given number of basis points, away from their spline-implied yields are removed from the sample. A new fitting procedure is then conducted until the sample becomes stable. The obvious advantage of this approach is that it automatically deals with polluted price or bond static data[4]. The downside of outlier removal is that the comparison of spline curves from day to day will become tainted with sample changes. These are not always immediately obvious because increased noise can lead to an increase in the sample size when the outlier removal algorithm adopts a more lenient approach due to an increase in the observed standard deviation of spline spreads. In general, it is a bad idea to preserve tainted data and rely on post-processing to remove it. The better course of action would be to use outliers as suggestions for data that needs manual verification.

A related idea is the removal of bonds that are known to have distorted prices. This could be recently issued benchmark bonds, or futures contract CTDs. Such bonds can have sizeable repo or liquidity premia embedded in them, which makes them non-representative for the overall discount factor term structure. Again, there are arguments in favour and against such techniques. The main argument against removing bonds on the basis of systematic premia is that these tend to be the most liquid securities in the market. One could argue that their pricing responsed more to changes in economic factors than other bonds and instead of removing the benchmark, one might rather remove less liquid bonds from the sample. Also, it can be argued that the idea of a liquidity premium for the most active bonds is equivalent to an 'illiquidity discount' on the less liquid bonds. The 'true' discount factor curve is therefore somewhere between the curve formed by the most liquid bonds and that formed by the least liquid ones. While simply mixing all bonds equally in the sample recovers this 'true' curve is not obvious, but it should produce a closer result than either extreme.

---

[4]It is often the case that data sources contain errors that are hard to spot in very large data sets. For instance, a given bond may be callable but not marked as such in the incoming data set. The market price of this call option will generate a larger deviation from the spline curve if the bond is included under the assumption that no call option exists. Another common problem is the distinction between unsecured and secured or guaranteed liabilities of the same issuer. Outlier removal would catch most of such instances, or cases where supposed market prices are simply erroneous. This is not to suggest that polluted data is the reason why the ECB is using outlier removal.

CHAPTER 20

Curve Analysis

The preceding sections dealt with ways to represent curve shapes, and now is the time to consider why yield curves have the shapes they have. An insightful and influential series of papers by Ilmanen [49,50] broke down the drivers of the US Treasury yield curve into 3 categories, namely expectations, convexity bias and risk premia. It is prudent to add a fourth category, investor preferences (related to the preferred habitat concept in economics).

These 4 drivers will be discussed in more detail below but one statement can already be made upfront: While the aggregate result of them is the current shape of the yield curve, each individual component is unobservable. There are models that purport to be able to dis-aggregate yield curve changes into 2 or more of these drivers but such models generally rely on restricting the functional form of those drivers. The most commonly known such decomposition is the Fed's ACM model [2], named after the authors Adrian, Crump and Moench. It provides a separation of expectations from risk premia and this decomposition is available daily from the New York Fed. Like other such analyses, the decomposition is based on fairly restrictive assumptions of how risk should be priced, and those assumptions may not hold in practice. The general approach taken here is that, from time to time, one may be able to interpret a particular yield curve move as related to any of these 4 components, but mechanical quantitative decompositions should be treated with great care.

20.1   EXPECTATIONS

Market term interest rates should reflect expectations of future short-rate movements, and in most cases these will be related to central bank policy rate changes. Indeed, their influence on longer-term interest rates is an important factor in the transmission of monetary policy rates into the real economy. If no such influence existed, borrowers in the term fixed-rate market would not be affected by changes in monetary policy.

At the same time, expectations are unlikely to work over very long horizons. It is doubtful that the collective mind of the market has a concrete view on the monetary policy interest rate of the Fed or the ECB prevailing in 20 years, time. It is more reasonable to assume that very long-term expectations converge to some form of equilibrium rate like the Wicksellian natural interest rate [22,51]. This long-term neutral interest rate would then roughly correspond to the expected potential nominal growth rate of the economy. The expectations part of the term structure of interest rates should therefore be described by a path of short-term rates from their current levels towards this neutral rate. The Vasicek model introduced above contains the parameter θ that can be interpreted as such a long-run interest rate to which the short rate diffuses[1].

If monetary policy is the driver of short-term interest rates, then economic developments as drivers of monetary policy can give some guidance of how the expectations component of the yield curve shape should behave. As a simple illustration one can use the original Taylor rule [79]:

$$r = p + \frac{1}{2}y + \frac{1}{2}(p - 2) + 2 \tag{20.1}$$

r is the target rate, p is the rate of inflation and y is the deviation of GDP from target. This rule can generate a term structure of the impact on interest rates from a shock to macro-economic data if one assumes that the economic data itself has a mean-reverting nature.

To do this, one can fit a standard VAR model to the historical observations of y and p, and consider the impact of a change in either on the future evolutions of these variables. This impulse-response function can be viewed as a simple model of the change in assumptions investors will make in response to learning of the most recent observation of economic data relative to their pre-release assumptions. Using the GDP deflator to describe the price level (instead of the core PCE deflator apparently preferred by the Fed), the impulse-response functions for a 1% shock to GDP and prices are shown in Figure 20.1[2].

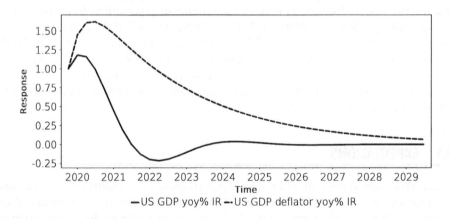

FIGURE 20.1   VAR model impulse-response functions of an assumed 1% shock to US GDP and GDP Deflator in Q4 2019. The models were calibrated to data from 1980 to 2019 and the lags are 4 for GDP and 2 for the deflator. Source: GDP data downloaded from FRED.

---

[1] Indeed, the Vasicek spline is the simplest in a family of affine models that are based on such drift processes. The ACM model is also of this family.
[2] Note that such a large shock is unlikely in reality but the models used are linear so that the impact of a surprise is proportional to the size of the surprise. The calibration period for the VAR models

The two impulse-response functions look very different in that the inflation shock is much more persistent. This shock can now be translated into a response of par interest rates by integrating the adjustment to the policy rate r in the Taylor rule Equation (20.1) mandated by these shock responses of the two macro variables. Using a US Treasury spline curve from February 2020, the par rate changes resulting from changed expectations under these assumptions is shown in Figure 20.2.

A change in growth expectations should be mostly reflected in the steepness of the front end of the curve (for instance, the 2Y–5Y spread), driven by changes in front-end yields. The inflation shock is more persistent but the increasing PVBP of longer bonds reduces the impact of this persistent response of policy rates on the par curve. Still, one could conclude that changes in the inflation outlook should lead to movements all along the curve.

Although the analysis is done here in terms of the quarterly real GDP and GDP deflator data, investors receive a multitude of other economic data releases that provide related information at higher frequency. For instance, growth estimates can also be informed by retail sales data, business confidence, new orders, unemployment and so on. Price developments are meanwhile visible in consumer prices, average hourly earnings, negotiated wage settlements, energy prices and the like. Not only are some of these indicators available at monthly frequency, but they arrive at different times so that growth and inflation estimates can be updated practically in real time.

This then raises the question why daily movements in the US yield curve, shown in Figure 31.9 on page 355, do not correspond to either of the two patterns shown in Figure 20.2. The main component of actual US yield curve changes is a nearly parallel movement of rates.

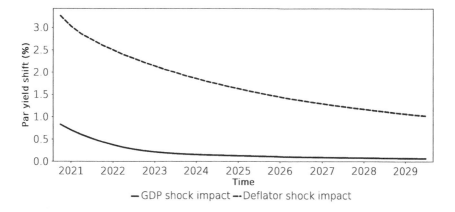

FIGURE 20.2   Projected par rate responses to a 1% shock to GDP and the GDP deflator using the 3 February 2020 UST Nelson-Siegel-Svensson spline for discounting. Source: GDP data downloaded from FRED, Treasury prices from TreasuryDirect.

has been chosen to be long, but not to include the oil price shock phase of the 1970s. Indeed, starting at 1980 means that some data predates the adoption of explicit inflation targeting in the US although the general idea of price stability was present before [9].

In the context of the expectations hypothesis, the prevalence of parallel curve shifts could be interpreted as meaning that investors assign a much higher degree of persistency to data surprises than is warranted by historical data. In addition, unlike the more sophisticated approaches taken in the modelling literature, no attention has been paid here to the difference between real and nominal returns.

However, these explanations retain the idea that investor decisions are based on constant long-term expectations. In other words, the modelling hierarchy assumed in the analysis so far has been that the long-term evolution of the economy remains the same, but that short-term surprises can occur, and these can have effects on asset prices:

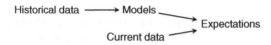

In reality, it could well be that current data also affects long-run expectations. For instance, various market commentators do at the time of writing cite factors such as shifting demographics to justify expectations of a 'low for longer' outlook on interest rates. In this view, expectations could change not just for the near-term outlook on monetary policy rates, but the equilibrium level of the natural real rate of interest r^*. Additionally, monetary policy rates are being set specifically with a view to influence the macroeconomic variables used here to derive rate expectations. Investors face, not only uncertainty about the evolution of these variables, but also about the reaction function of the central bank, and the transmission of central bank actions into changes of economic activity. For instance, some central banks have debated the notion of an 'overshooting commitment', meaning that they will tolerate higher inflation for some time after periods of below-target inflation. Investors therefore need to reassess whether the Taylor rule Equation (20.1) remains a good guideline for translating changes in economic data into yield curve expectations.

Indeed, the calibration time period for Figure 20.1 has been chosen somewhat maliciously. Persistence of an inflation surprise should be associated with a central bank that is perceived as unwilling or unable to maintain price stability. A credible inflation targeting central bank should be able to reverse any shock to prices rather quickly, namely within the standard monetary policy horizon of 12 to 18 months. Comparing models calibrated to different periods of history, as in Figure 20.3, shows that the persistence of price shocks has indeed changed over time. Investors would therefore be unwise to base expectations on long historical horizons. Consequently, changes of models and their parameters should be as important to changes in expectations as changes in model inputs.

More broadly, it is no longer the case that macroeconomic surprises feed through to bond markets only through changes in the expectations for monetary policy rates. Central banks now use a variety of tools to affect yield curves directly beyond the front end [65]. Investors therefore now must translate incoming economic data into a variety of other market rates, such as spreads or long-term yields. Capturing a functional form for such expectations is practically impossible.

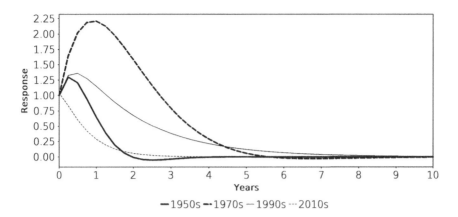

FIGURE 20.3   Changes in the impulse-response functions of the US GDP deflator through time. Each line represents the impulse-response function of a VAR model calibrated to two decades of data (1950–1969, 1970–1989, 1990–2009, 2010–2019). Source: GDP data downloaded from FRED.

20.2   CONVEXITY BIAS

The expectations hypothesis links the curve shape, and its dynamic, to changes in expectations for short rates. Convexity bias introduces an additional driver of curve shape, namely the volatility of interest rates. To understand this concept, it is useful to start with a butterfly position involving 3 bonds (this trade is explained in Section 31.1.3 on page 353):

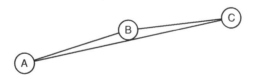

Under normal circumstances, the weighted average yield, including funding costs, of the bullet (Bond B) is higher than that of the wings A and C in a duration-neutral butterfly. The weighted average convexity of this position, meanwhile, is negative. The negative aggregate convexity arises from the rapid increase in convexity of longer-dated cashflows relative to duration (cf. Figures 16.10 and 16.11 on page 166, 167).

As Section 16.9 pointed out, positive convexity means that re-hedging a duration-neutral portfolio after yield changes will, subject to transaction costs, result in capital gains income, while re-hedging a negatively convex portfolio will result in losses when re-hedging. An investor would therefore normally not be willing to hold a negative convexity portfolio unless it provides some additional return. The idea of convexity bias is that the positive weighted average yield of the butterfly reflects its negative convexity. In other words, the convex shape of the yield curve is the result of the non-linearity of the price–yield relationship.

This proposition can be tested by regressing the net yield of a butterfly on its convexity value. This has been done in Figure 20.4 for the US Treasury curve. Because the cost of holding a negative convexity portfolio is not only a function of the amount of negative convexity but also of volatility, the chart uses the product of negative convexity and implied volatility. For the history period shown there is indeed a good correlation in evidence. Since then, increased central bank activity around the globe has reduced both implied volatility (and thereby the value of convexity) and affected yield curve shapes.

Because the value of convexity is a function of how much a random walk deviates from its mean, the convexity premium $c(t)$ is a function of the square root of maturity:

$$c(t) \sim \sigma\sqrt{t} \tag{20.2}$$

Convexity bias is responsible for the inversion of the very long ends of most yield curves. At maturities beyond 25 to 30 years, expectations and risk premia reach nearly steady states while the convexity of bonds, and the value of that convexity, continues to increase. Most yield curve models have difficulties reflecting this effect, leading to an apparent over-valuation of very long-dated bonds. This apparent misvaluation is a shortcoming of the relevant model, not a real trading opportunity.

It should be noted that not every investor views portfolios relative to a duration target, and therefore assigns significant value to convexity. That does not mean, however, that such investors can ignore convexity bias. As long as a sufficient market influence is being exerted by convexity-sensitive investors, curve analysis has to respect this effect.

Convexity bias cannot be clearly separated from expectations because when central bank policy rates are perceived as being 'in play', implied volatility increases at the same time as policy rate expectations shift. Using the butterfly in Figure 20.4 as an example, the 2Y–5Y spread can increase because the market expects a rate cut (lowering the 2Y

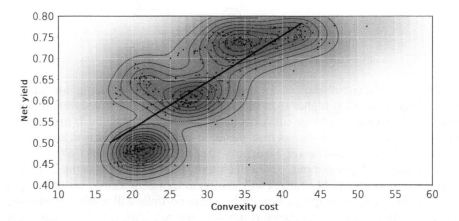

FIGURE 20.4 US Treasury 2–5–10Y butterfly yield pickup as a function of convexity cost (net convexity times implied volatility) Jan 2009 to Jun 2010. The one-year spline rate has been used to approximate the net funding cost; butterfly rates are also par spline rates. Source: Treasury prices from TreasuryDirect, volatility VXTYN downloaded from FRED.

rate), and because higher implied volatility increases the implied cost of being short the 5Y in this butterfly. Delineating these two effects is practically impossible.

20.3 TERM RISK PREMIUM

The notion of a risk premium is relatively straightforward. As an example, one can consider a game where a player can wager 100 coins on a single toss of a fair coin. If the coin comes up heads, the money is lost. If it comes up tails, the player gets 200 coins. No rational person would participate in this game because the expected outcome is to have 100 coins. The player can achieve the same outcome by not participating and so avoid the risk of losing those coins[3].

The game can be altered by raising the amount that can be won. If tails results in a payout of not 200, but 300 coins, it may be rational to wager the 100 coins for an expected profit of 50 coins. Of clear importance is the value of 100 coins to the total wealth of the player. The smaller this value, the readier the player should be to risk it for a small gain.

In terms of investment, one could imagine the following alternative game. An investor has the choice between investing cash for 1 or 2 periods of equal length. There is no difference in the expected interest rate of the second period versus the first. The market interest rate for the 2-period investment equals the compounded expected interest rates over these periods.

Again, an investor would be unwise to commit invested money for 2 periods on the expectation of earning the same as if the money was invested subsequently for the 2 periods in independent investments. Committing to the 2-period term investment amounts to foregoing the option of consuming, or investing in other ways, the money after the first period. The 2-period interest rate should therefore exceed the compounded expected interest rates of the 2 single-period investments. Otherwise investors should prefer to keep their money in 1-period investments.

This logic informs the Chicago school of economics, which models risk premia in terms of log-utility [23] and is therefore able to quantify risk premia exactly relative to expected returns and risks. This approach is also the basis of the risk/expectations decomposition of the ACM model. The merit of this approach is tied to the realism of the rational utility-optimising investor[4]. In addition, the choice of log-utility as the appropriate target quantity in some ways makes the risk premia so derived comparable to a convexity premium. This is because the functional shape of the risk premium is tied to the convexity of the presumed utility function of the investor. If investor

---

[3]Those not convinced by this type of argument participate in the various lotteries around the world.

[4]In other words, those investors not participating in the various lotteries around the world.

utility was simply a linear function of wealth, then risk premia in this approach would not exist.

In this world view, higher interest rate volatility should lead to higher term risk premia, and so to a steeper curve. This is indeed in line with market experience, but with a twist. At longer horizons, interest rate expectations should be affected by mean reversion, and so should longer dated volatility. Very long rates should therefore react less to higher short-term volatility then intermediate rates. As a result, one would look for a volatility dependency not on the 2Y–30Y slope, but on butterflies like the 2Y–5Y–10Y, as discussed in the previous section.

In many analyses, the expression 'risk premium' is used differently. Analysts tend to create fair value models of various kinds and then ascribe any deviations to risk premia. In essence, given a set of known variables (potentially including their histories) φ, one could construct a model of interest rates r and write the standard modelling equation:

$$\mathbf{r} = f(\varphi) + \varepsilon \qquad (20.3)$$

The measurement error term ε can then be considered a risk premium because it is that part of market pricing that is not explained by the model $f(\cdot)$. This interpretation of course is dependent on the assumption that one's model is indeed the appropriate yardstick for the yield curve. In this sense, the term risk premium in this usage amounts to the things one does not know, or at least things not included in one's curve model.

20.4 PREFERRED HABITAT

The notion of a preferred habitat is that certain investors have a structural bias towards particular types of investment. The implication is that their demand for certain assets will not be explained by economic factors such as expected risk-adjusted return (i.e., risk premia) or expectations. It is useful to take a broad view of this effect, and this section outlines the most relevant of them.

The effects discussed here have one thing in common, namely that they cannot be hedged. Depending on one's understanding of risk premia and convexity bias, one can replicate their non-linear effects through the use of interest rate derivatives. Similarly, the interest rate effect of monetary policy expectations can usually be replicated through other financial instruments, such as equities or inflation derivatives. Preferred habitat effects, meanwhile, may be predictable but difficult to offset. Large-scale buying of long-dated bonds by pension funds is difficult to offset by other means given that the activity of these funds may be large.

20.4.1 Asset–liability matching

Most financial institutions have a well-defined liability structure and choose assets with a view to matching these liabilities. This asset–liability matching (ALM) approach is not a strict necessity because similar effects could be achived through the use of derivatives; potentially, however, at a higher cost. For instance, retail banks tend to fund a large part of their balance sheet with deposits. The economics of deposit interest rates are a balance between their cost, which incentivises banks to offer lower rates, and their supply, which means that banks need to pay enough to prevent customers from pursuing other investments, including deposits at competing banks. The latter aspect links bank deposit rates to board market interest rates, and so to monetary policy rates. Banks therefore are natural investors in floating-rate notes. In some countries, such as Italy, an ecosystem has evolved where the sovereign issued floating rate notes (the CCTS) and banks absorb a large part of this supply.

Many insurance companies have long-dated liabilities linked to life insurance that in many cases have defined yield floors. Although the entire asset mix of the investment portfolio is designed to earn at least this guaranteed income, some life insurance companies aim to purchase long-dated bonds if and when their yields rise above this guarantee rate. This approach is known as target buying. In this case, the preferred habitat of these companies is the set of bonds that has the necessary yield, not one particular sector of the yield curve. This can have effects on yield curve shapes. For instance, the JGB market sometimes exhibits a fairly predictable steepening or flattening behaviour at the long end (e.g., the 20–30Y spread) as life insurance buying in effect caps interest rates in times of slow interest rates. As soon as yields in any one sector reach their yield targets, demand for JGB increases and prevents further yield increases. The long end of the curve then bear-flattens or bull-steepens. Figure 31.6 on page 352 shows this effect.

In the US market, mortgage convexity hedging has a comparable effect. Holders of large RMBS portfolios generally attempt to maintain a steady duration risk in their portfolio. When interest rates decrease, mortgage prepayment risk increases and RMBS durations shrink. Mortgage hedging then requires the purchasing of US Treasuries, which has the effect of depressing yields further. Conversely, rising interest rates lead to longer mortgage durations, and US Treasury selling from the same type of investor. Whether the effect of this activity is large or not depends on how the mortgage coupons in the market are distributed relative to new production coupons. An interest rate level that leads to large-scale mortgage hedging is known as a convexity trigger. It should be noted that the prepayment option of a callable mortgage is an option that financial markets have sold to the mortgage borrower. Financial market participants can trade options between themselves but such trading does not change the aggregate negative convexity position of the market as a whole. Convexity hedging is the only other alternative for the market to buy back this option, namely dynamic replication.

20.4.2 Regulatory constraints

The preferred habitats described above amount to more or less voluntary behaviour of some market participants. In addition, there are regulatory reasons for some investors to make investments which then influence market prices.

The largest such sector in the European fixed income markets is the pension system, particularly in Denmark and The Netherlands. Pension fund regulation has undergone several transformations over the last decades and moved along one axis in particular. Because pension funds invest for very long horizons, one could take the approach that over such long time spans, asset returns should mean-revert. The appropriate way to regulate such funds would then be to make some actuarial assumptions about longevity and compare the assets held by a fund to its future obligations. The alternative approach is to be agnostic about mean-reversion of returns and instead demand that a fund has sufficient assets to cover liabilities discounted at current market rates[5]. An intermediate approach is to assume mean reversion in the very long run, but to use market rates in the short to intermediate sector. This is known as the ultimate forward rate (UFR) approach where forward rates beyond a certain horizon (chosen as the end of the 'liquid' part of the yield curve, however defined) are assumed to converge to a constant[6]. Discounting liabilities with market interest rates means that pension funds need to hedge againt interest rate risk. The most straightforward hedge, namely a fixed income asset portfolio that exactly matches the liability, is unattainable in the market. Some governments are large enough borrowers to create a sufficiently large long-dated bond portfolio but have for cost reasons not chosen to do so[7]. In addition, because pension funds are long-term investors, it makes sense for them to hold riskier assets such as equities, real estate and commodities and so earn the associated risk premia. As a result, pension funds tend to see the values of the liabilities increase relative to their assets when interest rates fall, and are then sometimes forced to reduce their duration gap through buying bonds when yields fall. In this sense, pension fund regulation, combined with the structure of the bond market, imposes a form of short convexity on pension fund managers.

20.4.3   Passive investing

Investors with no leeway over their investments, such as Exchange Traded Funds (ETF) are a special form of preferred habitat investors where the preferred habitat is the entire market that the ETF is linked to. For risk management reasons and because they are not incentivised to to so, such funds are unable to under-invest in overvalued sectors, or over-invest in undervalued sectors. Although such behaviour is ostensibly passive, it can affect relative pricing. Bond indices are not free-float adjusted and ETFs therefore need to achieve market-weight exposures even in yield curve segments where other preferred habitat investors create excess demand. ETF demand can then amplify the relative shortage in such market segments.

Passive portfolio re-hedging is also responsible for large-scale trading activity at the points in time when index rebalancings become effective (usually the market close of

---

[5]It should be noted that this does not amount to a rejection of mean-reversion, but simply to the assumption that current market rates incorporate the best estimate of the economic value of such a mean-reversion.

[6]Douglas Adams, had he still been alive at the time, would undoubtedly have felt vindicated by the choice of 42% as the answer to the question about the ultimate forward rate in The Netherlands in 2012. That being said, the Dutch UFR has been revised since then (to 3.9%) which calls into question what the economic rationale of the UFR is. To be logically self-consistent, an ultimate forward rate should be constant.

[7]Aside from the argument about government funding costs, it should be borne in mind that a funded pension system holding only domestic government bonds is redundant. Because the government bond coupons that feed into the pension system would then be funded by taxes, it would be more efficient to eliminate the cost overhead of pension funds and make tax transfers to pensioners directly.

the last trading day in a given month). This rebalancing is not uniformly distributed across the market and instead requires the purchase of newly issued securities and selling of newly excluded securities. However, such trading is to some extent predictable and therefore arbitraged across time.

20.4.4 Central bank reserve portfolios

Some central banks hold large-scale foreign currency portfolios designed to be liquidated quickly when required. Such sales can be required when a country faces a sudden capital outflow or a drastic fall in the value of its own currency[8]. Reserve portfolios can be built in various ways, but tend to result from times when the opposite problem occurred (excessive money inflows and currency appreciation). As a guide to sizing and structuring such a portfolio, a country may examine its import-related external payments and attempt to match them with a reserve portfolio that allows it to fund these outflows from maturing reserve assets, asset sales and repos. Large internationally connected financial systems can create the need for additional reserves.

To ensure the ability to intervene rapidly, reserve portfolios need to be liquid and do therefore generally not carry much duration risk. The preferred habitat of a reserve portfolio is therefore the short-dated sector of highly rated bonds denominated in the international trade invoice currencies, such as US dollars, euros and yen.

Note that not all foreign assets held by sovereigns are held for FX intervention purposes. Some sovereigns have sufficiently large assets to invest a large part of them with a view to earning returns. In such investments, preferred habitats play a lesser role.

20.4.5 Market technicals

Markets do not always work perfectly and local supply–demand imbalances can lead to price distortions. These effects are known as market technicals. Such technicals can take various forms. For instance, when sovereigns offer post-auction non-competitive allocations, the price at which these allocations happen can act as a temporary anchor of prices around the time of allocation. Option trader positions can force them to buy or sell in a way that may amplify or dampen market volatility [77].

Aside from these effects, which are localised and reasonably well understood, there is a cottage industry of technical analysis which purports to be able to predict future market movements from historical prices more generally [61, 63]. Various theories are proposed why past prices should be sufficient for prediction, such as investor psychology and supposedly special numbers. Technical analysis has the hallmarks of a cargo cult, with its own language of resistance and support lines, retracement levels and the like. Multiple schools exist that follow diverse signals such as Fibonacci levels, Japanese candle sticks and market pictures. The large amount of financial data means that a large number of supportive examples can be found for every rule. However, no systematic analysis of false positives exists and some concepts defy common logic. For instance, given the close relationship between yields and bond futures prices, any 'special' level

---

[8]Usually both types of event are connected.

in yields should correspond to a special level in futures prices. Because the CTD of bond futures contracts often changes between deliveries, the yield–price relationship also changes, but this is not reflected in technical analysis.

While one might disagree with technical analysis on this basis, there is a possibility that it can become self-fulfilling. If a sufficient number of investors believes that a given price is a support level, they can end up buying at that level in sufficient volumes to indeed make that price level act as a floor. For this reason it can be useful to be aware of the outcome of technical analysis even though the analysis itself is based on questionable arguments.

CHAPTER 21

Carry and Roll-Down

A traditional way to assess the relative attractiveness of different curve sectors is the use of the forward curve. Figure 21.1 shows for introduction the par, zero and overnight rates of the German curve in August 2014. At the time, the ECB deposit facility rate acted as the effective policy rate and was set at −0.1% but purchases of German government bonds under PSPP had not yet started. The curves show a standard behaviour for upwardly sloped curves, namely the zero (spot) curve is above the par curve, and the overnight forwards are above the swap curve. The only exception is the very front end of the curve where this relationship is inverted because the curve was sloping downward in this sector[1].

Before discussing the implications of this relationship in more detail, it is worthwhile discussing why this relationship is as it is. The zero rate is the constant term interest rate that, when compounded at the appropriate frequency, delivers the same discount factor as compounding the time-varying overnight interest rate over the same time horizon. An upward curve slope means that interest rates are rising for longer and longer horizons. Conceptually, the zero rate is an average of overnight rates, bar compounding and daycount differences. If nearer-dated overnight rates are below this average, then further overnight rates must be above it in order to catch up. Therefore, the overnight forward curve must have a larger slope than the zero rate curve. Put differently, because the zero curve measures the average overnight discount rate over a given period, it must be below the last value of that rate if the values are in ascending order. In the same way, the par curve can be thought of as the average coupon on a package of zero-coupon instruments. The average rate must be below the zero rate applicable to the maturity point when the intervening zero coupon instruments have lower yields.

According to [49, 50], the forward curve can be seen as an indicator of the most attractive curve points. This curve shows the incremental return of leaving one's money invested for an extra day. If the current curve shape is the best predictor of future curve shapes (for which there is some evidence), the forward rate is also a measure of return for holding a bond until the next day.

---

[1]One reason for this slope was the then expected cut in the deposit facility rate which occurred on 10 September 2014.

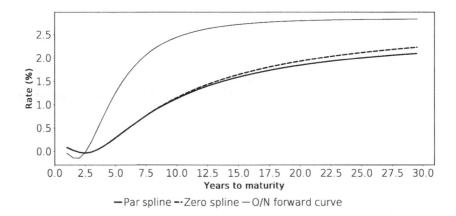

— Par spline **—·** Zero spline **—** O/N forward curve

FIGURE 21.1   Par, spot and overnight forward curves on a Nelson-Siegel-Svensson German government bond spline in August 2014, before the start of PSPP. Prices from Bundesbank. Note that the overnight rates are quoted in actual/360, the other rates are actual/actual.

Instead of this formalism, a different analytical approach is now more common.

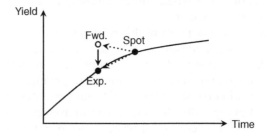

For each bond, if a curve is to hand, the expectation should be that, after a given holding horizon, the yield of that bond should have changed in line with the curve shape, i.e., declined in a normal yield curve environment. At the same time, the carry of each bond should be positive as (short-term) funding costs are lower than (long-term) coupon income. So, the forward price over the same period should be lower, and the forward yield therefore higher than the current yield. The holding-period return is therefore composed of two components, namely the difference between spot and forward price (the carry), and an expected decline in yield (the roll-down). One can see these two components as the funding-adjusted coupon income, and the expected capital gain, respectively.

As a concept this holding period return has the drawback of being a mix of price and yield concepts. Roll-down in particular has a cash value that depends on the forward DV01 of the bond. This implies that while a bond will eventually roll down to the overnight rate, no overall capital gain is associated with this process because the DV01 of the bond will at that point have fallen to zero.

Computationally, one works out the forward yield from the forward price, and the expected yield from the spot yield, and the change in fair value yield on the curve for the spot and forward date. Using the change in fair value yield together with the spot

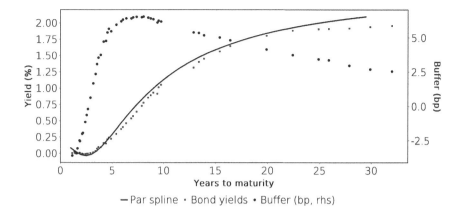

FIGURE 21.2   Carry and roll-down of German government bonds in August 2014. Note that due to coupon effects, bond yields to not coincide with par yields at all maturities. Prices from Bundesbank.

yield accounts for the fact that the spot yield may not be exactly on the curve. The result of this analysis is a yield difference called the buffer. The buffer, the difference between forward yield and expected yield on the curve, can be interpreted as the amount by which the current yield curve needs to shift up by the end of the holding period to eliminate the carry income of the bond.

The result of the analysis is a projected holding period return for each individual bond, expressed as a break-even yield shift. This return calculation takes into account all information about this security, including its specific repo rate, pull-to-par and pricing relative to other bonds, making this calculation superior to an analysis of the forward rate alone. Figure 21.2 shows the result of this calculation for the German market on a given day. Some features of the result are noteworthy. First, it is possible to have positive holding period returns even when yields are negative. A positive roll-down can offset negative carry. Second, the buffer first increases with maturity but then declines even as yields increase. Two effects play a role in this observation. On one hand, the curve becomes flatter towards longer maturities and roll-down therefore diminishes. On the other hand, the buffer is expressed in yield terms and the impact of higher carry is dominated by the division by an increasing DV01. Interestingly, the expected return is highest in the 4- to 9-year area, i.e., the bullet of the curve. This echoes some of the arguments made on convexity bias earlier (cf. Figure 20.4 on page 210).

One caveat should be mentioned for this type of analysis and that is the impact of the curve model used. The curve model in [49, 50] was a market model where forwards were obtained by bootstrapping. Such a model is in principle completely flexible but may sometimes be affected by idiosyncratic valuation effects of individual securities. Here, a Nelson-Siegel-Svensson spline provides the roll-down curve and the functional shape of the roll-down is constrained by the flexibility of that spline. Because the spline has only two 'humps', it is not possible to have a multitude of turning points in the roll-down curve. The apparent richer structure of the individual roll-down estimates in Figure 21.2 is the result of security-specific pricing effects.

CHAPTER **22**

Curve Spreads

The previous chapters introduced curves as the theoretical reflection of maturity-dependent discount rates, and therefore as a generalisation of the yield concept. It framed this generalisation in the idea that a curve can be calibrated to a set of instrument prices, and then be used to price instruments.

In general, the curve-implied price of an instrument need not match the actual market price the instrument unless the curve model is a market model and the instrument is part of the calibration. This potential difference in price raises the question of how to express it. In general, the topic of this chapter is how to measure the distance between a curve and an instrument.

The most straightforward approach is a simple price difference:

$$d = P - \sum_i Cf_i Df(t_i) \tag{22.1}$$

where P is the market price of the instrument, Cf_i are its cash flows and $Df(t_i)$ the discount factors implied by the curve. As usual, the shortcoming of this price difference is that it does not reflect the duration risk of the instrument in question.

The following sections introduce various curve spread measures used in the market. These spreads are generally expressed in basis points.

22.1 Z-SPREAD

The most natural way to construct a risk-adjusted curve spread from a discount factor curve is to translate the difference between curve-implied and market price into a yield spread, namely by taking the difference in yields calculated for the two prices:

$$s_z = y(P) - y\left(\sum_i Cf_i Df(t_i)\right) \tag{22.2}$$

The term z-spread for this expression is related to the use of cashflows, which are in essence zero bonds. This property makes z-spreads the natural choice of relative value measure for complex cashflow structures, and they are used extensively in the analysis of inflation-linked bonds. When the curve used to generate the discount factors $Df(t_i)$ is a spline, the same measure is also often called a spline spread.

At the same time, z-spreads are difficult to calculate for users who are unable to break down an instrument into its constituent cash flows. This should be a surprising problem but is related to the use of readily available libraries which can provide such calculations as yields, but do not provide cash flow extraction.

Like all spread discussed in this chapter, higher spreads imply cheaper pricing of the instrument relative to the curve. In Europe and Japan, this usage is uniform across spread measures. In the US, however, swap spreads are quoted as par spreads (discussed below) of swaps over US Treasuries. This means that a higher swap spread in the US implies a more expensive (relative to swaps) US Treasury. Unfortunately, the situation is muddled further by commercial data providers who use the US convention also for European and Japanese spread series.

22.2 PAR SPREAD

The par spread is a simple comparison between the yield of an instrument and an appropriately measured par rate on the curve. The most common example of such spreads are the swap spreads in the US and the Australian EFP (exchange for physical) spread.

Rather than defining the price of a bond relative to a curve, par spreads are often used to define a curve relative to the price of benchmark bonds, or other instruments. In those cases, the liquidity of the bonds is so high that it provides superior price discovery relative to that of the curve. An additional incentive to quote curve points versus benchmark instruments is that traders can agree to exchange a position in the curve point (e.g., a paying position in a swap) against the offsetting position in the benchmark (a long position in this example). Such exchanges, which are equivalent to basis trades in a futures contract, have very little outright interest rate risk and can therefore be held for a longer period than each of the two legs alone. As a result, the bid–offer spreads on these trades are tighter for the same notional amount.

In the US case, swap rates are defined by their spread over the relevant on-the-run US Treasury. This market convention has the consequence that swap spreads can jump as a result of new Treasury issuance, namely when the relevant benchmark changes. As in Figure 31.5 on page 351, the driver of such jumps is the yield difference between the old and new benchmark. Because different points on the US swap curve use different benchmarks, which are changing at different times, such jumps occur at different times and in different amounts across the swap curve.

In the Australian swap market, the Australian bond futures are used as reference instruments. Swap rates are often represented as EFP spreads, and trading a swap at the same time as the offsetting position in a futures contract is a common inter-dealer trade. It should be recalled from Section 28.8 that the Australian bond futures contracts are cash-settled basket futures which are quoted in yield terms already. This makes the calculation of the EFP spread very easy and transparent.

The main drawback of par spreads is that they can be affected by differences in coupon conventions between the curve and the instrument that is compared to the curve. For instance, EUR swaps with maturities over two years have an annual fixed payment, which is in line with the coupon frequencies of all euro area government bond markets with the exception of Italy. The par spread between an Italian government bond (BTP) and EUR swaps is therefore misleading because a par BTP with the same coupon rate as a swap has a shorter duration due to half the coupons being paid out half a year earlier.

22.3   SWAP SPREADS

When spreads are measured against a swap curve, they can be expressed against the fixed or the floating leg of the swap. A first important difference between these two choices is that both legs usually have different daycount conventions because the floating side is a money market rate while the fixed side is a bond rate. In addition, the two legs can have different payment frequencies (for instance, semi-annual floating against annual fixed in EUR), so that the DV01 associated with a basis point of spread on the floating side is not identical to that on the fixed side. The spreads discussed in the previous section are expressed on the fixed side which a swap curve shares with other curve model. This section adds spread measures that are more specific to the swap market.

22.3.1   Asset swap spreads

An asset swap is a trade where two counterparties exchange a floating-rate payment against the cash flows of an asset. Such trades had in the past the connotation of a credit derivative because paying the fixed side in the trade removes all duration risk for the holder of the asset, leaving him or her exposed mainly to the credit risk of the asset. At the same time, asset swaps are used by issuers to remove the duration component of their own liabilities.

In principle, an asset swap amounts to a transfer of all cashflows from the asset from the investor to the counterparty, while the counterparty pays the investor the flows on the floating side of a swap with a floating leg of Libor plus a spread x, including a virtual upfront payment of par which is offset by a payment of a reference price of the asset. The asset swap spread is the spread x that makes the package worth zero at inception. Put differently, the investor transfers, in economic terms, to the counterparty the bond at the reference price and receives back a package of floating rate cash flows of equal value. The bond in question need not be a fixed-rate bullet bond but can have any structure (including an FRN).

Asset swaps of this form, also more specifically called par–par asset swaps, involve some degree of upfront balance sheet commitment. The difference between the reference price of the bond and par is an upfront transfer from the investor to the counterparty. If this is positive, then the investor is in effect granting a loan to the counterparty

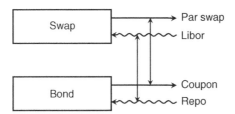

FIGURE 22.1 Simple fair-value asset swap spread model.

which is amortised via the spread x over the lifetime of the asset. If the price is below par, the loan is from the counterparty to the investor and is equally amortised via the spread.

Because the balance sheet exposure can be expensive, an alternative form of asset swap, the proceeds asset swap exists. In this type of trade, the notional of the swap is not equal to the par amount of the bond, but its price (the proceeds). This structure reverses the credit exposure because the bond will redeem at par while the notional payment of the swap is not par.

Because asset swaps are very bespoke structures, they do tend to be less easy to enter or unwind than standard swaps.

For low-risk bonds, a fair value asset swap spread can be constructed from an analogy (cf. Figure 22.1). To a speculator, a bond is a contract that pays a periodic coupon in return for regular payment of the repo rate required to fund the bond. A swap resembles this arrangement in that a regular swap coupon is paid in exchange for a regular Libor payment. This analogy implies that the asset swap spread of a bond should reflect the expected spread between the repo rate of the bond and Libor over the lifetime of the bond.

While compelling, this argument has some flaws. The future repo-Libor spreads are unknown and it may well be argued that the asset swap spread is an informative guess of how this spread will evolve, rather than that an assumed repo-Libor spread provides information about the fair value of asset swap spreads. At the same time, no bond is truly free of default risk. The Libor leg of a swap has a built-in survivorship bias (cf. page 337) that is not present in bond repo rates because a defaulted bond has no value as repo collateral. In summary, this analogy is most likely to provide only a floor to asset swap spreads but no point estimate.

22.3.2 I-spreads

The interpolated, or I-spread, is a simplified version of an asset swap. Instead of modelling the flows of the bond on the swap curve, one interpolates a rate on the swap curve at the correct maturity point. The interpolated swap spread is then the difference between yield of the bond and the interpolated swap rate. Unlike the asset swap spread, this makes it a fixed-side spread in the fixed-side daycount and compounding convention. In line with standard practice elsewhere, the interpolated swap has a short first, rather than a short last, coupon if the maturity of the bond does not fall on the maturity date of a standard swap. This tends to also involve a short first coupon on the floating rate leg of the swap.

I-spreads are of greater relevance to short-term hedges than asset swaps because the swaps used are par swaps at inception and so are faster to price and have a lower balance sheet cost. At the same time, the potential coupon differences between the bond and swap mean that larger curve movements will create a larger drift between bond and swap value. The trade-off between asset and interpolated swap is therefore one between liquidity and hedge quality.

22.3.3   The TED spread

The TED spread, also sometimes called the option-adjusted spread (OAS) is fundamentally different from the spreads discussed so far. It takes its historical name from 2 futures contract strips, namely the 13 week (91 day) T-bill contracts (T) and the 3 month eurodollar contracts (ED), both traded in the Chicago Board of Trade. The TED spread is the amount by which the ED curve needs to be shifted in oder to reprice a given bond. Illustratively speaking, it is the distance by which the ED curve needs to shift to obtain the T curve. The T-bill contract was delisted in July 2014 and the TED spread is now decribed by the CBOT as the Treasury-Eurodollar spread.

Unlike all the spreads discussed thus far, the calculation of this spread requires a change in the discount curve itself, rather than changes in intrument rates or spreads. In practice, this creates difficulties for non-US markets because the contracts equivalent to the Eurodollar contracts (Euribor on ICE, 3M Euroyen on TFX) have only a limited amount of liquidity in reds or further out contracts. TED spreads can therefore not be calculated from the money market futures curve alone. Instead, one shifts the implied forward rates in a market model, and rebuilds the discount curve from these shifted forward rates.

Three

Inflation-Linked Debt

CHAPTER 23

Inflation-Indexed Bonds

23.1 INTRODUCTION

The importance of inflation-linked debt (instead of, say, debt linked to the weather[1]) lies in the basic meaning of the word 'fixed income security'. While a nominal bond provides a fixed income in the sense of a fixed cashflow, what investors are usually interested in is not income *per se*, but consumption. The advantage of a fixed income is that if prices are stable (or at least move predictably), it will provide a steady (or at least known) stream of goods. For most of human history, this happy state of affairs has indeed been present and therefore fixed income securities have established themselves in the economy. However, at times prices can move quite sharply and unpredictably and thereby call into question the usefulness of a fixed nominal income. At such times, borrowers find more willing investors if they issue debt where cashflows are explicitly linked to prices. In doing so, they commit to compensate the lender for any loss in purchasing power experienced by the currency in which the bond cashflows are being paid. The most ready explanation for the existence of inflation-linked debt therefore is uncertainty about price developments.

The first inflation-linked bond known to the author was issued in what is now the US State of Massachusetts in 1780. At the time, the guardian of the currency used in Massachusetts was the Bank of England, which may be presumed to have been somewhat unconcerned with the purchasing power of bond coupons paid in what was a far away part of Britain that was waging its War of Independence. The bond in question, therefore, while nominally paying in pounds sterling, actually paid in what one would now call a basket of consumer goods. The statement of currency is therefore almost redundant and indeed kept open through the use of 'to be paid in the then current Money of said State'. Modern inflation-linked bonds do no longer spell out the underlying basket and instead refer to well-known indices published by respected statistics offices. However, this bond actually has a structure that is virtually identical to what is now generally known as the TIPS structure, so in order to prepare for working with the modern security, it's useful to spend some time analysing this one.

---

[1]Debt linked to weather exists but is a niche product.

The inscription of the bond, for one sample, reads:

In behalf of the State of Massachusetts-Bay, I the Subscriber do hereby promise and oblige Myself and Successors in the Office of TREASURER of said STATE to pay unto [name] or to his order, the SUM of Four hundred & seventy Pounds 8/9 on or before the First Day of March, in the Year of our Lord One Thousand Seven Hundred and eighty one with Interest at *Six per Cent.* per Annum: Both Principal and Interest to be paid in the then current Money of said State, in greater or less Sum, according as Five Bushels of *CORN*, sixty-eight Pounds and four-seventh Parts of a Pound of *BEEF*, Ten Pounds of *SHEEPS WOOL*, and Sixteen Pounds of *SOLE LEATHER* shall then cost, more or less than *One Hundred and Thirty Pounds* current Money, at the then current Prices of said ARTICLES — This SUM being THIRTY-TWO TIMES AND AN HALF what the same Quantities of the same Articles would cost at the Prices affixed to them in a Law of this STATE made in the Year of our Lord One Thousand Seven Hundred and Seventy-seven, intitled, *'An Act to prevent Monopoly and Oppression'.* The current Prices of said Articles, and the consequent Value of every Pound of the SUM herein promised, to be determined agreeable to a LAW of this STATE, intitled, 'An ACT to provide for the Security and Payment of the Balances that may appear to be due by Virtue of a Resolution of the GENERAL ASSEMBLY of the Sixth of *February* One Thousand Seven Hundred and Seventy-nine, of *this* STATE'S Quota of the CONTINENTAL ARMY, agreeable to the Recommendation of CONGRESS, and for Supplying the TREASURER with a SUM of Money for that Purpose'.

While this may sound somewhat obscure at first, it is relatively simple. First, the obligation is for the Treasurer of the State of Massachusetts to pay a certain sum to the person inscribed on the bond, or any other person if the original owner so wishes. The latter clause makes the obligation transferrable and thereby a bond. Without the addition of 'or to his order', the bond holder would have to claim the payment in person, which, given that this is soldiers' scrip, would devalue the obligation significantly. The payment is for 470 8/9 pounds (at the time still English pounds) plus 6% interest per annum, both adjusted for a price level. Assuming for simplicity that the bond pays interest for exactly one year, the final obligation will be 499.14 pounds, adjusted for the price level.

The price level adjustment to be made on payment is documented as follows. First, the prices of a bushel of corn (p_c), a pound of each of beef (p_b), sheeps wool (p_w), and sole leather (p_l) are to be established according to a law passed in 1779 which deals with financing the contribution of Massachusetts to the continental army for fighting the British. Second, the quantity:

$$I_M = 5p_c + 68\frac{4}{7}p_b + 10p_w + 16p_l \tag{23.1}$$

is to be calculated. The payment to be made is then 'a greater or less sum ... than 130 pounds current money'. In other words, the payment obligation will move up and down together with I_M and if $I_M = I_0 = 130$ pounds, then the sum to be paid will be the one calculated above, i.e., 499.14 pounds. Written as a formula, the treasurer would have to pay the sum of S pounds where:

$$S = \frac{I_M}{I_0} 499.14 \qquad (23.2)$$

The ratio I_M/I_0 is what is now referred to as an index ratio, i.e., the ratio of current to historical price level. Note that the expression 'in the then current money of said state' is almost superflous since the prices, and hence I_M, would presumably measured in current money. Using hindsight and calling the 'then money' dollar,

$$S[\text{dollar}] = \frac{I_M[\text{dollar}]}{130[\text{pounds}]} 499.14[\text{pounds}] \qquad (23.3)$$

so that the pound can be eliminated from the equation and only the dollar remains.

The convention to adjust payments by multiplication with an index ratio is the TIPS convention referred to above.

As a last send-off to this interesting document, we note that Massachusetts apparently passed a law fixing the prices of these items in 1777, but within the span of 3 years inflation had eroded the currency so much that prices had increased 32.5 times, i.e., annual inflation was running at 220 percent.

Seeing inflation-linked debt only as the last resort of debtors in countries with high and/or unstable inflation is misleading, however. An alternative is to issue bonds in a foreign, more stable currency. While indeed many emerging market economies issue inflation-linked debt to address the issue of currency stability worries, the biggest issuers of inflation-linked bonds are large economies with relatively stable rates of inflation. Therefore, there must be other reasons to issue and invest in such debt.

For sovereign issuers with progressive income tax systems, an important incentive to issue is the so-called tax creep. If all prices were doubled overnight and with it, all salaries were doubled, too, so that overnight the currency has been devalued by 50% in real terms, assuming for argument's sake with full compensation for savers. If all taxes were proportional to prices and wages, all these things taken together should not make a difference to the economy. With progressive income tax, however, the price doubling means that everybody would be in a higher tax band and as a result, the government's tax take as a share of gross domestic product would increase. Of course, the government would eventually be forced to adjust the tax bands upwards to take into account the new price level, but this is generally done retroactively. Overall, therefore, governments with progressive income tax have a long position in inflation and, depending on tax progression, this can be significant. Of course, tax officials are aware of this fact and budget projections incorporate tax creep. However, because the state treasuries and the central banks of the larger economies tend to be more or less independent, inflation is not under the control of the government and the government may therefore be inclined to hedge the long inflation position brought about by tax creep through a short position created by selling inflation-index bonds.

An increasingly important second reason is that sometimes there is strong demand from investors for inflation-linked debt, leading to a valuation effect known as the inflation risk premium. A number of investors have explicitly inflation-linked liabilities, such as insurance contracts or pension promises, so they are interested to hedge this exposure. More importantly, because the performance of nominal and inflation-linked debt is not perfectly correlated, inflation-linked debt can be seen as a different asset class which is interesting for diversification purposes.

23.1.1 Cashflows of inflation-linked bonds

There are 2 structures that are commonly used in the market to compensate investors for inflation. The apparently simpler of the 2, called the TIPS structure, pays fixed coupons, but adjusts every cashflow for inflation. This is done through multiplying each cashflow, be it a coupon or redemption flow, or the invoice price for settling a bond purchase, by a so-called index ratio R_t defined as the ratio of the reference index I_t (explained below) for the settlement date t and a fixed base index I_0, i.e.,

$$R_t = \frac{I_t}{I_0} \tag{23.4}$$

There is no particular reason to prefer one I_0 over any other because only the change in I_t affects the purchasing power, but in most markets the convention is to use the reference index for the first settlement date t_F of the bond so that $R_F = 1$. An exception is Sweden where most bonds use the same I_0. Because the adjustment for inflation means that all coupons have effectively a constant purchasing power, they are referred to as real coupons and the bonds in general as real bonds.

The reference index can technically not be the inflation index itself because measuring and publishing inflation numbers is costly and takes time. Daily levels are therefore not available. If one were to rely on inflation indices only, I_t would change only once a month. In most markets, therefore, interpolation of lagged inflation numbers is used. In this setup, the reference index is based on the theoretical inflation level present at a fixed time before the settlement date of the relevant cashflow. This period is the inflation lag. When no actual inflation level for this day has been published, the theoretical level is calculated by linearly interpolating between the two closest published values, as shown in Figure 23.1. The minimum length of the lag period is therefore the time it takes to publish a new index value, plus about one month.

In most markets, R_t is floored at the level of R_0, at least for the purpose of calculating the redemption cashflow. Note that the bond from 1780 cited above does not have such a floor because it uses the phrase 'in a greater or less sum'.

An important point to realise about the TIPS-style adjustment of cashflows is that it is exactly identical to the treatment of cashflows of a foreign currency investment. In this setting, I_t plays the role of an FX rate. The foreign currency here is not one that exists in the real world. Instead, it is a hypothetical currency defined as having constant purchasing power in terms of the inflation index used for adjusting the cashflows. This analogy is extremely fruitful for understanding return and risk measures for index-linked bonds. It also explains the near-equivalence between foreign currency issuance and index-linked debt for small and open economies.

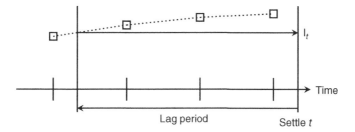

FIGURE 23.1 Reference index interpolation. The index level applied at time t is the interpolated level of the actual index at a given lag.

Because TIPS-style inflation-linked bonds adjust every cashflow for inflation, the loss of purchasing power on the principal is returned at the maturity of the bond. This means that the inflation-compensation component of interest rates is largely absent from the coupon payments and the coupons paid by TIPS-style inflation-linked bonds accordingly usually are lower than those paid by nominal bonds but the principal repayment is higher.

The alternative to the TIPS-style inflation link, used mostly in the corporate bond market and for the Italian retail BTP Italia, is to have a floating rate coupon defined as rate of inflation plus a spread. This type of adjustment, known as pay-as-you-go, means that coupons are usually higher than those of TIPS-style inflation-linked bonds, but the principal is repaid at par. Because the coupon rate is determined at the start of the coupon period, investors face some inflation risk but settlement is simpler than for TIPS-style bonds.

Given a term structure of inflation expectations, it is possible to compare the pricing of TIPS-style and floating rate note inflation-linked bonds, so at the outset there is no difference between the two types of link. However, the risk characteristics of the two types of bond are of course very different.

In the standard text [29], the TIPS convention is introduced as capital-indexed bonds while the floating rate note structure is called interest-indexed bond. This chapter deals almost exclusively with TIPS-style bonds because, despite their simple structure, they are more complex to analyse than pay-as-you-go schemes, and they are by far the most common.

Euro-area inflation-linked bonds tend to be linked not to the overall inflation index (usually euro-area HICP or, in the case of some French linkers, French CPI), but the index with tobacco removed from the index basket. The origin of this custom is the French loi Évin which bans tobacco advertising and promotion. France was the first euro-area country to issue inflation-linked bonds in large volumes[2]. Later issuers found

---

[2]It is not entirely unfair to argue that retail tobacco prices are mostly taxes and it would be counter-intuitive for a government to pay out on government debt a cost that it imposes on its citizens. That being said, the French famously manipulated historical photographs to eliminate cigarettes from the images of well-known personalities at the same time as this convention was established. A health-related aspect of this convention can therefore not be ruled out.

that the inflation swap market had developed most liquidity in the ex-tobacco indices and followed this lead.

23.1.2 Quotation of index-linked bonds

Inflation-linked bonds are usually quoted with a clean price and net of inflation adjustment. In other words, the quoted price will, to first order, not change due to passage of time (affecting accrued interest) or inflation. To the extent that clean prices are a natural way of quoting bonds because they exclude predictable performance elements from the price quote, also excluding inflation, is a sensible convention. Despite, or perhaps because of, this the UK market quotes inflation-linked bonds including inflation.

The nominal prices of inflation-linked bonds are therefore given by scaling the real price by the index ratio applicable to the settlement date t, i.e.,

$$P(t) = R_t \hat{P}(t) \tag{23.5}$$

The invoice price, i.e., the consideration paid for an inflation-linked bond for settlement t is then:

$$V = NR_t(\hat{P} + Accr_t) \tag{23.6}$$

where accrued interest is calculated as it would be for a nominal bond.

In the FRN-style inflation-linked bonds, the invoice price is simply:

$$V = N(\hat{P} + Accr_t) \tag{23.7}$$

but the accrued interest is calculated from a floating-rate coupon that includes an inflation component.

23.2 REBALANCING, REBASING AND REVISION OF CPI INDICES

A CPI index is a chain-weighted average price of consumption items with the weights determined by their share in the consumption expenditure of individuals. As consumption patterns change over time, these weights also need to be revised. In addition, changes in fashions and technology also require adjustments in the items that are used to sample the prices of certain consumption items. For instance, flat-screen television sets used to be luxury items but have now completely replaced CRT-based devices, and mobile communication plays a much larger role than fixed-line telephony.

The statisticians compiling a CPI respond to such changes in two ways. The first are constant small adjustments in sampling methodology and sample items. Such adjustments tend to have only a marginal effect on the inflation rate. Because CPIs are chain-weighted, the replacement of one item with another has no impact on the level of the index, while the impact of the replacement on the rate of change of the CPI depends on the item weight and the difference in the rate of price change between the old and new item. For regular adjustments, both of these numbers tend to be small, although on occasion they can be substantial.

Over longer horizons, it is necessary to revise weights in a more fundamental way by reassessing actual spending habits. These are sampled by consumer expenditure surveys which are costly to conduct. Such surveys therefore do not occur very often, roughly every 5 years or so, depending on the country. Consumer expenditure does not exactly match consumption expenditure because people spend cash on non-consumption items such as transfers (e.g. child support) or savings (including pensions and capital life insurance), and not every spending item might be included in the CPI index. For instance, a number of consumer price indices do not include the cost of owning a home (the so-called owner-equivalent rent) due to difficulties in accurately measuring this cost[3]. Certain cash spending items may, on the other hand, also relate to other consumption items. School fees, for instance, may include food items that are unrelated to education itself. Changing the measurement basket for the inflation index is known as rebalancing.

When index weights are revised on a broad basis, statistics offices may choose to let the index start from a new level. This is known as an index rebasing. In Japan, the quinquennial index revisions include a rebasing where the new index is scaled to that its average reading over the twelve months of the base year is equal to 100. Japanese CPI may therefore be referred to as, for instance, the 'base-2010 CPI' to distinguish it from the 'base-2015 CPI' with different index weights *and* a different base level. To the extent possible, a CPI index can be backfilled with weights of a later index vintage which makes indices comparable across time. Because the weight revision involved in a rebasing simultaneously affects the weights of many items, it can have a measurable impact on the inflation rate. Figure 23.2 shows the difference in the cumulative price change of the base-2010 and base-2015 nationwide all-items Japanese CPI between 2005 and 2015, the last year for which the base-2010 index was produced. Although quantisation noise disturbs the comparison, a different run rate is evident.

For inflation-linked bonds, index rebasing has two consequences. The first is that after a few years, the index vintage in which the base CPI is measured is discontinued. This means that the base index needs to be adjusted to the new index vintage. This could be done by either resetting the base index to the back-filled value of the new vintage index applicable to the date the original base index was set, or chaining the old and new index together during a transition period and converting the index ratio with the ratio of old and new index during that period. Specifically one uses:

$$I_{old}(t) = I_{new}(t) \frac{<I_{old}>}{<I_{new}>} \tag{23.8}$$

---

[3]Real estate transactions do not occur frequently or transparently, and part of the cost of purchasing real estate is related to the financing cost of mortgages, rather than the cost of property as such.

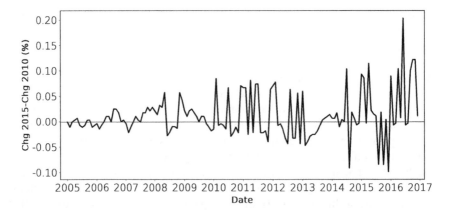

FIGURE 23.2 Difference between the Japanese CPI (all items) changes since January 2005 for the base-2010 and base-2015 indices. Note that index levels are reported with one decimal so quantisation noise is in the order of 0.1%. Source: MIC, e-stat.co.jp. Licenced under CC BY 4.0.

where the averages $< \cdot >$ are taken over the base year of the new index vintage. In Japan this implies that $< I_{new} >= 100$. When indices are rebased more than once, such adjustments can be chained. Note that the value of the fraction never changes.

This method has the advantage of leaving historical index ratios unchanged. Some data providers, like Bloomberg, incorporate this adjustment in the base CPI. This means that the base CPI of a given bond appears to change, contrary to how indexation has been introduced here. However, the value of the index ratio for any given day is unchanged by this approach.

The second consequence of rebasing is that the near-term run rate of inflation can be affected, which should then affect the fair value of breakeven inflation. This potential effect on breakeven is why index-linked bond analysts take a keen interest in rebasings which would otherwise be a rather niche subject[4].

In other jurisdictions, such as Europe and the US, large-scale index weight changes are reflected not through the publication of a rebased new index vintage with a new base year, but through a revision of the existing index. In essence, past values of the CPI are recalculated using the new methodology, and scaled such that the current value of the index remains unchanged. While this approach avoids the potential confusion of multiple base-year indices, it breaks the idea that a past index level is immutable.

23.3 INFLATION SEASONALITY

Inflation figures are generally quoted in the press as annual rates of change and this is for most purposes the appropriate way of referencing price stability. Central banks also

---

[4]This statement should be taken in relative terms. Inflation-linked bonds are not exactly mainstream.

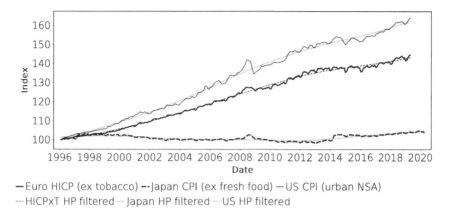

FIGURE 23.3   German, US and Japanese inflation indices over time. Sources: Data from ECS, BLS, MIC.

express price stability targets in terms of annual rates of change, with a 2% annual rate of change being a usual target point.

This convention obscures, however, persistent seasonal patterns in inflation. Figure 23.3 shows the main German, US, and Japanese price indices together with a Hodrick-Prescott (HP) filtered version that removes short-term fluctuations. The HP filter is used here for simplicity rather than accuracy[5] and realistic seasonality adjustments usually use more complex filters such as the X12-ARIMA filter [76] which better reflect the impact of, for instance, movable feasts such as Easter.

The average differences between the actual monthly inflation readings and the smoothed index levels provides an estimate of the seasonality effects present in inflation[6]. Using the data in Figure 23.3, one finds the seasonal deviations (expressed as average percentage deviations from trend) shown in Figure 23.4.

Notably, the seasonal fluctuation in price levels is of an order of magnitude that is comparable to that of the underlying inflation itself. The Japanese CPI excluding fresh food in particular shows a seasonal variability well in excess of the long-term average of the inflation trend. This means that over any reasonable active investment horizon the inflation return of Japanese inflation-linked bonds is tied to the, more or less predictable, seasonal fluctuation in prices rather than the underlying inflation trend. Even for other inflation markets, the seasonal patterns are significant sources of returns.

The large seasonal fluctuations of inflation indices are driven by more or less predictable events such as seasonal sales campaigns and holiday dates. Figure 23.5 shows

---

[5]The main epistemological drawback of the HP filter is that adding new data can change the filtered value of older observations. This problem has not hurt its ubiquity in econometrics. For the purposes of the present analysis it is sufficiently accurate.

[6]There are two sources of errors in this estimate. The first is that over a finite observation period the effects of one-off events, such as strikes or transport disruptions, may not be averaged out completely. At the same time, longer observation periods may obscure time-variant phenomena such as the 'Black Friday' sales that are a recent phenomenon in retail pricing.

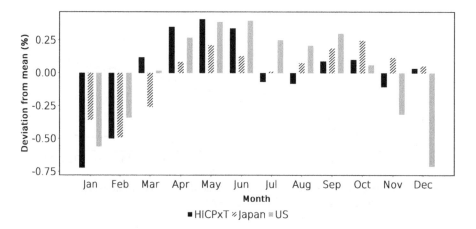

FIGURE 23.4 Seasonality factors (percentage deviations from trend developments) for the 3 inflation indices shown earlier. The trend is the HP-filtered monthly data shown earlier.

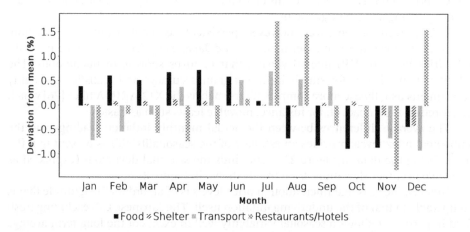

FIGURE 23.5 Seasonality factors (percentage deviations from trend developments) for the 4 main components of German HICP, ordered by their weight in the overall HICP index.

the seasonality factors of the 4 main components in German HICP, extracted in the same way as in Figure 23.4 from HP-filtered data. Notably, the German HICP component related to restaurant food and hotel stays shows clear peaks in the main holiday periods of summer and Christmas. Although the weight of this component in the overall HICP is less than 10%, the high volatility of this sub-index means that it contributes significantly to the overall seasonal pattern in the overall index. This observation explains the importance of using somewhat more sophisticated time-series filters than the HP filter used here. Movable feasts can affect highly volatile components of inflation at different times of the year and simple filters will treat these predictable effects as noise instead.

At the same time, highly volatile inflation index components raise an important concern about price indices. In some case, prices follow demand and the spikes in hotel prices during holiday seasons are probably due to such demand peaks. Other price fluctuations are driven by supply, however. For instance, higher demand for light oil distillates such as gasoline during the summer driving season tends to create higher supply in heavier distillates such as heating oil and diesel because a given barrel of crude oil contains a fixed mix of both (see [54] for a good introduction to this topic). Many consumers are aware of attendant seasonal price fluctuations and are able to adjust their consumption schedules to these patterns. For instance, European households that use heating oil tend to buy this fuel in summer when it is cheap because they have sufficient storage capacity to carry the oil into the winter season. The inflation index, however, assigns a fixed weight to the heating component of the sub-index related to shelter. The effect of this fixed weight is that the absolute level of heating costs is over-estimated in the price index. However, because households are unable to carry substantial amounts of fuel over several years, the rate of change in the price index is unlikely to be significantly affected as long as the seasonal price and consumption patterns remain unchanged[7].

The value of an inflation-linked bond is given by its dirty price multiplied by the index ratio R_t. Given that seasonality of inflation leads to a seasonal pattern in R_t, and that short-term expected returns on bonds should follow short-term interest rates which do not have such a seasonal pattern, the clean prices of inflation-linked bonds must somehow absorb that seasonality. Before going into the theoretical details, one can look at empirical evidence. Figures 23.6 and 23.7 use a simple cyclical cubic smoothing spline (cf. e.g. [87]) fitted to the clean prices of every inflation-linked bond in their market. The prices of each individual bond have been normalised to 100 at the start of each year to reduce the impact of coupons on the absolute price range.

The fit does not address any non-seasonal patterns such as changes in long-term inflation expectations. Such patterns can be assumed to approximately average out over the observation periods used here (around 10 years for the US and 7 years for the German data).

The charts suggest that by and large the market for inflation-linked bond rationally reflects seasonality in the underlying index through adjustments in the (not inflation-adjusted) clean prices. However, while the amplitude of seasonal price fluctuations in the US more or less matches the swing in the seasonality, the price swing is much larger in German bonds.

Because the clean prices affect real yield calculations (addressed below), and real yields drive breakeven inflation, breakeven inflation also has a seasonal pattern. This

---

[7]As an aside, the ability to engage in this form of strategic consumption timing is tied to sufficient idle assets. Only consumers who are not constrained by liquidity can choose to purchase items when they are cheap. Others will purchase these goods as and when they are required, subject to necessary funds. This suggests that the absolute level of prices paid for the same goods can be lower for consumers with sufficient wealth than for less wealthy members of society, at least as long as price patterns are reasonably predictable. Whether this is a social problem is debatable given that the contents of consumption baskets are also determined by wealth and the total consumption tends to increase with income.

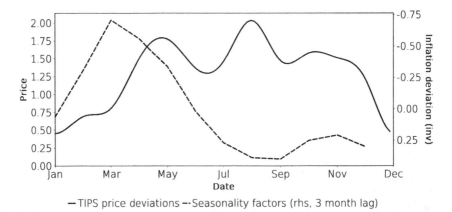

- TIPS price deviations --Seasonality factors (rhs, 3 month lag)

FIGURE 23.6   Seasonal patterns in the clean prices of US TIPS and lagged seasonality of CPURNSA (from Figure 23.4). The cyclical cubic smoothing spline is fit to 81,500 observations taken from treasurydirect.gov. Source: Data obtained from treasurydirect. Gov.

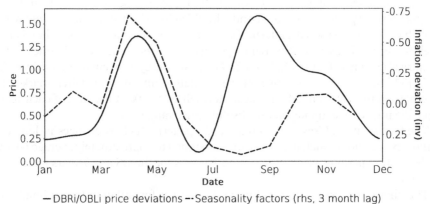

- DBRi/OBLi price deviations --Seasonality factors (rhs, 3 month lag)

FIGURE 23.7   Seasonal patterns in the clean prices of German DBRi and OBLi prices with the lagged seasonality of HICP (cf. Figure 23.4). The cyclical cubic smoothing spline is fit to 8,500 observations taken from the Bundesbank. Source: Data obtained from the Bundesbank.

realisation is important for the interpretation of breakeven inflation as a measure of long-term inflation expectations.

23.4   PRICE FORMATION IN INFLATION-LINKED MARKETS

The relatively stable seasonality patterns in inflation indices and their influence on the pricing patterns of inflation-linked fixed income products can provide some clues on the price discovery process.

Figure 23.8 shows the seasonality in zero-coupon inflation swap rates, extracted in the same way as elsewhere in this chapter through the comparison of a

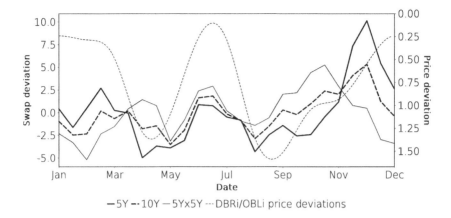

FIGURE 23.8 Seasonal patterns in the clean prices of German DBRi and OBLi prices (inverted) with the seasonality of HICP swaps. Sources: Data from ECS SDW, Bundesbank.

Hodrick-Prescott-filtered time series with the original data. The inflation swaps cover an integer number of years and should therefore not incorporate any seasonality. Furthermore, the chart shows not only the spot-starting swap rates but also the 5Yx5Y forward inflation swap rate[8]. This forward rate should not only not exhibit seasonality, but should also be covering inflation expectations beyond the forecast horizon of realistic economic observers. Despite this, the forward rate has a seasonal pattern is driven more or less by the two spot rates. To some extent, this pattern also seems to correspond to the one observed for index-linked bond prices.

A possible explanation for this somewhat non-intuitive outcome is that the breakeven inflation rates seen in the market are driven at least partially by short-term considerations, rather than solely by rational expectations of future realised inflation. In particular, the inflation swap market differs from the inflation-linked bond market in that transactions are generally symmetrical in that for each inflation payer in the swap market there is an equal receiver. The bond market, meanwhile, has a relatively constant outstanding volume while the market appetite for such bonds waxes and wanes over time. For speculative holders of inflation-linked bonds, short-term income is an important consideration because limits on P&L drawdowns usually prevent traders from holding losing positions for long periods. A trader with a firm view on inflation five years from now will find it difficult to express such a view with a 5Yx5Y inflation swap because a 10-year investment is beyond the usual career planning horizon in most financial firms. At the same time, the inflation-linked bond market provides a natural source for paying interest in the inflation swap market in that a trader can buy an inflation-linked bond, pay fixed in the nominal swap market to hedge out the real coupons, and pay inflation in the zero-coupon inflation-swap market to offset the index link of the bond.

---

[8]In line with market convention, this rate is calculated from the 5Y and 10Y zero coupon rates r_5 and r_{10} with the approximation $r_{5x5} = ((1 + r_{10})^{10}/(1 + r_5)^5)^{0.2} - 1$.

This market structure then implies that short-term developments in the carry on inflation-linked bonds drive their pricing to some extent, and so interfere with the rational expression of long-term inflation expectations. Then main source of noise in these short-term carry developments are related to changes in the oil price because energy prices are at the same time volatile and have a high weight in the inflation indices. Because traders generate inflation swap paying interest from the inflation-linked bond markets, seasonal and short-term fluctuations affect inflation swaps although the swap rates, particularly the longer-dated forwards, have no fundamental reason to reflect these fluctuations.

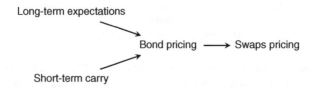

As a result, inflation seasonality and changes in energy prices affect ostensibly long-term measures of inflation expectations. The extent to which this happens depends on a number of other market factors, such as the general availability of arbitrage capital, that are difficult to quantify.

23.5　RETURN MEASURES OF INFLATION-LINKED BONDS

Even allowing for the fiction that the concept of yield for nominal bonds reflects the reasonable assumption of a constant rate at which cashflows can be reinvested, inflation-linked bonds present a problem. Inflation is clearly not fully predictable (otherwise inflation-linked bonds need not exist), so the inflation uplift experienced by reinvested real coupons is uncertain.

The first solution is to simply ignore the idea of inflation altogether and treat Equation (16.10) as referring to the real coupons and the real (not inflation-adjusted) price of the respective inflation-linked bond. This gives rise to the idea of the real yield ρ of inflation-linked bonds.

At this point, it is useful to refer back to the assertion that TIPS-style inflation-linked bonds can be treated, mathematically at least, like foreign currency bonds. In this setting, the real yield is the equivalent to the yield of the bond calculated in its domestic market. In other words, if a USD-based investor were to purchase a JGB, the yield of the JGB calculated the normal way in Japanese Yen would play the role of the real yield of a TIPS, while the nominal yield of the equivalent US Treasury bond would be the best stimate of the USD return of that JGB. Both return measures have no direct bearing of the return in nominal terms for the investor because FX or inflation risk, respectively, would introduce additional return components.

If an investor is instead searching for a nominal return measure for inflation-linked bonds, one solution is to forecast inflation up to the maturity of the bond, calculate the expected nominal cashflows based on the resulting values for I_t on the relevant cashflow dates and calculate the yield using Equation (16.10). Naturally, this yield forecast will depend on each individual investor's inflation forecasts. In a world of efficient markets and risk-neutral pricing, however, this effort will be in vain because the best possible estimate for the nominal return r corresponding to the investment horizon of the respective inflation-linked bond is already known, namely, it is the yield of the nominal bonds of the relevant horizon. One therefore postulates the existence of a nominal yield of inflation-linked bonds and assumes it to be equal to the (possibly interpolated) yield of the comparable nominal bonds.

Of course, some of the assumptions stressed here are totally unrealistic and so nominal yields of inflation-linked bonds are to be interpreted with caution. Turning back again to the foreign currency analogy and the USD/JPY example, it is indeed possible to make an efficient market argument that the expected unhedged return on a 10Y JGB investment for USD-based investors is equal to the 10Y Treasury yield. However, given the heroic assumptions underlying this argument, few would elevate this return measure to the status of a yield which, though flawed (cf. Section 16.7), is at least based on a firm mathematical formula.

23.6 BREAKEVEN INFLATION

Arguably, the main use of the nominal yield of an inflation-linked bond is as an input for the calculation of breakeven inflation. Simply speaking, breakeven inflation ι is the rate of inflation that will make the internal rate of return of investing in an inflation-linked bond identical to that of a nominal bond of identical maturity.

There are 3 usual methods to express breakeven inflation. They are given below together with mnemonics referring to well-known relationships in other areas where they exist.

> **Fisher hypothesis** The simplest, and most common, calculation of breakeven inflation $\iota = r - \rho$ corresponds to the idea that nominal rates are the sum of growth and inflation expectations. The main drawback is that this equation neglects any compounding effects.
>
> **FX points** Using the real and nominal interest rates as interest rates in two different currencies, breakeven inflation can be interpreted as the annual change in the exchange rate that will make the returns in either currency identical. Breakeven inflation is therefore given by the well-known formula for FX forward points:
>
> $$\iota = \frac{1+r}{1+\rho} - 1 \qquad (23.9)$$
>
> used here with the tacit assumption of a 1-year horizon.
>
> **Exact** The exact way to calculate breakeven inflation assuming a constant rate ι is to use a given ι, calculate the resulting nominal cashflows from the inflation-linked bond and then calculate the internal rate of return of these cashflows using the equivalent of Equation (16.10). Then, ι is adjusted until the internal rate of return so obtained matched the nominal yield of the index-linked bond. This corresponds to

a two-stage iteration process (the calculation of y in Equation (16.10) is an iteration process, and this iteration has to be repeated for each trial value of ι). Unless this calculation is done using a proper seasonality adjustment, the added precision of this calculation is somewhat illusory.

Markets generally use the first definition but data providers also offer the third. A consequence of the different risk characteristics of inflation-linked and nominal bonds is that breakeven inflation is directional with the level of nominal yields.

Breakeven inflation as calculated here suffers from seasonality effects when used as an indicator of inflation expectations. Because bond returns are measured between settlement date and maturity, settlement on a date when the reference index is seasonally low would push breakeven inflation upwards, while a maturity date on a seasonally low breakeven index would push it downwards. Simply speaking, breakeven inflation should measure the average annual rate of change in the underlying inflation index between settlement and maturity, subject to the interpolation lag (cf. Figure 23.1). If the intervening period between these 2 dates is not an integer number of years, seasonality can distort this interpretation.

Figures 23.9 and 23.10 show this effect in a very simple way. They are based on a constant HICP ex-Tobacco inflation of 2% with the historical seasonality pattern added to the observed index levels. In the first example, two different end dates differing by three months are chosen and the average inflation rate between a common settlement date and these two maturity dates are shown[9].

The average inflation to the maturity date falling on a seasonally high index reading appears higher although the underlying inflation path is the same as for both bonds.

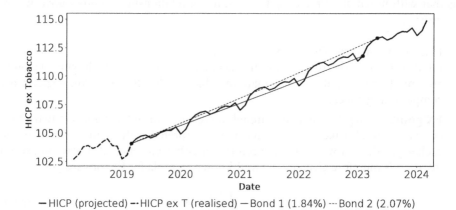

— HICP (projected) --·HICP ex T (realised) — Bond 1 (1.84%) ··· Bond 2 (2.07%)

FIGURE 23.9   Effect of seasonality on breakeven inflation. Average annual inflation is 2% in this example but the seasonality of HICP ex-Tobacco is added to the projected inflation path. When the maturity date falls on a seasonally low index level (Bond 1), breakeven inflation appears to be lower.

---

[9]This chart, and the next, ignores the inflation lag for simplicity.

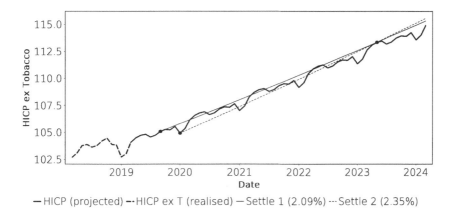

FIGURE 23.10 Effect of seasonality on breakeven inflation. Average annual inflation is 2% in this example but the seasonality of HICP ex-Tobacco is added to the projected inflation path. When settlement occurs on a seasonally high index level (Settle 1), the apparent breakeven inflation rate is lower.

This effect complicates the comparison of bonds linked to the same index but maturing in different months, such as different Japanese inflation-linked government bond series, or between French and German government bonds linked to HICP ex-Tobacco.

At the same time, even for an unchanged inflation path breakeven inflation can change as a result of changing settlement days. In Figure 23.10 the maturity date and underlying inflation is the same but the settlement date changes. The average inflation rate between settlement and maturity changes significantly even though the actual underlying annual inflation remains constant.

The effect of seasonality on breakeven inflation diminishes with increasing bond maturity because the same absolute change in the price level is amortised over a larger time horizon. Figures 23.9 and 23.10 were drawn for relatively short maturities to make the seasonality effect more visible. Also, the reason why Figures 23.6 and 23.7 use the price, not yield, changes of bond prices throughout the year is that the seasonality effect is an absolute price shift which has a smaller effect on the yields of longer-dated bonds.

An important question is whether breakeven inflation is in any way related to inflation expectations. In theory, the expected inflation rate over the lifetime of an inflation linked bond should be decisive in deciding whether to buy a linker or the equivalent nominal bond. In practice, this argument assumes a balanced market and inter-temporal substitution of future returns. An investor buying an inflation-linked bond at a time of low inflation because she or he expects inflation to rise will initially underperform an investor in the nominal bond. Until the time this asset allocation decision is vindicated by either a change in market prices (higher breakeven inflation) or realised returns (higher index ratio), this underperformance needs to be justified. Doing so is complicated by the ready convertibility of nominal into inflation-linked bonds which argues against early hedging of rising inflation[10]. In addition, the amount

---

[10]The vernacular summary of this argument is 'Nobody buys an umbrella until it rains.'

of inflation-linked bonds circulating in the market is independent of the demand for them given that developed-market inflation-linked debt has long maturities[11]. At times, there may be a surfeit of such bond circulating, which will depress their prices and thereby breakeven inflation. At other times, investors may be scrambling to find real assets for fear of imminent inflation, and breakeven inflation may be elevated relative to expectations because short-term fears override long-term expectations.

Put differently, using breakeven inflation of bonds as a measure of future expected inflation is equivalent to relying on the rationality of others, and their willingness to risk capital in the expression of their views. The deviations between inflation expectations, and market-based inflation rates arising from the cost of expressing expectations are known as the inflation risk premium.

23.7 CARRY ON INFLATION-INDEXED BONDS

Carry on inflation-linked bonds at first sight is no different from the carry on nominal bonds. For an initial cash outlay of P_0 at t_0, the arbitrage-free forward nominal cash price of the bond at t_f is $P_f = P_0/Df(t_0, t_f)$. The complication arising is that inflation-linked bonds are usually not quoted in nominal, but real terms. In other words, the invoice price P_0 is given by $P_0 = R_0\hat{P}_0$ where $\hat{P}_0$ is the quoted real price (including accrued interest). Correspondingly, $P_f = R_f\hat{P}_f$ and so:

$$\hat{P}_f = \frac{R_0}{R_f} \frac{\hat{P}_0}{Df(t_0, t_f)} \tag{23.10}$$

This expression allows some insight if one writes $R_f = (1 + DCF(t_0, t_f)i(t_0, t_f))R_0$ and also expands $Df(t_0, t_f) = 1/(1 + r(t_0, t_f)DCF(t_i, t_f))$. The rate $i(t_0, t_f)$ here is used as an interest rate but is in fact the (lagged) inflation rate between t_0 and t_f. This gives:

$$\hat{P}_f = \frac{1}{1 + DCF(t_0, t_f)i(t_0, t_f)}\hat{P}_0(1 + r(t_0, t_f)DCF(t_i, t_f)) \tag{23.11}$$

and for small values of $DCF(t_0, t_f)$, $i(t_0, t_f)$, and $r(t_0, t_f)$ this can be simplified to:

$$\hat{P}_f = \hat{P}_0(1 + (r(t_0, t_f) - i(t_0, t_f))DCF(t_i, t_f)) \tag{23.12}$$

This is formally very close to Equation (16.20) but instead of the repo rate $r(t_0, t_f)$ one has the strange expression $r(t_0, t_f) - i(t_0, t_f)$, i.e., the difference between the repo rate r and the inflation rate i. This rate is called the real short rate. Unfortunately, some economists have the tendency to sportingly call the difference between practically any inflation rate and any nominal interest rate real rate, so this term may be confusing.

---

[11] Because near-term inflation can be predicted with reasonable accuracy, there is no need to buy inflation-linked bonds to hedge it, and hence no natural demand for short-dated inflation-linked bonds.

However, the meaning of $r(t_0, t_f) - i(t_0, t_f)$ should be obvious. If there was a market for short-term funds in which payments are adjusted according to inflation in the same way as for inflation-index bonds, one could use Equation (16.20) directly and would not have to worry about the inflation-linked nature of the bonds. As it is, one needs to use nominal repo interest rates and adjust for inflation explicitly.

So far, these formulas have ignored a little technical problem, namely that there is no general way to know either R_f or $i(t_0, t_f)$. Note that these are hard quantities in the sense that they are defined by the bond issuer and the respective statistics office. They are not things that can be decided by negotiation market counterparties, as for instance $r(t_0, t_f)$. There is no solution to this problem, but what is generally done is to use forecasts of I_f or $i(t_0, t_f)$ to estimate $\hat{P}_f$. This means, of course, that market participants have no problems agreeing on P_f for an inflation-linked bond (because they have to agree only on the repo rate $r(t_0, t_f)$ which is likely to be easily observed), but in order to agree on $\hat{P}_f$ they would have to agree in their inflation outlook as well. In many developed markets, there are forward contracts for I_f which can be used to hedge this risk, usually for up to about one year.

23.8   COMPREHENSIVE INFLATION MODELLING

The starting point of any model for the valuation of inflation-linked instruments is the nominal discount curve. Nominal rates products are more liquid than index-linked ones, and monetary policy, which ultimately governs the funding costs in an economy, is implemented in nominal terms.

Given the strong influence of seasonality on pricing, simple measures such as yields or breakeven-inflation do not suffice to analyse the relative valuation of index-linked bonds and inflation swaps. The only way to encapsulate all available information is to construct and calibrate a comprehensive model of the relevant inflation index in the future, and then use the nominal rates curve to discount these projected nominal cash flows. A very simple model for the inflation index I_f at a future date f has the form:

$$I_f = I_t \frac{s_f}{s_t} e^{\iota(f-t)} \tag{23.13}$$

where s_f and s_t are the seasonality factors applicable to settlement at spot (t) and the forward date f. The rate ι is essentially a zero-coupon breakeven inflation rate and the exponential term in which it is incorporated reflects the geometric nature of a fixed inflation rate in terms of the development of the underlying index. One would normally specify this model in terms of the monthly index readings, and then apply the lag and interpolation rules pertaining to the bonds in question.

If sufficient data is available, it is possible to make ι time-dependent (i.e., introduce a function $\iota(t)$) with a reasonably simple functional form rather than using a constant. This avoids a jump in the overnight inflation rate from its current value to the new constant ι. For instance, one could model a gradual convergence of the inflation rate to a long-run value with the two-parameter function:

$$I_f = I_t \frac{s_f}{s_t} \exp\left((f - t)(\iota_0 + \iota_l) \frac{(f - t)/\tau}{1 + (f - t)/\tau} \right) \tag{23.14}$$

The long-run inflation rate would be $\iota_0 + \iota_l$ in this model, where ι_0 is the most current reading of the annual inflation rate. The time scale parameter τ defines a convergence speed from the current inflation but although this parameter is useful for curve fitting, it has little economic significance. In particular, when $|\iota_l| \ll 1$, the actual value of τ has no impact. Examples of the evolution of the assumed annual inflation rate and the projected index are shown in Figures 23.11 and 23.12.

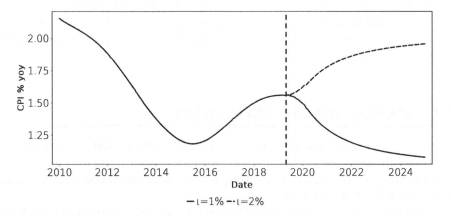

FIGURE 23.11 Examples of inflation rate dynamics of the model Equation (23.14). The two curves separate at the last known reading of the actual inflation index.

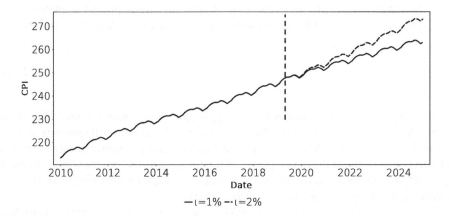

FIGURE 23.12 Examples of inflation projections for the purpose of modelling inflation-linked bond prices using two different ι values and $\tau = 3$ in Equation (23.14). The 2 curves separate at the last known reading of the actual inflation index.

Time-dependent ι assumptions are particularly important when there are future events that lead to jumps in the inflation index, for instance as a result of announced or expected tax increases[12]. In more developed markets, the exigencies of repo trading in inflation linked bonds have created a more or less liquid market in near-term index forwards extending about 1 year into the future. Such forwards permit the extension of the starting point of the extrapolation Equation (23.13) into the future.

Having modelled the nominal cash flows, one can then use the standard equation linking them to the nominal spot price of the corresponding bond:

$$P = \sum_i Df(t_i)Cf_i \tag{23.15}$$

Using the definition in Equation (23.13), for example, this can be re-written (with an appropriate change of variables) as:

$$P = \sum_i Df(t_i)\hat{C}f_i \frac{I}{I_0} \frac{S_{t_i}}{S_0} e^{\iota t_i} \tag{23.16}$$

This only holds if the bond in question has no indexation floor at I_0 for either coupons or principal, or if that floor is well out of the money. If the floor exists and is close to the money, then the cash flow at time t_i can be higher than the linear function shown here.

Equation (23.16) has a very useful form because the ι term is unrelated to the structure of a particular bond. By introducing a real discount factor:

$$Rf(t) = Df(t)\frac{S_t}{S_0}e^{\iota t} \tag{23.17}$$

Equation (23.16) becomes:

$$P = \frac{I}{I_0} \sum_i Rf(t_i)\hat{C}f_i \tag{23.18}$$

The analytical significance of this re-casting is that $Rf(t)$ can be represented as a composite curve model along the lines of Section 19.4.5 (page 202). A modelling hierarchy for an inflation-linked bond curve would therefore start with a spline for the nominal curve, and then stack an inflation model along the lines of Equations (23.13) or (23.14) with appropriate seasonality corrections on top of that nominal model to arrive at an appropriate real discount curve. A standard curve fitting algorithm can then use the ι parameter, or the two parameters (ι_l, τ) to match observed market prices. This has been done to produce the forward rate curve shown in Figure 23.13. Note that the forward rates show a strong seasonal pattern which is essentially the annualised slope of the seasonality of the underlying consumer price index. Such behaviour of the real rate contradicts the economic intuition of interest rates as consisting of a real return expectation plus some inflation compensation. However, seasonality in the index ratio calculation exists but nominal rates do not show a seasonal pattern. The real rate curve is therefore simply the only place where seasonality can be reflected in a yield curve model.

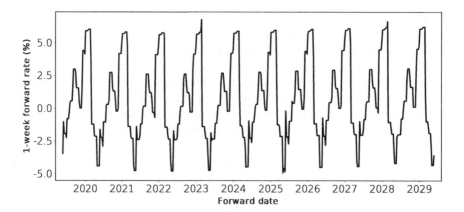

FIGURE 23.13   Real 1-week forward rates in a seasonally adjusted model using a standard Nelson-Siegel spline for nominal US Treasuries and the inflation model Equation (23.14) on 20 February 2020. Source: Prices from TreasuryDirect.

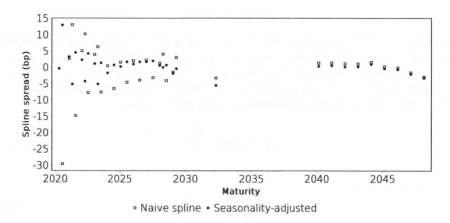

□ Naive spline • Seasonality-adjusted

FIGURE 23.14   Spline spreads of US TIPS against a naive (not seasonally adjusted) and a comprehensive (seasonally adjusted) curve model. Source: Data from TreasuryDirect, inflation modelling using the model above.

With this apparatus of a real discount curve that reflects inflation expectations as well as seasonality, it is possible to construct an accurate rich-cheap model for individual inflation-linked securities. Figure 23.14 of US TIPS spline spreads shows that this approach is warranted. The July maturity TIPS appear substantially overvalued in a naive (not seasonally adjusted) model, but that is because they pay on the comparatively high April CPI reading. The April maturities, paying on the January CPI reading, look cheap in comparison. This effect was visualised conceptually in Figure 23.9 and

---

[12]The consumption tax hikes in Japan in 2014 and 2019 were examples where a functioning inflation-linked bond market had to properly reflect one-off jumps in the price level.

is here demonstrated with actual bonds. The solid markers are the spline spreads calculated with the seasonally adjusted real curve of Figure 23.13 and the substantially smaller range of spreads demonstrates the impact of seasonality on market valuations. The market does appear to retain some deviations from fair value even in this model, but that reflects the parsimony of the approach taken in Equation (23.18). New TIPS have a higher value of their deflation floor but the model does not reflect this value. It may also be that the market consensus seasonality model is different from the one used here (a Hodrick–Prescott filter using data since 2000).

23.9   INFLATION MODELS AND EXPECTATIONS

The discussion of the preceding section centred on the appropriate structure of an inflation model for the relative valuation of individual inflation-linked securities. An ancillary result of this modelling effort is a long-run inflation estimate and it can be interesting to treat it as an economic forecast. It is not immediately obvious that this model parameter should be a useful economic estimate. First, market prices contain risk premia in addition to pure expectations. In the absence of an explicit model for the risk premia one needs to consider this model estimate as biased. Second, if the number of observable inflation-linked bonds is small, the estimate of the long-run inflation rate can be subject to a large measurement error. In essence, each bond provides one sample for future inflation developments and only a large set of samples can make the aggregate estimate reliable. Third, unlike the inflation swap curve, the two models presented in Equations (23.13) and (23.14) do not have any pretence of having a meaningful term structure. Instead, the term structure of real yields in these models is inherited largely from the respective nominal yield curve[13].

With these caveats in mind, Figure 23.15 shows the history of the long-run inflation estimate obtained from US TIPS prices. Each daily data point is the result of fitting splines to the nominal US Treasury curve and then calibrating a TIPS model using the definition Equation (23.14). The result suggests that inflation priced into the TIPS market is reasonably well anchored to the Fed's inflation target and fluctuates only mildly around 2%. This, from a central bank's point of view, benign picture only changed with the unprecedented decline in energy prices in March 2020.

For European inflation, the German linker market can be used to obtain a similar estimate but the smaller number of bonds makes this estimate more subject to volatility[14]. Figure 23.16 shows these estimates together with the HICP inflation swap 5Yx5Y forward rate which should in theory be a comparable estimate of long-run steady-state inflation[15]. Investors should be indifferent to holding German nominal

---

[13]It is of course debatable whether the term structure of inflation swaps provides any extra information about inflation developments or is also simply based on the relative levels of the real and nominal curves.

[14]The French OAT€i market would provide better estimates.

[15]There should be a convexity adjustment applied to the inflation swap forward. See footnote on page 239.

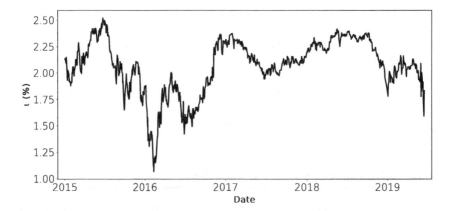

FIGURE 23.15 History of the long-run inflation obtained from fitting a TIPS spline. Source: Data from TreasuryDirect, inflation modelling using the model above.

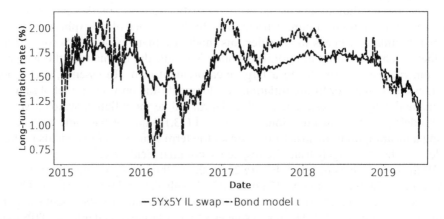

FIGURE 23.16 Model-based long-run HICP ex-tobacco estimate from German OBLi/DBRi prices and 5Yx5Y forward inflation swaps. Source: Prices from ECB SDW and Bundesbank.

bonds, and swapping the coupons into inflation, or holding inflation-linked bonds directly. The two measures indeed show a remarkable degree of correlation but also phases of divergence. If one subscribes to the pricing hierarchy shown on page 240, then the degree to which the bond-based inflation measure diverges from the swap measure would be an indication of the width of the arbitrage corridor around this equivalence. The average absolute deviation between the two series in the figure is about 15 bps which implies an arbitrage corridor of around 30 bps. This may not be an unrealistic estimate for the implied balance sheet cost of carrying an inflation-linked bond asset swap position that needs to be held for a long time to accrue an arbitrage profit. It also implies that either estimate of long-run inflation faces a comparable degree of uncertainty.

This should not be seen as a significant problem because the measurement of the price level itself is also subject to measurement errors. The German statistics office aims for a 0.1% percentage point accuracy [31] in its measurement of the German HICP. In other words, assuming that there is a consensus path of HICP inflation, then it appears that financial markets indicators of this path may be deviating by around 15 bps from this path due to the cost of arbitraging the relevant instruments. At the same time, the published levels of inflation may also be deviating from its true level by up to 10 bps.

Defaultable Claims

CHAPTER 24

Credit Risk

Credit risk is the general term for the risk that a counterparty in a contract or security does not perform as required by the contractual obligation, leading to unexpected losses for the other counterparties or security holders. This type of risk must be distinguished from other types of risk, for instance that the value of a claim is less than expected due to some adverse development in the price of a given commodity. As will be discussed in Chapter 26, the distinction between the deterioration of the value of a claim and the ability of a counterparty to perform under a claim is very important. Some ABS will in many circumstances not fully repay without such failure to pay being an event of default.

24.1 DEFAULT, INSOLVENCY, AND BANKRUPTCY

Debt contracts, be it loans or bonds, usually bind the debtor in more ways than a simple payment obligation. It is therefore possible that a debtor violates the terms of a debt contract in ways other than not paying cash when due. This makes it important to distinguish between the various forms of of contract violations collectively usually listed as events of default in the respective contract.

For instance, the covenants of a loan or bond may restrict the gearing, or leverage, of a company. If the company exceeds the maximum permitted leverage, it is in default even though it may still be current on its payment obligations. How such a situation is resolved will depend on the debt contract or prospectus and may involve significant transfers of decision-making powers to creditors.

Generally, the concept of default is wider than that of insolvency. Insolvency refers to an inability to pay amounts when due, which may include payments for goods and services received, not only payments on money borrowed. Insolvency need not necessarily mean that a debtor has insufficient assets to cover its liabilities because some assets may be valuable, but hard to turn into cash in the time required to meet upcoming payments.

Bankruptcy is usually the final stage in a company's existence when it is insolvent and beyond rescue. For creditors, bankruptcy entails a number of disadvantages beyond delays in the recovery of money lent. Companies can have assets that only have value while the company operates, such as brand recognition and business relationships, that will be less valuable or even worthless in bankruptcy. This creates an incentive for creditors to work with a debtor to maximise the recovery value of a company's assets. In this sense, debt restructuring and debt forgiveness lead to losses for the creditors but such certain losses can be preferrable to the uncertainty of going through a court-administrated bankruptcy process.

24.2 SENIORITY AND SUBORDINATION

When a debtor is unable to repay monies borrowed, not all creditors have equal ranking in their claim to be paid. In essence, failure to pay means that there are insufficient assets to make payments and claimants to these payments will have to compete for the assets that can be distributed. According to their relative ranking, creditors are called senior or subordinated depending on the cardinal ranking of their claims. Relative seniority is a function of several factors.

24.2.1 Time subordination and acceleration

The most obvious form of subordination is time subordination: creditors who get paid first have a higher likelihood of recovering their money.

To prevent time subordination from overriding all other forms of creditor ranking, insolvency legislation in most countries ensures that all debts of a debtor normally become due and payable, including accrued interest, when a default occurs on a given class of debt. This acceleration protects holders of longer-term debt from time subordination, but can dramatically worsen the liquidity situation of the debtor. When a borrower uses multiple entities and governing laws to borrow, acceleration is usually made explicit through cross-default clauses in the relevant documentation. Such clauses reduce the risks related to situations where a debtor is insolvent in one jurisdiction, leading to a distribution of assets to debtors in that jurisdiction while holders of comparable debt elsewhere are time-subordinated.

While time subordination is undesirable in straight debt, it is being used to improve the credit tiering in some ABS transactions. In such structures, repayments of principal of the underlying loans is directed first to the most senior tranche so that this tranche has the shortest-weighted average life.

Some jurisdictions, e.g. Austria, limit time subordination in statutory terms by allowing for clawbacks of debt repayments in certain situations. In particular when a lender should be aware of the financial situation of a borrower and receives a payment shortly before bankruptcy, courts may order a return of such payments to the bankrupt estate for distribution to other creditors. The assumption behind such clawbacks is that the lender took advantage of superior information to extract early repayment to the disadvantage of less privileged creditors.

24.2.2 Contractual subordination

Private debtors can freely negotiate debt contracts between themselves, including a ranking of claims. In general, a debtor will offer a higher rate of interest on lower-ranking claims and a lender can choose to accept the additional risk inherent in a subordinated claim for this higher rate of interest.

Contractual subordination can take multiple forms. The most straightforward approach is to spell out seniority directly in the debt prospectus. However, other contractual clauses can have similar effects to explicit seniority/subordination specifications. For instance, certain classes of high-yield debt may offer the borrower the option to 'pay in kind' (PIK), i.e., pay with new debt instead of cash when coupons are due. This establishes a contractual time subordination of PIK bond holders because their claim to cash payment is in effect delayed while other debt holders may be receiving cash.

Some high-grade corporate bonds contain rating triggers on the coupons that increase the interest payable when the credit rating of the debtor falls below certain thresholds. Such rating triggers can increase stress in the free cashflow for the borrower just at the time when rating agencies are taking a negative view on the financial outlook of the debtor. Holders of bonds with rating triggers are affected to a lesser degree and are therefore somewhat senior to equivalent bonds without the rating trigger.

Lenders have a strong interest in their exact position in the seniority hierarchy of the borrower's debt. This implies that the hierarchy should stay largely unchanged over the lifetime of the bond. Covenants such as limits on leverage and limits to subordination of existing claims work to establish such stability.

24.2.3   Statutory subordination

Most countries' jurisdictions impose subordination on certain classes of creditors. The most prominent example is the statutory bail-in of certain bank creditors as part of the European Bank Resolution Directive and the TLAC[1]/MREL[2] requirements for bank funding.

Banks have traditionally relied on very low levels of equity, augmented by similarly low levels of subordinated debt, to finance their operations. This implied a very high share of senior debt, including deposits, in funding bank assets. When bank asset valuations declined drastically in the financial crisis that started in 2008, public authorities had the unpalatable choice of either accepting bank defaults on very large swathes of senior unsecured bank liabilities with unforeseeable consequences, or injecting additional equity through tax-funded bailouts. One of the results of this experience is that some form of bank debts can now be 'bailed-in', i.e., forced to share losses, even when there is no explicit contractual provision for this to occur.

Depending on the jurisdiction, the write-down features can be contractual (embedded in the bond prospectus) or statutory (enforced by national legislation across a class of debt instruments). It is not immediately obvious which of the two is preferable. Contractual subordination allows banks to issue non-subordinated debt that is distinct from the subordinated debt. On the downside, investors are reminded by each prospectus that certain bonds are riskier than others and may require excessive compensation for

---

[1]Total loss-absorbing capital.
[2]Minimum Requirement for own funds and Eligible Liabilities.

this risk. Statutory subordination in effect moves the risk warning to legislation and so applies it equally across banks and a given instrument class.

A similar aim is achieved with conditionally convertible bank debt, also known as CoCo. CoCo bonds turn into equity automatically when certain capital thresholds are broken, usually related to the total tangible equity ratio relative to risk assets. CoCo conversion is therefore triggered by accounting events rather than supervisory action, and a CoCo holder receives equity rather than a given write down of her or his claims against the bank. The valuation of CoCos is complex, especially when one considers that the share price of a bank is likely to fall in a situation where capital is insufficient. Even if earnings expectations were unchanged, equity investors would consider dilution through CoCo conversion and potential additional equity issuance.

Statutory seniority is a much older concept, however. Most covered bond legislative frameworks protect certain counterparties of the cover pool more than other creditors of a covered bond issuer. Lenders to companies undergoing court-protected restructuring usually have certain protections ('lender in possession') and so on.

24.2.4   Joint liabilities and credit support

When debts are jointly owed by multiple debtors, the difference between joint and several liability and several liability is an important factor in default risk analysis. For several, but not joint, liability the default of any one borrower leads to a default on the debt[3]. The severity of this default (the loss given default LGD) may be low, however, given that only part of the debt is affected. For investors who apply historical cost accounting, such an event may trigger an impairment event, and hence force a re-marking of the position which may entail larger or smaller losses. Some rating agencies do not include LGD in these assessments and hence apply what is known as the weakest link approach: The credit rating of the joint debt instrument is in essence driven by the rating of the weakest borrower in the pool.

For joint and several liability, the debt only defaults if all borrowers default because the lost payments from any one borrower are covered by the others, up to the point where a single borrower is liable for the entire debt[4]. While this appears safer, it is often the case that no single borrower in the pool can in fact support the entire structure. Defaulting borrowers increase the burden on the non-defaulting borrowers, which in turn makes them more likely to default. Still, the credit risk of a joint and several liability is most affected by the risk of the strongest borrower in the pool.

In some cases, borrowers receive explicit or implicit debt support from a larger entity. For instance, Japanese regional entities are seen as benefiting from credit support by the central government or prefecture. This can result in a risk structure resembling a joint and several liability. An important question in such cases is the form of this support. The spectrum ranges from first-call unconditional guarantees, where the support provider makes an unconditional promise to immediately cover any missed payment from the debtor, to sufficiency support, where the support provider makes only a general

---

[3]In Boolean logic, this would be an OR relationship.
[4]In Boolean logic, this amounts to an AND relationship.

commitment to ensure the economic viability of the borrower. In such structures, debt holders may face delays on collecting due payments, or even the risk of reduced payments.

24.2.5   Sovereign debt

Sovereign debt differs fundamentally from private sector debt because the assets of a sovereign, such as taxes, levies and mineral rights, are only enforceable by the sovereign itself. This precludes the idea of liquidating a sovereign and distributing the assets to the creditors[5]. The sovereignty of a sovereign also precludes a court-directed asset distribution[6]. Put differently, what sets sovereigns apart from private borrowers is that they have a virtually infinite lifespan. While a private borrower can be wound down or dissolved when they fail to repay debts, sovereigns remain. This means that sovereign borrowing is a repeat game. Lenders to a sovereign will be aware of past defaults and accept debt on worse terms from repeat defaulters. Such experience is unavailable to lenders to private borrowers, and acts as a deterrent to capricious defaults by sovereigns.

In the course of the crisis in the euro area debt market, some solutions were proposed that rely on an effective mechanism to create senior and subordinated sovereign bonds. In practice, such ideas may clash with the very notion of sovereignty. Subordinaton of private debts is a fairly reliable concept because it can be pursued through the courts, and courts can also oversee the liquidation of private estates. Sovereigns, in contrast, have no or little distributable assets that can be liquidated by courts that are not also subject to legislation by the same sovereign. The freedom to decide which monies to pay to which creditor, meanwhile, is an essential ingredient of sovereignty.

Seniority in the absence of a court to enforce it is essentially only a promise by the issuer. Given that debt itself is a promise (namely, to repay money borrowed), senior sovereign debt is only more valuable than subordinated debt if the issuer breaks one promise (the promise to pay) but keeps another (to pay some creditors more than others).

24.3   THE DEFAULT PROCESS

The default of a debtor generally gives creditors the right to enforce their claims with a level of control that exceeds that present in performing lending relationships. The first

---

[5]It should be noted that this is the modern state of affairs. In history, taxation rights have been sold by sovereigns (cf. e.g. [41, 60]), and mining rights were granted in lieu of debt repayments [35].

[6]It should be noted that in modern democracies the executive branch of government is subject to the courts, but the sovereign itself is not. Courts can hold the executive to account when it fails to honour the law as it stands, but they have only limited jurisdiction about changes to the law through the legislative process. This process is only restricted by a country's constitution. A sovereign may also have bound itself through international treaties in a way that could restrict some commercial decisions. However, whether a government is able to bind the country in ways that restrict the application of its constitution is a perennial subject before the German constitutional court.

question for creditors is usually whether or not it is advantageous for them to allow the debtor to continue operating, possibly with some alterations to the business model, or alternatively wind down the debtor and realise the assets in a liquidation. The distinction between these two options is not always very sharp. For instance, a debtor may have a business that can be sold off in its entirety without suspending operations. In this case the operating business is comparable to an asset in its own right.

Under normal circumstances, asset sales are likely to incur substantial discounts to their carrying value. This is because production processes are usually very specialised and the default of a debtor is usually a sign that the specific approach of the debt was unviable. Potential buyers would need to integrate the assets into their production process, and may not have demand for the extra output that could be achieved through their use. Additional discounts are likely to arise in expedited sales processes ('firesales') when buyers perceive an opportunity to achieve lower prices because the seller can only choose between low valuation or no sale at all.

These factors often create a strong incentive for creditors to conduct the resolution of defaulted claims in a way that is non-antagonistic versus the debtor and involves a continuation of the debtor's business activities. The aim of such a process is an eventual recovery of the debtor to such a degree that liabilities can be serviced, potentially after reducing them by some amount. When this managed default approach is not feasible, a debtor might be wound down. Bankruptcy codes refect these different approaches by specifying multiple procedures. For instance, the US bankruptcy code[7] specifies a managed default (reorganisation) in Chapter 11 for private companies and Chapter 9 for municipalities, while a liquidation follows Chapter 7 of the that code for private enterprises.

Debtors usually have multiple debt instruments outstanding, and the preferred way to resolve a default depends for each investor on the specific nature of the instrument they hold. For instance, an investor who recently bought a low-coupon security well below par might prefer an immediate wind-down (resulting in an imminent cash payout perhaps in excess of the purchase price) while a holder of a high-coupon security would prefer a maturity extension and continuation of debt service rather than losing the coupon income.

In general, default proceedings have the potentially conflicting aims of respecting contractual priorities of different debt classes, and at the same time ensuring equitable treatment of debtors of equal rank. The specific quantification of 'equitable' alone is a challenge. To value claims of owners of securities with different coupons and maturities, one would have to resort to an appropriate discount curve. How to calibrate such a curve, and what valuations to use for such a calibration, can easily be subject to dispute.

The usual venue to resolve conflicts are the courts that have jurisdiction over the liabilities in question. However, the same debtor might have debt issued in multiple jurisdictions and hold assets that are distributed across yet a different set of jurisdictions. This creates the problem of multiple courts granting conflicting access to assets to different creditors. There is no obvious solution to this problem.

---

[7]Technically, Title 11 of the United States Code.

Related to the problem of multiple jurisdictions is the problem of hold-out creditors. Most debt holders are averse to holding illiquid securities such as debt instruments that are subject to default proceedings. They therefore tend to prefer a speedy resolution of default situations, even at the expense of maximising the recovery value. Sometimes this preference is abused by so-called hold-out investors[8] who delay the final resolution of a default through prolonged court actions with the aim of achieving a higher payout for themselves. In essence, a multiplicity of debt instruments and jurisdictions can create the preconditions for a Nash equilibrium that delays final resolution of claims in a manner that is equitable to all debt holders across all jurisdictions.

24.3.1 Collective action clauses

Collective action clauses, usually abbreviated to CAC, are an avenue to circumvent the problems related to court-directed debt restructurings. CAC are included in bond documentation and so form part of the legal framework of a debt security. A restructuring using CAC is a credit event as would be a restructuring in any other way.

Under a CAC, the issuer can propose certain modifications of debt instruments and bond holders can then vote on whether to accept those terms. The essence of the CAC process is that all bond holders agree to be bound by the outcome of this vote ahead of time by having invested in the bond. This differs from a court-directed default process where there is a risk that some creditors refuse a proposal from the issuer and try to achieve better terms in a court. Such court proceedings may hold up the default process and delay payments.

Multiple variations of CAC exist. The voting threshold for accepting modifications is usually high (generally 2/3 or 3/4 of nominal held), and various prescriptions for the determination of a quorum, and the procedure for dealing with the absence of a quorum exist. Some CAC require dual majorities when multiple bond series are to be restructured, namely majorities for both each affected series and across all series. Such cross-series modifications are a useful tool for ensuring equity between debt classes, and CAC requiring dual majorities, known as dual-limb CAC face a higher risk of failing. The alternative single limb CAC require only a majority across series.

It must be borne in mind that CAC merely govern the procedure to follow in a default situation to prevent adverse Nash equilibria from emerging. CAC do not cause defaults, and CAC do not cure defaults. If a CAC-based restructuring turns out to be unfeasible, and even improved offers from the debtor do not suffice to convince investors to agree, then a default will still go ahead. The way in which this happens will then resemble a court-ordered default with the potential delays that may arise if multiple courts rule on multiple debt instruments.

Euro area government bonds with original maturities longer than one year issued since January 2013 carry so-called model CACs due to a clause in the ESM Treaty. These dual-limb CACs were proposed by the Economic and Financial Committee of the EU and are included either in bond documentation, or the respective national law for bonds

---

[8]When investors acquire debt in near-default or default situations to then act as hold-outs, they are less charitably known as vultures.

issued without a specific prospectus under domestic fiscal legislation. The purpose of these clauses is to streamline any potentially required debt adjustment before the ESM engages in economic support for a euro area member state. The introduction of these CACs was an interesting practical experiment in having a coexistence of two types of otherwise comparable types of debt from the same issuer that only differ in the CACs. Market pricing normally does not distinguish between these debt types, which could be seen as a signal that CACs are of little relevance. There are two reasons to treat this conclusion with some caution, however. The first is that newer bonds are more liquid, which should attract a liquidity premium. This liquidity premium may offset any discount applied as a result of CAC. Second, and probably more significantly, it is not obvious that domestic law bonds without a CAC would be treated differently from CAC bonds if a restructuring were required. The issuer could in theory retro-fit CACs on bonds without such clauses through a change of domestic law, and this is what happened for the Greek 'private sector involvement' in 2012 [30]. A more educational experiment would therefore be the co-existence of CACs of different types.

24.3.2   Debt exchanges and consent solicitations

Not every case where a bond is not repaid as scheduled, or where bond terms are violated, is a default. Bond issuers can ask bond investors to accept changes in the terms of a bond, or to exchange their bonds, voluntarily. Such changes need not have a direct economic impact on bond holders, and may even serve to improve the probability of receiving the expected cash flows.

When an issuer needs to change certain terms of a bond, it can launch a consent solicitation where investors are asked to consent to this proposed change in terms. Usually in such cases, an issuer seeks to obtain a relaxation in some covenants that have turned out to be more onerous than expected. Investors can withhold consent, but may then face a higher risk of default. Because a consent solicitation modifies an existing instrument, the terms of the solicitation are usually prescribed, at least in general terms, in the bond prospectus.

An exchange offer, on the other hand, is a more comprehensive event because it involves a change in instrument. The issuer will typically propose an exchange of one bond into another, and offer some incentives to participate in this exchange. Typically, an issuer will offer an exchange of instruments with incentives paid to participating investors. Investors are free not to participate in the exchange, but those not taking part face two risks. The first is losing out on the incentives, the second is the reduced liquidity of the instruments that have not been exchanged if a large majority of investors agrees to the exchange.

Transactions of this kind are therefore prime examples of game theory. Investors have no a-priori interest to agree to any exchange that may leave them worse off in their claims versus the issuer. If investors as a whole resist the exchange, it will not succeed. The issuer, and its advisors, design the terms of the exchange such that a sufficient number of investors agree to it, and so in effect enforce the terms of the exchange on other investors.

An important consideration of events described in this section is that it is not correct to view them through the lens of an antagonistic relationship between investors and borrower. Investors rely on a borrower to use their funds in such a way as to earn them returns. The borrower is restricted in how these funds can be used by the terms of the debt instruments that the borrower has issued. When circumstances change, it may be acceptable to all parties to amend the terms of such instruments in such a way as to reflect the change in circumstances. The absence of antagonism is of course not the same as fraternity. Investors need to consider their own interests, and those of their fiduciaries, first.

Whether a bond exchange has an impact on a credit rating, or triggers credit default swaps, depends on the terms of the exchange. If it occurs under stressed conditions and results in a reduction of claims against the issuer, rating agencies may decide to treat the event as a default. Credit default swaps might also be triggered in this case. If the exchange does not reduce the economic value of the bond, there may be no impact on the rating.

24.3.3 Managed defaults

A managed default process starts with the decision not to pursue an immediate wind-down and requires a court decision to halt proceedings in this direction. The suspension of the wind-down is known as a stay. During the stay, debtors and creditors can conduct negotiations about potential debt restructuring, i.e., reduction or rescheduling of interest and principal payments. Debtors are also often able to incur new debts to cover working capital requirements[9]. Lenders advancing such funds are then subject to special protection (higher seniority). Ideally, a managed default results in a preservation and recovery of the business that the borrower engaged in, and creditors achieve the recovery of a higher share of their initial investment than would be coming out of a wind-down.

A managed default can fail if initial assumptions turn out to have been too optimistic. In such cases, a managed default will transition into a wind-down, a scenario discussed below.

24.3.4 Wind-downs

A wind-down is the last stage in the life of a corporate debtor. When there is no realistic prospect of a recovery in the entity's business, it may be preferable to sell any remaining assets and pay out creditors with the proceeds. In rare cases, there may even be leftover funds that can go to erstwhile equity holders.

A wind-down is not necessarily a fast process and can take years. Banks in particular have assets that are contractual relationships which can span many years and are difficult to liquidate. The case of the German Herstatt Bank (which created the term Herstatt risk) is a good example. The wind-down of the bank started in 1974 and ended only in 2006.

---

[9]US law describes this situation as 'debtor in possession'.

24.4 CREDIT RATINGS

Given the difficulty faced by investors when trying to assess the credit risk of a given debt instrument, it is unsurprising that an industry has developed that provides credit risk analysis services. These companies, generally called rating agencies[10], issue opinions and express relative credit risks in the form of credit ratings. The ratings from any one agency form a scale, and examples of comparable long-term ratings from five major rating agencies are given in Table 24.1. Similar ratings, but with simpler scales, exist for short-term debt instruments. The best possible rating is AAA/Aaa while issues in default are rated C or D. While ratings are generally public, the reports that support and explain these ratings usually require additional access fees. Ratings above the BBB-/Baa3 level are usually called investment grade and this threshold is reflected in the inclusion criteria for investment-grade debt indices. Debt with lower ratings is called variously 'sub-investment grade', 'high yield', 'speculative' or 'junk'.

Ratings can apply to issuers, classes of debt by one issuer, or individual issues. Issuer ratings generally have one additional category, namely 'selective default' which describes a situation where the issuer has chosen not to service some debts but is still current on others.

Rating agencies update ratings either on a regular schedule or in response to incoming data. Such rating changes, at least those undertaken by the leading agencies (the three leftmost agencies in Table 24.1) are generally watched closely by the market. As part of this process, agencies sometimes given an indication that a rating change is imminent through such qualifiers as 'review for upgrade' or 'negative outlook'. Markets react to the publication of such qualifiers and to their removal just as they react to changes in ratings themselves. Actions by the smaller agencies attract less attention in international markets but are still relevant. DBRS is recognised by the Eurosystem General Framework [6] and therefore relevant for euro area collateral eligibility while R&I is the leading agency opining on Japanese domestic issuers.

Credit ratings generally refer to the likelihood of full and timely payment of principal and the full payment of interest[11]. Some rating agencies also take into account the likely loss in case of a default event. Significantly, credit rating scales are ordinal, but not cardinal, scales. Higher ratings imply a lower likelihood of loss than lower ratings, but no rating implies a given level of credit risk. This means that credit ratings should not form an input to quantitative risk models although they invariably are used in this way. For instance, Article 59 of the Eurosystems General Framework uses one-year probabilities of default to translate external ratings[12] into Eurosystem quality steps.

Every rating agency publishes a number of reports outlining its rating methodology for different types of instrument. Usually, these start with a stand-alone issuer rating

---

[10]Some people take issue with the use of the word 'agency' in this context because this term is usually reserved for public institutions, not private companies. As will be explained later, of all the concerns surrounding rating agencies, this one is probably the least significant and the term 'agencies' is used here throughout.

[11]Note that timeliness of payment of interest is not part of this definition.

[12]A rating agency is called external credit assessment institution (ECAI) in this framework.

TABLE 24.1 Comparable long-term debt rating scales of five major credit rating agencies (Standard and Poors, Moody's, Fitch, DBRS and Ratings & Investment). The horizontal line below BBB- delineates the investment grade from lower ratings.

S&P	Moody's	Fitch	DBRS	R&I
AAA	Aaa	AAA	AAA	AAA
AA+	Aa1	AA+	AA (high)	AA+
AA	Aa2	AA	AA	AA
AA-	Aa3	AA-	AA (low)	AA-
A+	A1	A+	A (high)	A+
A	A2	A	A	A
A-	A3	A-	A (low)	A-
BBB+	Baa1	BBB+	BBB (high)	BBB+
BBB	Baa2	BBB	BBB	BBB
BBB-	Baa3	BBB-	BBB (low)	BBB-
BB+	Ba1	BB+	BB (high)	BB+
BB	Ba2	BB	BB	BB
BB-	Ba3	BB-	BB (low)	BB-
B+	B1	B+	B (high)	B+
B	B2	B	B	B
B-	B3	B-	B (low)	B-
CCC+	Caa1	C	CCC (high)	CCC+
CCC	Caa2	C	CCC	CCC
CCC-	Caa3	C	CCC (low)	CCC-
CC/C	Ca	C/DDD	CC/C	CC
D	C	DD/D	D	D

(which need not be on a scale comparable to the final rating scale) to which upward and downward adjustments are made to reflect external support or unfavourable environments. For each rated instrument or instrument class, further adjustments are made to reflect rank in the liability structure of the issuer, as well as presence, quantity and quality of any collateral. In many cases, a sovereign ceiling is then applied so that no debt instrument of a domestic issuer can have a higher rating than the sovereign in which it is incorporated.

A credit rating is normally issued on request, and against payment from, the issuing entity. Such a solicited rating creates a conflict of interest between the agency's economic interests and its objectivity. To manage this conflict, agencies generally opine only on concrete structures rather than advising on what steps an issuer would have to take to achieve a given target rating. This service of ratings advisory is instead performed by investment banks. There is as a result no process of negotiation of rating versus payment between issuer and agency. On the one hand, this limits the scope for ratings of convenience, but on the other hand also protects the agencies from responsibility for issuer structures that later turn out not to be stable. Because some ratings, particularly those of banks and sub-sovereign entities, depend on the ratings of other entities, namely those of their sovereigns, agencies can also issue an unsolicited rating in order to have this required input. Sovereign ratings of developed economies tend to be unsolicited because these issuers have no need to pay for a credit rating to achieve investor participation. Although an unsolicited rating has less scope for conflicts of interest, rating agencies have usually privileged access to financial information of the issuers with solicited ratings. The absence of that additional information could negatively affect the quality of unsolicited ratings. Of course, for developed economy sovereigns there is a plethora of publicly available information far in excess of what would be available for a typical bank, for instance. As a result, there is no unequivocal difference in quality between solicited and solicited ratings. Some regulators, however, insist on a clear delineation between the two types of rating.

Issuers can choose to discontinue their ratings from a given agency. This of course may be perceived as taking evasive action ahead of a looming downgrade, and, to the extent that ratings are required by some investors, may lead to a loss of potential demand. On the other hand, an issuer may have a substantiated difference of opinion with a rating agency over methodology and may use this to justify such a step.

The perhaps more serious concern of an issuer-funded ratings system is not that an individual issuer obtains favourable ratings in exchange for cash, but that entire debt classes are rated inconsistently relative to other debt classes. This is because a ratings agency may forgo the income from a single transaction to protect its reputation but may be more conflicted when having to choose between assigning non-viable ratings to a whole class of debt, or securing a larger income stream. Some of the ratings issued for structured products ahead of the financial crisis in 2008 were based on rather simple models; one could argue that a more critical stance from the agencies would have prevented some of the excesses in leverage at the time. However, one should not neglect the co-dependency of issuers and professional investors who typically act as agents, not principals, in the investment process. As long as fund managers are incentivised to achieve certain returns with a given credit rating, they have limited interest in setting aside overly optimistic assessments from a rating agency, at least not in a structural way.

24.4.1 Rating migration

Credit ratings present an apparent contradiction: it is clear that longer-dated debts have a higher probability to default than shorter-dated debt (because there is more time for them to default in), but ratings are assigned uniformly to all comparable liabilities of the issuer. This contradiction is resolved by rating migration. Credit ratings reflect the information available at the time they are assigned but it is understood that they can change. While a longer-dated bond has the same rating as a shorter-dated bond by the same issuer, this rating can change, possibly for the worse, over time, including after the shorter-dated bond has matured.

The migration of ratings is an additional reason to treat ratings as ordinal rather than cardinal rankings. Lower rated securities can be less risky than higher rated ones,

TABLE 24.2 Global one-year corporate average transition rates (1981–2017, in %) published by Standard and Poors (from Table 21 in [83], transposed). NR stands for Not Rated. Source: Data from Diane Vazza and Nick W Kraemer. 2017 annual global corporate default study and rating transitions. Technical report, S&P Global Ratings, 2018.

To/From	AAA	AA	A	BBB	BB	B	CCC/CC
AAA	86.99	0.51	0.03	0.01	0.01	0	0
AA	9.12	86.95	1.72	0.1	0.03	0.02	0
A	0.53	7.91	88	3.45	0.12	0.08	0.12
BBB	0.05	0.5	5.22	85.79	4.88	0.18	0.21
BB	0.08	0.05	0.3	3.73	77.19	5.05	0.59
B	0.03	0.07	0.12	0.49	6.79	74.34	13.18
CCC/CC	0.05	0.02	0.02	0.11	0.58	4.44	43.46
D	0	0.02	0.06	0.17	0.68	3.59	26.82
NR	3.15	3.97	4.52	6.16	9.72	12.28	15.63

but an assessment of absolute risk involves more characteristics than just a rating. Ratings are generally meant to apply 'through the cycle', i.e., be independent of the current state of the business cycle. However, because business cycles are not fully predictable, rating transitions can have cyclical components. That being said, investors also have only partial insight into business cycle dynamics. The informational value of ratings is therefore not diminished by the potential errors in business cycle assessments by the rating agencies.

Rating agencies generally publish statistics about rating changes (cf. e.g. [66, 83, 85]) which serve to underpin the reliability of their ratings. These statistics generally include annual default rates as well as annualised rating change probabilities. An example is shown in Table 24.2.

Rating migration means that care needs to be taken in interpreting these statistics. For instance, a given rating agency may show that a AA-rated security has a one-year default probability of $p_{AA,D}$, meaning that a security with this rating will default within the year with a probability of $p_{AA,D}$. The default probability over two years $p_{2,AA,D}$ could therefore assumed to be given by the sum of the probabilities of defaulting in the first year and surviving the first year but defaulting in the second, i.e.,

$$p_{2,AA,D} = p_{AA,D} + (1 - p_{AA,D})p_{AA,D} \approx 2p_{AA,D} \tag{24.1}$$

This interpretation would be incorrect because it neglects the possibility of surviving the first year, but having a different rating at the end of it, and then defaulting with the probability implied by the new rating. The correct approach would therefore be:

$$p_{2,AA,D} = p_{AA,D} + (1 - p_{AA,D})\sum_k p_{AA,k}p_{k,D} \tag{24.2}$$

where k runs a sum over all non-default ratings that the security can have after the first year. Comparing this to the previous equation shows that the two are identical if, and only if, $p_{AA,k} = \delta_{AA,k}$, i.e., if the rating cannot change.

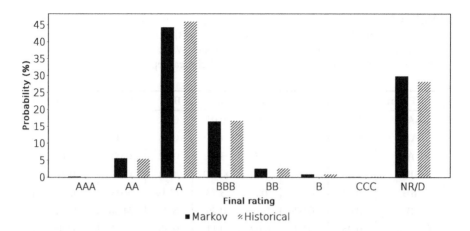

FIGURE 24.1 Comparison between the seven-year Markov-implied and actual probability distribution of the rating of an A-rated issuer after 7 years. Data from SP RatingsDirect [83].

The most basic assumption on credit ratings is that they follow a Markov process determined by a transition matrix as implied by Table 24.2. This approach underpins the Jarrow–Lando–Turnbull credit model [73]. The raw transition matrix is augmented by an additional column that makes the default states (D and NR in this classification scheme) absorbing. Multi-year ratings transition probabilities are then given by the powers of this one-year transition matrix. The Markov assumption amounts to the postulate that the transition process has no memory and is homogeneous over time. In practice, there are reasons to assume that this postulate may be violated. The business cycle can drive unforeseen changes in ratings, and companies actively manage their credit rating through changes in their capitalisation. A company may choose to increase gearing by distributing capital through dividends or share buybacks, or reduce gearing through retaining earnings or raising additional equity. The Miller–Modigliani theorem that the gearing of a company is irrelevant is not only contradicted by the tax effect on debt financing [46], but also because there is a non-linear relationship between debt financing cost and credit ratings. While an issuer may be forgoing tax benefits by keeping gearing low enough to maintain a very strong rating, increasing gearing may lead to such a low credit rating that the borrower would be required to pay very high coupons, or post collateral for borrowing and bilateral derivative transactions. This would suggest that the rating of a single company may exhibit mean-reverting behaviour.

It is possible to test the Markov assumption because rating agencies publish not only one-year transition probabilities but also track ratings transitions over longer periods. If the ratings process were non-Markovian, a comparison between the Markov-implied multi-year transition matrices and the actual multi-year transitions would show a difference.

Figure 24.1 shows a simple example of such a calculation. The one-year transition matrix derived from Table 24.2 is used to construct a seven-year transition matrix which can be compared directly with the actual seven-year transition matrix produced by the

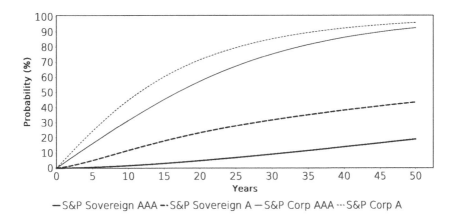

FIGURE 24.2 Cumulative probability of losing an investment grade rating over time for two different initial ratings and issuer types. Sources: Data from Diane Vazza and Nick W Kraemer. 2017 annual global corporate default study and rating transitions. Technical report, S&P Global Ratings, 2018; Lawrence R Witte. 2017 annual sovereign default study and rating transitions. Technical report, S&P Global Ratings, 2018.

same rating agency for the same issuer types. Shown in this example are the probabilities of an initially A-rated issuer to find itself 7 years later in any rating band under both approaches. Although some probabilities differ slightly, overall the Markov assumption does not perform too badly in this example[13].

The no-memory property of the Markov process implies that the initial rating is irrelevant for the credit risk of an issuer over very long horizons. Simply speaking, over a long enough time, any rating will migrate to any other rating with sufficient probability. This is unless the issuer gets trapped in the absorbing default state from which there is no return.

For a sovereign issuer, the default state is not absorbing because, as outlined above, it cannot be wound down. A rating agency may be tempted to conclude that sovereign ratings should reflect the possibility of strategic defaults. On the other hand, sovereigns may be more inclined to preserve good ratings given that there is no tax effect rewarding gearing and investment by domestic companies may be constrained by a low sovereign ceiling. An interesting comparison is therefore between the transition matrices of sovereign and corporate issuers, as done in Figure 24.2. The projected 50 year risk evolution of the corporate issuers shows an appreciable convergence at long investment horizons, i.e., the expected irrelevance of the initial rating. For sovereign issuers, this convergence is not reached in the time horizon shown here. Note that transition to Not Rated status is a large contributor to the significantly higher probability of losing investment grade ratings for corporate issuers (cf. the last row in Table 24.2) while sovereigns tend to preserve at least unsolicited ratings. For an investor, the loss of an investment grade rating may lead to forced selling but the associated losses may be

---

[13]Note that because the observation horizon is finite, there is a small sample bias between the historical 1-year and 7-year transition matrices.

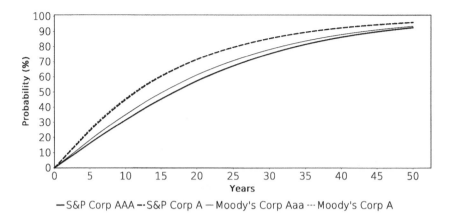

FIGURE 24.3 Comparison of cumulative probabilities of losing an investment grade rating (same definition as in Table 24.2) for two different initial ratings and two different rating agencies. Sources: Based on Sharon Ou, Sumair Irfan, Yang Liu, and Kumar Kanthan. Annual default study: Corporate default and recovery rates, 1920–2016. Technical report, Moody's Investor Services, 2018; Diane Vazza and Nick W Kraemer. 2017 annual global corporate default study and rating transitions. Technical report, S&P Global Ratings, 2018.

much less than in the case of a default. It is also notable that the difference between sovereign and corporate issuers is much larger than the difference between AAA and A ratings.

At the same time, one can compare the ratings evolutions across different rating agencies, as in Figure 24.3. Note that this comparison is not entirely meaningful because the historical rating transitions refer to distinct (albeit largely overlapping) pools of obligors, there is a slight difference in the observation period, and the two agencies may use slightly different definitions for a given rating. On this evidence, the risk characteristics of equal ratings assigned by the two agencies shown here are not materially different. While there is some divergence in the AAA rating evolution, the two A ratings follow a virtually indistinguishable path. This can be interpreted as a sign that ratings do reflect all available information in a rational way. It also supports the judicious use of ratings for the quantification of credit risk. Detractors might instead argue that ratings are not sufficiently independent. This will be discussed below.

24.4.2 Alternative rating approaches

The credit rating business is a natural oligopoly with high barriers to entry. For a new entrant to obtain the attention and trust of investors it is not sufficient that it is correct in its credit assessments, however defined. It would also require existing agencies to be wrong to such an extent as to make investors look for alternatives. To demonstrate superiority, a new pretender would have to demonstrate over a sufficient number of defaults (which translates into a sufficiently long period of time) that its own ratings were better predictors of default risks than those of the existing providers. To conduct the necessary analysis, it would have to rely on funding and data from issuers for this extended period of time. Additionally, regulators have placed additional burdens on rating agencies that require costly compliance mechanisms to implement.

In the European Union, a feeling that the major rating agencies, which tend to be incorporated outside the EU, had been unduly harsh in their assessment of European issuers, led to calls for new approaches to credit risk assessment. The idea that a domestic agency might take different views on domestic issuers is not completely absurd. The Japanese R&I rating of the Japanese sovereign is AAA, far above the single-A ratings assigned by Western rating agencies. Fitch was also the last of the three major agencies to strip France of its AAA rating at a time when it was the last of the three major agencies to still have a large European ownership interest.

Two potential alternatives to the current setup have been discussed. The first is to set up rating agencies that are funded by investors or the public sector, the second is to reduce the usage of ratings in financial markets.

The analysis services provided by rating agencies are valuable, which exposes them to the curse of the commons: Every potential user values the product but not every user is willing or able to pay for the service. The unwillingness of some users to pay for the product reduces the incentives of those who are able to pay. Issuers are paying for this part of market infrastructure because it supports their own funding levels, leading to conflicts of interest. If the users of ratings wanted their own ratings service, they could have set it up a long time ago.

To break the curse of the commons, one could introduce publicly funded rating agencies. The problem with that approach is that the public sector itself may be perceived as conflicted. Few governments are expected by investors to encourage a publicly funded company to opine objectively on that government, regional entities or significant banks under its jurisdiction, if such opinions were to require negative judgement. If the problem of 'he who pays the piper calls the tune' exists for issuer-funded ratings, it might well be that 'he who pays and regulates the piper calls the tune'. Taxpayers might also view ratings as too narrow a common good to warrant public funding.

Alternatively, the use of agency ratings could be discouraged. This is the course of action taken by the European Union which is trying to regulate greater reliance on internal ratings analysis by banks and asset managers. Aside from avoiding any biases in the analysis of agencies, this would reduce the impact of correlated selling or buying decisions that can result from rating changes by a single rating provider when it is being used to define index memberships or collateral eligibility. The essential problem with this solution is cost. There is not much added value in analysing the same public accounting information $n + 1$ times when it has already been analysed n times by competent analysts, or, worse, by assigning a less than competent analyst to conduct additional analysis that then influences investments. To date, therefore, while over-reliance on agency ratings is being discouraged, these ratings still form a very important part of the credit investment process.

CHAPTER 25

Covered Bonds

Covered bonds are a class of secured bonds issued by financial institutions. The covered bond segment is a large part of the European fixed income universe, and in Denmark exceeds the size of the domestic government bond market. Unlike most other bank bonds, covered bonds tend to have fixed coupon bullet structures to make them more similar to government bonds. This type of bond evolved from mortgage lending, and played an important role in funding large-scale real estate developments, for instance the rebuilding of Copenhagen after a large fire in 1795.

Essentially, a covered bond is a means to reduce the funding cost of banking assets by providing the clients providing the funds with better security than a normal bank debenture or deposit. For a lender to a bank, the funding and risk picture looks like this:

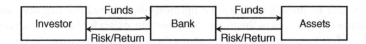

An investor putting money into a bank is exposed to the risks of the bank's assets, as well as additional risks related to the management of the bank. Because the assets of the bank are not directly visible to an investor, some assumptions will be made by the public which may be or not be accurate. If a bank can be set up so that a) investors are well informed about the assets held by the bank, b) these assets are of a high quality, and c) investors have access to these high-quality assets if the bank should fail, then investors should require lower risk premia for their invested money. This is the guiding idea behind the concept of covered bonds which were introduced as a way to source funding for real estate investments at a low cost that reflects the value of having real estate collateral.

Covered bonds are debt instruments issued by banks which are secured by specific collateral of high, and prescribed, quality. Should the issuing bank fail, investors in these bonds gain rights to the assets securing the covered bonds. In addition, covered bonds are excluded from regular insolvency proceedings and do therefore not accelerate in case of default of the issuing bank.

The name 'covered bond' stems from the existence of a cover pool which is a segregated pool of assets on the issuer balance sheet that serves as collateral for the bond. Issuers tend to maintain cover pools that collateralise more than one bond. In

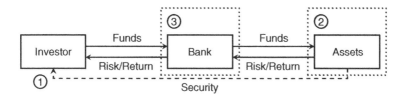

FIGURE 25.1 The essential safety features of a covered bond: Security pledge (1), Cover asset quality (2) and specific bank supervision or specialist bank principle (3).

the Danish market, cover pools are also known as capital centres. The three essential safety features of covered bonds are outlined in Figure 25.1. The particular safety of these bonds arises from the combination of them being secured by collateral, the legally prescribed high quality of that collateral, and a specific supervisory regime. The latter can go as far as business restrictions for covered bond issuing banks, known as the specialist bank principle.

Covered bonds provide banks with funding at levels that are far cheaper than their senior unsecured bonds, sometimes by several hundred basis points. Weaker banks can sometimes issue covered bonds even when there is no market for their unsecured debt. In turn, this allows banks to lend at cheaper levels when the loans qualify as cover assets. Seen as a system, covered bonds channel investor funds to specific borrower types at lower rates than the general banking system would be able to. This is the motivation for governments to create covered bond legislation.

Two basic varieties of covered bond exist. The first, statutory covered bonds, rely on specific legislation and supervision to ensure the integrity and asset quality of the cover pool as well as the structure of the covered bond. Covered bond legislation now exists in most developed economies, and several countries have multiple legal frameworks for covered bonds. In countries where covered bond legislation does, or did, not exist, or where issuers find it hard to comply with such legislation, so-called structured covered bonds have been issued. These bonds replicate the core features of a covered bond through contractual means, similar to asset-backed structures. Note that 'structured' in this context does not refer to the coupon structure of the security but the underlying collateral structure. Both statutory and structured covered bonds have evolved over recent years and adopted credit-enhancement features of ABS. The core difference between covered bonds and ABS, however, remains in place: covered bonds are bank liabilities, and the assets that secure these liabilities remain on the balance sheet of the issuer.

The covered bond market traces its existence to the German Pfandbrief, a class of privileged bond introduced in 1770. The Pfandbrief was initially designed as a way to syndicate mortgage loans. Given that mortgage credit had been in existence in bilateral non-bank lending between private individuals, the Pfandbrief can be seen as an industrialised version of a pre-existing form of mortgage lending. The lower interest rates on bank mortgages that are refinanced with Pfandbriefe incentivised replication of this model. The Great Fire of Copenhagen 1795 required a substantial reconstruction effort and the necessary funding was raised with the first Danish covered bonds.

The Pfandbrief structure has since been applied to public sector loans as well. During the halcyon days of the German Pfandbrief in the first few years after the

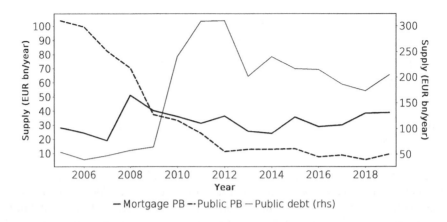

FIGURE 25.2 Annual issuance volumes of mortgage Pfandbriefe, public sector Pfandbriefe, and public sector bonds, excluding German federal government bonds. Source: Data from Bundesbank capital market statistics and German Federal Debt Management Agency.

introduction of the euro, public Pfandbriefe (covered bonds backed by public sector assets) far outstripped the volume of mortgage Pfandbriefe. Two events changed this picture. The first is the expiry of state guarantees ('Gewährträgerhaftung') of liabilities of German state banks (Landesbanken). These were grandfathered in a settlement between Germany's private and public banks that was reached in 2001 and applied mostly to liabilities originated before 18 July 2005 and maturing before the end of 2015. This expiry rendered a large volume of state bank liabilities ineligible as covered bond cover assets. The second was the financial crisis starting in 2007 which reduced the ability of banks in general to intermediate the funding of high-grade public sector debtors through loans. Instead, these public sector borrowers turned to direct capital market financing. While banks continued to purchase such securities, their funding costs no longer gave them a comparative advantage in funding such debtors. The result was a decline in public sector Pfandbrief issuance while public sector bond issuance surged (cf. Figure 25.2). In comparison, mortgage Pfandbrief issuance volumes remained comparatively stable over the years, confirming the importance of this asset class for the German housing market. The Spanish equivalent of the public sector Pfandbrief, cédulas territoriales, is now also inactive while the market for mortgage cédulas hipotecarias remains vibrant. Some other countries did not develop a public sector covered bond instrument because they already had an existing funding instrument for non-government public sector debt through specialised lenders, such as Kommunekredit in Denmark and MuniFin[1] in Finland.

Following the introduction of the euro, the importance of competitive bank refinancing channels became more of a focus of legislators and other euro area countries either revived existing legal frameworks or created new ones to provide access

---

[1]The actual name of this institution is Kuntarahoitus, often referred to as Kunta.

to the covered bond market to their banks. The resulting instruments are collectively known by the generic term 'covered bond' because the national designations are generally legally protected. It is illegal in Germany (as well as Austria and Switzerland) to label a French Obligation Fonciere a 'Pfandbrief' even though this bond type has many features in common with a German Pfandbrief. Conversely, a German Pfandbrief cannot be labelled an Obligation Fonciere in France.

There is no cross-country, or even EU-wide, standard definition of what exactly constitutes a covered bond. In response to the size constraints of the Danish fixed income market[2], the European Union has introduced a concept into European legislation that reflects the salient features of most covered bond laws. Generally speaking, the securities satisfying this definition:

- are issued by specialist banks,
- under special supervision by their regulator,
- offer special protection to their holders, and
- are secured by high-quality assets.

Structured covered bonds, by definition, do not satisfy the first two requirements because they rely on contractual means, rather than specific legislation, to provide the last two features.

One of the features that is now generally accepted as necessary in covered bonds is that they should not fall due in case of insolvency of the issuer. Instead, bond holders look to continue receiving the cashflows they originally expect because the security pledged as collateral is expected to generate the necessary cash. This aim requires not only fairly strict asset-liability matching from the issuing bank, but also presents important problems for the legal system under which these bonds are issued. In particular, the applicable bankruptcy code must recognise a situation where insolvency occurs but some creditors remain outside the normal bankruptcy proceedings. This means that the security structure of covered bonds cannot easily be created without close involvement of the sovereign.

Beyond the commonalities lie various differences. Table 25.1 shows examples of differences in such important parameters as maximum permissible loan-to-value (LTV) ratios, lending areas, permissibility of MBS collateral, and so on. The purpose of this table is not to define the various frameworks, but to highlight differences. These differences result in varying degrees of risk and diversification across the different covered bond structures. As will be discussed later, investors need to weigh these differences against other parameters, such as over-collateralisation and maturity profiles, to arrive at a risk assessment.

One driver of an evolution in covered bond structures has been the competition of the ABS market. Because ABS issuing vehicles are capital-light, investors insist on detailed protection mechanisms againt risks that could normally be expected to

---

[2]The covered bond market in Denmark is much larger than that for government bonds, and therefore covered bonds dominate the positions of domestic asset managers. The resulting levels of issuer concentration are higher than what is normally considered permissible for fund managers.

TABLE 25.1 Simplified comparison of selected features of statutory mortgage covered bond frameworks. In some fields the most relevant value has been selected from multiple options (Source: European Covered Bond Council).

Framework	Max. LTV	Lending area	Substitute	MBS
German Pfandbrief	60%	EEA, Switzerland, US, Canada, Japan, Aus, NZ	20%	×
French Obligation Foncières	80%	EEA, others	15%	•
French Obligation à l'Habitat	80%	France	–	•
Spanish Cédulas Hipotecarias	80%	EU	5%	o

TABLE 25.2 Outstanding volumes of covered bonds by country at the end of 2018 absolute and per head of the population (Source: Based on European Covered Bond Council, OECD).

Country	Total outstanding (EUR m)	Per capita (EUR)
Australia	65,855	2,677
Austria	58,928	6,717
Canada	107,496	2,949
Denmark	405,991	70,622
Finland	37,257	6,770
France	321,311	4,810
Germany	369,747	4,481
Iceland	3,123	9,231
Ireland	23,319	4,874
Italy	168,936	2,788
Japan	1,000	8
Luxembourg	6,103	10,332
The Netherlands	94,797	5,550
Norway	121,182	23,046
Spain	231,615	4,978
Sweden	217,979	21,808
Switzerland	119,422	14,184
United Kingdom	98,192	1,491

be addressed by a reasonably well-capitalised bank, such as short-term cashflow mismatches, derivatives counterparty risks, etc. Covered bond legislation has added comparable features for cases where the issuing bank is no longer viable, and the protection afforded by its capital is no longer meaningful. The process of managing the cover pool for the benefit of covered bond holders, for instance, is now more regulated than it was a few decades ago.

Aside from the stability of the covered bond product itself, one should be aware that there is strong systemic support for these debt instruments in several countries. Table 25.2 compares outstanding volumes of these bonds to the population. Where covered bonds form a substantial part of the total debt structure in a country, the contagion risk that would arise from the default of any one issuer may make it preferable for other actors to step in with a support package rather than accept such a default. Such support may take the form of mergers or takeovers between weaker and stronger issuing banks, for instance.

The recent financial crisis has called into question the ability of issuing banks to maintain the cash flow structure required to pay off the covered bonds outstanding at the time they encounter financial difficulties. As a result, some banks have modified their outstanding covered bonds in such a way that the redemption structure can change according to incoming cash flows from the underlying loan pools. In these conditional pass-throughs, the cash flow timing and credit risk passes to investors when the situation of the covered bond issuer no longer permits the assumption of this risk. Another structure that emerged from the crisis are soft bullet covered bonds, structures that can extend maturity under specific circumstances to ensure that redemption cash needs do not lead to an insolvency of the structure. Both conditional pass-throughs and soft bullets should be recognised as forms of credit rating arbitrage. By softening the obligations of the issuer, it is more likely that the issuer can satisfy them, which results in better ratings. For investors, however, very egregious forms of rating arbitrage can create substantial uncertainty about future cash flow timing.

25.1 STATUTORY COVERED BONDS

In a classic, statutory covered bond structure, cover assets are held on the balance sheet of the bond issuer in what is called the cover pool. A special registrar maintains lists of assets held in the cover pool as collateral against the covered bonds and the outstanding bonds secured by these assets. The registrar is responsible for ensuring that the volume of cover assets at all times suffices to cover the outstanding bonds, and that the asset quality is of the reuired standard. Depending on the jurisdiction, public sector loans and mortgage loans serving as cover assets can be held in the same cover pool or must be in segregated pools. Covered bond issuers are required by law to publish regular updates on the amount and composition of cover assets to allow investors a minimum degree of credit analysis of the pool.

Most jurisdictions permit the limited use of substitute collateral which are assets that are outside the general definition of eligible cover assets. The purpose of substitute collateral is cashflow management and liquidity of substitute assets should generally be very high. For instance, mortgages tend to have monthly amortising structures while covered bonds have annual or semi-annual coupon and bullet structures. The cover pool maintainer may therefore use cash or cash equivalents in the pool to retain cash received from the underlying loans until the next upcoming cash outflow for bond servicing. Over the years, regulators and rating agencies have tightened their scrutiny of substitute collateral.

Cover pools generally contain more cover assets than required to collateralise the outstanding bonds, in a practice called overcollateralisation. The excess collateral is therefore usually called OC. Legislation defines a minimum level of OC, but issuers routinely exceed this legal minimum. The amount of OC, together with the cover pool asset quality and the credit strength of the issuer, largely determine the credit quality of the covered bond. It should be borne in mind that OC is by definition funded

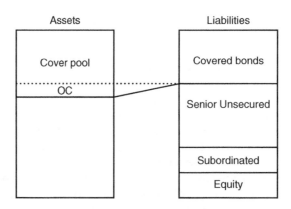

FIGURE 25.3   Balance sheet structure of a covered bond issuer.

by liabilities other than covered bonds, but is pledged to covered bond holders. This asset encumbrance lowers the likely recovery values for unsecured creditors of the issuing bank, including depositors. Some regulators therefore take a rather dim view of covered bonds and severely restrict the volume of covered bonds that can be issued by banks. In other jurisdictions, covered bonds tend to be issued by specialist banks and it is assumed that the other creditors of such banks are aware of the amount of assets that are so encumbered and factor this into their investment decisions. In any case, OC is funded at a cost that usually exceeds the cost of covered bond funding. An issuer must therefore optimise the OC level to be high enough to succeed in placing covered bonds at low interest rates, but not so high as to lead to higher unsecured funding costs due to excessive encumbrance, and higher overall funding cost for the total collateral pool.

Issuers are required to maintain the quality of the cover pool at all times. In practice, this requires the replacement of deteriorated assets with others over time. For instance, an issuer experiencing arrears on a mortgage used in the cover pool must, by law, remove that mortgage from the pool and replace it with a performing loan, under the scrutiny of the cover pool registrar.

The type of loan eligible as a cover asset is restricted by law. Such restrictions take the form of geographic limits for the obligors, as well as loan details. For mortgages, this might be the type of property that secures the mortgage as well as the loan-to-value ratio[3] including applicable valuation criteria. Cover pool eligible mortgages are generally first-lien mortgages only. In public sector loans, restrictions can apply to the type of public sector borrower, for instance whether or not the borrower has the right to levy discretionary taxes or fees. As a result of cover pool eligibility criteria, some retail mortgage markets are segmented. Banks would offer first-lien mortgage loans up to the

---

[3]This ratio, usually abbreviated as LTV, is the ratio of loan value to the most recent assessed property value. Property values are assessed by valuation experts using statutory valuation approaches. Some jurisdictions use indexation to regularly adjust property valuations on existing loans without a full assessment.

statutory LTV limit at one set of terms that reflect the covered bond funding costs, while the share of a mortgage loan that exceeds this LTV limit would be offered as a more expensive loan secured either by the same mortgage or an additional second lien mortgage[4].

It is not immediately good or bad to have wider or narrower ranges of eligible collateral. A narrow eligible collateral range will lower the default risk in the cover pool but tend to result in higher asset concentration and lower net interest margin for the pool.

Unfortunately, national legislators have seen fit to create a proliferation of covered bond frameworks across even a comparatively harmonised financial landscape like the euro area. There are explanations for having different national frameworks, namely the interaction between insolvency law and covered bonds on one hand, and the long-term nature of cover pool assets on the other. German retail mortgages, for instance, tend to have contractual maturities of 30 years and are structured to match German cover pool criteria[5]. Harmonising frameworks across multiple countries would therefore require a wholesale switch in retail product designs. Such explanations are somewhat insufficient, however, for explaining multiple competing legislative frameworks in the same country.

25.2   DANISH COVERED BONDS

The Danish covered bond market is one of the oldest statutory markets in the world. While it has seen its share of innovation, some features make it very different from other markets.

The core distinguishing feature of Danish covered bonds is the balance principle which means that the underlying mortgages are closely related to the bonds with which they are being refinanced. A Danish borrower can therefore derive the likely terms of a new mortgage by observing the market prices of covered bonds[6]. In other markets mortgages of different types are bundled into the same cover pool and refinanced by portfolios of covered bonds so that this linkage in economic terms does not exist.

On the basis of the balance principle, Danish borrowers have an additional way of refinancing a mortgage through a process known as delivery. A borrower can purchase the specific bond that refinances her or his mortgage, and deliver this bond to the issuing bank in return for a full or partial cancellation of the mortgage loan. In addition,

---

[4]Jurisdictions differ in the precise legal definition of a mortgage and the existence or not of second-lien mortgages. In some cases a lender can take security over a property without a mortgage as such. Such differences are reflected in national covered bond frameworks.

[5]A German mortgage usually has a first-ranking portion covering up to 60% of the lending value eligible for Pfandbried refinancing, and a second-ranking portion for amounts about this threshold which is refinanced in other ways, with a higher cost attached.

[6]One of the results of this close match is that Danish regulators were among the first to push for high price transparency for bonds which, as in other markets, trade largely over the counter (OTC). High transparency in this context means fast disclosure of a large subset of all trades conducted.

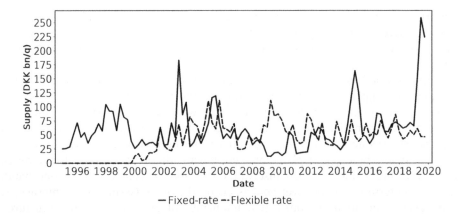

FIGURE 25.4 Quarterly gross Danish covered bond issuance volumes for fixed-rate and variable rate mortgages. Note that the shorter maturity of variable-rate refinancing bonds requires more frequent refunding.
Source: Finans Danmark Udlånsstatistikken.

borrowers can prepay the loans early, as is the case in US mortgages. In this case, the issuing bank will partially call the covered bond that refinances the mortgage that has been prepaid. These two prepayment mechanisms have opposing effects on a mortgage loan if done with the aim of refinancing the mortgage at current conditions with a new loan. Delivery does not change the present value of the mortgage, but when interest rates are higher than when the loan was originated, the mortgage can be restructured to a lower principal amount but a higher coupon. The main reason to conduct such a restructure is that it increases the economic value of the prepayment option. If interest rates fall again, the option to refinance the mortgage through prepayment, i.e., restructure the mortgage with the same principal but a lower coupon, usually has a positive value (cf. Section 27.1 on mortgage repayments on page 290).

The standard Danish mortgage contract is a 30Y annuity but this structure has been modified over the years. It is now common to have amortisation holidays within the contract, i.e., phases where the borrower makes only interest payments, to allow for lower income periods. The total length of such holidays is limited. Because long-dated annuities mean that borrowing rates are determined by the long end of the yield curve, a competing product has existed since 2000 that allows the borrower to save on the term risk premium at the expense of higher interest rate volatility. These contracts, known as Flexlån, have variable rate coupons with fixing periods of up to 10 years. The balance principle is implemented for such loans by re-fixing the coupon rate through auctions of the fixed-rate bonds that refund such mortgages. The relative share of fixed and variable-rate mortgages fluctuates over time in responce to changing interest rates (see Figure 25.4).

Interestingly, although euro-denominated mortgages exist in Denmark and the Danish Krone is being kept in a very tight relationship with the euro through Denmark's membership in ERM II, the take-up of such euro-denominated mortgages is comparatively low.

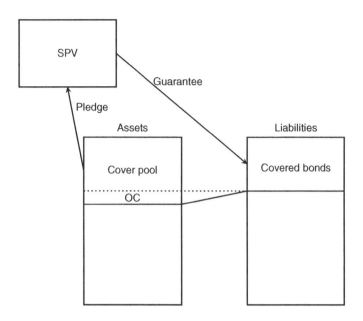

FIGURE 25.5   General structure of a structured covered bond issuer balance sheet and the guarantor SPV.

25.3   STRUCTURED COVERED BONDS

As mentioned above, structured covered bonds are private law arrangements that look to achieve the economic features of a covered bond. They are useful when a covered bond framework does not exist in the jurisdiction of a potential issuer, when the framework that does exist is unsuitable, or when there are specific circumstances that prevent an issuer to use an existing framework. An example of an unsuitable framework would be the absence of a carve-out of covered bond cover pools from standard insolvency procedures. Without this carve-out, covered bond investors would immediately join the general insolvency procedure and face an acceleration of their claims. An example of specific circumstances would be non-subordination language in an issuer's senior unsecured bond documentation that prevent pledging assets to the cover pool.

The standard design pattern of a structured covered bond is a senior unsecured bank bond that is guaranteed by a special-purpose vehicle holding cover assets. Possible variations are in the funding of the assets on the SPV balance sheet, which is commonly done through an intercompany loan. In essence, the bank sets up the SPV, loans its funds and the SPV uses these funds to purchase the cover assets from the bank. The bank funds the loan through the issuance of a structured covered bond which is guaranteed by the SPV. Should the bank default on the bond, the SPV can use or liquidate the cover assets to fund payments under the guarantee it has extended to the holders of the structured covered bond. The terms of the intercompany loan are designed such that, while the banks, other creditors have a claim to repayment of the loan after insolvency of the bank these claims rank behind the guarantee. In this way, the residual value of the cover pool (the economic equivalent of OC) falls to the unsecured creditors of the bank, just as in any other covered bond structure. This distribution only takes place after the maturity of the covered bond, in line with most statutory covered bond frameworks.

In some jurisdictions, the asset transfer to the guarantor SPV is only perfected at the time of default of the issuer. In this case, the intercompany loan does not occur at the time of bond issuance, and the delay in the asset transfer can reduce tax or accounting issues that would be faced by the issuer if the asset transfer happened at the time of bond issuance.

An important use of structured covered bonds is the 'recycling' of suitable loan pools that were not originated with covered bond issuance in mind. Statutory covered bond frameworks specify features for eligible loans while structured covered bonds can use loans that vary in some respects, such as geographical location, type of collateral, or loan-to-value ratios. Because the assets of structured covered bonds are transferred to the SPV rather than being pledged, structured covered bonds are also a possible avenue for issuers with negative pledge clauses on existing senior unsecured debt to issue covered bonds.

25.4 COVERED BOND CREDIT RISK ANALYSIS

The credit risk of a covered bond is driven by three factors in addition to its maturity: The strength of the issuing bank, the quality of the cover pool assets, and the amount of OC. Simply speaking, a perfectly safe bank will never default, so the existence or quality of the cover assets is irrelevant[7]. If the bank is not perfectly safe, then the credit quality is determined by the likelihood of cover assets sufficing to generate the cash payments due under the bonds, even after the issuer is no longer in a position to replace deteriorated cover assets. Again simply speaking, the faster the cover assets deteriorate, the more OC is required to preserve sufficient cover assets until the maturity of the covered bond. Also, with equal cover asset quality, the earlier the issuing bank is expected to default, the more OC will be used up before the covered bonds mature. Figure 25.6 illustrates this logic.

A crucial feature of a covered bond is that, in contrast to an ABS, the collateral pool is constantly replenished through asset substitution by the issuing bank. This replenishment stops when the issuing bank defaults. At that point, the value of the cash flows from the collateral pool declines through credit deterioration, similar to the rating evolution shown in Figure 24.2 on page 256.The speed at which this deterioration happens is a function of the quality of the credit pool. What matters for the credit quality of the covered bonds is whether this deterioration process erodes the collateral value below the payment obligation of the bond before the bond matures. Aside from the quality of the cover pool, this is determined by the expected time between the default and the

---

[7]In the Japanese market, where the large banks are traditionally seen as very safe (or at least too big to fail), covered bond development was held back by very tight senior unsecured pricing. The market simply had not developed a demand for cover assets.

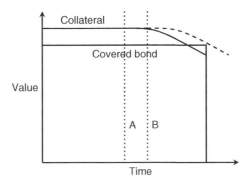

FIGURE 25.6 Illustration of the three drivers of covered bond default risk for two default timing scenarios of the issuing bank for a single outstanding covered bond. In the case of an earlier default (A), the excess collateral is exhausted before the maturity of the bond and bond holders face losses. In the case of a later default (B), the excess collateral declines at the same speed after default but is still sufficient for repayment of the bond.

maturity of the bond, which is a function of the stand-alone credit quality of the issuing bank, and the amount of excess collateral. Therefore, simply speaking, a riskier collateral pool, longer-dated covered bonds, and a lower stand-alone credit quality of the bank require more excess collateral to achieve the same credit quality for the covered bond.

It should be borne in mind that the choice of cover assets is a business decision of the issuing bank. A given bank may opt to finance riskier loans, and so deliberately include lower quality assets in the cover pool, than other banks. As long as the amount of excess collateral appropriately reflects this choice, this difference in cover assets need not affect the credit quality of the covered bond. This means also that more excess collateral is not necessarily a sign of a weaker quality of the bank, although it might be.

The issue of asset encumbrance also affects the structuring choices of the bank. Pledging more excess collateral potentially increases the riskiness of lower-ranked debt like senior unsecured bonds. As long as markets price this risk, issuing more senior unsecured debt to fund the excess collateral becomes more expensive as a result of this encumbrance. This affects the economics of the covered bond issuance, and in effect provides a cap on credit enhancement of covered bonds through the use of excess collateral. Using low-quality collateral for covered bonds is uneconomical due to the cost of funding the excess collateral with senior unsecured debt and equity.

CHAPTER 26

Asset-Backed Securities

The term asset-backed securities encompasses a wide range of securities that share a common characteristic. The securities are issued by a corporate entity set up specifically to hold a certain pool of assets, issue refinancing instruments against it, and manage the flow of cash between assets and the refinancing instruments. The process of turning assets into securities is called (unsurprisingly) securitisation. The special entities are known as special-purpose vehicles (SPVs) or (less commonly) special-purpose entities (SPEs). ABS allow the refinancing of cash-generating assets without resorting to loans or other on-balance sheet forms of financing. The entity that uses ABS to refinance assets is generally known as the originator of the transaction. In contrast, the arranger of the transaction is the entity that defines the transaction structure, sets up the SPV, etc., and it is of course possible that the originator and the arranger of a transaction coincide.

SPVs commonly have very little equity capital relative to their asset bases, have no employees, are lightly regulated and often located in tax-efficient jurisdictions. The rights of the creditors of an SPV are governed by the prospectus of the SPV securities issues which typically also defines the corporate structure of the SPV itself. Note that for securities issued by banks or standard corporations, the prospectus would be significantly less descriptive on the corporate structure as such, and only define certain restrictions (covenants) on financial parameters. This issuer structure sets ABS apart from the much older covered bond structure (see Chapter 25) where the issuer has traditionally been a fully regulated bank.

Because the SPVs have very little corporate structure themselves, they need to rely on third parties to manage their daily operations. These parties are compensated for their services by the SPV with part of the cash generated by the assets that the SPV holds. The key party in this is the servicer of the assets. For ABS backed by loans for example, this would be the company that collects payments from the debtors, manages late payments and defaults, etc. The business of servicing can be quite attractive because it is essentially free of direct credit risk. The holders of ABS, however, have some exposure to the credit of the servicer. These aspects will be discussed in more detail later.

When the Basel Committee on Banking Supervision introduced a first risk-based framework of bank capital requirements ('Basel I') in 1988, it created an opportunity for capital structure arbitrage where banks could choose to structure their asset base so as to reduce the regulatory capital required to be held against these assets without significantly changing the economics of the assets themselves. The comparatively simple nature of the risk weights made it attractive to repackage assets into ABS and retain riskier elements of the securities issued by the SPV. Over time, other incentives to issue have emerged and this explains why the market is still thriving despite the much more realistic capital framework in place now.

The European Union has established a regulatory framework for ABS transactions known as the STS (simple, transparent, standardised) label. This regulation sets a higher standard of information disclosure for securitisation transactions seeking to obtain the STS label. Such efforts to make securitisations less opaque have some tradition in the euro area where the ECB has insisted on loan-level data disclosure for ABS to be acceptable as collateral for ECB operations.

26.1 THE ABS ISSUANCE PROCESS

ABS are created by setting up a corporate entity, the SPV, and then transferring certain assets to the SPV by way of a sale. At the same time as the sale of assets closes, the SPV sells securities to a consortium of investors to finance the purchase of the assets. The assets underlying an ABS transaction can be loans, leases, bonds, royalties, etc. In general, any set of assets that generates regular cash flows can be used for an ABS transaction.

An important aspect of this process is that the originator of the assets, which is often a bank but can be any corporate entity that has claims to certain assets, transfers the assets with a certain degree of finality, namely in a way that allows them to be de-recognised on the balance sheet of the originator, usually by way of a true sale. What constitutes an asset transfer in this context is somewhat dependent on the applicable local law and accounting rules. For instance, some jurisdictions recognise transfers for balance sheet purposes even when the seller still has some interests in the assets but transfers them to the SPV in case of default of the originator (perfection). In any case, with the transfer of assets to the SPV, the SPV and therefore the creditors of the SPV have no further claims on the originator. This is known as the non-recourse condition.

The arrangers of the ABS will typically set up two counterparties for the SPV that aid the cash flow management of the structure. The first is the swap provider which conducts swap agreements with the SPV that allow, for instance, fixed rate loans to be used for the issuance of floating rate liabilities. The second counterparty is the GIC provider who maintains a guaranteed interest account where the SPV can hold cash collected from the assets before it is distributed to the holders of its liabilities. Swap and GIC providers have an effect on the overall credit risk of the SPV and it is therefore common to have mandatory minimum credit ratings for both, and stipulations to replace them if these minimum ratings no longer apply.

ABS are marketed and sold before the SPV structure is fully in place, and particularly before assets are transferred to the SPV. This creates certainty for the originator that the securitisation will actually go ahead, but also means that the time between the primary market sale of ABS and the settlement is usually longer than for standard securities.

26.2   DEFAULT RISK OF ABS

The concept of an ABS default is somewhat more complex than that of a normal debtor. The ABS is issued by an SPV that has no natural assets of its own, and therefore carries very few risks that are not connected to the asset pool that is being repackaged. This means that the ABS default risk stems mostly from the default risk of the underlying assets, rather than the risk of default of the issuer itself.

This general statement needs to be qualified somewhat, however. Failure to pay is not the end of a default process, instead the lender normally attempts to recover as much as possible of a loan through the legal process, or by selling the defaulted loan. When a loan has been repacked in an ABS structure, the economic interest in the loan has been redistributed to the holders of the ABS tranches but these investors have no legal basis on which to pursue either avenue. The onus to pursue recovery is on the ABS issuer, which typically subcontracts this task to the loan servicer, i.e., the legal entity that collects payments on behalf of the ABS investors during the normal performance of the loan pool.

Before going into more detail of what this means for investors, it may be useful to address issuer default risk of the ABS. This is the risk that the SPV loses money unrelated to losses in the underlying assets. Given the sparse SPV structure, such risk is generally related to ancillary activities, namely the GIC and swaps, or from legal risks incurred in the process of issuing and servicing the transaction. It is possible, but very unlikely, that the SPV loses cash deposited into the GIC, or faces losses from swap activities. SPVs are generally structured so that their stand-alone default risk is negligible in the absence of gross malfeasance. Achieving this level of security is one of the more difficult aspects of ABS structuring.

The exposure to the underlying asset risk is something that most investors find difficult to assess. Collateral assets tend to be bilaterally negotiated loans where the originator has a much better view on the loan quality than any outsider. To protect investors, loans in ABS pools tend to be collateralised and subject to screening criteria that are independent of the issuer. Such criteria can be credit scores, income levels, and the like.

The core strategy by which ABS manage default risk is through tranching. Tranching means that each ABS transaction involves the issuance of multiple bond series: cash coming from the transaction is distributed according to a priority waterfall. Losses from the loan pool are first deducted from the payments going to the equity tranche, then from those going to the mezzanine tranche, and only as a last resort are payments on the senior tranche reduced. Senior investors are therefore protected from losses by the assignment of such losses to the more junior tranches. Investors in the various tranches are compensated for the different amount of credit risks by different coupons. The senior tranche pays the lowest coupons while the equity tranche pays the highest, at least as long as it is not wiped out by losses in the pool.

While a detailed discussion of tranching is beyond the scope of this book (cf. [45] for more detail), some general remarks can be made. First, the equity tranche is sized to absorb the expected losses from the collateral pool, which means that it is designed to be more or less wiped out at the end of the transaction. The mezzanine tranche is

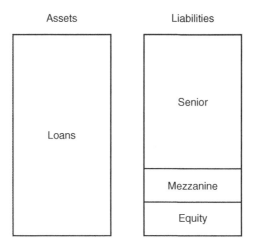

FIGURE 26.1 Standard tranche structure. In reality, the equity and mezzanine tranches would be much smaller compared to the senior tranche.

designed to be thick enough to protect the senior tranches from losses even in scenarios where losses in the pool are significantly above their expected level.

Simply speaking, the size and return on the equity tranche are determined by the expected losses on the pool while the size and return on the mezzanine tranche depend on the *uncertainty* about these losses. In option terms, the equity tranche is a long call option on the credit quality of the asset pool while the senior tranche is a far out of the money short put. The mezzanine is a short straddle and so shows the highest return volatility when the quality of the loan pool changes unexpectedly.

26.3   MATURITY OF ABS

Because an ABS is issued out of a specific structure set up to manage the transaction, there is a natural maturity date for each ABS known as the legal final maturity when the SPV is dissolved. No payments are made under an ABS after the legal final date. Unless there is an unconditional clean-up call (discussed in the next chapter), the legal final maturity is chosen to be longer than the longest loan maturity in the pool, plus some buffer to pursue potential insolvency procedures against defaulted borrowers.

When an ABS actually repays depends on the underlying loan pool and ABS do not usually have bullet repayment schedules. Instead, ABS are partially redeemed on each payment date as and when loan repayments occur in the underlying pool. To reduce the risk of time-subordination (see Section 24.2.1 on page 256), many ABS are structured so that principal repayments are directed at the most senior tranche.

In many cases investors wish to have some minimum duration in an ABS transaction. To satisfy such demand, an SPV can be structured that there are multiple senior tranches. Principal prepayments are then directed first at one of these senior tranches, then the next, and so on. Tranches initially protected from prepayments, or subject to a planned amortisation schedule, are known as planned amortisation certificates (PACs). In essence, prepayment risk like default risk can be tranched and so distributed between different security classes within the same ABS structure. More complex tranching structures do, however, require more complex valuation models, and higher risk premia stemming from the unavoidable uncertainty both about the appropriate models and their parameters. While designing a seniority and amortisation structure to suit one particular type of investor may make it possible to sell one tranche at a lower spread to such investors, there is a risk that other tranches absorbing more complex risks need to have significantly higher spreads. The overall funding cost of a structure may then be lower if a more straightforward structure is chosen.

CHAPTER 27

Residential Mortgage-Backed Securities

The largest class of asset-backed securities are structures that refinance pools of residential mortgages, called residential mortgage-backed securities or RMBS. Cultural or tax effects create widely different rates of home ownership across different countries. The US, The Netherlands and Denmark have very high rates of home onwership, while Germany has traditionally been a country of renters. Accordingly, the former three countries have large markets for securities that refinance individual property loans. In the case of the US and The Netherlands these are ABS, while in Denmark they are covered bonds. RMBS differ from commercial mortgage-backed securities (CMBS) in that RMBS portfolios are more fine-grained than CMBS, and their exposure to industry performance is less concentrated on single sectors such as retail.

The US market, where 30 year fixed-rate mortgages form the main financing vehicle for household purchases, has a large volume of loans known as conforming loans. Such loans are for single-family properties with a maximum size that depends on the location of the property. Conformance criteria are defined by the US Federal Housing Finance Agency. Crucially, conforming loans can be purchased, insured and refinanced by the so-called government-sponsored enterprises[1] (GSEs) Fannie Mae and Freddie Mac.

Trading in residential mortgage-backed securities dominates the private sector bond market in the United States. Over 80% of trade volume reported on TRACE relates to RMBS transactions. Specifically to the US, the bulk (around 90%) of trades are done in to-be-assigned (TBA) format. In this approach, new mortgages are traded on a forward basis and settled once the respective mortgage pool has been originated and securitised. Until assignment, the buyer has no information on the specific pool of mortgages. This type of trading works because the characteristics of conforming mortgages are highly standardised and pools therefore largely comparable. It is, however, possible that the mortgage origination speed is different from expectations. When fewer mortgages are originated than expected, the forward transaction may be

---

[1] In the US market, these entities are generally known as agencies despite being private companies. As with the term 'rating agency', as long as one does not take the market jargon as legal gospel, there should be no confusion.

impossible to settle because more new bonds have been sold than were originated. In this case, buyers and sellers can agree to a dollar roll which is equivalent to the old London market concept of a backwardation: The trade settlement is postponed to the next settlement cycle, and the purchase price adjusted for the value of the intervening carry. Alternatively, buyer and seller can agree on a coupon swap where securities with one coupon are exchanged against securities with a different coupon, with an attendant compensation payment. Such coupon swaps are particularly important when mortgage production rates shift between different coupons, and there is therefore a structural lack of certain expected coupons for the foreseeable future. Such a structural shift cannot be addressed through dollar rolls because the trades would consume balance sheet for some time, and because prepayments over time affect relative valuations of older and newer bond series.

27.1   RESIDENTIAL MORTGAGE PREPAYMENTS

The expected rate of mortgage prepayments is determined by a variety of factors, corresponding to the types of decisions made by mortgage borrowers over the duration of the loan. Below is a list of factors which are then incorporated in a mathematical model.

Non-economic prepayments (attrition) refers to early mortgage redemptions that do not have an economic motivation. These could be driven by defaults (leading to foreclosure auctions and therefore at least partial repayment), moves (for instance as families trade up to a larger property after having children), fire damage, or death of the borrower (some jurisdictions require life insurance coverage of loan amounts). An important factor that determines the rate of such prepayments is whether properties are sold with the mortgage in place, or sales require remortgaging. Jurisdictions where it is common to transfer properties together with an existing loan see correspondingly lower attrition rates of mortgage pools.

Non-economic prepayment rates can exhibit dependencies on macro-economic variables, for instance through higher default rates during economic downturns. They can also be somewhat seasonal because voluntary moves occur more often in summer than in the winter months. Even mortality rates in the general population have clear seasonal patterns in most climate zones.

In any case, non-economic repayments mean that the expected average life of a mortgage pool is shorter than the weighted average maturity of the pool independent of the future evolution of mortgage market conditions.

Economic prepayments are early redemptions of a mortgage loan due to economic incentives. This usually means that mortgages are available at a lower rate and the borrower decides to repay the existing mortgage early with cash raised in a new mortgage. Prepayments generally are associated with costs, such as notary fees and bank fees. Because some of these costs are fixed, rather than proportional to the loan size, larger loans tend to prepay faster than smaller ones.

Some jurisdictions allow the bank to charge the opportunity cost of losing the mortgage loan early which drastically reduces the economic benefits of early repayment. In other markets, for instance the US, the benefit of a lower mortgage rate needs to be weighed against the extension of the loan maturity. It needs to be kept in mind that the benefit of a lower rate depends on the remaining principal and amortisation schedule. A mortgage late in its life consists mostly of redemption payments and a lower interest rate has a diminished cash value.

Economic prepayments are subject to a phenomenon known as burn-out which is the observation that economic prepayments at a given refinancing rate decline over time. This is because cost-sensitive borrowers for whom refinancing is triggered at that rate are eliminated from the current mortgage pool[2] so that the pool becomes less likely to refinance at that rate. There can also be a drift higher in economic repayments due to an increased availability of information about refinancing terms, and the emergence of mortgage brokers who seek out borrowers that might refinance in return for a fee. A somewhat curious but significant aspect of economically driven refinancing is known as the newspaper effect: When interest rates have been low for some time but appear to be on the verge of a rise, newspapers tend to run articles in their weekend property sections that highlight the imminent loss of attractive refinancing options. This can lead to a spike in mortgage refinancing after the trough in interest rates is reached.

Some markets exhibit further special effects. In Denmark, for instance, speculative repayments can occur when borrowers deliver below-par mortgage bonds to their banks and refinance with current higher-rate mortgages. This type of refinancing reduces the mortgage principal and leads to a refinancing option at the new higher rate. In an ideal scenario, a Danish mortgage borrower would refinance a mortgage at the current principal amount at low rates through prepayment, and use times of higher interest rates to reduce the principal amount through delivery. During the 30 year lifetime of the standard mortgage in this market, this could lead to multiple savings occasions. The option to buy back one's mortgage below par does not exist in most other markets. In the Danish case, it also does not directly lead to an early redemption of bond held by other investors because the borrower has to purchase the mortgage bond in order to deliver it. An investor not selling the bond will therefore be unaffected.

Non-economic non-prepayments are situations where a borrower has a clear incentive and opportunity to refinance but does not exercise this option. Depending on the market, there can be multiple reasons for such behaviour beyond disinterest in one's financial affairs, or the time and effort involved in realising a potential reduction in mortgage costs. For instance, refinancing might require a re-appraisal of the property value, and that value may have declined, making refinancing unavailable. The same can be true for the credit rating of the borrower[3].

The modelling implication of this effect is that refinancing rates never reach 100% even in the most advantageous circumstances. More broadly speaking, this effect means that one does not model prepayment behaviour as a step function of

---

[2]These borrowers will of course appear again in a new pool with their refinancing loan.

[3]Most developed markets have some form of credit assessment of retail borrowers available, such as the Schufa system in Germany or the FICO score in the US. Banks would then typically consult such information before granting any loan, including a renewed mortgage.

the incentive (no economic prepayments below a threshold and 100% refinancing above it), but as a gradual saturation function.

Clean-up call is a feature in some RMBS transactions where the originator will repurchase the remaining asset pool at a set time and the SPV uses the proceeds of this purchase to redeem all remaining bonds. In essence, the mortality on the clean-up call date is 100%. Such a call is in essence a cost management strategy because it leads to a dissolution of the SPV structure at a time when only a small share of the original pool is left but a large part of the servicing cost remains.

Prepayments are observed in principle at each payment date and the share of mortgages that prepay are called the mortality, or single month mortality (SMM). It is sometimes more convenient to express the prepayment speed in an annual variable. This is known as the constant prepayment rate CPR [45], given by:

$$CPR = 1 - (1 - SMM)^f \qquad (27.1)$$

where f is the payment frequency ($f = 12$ for monthly, $f = 4$ for quarterly, etc.).

27.2 PREPAYMENT MODELLING

Investors in pre-payable mortgages need to carefully model the risk of early repayment. As the previous section has made clear, prepayment is largely driven by the availability of more favourable financing conditions relative to a current mortgage. This means that refinancing does not imply that a borrower ceases to pay interest on the financing of a property. Instead, the borrower ceases to pay interest on one loan, and instead pays interest on another. For the investor in the original loan, or the RMBS it has been repackaged into, that means a loss of interest payments. A mortgage valuation model consists of two components. The first is a model for the mortality of a mortgage at a single payment date (the SMM). This basic mortality model is then used to value the mortgage, taking into account prepayments at any future date.

In what follows, a simplified model will be used to illustrate the basic features of a prepayment model for hypothetical USD-denominated mortgages with a quarterly payment frequency[4]. At each payment date, the borrower has the choice to either make only the scheduled payment or additionally repay the entire remaining principal and take out a new mortgage for that amount at current conditions. The refinancing incentive is assumed to be the ratio between the cost reduction created by refinancing and the original mortgage amount. This cost reduction s is determined by the difference in the discounted value of cashflows on the original mortgage and a new mortgage used for refinancing that has the same original years to maturity as the existing mortgage. The discount curve is the current mortgage curve which is defined as the US Treasury

---

[4]This frequency, instead of monthly, is chosen to make Figure 27.4 more readable.

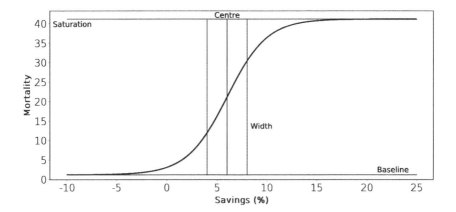

FIGURE 27.1 The prepayment model Equation (27.2) and its four parameters: Baseline b_k, centre c, width w and the saturation level $1 - m + b_k$.

zero-coupon curve[5] plus a flat spread. Lastly, to align this with the US market, the original years to maturity of a new mortgage is assumed to be 30 years.

The main simplification of the model is that it does not take rates volatility into account. The benefit of prepaying is determined only by the change in interest costs, not the value of the option that is being exercised by prepaying, or the option received by taking out a new mortgage.

The prepayment model has four parameters which in an actual modelling setting would be calibrated to historically observed prepayment data. Here, reasonable values have been chosen more or less at random for illustration. There is a baseline attrition rate (b_k) linked to non-economical repayments which is set at 5% per year. At a saving c of 6% of original mortgage amount, half of the interest-rate sensitive borrowers are expected to prepay. There is a 2% uncertainty interval w around this point, and a share m of 60% of borrowers are assumed not to be sensitive to interest rates (non-economic non-prepayments). These parameters are then put into a logistic function:

$$p_k = b_k + \frac{\exp((s-c)/w)}{1 + \exp((s-c)/w)}(1-m) \tag{27.2}$$

(shown in Figure 27.1) to yield the mortality at the payment date k as a function of the available saving from prepaying a mortgage on a given date. In a more realistic model, some of these parameters (particularly b_k) would be time-dependent.

The mortgage used as an example is a 4.5% coupon mortgage with a maturity date of December 2040. The original maturity of the mortgage is 30 years so at the time of analysis (May 2020) it is already ten years old. This information is then used to calculate the economic gain from prepaying, i.e., the parameter s of the model Equation (27.2).

---

[5]The US Treasury curve is represented by a Nelson-Siegel spline fitted to actual Treasury prices on the analysis date.

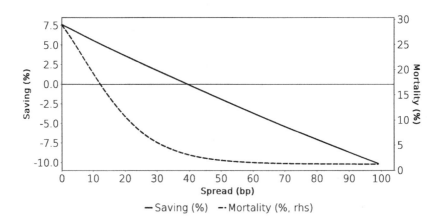

FIGURE 27.2 The basic mortality model used in this section. The control parameter of the model is the spread of mortgages over US Treasuries. As the spread increases, the cost saving from prepaying declines, and so does mortality.

Figure 27.2 illustrates this basic mortality model. The decisive variable is the spread of mortgage rates over the US Treasury curve. Higher spreads make new mortgages more expensive and it is therefore less attractive to refinance. The same effect would occur when US Treasury rates themselves increase. The spread parameter used here is therefore best thought of as a general shift in mortgage rates rather than as a mortgage spread. The general picture is then that when mortgage rates are lower, borrowers have a higher incentive to prepay an existing mortgage with a higher coupon. The connection between the cost saving of refinancing, and the actual refinancing rate is given by the logistic function Equation (27.2). This function needs to be understood as a statistical model. The choice of each mortgage borrower is the binary decision to prepay or not, and this decision is affected by many factors. The assumption of Equation (27.2) is that when averaging over a large pool of borrowers, their collective decisions combine to a deterministic relationship between refinancing conditions and refinancing rates.

This mortality model contains several simplifications compared to the considerations in the previous section. There is no notion of burn-out so that there is no path-dependency of the model. In other words, prepayments depend on current interest rates, but not on past levels. Second, there is no size dependence of prepayments because the saving is assessed purely on the basis of relative savings with no regard to potential fixed fees. Relative fees (fees proportional to the mortgage amount) would be expected to be reflected in the parameter c. There is an apparent problem with this function, namely that prepayments rise from the baseline level even when the refinancing incentive if zero or even negative, which for these parameter values happens at spreads of over 80bps. Because the logistic function is never exactly zero, this effect is unavoidable and it has no meaningful impact on the accuracy of the model. While it would be possible to cure this defect by introducing explicit cut-offs, the advantage of retaining the logistic function is that it is infinitely smooth. More complex valuation models that rely on yield curve scenario analysis tend to struggle with discontinuities.

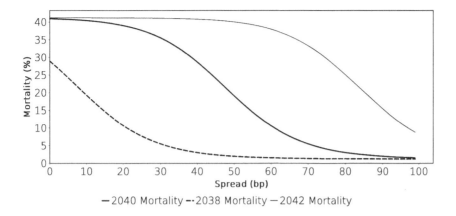

FIGURE 27.3 Comparison of the mortalities of three identical bonds with different seasoning. The solid line in the middle refers to the same bond as the one used in Figure 27.2.

As has been pointed out earlier, the incentive to prepay is dependent on the remaining life of the mortgage. To illustrate this, Figure 27.3 compares the mortalities of three bonds that are identical in all aspects except their origination and maturity year.

The mortality for a given spread is higher for longer mortgages simply because the longer remaining life means that the borrower pays an above-market coupon for longer when rates are low. At extremely favourable conditions, all three bonds prepay as fast as possible. At very high refinancing rates, meanwhile, none of these mortgages prepays and so all three mortalities converge to zero.

Having discussed prepayment models, it is time to turn to the valuation aspect of prepayments implied by these models. Simply speaking, prepayment means that an investor in an RMBS receives less cash faster than scheduled. The decline in total cash is the result of a loss of future interest payments on the part of the principal that has been repaid early. This principal, meanwhile, is being repaid ahead of schedule. These two effects have an opposing impact on the value of the mortgage because an earlier payment has (at positive interest rates) a higher present value than a later one. The purpose of a valuation model is to calculate the combined impact of these two effects.

Figure 27.4 compares the expected cashflows from the same mortgage under different rate assumptions. When market mortgage rates are very high, then no prepayment occurs and the expected cashflow structure matches the regular annuity that follows from the mortgage formula Equation (16.1) on page 141. When refinancing is attractive, prepayments add to the early cashflows while later cashflows are lower because the mortgage pool is then smaller than it is at the beginning as a result of prepayments.

Figure 27.4 shows only the next 20 cash flows. To value the mortgage, all subsequent cashflows need to be taken into account. This is done in Figure 27.5 which shows the simple sum of all cash expected from the mortage together with two sample discount factors, all as a function of the interest rate level. At very low rate levels, the mortgage prepays as fast as possible and the total cash received is essentially the remaining principal plus the next few coupons. At very high rate levels, the total cash paid converges

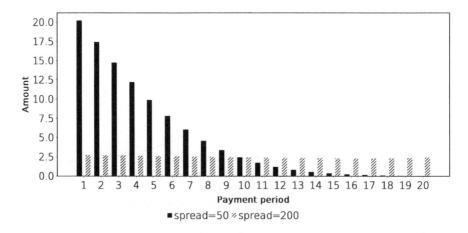

FIGURE 27.4 Total cashflows (interest, amortisation and prepayment) from the 2040 sample quarterly mortgage over the next five years (20 quarters) for different spreads. At a spread of 200, practically no prepayment occurs and the cashflow structure is simply the scheduled annuity. At a spread of 50, the mortgage prepays very fast.

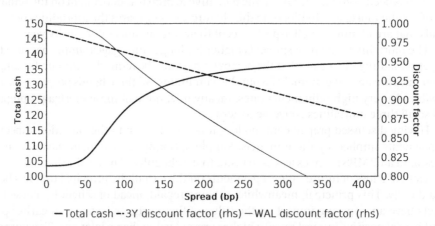

FIGURE 27.5 Total cash paid (as a fraction of the remaining principal) by a mortgage as a function of refinancing conditions, and two discount factors. The first has a fixed maturity of three years, the second has a maturity equal to the weighted average life of the mortgage.

to the sum of all scheduled payments because no early redemptions occur. Put differently, at high interest rates all the interest payments originally scheduled actually take place. The lower the interest rate, the more borrowers will refinance and their future interest payments will then go to the holders of the new mortgages that were originated for refinancing.

This figure shows that the non-linear shape of the mortality function Equation (27.2) means that the spread dependency of the cash payable and the discount factors are different. The slope of the cash amount is steepest where the prepayment option is most at the money which in this model is around the 80 bps spread level. At high

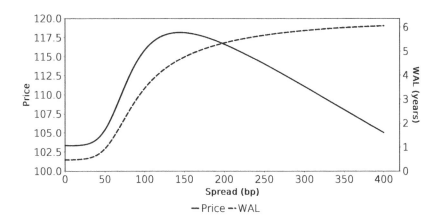

FIGURE 27.6   Price-yield (here, price-spread) relationship of a prepayable mortgage. The weighted average life of the cashflows is added for illustration.

rate levels, prepayments are more or less irrelevant and the amount of cash received converges to a constant. The discount factors, meanwhile, have the usual bond-like price-yield relationship. As a result, the total value of the mortgage is very sensitive to prepayment speeds where those speeds vary most, whereas it is more sensitive to discounting at higher rates. The figure also shows another effect. As prepayments decline, more of the cash is paid later, and therefore subject to discounting over longer periods than when prepayments are higher. To measure this extension, the figure uses the weighted average life (WAL) defined as:

$$\mathrm{WAL} = \frac{\sum_i CF_i t_i}{\sum_i CF_i} \tag{27.3}$$

The extension of payments in time happens when interest rates rise, so the cash flows from the mortgage have to be discounted over longer periods at higher rates. The discount factor applicable to the weighted average life of the mortgage therefore declines faster than than a constant-maturity discount factor as rates rise.

The end result of this analysis is the price-yield relationship shown in Figure 27.6. Unlike a standard bond, the price of this mortgage initially increases with rising yields because prepayments become less likely and the mortgage holders therefore receive more interest payments. This decline in prepayments is also leading to an increase in the weighted average life of the mortgage. Only at high yield levels, where prepayments are no longer relevant, and the weighted average life stabilises, does the mortgage behave like a normal bond and declines in price as a result of falling discount factors.

A rising price for a rising yield implies a negative duration, so in this example, the mortgage duration is negative up to a spread of around 140 bps. Around this spread level, duration increases from the initial negative value to a bond-like positive one as yields rise. A rising duration for rising yields implies negative convexity. To achieve a bond-like behaviour for a mortgage portfolio, portfolio managers have to buy and sell duration risk in response to yield movements on an ongoing basis. The standard duration instrument in the US market is the on-the-run Treasury and hedge activity in this bond is an important source of liquidity in this security.

The negative convexity of the US, and also the Danish, mortgage market is a reflection of the prepayment option that the RMBS and Danish mortgage market has written for mortgage borrowers. The trading required to hedge mortgage convexity is equivalent to the trading required to hedge any other short option position. What is unique to the mortgage market is the size of this options position and that the long side of this option is being held by ordinary households. Unlike options traded between financial market participants, this rules out one particular hedge for an option seller, namely to repurchase the option from the buyer.

In general, it should be noted that while the graphical examples here are based on a realistic prepayment model, they do not span the full universe of effects that can occur in RMBS. In particular, the relative impact of having more cash to discount as a result of lower prepayments, and the lower present value of future cash flows, depends on the baseline yield level and curve steepness which are very low at the time of writing. This current yield configuration emphasises the hump of the price-yield relationship.

Derivatives

CHAPTER 28

Bond Futures

28.1 INTRODUCTION

Traditional bond futures are exchange traded contracts where the seller (the short) commits to deliver a given notional amount of a bond out of a certain basket to the exchange and the buyer commits to buy such a bond from the exchange at a specified time. The notional amount to be delivered per futures contract is a fixed quantity, such as 100,000 euros or 100,000,000 yen. Most bond futures contracts are settled through the actual delivery of a bond, hence they are examples of physically settled contracts. This transaction is executed at a price that is given by the final trading price of the contract and a conversion factor that is specific to each bond in each contract. The invoice price for a bond on delivery is given as:

$$[\text{Invoice price}] = [\text{Futures price}] * [\text{Conversion factor}] + [\text{Accrued interest}] \quad (28.1)$$

There are bond futures contracts that are not settled by physical delivery but by simply closing out long and short positions through a cash payment calculated with reference to the yields of the bonds in the deliverable basket. Such cash-settled contracts usually follow a pricing formula such as:

$$\text{EDSP} = 100 - 100 * \sum_i w_i y_i \quad (28.2)$$

where w_i are the fixed weights and y_i the yields on the final trading day of each bond i in the deliverable basket, respectively. The EDSP (short for exchange-determined settlement price) determined the close-out price of the contract.

For both physical and cash settlement, the equivalence of contract and bond market at one point in time is the crucial link between futures contract and underlying market during the entire life of the contract.

The open interest is the total number of long positions in a contract which by definition is equal to the total number of short positions. On some exchanges, including Eurex, it is possible for a trader to hold both long and short positions in the same contract at the same time. This can happen for instance by first selling, and then buying back the same contract but not netting out the resulting position. When netting is not automatic, or implemented with a delay, the open interest will overstate the actual risk held in the contracts.

The motivation to trade futures contracts is that they are usually more liquid than actual bonds. Simply speaking, there are many bonds but only a few futures contracts, so trading in each of the contracts is more active. In the US, where trading in bonds is focused on only a few on-the-run issues, futures can be less liquid than those benchmark bonds. In some markets, such as the market for Japanese government bonds, there are other restrictions, such as taxation or reporting requirements, that cause some investors to use futures contracts instead of bonds to gain exposure to that market. In the bond market, the expression 'cash market' usually refers to physical bonds, as opposed to the futures markets.

The majority of bond futures contracts are designed to settle through physical delivery. Delivery can occur at any time during the delivery period. In the case of the older bond futures contracts (US and UK), the delivery period is an entire month. Newer contracts (those on Eurex and in Japan) have a single delivery day. Before delivery, the short in the contract notifies the clearing house of the exchange of the intended delivery and the delivered bond is then assigned to one or more long positions. The event of notification has implications for risk management, detailed below.

Physical delivery is also to some degree the default mode of exchange-traded contracts, dating back to the Osaka rice exchange. This settlement approach has a drawback related to surprising instances of insufficiently available supply in the deliverable bonds. Open interest for the most commonly used bond futures contracts tends to be equivalent to a bond volume that far exceeds the available supply of the bond that is most economical to deliver, or even the entire deliverable basket. Contract users relying on the simple cash-and-carry arbitrage to value and risk-manage futures positions therefore face risks related to the delivery mechanism. For many users, however, the actual delivery mechanics have no bearing on the purpose they used the contracts for. Indeed, the vast majority of contracts is closed out before delivery, usually by rolling the exposure into the following expiry (the futures roll is described below).

These difficulties do not arise in cash-settled futures. Whether this makes cash settlement a better design is, however, a complex question.

Physical settlement has a built-in deterrent of attempts to push the contract valuations to extremes. Assume a trader who is long the contract and pushes the price above its intrinsic value to increase the value of the position. The rest of the market can simply react by delivering the CTD to that trader who will end up owning this bond, potentially to maturity, at an inflated entry price. Conversely, a trader pushing the contract price down to support a short position might find that the market asks for delivery of the CTD at an artificially low price. Physical delivery, in other words, means that the economic lifetime of the contract does not end with delivery. Physical delivery simply exchanges the futures contract with a physical asset at a valuation determined by the final contract price. The future development of the price of this physical asset can cause problems for those looking to manipulate the futures contract. This being said, the increased cost of managing bond portfolios under more recent regulation also makes it more expensive for the market to actually implement the trades that act as deterrents to price manipulation of physically settled contracts.

Cash-settled contracts, in contrast, provide a clean exit from the contract life-cycle at delivery. While this eliminates the risk of insufficient availability of deliverable bonds, one of the lessons of the financial crisis is that this finality may be problematic. All Libor futures and FRAs are by definition cash-settled contracts, as are the floating rate resets of interest rate swaps. From the public information available from court cases surrounding the Libor issue, some traders allegedly manipulated the Libor fixings in order to move such cash-settled contracts in their favour on the days when contracts they held were expiring. The absence of any direct link of such derivatives to physical assets, such as a deposit with another bank at Libor, arguably reduces the hurdles to such behaviour. Better policing of the way in which reference rates are being set may reduce this problem of cash settlement but it will not eliminate it. For instance, a trader may be willing to make a deposit at an off-market rate in order to shift the fixing of a transaction-based deposit rate benchmark if the size of that deposit is small compared to the derivatives contracts held by the same trader that expire linked to the benchmark.

New information and changes in market composition will continue to change the relative merits of physical and cash settlement. At the same time, it is very difficult to create new futures contracts and attract sufficient trading interest to generate a deep and liquid market in them. For this reason, even somewhat sub-optimal contract designs can remain in use for a long time. Occasional squeezes in physically delivered bond contracts have not reduced the interest in them, just as manipulated fixings have not reduced the interest in trading cash-settled contracts on money market rates.

28.2 FUTURES TRADING PATTERNS

28.2.1 Open interest and trading volume

Exchanges widely publish aggregate activity measures for the contracts that they offer. Market participants use these to judge the liquidity, and thereby the suitability for hedging and trading, of a given contract. In addition, changes in trading activity can signal changes in investor attitudes. The two measures used are open interest (the total number of long positions which is equal to the total number of short positions) and volume (the number of contracts traded in a given period of time).

It should be noted that open interest figures are not easily comparable across exchanges. On a very basic level, contracts have different sizes. The JPX JGB contracts are for JPY 100 million notional while the German and US bond contracts are for 100,000 euros or dollars, respectively. At current exchange rates, this makes a single JGB contract around ten times larger in value terms than an equivalent US contract. Second, exchanges have different rules for the netting of exposures which are related to their clearing models. US exchanges, which typically operate on an agency clearing model, tend to automatically net long and short positions of the same end users so that a user is either long or short. European exchanges operating under the principal clearing model do not have the required information to do so reliably and may choose to permit the simultaneous existence of long and short positions in the same contract for the same account. This inflates the open interest figures and the degree to which this happens is related to the total amount of trading that takes place from the point in time when a contract is listed[1]. Open interest figures are usually available only with a delay of one or two business days while trading volume can be observed in real time.

Some market analysts closely watch changes in open interest to gauge changes in directional trading interest in the market. For instance, when open interest increases while contract prices fall, one could argue that new risk positions were established through selling of contracts, and that this represents an increase in short positions. Conversely, a decline in open interest in a falling price environment could signal a closing-out of long positions, and so on. While this type of argument sounds compelling enough at first, there are some problems. First, by construction, there is a long position for every short position. The market as a whole is therefore always neutrally positioned, and long or short positioning can at most refer to investors with a greater or lesser risk capacity[2]. Second, open interest is reported daily and market direction can change during a trading day. For instance, if prices fall in the morning, but then rise in the afternoon, any change in open interest during the day could have occurred during the price decline or increase. Using day-on-day price changes and day-on-day changes in open volume not only makes the assumptions outlined above between position changes and market moves, but additionally adds the assumption that the relationship between position changes and price moves is strictly linear. Third, futures contracts are hedge instruments for underlying markets. Even if it were true that higher open interest on a given day with price declines is the result of a new short position in the contract, this short position may be the hedge of a long position in bonds or swaps. It would therefore not have any signalling effect on overall market direction. Fourth, open interest has some seasonality related to roll activity, as further outlined below. One should therefore generally not base directional assumptions on open interest figures. Increasing open interest and volume signals more activity but, because each contract seller requires a contract buyer, the driver of that increased activity is not always clear.

Trading activity has a seasonal pattern related to futures rolls. Contracts only exceptionally go through to delivery and positions are instead rolled from the front contract into the back contract before delivery. Most exchanges have mechanisms that let traders execute rolls, i.e., simultaneous buying of the front contract, and selling of the back contract, in a single transaction. Where this is not desirable or possible, a roll can be 'legged', which means that a trader attempts to execute the two trades separately in a short period of time[3]. The roll activity can be seen in the evolution of open interest in the two contracts, as shown on two examples in Figure 28.1. The open interest in the back contract tends to increase some time before delivery and this process appears to be happening systematically earlier for the CBOT contract. As the back contract open interest increases, the front contract open interest declines. Note that at delivery, the

---

[1]Unkind minds might suggest that an exchange has an interest to report higher open interest figures given that some market participants views these as a sign of higher activity and better liquidity.

[2]In the US market, where the CFTC provides a breakdown of open interest by investor type, perhaps such differentiation could be analysed. See Section 28.2.2 on page 307 for more discussion of this topic.

[3]'Legging it' in some parts of London means 'running'.

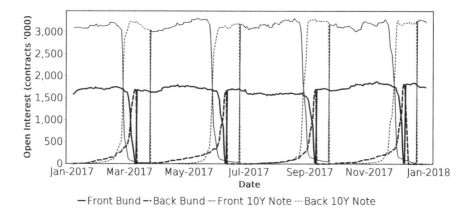

FIGURE 28.1 Open interest for the front and back contracts during 2017 for the Eurex Bund and CBOT 10Y Note contracts. Sources: Data from Eurex and CBOT.

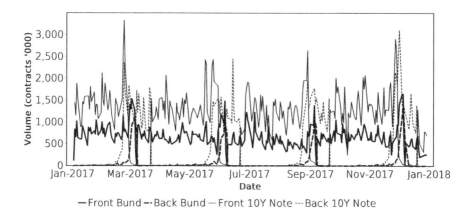

FIGURE 28.2 Daily trading volumes for the front and back contracts during 2017 for the Eurex Bund and CBOT 10Y Note contracts. Sources: Data from Eurex and CBOT.

erstwhile back contract becomes the front contract which explains the jumps in front contract open interest in this chart.

Because rolling is itself a trading activity, total trading volume and, to a lesser extent, total open interest tend to spike during the roll period without there being any associated change in market risk sentiment. As Figure 28.2 shows, both front and back contracts become more active during the roll period, and this increase in activity is particularly pronounced for the back contract which rarely trades ahead of the roll. Exchanges generally publish total trading volume for all expiries and these figures show large spikes before delivery.

One way to construct volume series that are adjusted for roll activity is to consider that a roll trade creates one trade each in the front and back contracts while any outright trade will only generate a single trade in the active contract. This means that the

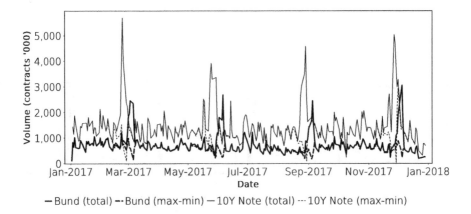

FIGURE 28.3 Daily trading volumes (totals and maximum-minimum measures) for the Eurex Bund and CBOT 10Y Note contracts. Sources: Data from Eurex and CBOT.

better measure of activity is the *difference* between the daily volumes in the front and back contract, at least as long as the whole market considers the same contract as active for each day. Because it is not clear whether the front or the back contract is the most active, one can simply subtract the smaller of the two volumes from the larger of the two. Figure 28.3 shows that this difference measure does avoid the spikes around delivery that appear in the total volume figures. This measure underestimates activity when both back and front contracts are used for outright trading, which happens when market participants differ in the timing of their roll activity.

Future roll activity can to some extent be predicted based on historical patterns. Some investor types, particularly futures specialists known as commodity trading advisors (CTAs) tend not to hold futures contracts when it could be possible that they would have to take or make delivery. They therefore execute their rolls before the start of a

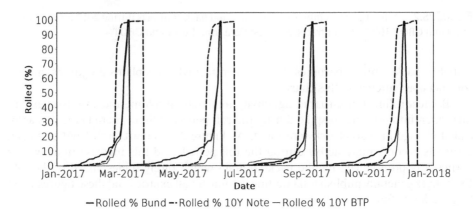

FIGURE 28.4 Roll progress histories for the Eurex Bund and 10Y BTP and CBOT 10Y Note contracts. Sources: Data from Eurex and CBOT.

delivery window. Monitoring the progress of the roll provides a gauge of how much there is still left to do. The standard way to monitor rolls is to calculate the share of back contract open interest in the total open interest, as in Figure 28.4. This chart shows that there are clear differences in behaviour between different contracts. Note that US contracts can be delivered on any good business day during the delivery month while the Eurex and JPX JGB contracts have only a single delivery day. This means that a CTA would have to have closed out front contract positions before the expiry month of a US contract to rule out having to take delivery. Further, the somewhat less active BTP contract on Eurex appears to be typically rolled later in the delivery cycle. It should be noted that this observation could partly be explained by the overstating of back contract open interest due to the absence of netting as mentioned above.

28.2.2 CFTC data for US futures contracts

The US market is peculiar in having a public system of position reporting by investor type. The Commodity Futures Trading Commission collects and published on its website weekly data on open futures positions. It is therefore possible to some extent to analyse the behaviour of some major investor classes in the market.

Some caveats should be borne in mind, however. Investors are broken down into four classes ('Dealer', 'Asset Managers', 'Leveraged Money', and 'Others') and reporting is by contract, but not by expiry. The data is published with a lag of about one week and does not cover all positions (adjustment series for 'non-reported' positions are part of the publication). From Figure 28.5 it is visible that the identified investor classes comprise between 35 and 45% of the total open interest in the 10Y note future used here as an example.

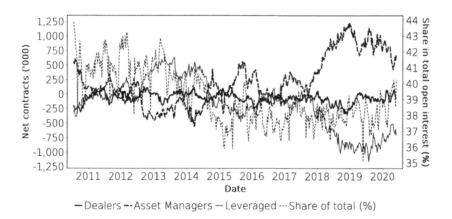

FIGURE 28.5 CFTC net positions (long minus short) in the CBOT 10Y note futures contract over time for three investor types. The thin dotted line, plotted against the right axis, shows the share of these positions in the total open interest (calculated as all longs plus all shorts of these three investor classes divided by the sum of all longs and all shorts). Source: From CFTC.

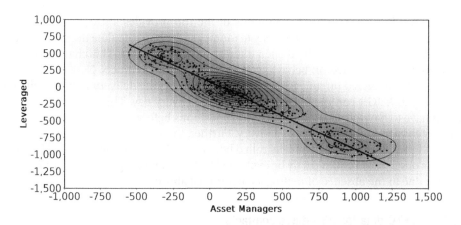

FIGURE 28.6   CFTC net positions (long minus short, in thousands of contracts) for Asset Managers and Leveraged Money in the 10Y note contract. Data period 2010–2019. Source: From CFTC.

Several details of these series are interesting. The net position of dealers is not uniformly short as would be expected in other markets (Europe and Japan), and it is indeed marginally long on average over the history shown here. Given that the default position of a European or Japanese dealer is to own bond inventory and sell futures to hedge this inventory, dealers should not normally have a net long position in futures contracts. In the US market, however, the on-the-run Treasury bonds are so liquid that they are used for inventory hedges to a much larger degree than in other markets. As will be explained further below, an additional factor may be misclassification in the split between dealers and speculators in the sense that some speculators are actually acting like dealers. Equally, the observation that asset managers are sometimes significantly short implies that futures contracts are not only used for the reduction of cash drag.

Despite the caveats of the CFTC data, the 'Leveraged money' (often called 'Speculators') series attracts some attention as a guide to future market developments. Market analysts are perennially looking for the 'pain trade' which is the speculative position that is crowded and therefore at risk of a fast unwind when prices move against it. The problem with using the CFTC series for this purpose is that the 'Speculators' position is not necessarily driven by active speculation.

Figure 28.6 demonstrates that the 'speculators' positioning follows more or less inversely the positioning of the asset managers. It is therefore conceivable that some speculators act as a bridge between the cash market and the futures market, i.e., provide liquidity in the futures basis.

This observation could also explain the developments in the US Treasury market during the well-publicised spike in repo funding rates in September 2019. This spike in rates occurred despite a significant level of liquidity[4] in the system, which meant

---

[4]Liquidity is here used in the European sense of current account holdings at the central bank. In the US, the term 'reserves' is used for the same concept.

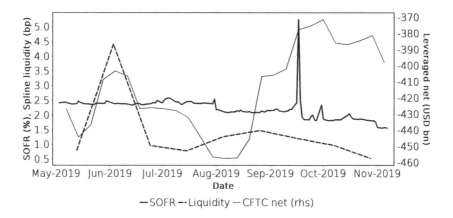

FIGURE 28.7 SOFR and CFTC positioning (speculator net positions across all US Treasury contracts) and US Treasury market liquidity (cf. Figure 18.3). Sources: Data from CFTC, TreasuryDirect, Federal Reserve Bank of New York.

that the Federal Reserve System waited one day before conducting liquidity-providing operations to address the funding stress. In essence, the spike in repo rates can be seen as the result of a demand for funds in the repo market that came from market participants outside the purview of the supervision exercised by the Federal Reserve. A good candidate group of participants is the so-called principal trading firms (PTFs) who are financial firms that trade for their own account on various trading platforms. PTFs usually hold themselves out as liquidity providers and post quotes on electronic platforms. PTFs can trade high volumes even with little of their own capital because the counterparty risk in Treasury trading is mitigated through central clearing and and very short settlement cycles. PTFs could be using US Treasury futures contracts for hedging just like dealers in other jurisdictions, but because they are not classified as dealers for CFTC purposes, these hedges show up as net shorts in the speculative positions.

Position funding for PTF takes place in the repo market, and increasingly via sponsored access clearing on FICC which limits the visibility of this funding for the Fed. In this setting, funding stresses in the repo market can have spill-overs into the market for US Treasuries because a given class of market makers, the PTFs, find it harder to operate.

Conversely, stresses in the funding market may manifest themselves in the liquidity of US Treasuries before they show up as spikes in repo funding rates. If this assumption is correct, then the spike in SOFR on 16 September 2019, which was followed by Fed liquidity injections from 17 September, was merely the climax of a deterioration in market conditions that started earlier in September and manifested itself in reduced hedge volumes in the futures contracts and more variability in US Treasury spline spreads. It should be noted, however, that the reduction in CFTC short positions over the course of was equivalent to USD 35bn while the size of Fed operations was significantly higher, namely USD 75bn initially, rising to over USD 250bn by the end of October. The PTF connection can therefore only be one part of the total picture.

28.3 VALUATION OF PHYSICALLY DELIVERED BOND FUTURES

Because a futures contract establishes the obligation to deliver a bond at a given point in time, at that point the contract and the bond that will get delivered are identical in economic terms. Out of a basket of bonds, usually one issue is most economical to deliver and this issue is called the cheapest to deliver (CTD). The sellers (shorts) of the contract can select which issue to deliver, so they will usually deliver the CTD. The convergence in value of the CTD and the contract is the essential feature of a futures contract. Only because of this convergence is there a pricing relationship between the futures contract and the bond market. Without such a relationship, futures would not be a useful hedge instrument.

A corollary of the requirement that CTD and futures contracts converge at the point of delivery is that there must be a well-determined relationship between the spot price of any deliverable bond and its forward price for the delivery period. This means that there must be a deep and liquid repo market in order for a futures market to exist. Put differently, a futures contract will fail to attract genuine trading interest unless there is an existing and working repo market for the underlying bonds. An example for such a failure was the Eurex medium-term Euro-Jumbo Pfandbrief contract launched in June 1999.

28.3.1 Basis and implied repo rate

There are three ways to express the difference in the current valuation of a futures contract and the underlying bonds, namely gross basis, net basis and implied repo rate. All three measures can be transformed into each other using market information, so they represent the same information in different ways. Which representation is the most appropriate depends on the application. These quantities are introduced first in schematic fashion and the exact mathematics will be delivered later.

The gross basis is the difference in price between a given bond and the price implied by the futures contract and it is calculated as:

$$[\text{Gross Basis}] = [\text{Spot clean price}] - [\text{Conversion factor}] * [\text{Futures price}] \quad (28.3)$$

Because the contract and the bonds both move with interest rates and in the same direction, the gross basis is a lot more stable than bond prices or futures prices themselves. The expression basis is also used for a combination of bond and future that is traded in a single transaction[5]. In line with the signs in Equation (28.3), 'buying the basis' means buying the bond and selling the equivalent number of futures contract while 'selling the basis' means selling the bond and buying the future[6].

---

[5]In practice, the two counterparties agree on the basis trade and then settle the bond leg in the usual way while the futures leg of the trade is given up to the futures exchange ('crossed' on the exchange), bypassing the public order book.

[6]A helpful mnemonic device for this sign convention is that bond and basis start with the same letter.

The gross basis of deliverable bonds is traded very actively and at relatively low bid–offer spreads. The high liquidity arises from the very low directional interest rate risk that is contained in a basis trade. It has become quite common in the European bond market to define conversion factors even for non-deliverable bonds so that basis trades can take place even for those securities. Such conversion factors are usually calculated using linear regression, rather than the exchange-defined formulas discussed earlier.

The futures price reflects the price to be paid for a bond on delivery date, i.e., a date in the future, so the gross basis contains an element of carry between the spot settlement date and the futures delivery date. Replacing the spot cash price in Equation (28.3) with the forward price of the relevant bond to delivery, gives the net basis:

$$[\text{Net Basis}] = [\text{Forward clean price}] - [\text{Conversion factor}] * [\text{Futures price}] \quad (28.4)$$

From this definition follows:

$$[\text{Net basis}] = [\text{Gross basis}] - [\text{Carry}] \quad (28.5)$$

The net basis of the cheapest to deliver (CTD) issue is usually very close to zero, at least when the CTD is relatively clear. This is because the market prices the spot price and the repo rate with the assumption that the CTD will get delivered and will therefore be equivalent to the contract on that forward date. On delivery day, net and gross basis are identical and reflect the profit or loss from delivering a bond into a short futures position. This profit or loss should be zero for the CTD, while delivering a different bond should lead to a loss equal to the net basis of that bond[7]. This provides a way to calculate the fair value of a futures contract, called the cash-and-carry arbitrage, explained below.

The third quantity expressing the relationship between futures price and bond prices is the implied repo rate (IRR). This repo rate is the financing rate that makes the net basis zero. In other words, it is given by solving the equation:

$$[\text{Carry}([\text{repo rate}])] = [\text{Spot clean price}] - [\text{Conversion factor}] * [\text{Futures price}]$$
$$(28.6)$$

for the repo rate. The intuitive interpretation of the implied repo rate is that it is the financing cost at which one can buy the relevant bond against the futures contract and later go into delivery without making any profit or loss. There is no reason why the implied repo rate of any given bond should be related to actual market repo rates and implied repo rates can have large negative values. The implied repo rate of the CTD is usually very close to the actual market repo rate while the other deliverable bonds have lower implied repo rates than their market repo rates. Intuitively, this expresses the same information as the net basis. A positive net basis means that with current prices and repo rates it would be uneconomical to deliver that bond. The implied repo rate shows where the repo rate would have to be to eradicate that loss while the net basis

---

[7]Note that physical delivery means that technical factors can influence the actual performance of this strategy. This is explained in more detail in the section on futures squeezes.

shows how much the spot price would have to move relative to the futures contract to achieve the same effect.

In the US market, where special repo rates for deliverable bonds do not move too much, it is quite common to use the implied repo rate as an indicator of CTD status and to call the bond with the highest implied repo rate the CTD [18]. This indirect argument can be misleading, however, and is frequently wrong in the euro area bond markets where CTDs can trade at very special repo rates.

28.3.2   Conversion factors and the notional coupon

So far, conversion factors were presented as abstract numbers but it is now time to explain them in more detail. The motivation to introduce conversion factors becomes clear if one sets the conversion factor for each bond in Equation (28.8) to 1. The futures price would then be a simple clean price and the bond with the lowest cash price at delivery would be the CTD. This would usually be the bond with the lowest coupon. In other words, the futures contract would in most cases be simply a forward contract on the deliverable bond with the lowest coupon. Such a situation is unsatisfactory because it negates the purpose of having a deliverable basket of bonds. At least in principle, all deliverable bonds in the basket should have some chance of getting delivered so that their pricing interacts with that of the contract.

Simply speaking, conversion factors are the mechanism to equalise bond prices in relation to the futures contract to make it more likely that multiple bonds are similarly economical to be delivered.

This aim is achieved by setting the conversion factor of a bond equal to the clean price the bond would have if it traded at a particular yield on the delivery day of the contract. Unfortunately, this particular yield is called the notional coupon of the contract, which causes a lot of confusion.

Starting on a more mathematical treatment of the futures contracts, one defines the conversion factor c_{i,t_D} of bond i in the basket of a contract with delivery date t_D and notional coupon C as:

$$c_{i,t_D} = \sum_k \frac{Cf_{i,k}}{(1+C)^{DCF(t_D, t_{i,k})}} - A_i(t_D) \tag{28.7}$$

which is nothing but Equation (16.10) using C instead of the yield[8].

One can then write the invoice price I_{i,t_D} from Equation (28.1) using the futures price F as:

$$I_{i,t_D} = Fc_{i,t_D} + A_i(t_D) \tag{28.8}$$

to find that if one inserts Equation (28.7) into this equation it becomes:

$$I_{i,t_D} = F\left[\sum_k \frac{Cf_{i,k}}{(1+C)^{DCF(t_D, t_{i,k})}} - A_i(t_D)\right] + A_i(t_D) \tag{28.9}$$

---

[8]Each futures exchange publishes its own specific formula for Equation (28.7) which may take account of local yield conventions, etc.

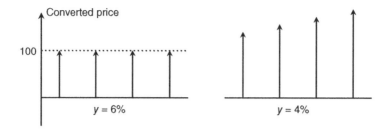

FIGURE 28.8 Behaviour of converted bond prices under a parallel downwards yield shift. The sample shows four bonds in the deliverable basket with different durations. The price of the bond with the lowest duration will react least to the yield shift, making it more likely to be CTD.

This equation becomes interesting when all bonds are in fact trading at a yield of C so that their invoice prices are equal to their market prices. One then finds

$$\sum_k \frac{Cf_{i,k}}{(1+C)^{DCF(t_D,t_{i,k})}} = F\left[\sum_k \frac{Cf_{i,k}}{(1+C)^{DCF(t_D,t_{i,k})}} - A_i(t_D)\right] + A_i(t_D) \qquad (28.10)$$

This equation permits only one solution, namely $F = 1$. In other words, if all deliverable bonds were trading at a yield equal to the notional coupon, the futures contract would be trading at a price of 100 (futures contracts are quoted in percent of notional just as bonds) and all deliverable bonds would be equally CTD. A bond would be more likely to be CTD if its forward price was below that of other bonds, i.e., the CTD status would indeed be associated with relative cheapness of a particular issue, not its coupon or other details. This is precisely the purpose of conversion factors.

However, the assumption that bond yields are always close to the notional coupon is not necessarily true and indeed not true for most contracts. Notional coupons on the world's main bond contracts are 6% and market yield levels are below this level. This has an impact on the CTD status of the bonds in the basket as shown in Figure 28.8. The left hand side shows the converted forward price, i.e., the forward price divided by conversion factor, of each of four bonds in a hypothetical basket under the assumption that the forward yields are equal to the notional coupon. In this situation, the future trades at 100 and all bonds are equal CTD.

The right hand side shows the same four bonds after a parallel downmove in yields. Intuitively, they are still equally expensive because they still trade at the same yield. However, they are no longer equal CTD because their prices have moved by different amounts but the conversion factors are still the same. The bonds with the highest duration will move most in price and therefore the bonds with the lowest duration are cheaper to deliver. When yields move down, therefore, low duration bonds are more likely to be CTD than higher duration bonds.

As mentioned above, the European market quotes bases for bonds that are not actually deliverable and therefore have no conversion factor as such. Instead of using the same Equation (28.7), which is of course valid for any bond regardless of deliverability, the market convention is to use a regression analysis to find the price sensitivity of the bond relative to the future. This means solving the regression equation:

$$P^{bond} = \alpha + \beta P_F \tag{28.11}$$

and using β as the conversion factor. Because bases are only comparable through time if the conversion factors stay constant[9], the time window across which the regression is run is usually fixed, often to some period before the futures contract becomes the front contract so the conversion factors can be used from the start of active trading in the contract. This procedure is not ideal because the regression β is not very stable, in particular because the liquidity of the futures contract during the time when the regression data is sampled is not very high. However, the procedure can easily be executed using just market data and avoids the necessity of conducting the analytical calculation outlined above.

28.3.3 The cash-and-carry arbitrage

The cash-and-carry arbitrage is the theoretical trading strategy that links the calculations done so far with actual market prices and repo rates. The strategy consists of buying a deliverable bond, selling an equal notional of bond futures against it, financing the bond in the repo market, and delivering the bond into the short futures position at expiry of the contract. Delivery is economically equivalent to selling the gross basis (which on delivery day is equal to the net basis) at zero, so the cash-and-carry arbitrage will break even only for zero net basis.

However, the strategy is the starting point for futures contract analysis and in particular for the valuation of the future relative to the cash bond prices. The standard way to do this is a so-called basis sheet which takes the deliverable basket of a contract together with all pricing data and calculates the necessary forwards. A sample basis sheet is shown in Table 28.1.

The sample shows an interesting point: The range of converted forward prices (106.554 to 106.946) is narrower than the range of spot prices (99.363 to 100.249). This is precisely the effect that conversion factors are there to achieve, namely to bring the deliverable issues closer in price relative to the future. The bonds shown here have very similar coupons and the effect of the conversion factors would be stronger for a wider coupon range.

For the purposes of a fair value calculation of the futures price, one would use the converted forward price of the CTD. This is the price at which one could sell the future today, buy the CTD bond at today's cash price, lend it out for financing at the specific repo rate, and go to delivery.

As will be discussed in more detail later, there are practical caveats to this calculation. The repo rates quoted for 'term' in the repo market are usually for bond lending until after the delivery. This means that a trader who obtains financing in a repo contract to 'term' will not have the bond available for delivery and therefore will fail towards the exchange. Even if the bond is lent out to just before delivery, a trader engaging in

---

[9]Equation (28.7) provides this because the spot settlement date does not enter the calculation.

TABLE 28.1   Sample basis sheet analysing a fictitious bond futures contract modelled on the Eurex contracts. CF stands for conversion factor, CFP for converted forward price (forward price divided by conversion factor), NBasis for net basis. The interest rate levels in this example are very far from actual interest rates on the analysis date.

Analysis date:	14 Apr 2020
Settlement date:	16 Apr 2020
Delivery date:	10 Jun 2020
Notional coupon:	6.0%
Futures close:	106.573
Fair value:	106.553
Quality option (cts):	0.2
Contract PVBP:	7.771

Bond	Price	Yield	Repo	CF	CFP	NBasis
D 4.875% 01/29	99.446	4.950	2.00	0.925874	106.946	36.3
D 5% 07/29	99.904	5.010	2.00	0.931507	106.781	21.1
D 5% 01/30	99.363	5.080	2.00	0.928327	106.554	0.0
D 5.125% 07/30	100.249	5.090	2.00	0.935186	106.711	14.6

cash-and-carry arbitrage faces the risk that the repo counterparty does not return the bond in time. Taking the arbitrage calculations shown here at face value is therefore not without risks. The structure of this chapter will therefore be to start from the simple concept of pure arbitrage and then introduce the deviations that arise from various features that deviate from an ideal market.

28.3.4   The quality option

In principle, it is unclear what bond will be cheapest to deliver at the time a bond future expires. If there can be a change in the CTD, it may be profitable to sell the contract and buy the current CTD. If the CTD changes, one can then sell that bond and instead deliver the new, now cheaper to deliver, issue.

The existence of this trading strategy means that the futures contract is less attractive to hold than the CTD. Therefore, the fair value of the CTD net basis should be slightly positive. In other words, the future should be slightly cheaper than the converted forward price of the CTD. This is equivalent to an option premium and this option is called the quality option[10].

Because conversion factors only partially compensate for differences in bond details (maturity date and coupon rate), and large shifts in yields have the effect on net bases

---

[10]This may not be an obvious name for the right to choose between bonds that are basically identical in quality. However, the name is carried over from commodity contracts where there are important economic differences between different varieties of deliverable products, such as lean hogs. In these markets, conversion factors or add-ons are applied to different grades of deliverable products in order to reduce the arbitrage opportunities between differing product grades.

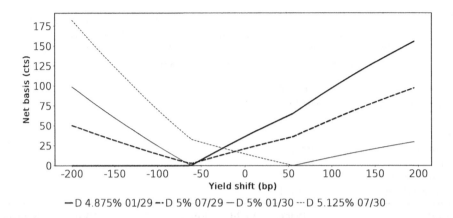

FIGURE 28.9 Net bases (in cents) of the deliverable bonds in a futures basket as a function of parallel yield shifts.

outlined in Figure 28.8 on page 313, the quality option is reflected in an option-like pay-off structure of net bases shown for an example in Figure 28.9.

At low yields, the CTD status is being pushed to the lowest duration bond, so that the net basis of this bond looks like a call option on yields (or, equivalently, a put option on bond prices). At high yields, the CTD status shifts to the highest duration bonds so that the net basis of that bond appears like a put option on yields. The net bases of the two bonds with intermediate durations look like straddles.

Because every net basis has the pay-off of an option, the net basis of any bond must in theory always be strictly positive, i.e., larger than zero. In practice, the probability of a yield shift induced CTD switch may be so small that its value is close enough to zero not to be tradeable. In this case, the net basis of the CTD is zero and that is indeed how the fair value of futures contracts is calculated by many market participants. Note also that, when there is a perceived risk of delivery failure, the net basis of the CTD can be negative. The section on squeezes below explains this in more detail.

Because the quality option embedded in a future has itself an interest rate sensitivity, the total interest rate sensitivity of the future can have interesting properties. This is relevant for hedging with futures and will be discussed in the next section.

28.3.5 Hedging with futures

The high liquidity of bond futures contracts in most markets makes them an ideal hedge instrument. To construct a hedge for a given bond means to find the number of futures contracts that provides the same, but opposite exposure to interest rate movements. Assuming that there is a single yield y that drives the movements in price of both the bond and the future, this means finding the number λ so that:

$$N\frac{\partial P}{\partial y} = \lambda N_F \frac{\partial F}{\partial y} \tag{28.12}$$

Here, N_F is the notional amount of the futures contract.

The bond's sensitivity to yield changes is given by the PVBP of the bond. So far, however, it is not clear what the interest rate sensitivity of the futures contract price F is, because a futures contract does not have a yield. The essence of this section is therefore to discuss the calculation of the PVBP of a futures contract.

If there is a clear CTD situation, the futures contract is a simple forward contract on the bond, so one can try to extract the future's price sensitivity from information about the CTD. It is possible to calculate the sensitivity of the forward price of the CTD with respect to changes in the forward yield on the delivery date, i.e., one can calculate the quantity:

$$PVBP_f^{CTD} = \frac{\partial P_f^{CTD}}{\partial y_f^{CTD}} \tag{28.13}$$

for the CTD forward price and yield. In a clear CTD situation, the futures price is given by:

$$F = \frac{P_f^{CTD}}{c_{CTD,t_D}} \tag{28.14}$$

so, by combining the last two equations:

$$\frac{\partial F}{\partial y_f} = \frac{PVBP_f^{CTD}}{c_{CTD,t_D}} \tag{28.15}$$

This links the futures sensitivity to changes in the forward yield of the CTD to the forward PVBP of the CTD. While this is already close to what is needed, it still does not give much information about the spot sensitivity. In common market practice, this problem is simplified by assuming that:

$$\frac{\partial P_f^{CTD}}{\partial y_f^{CTD}} = \frac{\partial P^{CTD}}{\partial y^{CTD}}, \tag{28.16}$$

in other words, that the sensitivity of the forward price of the CTD with respect to changes in the forward yield is equal to the sensitivity of the spot price to the spot yield. This assumption is not totally wrong because the impact of a 1 cent price change in the spot price is equal to a $1 * (1 + r * DCF(spot, forward))$ cent price change in the forward where r is the applicable repo rate. This means that:

$$\frac{\partial F}{\partial y} = \frac{PVBP^{CTD}}{c_{CTD,t_D}} \tag{28.17}$$

The quantity $PVBP^{CTD}/c_{CTD,t_D}$ is called the converted PVBP of the CTD and Equation (28.17) implies:

$$\lambda = c_{CTD,t_D} \frac{N}{N_F} \frac{PVBP}{PVBP^{CTD}} \tag{28.18}$$

This means in particular that the hedge ratio for the CTD itself is simply given by the conversion factor. Note that this implies that the cash-and-carry arbitrage trade has interest rate risk because the delivery mechanism implies a hedge ratio of 1.

When the quality option of the futures contract plays a role (i.e. if there is a meaningful chance of a CTD switch) Equation (28.17) is no longer appropriate. Indeed, because lower yields tend to favour lower duration bonds for CTD status and higher yields favour higher duration bonds, the futures contract can exhibit a phenomenon known as negative convexity, i.e., a rising PVBP when yields decline, and vice versa. This is the opposite of a bond.

The following examples use a stylised deliverable basket containing four bonds for a futures contract with a 6% notional coupon expiring on 10 Jun 2020. The bond details with pricing are given in Table 28.1 and, unless stated otherwise, the analysis takes place for settlement on 16 April 2020. Yield volatility is assumed to be 40% lognormal annualised.

Figure 28.10 shows the PVBP of the futures contract given in Table 28.1 as a function of parallel yield shifts. At very low yields (high futures prices), the contract CTD is clearly the lower duration bond and the future behaves more or less like that bond, in line with Equation (28.17). Conversely, at higher yields, the higher duration bond is CTD and again the contract tracks this bond so that Equation (28.17) can be used. Around the yield level where the CTD situation is less clear, however, the futures contract duration falls when the futures price increases, which is the opposite of how a bond behaves.

This negative convexity is a problem for hedging because it leads to a drag on hedge performance. Starting from a perfectly hedged position of short bond, long futures contracts with a zero net PVBP in a negative convexity situation as described above, a decrease of bond prices will drive a decrease of the futures price and the two effects cancel out. However, while the decrease in the bond price would decrease the duration of that bond, the PVBP of the futures contract would increase. The position would therefore no longer be hedged and instead have a long duration. Futures contracts could

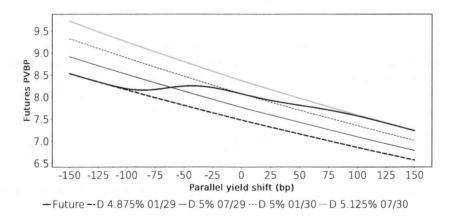

FIGURE 28.10 Spot PVBP of a futures contract for a simple deliverable basket. To highlight the role of the CTD switch, the spot PVBPs of the individual bonds are shown as well.

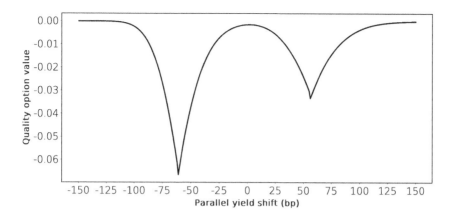

FIGURE 28.11   Fair value of the quality option for the standard basket Table 28.1 as a function of parallel yield shifts.

be sold to re-adjust the hedge but note that these sales would take place at the new, lower price. If bond prices then move back up to their original level, the hedge would be short duration. Futures contracts would have to be bought back, at the new higher level. For both upwards and downwards moves, the long future-short bond position loses money every time the hedge is adjusted to remain PVBP-neutral.

The conclusion is that a trader would ask to be paid to enter this type of position in anticipation of the convexity drag. In other words, the trader would pay less for the future than implied by the cost of the bond. This statement is equivalent to the one made when discussing the quality option: the net basis of any bond is in theory strictly positive. The equivalence here is the same noted by the Black–Scholes theorem, namely that the price of an option is equal to its expected hedge costs. Figure 28.11 shows the yield dependency of the fair value of this option, seen from the perspective of a long CTD basis position. At very high and very low yields, the quality option is worthless. In the negative convexity area, it becomes meaningful. The reason that there are only 2 local minima in this chart, despite 3 CTD switches in Figure 28.9, is that the economic value of a CTD switch between the middle 2 bonds happens to be relatively low in these examples.

Most contract users do not conduct detailed analyses of futures PVBP because the computational effort is substantial. At the time of writing, market yields are also so far below notional coupons that the chances of CTD switches are very low. The standard approach is therefore to simply treat the future as a forward contract on the CTD and equate the futures PVBP with the PVBP of the CTD, divided by the CTD conversion factor. This adjustment is essential given how the invoice price of a contract is calculated. As long as no CTD switches occur, the approach is unproblematic.

Alternatively, at least one large data provider takes a more direct approach to futures PVBP (and yields) by taking the contract definition literally and treating the future as a forward contract on the notionally deliverable bond. For instance, since the Eurex Bund contract is a 10Y contract with a 6% notional coupon, the future is treated analytically as a forward on a fictitious 10Y bond with a 6% coupon at time of

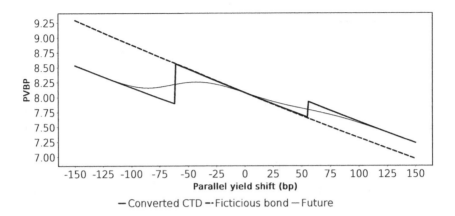

FIGURE 28.12 Futures PVBP approximations as a function of yield shifts. The converted CTD PVBP performs well in clear CTD situations (very high and very low yields) while the fictitious bond approximation is usually incorrect, particularly at low yields.

delivery. This approach has the advantage that a yield for a futures contract can easily be derived (it is simply the yield of the fictitious bond). The disadvantage is that what is actually deliverable is someting completely different. In the case of the Eurex Bund contract, the actual CTD has a maturity of between 8.5 and 9 years at delivery (longer bonds are deliverable but unlikely to be CTD at current market levels). The shorter maturity of the actual CTD means it has a lower PVBP than the fictitious bond. This effect is somewhat counteracted by the higher coupon of the fictitious bond relative to actual current coupons. However, as Figure 28.12 shows, these two errors do not quite compensate for each other.

Aside from hedge costs, negative convexity has a second effect related to the time decay of the quality option. As time approaches the delivery date there is less of a chance for yields to move so much as to cause a CTD switch. It therefore becomes more likely that the CTD becomes relatively obvious and the futures contract PVBP moves towards the converted PBVP of that likely CTD. Figure 28.13 shows this effect.

The setting of Figure 28.13 is somewhat arbitrary in that the futures price is assumed to remain constant to isolate the time decay of the quality option. The evolution of the converted PVBP of the 2 bonds is shown for the futures price level where they are the CTD. Both decline over time as they move closer towards their own maturity. Far from delivery there is a high chance of a CTD switch and the contract has a PVBP roughly between those of the 2 bonds. As time passes, the contract drifts towards either of the 2 deliverable bonds, finally converging to what is implied by Equation (28.17). This means that hedges need to be adjusted even though Equation (28.17) would suggest that they do not.

At the time of notification, a position in the futures contract irrevocably turns into the corresponding notional amount of the delivered bond. This creates a significant change in interest rate risk for the position. Prior to notification a 1 bp move in interest rates creates a profit or loss equal to the *converted* DV01 of the CTD times the size of

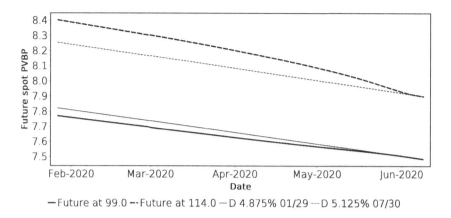

−Future at 99.0 --Future at 114.0 −D 4.875% 01/29 ---D 5.125% 07/30

FIGURE 28.13 Spot PVBP of the futures contract from Figure 28.10 but as a function of time for just two different price levels in the negative convexity area.

the notional position as given by Equation (28.15)[11]. After notification, the P&L is simply equal to the *actual* DV01 of the notified bond times the delivered amount. If, as is currently the case in most markets, notional coupons are far from actual coupon rates, and conversion factors therefore are very different from 1, this creates a sizeable jump in risk.

28.4 FUTURES ROLLS

Usually, only a small share of bond futures contracts (small single digit percentages) are held to expiry and go through the delivery process. The bulk of positions is closed out by a process called rolling: holders of the contract that is about to expire simultaneously close this position through offsetting trades and re-establish the same risk exposure in the next expiry of the same contract. Most exchanges therefore allow the trading of the spread between different contract expiries, for instance between the March and June expiries, in a single trade.

The roll of a futures contract is the spread between the first and second expiry contracts, also known as the front and back contracts. In the parlance of exchange trading, the roll is known as a calendar spread[12].

The roll is given by the equation[13]:

$$\text{Roll} = \text{Front} - \text{Back} \tag{28.19}$$

---

[11]Notification is for spot delivery and the likelihood of a CTD switch should be zero at that point for contracts with a single delivery day, or close to it in case of contracts with a longer delivery window.

[12]Calendar spreads are a slightly more general concept because the contracts involved need not be sequential.

[13]The mnemonic of this equation is that the front contract is infront of the back contract in this subtraction.

Because the carry on deliverables is positive in normal curve environments, bond futures usually trade in backwardation, i.e., the back contract is cheaper than the front contract and the roll is positive. The futures roll can be in contango when the CTD of the back contract is a different bond from the front contract CTD.

Because so many contracts are rolled rather than settled at expiry, the accurate valuation and risk management of the roll is essential for bond futures users. Fortunately, the roll is simply the difference between two contracts, and the valuation and risk calculations for these contracts have been dealt with in detail already. The main feature to look out for in any futures roll is whether there is a change in CTD because the front contract CTD falls below the minimum maturity specified in the contract specification. In addition, newly issued bonds may enter the deliverable basket of the back contract before its expiry. This analysis uses the delivery basket of Table 28.1 for front and back contracts but removes the shortest bond (D 4.875% 01/29) from the back contract basket for the examples involving a CTD switch. The delivery date of the back contract is assumed to be 10 September 2020, i.e., 3 months after the front contract delivery.

The quality option affects the roll even when the front and back contract have the same CTD because the probability that the CTD changes is usually higher for the back contract given that there is more time for yields to move. This means that even if all inputs to the carry calculation remain unchanged (or rather, move in line with the implied forwards), the roll should change through time because the time decay of the quality option is different for the 2 contract expiries (Figure 28.14).

Importantly, the roll fair value is sensitive to changes in the overall yield level for 2 reasons. The first is that the discount rate applied to deliverable bond cash flows for the purpose of calculating the conversion factors is the notional coupon. When this notional coupon differs from actual market yields, the time difference between front

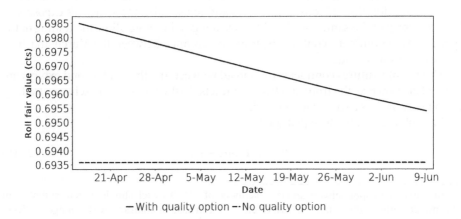

— With quality option --·No quality option

FIGURE 28.14 Futures roll with CTD change (shortest bond drops from the basket) through time. Disregarding the CTD switch option, the roll fair value is constant through time in this simulation where spot prices and repos simply follow the forwards. The time decay of the CTD switch option, however, means that the roll fair value changes through time when the option is taken into account.

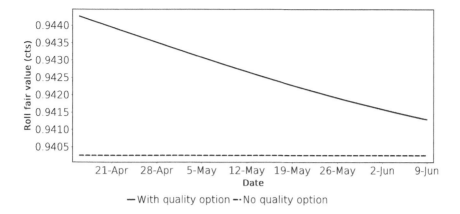

FIGURE 28.15 Futures roll without CTD switch through time. Essentially the picture is unchanged relative to Figure 28.14 but the option-free roll value is different and here simply reflects the carry of the front and back contract CTD over the period between the 2 delivery dates.

and back delivery creates a valuation difference (cf. Figure 28.15). The second is that if the CTD in the front contract is not the same as in the back contract, usually because the front contract CTD is not deliverable in the back contract, the duration risk of the CTDs will be different. Figure 28.16 shows this second sensitivity for the standard basket used here in the 2 roll scenarios (shortest bond drops out or not). In higher yield scenarios, the longest bond in the deliverable basket is CTD so the removal of the shortest bond has no impact. In low yield scenarios, the shortest bond is CTD in the front contract. Its absence in the back contract then leads to a larger difference in the roll fair value.

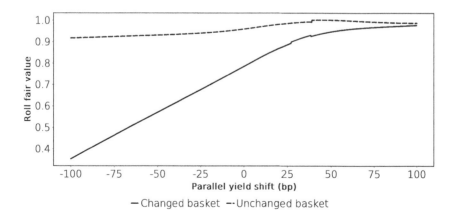

FIGURE 28.16 Sensitivity of the futures roll to parallel yield changes. The kinks in the lines correspond to spikes in the quality option valuation due to the limited number of simulations used.

The difference in yield sensitivity between front and back contracts means that a contract user will not normally roll a position one for one. After all, the total futures position normally corresponds to a fixed amount of risk that needs to be hedged. When the back contract has a higher PVBP than the front contract, fewer back contracts need to be bought or sold than front contracts are sold or bought. The PVBP-neutral roll ratio is simply the ratio of the front and back contracts (cf. next section).

An alternative yield sensitivity measure of the roll is the amount by which yields have to move to change the fair value of the roll by 1 cent. This yield difference Δy is simply:

$$\Delta y = \frac{1 cent}{PVBP_{Front} - PVBP_{Back}} \tag{28.20}$$

Note that this measure is undefined when both contracts have the same PVBP as is for instance the case for cash-settled futures.

28.4.1 Roll ratios

While the value of the roll is expressed as a price difference, a futures hedge position is not usually rolled one for one. As the previous section has discussed, the difference in PVBP of front and back contracts means that the roll itself is directional. A PVBP-neutral roll strategy requires that the risk in the front contract is matched with the risk in the back contract, not that the amounts match. In essence, the necessary condition is:

$$N_{Front}PVBP_{Front} = N_{Back}PVBP_{Back} \tag{28.21}$$

which means that the PVBP-neutral roll ratio is:

$$\frac{N_{Back}}{N_{Front}} = \frac{PVBP_{Front}}{PVBP_{Back}} \tag{28.22}$$

Typically, the roll ratio so defined is lower than 1 which means that the number of back contracts that need to be bought or sold to offset a given position in the front contract is less than the number of contracts in the front contract. This is because the back contract CTD tends to be the same or a longer bond than the front contract and so the back contract PVBP is usually higher than the front contract PVBP.

Before moving on, this observation raises a question: namely, Why if rolling futures contracts results in a reduction in positions due to a roll ratio of less than 1, do futures contracts still have any open interest? After all, a geometric series with a multiplier of less than 1 should converge to zero. The answer is that while existing bonds, including the CTDs of future contracts, have diminishing duration risk, new bonds appear all the time. In the long run, the average duration of new bonds must exceed the average duration of existing bonds or else the total market duration would shrink over time. Hedging these new bonds requires selling more futures contracts. The hedging of these new bonds is one reason why the open interest of individual bond futures contracts increases gradually over time, as shown in Figure 28.1[14].

---

[14]Depending on the exchange, a second reason can be deferred netting of long and short positions held by the same investor.

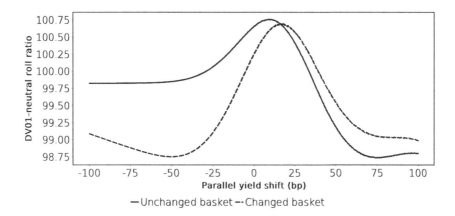

FIGURE 28.17 Sensitivity of the futures roll ratio (back contracts per 100 front contracts) to parallel yield changes. Shown are 2 scenarios, one where the delivery baskets are identical and one where the shortest bond of the front delivery basket is no longer deliverable into the back contract.

This equation for the roll is simple in principle but complex in the presence of a CTD switch option. As shown in Figure 28.10, the PVBP of a futures contract changes near the price levels where the CTD switches. If both front and back contracts are close to CTD switches, the price levels where these switches happen are unlikely to be exactly the same. As a result, the PVBP-neutral roll ratio can fluctuate in complex ways.

Figure 28.17 shows the PVBP neutral roll ratios for the 2 types of contract roll used so far, 1 where the baskets of front and back contract are identical, and 1 where the shortest bond in the front contract is not deliverable into the back contract. For the changed basket at low yield levels (when the convexity bias of the contract favours shorter bonds for CTD status), the roll ratio is less than 1 because the shortest bond in the back basket is longer than the shortest bond in the front basket. This is the effect of basket changes on roll ratios discussed above. For the unchanged basket, the same bond is CTD in front and back contract and the roll ratio is therefore very close to one-for-one. Only the discounting effect embedded in the conversion factor calculation creates a small difference in contract PVBPs. At higher yields, the CTD switches to longer bonds, and these longer bonds are present in both the front and the back contract baskets. The roll ratios of both unchanged and changed contracts converge to each other, and also towards one-for-one. Only at much higher yields is there again a deviation from a one-for-one roll ratio, this time caused by convexity effects.

28.4.2 Advanced futures delivery models

The delivery option model used in this section is a simple 1-factor model where CTD switches arise only from the effect parallel yield shifts have via the basis effect. In general, 10,000 simulations of future yield scenarios have been used to generate the charts seen so far. Such a model is appropriate for a textbook but not for real risk management systems. In reality bonds exhibit idiosyncratic movements that increase the probability of CTD changes. Particularly for very long futures delivery baskets, like the US Long

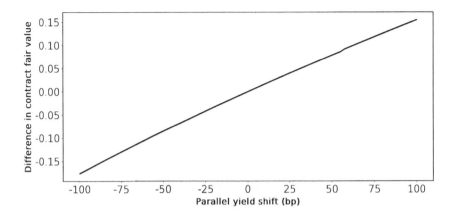

FIGURE 28.18   Difference in contract fair value between a model that assumes repo rates to move in parallel with bond yields and one that assumes constant repo rates. For higher rates, the model with parallel rate shifts would give a higher contract value than one assuming constant repo rates.

bond contract (US Treasuries between 15 and 25 years remaining maturity), various curve shape changes are also sources of additional CTD switch risks. Linear models like the one used here can be extended to higher numbers of risk factors. In principle, the number of required factors is equal to the number of deliverable bonds but these factors are highly correlated. Sampling a high-dimensional space of correlated random variables in turn raises questions of computational efficiency and stability. A natural compromise is to use dimension reduction techniques such as PCA to achieve a good mix of accuracy and stability.

Another important shortfall of this type of model is that it ignores the correlation between repo rates and bond yields. For short-term (e.g. 2 year) bond futures contracts in particular, central bank actions will affect both the current level of bond yields and the repo rates until delivery. Higher bond yields mean lower spot, and therefore lower forward, prices, but higher repo rates will mean higher forward prices relative to spot prices. The interplay between these two factors needs to be analysed. The simplest approach is to assume the 2 extreme cases of either repo rates move in parallel with bond yields or constant repo rates (as was assumed so far). Reality would then be between these 2 cases. Figure 28.18 shows the impact these approaches have on fair value estimates of the standard basket Table 28.1.

28.5   DELIVERY WINDOWS

So far the delivery process has been discussed in the context of a known delivery date. For the Eurex and Japanese futures contracts, that day is the 10th of the delivery month, or the next good business day if the 10th is not a business day. The US and UK bond futures contracts allow for delivery on any good business day during the delivery month. The choice of delivery day, as with the bond to be delivered, is with the short, and the exchange will automatically assign a randomly selected long to take delivery for each contract that is notified for delivery.

This additional option of delivery timing complicates the valuation of the contract. Given that the bond future has a given price at any point in time but bonds tend to have positive carry in a positively sloped yield curve, the short has a natural interest to delivery as late as possible in the delivery window so as to earn that carry before letting go of the bond at the futures-implied price. In practice that means that deliveries tend to be concentrated late in the delivery window. However, 2 effects can change this simple analysis. The first is the quality option which, like any option, decays in value as time passes. Because the short in the future is long the option, it may sometimes be advantageous to monetise the time value of the option through delivery rather than letting it decay. At the time of writing, the quality option is sufficiently worthless to make this consideration meaningless. A second complication is the repo market. The cash-and-carry arbitrage relies on repo funding which has fails risk. A repo counterparty may not return the CTD lent out for funding in time for delivery to the exchange. A risk-reduction strategy is to give up 1 or 2 days of carry by delivering a little earlier.

In a downward-sloped (inverted) yield curve configuration, carry on the deliverable bonds can be negative. In this case, all 3 reasons above argue for early delivery.

28.6   INTERACTION BETWEEN FUTURES AND BONDS

Bond futures are the main avenue for price discovery in the European and Japanese bond markets and are growing in importance in the US. Futures trading volumes exceed the trading volumes in the underlying cash markets by a large amount in the euro area and this poses the question of how reliably the cash-and carry arbitrage can tie futures prices to the underlying cash market.

Two possible decouplings are imaginable. The first is that the futures contract valuation decouples from the arbitrage-free forward price of the cheapest-to-deliver bond. Where the future outperforms the CTD, this could be an example of a squeeze, discussed in the next section, leading to a negative net basis. The second type of decoupling would be where the CTD decouples from the surrounding bond market. In this situation, the pricing implied by the cash-and-carry arbitrage stays intact but the specific situation of the CTD, combined with the non-fungibility of different bonds by the same issuer, leads to the CTD trading as a separate asset.

For hedging purposes, either type of decoupling is unwelcome because it removes the strong correlation between changes in the price of the futures contract and the bonds that are expected to trade in line with it. However, the first type is more concerning from a market functioning perspective because it implies that standard arbitrage relationships are breaking down. Extraordinary pricing of individual bonds, meanwhile, is not in itself too concerning.

So far, the first type of decoupling has been rare but the second is relatively common. In stressed market situations, it is quite common for investors to resort to the most liquid asset, namely the futures contract, to reduce risk. This means that the dislocation between CTD pricing and surrounding bonds can be a useful proxy for measuring market stress.

In Japan, a somewhat special situation is created by the coincidence of a high market weight of Japanese government debt in global government bond indices and the persistently low yields in the JGB market. Global bond fund managers are faced with

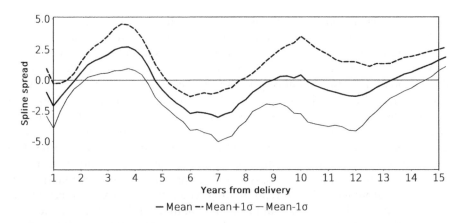

FIGURE 28.19 Average spline spreads, including the 1 standard deviation bands of JGB by years to maturity after the next 10Y JGB delivery during the years 2009–2013, before the start of QQE. The JGB CTD is a 7-year bond and this maturity point tended to be the least attractive on the JGB curve from a carry-rolldown perspective. Daily data, price source JSDA.

the dilemma of having to maintain a high exposure to the Japanese market while seeing little expected return from these bonds. The standard investment strategy has therefore been to proxy JGB exposure through futures contracts and instead invest cash somewhere else. This strategy means that buying JGB futures was not subject to relative value considerations and led to a structural expensiveness of the JGB future relative to surrounding cash bonds. Figure 28.19 shows the average spread of JGB to a Nelson-Siegel spline by maturity adjusted by the next futures delivery date. The 7-year point is the most expensive point on the curve in this metric.

The quantitative and qualitative easing programme of the Bank of Japan has disrupted this traditional pattern but it is still in evidence. Figure 28.20 shows the evolution

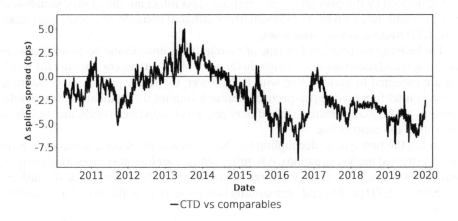

FIGURE 28.20 Average spline spread of the JGB contract CTD on the the JGB curve relative to the JGB 1 year shorter and longer on the same spline. Daily data, source: JSDA.

of the relative value of the JGB contract CTD versus surrounding bonds (bonds that are 1 year longer or shorter in maturity are chosen here to eliminate seasonality effects).

The opposite position in futures contracts relative to the long position of foreign investors is a structural short position of JGB dealers who hedge their long inventory. The structural richness of the contract results in subsidising the non-CTD bonds for domestic investors by improving the carry of these hedged inventory positions.

28.7 FUTURES SQUEEZES

A squeeze is a generic term for situations where the delivery of the futures contract is somehow affected by limited supply of the CTD. Different bonds are generally non-fungible and the delivery specifications and economics of bond futures contracts require that there is a sufficient amount of the right bonds available for the contract shorts to deliver through the exchange to the longs. Sometimes this sufficient supply is absent due to the actions of one or more market participants. More frequently, the mere prospect of insufficient supply affects trading in the contract and the underlying bonds ahead of the delivery period of the contract to such a degree that the actual delivery process becomes almost irrelevant. As will be explained below, the usual sign of an expected delivery problem is a negative CTD net basis.

The general principle of a futures squeeze predates the existence of bond futures and indeed the existence of futures exchanges. In [82], Mark Twain describes a short squeeze on railway shares so cursorily that he could evidently presume that his readers in 1889 would understand the strategy without much explanation. In a short squeeze, a trader will establish the right to receive particular securities in an amount that exceeds the total amount of such securities available in the market at that point. The traders who are under obligation to deliver the securities will be forced to either deliver alternative, more valuable, securities, or negotiate a settlement. In Mark Twain's fictional example, the delivery obligation was for newly issued shares and the obligation arose through a bilateral contract. In that case, a negotiated, if punitive, bilateral settlement was possible. In the case of bond futures, the delivery obligation arises through exchange rules and it is more likely that a different bond than the CTD gets delivered.

Futures squeezes are a prominent topic for discussion because the bond volume corresponding to the total open interest in most bond futures contracts usually exceeds the outstanding amount of the CTD by several factors and usually also exceeds the total outstanding amount of deliverable bonds. Because only a small portion of the open interest in a given contract is actually put through delivery, this volume mismatch is normally not a problem. However, it allows a trader to build up a large position with the intention to demand delivery without this showing up in open interest statistics in a meaningful way.

Somewhat more subtly, bond futures squeezes usually involve the repo market because the delivery window is fairly short. The deliverable bonds have to be delivered to the exchange to satisfy the delivery obligation and that means that the bonds do not have to be owned by the shorts, they just have to be in their possession; for instance, through repo borrowing. In order to restrict the ability of the shorts to borrow the bonds for delivery, it is therefore sufficient to buy up the supply in the repo market. This is usually cheaper and less risky than outright purchases of the CTD.

The following paragraphs provide a guide to analysing the economics of a squeeze situation. However, financial markets regulators have taken an increasingly dim view of such trades and it is unlikely that severe squeeze situations will occur in the future.

A trader could follow the example given by Mark Twain and buy futures contracts as well as the CTD so that delivery of that bond would be constrained. The trader would hedge this position by short-selling the next-to-CTD bond or the far contract. As shorts would find themselves unable to deliver the CTD, they would have to deliver the next-to-CTD at a much higher cost, allowing the trader to obtain this bond comparatively cheaply. Depending on which bond is CTD in the far contract, the trader could exit the position through delivering the bonds received in the near contract delivery into the short position of that far contract.

The market would reflect the likelihood of this scenario in a negative CTD net basis because the value of the futures contract increases with the probability of receiving a bond other than the CTD. In other words, while normally the CTD net basis would be non-negative and merely reflect the quality option, a potential squeeze implies that the cash and carry arbitrage for the CTD is no longer realistic.

The negative net basis of the CTD emerging in a squeeze situation translates into an implied repo rate (IRR) that is higher than the market term repo rate for this bond. Such a situation can be interpreted as reflecting the repo market view of a squeeze rather than the futures delivery view, namely that the reverse leg of a specials repo transaction in the CTD is likely to fail. Borrowers of the CTD might be shorts in the contract who prefer to deliver the borrowed bonds to the exchange rather than returning it to the lender because the penalties of the exchange for non-delivery are higher than those in the repo market. If this risk is substantial, a bond trader looking to make delivery would not fund the CTD in the specials market but with a trusted counterparty in a more generic market (such as central bank refinancing operations)[15] or even in the unsecured market. In other words, squeeze risk does not only manifest itself in a negative net basis, but equivalently in an IRR that approaches central bank or unsecured funding rates. As long as there is an expectation that sufficient amounts of the CTD are available in the market, these rates provide caps on the IRR, and thereby floors on the net basis, of the CTD.

An important aspect of futures squeezes is that they are inherently unstable. A single entity will find it hard to muster the balance sheet necessary to control a meaningful amount of deliverable bonds. Even if that were possible, exchanges can impose position limits in the near contracts to lower the risk of excessive deliveries. While in theory multiple agents could conspire, through explicit collusion or by independently happening to execute the same strategy, to act collectively to engineer a squeeze, it would always be the first such agent who exits the strategy that realises the largest profit. This form of a free-rider problem reduces the likelihood of squeezes.

---

[15] Eurex has recently established a segregated pooling basket for CTDs to enable users to employ this specific type of funding strategy.

28.8 CASH-SETTLED FUTURES

Contracts like the Australian government bond future are settled in cash using Equation (28.2). By definition, this means that the PVBP of the futures contract is equal to 1. As a result, the hedge ratio between future and deliverable baskets is not constant as shown in Figure 28.21. Other than that, the fair value estimate of a cash-settled future is exactly equivalent to the cash and carry arbitrage described in Section 28.3.3. The only difference is that every deliverable bond plays a role in the calculation of the contract fair value at all times whereas in a physically settled future the CTD is usually sufficient.

Given that price changes are the integral of PVBP over yield changes, it should be unsurprising that the price development of the future will not be reflective of the volume-weighted average price change in the deliverable basket. Figure 28.22 shows this effect.

Optically at least, cash-settled futures are not prohibitively inefficient. The divergence between the fair values of future and deliverable baskets is an example of convexity[16]. As mentioned in the introduction to this section, the choice between cash and physical settlement is essentially undecidable. Both delivery methods have substantial merits but are also problematic. The high switching cost between contract specifications is likely to remain an essential factor in keeping both models active in the market.

A cash-settled bond futures contract should require a convexity adjustment in line with that for money market futures Equation (13.17) to reflect the daily margining requirement. However, because the contracts have a short time to expiry, this convexity adjustment would be very small and is not applied in practice.

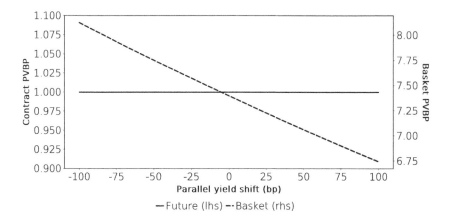

FIGURE 28.21 PVBP of a cash settled future with deliverable baskets as in Table 28.1 versus the volume-weighted PVBP of the basket itself.

---

[16]This divergence is also an example of the broad use of the word 'convexity' in the fixed income context.

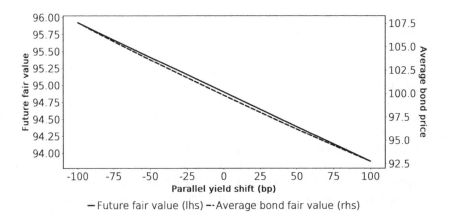

FIGURE 28.22 Fair value of a cash settled future with deliverable baskets as in Table 28.1 versus the volume-weighted price of the basket itself.

28.8.1   Exchange-for-physical transactions

An exchange-for-physical, or EFP, means in the commodity markets that two counter-parties agree to exchange a given position in a futures contract for an equivalent size of the underlying, or a related, physical commodity. The exchange is then notified of this off-exchange transaction so that clearing of the residual futures contract positions can take place as usual.

In the Australian rates market, an EFP refers to an exchange of a position in an Australian government bond futures contract against entering an interest rate swap with an equal notional amount. As in a commodity EFP, the transaction takes place outside the futures exchange but is then given up to the exchange for clearing. Because the Australian bond future is a cash-settled contract trading on yield terms, it is fairly straightforward to value the transaction. In some ways, it can be compared to trading on a bond basis in a physically settled futures market, with a similarly low residual interest risk. The spread between the swap curve and the implied yield on the futures contracts is known as the EFP spread.

28.9   NEW BOND ISSUES

The analysis of bond futures, both physically and cash-settled, has to incorporate expec-tations of bonds that will be issued between the analysis date and the delivery date. Depending on the contract, two approaches can be differentiated. In either case, the new issues would be included in the projected deliverable basket.

In the more simple case, the newly issued bond is clear CTD. This could be due to its duration relative to the rest of the basket or due to other features. In this case, an analyst would take the market price of the future as given and infer a price for the new issue from the pricing of the future. This information might then inform an opinion about the new bond, such as that it is expensive or cheap.

In a more complex setting, the new bond is not obviously the CTD. An analyst would derive a price estimate for the new bond based on historical experience and then see what this projected pricing would mean for the deliverable basket. If the new bond happens to be CTD, the market may already be pricing the future as a proxy for the new bond, as in the case above, or be reflecting a compromise between different delivery scenarios.

In either case, expert judgement is important to establish the fair value of the futures contract.

CHAPTER 29

Swaps

29.1 INTRODUCTION

Swaps have already been mentioned briefly in the context of overnight index rates. Generally, a swap is a transaction where two parties bilaterally agree to exchange (swap) cash flows in the future.

Essentially there are only two rules governing the swaps market:

First, if it moves it can be swapped;

Second, cash payments in the same location, currency and on the same day are netted.

The first rule means that there are swaps not only on fixed income benchmarks but also on oil prices, the number of sunny days, the degrees and number of days that temperatures fall below a certain level in a given area (so-called heating degree swaps), etc. A corollary to this rule is that things that do not move do not get swapped. The second rule is essentially a risk management measure.

The first ever interest rate swap was conducted in 1981 between IBM (then a triple-A rated bond issuer) and the World Bank (properly named the International Bank for Reconstruction and Development, IBRD) and the transaction was arranged by Salomon Brothers. At the time, IBM wished to raise dollars but found little demand in the USD market for new IBM bonds. At the same time, the World Bank wanted to raise Swiss francs but lenders in this currency already held a lot of World Bank debt. Therefore, IBM issued a Swiss franc bond and the World Bank a USD bond. IBM and the World Bank then agreed to swap the cashflows from these two bond transactions, so IBM ended up borrowing in USD and the World Bank effectively borrowed Swiss francs.

The structure of this first swap would today be considered unusual because it amounts to a cross-currency fixed-versus-fixed swap. However, that swap illustrates the immense transformation swaps have introduced in the fixed income world. Before swaps, a foreign buyer of a 10Y dollar-denominated corporate bond issued by corporation X was assuming the following risks:

- 10Y interest rate risk
- Dollar currency risk
- Default risk of X

Swaps, in conjunction with special purpose vehicles (SPVs), changed this picture completely. A buyer could transform the USD bond into a CHF bond (which is basically what happened in the first swap), hedge out the default risk (with a credit default swap), remove the 10Y interest rate risk (with an asset swap), etc. For that matter, the investor could turn the economic risk characteristics of the USD bond investment into that of holding a Peruvian equity portfolio (with a total return swap), or running the local brewery (with a cooling degree day swap). Swaps allow the extraction, and transformation, of selected risks in a given asset. As such, trading swaps can be seen as ways to trade pure risk whereas trading of actual assets commingles the trading of risk with the trading of investments.

In essence, swaps release some of the frictional losses embedded in preferred habitats (cf. Section 20.4). The existence of preferred habitats implies that investors buy assets with sub-optimal risk–return characteristics because those assets have certain features that outweigh their risk-adjusted returns. With a swap, an investor can modify the risk of a given asset to suit her or his preferred habitat. As such, swaps can add value to the total economy via more optimal capital allocation, even though each swap is a zero-sum game between two counterparties.

Swaps used to be pure bilateral instruments but have changed in nature over time. Standard swaps between banks were among the first instruments, after futures and FX transactions, to be centrally cleared. This turned out to be helpful in the financial crisis, and central clearing is now mandatory for standard swaps in most jurisdictions. In addition, swap-like futures contracts, which have been around since the 1990s, have seen a somewhat larger take-up in recent years.

The volume of swaps transactions is huge and far exceeds trading in bonds. The Bank for International Settlements estimates that around USD 341 trillion notional of interest rate swaps were outstanding in H2 2019. This accounts for almost a third of the total OTC derivatives of USD 558 trillion at the same point in time. Note that, at the same time, the total size of the global debt market was only around USD 120 trillion, also according to the BIS. However, the market value of these swaps was only 7.5tr. Although still a large number, it implies that the average market value of an interest rate swap is only about 2.2% of its nominal amount. As will be discussed further below, there are strong incentives to keep the market value of a swap low, and there are ways to achieve that. Because most investors have portfolios of partially offsetting swaps, neither total gross value, nor market value are necessarily reliable indicators of the size of the swap market.

Trading in the swaps market is usually done using standard documentation based on the ISDA Master Agreement drawn up by the International Securities Dealers Association and normally two counterparties wishing to trade swaps just sign an ISDA Master (perhaps adjusting minor details to suit their particular situation) and then trade swaps using a simple short-form confirmation each time a new swap contract is concluded. In bilateral contracts, parties usually agree on a standard Credit Support Annex (CSA) to the ISDA Master that requires the swap to be marked to market every trading day. Depending on the outcome of the mark-to-market, the party which faces a loss in the transaction has to deposit collateral (cash, bonds, or cash or bonds, depending on the CSA) with the counterparty to protect the counterparty from default risk. The use of CSAs has largely been superseded by central clearing but some exceptions remain. Some market participants, particularly pension funds, tend to have assets but not cash on hand to make daily margin payments in cash. They therefore tend to prefer trading with bond CSAs. Some sovereign treasuries, meanwhile, find it difficult to post collateral under CSAs and therefore use one-sided CSAs where they receive collateral when their swaps are in the money, but do not post collateral when they are not[1]. In recent years, however, even sovereigns have moved towards central clearing to reduce the xVA costs associated with other clearing arrangements (cf. Section 12.3 on page 108).

What sets swaps apart from securities is that they can be, and frequently are, tailored to the specific needs of particular users. For instance, swaps can use a multitude of calendars for the observation of the reference indices on a floating side, the payment of any cash due, possible termination dates, and so on. In a trade between counterparties in London and Athens, for example, it may be useful to use the combined holiday calendars of both locations because many public holidays in one location are not holidays in the other[2].

29.2 PLAIN VANILLA SWAPS

Plain vanilla swaps are the essential building block of the fixed income swaps market. These swaps have the two counterparties exchange a fixed versus a floating rate payment. The fixed side generally matches the daycount convention and payment frequency of the local sovereign bond market (actual/actual in most cases, and semi-annual in the US, the UK, and Japan, annual in the euro area). The floating side is traditionally given by quarterly or semi-annual payments equal to the local Libor, quoted in the appropriate money market convention (actual/360 or actual/365). This makes plain vanilla swaps hybrids between the bond and money markets. Both sides are expressed in percentages of a fixed amount which is the nominal amount of the swap.

Swaps have a tenor (the time between settlement date and maturity) and can be forward starting. A forward swap is usually written in the form 5Yx10Y which would be a swap starting in 5 years' time and then running for 10 years[3]. This notation is subtly different from that for FRAs, where there is no 'x' and the second period is not the tenor but the maturity.

The market is most liquid in par swaps, which is a swap that at inception has zero fair value (before xVA adjustments). Par swap rates are the natural ingredient for bootstrapping a discount factor term structure of swap rates (cf. Section 19.3.1).

On balance, convention comes down on the money market side because the fixed side of the swap is treated as the borrowing side. Swap rates are quoted in terms of the fixed rate given while the floating side is simply the Libor rate. A swap trader saying 'mine' on a swap agrees to pay the fixed side, whereas a bond trader saying 'mine' will

---

[1] Because swap dealers still have to manage the risk associated with sovereign counterparties that have net obligations under swaps, they tend to buy protection in the form of sovereign CDSs. This is an important reason for sovereign CDSs to exist.

[2] In this specific example, even Easter falls on different days.

[3] For a swap like this in EUR, the first fixed cash flow would occur after 6 years, and the last after 15. In USD, GBP or JPY, the first fixed cash flow would be after 5 years and 6 months.

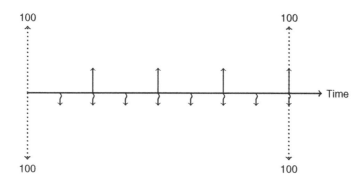

FIGURE 29.1   Cash flows in a 4Y plain vanilla swap in euros (annual fixed against semi-annual floating) for a notional of 100. The dotted lines refer to the exchanges of nominal which are netted out. Fixed payments are also netted against the floating payments occurring on the same day.

receive the fixed coupon on the bond that was quoted. The swap convention stems from the money market convention of taking the money ('mine') in exchange for paying the quoted interest rate on it.

There are manifold reasons to use interest rate swaps. For instance, corporate earnings tend to be closely correlated with the economic cycle, which in turn is closely correlated with short-term interest rates. Corporates therefore are natural borrowers in the floating rate market. At the same time, most investors tend to favour fixed-rate bonds. By using an interest rate swap, a corporate is able to issue such fixed rate bonds but in reality maintain a floating rate exposure. Banks, meanwhile, are natural receivers of floating rate coupons to defease floating rate liabilities (cf. Chapter 17). Where banks buy fixed-coupon assets, they therefore tend to swap them down to floating rate. Some sovereigns use swaps to hedge long-dated issuance down to their preferred issuance duration. Overall, the natural fixed rate payer and receiver sides of the market are roughly distributed as shown in Table 29.1.

There is a persistent myth that the term structure of swap rates is linked to the senior unsecured funding costs of prime banks. The source of this belief is that the floating side is the short-term funding cost of prime banks, and the present value of the fixed side payments should equal the expected value of the floating side payments to make the swap fair. A simple examination of the interest rates on newly issued senior unsecured bank

TABLE 29.1   Natural positions in the plain vanilla swap market for different investor types.

Sector	Payer	Receiver
Intermediate	Banks	Corporates
	Sovereigns	Banks
Long end	Banks	Pension funds
	Asset swappers	Life insurers
	Mortgage lenders	Sovereigns

bonds shows that they are usually higher than the swap rate of the same maturity. Aside from the term premium in interest rates (cf. Section 20.3), an important source of this difference is survivorship bias in the swap rate. The yield to maturity of a bond reflects that buyer of a bond is in principle exposed to the borrower until the bond matures. The receiver of a swap, however, pays a Libor fixing that *at the time* reflects the funding costs of prime banks *at that time*. If any one bank should decline in creditworthiness, it will be removed from the Libor panel, but its bonds remain outstanding.

A specific form of a plain vanilla swap are IMM-dated swaps which are forward-starting swaps with a start date that equals the next IMM date (cf. Section 13.9.1). Using IMM swaps is in the first instance a way of ex-ante trade compression because there are only 4 possible start dates per year. In addition, the floating leg of an IMM swap is fixed on a money market futures expiry date so that the fixing is easier to hedge.

29.3 TRADE COMPRESSION AND RE-COUPONING

Swaps can be closed out by mutual agreement, usually against a final payment to settle the remaining valuation. In case of bilateral swaps, it is also possible to use a technique called novation where 3 counterparties agree that 1 counterparty steps into an existing contract, replacing 1 other. The default mode of removing the economic risk of a swap, however, is to enter a new, offsetting swap. The reason for this development is that the new swap can be executed with any counterparty and the rate on the offsetting swap may therefore be more competitive than the close-out rate offered by the original counterparty.

As a result of this practice, swap users tend to end up with large portfolios of partially offsetting swaps. In the first instance, this inflates the total gross volume of swaps outstanding. This practice also creates unnecessary settlement risk because the cashflows on these swaps do not fully align[4]. Regulators now require in some jurisdictions that counterparties analyse the swaps they have and attempt to reduce them. For instance, if bank A pays in a 10Y and 8Y6M swap to bank B, and receives in a 9Y3M swap from the same bank, then it may be possible to collapse the economic exposure into 1 or 2 swaps, for instance by eliminating the 9Y3M swap. This process is known as trade compression. Commercial providers, such as the CME-owned TriOptima, offer the service to compress trades across multiple counterparties. As a result of better trade compression, the global total gross volume of swaps may be declining as the impact of compression outweighs the flow of new trades. Note that compression is difficult for asset swaps because these are specific to securities, and compression may have consequences for users who apply hedge accounting.

In addition to trade compression, swap users can reduce the amount of margin tied up in a transaction by restructuring it. When an existing transaction has moved away from fair value, one of the counterparties has to post margin to the other. This margin, and the fair value of the swap, consume balance sheet of both counterparties.

---

[4]As mentioned above, this is one reason to use IMM swaps.

The two counterparties may therefore agree to terminate the existing non-par swap and immediately conclude a new swap with the same cashflow dates but a new, par, coupon. This is known as re-couponing. Because swaps can be re-couponed at any time, the total net value of swaps in existence is a relatively meaningless number because swaps with a non-zero net value are those that have not been, and perhaps cannot be, re-couponed. Reasons not to re-coupon can include taxes (margin crystallises as profit and loss on such a transaction), and non-standard clearing arrangements.

Because a re-couponing is technically a combination of 2 transactions (1 swap exactly offsetting the existing non-par swap, and a second replacing it with a new par swap), reported swap transaction volumes are inflated by this practice. A 30Y swap can be re-couponed many times throughout its long life, but would be initiated only once. As a result, the re-couponing volume may completely dominate the observed trade universe.

Standard Trading Strategies

CHAPTER 30

Trading Principles

30.1 DEFINITIONS

A trade is a voluntary and deliberate assumption of market risk with the aim of closing out this position at a profit. Given the fallibility of human intelligence, a trade can also result in a loss. A trade need not be related to a new position in financial instruments, but can also be the deliberate decision *not* to adjust a position in the face of new risks or information.

The profit and loss (P&L) of a trade is the valuation gain or loss associated with that trade, including any cash income or payments during the lifetime of the trade.

Investors make a finite number of trading decisions and the number of investors is large. It is therefore possible that 1 or more investors achieve a very high share of successful trades simply throgh the operation of the law of large numbers (a fraudulent way of achieving a perfect streak of success is outlined in [78]). This creates a natural limitation to how much one can learn from the trading experience of others. The success of a successful trader may be the result of sheer luck and replicating the same strategy might not be successful.

With this caveat, some ingredients to a successful trading strategy can be identified, as follows:

Rationale A trade should have a clearly defined rationale, i.e., a clearly articulated justification for the expected outcome.

Profit target and stop-loss The trader should define an envisaged profit target and a loss level at which the trade will be closed out to prevent further losses.

Exit strategy At the time the trade is entered into, it must be clear how to exit it, with a rational assessment of the costs involved.

Consistency The motivation for the trade will be the expectation of some market price changes. The actual instruments chosen by a trade to express this view, and their position sizes, should match the analysis done.

The need for a clear trade rationale is the essential motivation for all preceding chapters of this book. Taking risks requires an understanding of the valuation mechanisms of the instruments involved. While this may at times be tedious, it is a prerequisite for understanding opportunities to take calculated risks.

Clearly stated profit targets and stop-loss levels allow a simple probabilistic calculation of capital risked for a given expected return. An old trader rule, 'let profits run and

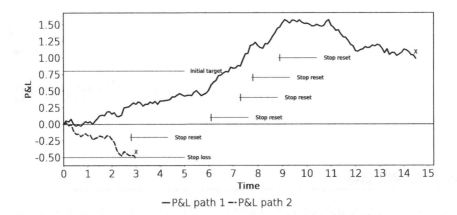

FIGURE 30.1 Illustration of the use of stop-loss levels and adjustments. X marks a stop-loss closing of the trade, the vertical lines in the stop loss adjustments denote the time of the adjustment. Time units are arbitrary.

cut losses short' translates into the idea to regularly revise stop-losses to follow *positive* gains from the trade. Instead of leaving the stop-loss at the initial level, an adjustment of the stop-loss to follow profit means that not all gains will be lost if the trade first moves into one's favour and then against it. Target levels can be similarly adjusted. If a target level has been reached, most traders would move their stop-loss to that level and leave the trade in place with a new target.

An illustration of systematic adjustment of stop-loss levels is given in Figure 30.1. The trade is assumed to start at a P&L of 0 and 2 sample evolutions are shown. In Path 1, the trade is successful and every time the P&L has moved up by a fixed amount, the stop-loss is moved up by this amount. The trade is not closed even after the initial target is reached and eventually the stop loss is higher than that target. Variations of this approach would be to adjust the stops periodically or to set them in terms of the underlying variable (e.g., yield or spread level) rather than P&L. At the same time, trades can be closed out without waiting for a stop loss. In this illustration, since P&L moves sideways between Time 9 and 11, a trader might decide to redeploy balance sheet and close out a trade with static performance.

A commonly assumed exit strategy is the 'greater fool' approach, namely the assumption that prices will continue to move in their current direction and there will be a new investor willing to take on one's position later. The name of this strategy stems from the phrase 'Who is more tool, the fool or he who follows the fool?' and it is usually related to late stages in a bubble. In these situations, there is no obvious justification for current valuations other than the observation that new buyers (or sellers) appear to be emerging. While money has been made with this approach, it does not require much in the way of analysis and will therefore not be discussed here.

In many cases, liquidity conditions can be correlated with market outcomes. For instance, a trade that is designed to inoculate a portfolio against large market swings needs to be designed with the understanding that such large market swings will probably lead to wider bid–offer spreads, or impaired access to repo funding. Trades that involve many legs, or borrowed positions in rare securities would then be subject to higher frictional costs.

Consistency tends to be the most common problem with trade implementation in fixed income markets because most fixed income instruments have a finite lifetime. A non-exhaustive list of examples is given below:

Model error A spline model is used to identify rich and cheap curve sectors and a trade is designed to benefit from this mispricing. Because the trade involves actual bonds, it could be that in the cheap sectors in the spline model all bonds appear rich, or that in the rich sectors of the model all bonds appear cheap. This would be a sign that the model simply does not fit the curve, rather than that bonds are mispriced.

Basis Instead of implementing a trade in cash bonds, one could use futures contracts to minimise entry and exit costs. If the analysis is done in bonds, however, one needs to check that the basis is at fair value. It could be that the evolution of the basis will counteract the anticipated performance of the underlying bonds.

Sample bias An investor concluding that a certain type of asset class (for instance, AA-rated bank bonds) is rich or cheap may implement a trade using a subset of this asset class (for instance, a single bond issued by an AA-rated bank). This exposes the trade to the idiosyncratic risk of this single bond in addition to the generic risk of this asset class.

Carry A trader may conduct an analysis that suggests a spread trade and then adjust the risk-neutral weights of the trade so as to achieve zero or positive carry when the original weights would result in negative carry. Because the adjusted weights do not reflect the original spread analysis, the trade is inconsistent with its rationale.

30.2   TRADE IDENTIFICATION

The identification of potentially profitable trading strategies is of course the crux of trading. The simplest approach is to simply collect a sufficient amount of data and then mine this data for significant deviations from the historical mean. This approach, optimistically called statistical arbitrage[1] [86], or stat arb, is comparatively straightforward. Because it is so straightforward, one could argue that it has limited potential because too much money is being wagered on it already. In fact, automated portfolio strategies (sometimes called smart beta strategies) are being offered by various providers. These strategies follow pre-defined statistical arbitrage algorithms which have been back-tested and optimised. A trader looking to exploit statistical arbitrage therefore competes with a number of computers watching the same relationships. An often overlooked limitation of statistical arbitrage is that, by construction, it misses half of the potential opportunities to make profits. Waiting for a given spread to be away from its

---

[1]Strictly speaking, 'arbitrage' is a term reserved for riskless strategies. Because statistical arbitrage relies on past probability distributions remaining unchanged; it is not riskless, and therefore not arbitrage.

perceived equilibrium level, and then putting on a trade that benefits from the reversal is statistical arbitrage. That approach means, however, passing up the chance to profit from the initial move away from the equilibrium level. This is not to say that statistical arbitrage does not work, but one should be aware of its constraints.

An alternative approach is to establish positions ad hoc, based on some perceived insights into near-term market moves. The difference to statistical arbitrage is that ad hoc strategies can take into account information outside market rates while statistical arbitrage usually only considers market rates themselves. One would hope, albeit perhaps falsely, that additional information and human intellect can create an edge over purely statistical strategies.

The synthesis of these 2 approaches is common sense. If one has a reason to expect a given market move, one can consider a trading strategy. If a certain spread is far from its mean, that could be an indication that it will be reverting to that mean. That said, even when one detects such a statistical anomaly, one should first try to understand why it happened in the first place. Investor behaviour could have changed, and so could the regulatory environment. Different macro-economic environments affect curve shapes in different ways. Seen in this way, a small dislocation might be a harbinger of bigger things to come and expecting a continuation might be more profitable than positioning for a reversion.

Deciding on a trading strategy is only the first part of the process. The next step is the selection of specific instruments and the notional positions that will be held in each instrument. The determination of nominal amounts depends on the risks (PVBP) of each instrument and may also incorporate other factors as discussed below. The specific instruments to be used depends on the trade strategy but can also be influenced by other considerations such as liquidity of relative valuations. A long position in 10Y bonds would by default be established in the most liquid 10Y bond, but a trader might decide that a nearby comparable bond is relatively cheap and therefore purchase this alternative bond instead.

30.3 TRADE PORTFOLIOS

Few reasonable traders would commit all available risk capital to a single trade. This means that for a given risk capital budget, multiple trades compete for risk capital, bearing in mind that different trades may partly compensate inherent risks. Risk therefore has to be rationed across active trades.

While models exist for this purpose, notably the Black–Litterman model [56], there are some fundamental challenges to doing so in an epistemologically consistent manner. Mean-variance optimisation, for instance, is a single-period approach that is hard to reconcile with portfolios of trades that have diverse expected horizons. In addition, complex trades tend to have strongly non-normal return distributions so that mean and variance are insufficient to describe their risk profiles. Last but not least, trades tend to be determined on the basis that a recent development will revert (statistical arbitrage), or that a trend will change. This would normally imply adjusting one's expectations, not only of expected returns (means) but also of correlations (variances), not to mention higher-order moments of the relevant multi-dimensional distributions.

CHAPTER 31

Curve Trading

Curve trading is the summary term for trading strategies that are based on the anticipation of changes in the bond or swaps curve shape. Two important preliminaries must be remembered before going into the details of such strategies. First, although the strategies are analysed in terms of changes of the curve shape, they are implemented with specific instruments. The idiosyncratic valuation of these instruments relative to the overall curve shape creates additional risk in such strategies that should be borne in mind. The valuation of individual bonds or futures contracts in particular can deviate from surrounding bonds in the same curve segment. Second, carry in different parts of the curve is different and that means that a certain change in the curve shape is already priced into the current curve shape. Any risk position must be viewed relative to the forward curve on the analysis horizon, not the current curve.

There are a number of curve trading strategies and they can be visualised as in Figure 31.1. There, risk positions in bonds in four points A, B, C, and D are shown. Upwards arrows are meant to imply long positions, downward arrows short positions. Seen by themselves, A and C are outright longs, while B and D are outright shorts. Such individual positions can be combined, however, to express more complex views on curve movements. The possible combinations are shown in the following table.

Legs	Combination	Name	Positions for
1	A, C	Outright long	Falling yields
	B, D	Outright short	Rising yields
2	AB, AD, CD	Steepener	Long-term yields rising more, or falling less, than short-term yields
	BC	Flattener	Long term yields fallong more, or rising less, than short-term yields
3	ABC	Butterfly	5Y ('bullet') yields rising more, or falling less, than 2Y and 10Y ('wings') yields
	BCD	Butterfly	10Y ('bullet') yields falling more, or rising less, than 5Y and 30Y ('wings') yields
4	ABCD	Condor	5Y–10Y spread flattening relative to the 2Y–30Y spread

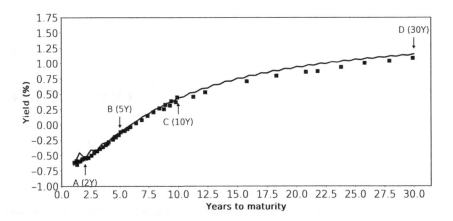

FIGURE 31.1 An example of four curve positions on the German spline, shown here for 18 September 2018. The maturities for the positions have been chosen for illustrative purposes. Upwards arrows imply a long position, downwards arrows a short position. Source: Data from the Bundesbank.

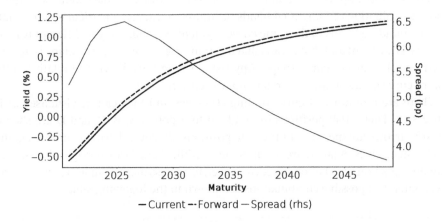

FIGURE 31.2 Current par curve and implied 6 months forward par curve for the German Nelson-Siegel spline on 18 September 2018. Source: Data from the Bundesbank.

The carry (cf. Section 16.11 on page 167) and rolldown of a curve position is simply the weighted sum of the carry and roll-down of the individual legs. Naturally, a simple outright position has the largest carry and roll-down because the individual legs in higher-order trading strategies partially offset each other in this respect. However, an implication of Figure 31.2 is that curve positions have non-zero net carry. Because the forward par curve tends to be flatter than the current curve, a steepening trade has positive returns even in an unchanged yield curve scenario, for instance.

In general, a strategy with n legs requires the determination of n notionals and therefore a system of n equations. The first of these equations sets the size of the trade and there are two common ways of specifying this size. One is to simply select one notional amount. The more appropriate alternative is to specify the trade size in terms of risk, such as in currency units per 1 bps yield change. These representations are mathematically equivalent. For an outright trade with notional N, the risk R is simply:

$$R = N * PVBP \tag{31.1}$$

For more complex trades, the remaining equations are usually derived such that a trade with n legs is hedged against the risks of all trades with up to $n-1$ legs. For example, a butterfly trade ($n = 3$) would therefore generally be set up so that it is hedged against outright yield moves ($n = 1$) and steepening/flattening moves ($n = 2$). The logic of this approach is that if one wanted to have steepening exposure in a butterfly, one could implement it in a separate additional trade. Hedging against $n-1$ exposures contributes $n-1$ equations so that together with the trade size, all n notionals can be determined. Details are discussed in the following subsections with sketches that show curve positions and an illustration of curve shifts, in dotted lines, that would lead to a positive P&L from the respective trades. Trades that profit from the opposite curve shift can be set up by inversing the positions.

As will be seen later on, higher order curve movements (butterflies and condors) are smaller in absolute size than lower order movements (outrights or steepeners and flatteners). Given that the trading strategies aimed at profiting from correctly predicting these movements increase in transaction costs with each added leg, lower expected profits due to the smaller expected movement run against higher expected transaction costs.

The main reason to be interested in higher-order trading strategies, aside from the simple fact that there are a lot more possible trades, is therefore related to information advantage or preferred habitat structures. Most taxi drivers have an opinion about the outright direction of interest rates and practically all investors have ways to express such views in their portfolios. A trader entering an outright position needs to question whether he or she has information that is not available to the general public, and therefore not already reflected in current market prices given the ease with which such a position can be established.

Higher-order curve positions tend to be related to more predictable short-term market dislocations, such as auctions or other supply events. They can also arise implicitly from hedging of outright positions. A trader who bought an illiquid 7 year security as part of market making might be hedging it with 5Y and 10Y futures. This creates a butterfly position which is likely to have little curve risk. The same trader might hedge all of the 7Y risk by selling 10Y futures to deliberately enter a steepening trade, or build a flattener by hedging with 5Y futures only. Because so many possible combinations of two, three or more legs exist, there are more ways in which specific information can be optimally expressed in trades.

It is sometimes assumed that higher order strategies lend themselves to more active trading because they show more volatility. After all, economic theory would predict that outright moves in interest rates should more or less follow the business cycle and therefore take around 8 years on average to change direction. The reality is more complex. As will be discussed later (on page 356), outright moves in fact tend to dominate daily yield curve dynamics. What sets more complex strategies apart is the difference in risk–return dynamics. In any case, the income volatility of a trading book is not determined solely by the volatility of the rates it is exposed to, but also the size of that exposure.

It is now relatively common to combine outright strategies in fixed income with outright positions in other asset classes, such as equities or commodities. This is very similar to building higher-order strategies in fixed income alone because the general aim is to hedge out common economic factors and target specific discrepancies in pricing of what is assumed to be similar risk.

31.1 SIMPLE CURVE TRADES

31.1.1 Outright Trades

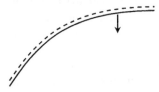

FIGURE 31.3 Outright short

Outright trades reflect expectations of general upwards or downwards yield movements. They are easy to set up and are in many cases combined with positions in other asset classes, notably FX and equities. In order to reduce transaction costs, some investors implement these trades with futures rather than cash bonds. This can lead to dislocations between the futures CTD bonds and surrounding bonds in the same market when liquidity in the cash bond or repo market prevents efficient arbitrage between these market segments.

31.1.2 Steepeners and Flatteners

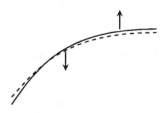

FIGURE 31.4 Flattener

The basic form of curve trading are steepening and flattening trades. To measure the steepness of the curve, one generally uses spreads between the benchmark bonds at certain maturities, usually those where a sovereign is actively issuing. Two examples of such spreads for the German curve are shown in Figure 31.5. They are simply the differences in yields of the benchmark bonds.

Higher order curve shape indicators can be constructed in a similar fashion. Before discussing how to set up trades, one drawback of benchmark spreads should be pointed out. Benchmarks change over time, here because the sovereign issues new bonds. Typically, a new bond will have a slightly higher yield than the previous benchmark at the same maturity point because it will have a longer maturity and curves have a positive slope. The change in benchmark therefore usually creates an upward jump in the benchmark yield. While this jump may be small to outright yield levels, it still signals a change in market rates that is not related to a change in prices of any of the outstanding

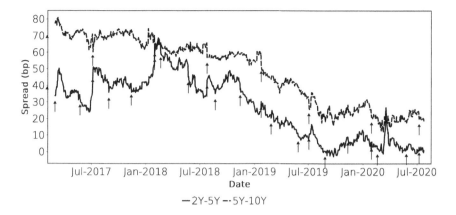

FIGURE 31.5 German government curve benchmark spread examples. The arrows mark the switches of benchmarks where they affect the respective spread. Source: Data from the Bundesbank.

bonds (a change in prices may of course happen at the same time as the benchmark change). For spreads, the impact may seem larger, and a good example is the issuance of a new OBL (German 5Y benchmark) on 25 July 2018. As Figure 31.5 shows, on this day the 2Y–5Y spread apparently steepened while the 5Y–10Y spread flattened. The actual driver of this apparent curve shape change was the change in 5Y benchmark from the older OBL177 to OBL178, with a maturity extension of about half a year.

A steepening or flattening trade should be hedged against outright yield movements. For the two notional N_1 and N_2 this means:

$$N_1 \text{PVBP}_1 = -N_2 \text{PVBP}_2 \qquad (31.2)$$

For the second equation one could simply select a fixed value for N_1 or N_2, but it is better to express the exposure in terms of risk. A fall in the yield at leg 2 by 1 bp with an unchanged yield in leg 1 creates a P&L of $N_2 \text{PVBP}_2$. By Equation (31.2), the same P&L arises when the yield in leg 1 increases by 1 bp for an unchanged yield in leg 2. This means that a risk R determines the notionals of a flattening or steepening trade as:

$$N_1 = \frac{R}{\text{PVBP}_1} = -\frac{R N_2 \text{PVBP}_2}{\text{PVBP}_1} \qquad (31.3)$$

A flattening trade has the same notional amounts but with opposite signs as a steepening trade. For the steepening trade, the longer maturity leg has a negative notional, for the flattening trade it is the shorter maturity leg.

Like all trades in this and the following sub-sections, one needs to be aware that the relationship Equation (31.2) will change over time because the two PVBP will

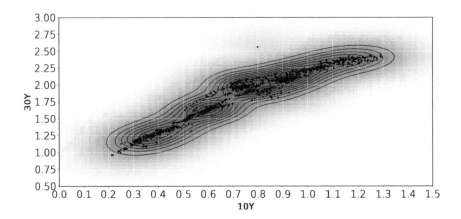

FIGURE 31.6 Japanese 10Y and 30Y rates 2010–2015. Nelson-Siegel par yields with prices from JSDA.

decline over time. In relative terms, the decline will be faster for the shorter maturity leg. This implies that the hedge will have to be continuously adjusted over time, or should be executed in forward PVBP in the first place, with a forward horizon set in relation to the expected holding period.

Somewhat inevitably, steepening and flattening positions are also sometimes expressed in ownership terms. Being 'long the curve' is a steepener, 'short the curve' is a flattener [86]. Helpful mnemonics for this convention are that it is consistent with futures terminology (long the roll means long the front, short the back contract), and being long the curve means wishing that it goes up (steepens).

Although steepeners and flatteners are linear trades, they can sometimes exhibit non-linear behaviour. For example, Figure 31.6 shows a scatterplot of the Japanese 10Y and 30Y JGB yields and there is a clear change in the slope between the two variables at around 0.75% in 10Y yields and 2% in 30Y yields. The explanation for this behaviour is that in the JGB market is largely domestic and some local investors base their behaviour on fixed yield targets related to life insurance liabilities. This creates strong demand for long-dated bonds above these target yields. In a sell-off, the long end of the curve is thereby supported at a certain level.

For a trader, such changes in behaviour create interesting opportunities, namely linear trading strategies that have an option-like non-linear pay-out when yields are near their pivot point. Of course, while it is possible to mine historical data for such opportunities, trading decisions require more structural analysis. The reason why Figure 31.6 presents data before 2016 is the change in JGB curve dynamics induced by the Bank of Japan quantitative easing policy. Interest rate levels in Japan are now far below most investors' target levels and BoJ operational implementation is now more significant for curve movements than before.

31.1.3 Butterflies

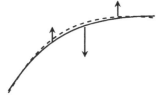

FIGURE 31.7 Butterfly

A butterfly trade is exposed to the performance of one instrument relative to two instruments of shorter and longer maturities. The centre instrument is known as the bullet (less often as the body), the other two are the wings. A difference exists between the conventions in the swap and bond markets when it comes to the measurement of butterfly spreads. While bond traders quote butterflies as bullet yield minus half of the sum of the two wing yields, swap traders quote the sum of the two wing rates minus twice the bullet rate. For identical interest rates, a bond butterfly spread is therefore half the number, with the opposite sign, of the swap butterfly spread. This inconvenience stems from the idea that swap rates are imagined as borrowing rates whereas bond yields describe incomes.

For bond butterflies, the benchmark change problem becomes more acute because it applies to three legs of a trade that tends to have little volatility. The standard remedy is to use spline yields instead of actual bond yields for analysis although the actual trade would still have to be implemented with specific bonds.

The weights of the legs follow from the principle outlined above that the trade should not have directional or steepening risk. These translate into the two equations:

$$N_2 \text{PVBP}_2 = -(N_1 \text{PVBP}_1 + N_3 \text{PVBP}_3)$$

$$N_1 \text{PVBP}_1 = N_3 \text{PVBP}_3 \tag{31.4}$$

An alternative way to interpret these equations is to visualise a butterfly as a combination of a steepener and a flattener with identical risks and a shared leg that forms the bullet. Each of the two trades is duration neutral, and if they have equal but opposite exposure to steepening risk, the butterfly will also be hedged against this type of risk. In terms of equations, one can split the bullet position N_2 into two parts N_2^a and N_2^b ($N_2 = N_2^a + N_2^b$) and specify the trade as follows:

$$N_2^a \text{PVBP}_2 = -N_1 \text{PVBP}_1$$

$$N_2^b \text{PVBP}_2 = -N_3 \text{PVBP}_3$$

$$N_1 \text{PVBP}_1 = N_3 \text{PVBP}_3 \tag{31.5}$$

where the last equation is equivalent to $N_2^a \text{PVBP}_2 = N_2^b \text{PVBP}_2$, i.e., $N_2^a = N_2^b$ which means an even split between the two components of the bullet.

A variation of the equal-weighted butterfly is to adjust the wing risks to the maturity difference between each wing and the bullet. This corresponds to the assumption that the curve steepening or flattening is mostly linear, and Equation (31.4) is then replaced by:

$$N_2 PVBP_2 = -(N_1 PVBP_1 + N_3 PVBP_3)$$

$$(m2 - m1)N_1 PVBP_1 = (m3 - m2)N_3 PVBP_3 \tag{31.6}$$

This butterfly will have a higher absolute weight on the wing closer to the bullet. It should be borne in mind, however, that the risk characteristics of very unevenly weighted butterflies are essentially those of steepening or flattening trades. It is therefore rare to see recommendations like a 2Y–4Y–30Y butterfly.

31.1.4   Condors

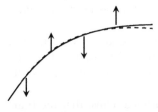

FIGURE 31.8 Condor

A condor is a comparatively rare strategy involving 4 positions along the same curve with equal risk amounts. The simplest way to conceptualise this strategy is as a combination of a steepener and a flattener with equal risks. The 2 legs of 1 of these strategies are outside 2 legs of the other. While multiple positions across the curve are common in most trading books, the specific choice to make the risks of the 2 constituent strategies equal sets the condor apart.

The equations determining the notionals follow those of a simple steepener and flattener Equation (31.2) for each of the two basic strategies, and an additional equation ensures the equality of the risk of these two strategies:

$$N_1 PVBP_1 = -N_4 PVBP_4$$

$$N_2 PVBP_2 = -N_3 PVBP_3$$

$$N_1 PVBP_1 = -N_2 PVBP_2 \tag{31.7}$$

31.2   INTRINSIC CURVE MOVEMENTS

Curve spreads describe the curve shape in terms of standard yield differences. As pointed out in the previous section, such spreads can be subject to various correlations that need to be taken into account before judging the appropriateness of their levels. This suggests an alternative approach, namely to extract characteristic curve movements from the historical data instead of imposing them ex-ante. A useful, but by no means exclusive approach to that is a PCA of par yields as demonstrated in Figure 31.9. A number of par yields are put into a PCA and the 3 factors (eigenvectors) corresponding to the largest three eigenvalues are shown[1].

---

[1]Note that, even with normalisation, eigenvectors are invariant to a change of sign on each component. The signs PCA factors shown here have been adjusted so as to correspond to standard curve strategies.

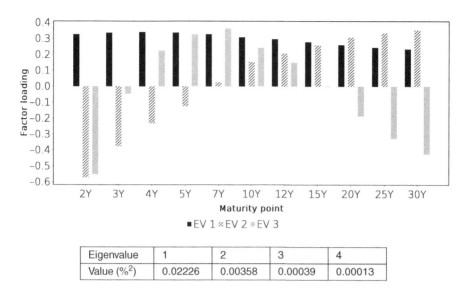

Eigenvalue	1	2	3	4
Value (%²)	0.02226	0.00358	0.00039	0.00013

FIGURE 31.9 Normalised PCA factor loadings for the US Treasury Nelson-Siegel spline. History 2014–2018, PCA on daily first differences. Source: Data from treasurydirect.gov.

PCA is often used in this context because the preconditions for PCA to give meaningful results are aligned with those of a good trading strategy. Yield movements are assumed to be driven by independent factors that follow stationary normal distributions, and the contributions of these factors are additive. Under these conditions, hedging against 1 or more factors will present an optimal reduction in market risk.

In the examples used here, as in some other studies, an additional issue should be borne in mind. Bond yield curves extracted from parametric models are very convenient as PCA inputs because they avoid the problems created by the aging of underlying bonds. That said, the underlying curve model imposes a correlation structure on the yields at various horizons and reduces the number of independent variables in the system. Logically, there cannot be more independent factors driving those model yields than the model has parameters, no matter how many bonds are used to fit the model. A PCA may, however, show a larger number of independent factors because the model parameters have a non-linear impact on model yields.

Once PCA factors have been calculated, one can calculate the residuals of the yield curve after removing a given number of factors. Assuming the input yields are given as the vector $\mathbf{y}(t)$, the residual curve $\mathbf{y}_k(t)$ after removing the first k factors $\mathbf{e}_i$ is simply:

$$\mathbf{y}_k(t) = \mathbf{y}(t) - \sum_{i=0}^{k} \mathbf{y}(t)\mathbf{v}_i \tag{31.8}$$

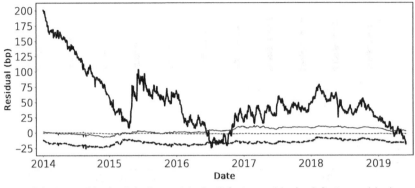

—0-factor residual --1-factor residual —2-factor residual ---3-factor residual

FIGURE 31.10 k-factor residuals of the 10Y point on the German Nelson-Siegel spline. The 0-factor residual is simply the 10Y yield. Because PCA factors have been calculated based on yield changes, residuals are not centred at 0. Source: Data from Bundesbank.

The time series of the products $\mathbf{y}(t)\mathbf{v}_i$ are the factor realisations of the factors i. Figure 31.10 shows the residuals of the 10Y point on the German spline. As expected, the volatility of the residuals declines as more and more factors are removed. The incremental reduction in volatility declines because successive factors contribute less and less to total variance.

The structure of the main factors tends to be fairly invariant across markets although some less liquid curves show less structure in higher eigenvectors. The PCA decomposition of the German curve, shown in Figure 31.11, is very similar in overall structure to that of the US curve.

In general, the first PCA factor tends to have identical signs in all components which means that it describes a general upward or downward movement in interest rates. That such movements should contribute the main variance to overall interest rate dynamics is the empirical justification for the use of duration as a risk measure, and the attention to short-term directional changes when managing portfolio risk. The main theoretical drawback of yield as a return measure, and by implication of duration as a risk measure, is that they assume a flat discount rate structure. While the existence of a yield curve negates the existence of such a flat discount rate structure, the nearly flat structure of actual yield *changes* suggests that duration is useful for describing portfolio *risk* in practice.

There tends to be a sporadically high degree of correlation between the first factor realisations across economies, reflecting market dynamics that are driven by common global factors, such as the outlook for energy prices or global growth. Investors can move capital freely between markets and so create a weak form of arbitrage between them.

Consequently, the first PCA factors measuring general changes in interest rate levels react in parallel, if not always to the same degree. Figure 31.12, comparing the first

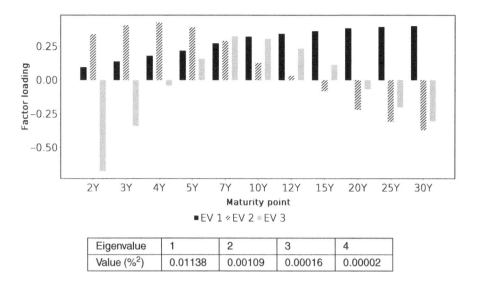

Eigenvalue	1	2	3	4
Value (%²)	0.01138	0.00109	0.00016	0.00002

FIGURE 31.11 Normalised PCA factor loadings for the German government bond Nelson-Siegel spline. History 2014–2018, PCA on daily first differences. Source: Data from Bundesbank.

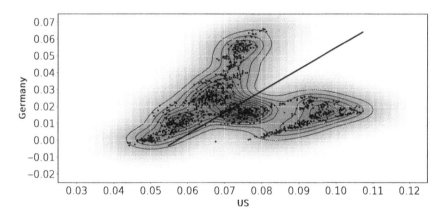

FIGURE 31.12 First PCA factor realisations for the US and Germany. History 2014–2020. Source: Data from treasurydirect.gov and Bundesbank.

PCA factors of the US and German curves, shows essentially two different correlation regimes. One is a nearly one-for-one correspondence of changes, the other has a nearly static German first factor against a volatile US one. Given that during the observation period the ECB started a sizeable public sector bond purchase programme that had a significant dampening effect on yield levels in the euro area, while the Fed started

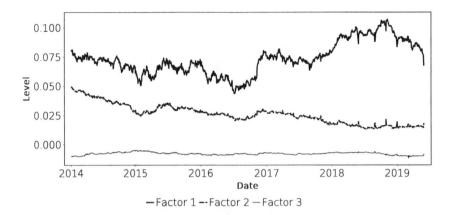

FIGURE 31.13 PCA factor realisations for the US Treasury Nelson-Siegel spline. Because the factors are normalised, their realisations show a good measure of their actual yield impact. History 2014–2020. Source: Data from treasurydirect.gov.

a reduction in the bond portfolio it had accumulated earlier, such changes in correlation should not be surprising[2].

The second PCA factor tends to describe relative yield changes between the front and back end of the yield curve, i.e., a steepening or flattening of the yield curve. The relationship between maturity and yield change is only rarely linear. Also, the first PCA factor tends to already incorporate some degree of yield curve shape change rather than a parallel move. A correlated movement of yield levels and curve slope is known as bear-steepening, bear-flattening, or their opposites bull-flattening and bull-steepening, respectively. The steepening or flattening captured by the second factor therefore is a movement that is uncorrelated by the steepening or flattening already incorporated by the first factor.

The third PCA factor also tends to have a characteristic shape, namely an under- or out-performance of the centre of the curve relative to the short and long ends. Because every duration-neutral butterfly with a short bullet position has positive convexity, re-hedging the trade after every outright yield shift should over time result in a positive P&L, at least before transaction costs. To the extent that volatility is expected by the market, this positive P&L should be reflected in the carry of the trade which is determined by the shape of the yield curve. By implication, therefore, the yield of the bullet should be higher than the straight-line interpolated yield of the 2 wings at the bullet maturity point. This means that the usual convex shape of the yield curve is related to the convexity of butterfly trades. Although it is unlikely that this is the

---

[2]Non-standard monetary policy tools affect the formation of market prices. If different markets can reflect changes in economic fundamentals only to a limited degree, than this should suppress the correlation between their yield movements.

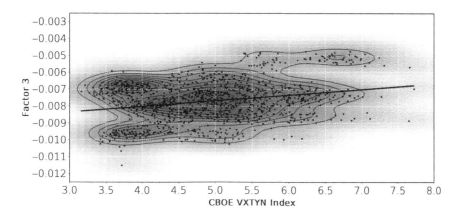

FIGURE 31.14 Scatter plot of the PCA factor 3 realisation versus the CBOE VXTYN volatility index. US Treasury Nelson-Siegel spline. History 2014–2018. Source: Data from treasurydirect .gov, index data downloaded from FRED.

sole explanation for the yield curve shape, the convexity of the yield curve does tend to be connected with volatility. Because curve convexity tends to be captured by the third eigenvector of a curve PCA (cf. Figures 31.9 and 31.11), this connection is visible when plotting the realisation of this factor against implied volatility. This is done in Figure 31.14 for the US Treasury market (as in Figure 31.13) against a measure of fixed income volatility, namely the VXTYN index produced by CBOE.

The correlation is positive in this dataset but clearly not strong enough to argue that implied volatility is the sole driver of curve convexity. Again, the nature of PCA is such that if implied volatility were itself very volatile and responsible for very significant changes in curve shape, the effect would show up already in the lower eigenvectors. In addition, the convexity effect on curve shapes tends to be fairly localised, and is therefore more clearly evident in analyses such as Figure 20.4 on page 210.

It should therefore not surprise that there is also not too much of a relationship between the model volatility of a structural curve model such as the Vasicek model and realised curvature (cf. Figure 31.15).

While the Vasicek spline parameter k does change curvature (cf. Figure 19.5 on page 201), the way in which this occurs need not coincide with how curvature is captured by the PCA analysis. An important contributor to this discrepancy is the correlation between the various parameters of the Vasicek spline, or indeed generally the parameters of structural curve models.

At the time of writing, the yield curves in major markets, and the implied volatilities of interest rates, are heavily influenced by direct central bank actions, namely large-scale asset purchase programmes or portfolios, and relatively clear forward guidance of interest rates. To some degree, this limits the impact of economic factors, such as the relationship between volatility and convexity, on the curve shape.

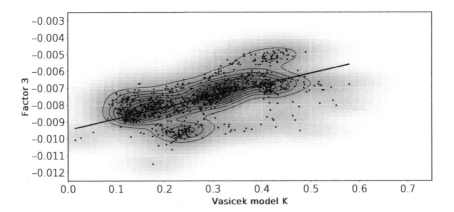

FIGURE 31.15 Scatter plot of the PCA factor 3 realisation against the k parameter of a Vasicek spline fitted to the US Treasury curve. History 2014–2020. Source: Data from treasurydirect.gov.

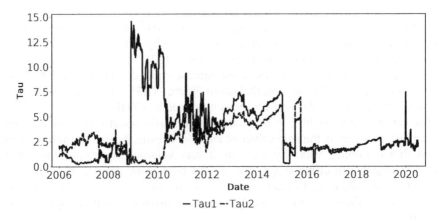

FIGURE 31.16 History of the λ parameters of the daily ECB AAA Nelson-Siegel-Svensson spline. Source: Based on ECB SDW. Note that the ECB specification refers to these parameters as τ_1 and τ_2.

31.2.1 Alternative specifications

As mentioned above, it is by no means clear that PCA is the most appropriate way to extract patterns of curve shapes and measure their changes. The Nelson-Siegel and Nelson-Siegel-Svensson splines are explicitly designed to reflect standard yield curve changes ('level', 'slope' and 'hump') through different β parameters (cf. Figure 19.3 on page 197). Without going through the circuitous route of fitting a spline to market yields, and then running the resulting spline par yields through PCA, one could directly use the relevant parameters of these models.

While this is an interesting thought, there are 2 problems with it. The first is that the λ parameters of the Nelson-Siegel splines tend to be very volatile, as shown in Figure 31.16. The parameters β_3 and β_4 measure the size of humps but it is not possible to consistently express the size of such a hump through a butterfly trade because the location of that hump is shifting. The second difficulty is that the β_i are correlated through time. A butterfly trade with 3 legs has 2 free parameters for hedging and finding the corresponding 2 equations requires bumping each of the β parameters to establish model sensitivities[3] and a historical correlation analysis of the β.

---

[3]One might argue that the β linearly determine interest rates and model sensitivity should therefore be straightforward. This would be true if the trade was implemented with zero-coupon instruments. Usually that is not the case, however, so the non-linear dependencies of par instrument prices need to be used.

CHAPTER 32

Bond Trading

Bonds tend to be traded to express views on yield developments. In this respect, trading bonds is not different from trading swaps or interest rate derivatives. How to analyse and implement such strategies has been discussed in the previous chapter. This chapter will instead focus on trading ideas that are not expressible in these ways.

That being said, some of the concepts presented here also affect some curve trading strategies. When putting on a 2Y–10Y curve steepener through bonds, it may be useful to sell an expensive 10Y and buy a cheap 2Y. In this respect, a curve trade is overlayed with 2 bond relative value trades. The focus of this chapter is on such relative value ideas.

32.1   BOND RELATIVE VALUE

The start to trading individual securities is valuation. Yields alone are insufficient for this purpose because the yield concept suffers from a number of drawbacks that were discussed in the relevant Chapter 16.7. Instead, curve spreads of various kinds are used to identify the relative valuation of bonds.

Given that multiple spreads can be calculated for each security against multiple curves (G-spreads against government curves, I-spreads against the swap curve, Z-spreads against an issuer-specific spline, etc.), a first question is which is the most appropriate. The simple answer is that usually the most sensible spread is the 1 that reflects the usual hedge strategy for the bond in question.

> **Government bonds** are hedged with other government bonds and a Z-spread against government bond spline is the natural first choice for a relative valuation measure.
>
> **Sub-sovereigns, supranationals and agencies** tend to be hedged with sovereign bonds and G-spreads would appear the natural first choice. However, G-spreads are not directly comparable between bonds that reference different benchmarks, and G-spreads do not correct for duration differences. A Z-spread against a government

spline is therefore more meaningful. In the euro area, most SSA bonds are traded against French government bonds rather than the German curve. Constructing issuer-specific splines in the SSA segment is usually difficult given the lower number of outstanding securities, but the composite spline curves outlined in Section 19.4.5 on page 202 can be used in many cases.

High-grade corporate bonds, covered bonds and senior secured bank debt are usually hedged with swaps, so an I-spread or asset swap spread is a good first choice.

Corporate debt in general is subject to wide, and potentially steep, credit curves. A fair value model based on a risk free curve (usually the swap curve) and credit default swaps is a more approriate choice than the swap curve alone. Such models are beyond the scope of this book, cf. for instance [73].

Splines tend to be calibrated with no reference to repo rates. They therefore neglect the additional value that securities lending (collateral swaps) can bring to holding a bond that is special in the repo market, or the higher cost of shorting such a bond. The logically consistent way to incorporate this information would be to calibrate the spline not to spot prices, but to some form of forward. The reason this is not done widely is that on one hand it is not clear over what horizon the forward should be calculated, and that repo rates beyond the overnight horizon are very opaque. Calculating forwards over short horizons does not make much of a difference, and over longer horizons one would have to make some assumptions about the evolution of the overnight repo rates.

Beyond the simple answer that hedge strategies determine valuation benchmarks lies a more complex one. Hedging determines near-term price changes with reference to the more liquid hedge instruments. This is the appropriate frame of reference for identifying temporary misalignments in valuation patterns. However, if the aim is to identify underlying value, then these curve spread measures do not help so much. Seeing a KFW bond trade at 2 bps over a composite KFW spline means that the bond is cheaper than other KFW bonds, but not that it is a good investment. To determine whether it is a good investment, one would have to compare its spread to other substitutes (other German agencies, other euro area agencies), outlook for supply, trends in investor demand and so on.

32.2 RELATIVE VALUE STRATEGIES

32.2.1 Spread Widener/Tightener

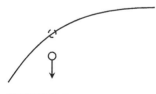

If one expects a bond to underperform a curve, one can express this view with a spread widener. This involves selling the bond and receiving the appropriate curve. The default strategy would be to sell the bond in an asset swap and so hedge virtually all of the individual cash flow risk of the bond. Given the expense

FIGURE 32.1 Spread widener   of executing such a non-standard swap, one might instead execute a matched (interpolated) swap. A spread tightener, the opposite trading view, involves the opposite positioning: Long the bond and paying the curve.

An area of uncertainty is the nomenclature. If the bond is trading above the curve, an underperformance of the bond will widen the spread to the curve. If the bond instead is below the curve, an underperformance will tighten it. The choice made here is to be consistent in terms of positioning and associate a short bond position with spread widening, even if it means a negative spread becoming less negative (as shown in the sketch). This is appropriate in a global curve environment where some government bond markets trade below and above the corresponding swap curves.

If one uses a spline curve to identify bond valuations, then positive spline spreads signal relative cheapness and so potentially a signal to put on a spread tightener. Negative spline spreads, correspondingly, might be a signal for future underperformance to correct relative richness. While the interpretation of this spread is straightforward, its expression in a trade is not because unlike swaps, spline curves cannot be traded directly. The solution is to embed the widening or tightening trade in a bond spread or butterfly position against one or two other bonds with the opposite valuation signals. The incentive to use a butterfly instead of a simple spread is a potential duration difference between the 2 bonds which exposes the trade to curve steepening or flattening risk. A butterfly removes this curve risk while butterfly risk is smaller in magnitude (cf. Figure 31.10 on page 356).

For bond portfolio managers tracking an index, the benchmark acts like a short position in the entire curve (cf. Section 38.1.3 on page 405). A spread widener can then be implemented through an underweight in this specific bond, while a spread tightener would suggest an overweight.

32.2.2 Basis Trade

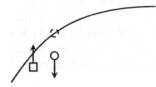

FIGURE 32.2 Short basis trade

The alternative to paying or receiving a curve, where possible, is to be short or long a futures contract against a bond, i.e., a basis trade. In the example here, the short position in the bond is hedged with a long in a futures contract. This approach assumes that the futures contract will move in line with the curve in question, and that the futures contract CTD is close in maturity to the bond so that curve risk is not relevant.

The hedge equation is simply that the bond risk should be matched by the futures risk, with an opposite sign:

$$N_B \text{PVBP}_B = -N_F \text{PVBP}_F \qquad (32.1)$$

Because a DV01-neutral package of a bond and a future has no duration risk, it is often tradeable with a lower bid–offer spread than an outright trade in the bond[1].

Should bond and futures CTD differ significantly in maturity, then two different futures contracts can be used to eliminate the curve risk in line with a usual butterfly position. A useful assumption is that any yield curve steepening or flattening is linear, so the futures should be weighted according to their distance to the bond:

$$N_B \text{PVBP}_B = -(N_{F1} \text{PVBP}_{F1} + N_{F2} \text{PVBP}_{F2})$$

$$(m_B - m_{F1})N_{F1} \text{PVBP}_{F1} = (m_{F2} - m_B)N_{F2} \text{PVBP}_{F2} \tag{32.2}$$

where m_B etc. are the times to maturity (in any unit) for the bond and the futures CTDs. This equation will lead to a higher hedge weight assigned to the future that is closer to the bond. Note that it is not necessary for the futures to bracket the bond ($m_{F1} < m_b < m_{F2}$) and if the bond is outside the maturity points of the CTDs, the signs of N_{F1} and N_{F2} will differ.

32.2.3 Bond Spread

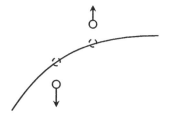

FIGURE 32.3 Bond spread trade

A bond spread trade is a simple long position in one bond and a short position in another. The mathematics match those of a curve steepener or flattener trade as discussed in Section 31.1.2. The difference is one of motivation, and that provides the link to bond relative value analysis.

In a steepening/flattening trade, the expectation is that curve shape changes and the bonds are chosen to implement this curve view. The trade suggested here is driven by an expectation that the relative valuation of two bonds changes but the overall curve shape does not.

32.2.4 Bond Spread with Curve Hedge

The bond spread in the previous example is exposed to overall curve steepening/flattening risk. If the bond maturities are sufficiently far apart, this risk can negatively affect the risk/reward characteristics of the trade.

---

[1]In this type of trade, the counterparties agree to cross the appropriate number of futures contracts on the exchange immediately after the trade.

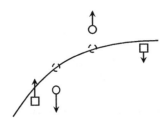

FIGURE 32.4 Curve-hedged bond spread

Where suitable futures contracts are available, this curve risk can be hedged out by entering an opposite flattening/steepening position to the one formed by the spread trade. For instance, a spread trade between a 3Y and a 4Y bond could be hedged with 2Y and 5Y bond futures. Futures contracts, or in the US market the on-the-run benchmarks, have very tight bid–offer spreads compared to cash bonds so that the extra cost of entering or unwinding the hedge is comparatively low.

The appropriate amounts follow in essence the calculation for a curve steepener or flattener (cf. Section 31.1.2). For the 2 bonds and 2 futures, Equation (31.2) must hold, and in addition the risks on the bond leg must be the opposite as for the futures leg. This yields a system of 3 equations for 3 unknowns, in addition to the fourth parameter determining the aggregate risk:

$$N_1 \text{PVBP}_1 = -N_2 \text{PVBP}_2$$

$$N_{F1} \text{PVBP}_{F1} = -N_{F2} \text{PVBP}_{F2}$$

$$N_1 \text{PVBP}_1 = -N_{F1} \text{PVBP}_{F1} \tag{32.3}$$

Even with this hedge, the curve risk may not be fully hedged. For instance, if the 2 bonds in question were Dutch government bonds and one were to use German bond futures to hedge the curve because there are no futures on Dutch bonds, then the hedge would still be at risk from a relative steepening or flattening of the Dutch versus the German curve. This risk should be substantially lower, however, than the steepening risk of the Duch curve alone.

Note also that the configuration shown here, where the futures contracts surround the bonds in question, is not the only possible one. One can equally, and with the same equations, hedge a spread between a 3Y and 4Y bond using 5Y and 10Y futures. However, the more the futures diverge from the bonds in terms of curve sectors, the higher the residual curve risk of the trade.

32.2.5   Alternative Strategies

More complex trading strategies than the ones used here are possible, and more will become available with the development of new instruments. Swap futures are gradually building more liquidity and may at some point become a more natural way to express spread views than bilateral swaps. Money market futures strips already provide this opportunity in some cases (for instance, Euribor contracts against the Eurex Schatz futures, or Eurodollars against the US 2Y and 5Y Note futures). The essential designs of these trades are similar to the examples shown here and should not be too difficult to quantify for the reader.

One point that should be borne in mind, however, is that simplicity is a virtue for active trading strategies. An over-engineered trading strategy with too many parts tends to require a lot of re-adjustment during its lifetime which blurs the performance attribution.

Seven

Risk Management

CHAPTER 33

Principal Component Analysis

Principal component analysis (PCA) is a useful statistical technique for dimension reduction of multivariate normally distributed data that can easily be implemented using standard statistics packages. A useful starting point are mean and standard deviation of a univariate normal random variable. While the mean is the centre of the distribution, the standard deviation provides a measure of how far the data is spread around the mean.

PCA is used throughout this book but presented here in the risk management section because it is particularly convenient for reducing the dimensionality of a complex system.

In 2 dimensions, standard deviation becomes a less well-defined concept. If one were to use a ruler to measure the extent of the distribution, it is clear that one point of the ruler should coincide with the mean, but it is not obvious in which direction the ruler should point. It turns out that if the standard deviation is measured and marked with the ruler in all possible directions, the resulting marks form an ellipse (cf. Figure 33.1).

This is related to a different problem which can be described in terms of the usual characters in cryptography: If Alice, after an initial transmission of some information, had to repeatedly describe to Bob a sample of a bivariate distribution (x_i, y_i) with a single number z_i, how should she calculate that number? One possibility would be to choose 1 of the dimensions, e.g. $z_i = x_i$. For any given value of x, however, there is a range of likely values of y, and vice versa. Could there be a linear combination $z_i = \alpha x_i + \beta y_i$ so that Bob has the lowest uncertainty about (x, y) when receiving only z_i from Alice?

The relationship between the 2 problems is that the optimal α and β will reduce the standard deviation of the estimate (x', y') made from the value z to a minimum. As such, the problem of reducing dimensionality (here from 2 to 1) can be expressed as an estimation problem.

Before moving on, the next question is why it should be sufficient to consider linear models given the multitude of non-linear relationships discussed throughout this book. The answer is that one is often faced with risk analysis around a given point (usually the current set of market rates ϑ), and risk is then the change in portfolio value for small

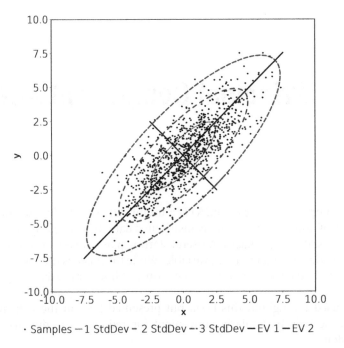

· Samples — 1 StdDev - 2 StdDev −·3 StdDev — EV 1 — EV 2

FIGURE 33.1 Standard deviations of a highly correlated bivariate normal distribution of 2 variables x and y with the 2 eigenvectors of the covariance matrix (EV1 and EV2). The somewhat unusual chart format was chosen to preserve the right angle between the 2 orthogonal eigenvectors.

changes $\Delta\vartheta$ in these rates. One therefore has a problem that can be represented by a Taylor series:

$$P(\vartheta + \Delta\vartheta) = P(\vartheta) + \Delta\vartheta \nabla P + \dots \qquad (33.1)$$

Having a linear term therefore is valid as the first step in the approximation.

Conceptually, PCA can be explained as the process of extracting the single linear combination of variables $\sum_i \beta_{1,i} x_i$ that explains most of the variance of the data set. In this case, β_i would be the first PCA factor. The projection $\beta_1 x = z_1$ is known as the realisation of this factor. The next PCA factor is then the combination of variables that explains most of the variance of $x - z_1\beta_1$. The third PCA factor then explains most of the variance remaining after the first two factors $x - z_1\beta_1 - z_2\beta_2$ etc. In the communication problem above the best single variable for Alice to communicate to Bob is z_1, if he could communicate 2 numbers, the optimal choices would be z_1 and z_2, etc. For a hedger, the most important risk to hedge against is a change in z_1, once this is hedged, the next most important risk is z_2 and so on.

Instead of using this iterative process, one can obtain all PCA factors in a single step because they are simply the eigenvectors of the covariance matrix of the observations x_i. To recall, eigenvectors are the vectors β satisfying the equation:

$$M\beta = \lambda\beta \qquad (33.2)$$

The eigenvector corresponding to the largest eigenvalue λ is the first PCA factor and so on. The eigenvalues λ measure the standard deviation of the data set in the direction of the corresponding eigenvector as shown in Figure 33.1. Most standard numerical libraries contain ready-made routines for the simultaneous calculation of eigenvectors and eigenvalues.

Two considerations need to be made when producing a PCA: whether to construct the covariance matrix from levels or changes, and whether to normalise the covariance matrix, i.e., use the correlation matrix.

The levels versus changes choice is essentially related to the unit root problem in ordinary least squares regression analyses. If the series under consideration is stationary, levels and changes will produce the same eigenvectors. If the series are not stationary, then taking first differences makes them stationary. On the face of it, therefore, one should always conduct PCA on levels rather than changes. That being said, if the series is not stationary, then some assumptions related to the use of PCA may not hold.

The choice between covariance and correlation matrix similarly depends on the problem at hand. When constructing yield curve hedges, there is no point in normalising volatility at different points of the curve because the point of the analysis is precisely to adjust to such variations in volatility. When considering performances of equity and bond indices, however, the index levels or changes depend largely on the scale of the index, and these are largely a function of when the index in question was established. Normalising away such historical artefacts is a useful first step.

33.1 PCA AS GENERALISED REGRESSION

As in other disciplines, it is often necessary in finance to relate 2 variables in a linear equation, i.e.,

$$y = \beta x + \alpha \tag{33.3}$$

One can estimate α and β from N pairs of observed data (x_i, y_i) using standard regression equations:

$$\beta = \frac{N \sum x_i y_i - \sum x_i \sum y_i}{N \sum x_i^2 - \left(\sum x_i \right)^2}$$

$$\alpha = \frac{\sum y_i - \beta \sum x_i}{N} \tag{33.4}$$

The problem with financial variables is that it is usually not obvious which variable is dependent or independent. For example, when estimating a hedge ratio between 2 different bond yields, none of the 2 is obviously the independent variable. The problem is that when Equation (33.3) is re-formulated as the inverse problem:

$$x = \beta' y + \alpha' \tag{33.5}$$

one would expect that because changing x by 1, Equation (33.3) implies a change in y of β, that β' in Equation (33.5) would be equal to $1/\beta$. Running the regression Equation (33.4) given above with exchanged variables x and y will, however, not yield that result with real data.

The problem is that Equation (33.4) makes an implicit assumption, namely that x can be measured with certainty while y may be subject to noise, i.e.,

$$y_i = \beta x_i + \alpha + \varepsilon_i \tag{33.6}$$

The more realistic approach for financial variables is usually that there is an underlying factor z that drives the evolution of both x and y but both these 2 dependent variables are subject to additional, unknown noise:

$$x_i = \beta_x z_i + \alpha_x + \varepsilon_{x,i}$$
$$y_i = \beta_y z_i + \alpha_y + \varepsilon_{y,i} \tag{33.7}$$

One can write this in matrix form if the 2 noise terms are correlated:

$$(x_i \ y_i) = \begin{pmatrix} \beta_x & w_x \\ \beta_y & w_y \end{pmatrix} \begin{pmatrix} z_i \\ \varepsilon_i \end{pmatrix} + (\alpha_x \ \alpha_y) \tag{33.8}$$

where neither z nor ε are directly observable but z is assumed to be the signal while ε is noise. Under the additional assumption that the signal term z dominates the variance of x and y, one arrives at a PCA problem: The eigenvector of the covariance matrix of x and y corresponding to the largest eigenvalue, i.e. the ratio β_y/β_x will provide a better estimate for the regression coefficient between y and x than Equation (33.4), and trivially one finds that the inverse relationship holds true when swapping x and y. The evolution of z would then be interpreted as that of the common factor driving both x and y.

Because the characteristic polynomial of a 2x2 matrix is quadratic, there is a closed-form solution for this problem:

$$\begin{vmatrix} \text{var}_x - \lambda & \text{cov}_{xy} \\ \text{cov}_{xy} & \text{var}_y - \lambda \end{vmatrix} = 0 \tag{33.9}$$

so:

$$\lambda_{\pm} = \frac{\text{var}_x + \text{var}_y}{2} \pm \sqrt{\frac{(\text{var}_x + \text{var}_y)^2}{4} - \text{var}_x \text{var}_y + \text{cov}_{xy}^2} \tag{33.10}$$

The required eigenvector is the one corresponding to the larger eigenvalue λ_+. Without normalisation:

$$\mathbf{v}_+ = \begin{pmatrix} 1 \\ \frac{\lambda_+ - \text{var}_x}{\text{cov}_{xy}} \end{pmatrix} \tag{33.11}$$

The second component of $\mathbf{v}_+$, $(\lambda_+ - \text{var}_x)/\text{cov}_{xy})$ in this equation, is comparable to the β in Equation (33.3). The associated α is easily recovered from $< y >= \beta < x > +\alpha$ as:

$$\alpha =< y > -\beta < x > \tag{33.12}$$

33.2 MEASURING DATA COMPLEXITY WITH PCA

A somewhat unconventional but nevertheless edifying use of PCA is the measurement of the complexity of curve dynamics. To recall, the eigenvalues of the covariance matrix measure the contribution of the corresponding eigenvector to the total variance of the sample. This suggests two uses of these eigenvalues. The standard one is the measurement of curve volatility, which utilises the absolute values of these eigenvaues. An alternative use of eigenvalues is to consider their relative magnitudes. If a single eigenvalue dominates total sample volatility, then the dynamic of the entire curve is largely determined by a single factor. Independently of whether the curve is volatile or not, such a single-factor curve would be considered somewhat uninteresting. In contrast, finding several eigenvalues with higher values signals a more complex curve dynamic.

To use this approach, one conducts PCA on rolling data windows, as shown in Equation (33.2). The yields shown are the raw spline yields at various maturities that enter the PCA. Instead of using the complete sample, a rolling window is pulled across time and PCA is applied on the covariance of changes inside this window as it moves along the time axis. This means that the covariance matrix becomes a time series, as do derived quantities such as the eigenvalues.

Furnished with the time series of eigenvalus, one can proceed to construct complexity measures. The standard quantity to express the degree of dominance in economics is the Herfindahl index, which is the sum of squares of market shares of firms in a given market. One can easily apply the same ideas to PCA eigenvalues and construct the quantity:

$$H = \frac{\sum_i e_i^2}{\left(\sum_i e_i\right)^2} \tag{33.13}$$

from the eigenvalues e_i. Figure 33.3 shows the evolution of this quantity when calculated on a rolling basis for two different yield curves. The high volatility of the curve after the outbreak of the Corona crisis in 2020 is shown clearly in the drop in the German Herfindahl index which implies that curve movements became less dominated by a single factor.

An alternative interpretation of this quantity is that it gives guidance on the appropriate hedge strategy for a given portfolio. A high value of the index suggests dominance of a single PCA factor which implies that a single hedge instrument should suffice to cover the bulk of portfolio risk. A lower value means more complex dynamics and the requirement for more hedge instruments.

Instead of calculating this index for different points of a single curve, as done above, one can conduct the same PCA on the same points of multiple curves, for instance,

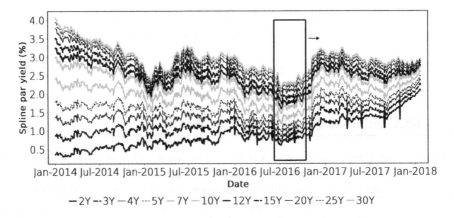

FIGURE 33.2   Spline par yields of the US Treasury curve through time. Source: Data from treasurydirect.gov.

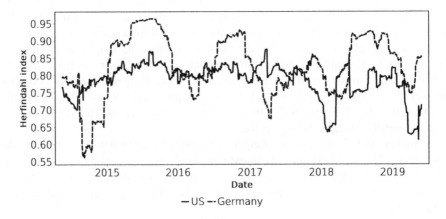

FIGURE 33.3   Herfindahl indices calculated from a rolling PCA of the US and German spline yields. History 2014–2020, rolling 90 business day window. Source: Data from treasurydirect.gov and Bundesbank.

the yields of multiple issuers. The resulting Herfindahl index would then help identify 'interesting' spread dynamics (bouts of name-specific risk aversion) that require complex hedge strategies.

This is done in Figure 33.4 for various Japanese issuer curves at two different maturity points (5- and 10-year) although the data shows that there is a fair degree of correlation between the spreads at these 2 points. Again, one would use such analyses as guidance to either the times when spread dynamics turn interesting, or to the required complexity of a hedge structure.

Relying on rolling correlation matrices is not without problems, however. Choosing long window lengths means that new data has a low weight in the estimation of the correlation matrix so it takes some time for structural changes in dynamics to be visible

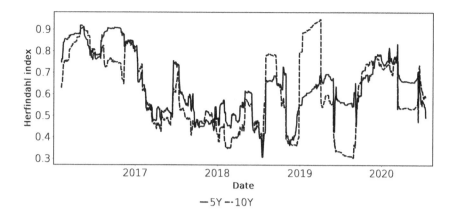

FIGURE 33.4 Herfindahl indices calculated from a rolling PCA of Japanese government bond and other issuer spline yields (issuers are Tokyo Metropolis, Osaka Prefecture, Kanagawa, JFM, Japan Expressway, JR East, JR West, Tokyo Electric, Kansai Electric, Chubu Electric). Source: Data from JSDA.

in the analysis. On the other hand, shorter windows usually lead to more volatility in the observed matrices. If the results are to be used for designing appropriate hedge strategies, such volatility could create unwarranted frequent adjustments.

CHAPTER 34

Bond Index Mechanics

A bond index is a default portfolio designed to represent an investable market subset. Multiple index providers compete in providing indices that represent, as well as possible, potential investment universes and the actual risks and returns available in these universes.

34.1 BOND INDEX PRINCIPLES

The fundamental requirements of any market index are threefold:

Ex-ante definition means that the index universe should be known ex-ante and not only ex-post. This rules out index definitions like 'the ten best-performing stocks of the current month', or return definitions like 'the top decile of actively managed funds'. This requirement ensures that an actual portfolio manager is able to make investment decisions based on information available at the time of investing.

Replicability adds the requirement that the index can actually be bought in the market. This constraint is particularly important when instruments included in the index differ in liquidity.

Broad bond market indices tend to include the entire universe of bonds satisfying the index criteria. Corporate bonds older than one year, however, tend to be virtually unattainable under normal market conditions. An index including them is therefore relevant to long-running bond portfolios but practically impossible to replicate with newly invested money.

An important qualification to the replicability criterion is that it refers to replication *within* the index universe itself. More complex indices virtually rule out replicability through return calculations that are unrealistic. The REX index of German government bonds produced by Deutsche Börse involves theoretical bonds with coupons that do no exist in the market at the time of writing. However, investors are able to replicate REX index returns by resorting to substitute bonds outside the German government bond market such as German Pfandbriefe. Such investment strategies do expose investors to off-index risks, in this case for instance the spread and relative liquidity risks of government and covered bonds.

Measurability requires that the index can be valued at a reasonable, for instance daily, frequency. This requirement ensures that any portfolio can be compared to the index at all times.

Measurability is one of the reasons why real estate and private equity indices are comparatively uncommon. These less liquid assets tend to trade rarely, and at prices that are not always fully transparent. It would therefore be unreasonable to offer an investment product that tracks the performance of such illiquid assets.

A bond index offering therefore consists of 2 independent elements. One is the time-varying set of bonds that constitute the index members, with the index provider warranting that eligible bonds are reliably identified and screened, and their outstanding amounts known. Mathematically speaking, this information amounts to a map of bond identifiers to outstanding amounts:

$$i \longmapsto N_i \tag{34.1}$$

where $N_i = 0$ when bond i is not included in the index. The second is a realistic pricing for the constituent bond set, which should be as close as possible to executable prices. This also amounts to a map from bond identifiers to prices:

$$i \longmapsto p_i \tag{34.2}$$

where p_i is the market price of a given bond i. As bond performances are calculated, other return factors, such as coupon payments, accrued interest, and inflation uplift (if applicable) would be taken into account. These return elements are, however, independent of market developments and can therefore be processed in a mechanical way.

As described in Chapter 18 on liquidity, the idea of a universally applicable price for a given asset at a given time is unrealistic. Pricing depends not only on the asset or the time, but also on the execution venue, the set of available counterparties, and the client in question. Index providers tend to resolve this ambiguity through averaging across multiple price providers, observed trades and so on. As a general principle, because index prices tend to be used to value portfolios, the relevant prices are bids because accounting standards require valuations of long positions on the basis of a liquidation trade. An exception is that bonds entering an index are valued at the ask side because the presumption is that a portfolio tracking the index will have to purchase, rather than sell, these bonds. As a result, indices incorporate an implied bid–offer spread that makes tracking errors more realistic.

Bond indices tend to be constructed such as to encompass multiple markets. This creates a fundamental problem for cross-market portfolios that attempt to reallocate investments from one market to another because there are different settlement conventions in different markets. For instance, an investor looking to sell a Japanese government bond portfolio to reinvest in US Treasuries is faced with the problem that JGBs settle T+2[1], so the cash obtained from selling the Japanese bonds will come due only

---

[1] Note that T+2 does not apply during the coupon period of JGB. Depending on the transaction date and the bond in question, settlement might occur later.

2 business days after the sale. This matches the T+2 settlement of the FX transaction turning the Yen received into US dollars. However, US Treasuries settle T+0 or T+1 so that the the cash to pay for the purchase is not available in time to settle this leg of the trade. The standard solution to this problem is to ignore it. Bond index returns are calculated on a common T+0 settlement basis across all markets. This makes virtually all derived information of the bond pricing incorrect in virtually all markets but leads to a consistent outcome for global indices. In practice, fund managers are able to negotiate trades on non-standard settlement in any case. In the example above, a fund manager could negotiate the US Treasury purchase on a T+2 settlement and the trader offering the pricing would simply repo the bonds in question for one or two business days before delivering to the fund manager.

34.2 INDEX REBALANCING

Bonds are being issued, and mature, on a daily basis. This would normally imply that a bond index-linked to market capitalisation changes on a daily basis as well. Rebalancing a bond portfolio tracking a few hundred securities every day in response to such supply events would lead to excessive transaction costs given the large number of required daily transactions. Because that approach is untenable, indices generally concentrate adjustments to the set of index constituents, and their outstanding amounts, usually to the last day of a trading month. Indices of less liquid markets may be rebalanced less frequently (usually quarterly) while daily rebalanced indices are available for comparison purposes at some index providers.

CHAPTER 35

Portfolio Risk Management

35.1 RISK-NEUTRAL PORTFOLIOS

A portfolio is a collection of assets that are managed for a common purpose. Assuming N assets, each held in a nominal amount of w_i and a price (including accrued interest, where applicable) of P_i, the total value V of the portfolio is simply the sum of its parts, i.e.,

$$V = \sum_{i=1}^{N} w_i P_i \tag{35.1}$$

The essential idea of risk management is to minimise the sensitivity of V to instantaneous changes in so-called pricing factors. Essentially, one assumes that all asset prices are functions of certain variables v_k:

$$P_i = f_i(v_1, v_2, \ldots v_k) \tag{35.2}$$

and therefore risk management consists of solving the problem:

$$\frac{\partial}{\partial v_k} V = 0 \forall k \tag{35.3}$$

This task is not trivial, unless one allows for the pathological case $w_i = 0 \forall i$ (the empty portfolio). To see why, assume the most simple functional form for Equation (35.2), namely that the are N pricing factors and $f_i(v_1, v_2, \ldots v_N) = P_i$. In words, each asset price is itself a pricing factor or, equivalently, the price of each asset follows an idiosyncratic path. In this case $\partial V / \partial v_i = \partial V / \partial P_i = w_i$ and the only way to solve Equation (35.3) is $w_i = 0$. Only an empty portfolio is completely riskless.

Somewhat less trivially, Equation (35.3) is a system of k equations and this implies that in a world with k pricing factors, a portfolio must contain at least $N = k$ assets to allow a solution for Equation (35.3). For most institutional portfolios, $N \gg k$ so this is not a problem.

Even with sufficient degrees of freedom, 2 more problems arise. The first is risk stability. Equation (35.3) ensures that the portfolio will not change value in cases of an instantaneous, infinitesimally small shock to the pricing factors v_k. This does not rule out that the values of the partial derivatives change through time of that asset prices are non-linear functions of the pricing factors. In either case, Equation (35.3) can be violated for an initially risk-neutral portfolio either through the passage of time or because pricing factors change. In option literature, the latter effect is known as γ whereas in fixed income it is generally referred to as convexity.

For instance, if one treats the level of a given interest rate as a pricing factor, then the sensitivity of the bond price to that pricing factor is its DV01[1]. The DV01 declines as the bond ages and approaches maturity, so that the sensitivity of the bond price to rate changes declines. As discussed above, the DV01 of a bond also declines when interest rates rise (positive convexity). A risk-neutral portfolio involving bonds will therefore generally change its risk sensitivity over time and in response to interest rate changes. A portfolio manager aiming to maintain a given portfolio risk will therefore have to execute trades over to actively preserve that risk exposure.

In the sections on RMBS (page 297) and bond futures contracts (page 318), it was pointed out that these instruments can, in some yield configurations, exhibit negative convexity. These are extreme cases of changes in the risk sensitivities that will cause problems with hedges structured using Equation (35.3). This can be the result of an implicit, rather than explicit, equivalence assumption. A portfolio manager benchmark against a fixed-rate index can use mortgages as an alternative with better carry. However, matching the risk characteristics of the benchmark is then a challenging task.

The second hurdle to risk stability is that portfolio risk parameters do not only change due to the passage of time and convexity effects, but also in response to other market parameters; most notably, changes in FX rates. Portfolio managers are generally measured on their return in one currency (the home currency) but may hold assets denominated in other currencies. When currency valuations change, the portfolio exposure to the risk factors linked to those assets changes proportionally. The same is true for inflation-linked debt holdings which are in many ways mathematically equivalent to holdings in an inflation-free foreign currency. However, price index levels tend not to change as rapidly as FX rates. Such effects are part of a phenomenon known as cross-gamma. More generally, cross-gamma refers to second derivatives of price with two different independent variables. Standard gamma is simply:

$$\gamma = \frac{d^2 P}{dy^2} \tag{35.4}$$

whereas cross-gamma has the form:

$$\gamma = \frac{d^2 P}{dy dz} \tag{35.5}$$

where z is another variable, such as an FX rate, inflation index, etc.

A long-only portfolio is constrained to have strictly positive asset weights $w_i > 0 \forall i$. Liability managers sometimes face the mathematically equivalent but opposite problem of a short-only portfolio $w_i < 0 \forall i$.

The long-only constraint means that the existence of a solution to Equation (35.3) is only possible under certain conditions satisfied by the factor sensitivities $\partial V / \partial v_k$. In

---

[1]This argument neglects the term structure of interest rates for illustrative purposes.

particular, there must be assets that have opposite signs in their sensitivities to each factor:

$$\forall i \exists k,j \: : \: \frac{\partial}{\partial v_i} P_k \frac{\partial}{\partial v_i} P_j < 0 \qquad (35.6)$$

This condition is similar but not equivalent to a negative correlation between assets k and j. There is a mathematical apparatus that formalises these ideas (M-matrices) but there is an additional constraint that needs to be respected in practical applications: The individual asset weights w_i need to be meaningfully large, where 'meaningful' is defined relative to trading costs. It is therefore very hard to formulate a consistent mathematical framework around the practical constraints of long-only portfolios.

For fixed income assets, which with very few exceptions have a non-negative interest rate sensitivity, the condition in Equation (35.6) is practically impossible to satisfy. Long-only bond portfolios are therefore generally not risk-free. For equities, there can be opposing sensitivities to risk factors so that it is possible to a larger extent to construct low-risk portfolios in this manner. However, given that equity prices tend to be positively correlated (if only through the actions of investors who trade entire market indices through the futures markets), completely riskless equity portfolios are also unrealistic.

This leaves open the beguiling idea of portfolios comprised of multiple asset classes (bonds, equities, commodities, etc.) that employ relationships of the type in Equation (35.6) to achieve very low risk along all pricing factors. Such portfolios are sometimes marketed as all-weather portfolios.

35.2 INDEX TRACKING

Index tracking, index replication or passive investing is the idea of replicating a market portfolio more or less exactly. Index tracking has become very popular due to the failure of active portfolio managers to consistently beat their target benchmarks after cost. The argument has been made that all asset managers combined hold the market portfolio and therefore the average manager can only achieve the market return. For an investor who is unable to identify ex-ante which particular manager will outperform the market over the relevant horizon, it therefore makes sense to simply aim to buy the market portfolio in the cheapest possible way by investing with a low-cost passive manager who does not spend any resources on sophisticated asset selection strategies. The advent of exchange-traded funds (ETFs) has provided further momentum to passive investing because passive funds are easier to document in the listing prospectus. Note, however, that not every ETF follows a passive strategy.

It should be noted that the arguments in favour of passive tracking have some logical gaps, particularly in the area of bond markets. First, it is not true that all private portfolio managers in aggregate hold the market portfolio. Instead, substantial parts of the bond market are being held by investors such as central banks with very specific investment preferences. The part of the market that remains available to private investors has therefore a risk structure that is different from the total market structure. More generally, the idea of passive investing amounts to the assertion that an asset included in a given index should be bought because it exists. This is only true under the assumption that every asset if fairly prices given all publicly available information, i.e., the efficient market hypothesis (EMH). Even if one accepts this hypothesis as broadly accurate, there is a sleight of hand involved: Information has to be incorporated in market prices in some way, and the EMH is silent as to how this happens. In practice assets are fairly priced because over-priced assets will be sold by active investors acting on information received and analysed, depressing their market prices, while under-valued assets will be bought by such investors, inflating the market prices. Efficient markets, in other words, are not a given; instead, they result from active decision-making of at least a subset of investors. Such investors are unlikely to remain in the market for long unless they are able to derive returns from this activity. In a market containing only passive investors, mis-priced assets would never correct. This raises the question, to be tested in the future, of whether the rise of passive investing will increase the excess returns available to active investors.

In the case of equity indices with few, liquid constituents, such as the DAX 30, passive tracking can be achieved by simply buying each constituent equity in proportion to the index weight (see, however, the section on friction effects), in an approach known as full replication. For larger equity indices and bond indices, which generally contain hundreds or thousands of securities with varying liquidity profiles, index tracking is more challenging. Fund managers tend to opt for partial replication where the actual fund portfolio contains fewer securities than the index.

One can start with the stylised balance sheet of an asset manager purporting to replicate an index (Figure 35.2).

Before any investment has taken place, the asset side consists of cash while the liability side will always comprise of all securities in the index. This initial situation is equivalent to an active trading book where a trader has borrowed and sold short every security in the index. The task of the asset manager is now to replace cash on the asset side with securities and derivatives so that the performance of the asset side mimics that of the liability side.

The easiest way to do this is to enter into a total return swap (TRS) on the index so as to transform the carry income of the cash holding into that of the desired index. This amounts to simply outsourcing the index replication task to the TRS provider and exposes the investors in such a fund to various risks, such as failure of the counterparty, or costs related to early unwinds of the TRS. Somewhat less trivially, the fund manager may be able to buy index futures (if they exist for the target index) and then only manage the roll process of these exchange-traded instruments. Both strategies are called synthetic replication. Synthetic replication with futures is commonplace in ETFs to avoid cash drag, explained below.

Assets	Liabilities
Some securities	All securities in the index

FIGURE 35.1   Asset–liability structure of a passive manager.

The bulk of passive investing is done through physical replication, however, which means that the asset manager buys actual bonds, equities, etc. to replicate the performance of the index. Typically, but not always, the assets in the replication portfolio will be part of the index. Including securities from outside the index universe is sometimes unavoidable, particularly when the index itself is not replicable, but some management mandates restrict the use of non-index securities.

Portfolio management essentially reduces down to three questions: Which securities should be in the portfolio?; How much of each security should be bought?; and, When should trading take place? Full replication of an index is fairly straightforward because the answers to these questions are trivial: buy all securities in the index, weigh each of them in proportion to its index weight, and trade whenever the index changes.

Partial replication is more complex because the first question becomes an optimisation problem. The more securities from the index are selected for the replication portfolio, the lower the performance divergence between tracking portfolio and index. However, more securities involve more trading costs, especially when the overall portfolio size changes, for instance due to fund inflows or redemptions. A portfolio manager will therefore strive to achieve a given tracking error with the minimum number of securities. Another systematic way of decribing this optimisation is finding a number of securities n so that the expected incremental trading costs caused by adding one more security exceed the expected reduction in tracking error gained by having $n + 1$ securities in the portfolio.

When the set of securities in the tracking portfolio is only a subset of the securities in the index, optimum tracking will normally also require that the relative asset weights in the portfolio are not proportional to the index weights. It is therefore also no longer obvious that trading should take place in response to changes in the index itself. Instead, trading might have to take place to restore some predetermined risk limits, which may be caused by a number of events not limited to changes in the index itself.

35.2.1 Factor Analysis and Spanning Sets

When one has decided on a factor analysis to risk modelling, which is the common course of action in equity portfolio management, then there is a mathematical tool at hand called a spanning set. A set of vectors $\mathbf{r}_i$, $1 \leq i \leq N$ is spanning a k-dimensional space $\mathbb{R}_k$, $k \leq N$ if and only if for every $\mathbf{e} \in \mathbb{R}_k \exists \{\lambda_i\} : \vec{e} = \sum_i \lambda_i \mathbf{r}_i$. Once one has chosen a k-factor model of the world, one can select a set of $N \geq k$ assets, measure their sensitivities to changes in each of the risk factors and verify that they form a spanning set. Note that correlations between the individual assets will reduce the effective dimensionality of their risk factors below their cardinality N. Once a spanning set is determined, the optimal weights of each asset can be determined, for instance through a Lagrange optimiser. The problem of replicating an index is therefore reduced to a three-step procedure:

1. Identify the relevant risk factors
2. Find a spanning set of assets that cover these factors, and
3. Calculate the optimal portfolio weights

The Lagrange formalism provides a set of linear equations that combine hard constraints with optimisation targets. In this case one would define the Lagrangian for assets i with weights w_i and prices P_i as:

$$\mathcal{L} = \sum_{j=1}^{k} \beta_j \left(\sum_{i=1}^{N} w_i \frac{\partial}{\partial f_j} P_i - F_j \right) + \sum_{i=1}^{N} \left(w_i - \frac{\overline{w}_i}{\sum_j \overline{w}_j} \right)^2 \tag{35.7}$$

Here, the partial derivatives $\partial P_i / \partial f_j$ are the factor sensitivities of asset i with respect to factor j and the first sum of the Lagrangian are the constraints that make the total portfolio sensitivity with respect to changes in factor j equal to the market sensitivity to that factor, here represented by F_j. The second part of the Lagrangian is the optimisation target, here chosen to be the sum of squares of the deviations of portfolio weights from their market weights $\overline{w}_i$, scaled to include only the assets in the portfolio. This is essentially a soft liquidity constraint on the portfolio construction. While factor analysis alone does not prevent an outcome where the total sensitivity to a given factor is represented by exposure to one rare asset, this version of the Lagrangian would lead to a high cost assigned to such a portfolio. This liquidity constraint will only be satisfied to the extent that the β_k constraints are satisfiable with reasonable, which usually means positive, weights. In essence, that amounts to a lower bond on N that is higher than the mathematical minimum $N \geq k$. Higher N will in general lead to less extreme weights, and this formalism recovers market weights exactly when N is equal to the number of assets in the market.

As usual, the system of equations that determine the portfolio weights is derived by differentiating $\mathcal{L}$, i.e.,

$$\frac{\partial}{\partial \beta_j} \mathcal{L} = 0$$

$$\frac{\partial}{\partial w_i} \mathcal{L} = 0 \tag{35.8}$$

The resulting weights w_i do, as has been hinted at, not necessarily match their market weights, or even achievable portfolio weights in the light of liquidity constraints. After they have been calculated, a useful cross-check is to verify that all weights are positive, and that the second term of the Lagrangian Equation (35.7) is indeed small. If that is not the case, then one can add other assets, or replace some of them, to try and rectify this problem.

In bond markets, the factor sensitivities would not, as in the equity world, be obtained by historical regressions. Bond risk characteristics change over time in a predictable way as a result of aging (cf. for instance Section 16.10). Historical regressions would capture the average state of this aging process in the past. Instead, the useful risk factors are yields, and the factor sensitivities are durations. Hence, a one-factor version of Equation (35.7) for bonds would naturally be:

$$\mathcal{L} = \beta \left(\sum_{i=1}^{N} w_i D_i^* - D_m^* \right) + \sum_{i=1}^{N} \left(w_i - \frac{\overline{w}_i}{\sum_j \overline{w}_j} \right)^2 \qquad (35.9)$$

where D_i^* is the duration of bond i and D_m^* the duration of the market[2].

More complex versions of Equation (35.9) could for instance compartmentalise the duration matching so that duration is not matched for the entire portfolio, but also for market segments, like 1–5Y, 5–10Y, etc., so that:

$$\mathcal{L} = \sum_c \beta_c \left(\sum_{i=1}^{N} w_i I(i,c) D_i^* - D_c \right) + \sum_{i=1}^{N} \left(w_i - \frac{\overline{w}_i}{\sum_j \overline{w}_j} \right)^2 \qquad (35.10)$$

where $I(c,i) \to (0,1)$ is an indicator function signalling whether bond i is in the maturity bucket c and the D_c are the weighted average durations of the market in bucket c. Note that, because the weighted average market duration equals the weighted duration of each bucket, Equation (35.10) recovers Equation (35.9) when the entire market is treated as a single maturity bucket. Portfolio managers tracking corporate bonds will in general be less concerned with curve risk than sector risk, so for them the split into sub-universes that should be duration-matched would be along industry sectors.

An interesting variation on this Lagrangian is to also change the optimisation term. Instead of using remaining degrees of freedom to tie asset weights to their market weight, one can add terms that systematically skew these weights. For instance, one could add a term that punishes high weights for expensive assets, where 'expensive' could be proxied by an appropriate spline spreads, or skew weights towards assets with high carry and rolldown. The algorithm would then systematically skew the portfolio towards higher ex-ante carry. Whether this leads to an actual outperformance, and whether the increased tracking error versus the benchmark that is induced by such skews is acceptable, are complex questions, and the answer depends very strongly on the market at hand.

35.2.2 Friction Effects

Portfolio management incurs costs, and the spanning-set approach to replication, leaves unhedged exposures to risk factors that are not considered in the construction of the spanning set. In practice, most portfolio managers need to hedge an additional risk, namely that of redemptions of fund shares.

---

[2]Note that this expression implies that the w_i are defined in market value, not nominal value, terms. This would be the usual case for a portfolio manager. For nominal weights, DV01 needs to be used instead of duration.

Index providers incorporate into the index level calculations some, but not all, of the frictional costs associated with index replication. For instance, coupon payments are not simply added to the daily index performance (which would imply that they are immediately re-invested in the index), but use a virtual money market account where such cash is accumulated and reinvested at the next index rebalancing date. Also, while bonds are usually evaluated on the bid side, newly added bonds are brought in on the ask side of the market pricing.

These calculation rules cover the cost of full replication in a reasonably frictionless market. Partial replication usually requires trading outside the rebalancing window and the associated costs are not included in the index calculation.

The largest hurdle to replicating index performance in most cases, however, tends to be the cost of holding cash, known as the cash drag. To give an example, the ECB's government yield curve on 10 June 2020 had a 5Y yield of −0.113%. €STR on that day was −0.548%, equivalent to −0.556% in the actual/actual yield convention used for euro-area government yields. Assuming that a fund manager tracks an index with an average yield given by that 5Y yield, and can invest cash at €STR, then the cost of carry of cash held to match short-term redemptions is −44.3*bp*; i.e., the difference in yield between benchmark and actual return. A 5% cash balance would therefore translate into an underperformance of just over 2bps versus the benchmark.

In theory, an asset manager could run a 0% cash balance and pay any redemptions by borrowing cash in the repo market against portfolio assets. To the extent that outflows are not compensated for by near-term inflows, the manager could close out the repo transaction with cash raised from an actual asset sale. While attractive in theory, this approach is illegal in most jurisdictions because it means that the manager is actually leveraging the portfolio. If outflows were to continue over some time in an environment of declining asset prices, this repo strategy would imply increasing losses for investors who keep their assets in the fund.

In practice, fund managers eliminate cash drag through the use of derivatives. Equity, ETF usually contain equity futures to achieve 100% index exposure despite cash holdings.

A separate class of frictions concerns indices that are not actually investable. Such indices are now rare, but even supposedly investable indices may in practice be difficult to replicate. For instance, broad bond indices in Japan are hard to replicate with new cash because secondary market liquidity of spread products (corporate bonds and municipal debt) is poor. The same is true for some broad European indices. Fund managers receiving fund inflows tend to find it hard to source older bonds, and so tend to have to accept higher tracking error risks to match the index carry.

CHAPTER 36

Hedging

36.1 INTRODUCTION

Hedging means adding instruments to an existing portfolio in order to neutralise the overall position against expected shifts in the market. In the simplest case, this may mean selling a futures contract against an existing bond position, or receiving in a swap against a short position in a money market futures strip. In a more complex setting, it may involve selling or buying different futures contract to adjust a large portfolio in order to follow changes in a benchmark index.

In general, hedging is done with a more liquid instrument, i.e., a government bond is hedged with a bond or money market futures contract, a sub-sovereign corporate bond with a sovereign bond, and so on. This is because the idea of a hedge is to voluntarily assume a new position in order to reduce the risk of an existing one. The cost of entering and unwinding this additional position should therefore be low.

The fundamental precondition for hedging is that the instruments involved need to have a stable relationship. In other words, their price changes in reaction to market movements need to be related to such a degree as to make it possible to offset the exposure inherent in one instrument with the exposure of another. Naturally, the offset cannot be perfect, but we can hope that the residual risk after hedging is small compared to the outright risk with no hedge. Using the simple example of a long bond position hedged with an appropriate futures contract, the outright exposure of the bond alone would translate into daily movements in the order of a few tens of ticks to perhaps a point or two, whereas the basis should normally move only a few cents per day. Hedging therefore reduces risk.

How an instrument is commonly hedged affects how it is priced. A trader views inventory in terms of its hedged cost. For instance, having bought a bond and hedged it with swaps at an I-spread of x bp, the trader will break even on the position when selling it at an I-spread of $x - \delta$ where δ is the bid–offer spread on the swap leg. This cost will therefore form an anchor for the price the trader will show to potential buyers and movements in the swap curve will be a decisive driver in the cash price of the bond. In other words, the hedge creates a correlation between swap rates, and the bond's yield in the profit-and-loss calculation of the trader. If traders generally agree on hedge strategies, then this correlation will be reflected in market prices more widely.

Hedging does not necessarily rely on linear assumptions such as stable correlation matrices, but normally this assumption is made. Even allowing for a general form of the relationship between instruments, there will always be idiosyncratic movements in a given position that are impossible to hedge against. In most cases, a trader will design a hedge position precisely in order to take a view on such movements. However, the implication is that only a completely flat portfolio is truly risk neutral. Any other portfolio is exposed to some form of risk.

The stability of the yield curve is the main reason why hedging is such an important topic in rates trading as opposed to equity and, to some degree, credit trading. The individual company risk in a share price is usually as large, if not larger, as the overall market risk, so effective hedging is a lot more difficult. In the credit markets, the existence of different bonds by the same issuer and of credit default swaps and other derivatives usually provides a larger spectrum of possible hedge instruments.

36.2   DURATION-NEUTRAL HEDGES

The simplest form of hedging is the duration-neutral hedge. Here, one starts from the mathematical relationship between price and yield movements of a fixed-coupon bond given by the DV01 $\overline{D}$:

$$dP = \frac{\partial P}{\partial y}dy = \overline{D}dy \tag{36.1}$$

Assuming 2 bonds with notionals N_1 and N_2 in the portfolio, the hedge condition is that the total price change under a yield movement should vanish, i.e.,

$$dV = (N_1\overline{D}_1 + N_2\overline{D}_2)dy = 0 \tag{36.2}$$

from which follows:

$$N_2 = -N_1\frac{\overline{D}_1}{\overline{D}_2} \tag{36.3}$$

At this point it is useful to remember that the DV01 $\overline{D}$ of a bond is the product of dirty price P and modified duration D^*, so one could write the same equation in terms of the market values M_1 and M_2 as:

$$M_2 = -M_1\frac{D^*_1}{D^*_2} \tag{36.4}$$

The equations are totally identical, but real money managers usually tend to think about positions in terms of market value whereas trading desks generally use nominal amounts.

The problem with both Equations (36.3) and (36.4) is that they were derived using dy as a non-indexed variable. In other words, they implicitly assume that there is a single yield variable that explains the movements in both bonds. While that might be the case if both bonds have almost the same maturity and are in the same market; it is most likely to be very wrong if the bonds are in different markets or have very different maturities. In these cases, duration neutral hedges have little meaning.

36.3 REGRESSION HEDGES

One way of curing the deficiencies of Equations (36.3) and (36.4) is to start from the slightly more general equation:

$$dV = N_1\overline{D}_1 dy_1 + N_2\overline{D}_2 dy_2 = 0 \tag{36.5}$$

and impose the linear relationship:

$$dy_2 = \beta dy_1 \tag{36.6}$$

to find:

$$dV = N_1\overline{D}_1 dy_1 + N_2\overline{D}_2\beta dy_1 = 0 \tag{36.7}$$

which then results in the equivalents:

$$N_2 = -N_1\beta\frac{\overline{D}_1}{\overline{D}_2} \tag{36.8}$$

$$M_2 = -M_1\beta\frac{D_1^*}{D_2^*} \tag{36.9}$$

As should be expected, these equations revert to Equations (36.3) and (36.4) for $\beta = 1$.

Once a β parameter has been introduced, there is little need to actually still use yields as the basic variables for the hedge construction. Instead, we could instead absorb the terms $\overline{D}dy$ into a simple dP and assume a relationship like:

$$dP_2 = \beta dP_1 \tag{36.10}$$

and construct the hedge based on price regression. Not only is this simpler, but it is also possible to use hedge instruments for which a yield cannot be defined, such as futures contracts or derivatives of othe underlying assets such as crude oil. Hedges so constructed are called price regression hedges.

Again, there is a fundamental problem in the background. The regression Equation (36.6) implies:

$$dy_1 = \frac{1}{\beta}dy_2 \tag{36.11}$$

i.e., the regression coefficient of the reverse regression should just be the inverse of the original β. However, when one actually does the standard linear regressions of the 2 variables in both directions, the regression coefficients will usually not be the inverse of each other. This is a sign that the regression equation is misspecified, in particular that the assumption that the independent variable contains no noise is incorrect. The most general way to address this problem is through the use of principal component analysis, discussed in Chapter 33.

36.4   YIELD CURVE MODEL HEDGES

Once the term structure of interest rates has been captured in a yield curve model, that model can be used to generate hedge coefficients that are appropriate for the type of curve movements that are consistent with the model. Different curve models generate different curve movements, so the hedge structures in model-based hedges will depend not only on the instruments, but also on the model. To give a very simple example, one can assume a curve model where the yields of all bonds are equal to the same number y. In this model, the only possible yield change is one where y changes, i.e., a parallel shift of the whole curve. One can then calculate the change in the value of a portfolio of n bonds under such a change:

$$dV = \left[\sum_{i=1}^{n} N_i \overline{D}_i\right] dy \qquad (36.12)$$

The hedge condition is $dV = 0$ and one can try to solve this equation given a fixed position in 1 of the bonds. Without loss of generality it can be assumed that N_1 is fixed, so the portfolio will be hedged if:

$$N_1 \overline{D}_1 = -\sum_{i=2}^{n} N_i \overline{D}_i \qquad (36.13)$$

This equation has an infinite number of solutions if $n > 2$. For $n = 2$ is simplifies to:

$$N_1 \overline{D}_1 = -N_2 \overline{D}_2 \qquad (36.14)$$

which has the solution Equation (36.3). In other words, in a flat yield curve model, duration neutral hedges are the natural model-implied hedges.

Generally, calibrating a given model with a view to using it for hedging is different from calibrating it for other purposes, such as the best possible fit of current yields, or prediction of future interest rates. The main criterion for a good hedging model is that the amount of unexplained profit and loss from a hedged position should be as small as possible. For trading desks, this generally means that on an overnight basis, the model should explain as much as possible of the price movements of the individual bonds in the market. In contrast, a simple curve fit will aim to reduce the current residuals as much as possible, i.e., there is no relationship to carry and rolldown on the position.

The simple model used above had a single parameter and that parameter directly explained the yield of each bond, so price changes are most naturally expressed via the DV01 of the bonds. Most structural curve models will instead generate a term structure of discount factors, so the natural approach to hedges is directly through price changes. One starts from the fact that the model price of a bond is the function of the bond and two sets of parameters:

$$\hat{P}_i = \varphi(i, \mu(t), \omega) \qquad (36.15)$$

The assumption is that the vector $\mu(t)$ is a time-dependent set of k state variables whereas the structural parameters ω are unchanged through time. In the simple model above, $\mu = (y)$ and $\omega = \emptyset$.

To hedge a portfolio in a model context means making the portfolio value independent of changes in the state variables $\mu(t)$. Aside from noise, the evolution of $\mu(t)$ is usually explained by the model and the parameters $(\mu(t), \omega)$. The change in the portfolio value can be written as a total derivative:

$$dV = \sum_{j=1}^{k} \left[\sum_i N_i \frac{\partial P_i}{\partial \mu_j} \right] d\mu_j \tag{36.16}$$

In order to be hedged against an arbitrary move in the state variables, all the terms in the square brackets of the equation above must vanish. This gives k linear equations of the form:

$$\sum_i N_i \frac{\partial P_i}{\partial \mu_j} = 0 \tag{36.17}$$

for the notional amounts N_i in the hedged portfolio. In general, therefore, a portfolio of k instruments is necessary to completely hedge against movements in a k-factor curve model. The number of instruments can be smaller if this system of equations is degenerate. Such a situation can occur if, for instance, some of the derivatives vanish for all the instruments in the portfolio.

If there are more instruments than model factors, there is an infinite number of hedged portfolios. To isolate a single set of portfolio weights, additional conditions have to be specified. The most important case is one where there are $k + 1$ instruments in the portfolio and one of the notionals, say N_1 is specified. This represents the common case where a trader is given a particular position N_B in a given bond from a client trade and needs to establish a hedge using liquid market instruments, such as futures contracts. Assuming that the trade is using a 2-factor model, 2 hedge instruments are needed in general to neutralise the position. Given the easy availability of linear equation solvers, it is easiest to write the hedge condition as a set of 3 equations for the 3 notionals $N_1 = N_B$, N_2, and N_3, namely:

$$\begin{pmatrix} 1 & 0 & 0 \\ \dfrac{\partial P_1}{\partial \mu_1} & \dfrac{\partial P_2}{\partial \mu_1} & \dfrac{\partial P_3}{\partial \mu_1} \\ \dfrac{\partial P_1}{\partial \mu_2} & \dfrac{\partial P_2}{\partial \mu_2} & \dfrac{\partial P_3}{\partial \mu_2} \end{pmatrix} \begin{pmatrix} N_1 \\ N_2 \\ N_3 \end{pmatrix} = \begin{pmatrix} N_B \\ 0 \\ 0 \end{pmatrix} \tag{36.18}$$

The bond position is recovered from the first of these 3 equations, while the other 2 establish the neutrality against changes in the 2 model state variables μ_1 and μ_2. Note that, although the price sensitivities of the model are expressed here in terms of partial derivatives, it will in most cases be necessary to calculate these derivatives numerically because a closed form does not exist.

One can use the same formalism to derive PCA-neutral butterfly weights. In this case, the model describes yields, not prices, so with the DV01 of each bond:

$$dP_i = \overline{D}_i \frac{\partial y_i}{\partial \mu_j} d\mu_j \tag{36.19}$$

Here, the state variables μ_1 and μ_2 are simply the current factor values for the first 2 principal components given by the scalar products $\mu_1 = y \cdot f_1$ and $\mu_2 = y \cdot f_2$. The partial derivatives are simple constants given by the factor loadings, namely:

$$\frac{\partial y_i}{\partial \mu_j} = f_{ji} \tag{36.20}$$

Equation (36.18) then takes the form:

$$\begin{pmatrix} 0 & 1 & 0 \\ \overline{D}_1 f_{11} & \overline{D}_2 f_{12} & \overline{D}_3 f_{13} \\ \overline{D}_1 f_{21} & \overline{D}_2 f_{22} & \overline{D}_3 f_{23} \end{pmatrix} \begin{pmatrix} N_1 \\ N_2 \\ N_3 \end{pmatrix} = \begin{pmatrix} \pm 100 \\ 0 \\ 0 \end{pmatrix} \tag{36.21}$$

The sign of the bullet notional of course depends on whether the bullet is rich or cheap.

CHAPTER 37

Mean-Variance Optimisation

The simplest framework in which to analyse and optimise portfolio performance is to consider only a single investment period. By implication, this means that auto-correlation of asset returns is irrelevant. If one further assumes that asset returns are normally distributed, then the only 2 parameters describing portfolio returns are the expected return and the uncertainty around this return, i.e., the risk of the portfolio. The idea of optimising the balance between return and risk is therefore equivalent to optimising the mean and variance of the expected portfolio returns. The presentation here follows essentially [56].

Given the expected returns $\mathbf{m}$ and the covariance matrix $\mathbf{V}$ of a portfolio with asset weights $\mathbf{w}$, return and return variance of the portfolio are:

$$r = \mathbf{wm}$$
$$\sigma^2 = \mathbf{wVw} \tag{37.1}$$

In the following, 2 related examples are used. They use 3 hypothetical assets which have the same expected returns in both examples but different covariance matrices. Two of the assets are supposed to represent riskier investments while the third is a close cash equivalent. The expected returns are:

$$\mathbf{m} = (\,2.215\ \ 2.065\ \ 0.995\,) \tag{37.2}$$

while the 2 covariance matrices are:

$$\mathbf{V}^P = \begin{pmatrix} 6.0 & 2.0 & 0.0 \\ 2.0 & 5.0 & 0.0 \\ 0.0 & 0.0 & 0.5 \end{pmatrix} \quad \mathbf{V}^N = \begin{pmatrix} 6.0 & -2.0 & 0.0 \\ -2.0 & 5.0 & 0.0 \\ 0.0 & 0.0 & 0.5 \end{pmatrix} \tag{37.3}$$

Although the variances of the 3 assets are the same in both covariance matrixes, the first one has positive correlations between the returns of the 2 risk assets while the second has negative correlations. The expected return of each asset in these examples is related to its riskiness which should also be the case for actual market assets. The expected return on the third asset is close to the risk-free rate which is here assumed to

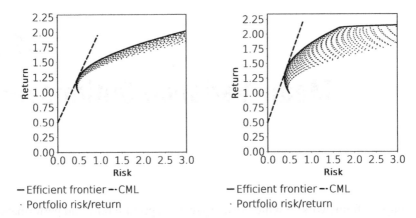

FIGURE 37.1 Expected portfolio returns and variances for different asset weight combinations. The left-hand chart is for the positive covariance matrix $\mathbf{V}^P$, the right for $\mathbf{V}^N$. The convex hull of each set of risks and returns is labelled 'Efficient frontier' and the tangent on that line through the riskless asset as the capital markets line (CML).

be 0.5. For now, portfolios are assumed to be constrained to full investment across the three assets and no borrowing, which translates into:

$$\sum_i w_i = 1 \tag{37.4}$$

and:

$$\forall i : 0 \leq w_i \leq 1 \tag{37.5}$$

There is an infinite number of possible portfolio combinations, even with these constraints. Selecting a regular grid of weights from the possible ranges and calculating the expected portfolio returns and risks results in a data set that is known as the 'Markovitz bullet', shown in Figure 37.1.

Both data sets share the same minimum risk point which corresponds to a portfolio consisting only of the least risky asset. Beyond that, there is a clear difference in the 2 expected risk and return distributions. Negative correlation between assets increases the chance that negative returns in one asset are compensated for positive returns in another. As a result, the negative correlation portfolio shows higher returns for the same risk. Put differently, a positive correlation between the 2 risk assets makes them partial substitutes which is why for a given amount of risk, there is a lower dispersion of returns in the left data set where the risk assets are positively correlated.

A portfolio (set of asset weights) A is said to dominate a portfolio B if A has a higher return than B but the same risk, or if A has lower risk but the same return. In the geometry of Figure 37.1, A dominates B if it is above B or left of B. For an investor, A would always be preferable to B. From this it follows that the convex hull, i.e., the points forming the boundary of the data set, of the set of possible risk and rerun combinations has a special meaning for portfolio allocation. Every portfolio inside the convex hull is dominated by 2 portfolios in the hull, namely a portfolio to the left (lower risk but same return) and 1 above it (same risk but higher return). This means that only portfolios in the hull, and specifically those in the upper part of the hull, are sensible investment allocations. These portfolios are said to form the efficient frontier of the set of assets available for investment. Constructing an investment portfolio therefore amounts to picking the desired spot on the efficient frontier.

If restriction Equation (37.4) is relaxed, the investor can invest in the riskless asset or borrow the riskless asset to invest more. This provides a special meaning to the point where a line through the riskless asset return forms a tangent on the efficient frontier. The tangent is marked as the capital markets line (CML) in the chart. An investor can hold a combination of the riskless asset and the portfolio corresponding to this tangent point on the efficient frontier. The tangent itself then denotes all the risk–return combinations that are possible with such a combined portfolio. All points of this line to the left on the tangent point represent partially invested portfolios, where some of the investment is held in the riskless asset, while all points to the right correspond to portfolios where the riskless asset has been borrowed to invest more in the risk assets. Because the efficient frontier is convex, every point of this tangent represents a portfolio that dominates every other point on the efficient frontier.

This concept of mixing the riskfree asset with risk asset portfolios is related to the Miller–Modigliani theorem according to which, in the absence of taxes and frictional costs, an investor can choose to adjust any investment to his or her risk preference by choosing to hold the riskless asset or borrow. The risk–return choices of the manager of the risk asset portfolio should therefore not depend on that of the investor. This idea has an important implication for the meaning of this tangent point.

With a certain amount of handwaving, this tangent point is known as the market portfolio where every asset is held in direct proportion to its market weight. This handwaving is best explained in an indirect way and relies on what is known as the efficient market hypothesis (EMH). To begin with, it should be recalled that all assets are held by somebody. If it was possible to identify a market asset that should be held below its market weight, investors should underweight this asset. Such underweighting will lead to a surplus of supply over demand and will lead to a lower price of the asset which will increase its future returns. Conversely, prices that should be held above their market weight will see a surplus of demand over supply, leading to a price increase and lower future returns. This means that eventually all future returns should adjust, via an adjustment in market prices, so that holding the market portfolio becomes the optimal asset allocation. The Miller–Modigliani theorem then makes the optimality of this portfolio independent of investor risk preferences because those can be expressed through the split of investment between the riskless asset and the market portfolio.

There are several problems with this argument and the main one is crytallised in the preconditions of the Miller–Modigliani theorem. In the real world, taxes and friction costs do exist. These mean that investors are unable to simply hold the market portfolio and achieve the correct risk preference via allocation to the riskless asset, and in particular when this involves borrowing it (cf. the introduction to [20]). Instead, most investors face frictions that restrict their investment choices. Few investors can access every global market at the same cost. They are therefore more likely to skew portfolio allocations towards assets that are more easily accessible, which means that it is unclear what the market portfolio actually is. It is therefore optimistic to assume that relative returns adjust in order to make every conceivable market portfolio optimal. To give another example, General Motors, the car maker, underwent a Chapter 11 restructuring in 2009. As part of that restructuring bond holders received equity in a new post-restructuring entity. The EMH implies that this event shifted the optimal portfolio allocation for every investor in the world from bonds towards equities.

While the EMH may have some conceptual arguments against it, there is an alternative way to interpret the capital markets line. If investors are unconstrained in their investment decisions, then the return r they demand for investing in an asset with volatility V should be a function of V:

$$r = f(V) \tag{37.6}$$

One can then approximate $f(\cdot)$ through a Taylor series around the point marked by any given portfolio, and there is no reason not to use the market portfolio with its volatility V_m and expected return r_m as a reference point. Specifically,

$$r = f(V_m) + \left.\frac{\partial f}{\partial V}\right|_M (V - V_m) + \frac{1}{2}\left.\frac{\partial^2 f}{\partial V^2}\right|_m (V - V_m)^2 + \ldots \tag{37.7}$$

The CML can then be interpreted as the second, linear, term of this series, while the first is the expected return r_m of the market portfolio. This interpretation does however not explain why this CML should coincide with the expected return on the riskless asset for $V = 0$, or why it should be tangential to the Markovitz bullet rather than cut through its boundary. The arguments in favour of these 2 statements is first a geometrical consideration (a line is defined by 2 points as per Euclid's first axiom) under the assumption that the price of an additional quantum of risk is constant, i.e., if higher-order derivatives in Equation (37.7) vanish. The tangent property requires a weaker form of the EMH which is a local equilibrium argument: At any given time, deviating from the market-neutral allocation will increase portfolio risk. In other words, the market portfolio need not be the globally most efficient portfolio, it just needs to be a local optimum. This local optimum is then a global one as long as risk premia are constant.

This alternative interpretation of the capital markets line builds a bridge to the preferred habitat theory which then amounts to the statement that different investors have different risk preferences, i.e., different and potentially more complex functional forms of Equation (37.6).

If the riskless asset is not available for investment or borrowing, a different approach needs to be followed to construct optimal portfolios. In order to come to an optimisation problem for any individual investor, it is necessary to define a cost function. Given that investors tend to hold assets with a view to later consuming their monetary equivalent, the standard approach is to assume some risk–return preference for an investor based on a utility model. The utility of a portfolio return is assumed to be the return minus some representation of the risk of the portfolio, i.e., the portfolio variance:

$$U = \mu\mathbf{w} - \lambda\mathbf{w}\mathbf{V}\mathbf{w} \tag{37.8}$$

where λ expresses the risk aversion of the investor. A higher λ means that an investor is willing to sacrifice more expected return in exchange for a given reduction in portfolio

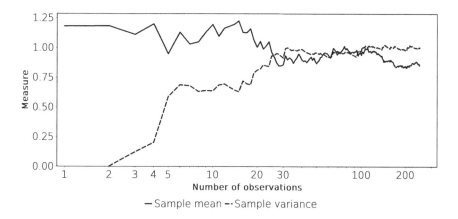

FIGURE 37.2 Example of sample mean and standard deviation of a normally distributed random number with mean 1 and standard deviation 1 as a function of the sample size.

risk. In other words, there is no overall optimal portfolio structure. Instead, the optimal portfolio structure is a function of the risk preference of each investor.

Equation (37.8) can be solved for the optimal weights $\mathbf{w}$ through a simple differentiation. At the $\mathbf{w}$ that maximises U, all derivatives with respect to $\mathbf{w}$ must be zero, so one has:

$$\frac{\partial U}{\partial \mathbf{w}} = \mu - 2\lambda \mathbf{V}\mathbf{w} = 0 \tag{37.9}$$

and:

$$\mathbf{w} = \frac{1}{2\lambda}\mathbf{V}^{-1}\mu \tag{37.10}$$

One needs to bear in mind the essential limitations of this framework. The first and foremost is that mean and variance are statistics of a probability distribution. That means that they describe random numbers but not determine them. Even if expected returns and variances are known exactly, and the statistical distribution of returns is completely determined by these numbers, the experience of any investor holding the assets, or a portfolio of them, will only over time *converge* to that given by these quantities. Figure 37.2, known in some form to most science students, shows the mean and standard deviation measured from samples of increasing size of a normally distributed random number sequence. Only over the course of many observations does that sample mean stabilise around the true mean of the distribution.

A useful test is therefore to study this effect on portfolio returns. Figure 37.3 shows the same efficient frontiers and capital markets lines as Figure 37.1. Instead of showing expected returns and variances, however, multivariate normal random number generators were used to draw samples from the return distributions of the 3 assets. These samples are then weighted with the weights given by the market portfolio and averaged over 12 observations to give a flavour of the return and risk experience of an investor with a monthly analysis horizon over the course of a year. Fifty such simulations are plotted in the chart.

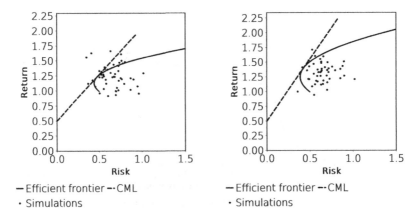

FIGURE 37.3 Simulated risk and return samples for the market portfolio in the positive (left) and negative (right) correlation examples (see Equations (37.2) and (37.3)). Efficient frontier and CML are the same as in Figure 37.1.

Over long periods, the actual return and risk experience will converge to the values expected by the mean-variance framework[1]. Over shorter periods, however, these simulations demonstrate that actual returns can differ substantially from predictions. Note, however, that the data in this simulation is much more dramatic than would be expected from a realistic portfolio because the small number of assets (3) limits the scope for diversification.

The result form portfolio managers is that, while the returns predicted by the mean-variance framework are the best possible predictor of actual returns, actual returns can differ substantially from these predictions. While a long investment horizon would seem sufficient to reduce this discrepancy through the operation of the law of large numbers, in practice the return and variance structure of the investment universe is likely to change over time due to changes in central bank policies, technological progress, etc. In other words, while the investor is waiting for actual returns to converge to their predicted values, those predictions will change[2].

For fixed income portfolios, an additional complication arises from the finite lifetime of most fixed income securities. As bonds approach their maturity or call date,

---

[1]Statistically speaking there is an alternative way to achieve a convergence, namely to sample returns across a large set of independent realisations. Given that each asset exists only once in this universe, this would require sampling across multiple alternative universes. While a many-worlds hypothesis exists as one possible explanation of quantum mechanics, the application of this theory to finance is unlikely to be fruitful. Investment managers tend to have to justify losses in the present universe without taking recourse to alternative universes where their investors made a lot of money.

[2]A dramatic example of this effect was the behaviour of airline bonds following the terrorist attacks of 11 September 2001. Airlines were large bond issuers given that they operated in a stable cashflow environment. The decline in passenger traffic following the attacks led to a drastic underperformance of these bonds. By the time passenger numbers recovered, the low-cost revolution in airline travel made earnings much more violatile.

their duration, and thereby their price sensitivity to yield changes declines. At the same time, expected carry and roll-down returns change over time as bonds move down the yield curve. A historical return covariance matrix of fixed income securities is therefore fairly meaningless for the prediction of future returns.

The usual solution to this problem is to abstract away from individual bonds any use bond indices to estimate returns. Sub-indices for several maturity bands are published by index providers so that one can in essence measure the expected return and variance properties of a generic 5Y euro-denominated A-rated corporate bond by observing an index like the iBoxx Euro Corporate A 3-5Y. This level of aggregation is generally suffi-cient for portfolio structuring, bearing in mind also that estimating a large covariance matrix with any confidence requires a lot of data. One should bear in mind, however, that index constituents change over time. For instance, corporate bond issuers tended to come mostly from stable industries like utilities, car makers, etc. Recently, technology companies have issued large bonds in response to changes in taxation. This changes the return characteristics of the relevant bond segments.

Somewhat more insidiously, most issuers tend to adjust supply to demand so that the relative weights of index components changes over time, and partly in response to market movements. For instance, several sovereigns used the unusually low interest rate environment created by the asset purchase programmes of the ECB from 2015 to issue extremely long-dated bonds with maturities of up to 100 years. On an index level, this increased the weight of longer-dated maturity buckets in the overall indices. This means that the structure of the market portfolio is changing, and this has implications for expected returns under the assumption of efficient markets.

The practical problems of mean-variance optimisation are that $\mathbf{V}$ is hard to estimate from sample data with any certainty for a larger number of assets, and that solving Equation (37.10) requires inverting $\mathbf{V}$ which can be numerically unstable.

One approach to fixing the numerical problems of mean-variance optimisation is, unsurprisingly, dimension reduction. The simplest way to achieve this is to replace individual asset return and variance data with that of asset classes (domestic equities, German bonds 2–5 years, etc.) and then optimising the portfolio structure in terms of these asset classes. Individual assets inside each class can then be assumed to follow natural weights, such as market capitalisation.

Alternatively, a reasonably low-dimensional set of risk factors can be postulated (such as industry-specific risks) or extracted from historical data through techniques such as PCA. One then constructs a mean-variance optimal factor portfolio and then maps the factor allocation back to an allocation to individual assets.

Both of these approaches side-step the numerical problems of inverting the covari-ance matrix $\mathbf{V}$ but introduce other issues at the same time. The return r_i of any given asset i in either approach is determined by a linear combination of k factors, i.e.,

$$r_i(t) = \sum_k \beta_{i,k} f_k(t) + \varepsilon_i(t) \tag{37.11}$$

In the case of asset class returns, each asset is mapped to a single return factor corre-sponding to the asset class it belongs to. The higher the number of factors, the more variance of each asset can be captured by the deterministic part of this equation. How-ever, the idiosyncratic risks of each asset, ε_i, remains. Whether a higher number of factors is better or worse is open to debate and depends on the problem at hand. For a bond portfolio in a liquid market, the performance of a subindex containing a given bond can be a good proxy for the performance of that bond. A low number of subindices can then give some stability to the solution Equation (37.10). Using a single common factor across multiple bonds is then feasibile. The experience in the equity market meanswhile suggests that a factor decomposition, i.e., a higher number of factors for each security, is a better solution for this asset class.

CHAPTER 38

Portfolio Rebalancing

An existing portfolio can at any time be adjusted. Such adjustments may become inevitable due to certain events, such as cash or equity distributions, occurring in any of the assets in the portfolio. This creates definitional problems around simple questions such as that of portfolio performance.

Consider the following simple question: Given a portfolio worth 100 invested in equal amounts in 2 assets A and B, where A has an expected return of 3% per year and B has an expected return of 5%, what is the expected value V of the portfolio in 5 years? Which of the following answers is correct:

$$V = 100 * (1 + 0.5 * 3\% * 5 + 0.5 * 5\% * 5) = 120$$

$$V = 100 * (1 + 0.5 * 3\% + 0.5 * 5\%)^5 \approx 121.67$$

$$V = 100 * [0.5 * (1 + 3\%)^5 + 0.5 * (1 + 5\%)^5] \approx 121.78$$

The correct answer is that all 3 formulas could be correct. In fact there is an infinite number of correct answers until one properly defines the strategy followed to invest asset returns. The first formula above is appropriate when any gains are extracted and held in a zero-return asset like physical cash. The second formula is correct when gains are collected on an annual basis and reinvested to re-establish the original 50%:50% portfolio mix. The third formula is accurate when any gains are reinvested in the asset they originate from. Note that in this third scenario the portfolio weight of asset B would be around 52.4% at the end of the 5-year period, while the weight of A would be only 47.6%. This example shows that portfolio rebalancing is an essential determinant of portfolio performance, and the calculation of portfolio performance depends on the rebalancing strategy.

Portfolio rebalancing is the adjustment of asset holdings w_i in response to certain events or on a periodic basis. The purpose of this chapter is to highlight that the choice of a portfolio rebalancing strategy implies a certain assumption about the autocorrelation structure of asset returns. In other words, the optimal rebalancing strategy depends on the correlation structure of the assets involved.

The first rule taught to traders tends to be 'cut your losses short, let your profits run'. The purpose of this rule is to avoid emotional attachment to particular trading views. What is interesting is that this strategy is, as will be shown below, halfway between a no-rebalancing and a constant asset allocation strategy.

38.1 PASSIVE AND SEMI-PASSIVE STRATEGIES

38.1.1 No Reallocation

The no-reallocation strategy is to simply buy a portfolio and never revisit the asset allocation at all. Incoming cash is assumed to be reinvested in the asset class it originated from or consumed. As time passes, the weight of underperforming assets in the portfolio declines because the better performing assets form a larger share of the total portfolio value. The adoption of this strategy amounts to some faith that the market valuations are rational and that it is indeed beneficial to be more exposed to assets that have performed well in the past.

The analytical drawback of this strategy, which also invalidates this theoretical argument, is that it is not time-invariant. The weight of each individual asset in the portfolio depends on the performance since the inception of the portfolio and therefore on the precise point in time when the portfolio was established. It is very unlikely that the future performance of assets should be dependent on the precise date when a given portfolio was established. Therefore, while past performance may sometimes be a good guide to future performance, expressing this view through a simple buy-and-hold strategy is likely to be suboptimal.

38.1.2 Passive Management

Passive management means that all assets are purchased in proportion to their outstanding amounts, or market weights. Portfolio rebalancing is only necessary to the extent that new assets appear in the market, that existing assets disappear, or that cash distributions from existing assets (coupons or dividends) need to be reinvested. Rebalancing is done periodically; usually monthly for bond portfolios. Given that several commercial data providers offer the service of collating the relevant information in the form of market indices, this type of strategy is also known as index tracking. Unlike the no-reallocation strategy above it avoids the problem of time-invariance and all passive portfolios targeted at a given asset universe with identical rebalancing periods have identical asset weights.

Passive management has a number of attractions. The most important one is cost: the analytical cost of following a market index is virtually zero and the only costs involved in running an index-tracking portfolio are transaction costs and custody feeds.

A purported second attraction is more theoretical. All assets in the market need to be held by somebody, and so the the idea that one investor holds more than the market weight of a given asset due to some superior insight into the future performance of that asset implies that another investor holds less than the market weight of the same asset, presumably also on the basis that this other investor expects an underperformance. Clearly, one of these 2 investors must be wrong, and averaged over many investors and over time, every investor will be right as much as they are wrong and every portfolio will more or less follow the market performance. A theoretical underpinning of this idea is the efficient market hypothesis (EMH) which in essence postulates that asset prices reflect at all times all available information.

The problem with this idea is that it makes several assumptions about the behaviour of all other investors in the market. These are in particular that all of them are unconstrained and rational in their investment decisions, and that they can react to incoming information at the same time. While the rationality assumption may be correct, some investor classes are clearly constrained in what investments they can make at any one time, and some investors cannot time their investment decisions optimally. Essentially, the idea that passive investment is rational amounts to relying on the rationality of all other investors to justify not undertaking independent analysis.

38.1.3 Index Replication

Perfect passive management is impossible due to liquidity constraints. Assets may exist in the market but be held by investors unwilling to sell, and managing a portfolio consisting of thousands of securities would require trading in minuscule quantities. Meanwhile, most portfolio managers need to manage cash inflows and outflows as investors put more money into a fund, or ask for redemptions. In practice, the strategy of passive investing means constructing a portfolio that mimics the performance of a market index as much as possible while consisting of only a manageable number of assets and preserving sufficient liquidity to manage redemptions. Portfolio assets also may or may not be part of the market index itself[1] if investment policies allow for such deviations.

The construction of an index-tracking portfolio introduces a new problem, namely that the actual portfolio will be exposed more to the idiosyncratic risks of the assets that are in the portfolio and not to the idiosyncratic risks of the assets that are in the index but not held by the portfolio. This means that the choice of the number of assets in the tracking portfolio, and the selection of the actual assets is an essential risk management consideration. Index replication is therefore not a purely passive investment strategy. Instead, the asset manager must make decisions as to the construction of the replicating portfolio, usually under the constraint that simply holding the index portfolio is practically impossible.

At the same time, the obligation to track an index can be seen as equivalent to holding a short position in the entire index portfolio. The hedge for this short position is the long position in the tracking portfolio held by the asset manager. This means that the asset manager is a natural relative value investor. Given that index performance calculations generally only consider the return on the index constituents but not their financing costs, there is usually a clear arbitrage opportunity created by the variability of repo rates applicable to different index constituents.

38.1.4 Constant Asset Allocation

Constant asset allocation is a strategy that consists of periodically rebalancing the portfolio to achieve a given allocation to the constituent asset classes. Assets that

---

[1]For instance, the German REX government bond index is practically uninvestable due to the peculiarities of its construction. Managers replicating this index therefore routinely invest in covered bonds (Pfandbriefe) to achieve the desired performance.

have increased in portfolio weight through outperformance are sold to purchase more of those assets that underperformed and therefore saw their weight in the portfolio decline. It should be stressed that this approach amounts to periodically selling the best-performing assets in the portfolio and using the proceeds to buy more of the worst-performing assets.

Unlike the no-rebalancing strategy, this approach leads to an asset allocation that is independent of the inception date of the portfolio.

The issue of rebalancing is particularly pertinent for portfolios consisting of assets denominated in multiple currencies due to the high volatility of exchange rates. A global equity portfolio managed to achieve a given asset allocation in euros might find itself selling dollar-denominated equities after a dollar appreciation even when these equities underperformed in dollars. A domestic fund in the US following the same strategy might therefore buy these same assets due to their dollar-based underperformance. It is not immediately clear which of the two funds takes the correct stance with regard to the asset class because their opposite actions are driven by changes in the exchange rate.

38.1.5   Trend-Following

Trend-following is a term for active management strategies that overweight assets that have shown an above-average performance and underweight underperforming assets. The rationale for such strategies is the positive auto-correlation of asset returns in subsequent periods observed for most assets. Trend-following can be seen as an amplified version of the no-rebalancing approach in that the weight of outperforming assets in the portfolio increases not just through the value gain of these assets, but also through additional purchases of these assets that are funded by sales of underforming assets. Trend-following is the usual investment model ascribed to a particular type of fund known as commodities trading advisors (CTA) which is a catch-all term for fund managers that operate in futures markets with a minimum of own capital.

Trend-following strategies are sometimes blamed for exacerbating market distortions because they create extra demand for assets that rise in price while selling assets that fall in price. When markets are inefficient, this is a valid concern when trend-followers are sufficient in volume to affect price formation. The catch with this accusation is that market inefficiency is not always easy to prove.

Perhaps more pertinently, trend-following strategies rely on the investment choices of others to determine their own trading strategy. As such, they may be active in nature, but are passive in their actual decision-making.

38.1.6   Mean Reversion

Mean reversion strategies are the natural opposite of trend-following strategies. Instead of overweighting outperforming assets, they underweight these assets in anticipation of asset returns reverting to their mean. Such strategies are sometimes called contrarian because they appear to run counter to current market sentiment. However, just as trend following strategies use past asset returns to guide future investment decisions and are therefore essentially passive, mean reversion strategies do not require fundamental analysis of the assets involved.

In practice, the inverse relationship between trend-following and mean reversion strategies is not perfect. Both strategies involve 2 principal time scales. First, the comparison of recent performance to trend requires the definition of the interval over which trend performance is measured. Second, the adjustment of portfolio weights in practice takes some time and this defines a time scale over which portfolio weights adjust to the moving targets defined by the strategy itself. It is in principle therefore possible for a fund manager to be both trend-following and mean-reverting at the same time, as long as the 2 timescales are sufficiently separated.

38.2   NUMERICAL EXAMPLES

The previous section has hinted that supposedly passive investment strategies like constant weights and no rebalancing can be understood to express views on the auto-correlation of asset returns. Given that active strategies like trend-following and mean reversion explicitly take views on the same auto-correlation properties, it is useful to compare the performance of these strategies in the controlled environment of simulations where mean reversion of asset returns can be set externally. Real world probability distributions have time-varying parameters that can obscure the contribution of the asset allocation strategy to the observed portfolio return.

The examples here are use a set of 3 assets which are intended to be identified with, for instance, bond, equities and cash. They have returns that follow a mean-reverting process in discrete time:

$$\mathbf{r}_t = \lambda \mathbf{m} + (1 - \lambda)\mathbf{r}_{t-1} + \mathbf{w}_t \tag{38.1}$$

The stochastic process $\mathbf{w}$ has zero mean and the covariance matrix $\mathbf{M} = \mathbf{w}^T\mathbf{w}$ is constant. To be consistent with the capital asset pricing model (CAPM), the mean return of each asset is defined to be proportional to its variance:

$$m_i = c + \beta \sigma_i \tag{38.2}$$

For illustration, Asset 3 has a low volatility while Assets 1 and 2 are more volatile. The main parameters that are used to show the effects of changing asset return characteristics on the performance of particular asset allocation strategies are the mean reversion speed λ and the covariance of the 2 most volatile assets $\sigma_{1,2}$. One sample price path for each asset is shown in Figure 38.1 for 4 different combinations of strong or weak mean reversion, and positive or negative correlation between the innovations $\mathbf{w}$.

The assets can be combined in a portfolio where each of them has a time-varying weight $w_{i,t}$ with the constraint $\sum_i w_{i,t} = 1$. For illustration, all weights are assumed to be equal at the inception of the portfolio $w_i = 1/3$. The next step is to then assume that portfolio managers apply one of 4 possible illustrative asset allocation strategies during a monthly rebalancing: No rebalancing, fixed weights, mean reversion, or trend-following. The mean reversion strategy implements a gradual decrease in the weight of an asset that exceeded its average return over the last period:

$$w'_{i,t} = w_{i,t-1} - k(r_{i,t-1} - m_i) \tag{38.3}$$

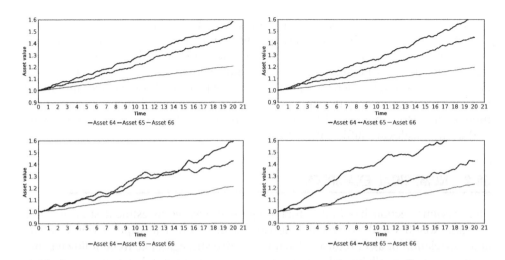

FIGURE 38.1 Asset returns for 4 different settings of mean reversion and covariance. Top row: fast mean reversion, bottom row: slow mean reversion. Left column: positive covariance, right column: negative covariance. Time is assumed to be in years with monthly returns.

subject to $w'_{i,t} > 0$ and after calculating all w', the weights are renormalised to 1:

$$w_{i,t} = \frac{w'_{i,t}}{\sum_i w'_{i,t}} \tag{38.4}$$

The trend following strategy implements the exact opposite approach by overweighting assets that outperformed:

$$w'_{i,t} = w_{i,t-1} + k(r_{i,t-1} - m_i) \tag{38.5}$$

Note that the only difference between Equations (38.3) and (38.5) is the sign before the strategy sensitivity parameter k.

Portfolio performances are caculated in the usual way, i.e.,

$$P_t = P_{t-1}\left[1 + \sum_i w_{i,t} r_{i,t}\right] \tag{38.6}$$

Figure 38.2 shows the outcome of 1 simulation path per choice of mean reversion and correlation between Assets 1 and 2. The asset return series are the same for each strategy, so the portfolio performance is only a function of how well the strategy performs for a particular type of covariance structure. The outcomes are somewhat as expected. For weak mean reversion, trend-following pays off and this strategy performs better than its logical opposite, the mean reversion strategy. The difference in outcomes is a function of the covariance between the 2 series. For a negative covariance, there

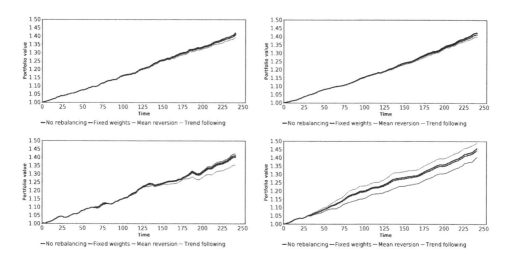

FIGURE 38.2   Portfolio performances of 4 different asset allocation strategies for different assumptions on asset returns. As in Figure 38.2, top row: fast mean reversion, bottom row: slow mean reversion. Left column: positive covariance, right column: negative covariance.

is more of a difference between being invested in one asset versus another, and therefore asset allocation decisions are more decisive for the overall outcome.

These examples give a flavour of the topic of dynamic asset allocation. Although the limitations of mean-variance optimisation for single-period investment analysis are there, the idea of systematic strategies that incorporate auto-correlation provides a natural extension. Of course, correlations change over time, and so do optimal strategies. As highlighted in Section 20.1, the expectations on central bank reaction functions do, and should, change over time. This should affect investors' asset allocation decisions.

FIGURE 38.2 Prediction ...

is one of a different asset being invested in one asset versus another, and therefore asset allocation decisions are more decisive for the overall outcome.

These examples give a flavour of the power of dynamic asset allocation. Although the limitations of mean–variance optimisation for single-period investment analysis is there, the use of systematic strategies that incorporate auto-correlation provides a natural extension, of course, correlations change over time, and so do optimal strategies. As established in Section 20.1, the expectations are central to asset allocation implications and should change over time. This should alter investors' asset allocation decisions.

Eight

References

Selected Global Bond Markets

The following section provides a short overview of the main global government bond markets. Individual bond series are given using their usual abbreviation (ticker symbol). Where Bloomberg uses different tickers, they are given as well. Local language names for each series are provided where feasible. The list is deliberately not trying to be exhaustive and some details are bound to change over time. Some additional markets are provided for illustration.

39.1 EURO AREA

The Euro area comprises the countries that introduced the common currency, the euro. Currently, these countries are: Austria, Belgium, Cyprus, Estonia, Finland, France, Germany, Greece, Ireland, Italy, Latvia, Lithuania, Luxembourg, Malta, The Netherlands, Portugal, Slovakia, Slovenia and Spain. The euro was introduced in 1999 and other countries joined later.

Each country in the euro area had its own debt market before the euro was introduced, and with the exception of the German market, where the role of the Deutsche Mark as a reserve currency had already brought in large foreign participation, most of these markets were largely (up to 95%) domestic. In order to satisfy the demands of the domestic client base, bond issues tended to be frequent and small because the low amount of secondary market trading made liquidity concerns unimportant. Bank trading desks tended to have specialised traders for each market. With the euro came a greater focus on cross-market trading, liquidity, and foreign investor participation. Two processes were initiated by the sovereigns in this context, and these were redenomination and reconventioning.

Redenomination refers to stating cash flows (coupons, redemption amound, and prices) in terms of euros instead of the legacy currencies. This was a largely symbolic step because the laws introducing the euro in the member countries retained the legal force of contracts stated in terms of the original currencies and effectively brought about redenomination anyway[1]. Reconventioning, on the other hand, was the very important

---

[1]Legally the legacy currencies still exist but are now non-decimal subunits of the euro. Saying 10,000 lire is now just an unusual way of saying 5.16 euro. The reason redenomination was undertaken is that exact instructions are required for the clearing of transactions. Computer systems

decision to make the bond markets more uniform by changing all daycount conventions to act/act and abolish minimum denominations. Given that the legacy markets used all kinds of conventions from 30/360 to act/act, this greatly aided the transparency of the market. Reconventioning was generally applied as of the first coupon payment date after the introduction of the euro, so each bond in theory was reconventioned on a different day. Note however, that there are still subtle differences in place between the markets, such as accrued interest rounding conventions in Italy. However, bond markets are clearly becoming more integrated and from around 2001 banks have started to reorganise their trading desks more along maturity-based splits than on issuer lines.

With the greater stability in short term interest rates brought about by the larger currency area, sovereigns have generally decided to lower the average time to maturity of their outstanding debt. Note that large issuers, such as sovereigns, have to make a conscious trade-off between long-term stability of financing costs (represented by long maturity bonds) and lower current interest rates (such as afforded by short maturity bonds). There is no hard and fast way of estimating the optimal maturity profile, but generally the ideal average time to maturity falls with decreasing rate volatility. By today, practically all sovereigns have started to use interest rate swaps as a tool to manage duration risk, but the sheer size of sovereign debt and the fact that practically all sovereigns are trying to manage their debt duration in the same direction, mean that there is limited scope for the market to absorb the risks. The French Trésor announced a large swap programme in 2001 only to find that the market almost immediately repriced the swap spreads of French government bonds.

With the exception of the German government, euro area sovereigns do not commit themselves to issue a certain amount of debt of a particular maturity far ahead of time. This gives them the flexibility to adjust the size, if not the maturity, of the issued bonds to the market environment at the time of the auction or syndication. Such flexibility can be both a good and a bad thing. The benchmark status of the German government debt is probably helped by the fact that the German agency does not attempt to time the market too much. However, only one issuer can be the benchmark issuer and, for the other governments, flexibility may therefore be more important. That being said, the bulk of issuance can be forecast with reasonable accuracy in most countries.

Supply in the euro area is generally through auction for the bigger issuers and syndication for the smaller ones. The EuroMTS interdealer trading system imposes a minimum size of EUR 5bn for bonds to be listed. This provides a strong incentive for debt managers to provide this amount of debt with the initial tranche of a new bond and restricts smaller sovereigns in terms of the number of bonds they can issue per year. Such smaller issuers will usually place the large initial tranche via syndication and then conduct regular tap auctions.

39.1.1 Austria

Austrian government debt is managed by the Austrian Federal Financing Agency (Österreichische Bundesfinanzierungsagentur, www.oebfa.co.at). Austrian government

---

are not given to analysing the economics of a transaction to decide whether instructions given in different currencies amount to the same economic value.

bonds used to be an example of having many small issues at very similar maturities, but quickly switched to issuing fewer, but larger benchmark bonds after the introduction of the euro.

RAGB (Bundesanleihe)

Maturities	10Y, 15Y, 30Y, 50Y, 70Y, 100Y
Coupon	Fixed annual, both decimal and 1/4% steps
Yield convention	True Street (annual compound)
Settlement, daycount	T+2 Vienna, act/act
Issuance	Monthly auctions or syndication
Usual volume	10bn
Strippable	Yes

RATB (Bundesschatzschein)

Maturities	7–365 days
Coupon	Zero coupon
Yield convention	Simple yield
Settlement, daycount	T+2, depending on market
Issuance	Irregular
Usual volume	Irregular
Strippable	No

Remarks:
Austrian T-bills are usually issued under English law even when denominated in euros. There is also no cross-default clause.

39.1.2 Belgium

Belgian government debt is managed by the Belgian State Treasury (treasury.fgov.be) which is part of the Ministry of Finance of the Kingdom of Belgium. The Treasury was an early adopter of exchange auctions with a view to consolidate illiquid product lines. In contrast to most other treasuries, Belgium also actively used exchange auctions to smoothen out the redemption profile of State debt. To this end, bonds within 1 year of maturity were exchanged against current long-dated benchmark bonds.

OLO/BGB (Obligations linéaires/Lineaire obligaties)

Maturities	2Y, 5Y, 10Y, 30Y, 50Y
Coupon	Fixed annual, 1/4% steps, now decimal
Yield convention	True Street, annual compound
Settlement, daycount	T+2 Brussels, act/act
Issuance	Monthly auction or syndication
Usual volume	7.5–15bn
Strippable	Yes

BGTB (Certificats de Trésorerie/Schatkistcertificaten)

Maturities	3M, 6M, 12M
Coupon	Zero coupon
Yield convention	Simple yield
Settlement, daycount	T+2 Brussels, act/360
Issuance	Biweekly auction
Usual volume	1.5–2bn
Strippable	No

Remarks:

Belgium was the only euro area money market that had to switch from act/365 to act/360 daycount convention. Note that Luxembourg had a currency union with Belgium before adopting the euro.

39.1.3 Finland

Finnish debt is managed by the State Treasury (www.valtiokonttori.fi) and has an EMTN programme that allows it to place public debt at short notice.

RFGB (Sarjaobligaation)

Maturities	5Y, 10Y
Coupon	Fixed annual, 1/8% steps
Yield convention	True Street, annual compound
Settlement, daycount	T+2 Helsinki, act/act
Issuance	Usually syndication followed by tap auctions. Although an auction calendar exists, scheduled auctions dates are frequently skipped.
Usual volume	5–7bn
Strippable	No

39.1.4 France

French government debt is issued by the Agence France Trésor (www.aft.gouv.fr), an agency of the French State set up in February 2001. AFT is active in the swap market and also conducts sporadic buy-backs of older French bonds. The issuance policy of the Tresor combines a fixed calendar with some flexibility as to the supply amount and the bonds supplied. France has in the past tapped off-the-run bonds which is otherwise fairly uncommon in any market.

France conducts two auctions per month, with a 10Y or longer OAT auction every first Thursday of every month and a 2Y, 5Y and inflation-linked OATi/OAT€i auction each third Thursday. These auction dates can be shifted if they coincide with national holidays. France has a primary dealer system called SVT (Spécialistes en Valeurs du Trésor) and a lending facility where SVT can borrow bonds to cover short positions.

OAT/FRTR (Obligations Assimilables du Trésor)

Maturities	10Y, 15Y, 30Y, 50Y
Coupon	Fixed annual, 1/4% steps
Yield convention	True Street (annual compound)
Settlement, daycount	T+2 Paris, act/act
Issuance	Usually two new 10Y issues per year, one 30Y, occasionally 15Y, and first 50Y in 2005
Usual volume	10–45bn
Strippable	Yes, coupon and principal strips are fungible

Remarks:

The Trésor is one of the more innovative global debt managers and the variety of OAT issues is evidence of that. France had issued Ecu-denominated OATs that were funged with French Franc OATs into euro issues, there were TEC10 10Y floating rate linked OATs, France issued the first 50Y government bond in euros, and so on. For a while, there was some effort to wrest benchmark status from the German 10Y sector through support of the Matif 10Y contract, but this failed due to a lack of market interest. The French curve remains an important reference or euro-area sub-sovereign issuers, in part due to the proliferation of French agency issuers.

OATi and OAT€i (Obligations Assimilables du Trésor indexées)

Maturities	10Y, 30Y
Coupon	Fixed annual, decimal 0.05% steps, linked to French CPI ex-tobacco (OATi) or Euroland HICP ex-tobacco (OAT€i)
Yield convention	True Street (annual compound), inflation-linked
Settlement, daycount	T+2 Paris, act/act
Issuance	Irregular
Usual volume	Irregular
Strippable	No

Remarks:

The French government was the first one to issue inflation-linked debt in the euro area and remains the benchmark issuer in this regard. Originally, the inflation link was to French CPI excluding tobacco costs, but bonds linked to euro area HICP inflation were first issued in 2001 and proved rather popular. Instead of switching completely to issuance of OAT€i, the Trésor still issues OATi and allocates supply opportunistically between the two.

BTAN/BTNS (Bons du Trésor à taux fixe et intérèts annuels)

Maturities	2Y, 5Y
Coupon	Fixed annual, 1/4% steps
Yield convention	True Street (annual compound)
Settlement, daycount	T+2 Paris, act/act
Issuance	Usually two 2Y and 5Y issues per year
Usual volume	20bn
Strippable	No

Remarks:
BTNS for a while held the 5Y benchmark status in euros and were commonly used to price new corporate supply. Quotation and settlement convention for BTNS differed from OAT but were gradually brought in line. France switched completely from issuing BTNS to FRTR/OAT.

BTF (Bons du Trésor à taux fixe et à intérèt précompté)

Maturities	13, 26, 52 weeks
Coupon	Zero coupon
Yield convention	simple yield
Settlement, daycount	T+1 Paris, act/360
Issuance	Weekly auction
Usual volume	4bn
Strippable	No

Remarks:
BTFs form the most liquid bill market in euros.

39.1.5 Germany

German government debt used to be managed by the German Bundesbank, but in 2001 the German Ministry of Finance set up a private company wholly owned by the German State to manage the debt instead. This agency is called the German Financing Agency (Deutsche Finanzagentur, www.deutsche-finanzagentur.de) and is located in Frankfurt.

The German Agency, like the Bundesbank before it, is very active in the secondary market (both outright and repo) through a process called market management, and retains part of each auction for this purpose. Market management is done mainly through anonymous interdealer platforms, so there is no way of gauging the Agency's actions. The Agency is also a fairly active user of interest rate swaps. Traditionally, Germany saw steady demand for its debt because the Deutsche Mark used to be a reserve currency, the German credit was perceived as very good, and supply was reasonably limited. With the introduction of the euro and the high cost imposed by the German reunification process, this uniquely benevolent situation is no longer present and the Agency is active in promoting German debt.

German bond auctions always happen on Wednesdays with the exception of Bubills which are issued on Mondays and inflation-linked bonds on Tuesdays. BKO auctions switched to Tuesdays in 2017. There is no primary dealer systems and bidding at the auctions is done by an auction bidding group that is in principle open to all dealers. Bidders are ejected from this group if they fail to take down at least 0.1% of the annual supply in duration-ajusted terms. The Agency publishes an annual issuance outlook from which it is generally possible to infer auction dates and auction amounts for the whole year with only marginal uncertainty. Towards the each quarter, the Agency publishes a detailed calendar for the following quarter. Deviations from the auction calendar (usually extra supply) can take place via non-public taps into the market management account of the Agency. Although they are announced in a timely fashion, it is impossible to gauge the market impact of such taps because it is not clear how long the Agency will retain these bonds.

Because the Agency can withold an arbitrary amount of debt at any auction, there is never a need to lower the amount issued at an auction. Because Germany typically tends to receive a large amount of noncompetitive bids and has complete freedom in allocating to these bids, it is not trivial to gauge the actual demand situation at an auction from the observed prices.

DBR (Bundesanleihe)

Maturities	10Y, 30Y, exceptionally 15Y
Coupon	Fixed annual, usually 1/4% steps
Yield convention	True Street (annual compound)
Settlement, daycount	T+2 Frankfurt, act/act
Issuance	Two 10Y issues per year, 0–1 30Y per year, typically 2–3 taps for each new 10Y
Usual volume	around 25bn
Strippable	Yes

Remarks:

DBR issues are the main benchmarks for European yields. This partly has historical reasons (some central banks still have restrictions for investing in other euro area sovereigns whereas the Deutsche Mark used to be a reserve currency), but is also supported by the dominance of the Eurex bond futures contracts in euro area trading. The world's most active contract, the Eurex Bund, is a contract on 10Y DBR, and the 5Y Eurex Bobl contract usually has a DBR CTD every other delivery. DBR issues tend to have long first coupons.

OBL (Bundesobligation)

Maturities	5Y
Coupon	fixed annual, usually 1/4% steps
Yield convention	True Street (annual compound)
Settlement, daycount	T+2 Frankfurt, act/act
Issuance	Two issues per year, typically two taps for each new issue
Usual volume	20bn
Strippable	No

Remarks:

The issuance procedures and maturity months for OBLs have changed several times since the introduction of the euro because these bonds were also important retail instruments. The current system is fairly transparent and fully adapted to the requirements of the wholesale market. The supply is now timed so that every other 5Y contract (Bobl) on Eurex will have an OBL as CTD.

DBRi (Inflationsindizierte Bundesanleihe)

Maturities	10Y, 30Y
Coupon	Fixed annual, decimal, linked to Euroland HICP ex-tobacco
Yield convention	True Street (annual compound)
Settlement, daycount	T+2 Frankfurt, act/act
Issuance	Irregular
Usual volume	10–16bn
Strippable	No

Remarks:

Inflation-linked contracts were severely restricted in Germany by the law that introduced the Deutsche Mark because such obligations were seen as inflationary feedback loops. This restrction was removed with the introduction of the euro, but the government did not start to issue inflation-linked bonds until 2006. For some time, there were also indexed 5Y OBLi. German break-even inflation trades very close to French break-even (when adjusted for seasonality) and the French inflation-linked curve remains the benchmark.

BKO (Bundesschatzanweisung, formerly Bundeskassenobligation)

Maturities	2Y
Coupon	Fixed annual, usually 1/4% steps
Yield convention	True Street (annual compound)
Settlement, daycount	T+2 Frankfurt, act/act
Issuance	Four issues per year, March, June, September, and December maturities
Usual volume	12bn
Strippable	No

Remarks:

Eurex Schatz contracts tend to have a BKO CTD and because the maturities tend to fall in the middle of the month, BKO swap spreads can be traded using Euribor contracts with little basis risk.

BUBILL (Bundeskassenschein)

Maturities	6M
Coupon	Zero-coupon
Yield convention	Simple yield
Settlement, daycount	T+2 Frankfurt, act/360
Issuance	Twelve issues per year
Usual volume	6bn
Strippable	No

Remarks:

The German government had a tacit agreement with the Bundesbank not to be overly active in the short-term debt market to avoid interference with the money supply targets of the central bank. With the introduction of the euro, the situation changed and Bubills became more active. However, their liquidity remains inferior to the French BTFs.

39.1.6 Greece

Due to problems with achieving the strict debt criteria needed to qualify, Greece joined the euro only in 2001, just in time for the introduction of euro cash. Due to excessive debts, Greece in 2010 needed a rescue package from the other EU member states who set up the EFSM and EFSF for this purpose. Greece restructured the bulk of its outstanding debt in 2012 as part of this rescue effort and remains sub-investment grade. The support for Greece was redesigned several times to achieve debt sustainability, and Greece has regained market access. The first post-restructuring bonds were issued already in 2014. The Greek bonds issued while Greece was receiving fiscal support from other euro member states had higher coupons than the interest charged by the public creditors. Somewhat uniquely, therefore, creditors willing to ease payment terms receive a lower interest rate than creditors with fixed claims.

Greek government debt is managed by the Public Debt Management Agency (www.pdma.gr). The market is essentially split between the 'strip', which is a series of bonds allocated to investors who participated in the 2012 'private sector involvement' (PSI), and the post-PSI bonds. The liquidity of the strip is poor while the newer bonds trade somewhat more actively.

GGB ($o\mu o\lambda o\gamma o\ \epsilon\lambda\lambda\eta\nu\iota\kappa o\upsilon\ \delta\eta\mu o\sigma\iota o\upsilon$)	
Maturities	3Y, 5Y, 10Y
Coupon	Fixed annual, 1/8% steps
Yield convention	True street, annual compound
Settlement, daycount	T+2 Athens, ISMA 30/360 or act/act
Issuance	Monthly auctions
Usual volume	5–10bn
Strippable	No
Remarks:	
Because the Bank of Greece operates a securities depository, transaction volumes of Greek government bonds are quite transparent.	

39.1.7 Ireland

Irish debt is managed by the National Treasury Management Agency NTMA (www.ntma.ie). Through a large bond exchange auction and listing in Euroclear in 2000, Ireland brought more liquidity into the market, and dispersion of liquidity across different instruments, such as CP, has also been reduced. Ireland issues both domestic euro debt and foreign currency bonds and also maintains an active CP programme. Ireland suffered heavily in the financial crisis due to an outsized financial system.

IRISH	
Maturities	2Y, 10Y, 15Y
Coupon	Fixed annual, decimal steps
Yield convention	True street (annual compound)
Settlement, daycount	T+2 Dublin, act/act
Issuance	Monthly auction (every third Thursday) or syndication
Usual volume	10bn
Strippable	No

39.1.8 Italy

The Italian Treasury (www.dt.tesoro.it) is part of the Ministry of Finance. Given the large size of Italy's debt relative to its GDP, Italy has been innovative in its debt management policy and has been one of the earliest adopters of derivatives. Italy has a highly liquid market in Treasury bills and when the floating rate CCTs are added to the actual zero coupon instruments, a large share of the total Italian government debt is short-dated.

BTPS (Buoni poliennali del Tesoro)

Maturities	3Y, 5Y, 10Y, 15Y, 30Y
Coupon	Fixed semi-annual, 1/4% steps and decimal
Yield convention	True Street, bond-equivalent
Settlement, daycount	T+2 Milan, act/act
Issuance	Two auctions per month, mid-month for for 5Y, 15Y and 30Y, month end for 3Y and 10Y
Usual volume	10–30bn
Strippable	Yes

Remarks:
The trading platform for BPT, MTS, is now the dominant interdealer platform in the euro area.

CCT/CCTS (Certificati di Credito del Tesoro)

Maturities	7Y
Coupon	Floating rate semi-annual, linked to most recent BOT auction yield plus margin
Yield convention	Not applicable
Settlement, daycount	T+2 Milan
Issuance	discontinued
Usual volume	not applicable
Strippable	No

Remarks:
CCT have been discontinued due to low liquidity and some questionable market practices. CCT used to be a conventient instrument for savings banks because both the variable coupon, and the 7Y maturity matches well the characteristics of a consumer deposit. Their role has been taken over by CCT€.

CCT€/CCTS (Certificati di Credito del Tesoro €)

Maturities	7Y
Coupon	Floating rate semi-annual, linked to Euribor plus margin
Yield convention	Not applicable
Settlement, daycount	T+2 Milan
Issuance	Monthly auction at month-end (together with 3Y and 10Y BTPS)
Usual volume	12–18bn
Strippable	No

Remarks:
CCT€ avoid some of the problems connected to the BOTS auction link of CCT but remain less liquid than BTPs.

CTZ/ICTZ (Certificati del Tesoro Zero Coupon)

Maturities	2Y
Coupon	Zero coupon
Yield convention	Simple yield
Settlement, daycount	T+2 Milan, act/365 (note: not act/360)
Issuance	Monthly auction
Usual volume	15–18 bn
Strippable	No

Remarks:
CTZ are exceptional in that they are included in bond indices despite being issued as bills.

BOT/BOTS (Buoni Ordinari del Tesoro)

Maturities	3, 6, 12 months
Coupon	Zero coupon
Yield convention	Simple yield
Settlement, daycount	T+2 Milan, act/360
Issuance	Monthly auction
Usual volume	6–10 bn
Strippable	No

39.1.9 The Netherlands

The debt of the Kingdom of the Netherlands is managed by the Dutch State Treasury Agency (www.dsta.nl). The Agency uses an auction method system called Dutch Direct Auction which is unique to The Netherlands. Auctions are done using an auction 'window' where the Agency continuously displays an offer price at which primary dealers can buy bonds[2]. The price is adjusted to dealer demand and market levels for up to one hour or until the desired bond volume has been sold. In such an auction, investment banks direct clients towards the DSTA. This is a mix between syndication (in that marketing is done by investment banks) and auction.

DSL/NETHER (Staatsleningen)

Maturities	3Y, 10Y, 30Y
Coupon	Fixed annual, 1/4% steps
Yield convention	True Street, annual compound
Settlement, daycount	T+2 Amsterdam, act/act
Issuance	Monthly auction on the Tuesday following the first Wednesday
Usual volume	10–18bn
Strippable	Yes

Remarks:
DSTA offers a repo facility for bonds with issue sizes smaller than 5bn to market makers in order to avoid squeezes in new bonds.

DTC/DTB (Schatkistpapier)

Maturities	3, 6, 9, 12M
Coupon	Zero coupon
Yield convention	Simple yield
Settlement, daycount	T+2 Amsterdam, act/360
Issuance	First Monday of each month
Usual volume	Irregular
Strippable	No

39.1.10 Portugal

The debt of the Republic of Portugal is managed by the Instituto de Gestão do Crédito Público (ICDO, www.igcp.pt). The Portuguese market remained fairly domestic even after the introduction of the euro because foreign investors could not clear government debt securities through either of the two major clearers Clearstream or Euroclear. Trading though electronic interdealer platforms also only started in earnest with the introduction of the Medip system which is operated by MTS Portugal. Nowadays, Portuguese government bonds can be cleared through Euroclear and the primary dealer group, Operadores Especializados en Valores do Tesouro, is fairly active.

---

[2]The expression refers to a time window.

PGB (Obrigações do Tesoro)

Maturities	10Y, 30Y
Coupon	Fixed annual, 1/8% and decimal steps
Yield convention	True Street, annual compound
Settlement, daycount	T+2 Lisboa
Issuance	Syndication and monthly auction each second Wednesday
Usual volume	5–12bn
Strippable	No

39.1.11   Spain

The debt of the Kindom of Spain is managed by the Tesoro Público (www.tesoro.es), part of the Ministry of Finance. Spain has a primary dealer system. Eurex launched a Spanish government bond future in 2015 but the contract remains illiquid, partly due to competing with the Eurex 10Y and 3Y BTP contracts as a hedge instrument for spread products in euros, and partly due to the stability of the Spain–France spread.

SPGB (Bonos/Obligaciones)

Maturities	3Y, 5Y (Bonos); 10Y, 15Y, 30Y (Obligaciones)
Coupon	Fixed annual, decimal 0.05% steps
Yield convention	True Street, annual compound
Settlement, daycount	T+2 Madrid, act/act
Issuance	Monthly except August, Bonos each first Thursday, Obligaciones each third Thursday
Usual volume	10bn
Strippable	Yes

Remarks:

Most Spanish Obligaciones used to have an unusual initial zero coupon period. The bonds were issued with less than one year to what would normally be the first coupon date but did not accrue any coupon during that period. Although the first coupon is therefore paid between one and two years after the bond is first issued, it is simply a full coupon, not a long first coupon. Put differently, the first accrual date is after the first settlement date. The bonds were therefore issued at a discount to the par price which effectively reflected negative accrued interest. This practice ended in 2006.

SPTB (Letras)

Maturities	3, 6, 12, 18 months
Coupon	Zero coupon
Yield convention	Simple yield
Settlement, daycount	T+2 Madrid, act/360
Issuance	Monthly auction
Usual volume	5–8bn
Strippable	No

Remarks:

The Spanish Letras are fairly liquid compared to the liquidity of Spanish coupon bonds.

39.2   ICELAND

The Icelandic debt market is unique in that practically all long-term debt is inflation-linked, while all short-term debt is issued in nominal terms. This makes the analysis of break-even inflation practically impossible. This structure is the result of being a small open economy which makes FX rates an important driver of domestic inflation. All trades by market makers have to be reported to the Nasdaq Iceland (www.nasdaqomxnordic.com, formerly Icelandic Stock Exchange) and there is therefore a reasonable degree of price transparency.

The national debt of the Republic of Iceland is managed by the National Debt Management Agency (Lánamál Ríkisins, www.lanamal.is). The actual government debt sector is only a small part of the total debt market while the biggest issuer in the Icelandic market is the government Housing Financing Fund Íbúðalánasjórður (www.ils.is). Icelandic Housing bonds form the core of the Icelandic long-term debt market. The bonds are annuities linked to Icelandic inflation, which reflects the structure of the underlying mortgage loans. The debt of the Housing Financing Fund carries a deficiency guarantee of the Icelandic State but is not explicitly state-guaranteed.

RIKS/ICEGB (Ríkisbréf)

Maturities	5Y, 10Y
Coupon	Annual fixed
Yield convention	True Street, compound
Settlement, daycount	T+2 Reykjavik, act/act
Issuance	Irregular auction
Usual volume	
Strippable	No

HFF/ICEHB (Íbúðalánasjórður Íbúðabréf)

Maturities	2014, 2024, 2034, and 2044 maturities
Coupon	Fixed semi-annual 3.75%, amortising annuity, inflation-linked
Yield convention	True Street, bond-equivalent (international), semi-annual compound (domestic)
Settlement, daycount	T+1 Reykjavik, 30/360
Issuance	Irregular auction, private placements
Usual volume	
Strippable	No

Remarks:
The current benchmark series of Icelandic Housing bonds was created in an exchange against older Húsbréf and Íbúðabréf bonds in 2004.

39.3 JAPAN

Japan has the highest debt load of all OECD countries and unless drastic measures will be adopted, this debt load is likely to rise further as a result of demographic trends. Unlike other developed countries, Japan never conducted a currency reform to hide the inflationary effects of past wars and therefore the smallest currency denomination, the sen, is now only used to quote securities prices. Japan introduced a primary dealer system in 2004 and at the time of writing, there are 21 primary dealers.

Although the Japanese Yen is a central bank reserve currency and Japanese government debt represents a large part of global bond indices, Japanese bonds tend to be underrepresented in global investor portfolios. This is mainly due to the combination of low yields with a central bank policy to keep the Japanese Yen weak against the US dollar.

Japanese government bonds have an ex-coupon period of three days, but no settlement of the relevant bonds occurs during these three days. Instead, settlement that would fall into the ex-dividend period is delayed until the day after the coupon has been paid.

Japanese government bonds are generally quoted on a simple yield basis. Exceptions are JF and JGBi bonds, which are quoted on the usual clean price basis, and when-issued JGB, which are quoted in compound yield. As in many Asian countries, it is common to refer to bonds by series number, and there are separate series for all JGB types and original maturities. Although it has no natural investor base, the 10Y JGB has benchmark status[3].

---

[3]The (simple) 10Y yield appears on the font page of the Nikkei newspaper (Nihon Keizai Shinbun) and was also the reference point when yield curve control was introduced by the Bank of Japan.

JGB

Maturities	2Y (JN), 5Y (JS), 10Y (JB), 20Y (JL), 30Y (JX), 40Y (JU)
Coupon	Fixed semi-annual, 0.1% decimal steps
Yield convention	Simple yield
Settlement, daycount	T+2 Tokyo, NL/365
Issuance	Auction (JS, JN, and JB monthly, JL bimonthly, JX quarterly)
Usual volume	2.1tr (JN), 5tr (JS), 6.5–7.5tr (JB), 3tr (JL), 2.1tr (JX), 2tr (JU)
Strippable	Yes

Remarks:

Bonds are reopened if they have the right maturity and a par coupon, otherwise a new bond is issued. This means in particular for 10Y (JB) issues that the final issue size depends on yield movements between the first and last auction of a new maturity point.

JF

Maturities	15Y
Coupon	Floating rate, semi-annual
Yield convention	Not applicable
Settlement, daycount	T+2 Tokyo, NL/365
Issuance	Quarterly auction
Usual volume	1.4tr
Strippable	No

Remarks:

The coupon of a JF is reset every six months to the simple yield of the most recent 10Y auction before fees, minus a spread called alpha. The higher the alpha of a bond, the lower the future coupons, but coupons are floored at zero. When dealers bid for new JF, bids are submitted in terms of alpha. Japanese yields are very low and there is a signficant probability that a 10Y auction happens at a lower yield than the alpha of a JF, so the coupon floor of a JF usually has a meaningful value. More importantly, because the coupon is reset to a 10Y rate, JF are highly convex products and the convexity adjustment represents a large part of the value of a JF. JF issuance ended in 2008 with JF48.

JGBi

Maturities	10Y
Coupon	Fixed semi-annual, 0.1% decimal steps, inflation-linked
Yield convention	True Street (bond-equivalent)
Settlement, daycount	T+2 Tokyo, NL/365
Issuance	Quarterly auction
Usual volume	up to 600bn
Strippable	No

Remarks:

JGBi are linked to non-seasonally adjusted Japanese CPI excluding fresh food. Unlike most other inflation-linked markets, JGBi redemptions up to JGBi16 are not floored at par. A new series of JGBi was launched in 2013 with a floor for the principal and the last coupon. In the absence of inflation, the JGBi market has been dormant since shortly after its inception in 2004.

JTB/JFB

Maturities	13 weeks, 6 and 12 months
Coupon	Zero coupon
Yield convention	Simple yield
Settlement, daycount	T+2 Tokyo (act/365)
Issuance	Weekly auctions
Usual volume	8tr
Strippable	No

39.4 SWEDEN

The debt of the Kingdom of Sweden has been managed since 1789 by the Swedish National Debt Office (Riksgäldskontoret, now Riksgalden, www.riksgalden.se) which is one of the oldest and most sophisticated debt managers globally. Sweden issues debt in Swedish krona as well as euros and dollars and inflation-linked bonds.

The Swedish market is an important diversification market for currency speculators who are at times fairly active at the front end of the market. Like most Scandinavian countries, Sweden greatly values transparency and timely market information is widely disseminated. The Swedish market generally trades on quotes in compound yield terms.

SGB (Statsobligationer)

Maturities	10Y, 25Y
Coupon	Annual fixed, 1/8% steps
Yield convention	True Street, annual compound
Settlement, daycount	T+2 Stockholm, ISMA 30/360
Issuance	Two auctions per month
Usual volume	40–100bn
Strippable	No

Remarks:

The euro-denominated eurobond issue SWED 5% 01/09 was fungible with the domestic SGB 5% 01/09 should Sweden adopt the euro instead of the Swedish krona.

SGBi (Realobligationer)

Maturities	10Y, 25Y
Coupon	Annual fixed, 1/8% steps, inflation-linked
Yield convention	True street, annual compound
Settlement, daycount	T+2 Stockholm, ISMA 30/360
Issuance	Two auctions per month
Usual volume	20–60bn
Strippable	No

Remarks:

Unlike many other markets, Swedish linkers do not always have their own specific base CPI.

39.5 UNITED KINGDOM

The United Kingdom arguably has the oldest intact government bond market by virtue of having avoided invasion by another sovereign. Occasional support from the Bank of England has also been important in keeping the government solvent. Britain has a long history of circulating capital, which has been conducive to the development of capital markets in general. While it used to be quite common in other countries for private persons to store surplus wealth in cash, real assets, or bilateral loans, Britain has had a history of institutional fund management and thereby a more active allocation of capital to profitable causes. This means that the UK has set a few trends for the global bond market.

Over the centuries, Britain has created a number of bonds that are not unique to the UK, but where the UK name is applied as a generic term. The main one is consol which these days is deemed by many to be identical to the term annuity but is in fact the short form of Consolidated, which was the name given to callable perpetual bonds issued by the UK government to consolidate a number of outstanding debt securities. Another one is war loan, which in the UK refers to specific securities, but is used globally to refer to debt securities with below-market interest rates issued by governments in times of war to solicit funds from patriotically spirited citizens.

The debt of Her Brittanic Majesty The Queen's Government is managed by the Debt Management Office (DMO, www.dmo.gov.uk), which is part of Her Majesty's Treasury but operates at arm's length. Government bonds in the UK are usually called gilt-edged securities, or gilts for short. Trading in gilts is done by gilt-edged market makers (GEMMs) which are securities houses that have applied for this status at the DMO. There are no significant restrictions to being, or ceasing to be, a GEMM, but once a house resigns from GEMM status, it cannot reapply for the status within a certain grace period.

The long end of the UK bond market is driven mainly by pension funds. The UK has one of the largest funded pension systems worldwide and any change in asset allocation by pension funds, whether forced by regulation or voluntary, tends to have a large impact on the UK curve.

UKT (Treasury stock, Gilt, Conventional)

Maturities	5Y, 10Y, 20Y, 30Y, 50Y
Coupon	Fixed semi-annual, 1/8% steps
Yield convention	True street, bond-equivalent
Settlement, daycount	T+0 or T+1 London, act/act
Issuance	Auction, 1–2 per month
Usual volume	10bn
Strippable	Yes

Remarks:
A futures contract on 10Y gilts is traded on ICE London.

UKTI (Index-linked Treasury stock, index-linked Gilt)

Maturities	10Y, 20Y, 30Y
Coupon	Fixed semi-annual, 1/8% steps, inflation-linked
Yield convention	True street, bond-equivalent
Settlement, daycount	T+0 or T+1 London, act/act
Issuance	Auction, roughly monthly
Usual volume	6bn
Strippable	No

Remarks:
Index-linked Gilts are linked to UK RPI with a 3 months, earlier an 8 months lag.

39.6   UNITED STATES OF AMERICA

The US bond market is the largest in the world and the creation of this market by Alexander Hamilton was a founding moment in the history the United States [14]. US government debt is issued by the US Treasury (www.treasury.gov). The maturity points of the curve where the Treasury issues are 2Y, 3Y, 5Y, and 10Y (collectively known as Notes), and in the past, 30Y (Bonds). The expression 'the bond' therefore usually refers to the most recent 30 year issue. The US also issues T-bills and inflation-linked bonds known as TIPS.

The US operates a Primary Dealer system which is unique in that the trading of bonds is also tied to the provision of central bank liquidity (Fed Funds) into the banking system. Actual liquidity provision in the secondary market has, however, spread across multiple firms thanks to easy access to anonymous matching platforms and, more recently, central clearing. The US bond market relies to a lesser extent than the European and Japanese market on bond futures contracts for price discovery although bond futures volumes are now considerable. The main price discovery takes place through the on-the-run benchmark securities. The US market has so far resisted decimalisation.

Tentative auction calendars are available some time ahead, but the actual size of supply generally becomes known through the Quarterly Refunding Announcement.

T (Treasury note/Treasury bond)	
Maturities	2Y, 3Y, 5Y, 10Y, 30Y
Coupon	Fixed semi-annual, currently 1/8% increments, decimal considered
Yield convention	True street, bond-equivalent
Settlement, daycount	T+1 New York (different for auctions), act/act
Issuance	Several auctions per month
Usual volume	40-50 bn
Strippable	Yes

TIPS/TII (Treasury Inflation-protected security)	
Maturities	5Y, 10Y, 30Y
Coupon	Fixed semi-annual, 1/8% steps
Yield convention	True street, bond-equivalent
Settlement, daycount	T+1 New York (different for auctions)
Issuance	Quarterly auction
Usual volume	15–40bn
Strippable	Yes

B (Treasury bill)

Maturities	4, 13, 26, 51 weeks
Coupon	Zero coupon
Yield convention	Discount yield
Settlement, daycount	T+1 New York, act/360
Issuance	Weekly auction (4 week bill Mondays, 13 and 26 weeks Thursday
Usual volume	30–120bn
Strippable	No

Remarks:

The close spacing of bills makes them bellwether instruments for market sentiment regarding timeliness of payment by the US Treasury during periods of shutdowns. These are times when Congress has not approved the bills required to fund the US government expenditure and the market therefore prices in the risk of temporary defaults.

Bibliography

1. Douglas Adams. *The Hitchhiker's Guide to the Galaxy*. Wings Books, New York, 1986.
2. Thomas Adrian, Richard K. Crump, and Emanuel Moench. Pricing the term structure with linear regressions. Technical Report 340, Federal Reserve Bank of New York, April 2013.
3. Liaquat Ahamed. *Lords of Finance*. Penguin, 2009.
4. Richard G. Anderson and Marcela M. Williams. How U.S. Currency Stacks Up-at Home and Abroad. *Central Banker*, 1(Spring 2007), 2007.
5. Walter Bagehot. *Lombard Street*. Wiley, 1873, 1999.
6. European Central Bank. Guideline (EU) 2015/510 of the ECB of 19 December 2014 on the implementation of the Eurosystem monetary policy framework. Technical report, ECB, 2014.
7. European Central Bank. Target 2 Annual Report 2017. Technical report, ECB, 2018.
8. Bank of Japan Study Group on Risk-Free Reference Rates. Report on the identification of a Japanese Yen risk-free rate. Technical report, Bank of Japan, https://www.boj.or.jp/en/paym/market/sg/rfr1612c.pdf, December 2016.
9. Ben S. Bernanke, Thomas Laubach, Frederik S. Mishkin, and Adam S. Posen. *Inflation Targeting*. Princeton University Press, 1999.
10. Ulrich Bindseil. *Monetary Policy Operations and the Financial System*. Oxford University Press, 2014.
11. Ulrich Bindseil. *Central Banking before 1800. A Rehabilitation*. Oxford University Press, 2019.
12. Martin Bohner. Fixed income models. Lecture notes retrieved from https://web.mst.edu/bohner/fim-10, Jan 2011.
13. Richard A. Brealey, Steward C. Myers, and Alan J. Marcus. *Fundamentals of Corporate Finance*. Irwin McGraw-Hill, 2 edition, 1999.
14. Hugh Brogan. *The Penguin History of the USA*. Penguin Books, second edition, 1999.
15. Bundesverfassungsgericht. Urteil des Zweiten Senats vom 19. Oktober 2006, 2006. 2 BvF 3/03.
16. Bundesverfassungsgericht. Urteil des Zweiten Senats vom 7. September 2011, 2011. 2 BvR 987/10.
17. Bundesverfassungsgericht. Urteil des Zweiten Senats vom 5. Mai 2020, 2020. 2 BvR 859/15.
18. Galen D. Burghardt and Terrence M. Belton. *The Treasury bond basis: An in-depth analysis for hedgers, speculators and arbitrageurs*. Probus Publishing, 1993.
19. Jeffrey R. Campbell, Charles L. Evans, Jonas D. M. Fisher, and Alejandro Justiniano. Macroeconomic Effects of Federal Reserve Forward Guidance. Technical report, The Brookings Institution, Spring 2012.
20. John Y. Campbell and Luis M. Viceira. *Strategic Asset Allocation – Portfolio Choice for Long-term Investors*. Oxford University Press, 1 edition, 2002.
21. Eurex Clearing. ISA Direct – Eurex Clearing's unique buy side membership. Technical report, Eurex Clearing AG, https://www.eurexclearing.com, 2016.
22. David Cobham. *Macroeconomic Analysis*. Addison Wesley Longman, 2 edition, 1998.
23. John H. Cochrane. *Asset Pricing*. Princeton University Press, 2005.
24. European Commission. Green Paper on the feasibility of stability bonds. Technical Report COM(2011) 818 final, European Commission, November 2011.

25. Markets Committee. Large central bank balance sheets and market functioning. Technical report, Bank for International Settlements, October 2019.

26. George Cooper. *The Origin of Financial Crisis*. Harriman House, 2008.

27. George Cooper. *Money, Blood and Revolution*. Harriman House, 2014.

28. Paul De Grauwe. *The Economics of monetary integration*. Oxford University Press, 3 edition, 1997.

29. Mark Deacon, Andrew Derry, and Dariush Mirfindereski. *Inflation-indexed securities*. Wiley, 2004.

30. Angelos Delivorias. Single-limb collective action clauses. Briefing, European Parliamentary Research Service, July 2019.

31. Destatis. Qualitätsbericht Preise (Harmonisierter Verbraucherpreisindex). Technical report, Statistisches Bundesamt, Wiesbaden, January 2018.

32. Umberto Eco. *The search for the perfect language*. Fontana Press, 1997.

33. Michael Ehrmann and Marcel Fratzscher. Transparency, Disclosure and the Federal Reserve. Staff Working Paper 2005, European Central Bank, March 2005.

34. Federal Reserve Act. https://www.federalreserve.gov/aboutthefed/fract.htm, 1913.

35. Niall Ferguson. *The House of Rothschild*. Penguin Books, 1998.

36. Michael J. Fleming. Measuring treasury market liquidity. Technical report, Federal Reserve Bank of New York, September 2003.

37. Milton Friedman. *Geld regiert die Welt*. Econ, 1992.

38. Tomoyuki Fukumoto, Masato Higashi, Yasunari Inamura, and Takeshi Kimura. Effectiveness of window guidance and financial environment. In *Bank of Japan Review 2010-E-4*. Bank of Japan, 2010.

39. Kenneth D. Garbade, Frank M. Keane, Lorie Logan, Amanda Stokes, and Jennifer Wolgemuth. The introduction of the tmpg fails charge for u.s. treasury securities. *Economic Policy Review*, 16(2), October 2010.

40. Dariusz Gatarek, Przemyslaw Bachert, and Robert Maksymiuk. *The LIBOR Market Model in Practice*. Wiley Finance, 2006.

41. Janet Gleeson. *The Moneymaker*. Bantam Books, 1999.

42. Charles Goodhart. *The evolution of central banks*. The MIT Press, 1988.

43. David Graeber. *Debt – The first 5,000 years*. Melville House, New York, 2011.

44. Friedrich August Hayek. *The Road to Serfdom*. The University of Chicago Press, 2007.

45. Lakhbir Hayre, editor. *SalomonSmithBarney Guide to Mortgage-backed and Asset-backed Securities*. Wiley, 2001.

46. Robert C. Higgins. *Analysis for financial management*. Irwin McGraw-Hill, 6 edition, 2001.

47. Patrick Honohan. Real and imagined constraints on euro area monetary policy. Peterson Institute Working Paper, Dec 2018. https://piie.com/publications/working-papers/real-and-imagined-constraints-euro-area-monetary-policy.

48. IASB. *International Financial Reporting Standards*. International Accounting Standards Board, 2005.

49. Antti Ilmanen. Market's rate expectations and forward rates. Technical report, Salomon Brother United States Fixed Income Research, June 1995.

50. Antti Ilmanen. Overview of forward rate analysis. Technical report, Salomon Brother United States Fixed Income Research, May 1995.

51. Otmar Issing. *Einführung in die Geldtheorie*. Vahlen, 13 edition, 2003.

52. Jessica James and Nick Webber. *Interest Rate Modelling*. Wiley, 2000.

53. David Kynaston. *Till Time's Last Sand*. Bloomsbury, 2017.

54. William L. Leffler. *Petroleum Refining in non-technical language*. PennWell Corporation, 3rd edition, 2000.

55. Les ordres fictifs sur le matif. http://www.liberation.fr/futurs/2000/08/26/des-ordres-fictifs-sur-le-matif_335237, August 2000.
56. Bob Litterman et al. *Modern Investment Management. An Equilibrium Approach*. Wiley, 2003.
57. James Macdonald. *A Free Nation Deep in Debt: The Financial Roots of Democracy*. Princeton University Press, 2003.
58. Hyman P. Minsky. *John Maynard Keynes*. McGraw Hill, 2008.
59. Ranald Mitchie. *The London Stock Exchange – A history*. Oxford University Press, 2001.
60. Antoin E. Murphy. *The Genesis of Macroeconomics*. Oxford University Press, 2009.
61. John J. Murphy. *Technical analysis of the futures markets*. New York Institute of Finance, 1986.
62. Arvind Narayanan, Joseph Bonneau, Edward Felten, Andrew Miller, and Steven Goldfeder. *Bitcoin and Cryptocurrency Technologies*. Princeton University Press, 2016.
63. Steve Nison. *Japanese Candlestick Charting Techniques*. New York Institute of Finance, 2nd edition, 2001.
64. Kjell G. Nyborg. *Collateral Frameworks*. Cambridge University Press, 2017.
65. Committee on the Global Financial System. Unconventional monetary policy tools: a cross-country analysis. Technical Report 63, Bank for International Settlements, October 2019.
66. Sharon Ou, Sumair Irfan, Yang Liu, and Kumar Kanthan. Annual default study: Corporate default and recovery rates, 1920–2016. Technical report, Moody's Investor Services, 2018.
67. Acta pacis westphalicae. http://www.pax-westphalica.de/, 1648.
68. Thomas Piketty. *Capital in the Twenty-First Century*. The Belknap Press of Harvard University Press, 2014.
69. Riccardo Rebonato. *Interest-rate option models*. Wiley, 2 edition, 1998.
70. William Roberds and Francois R. Velde. Early public banks. Atlanta Fed Working Paper 2014-9, 2014.
71. Thomas J. Sargent and Francois R. Velde. *The big problem of small change*. Princeton University Press, 1 edition, 2002.
72. Vivian A. Schmidt. The eurozone's crisis of democratic legitimacy. Technical report, European Commission Directorate-General for Economic and Financial Affairs, 2015. Discussion Paper 015.
73. Philipp J. Schönbucher. *Credit derivatives pricing models*. Wiley, 2003.
74. William Shakespeare. *The Complete Works*. Clarendon Press, Oxford, 1988.
75. Masaaki Shirakawa. *Mondern Monetary Policy in Theory and Practice*. Nihon Keizai Shinbun Shuppansha, 2008. In Japanese.
76. Time Series Research Staff. X-12-ARIMA Reference Manual Version 0.3. Technical report, U.S. Census Bureau, Washington, DC, 2011.
77. Nassim Taleb. *Dynamic Hedging*. Wiley, 1997.
78. Nassim Taleb. *Fooled by Randomness*. Texere, 2001.
79. John B. Taylor. Discretion versus policy rules in practice. In *Carnegie-Rochester Conference Series on Public Policy*, volume 39, pages 195–214. North-Holland, 1993.
80. Reiko Tokukatsu. *Negative interest rates*. Toyo-Keizai (in Japanese), 2015.
81. Toshiki Tomita. *Japanese Government Bond Research*. Toyo-Keizai, (in Japanese) edition, 2001.
82. Mark Twain. *A Connecticut Yankee in King Arthur's Court*. Oxford World's Classics, 1997. First published 10 December 1889.
83. Diane Vazza and Nick W Kraemer. 2017 annual global corporate default study and rating transitions. Technical report, S&P Global Ratings, 2018.
84. Clarita von Bernstorff, Hartwig von Bernstorff, and Emanuel Eckhardt. *Change is the only constant: Berenberg*. Hanser, 2015.
85. Lawrence R Witte. 2017 annual sovereign default study and rating transitions. Technical report, S&P Global Ratings, 2018.

86. M. Anthony Wong and Robert High. *Fixed-Income Arbitrage: Analytical techniques and strategies.* Wiley, 1993.

87. Simon N. Wood. *Generalized Additive Models – An Introduction with R.* Chapman and Hall/CRC, 2006.

88. Benedict XIV. Vix pervenit. http://www.papalencyclicals.net/ben14/b14vixpe.htm, November 1745.

Index

A

A. E. R., 116
ABS, 144
acceleration, 256
accounts payable, 28
accounts receivable, 28
Accrued interest, 158
actives, 123
agencies, 143
agency clearing, 106
algorithmic trading, 179
all-in price, 155
all-weather portfolios, 383
allocation process, 154
American auction, 155
amortising bonds, 141
annual effective rate, 116
annuity, 141, 432
arbitrage, 113
arranger, 284
asset encumbrance, 278
Asset-backed commercial paper, 112
asset-backed securities, 144, 284
auction, 155
auto-correlation, 406

B

BA, 29
back, 123
backwardation, 100, 322
balance principle, 279
bank, 17
Bank for International Settlements, 335
bank note, 14, 17
bank of issue, 35
bank run, 32
Banker's acceptance, 29

base index, 230
base money, 50
base prospectus, 137
Basel I, 284
basis sheet, 314
bearer security, 79
best effort basis, 98
best efforts, 154
best execution, 97
bid–ask bounce, 187
bid–cover ratio, 156
bidding obligation, 105
Big Bang, 177
bilateral contracts, 3
bills of exchange, 29
Bitcoin, 31
block trade, 97
blockchain, 31
blue, 122
Bond futures, 301
Bond-equivalent yield, 161
book-building, 154
book-entry, 80
bootstrapping, 192
bought deal, 154
Breakeven inflation, 241
brokers, 157
buffer, 219
bulldog, 148
bullet bond, 138
burn-out, 291
buy-in, 96

C

calendar spread, 321
call, 140
capital centre, 273

capital markets line, 397
capital structure arbitrage, 284
Carry, 167
carry, 218
cash drag, 384, 388
cash stub, 132
cash-and-carry arbitrage, 314
cash-settled contracts, 124, 301
CCP, 101
central bank, 34
central counterparty, 101
central limit order book, 86, 177
central securities depository, 80
certificate, 14
Certificate of deposit, 111
chartalism, 10
cheapest to deliver, 310
checking deposits, 17
cheque, 29
choice, 87
CIBOR, 117
clean price, 151, 159
clearer, 80
clearing, 85
clearing agent, 106
clearing house, 80
clearing member, 102
Clearstream, 81
clipping, 13
CLOB, 86, 177
CML, 397
CMS, 174
CMT, 174
co-lead, 154
CoCo, 258
collateral, 126
collateral swap, 129
collateral transformation, 129
collection period, 28
Collective action clause, 149
Commercial paper, 111
commitment fee, 112
commodities trading advisors, 406
commodity money, 11
competitive bids, 155
Compound yield, 215

compounding, 116
conditional pass-throughs, 277
conditonally convertible, 258
condor, 354
conforming loans, 289
consent solicitation, 262
consol, 140, 432
consolidated loan, 140
consolidated tape, 92
constant prepayment rate, 292
contango, 100, 322
continuous compounding, 116
contrarian, 406
conversion factor, 301
converted forward price, 313
converted PVBP, 317
convex hull, 396
Convexity, 164
convexity, 124, 382
convexity adjustment, 125
convexity hedging, 213
convexity trigger, 213
coupon, 138
coupon period, 138
coupon swap, 290
covenants, 148, 284
cover, 97
cover pool, 272, 277
Covered bonds, 272
CPR, 292
Credit Support Annex, 335
cross, 97
cross-default, 149, 256
cross-gamma, 382
cryptocurrencies, 31
CSD, 80
CTA, 306, 406
curve, 189
CUSIP, 81
custodian, 80
CVA, 109

D

dark pool, 86, 179
daycount convention, 114
daycount fraction, 114

debasement, 13
debt support, 258
default fund, 105
delivery, 279
demand deposits, 17
Deposit, 111
dirty price, 151, 159
discount factor, 30, 112
discount margin, 115, 173
discount rate, 30
discount window, 51
discounting, 30
dividend yield, 160
dollar roll, 290
domestic bonds, 147
drawer, 29
dual-limb, 261
Dutch auction, 155
Dutch Direct Auction, 155, 424
DVA, 110
DvP, 99
dynamic asset allocation, 409

E
EDSP, 301
Effective Fed Funds, 119
efficient frontier, 397
efficient market hypothesis,
    384, 397, 404
EFP, 332
EFP spreads, 221
EMH, 384, 397, 404
encumbrance, 283
Eonia, 119
ETF, 214, 383
Ethereum, 31
Euribor, 122
eurobond market, 148
Euroclear, 81
Eurodollar, 122
euromarket, 148
Euroyen, 121
events of default, 255
ex-dividend, 159
exchange offer, 262

exchange-determined settlement price,
    124, 301
exchange-for-physical, 332
exchange-traded fund, 383

F
fail, 95
fails charges, 95
fat finger, 98
Fed Put, 54
fee, 154
fiat money, 14
firm price, 86
firm underwriting commitment, 154
fiscal dominance, 65
fixed charge, 149
fixed income derivatives, 3
fixed income instruments, 3
fixed settlement, 100
fixed-equivalent yield, 173
fixed-price reoffer, 155
flipping, 153
floating charge, 149
forced money, 13
Forward rates, 131
FRA, 118
free banking, 37
FRN, 169
front, 123
full replication, 384
funding vehicle, 144
funge, 82
fungible, 153
FVA, 109

G
gamma, 124
GC, 126
GCSD, 80
general collateral, 126
gensaki, 130
GIC, 285
Gilts, 100
giro, 35
Girozentalbanken, 25
give-up, 101

global note, 80
gold, 122
greater fool, 344
green, 122
gross basis, 310
Gross-up, 150
GSE, 289

H
haircut, 128
Herstatt risk, 99
high-powered money, 32
home currency, 382
hybrid methodology, 120

I
I-spread, 223
IA, 103
Ibor, 118
IM, 103
IMM days, 122
IMM-dated, 338
immediate finality, 26
implied repo rate, 311
in competition, 89, 97
in-arrears, 170
independent amount, 103
index ratio, 229, 230
index replication, 383
index tracking, 404
indicative price, 86
infation risk premium, 244
inflation lag, 230
inflation targeting, 40
information leakage, 178
initial margin, 103
initial tranche, 153
inside money, 14, 20
inter-dealer brokers, 157
Interest Equalization Tax, 148
internal rate of return, 160
International Securities Dealers
    Association, 335
inverse floater, 171
investment grade, 264

invoice amount, 151
IRR, 311
ISDA Master Agreement, 335
ISIN, 81
issuance programme, 148

J
joint and several, 144
joint lead interest, 155

K
kangaroo, 148
KLIBOR, 117

L
lag, 170
Lagrangian, 386
Landeszentralbanken, 25
last look, 90
LCSD, 80
lead manager, 154
league tables, 154
legal final, 287
legal tender, 13, 15
lender in possession, 258
lender of last resort, 33
letters of comfort, 143
lex monetae, 13
LIBID, 117
LIBOR, 117
limit price, 177
liquidity, 176
liquidity premium, 86, 185
liquidity provider, 86
lit market, 179
Loan, 111
loi Évin, 231
LOLR, 36
Lombard lending, 51
long first coupon, 139
long-only portfolio, 382
loss given default, 258

M
margining, 102
mark-to-market, 128, 335

market indices, 404
market infrastructure, 101
market maker, 86
market portfolio, 397
master agreement, 88
meigara code, 81
merchant banking, 17
mezzanine, 286
mistrade, 98
mixed mandate, 40
model CACs, 261
modified duration, 163
monetary multiplier, 32
Money market futures, 121
money-centre, 25
month code, 122
Moosmüller yield, 160
mortality, 292
MREL, 257
MTS, 157
municipal, 142
mutan, 119

N

name giveup, 157
Negative pledge, 150
net basis, 311
netting, 22
new issue premium, 153
no-grow, 154
nominal bond, 227
non-competitive allocation, 155, 156
non-competitive bids, 155
non-recourse, 285
nostro, 23
notification, 302
notional amount, 301
notional coupon, 312
novation, 338

O

OAS, 224
OC, 277
off-shore, 148
off-the-run, 157
official rate, 133

OIS, 119
ON RRP, 49
on-the-run, 157
one-way, 87
open interest, 301, 303
open market operations, 51
open repo, 126
operational framework, 46
originator, 284
Ortoli facility, 145
OTC, 86, 177
outlier removal, 204
outright operations, 51
outside money, 14
over-the-counter, 86, 177
overcollateralisation, 277
overnight index swap, 119
oversubscribed, 154

P

P&L, 343
PAC, 288
pain trade, 308
par amount, 151
par spread, 221
par swaps, 336
par yield, 151
par–par asset swaps, 222
partial replication, 384
passive investing, 383
Passive management, 404
Pax Westphalica, 4, 13
pay in kind, 257
perfection, 285
perpetual bonds, 140
perpetuals, 140
Pfandbrief, 273
physically settled contracts, 124, 301
PIK, 257
plus, 152
policy rate, 133
positive money, 38
pot deal, 155
preferred habitat, 205
preliminary prospectus, 148
present value, 113

PRIBOR, 117
price level targeting, 40
price regression hedges, 391
pricing, 155
pricing factors, 381
primary dealers, 156
primary market, 153
principal clearing, 106
principal trading firms, 179, 309
proceeds asset swap, 223
programme, 137
project bonds, 143
prospectus, 137, 148
PTF, 179, 309
public exchange, 86
PVBP, 163

Q
quality option, 400
quoted margin, 170

R
rating migration, 266
Rating triggers, 202
ratings advisory, 265
re-couponing, 339
real bonds, 230
real coupons, 230
real rate, 244
real short rate, 244
real yield, 240
rebalancing, 233
rebasing, 233
reconventioning, 413
red, 122
redenomination, 413
rediscounting, 30, 51
reds, 148
reduced-form, 196
redundancy, 90
reference index, 230
registered securities, 80
registrar, 80
rehypothecation, 130
repackage, 144
repo, 51

repo market, 126
repo rate, 126
repurchase, 51
repurchase agreement, 126
request for quote, 177
reserve, 15, 21, 32
reserve ratio, 16
restructuring, 263
reverse inquiry, 112, 154
reverse yankee, 148
revision, 234
Revolver loan, 112
RFQ, 177
rinban, 130
RMBS, 289
roll, 321
roll ratio, 324
roll-down, 218
rolling settlement, 100
rolls, 304
Running yield, 160

S
samurai, 148
Schuldschein, 80
search costs, 178
secondary market, 157, 158
securities, 3
Securities lending, 128
securitisation, 284
seigniorage, 12
Sell-and-buyback, 129
sen, 153
serials, 123
servicer, 284
settlement, 85
settlement cycles, 99
settlement date, 100
settlement discipline, 95
settlement risk, 99
several liability, 144
shelf registration, 149
shinshōken kōdo, 82
short first coupon, 139
Short sterling, 122
short-form confirmation, 335

sight deposits, 17
simple interest, 115
Simple yield, 214
single limb, 261
single month mortality, 292
smart beta, 345
SMM, 292
SOFR, 119
soft bullet, 150, 277
solicited rating, 265
Sonia, 119
sovereign ceiling, 265
SPE, 284
special, 127
special-purpose entity, 284
special-purpose vehicle, 144, 284
specialist bank principle, 273
specie, 14
specific, 127
specifics, 123
spline spread, 221
spoofing, 179
spread guidance, 154
SPV, 144, 284, 335
squeeze, 329
SSA, 147
SSI, 92
stabilisation, 155
Standby facility, 112
stat arb, 345
statistical arbitrage, 345
stay, 263
sterilisation, 52
STIBOR, 117
STP, 91
straight-line amortising bonds, 142
straight-through processing, 91
streaming pricing, 177
street convention, 160
STRIPS, 140
structured covered bonds, 273
STS, 285
stub rate, 132, 173
sub-sovereign, 142
subject, 89, 97
substitute collateral, 277

sufficiency guarantee, 145
supranationals, 147
survivorship bias, 338
swap provider, 285
Swaps, 334
sweeping, 25
syndication, 154
synthetic replication, 384

T
T-bill, 111
T&Cs, 148
tail, 155
tap, 82
tap issues, 153
target buying, 213
tax call, 150
tax creep, 229
TBA, 289
TEC10, 174
technical analysis, 215
TED spread, 224
tegata, 111
term risk premium, 136
term structure, 189
terms and conditions, 138, 148
thirty-seconds, 152
TIBOR, 117
tick, 122
ticker, 81
ticker symbol, 413
time deposits, 17
TIPS structure, 227, 230
TLAC, 257
Tonar, 119
total return swap, 384
trade compression, 338
trade date, 100
trade lifecycle, 87
traded away, 97
trading, 85
trading on account, 29
tranches, 153
Treasury bill, 111
tri-party repo, 128, 129
trimmed mean, 117

TRS, 384
true sale, 285
turn, 133
turn premium, 133
two-way, 86

U
UFR, 214
ultra vires, 76
unsolicited rating, 266
uridashi, 148

V
valuation date, 99
variable-rate, 169
variation margin, 102
verb, 89
Vix pervenit, 4
VM, 102
Vollgeld, 38
volume, 303

W
WAL, 297
wampun, 13

war loan, 432
waterfall, 286
weakest link, 258
wealth effect, 54
white, 122
window guidance, 38
winner's curse, 89
WKN, 81
work an order, 98
wrong-way risk,
    128

X
xVA, 108

Y
yankee, 148
YCC, 60
Yield, 159
yield curve control, 60

Z
z-spread, 220
zero-coupon bond, 139

Printed and bound by CPI Group (UK) Ltd, Croydon, CR0 4YY

16/04/2025

14658507-0003